THE PAPERS OF

Alexander Hamilton

VOLUME XXIII
APRIL 1799–OCTOBER 1799

HAROLD C. SYRETT, EDITOR

Associate Editors

BARBARA A. CHERNOW

JOSEPH G. HENRICH   PATRICIA SYRETT

 COLUMBIA UNIVERSITY PRESS

NEW YORK, 1976

0231089260

FROM THE PUBLISHER

The preparation of this edition of the papers of Alexander Hamilton has been made possible by the support received for the work of the editorial and research staff from the generous grants of the Rockefeller Foundation, Time Inc., the Ford Foundation, the National Endowment for the Humanities, and by the far-sighted cooperation of the National Historical Publications and Records Commission, which administered the Ford Foundation grant during its ten years of existence, has continued its support of research and editing, and, in addition, has provided funds toward the cost of publication of this volume.

To these organizations, the publisher expresses gratitude on behalf of all who are concerned about making available the record of the founding of the United States.

745040

C

Columbia University Press
New York   Guildford, Surrey
Copyright © 1976 Columbia University Press
International Standard Book Number: 0-231-08922-8
Library of Congress Catalog Card Number: 61-15593
Printed in the United States of America

6001874006

Alexander Hamilton.
Oil painting by Ezra Ames, *circa* 1802

ACKNOWLEDGMENTS

SINCE THE PUBLICATION in 1975 of Volume XXII of *The Papers of Alexander Hamilton* the editors have incurred new obligations which they wish to take this opportunity to acknowledge. Of the many individuals who generously shared their specialized information or provided assistance, the editors are especially indebted to

Miss Ruth M. Blair, Manuscript Cataloger, Connecticut Historical Society, Hartford

Mr. John Catanzariti, Associate Editor, The Papers of Robert Morris, City University of New York

Miss Margaret Cobb, Assistant Editor, The Nathanael Greene Papers, Rhode Island Historical Society, Providence

Professor Joseph M. Conant, Emory University, Atlanta, Georgia

Mr. Walter A. Frankel, Librarian, Chair of Library Science, The Taft School, Watertown, Connecticut

Mr. Philip Gunn, Reeves & Sons, Ltd., Enfield, Middlesex, England

The Honorable James F. Hastings, Congressman, 39th District, New York

Mr. Allan Hecht, New York City

Mrs. Phoebe Jacobs, Rutherford, New Jersey

Miss Jean G. Johnson, Manuscript Assistant, New Hampshire Historical Society, Concord

Dr. Mary-Jo Kline, Editor, The Aaron Burr Papers, New-York Historical Society, New York City

Mr. John Knowlton, Washington, D.C.

Miss Mary Lou Lucy, Columbia University Libraries

Mr. Kevin MacDonnell, Special Collections, University Libraries, University of Houston

Dr. Douglas W. Marshall, Curator of Maps, William L. Clements Library of the University of Michigan

Mrs. Katherine Peckham, Middletown, Rhode Island

Mr. G. Simmons, Reeves & Sons, Ltd., Enfield, Middlesex, England

Mr. Eric Sloane, Cornwall Bridge, Connecticut

Miss Sara M. Solberg, New York City

Lieutenant Colonel J. E. South, Librarian, Royal Engineers Library, The Institution of Royal Engineers, Chatham, Kent, England

Professor David Syrett, Queens College, City University of New York

Professor John Syrett, Trent University, Peterborough, Ontario

Miss Helen Wallis, Map Librarian, The British Library, London

Professor Edmund P. Willis, York College, City University of New York

PREFACE

THIS EDITION of Alexander Hamilton's Papers contains letters and other documents written by Hamilton, letters to Hamilton, and some documents (commissions, certificates, etc.) that directly concern Hamilton but were written neither by him nor to him. All letters and other documents have been printed in chronological order. Two volumes of Hamilton's legal papers, entitled *The Law Practice of Alexander Hamilton*, have been published by the Columbia University Press under the editorial direction of the late Julius Goebel, Jr. The third and fourth volumes of this distinguished work are being completed by Professor Joseph H. Smith, George Welwood Murray Professor of Legal History of the School of Law, Columbia University.

Many letters and documents have been calendared. Such calendared items include routine letters and documents by Hamilton, routine letters to Hamilton, some of the letters or documents written by Hamilton for someone else, letters or documents which have not been found but which are known to have existed, letters or documents which have been erroneously attributed to Hamilton, and letters to or by Hamilton that deal exclusively with his legal practice.

Hamilton's significant legal opinions appear in *The Law Practice of Alexander Hamilton*, and they have accordingly been omitted from these volumes.

Because a large part of Hamilton's correspondence during the undeclared war with France concerns routine—and even petty and trivial—Army matters, such letters have been neither printed nor calendared. Instead, they are listed chronologically in an appendix with a key indicating the nature of the contents of each letter. There are, however, two exceptions to this rule. In the first place, all the correspondence between Lieutenant Colonel Nathan Rice, commandant of the Fourteenth Regiment of Infantry, and Hamilton has been

printed as typical of Hamilton's relationship with the commanding
officers of the twelve regiments of the Additional Army. Secondly,
an effort has been made to include as much as possible of Hamilton's
correspondence with the officers in the Regular Army on the ground
that letters and orders in this category may well have had some long-
term effect on the development of the United States armed forces.
In addition, such documents provide information for those scholars
who are interested in a comparison of the history of the United
States Army with that of other countries.

Army returns, warrants, and bonds are neither printed nor listed
in the appendix.

The notes in these volumes are designed to provide information
concerning the nature and location of each document, to identify
Hamilton's correspondents and the individuals mentioned in the text,
to explain events or ideas referred to in the text, and to point out
textual variations or mistakes. Occasional departures from these stan-
dards can be attributed to a variety of reasons. In many cases the
desired information has been supplied in an earlier note and can be
found through the use of the index. Notes have not been added when
in the opinion of the editors the material in the text was either self-
explanatory or common knowledge. The editors, moreover, have
not thought it desirable or necessary to provide full annotation for
Hamilton's legal correspondence. Finally, the editors on some occasions have been unable to find the desired information, and on other
occasions the editors have been remiss.

GUIDE TO EDITORIAL APPARATUS

I. SYMBOLS USED TO DESCRIBE MANUSCRIPTS

AD	Autograph Document
ADS	Autograph Document Signed
ADf	Autograph Draft
ADfS	Autograph Draft Signed
AL	Autograph Letter
ALS	Autograph Letter Signed
D	Document
DS	Document Signed
Df	Draft
DfS	Draft Signed
LS	Letter Signed
LC	Letter Book Copy
[S]	[S] is used with other symbols (AD[S], ADf[S], AL[S], D[S], Df[S], L[S]) to indicate that the signature on the document has been cropped or clipped.

II. SHORT TITLES AND ABBREVIATIONS

Annals of Congress	*The Debates and Proceedings in the Congress of the United States; with an Appendix, Containing Important State Papers and Public Documents, and All the Laws of a Public Nature* (Washington, 1834–1849).
Arch. des. Aff. Etr., Cor. Pol., Etats-Unis	Transcripts or photostats from the French Foreign Office deposited in the Library of Congress.

| ASP | *American State Papers, Documents, Legislative and Executive, of the Congress of the United States* (Washington, 1832–1861). |

Carter, *Territorial Papers* — Clarence E. Carter, ed., *The Territorial Papers of the United States* (Washington, 1832–1861).

Executive Journal, I — *Journal of the Executive Proceedings of the Senate* (Washington, 1828), I.

Gibbs, *Wolcott* — George Gibbs, *Memoirs of the Administrations of Washington and John Adams: Edited from the Papers of Oliver Wolcott, Secretary of the Treasury* (New York, 1846).

Godfrey, "Provisional Army" — Charles E. Godfrey, "Organization of the Provisional Army of the United States in the Anticipated War with France, 1798–1800," *The Pennsylvania Magazine of History and Biography* XXXVIII (1914: Reprinted, New York, 1965). Godfrey confuses the Provisional Army with the Additional Army.

Goebel ,*Law Practice* — Julius Goebel, Jr., ed., *The Law Practice of Alexander Hamilton: Documents and Commentary* (New York and London, 1964–   ).

GW — John C. Fitzpatrick, ed., *The Writings of George Washington* (Washington, 1931–1944).

Hamilton, *Intimate Life* — Allan McLane Hamilton, *The Intimate Life of Alexander Hamilton* (New York, 1910).

HCLW — Henry Cabot Lodge, ed., *The Works of Alexander Hamilton* (New York, 1904).

Heitman, *United States Army* — Francis B. Heitman, *Historical Register and Dictionary of the United States Army, From Its Organization, September 29, 1789, to March 2, 1903* (Washington, 1903).

JCC

Journals of the Continental Congress 1774–1789 (Washington, 1904–1937).

JCHW

John C. Hamilton, ed., *The Works of Alexander Hamilton* (New York, 1851–1856).

Journal of the House, I, II, III, IV

Journal of the House of Representatives of the United States (Washington, 1826), I, II, III, IV.

King, *The Life and Correspondence of Rufus King*

Charles R. King, ed., *The Life and Correspondence of Rufus King* (New York, 1894–1900).

Knopf, *Wayne*

Richard C. Knopf, ed., *Anthony Wayne: A Name in Arms; Soldier, Diplomat, Defender of Expansion Westward of a Nation; the Wayne-Knox-Pickering-McHenry Correspondence* (Pittsburgh, 1960).

Miller, *Treaties*, II

Hunter Miller, ed., *Treaties and Other International Acts of the United States of America* (Washington, 1931), II.

Minutes of the Common Council

Minutes of the Common Council of the City of New York, 1784–1831 (New York, 1917).

Mitchell, *Hamilton*

Broadus Mitchell, *Alexander Hamilton* (New York, 1957–1962).

Naval Documents, Quasi-War, November, 1798–March, 1799

Naval Documents Related to the Quasi-War Between the United States and France: Naval Operations from November 1798 to March 1799 (Washington, 1935).

Naval Documents, Quasi-War, April, 1799–July, 1799

Naval Documents Related to the Quasi-War Between the United States and France: Naval Operations from April 1799 to July 1799 (Washington, 1936).

Naval Documents, Quasi-War, August, 1799–December, 1799

Naval Documents Related to the Quasi-War Between the United States and France: Naval Operations from August 1799 to December 1799 (Washington, 1936).

Réimpression de L'Ancien Moniteur — *Réimpression de L'Ancien Moniteur Seule Histoire Authentique et Inaltérée de la Révolution Française* . . . (Paris, 1847).

1Stat.; 2 Stat. — *The Public Statutes at Large of the United States of America,* I (Boston, 1845); II (Boston, 1850).

6 Stat. — *The Public Statutes at Large of the United States of America* [Private Statutes] (Boston, 1846).

A Statement of Expenditures — *Message from the President of the United States, Accompanying A Statement of Expenditures from the 1st of January, 1797, by the Quarter Master General, and the Navy Agents, for the Contingencies of the Naval and Military Establishments, and the Navy Contracts for Timber and Stores.* . . . (Washington City: Printed by William Duane and Son, 1803).

III. INDECIPHERABLE WORDS

Words or parts of words which could not be deciphered because of the illegibility of the writing or the mutilation of the manuscript have been indicated as follows:

1. ⟨ – – – – – ⟩ indicates illegible words with the number of dashes indicating the estimated number of illegible words.
2. Words or letters in broken brackets indicate a guess as to what the words or letters in question may be. If the source of the words or letters within the broken brackets is known, it has been given a note.

IV. CROSSED-OUT MATERIAL IN MANUSCRIPTS

Words or sentences crossed out by a writer in a manuscript have been handled in one of the three following ways:

1. They have been ignored, and the document or letter has been printed in its final version.
2. Crossed-out words and insertions for the crossed-out words have been described in the notes.
3. When the significance of a manuscript seems to warrant it, the crossed-out words have been retained, and the document has been printed as it was written.

V. TEXTUAL CHANGES AND INSERTIONS

The following changes or insertions have been made in the letters and documents printed in these volumes:

1. Words or letters written above the line of print (for example, 9th) have been made even with the line of print (9th).
2. Punctuation and capitalization have been changed in those instances where it seemed necessary to make clear the sense of the writer. A special effort has been made to eliminate the dash, which was such a popular eighteenth-century device.
3. When the place or date, or both, of a letter or document does not appear at the head of that letter or document, it has been inserted in the text in brackets. If either the place or date at the head of a letter or document is incomplete, the necessary additional material has been added in the text in brackets. For all but the best known localities or places, the name of the colony, state, or territory has been added in brackets at the head of a document or letter.
4. In calendared documents, place and date have been uniformly written out in full without the use of brackets. Thus "N. York, Octr. 8, '99" becomes "New York, October 8, 1799." If, however, substantive material is added to the place or date in a calendared document, such material is placed in brackets. Thus "Oxford, Jan. 6" becomes "Oxford [Massachusetts] January 6 [1788]."
5. When a writer made an unintentional slip comparable to a typographical error, one of the four following devices has been used:
   a. It has been allowed to stand as written.

    b. It has been corrected by inserting either one or more letters in brackets.

    c. It has been corrected without indicating the change.

    d. It has been explained in a note.

6. Because the symbol for the thorn was archaic even in Hamilton's day, the editors have used the letter "y" to represent it. In doing this they are conforming to eighteenth-century manuscript usage.

1799

From Oliver Wolcott, Junior

Phila. Apl. 1. 1799

Dr. Sir (Private)

I have recd. your favour of March 21st. Mr. Wharton is a young man of virtue modesty and industry—he is pliant and docile—but I have observed no indications of invention or what may be called *Talents*. He is what I recommended him for, a proper person to copy and assist a man who has much business—but I do not think it probable that he could perform more than what is commonly expected of a clerk.

Genl McPherson it is said will march on Wednesday.[1] I am grieved when I think of the situation of the govt. An affair which ought to have been settled at once will cost much time & perhaps be so managed as to encourage other and formidable rebellions. We have no Prest. here,[2] & the appearance of languor & indecision are discouraging to the friends of govt. Mr. McH—— does the best in his power—yet his operations are such as to confirm more and more a belief of utter unfitness for the situation. The President has been informed of the disorders in that Dept. yet there appears no disposition to apply any correction. Expence, discord, and a general loss of confidence, will I fear be the only fruits of the regulations adopted by Congress[3] for the interior defence of the country.

In this State affairs bear an unpleasant aspect: the Governor[4] is habitually intoxicated every day & most commonly every forenoon. Dallas & Judge Kean[5] possess the efficient powers of the government. The former has written to several Magistrates, that setting up *Liberty Poles* as they are called is no Crime, if done peaceably. The Judge is in pretty open collision with the Mayor[6] who is a good Man. On Saturday night Brown &c were attacked in a most violent & cruel manner in their Houses.[7] The Mayor ordered the Men to Prison, but on Sunday Morning, they were enlarged by

order of Judge Mc.Kean. In short Mc.Kean & Dallas mean to have
it understood, that they are determined to support all the turbulent
& flagitious of the Community. I am not without hopes that this
violent conduct will open the eyes of the people, if it does not, we
shall soon have serious trouble in Pensylvania.

You know the state of things in the Country, the public opinion,
the disposition of the President. If any thing can & ought to be done,
and I can be of any service I will do it, however unpleasant.

I recd. the enclosed this morning & have shewn it to Mr. Mc.-
Henry—he says that the men are under your Orders & will leave
Windsor immediately.[8]

When you have read this be pleased to burn it—to prevent accidents.

I am Dr. Sir yrs. affectly   Oliv. Wolcott.

Genl. Hamilton

ALS, Hamilton Papers, Library of Congress.
    1. Brigadier General William Macpherson was in command of the troops
dispatched to suppress Fries's Rebellion. See James McHenry to H, March 13,
15, 1799; Macpherson to H, March 25, 1799.
    A veteran of the American Revolution, Macpherson had been an aide-de-
camp to Benjamin Lincoln and at the end of the war had attained the rank of
major. He had been appointed surveyor for the port of Philadelphia on September 11, 1789, inspector of the port on March 8, 1792, and naval officer for
the District of Philadelphia on December 30, 1793 (*Executive Journal*, I, 25,
111, 144).
    2. President John Adams had left Philadelphia on March 12, 1799, for his
home in Quincy, Massachusetts (*Gazette of the United States, and Philadelphia
Daily Advertiser*, March 13, 1799).
    3. This is a reference to "An Act for the better organizing of the Troops
of the United States; and for other purposes" (1 *Stat.* 749-55 [March 3, 1799])
and "An Act giving eventual authority to the President of the United States
to augment the Army" (1 *Stat.* 725-27 [March 2, 1799]).
    4. Thomas Mifflin.
    5. Alexander J. Dallas was Secretary of the Commonwealth of Pennsylvania,
and Thomas McKean was Chief Justice of Pennsylvania.
    6. Robert Wharton.
    7. On March 29, 1799, one or more "United Irishmen" attacked and injured
Andrew Brown, editor of the *Gazette of the United States, and Philadelphia
Daily Advertise*r because of allegedly derogatory remarks in his paper concerning a Saint Patrick's Day dinner (*Gazette of the United States, and Philadelphia Daily Advertiser*, March 30, 1799; [Philadelphia] *Aurora. General Advertiser*, April 1, 1799).
    8. This is a reference to the soldiers of the Second Regiment of Artillerists
and Engineers commanded by Lieutenant Nathaniel Leonard at Windsor, Vermont. H and McHenry had made arrangements for the transfer of these sol-

diers for possible use in suppressing Fries's Rebellion. See H to Leonard, March 24, 1799; H to McHenry, March 28, 1799; McHenry to H, March 30, 1799 (all listed in the appendix to Volume XXII).

From James McHenry [1]

War department 2d. April 1799

Sir

It being out of my power to send you copies of, you will herewith receive the following original letters from Brig. Gen. Wilkinson, which you will be pleased to return after taking such extracts from them as you may judge necessary.

Letter No. 1 dated 6 Decr. 1798 [2]

    Do No. 2   do   10 Jany. 1799 [3]

    Do No. 3   Do   31 Jany. [4]

    Do No. 4   Do   2 Feby. [5]

        No. 5 Circular letter to the officers commanding posts [6]

        No. 6 Correspondence with Govr. Gayoso [7]

        No. 7 Papers refered to in letter Jany 1799.

I have the Honor to be with the greatest respect   Your Obedient and Hum. Servt.   James McHenry

Major Gen. Alexr. Hamilton

LS, Hamilton Papers, Library of Congress.
    1. This letter is in reply to H to McHenry, March 29, 1799.
    2. See McHenry to H, March 19, 1799, note 2.
    3. In this letter Brigadier General James Wilkinson, commanding officer of the Western Army, discussed relations with the Spanish and enclosed a map showing "Christian Settlements" and Indian towns and a copy of a petition, dated January 1, 1799, from the people of the Mississippi Territory to Congress requesting that their Spanish land titles be legally recognized (LS, marked "Duplicate," Hamilton Papers, Library of Congress).
    4. In this letter Wilkinson reported that Zachariah Cox was in Tennessee, discussed relations with the Indians, and enclosed his correspondence with Manuel Gayoso de Lemos, governor of Louisiana (LS, Hamilton Papers, Library of Congress).
    Cox was one of the promoters of the Tennessee Land Company, which had received a grant of land at Muscle Shoals on the Tennessee River from the Georgia legislature in 1795. Wilkinson accused Cox of assembling and organizing an armed force on land which had been guaranteed to the Indians. Cox was also involved in the Blount Conspiracy, whose participants were trying to interest the British Minister, Robert Liston, in plans to establish a British colony

at Muscle Shoals. Wilkinson had ordered Cox's arrest in 1798, but Cox escaped. See McHenry to H, March 19, 1799, notes 1 and 2. For additional information on Cox's activities, see Isaac J. Cox, ed., "Documents Relating to Zachariah Cox," *Quarterly Publication of the Historical and Philosophical Society of Ohio*, VIII (1913), 29–114.

5. Letter not found.
6. Letter not found.
7. Wilkinson to Gayoso de Lemos, November 11, December 22, 1798; Gayoso de Lemos to Wilkinson, December 1, 1798, January 2, 1799 (copies, Hamilton Papers, Library of Congress).

To James McHenry

[*New York, April 2, 1799*. On April 4, 1799, McHenry wrote to Hamilton: "I have been honored with your letter of the 2d. Inst." *Letter not found.*]

To James McHenry

New York, April 3, 1799. ". . . More recruiting Instructions are necessary, there cannot be less than *thirteen* copies to each Regiment (one for each Company one for each field officer): you only sent ninety in the whole." [1]

Copy, in the handwriting of Philip Church, Hamilton Papers, Library of Congress.

1. See McHenry to H, March 21, 1799, note 10.

From John J. U. Rivardi [1]

Niagara [*New York*] *April 3, 1799*. Discusses the weaknesses of United States forts on the Great Lakes. Encloses "the Plan of Detroit." [2] Complains about contractors buying too much flour and about delays in settling quartermaster's accounts and lack of reinforcements. States: "Sir John Johnson having politely offered me To Take charge of whatever I Should want to Send To Detroit & Mackinac, I gave him the letters which you directed me To forward To the Officers commanding these two Posts. Major Burbeck [3] will receive his three Months earlier than he could by any other Conveyance. . . ." Cites other examples of friendship and cooperation between the British and American garrisons at Niagara and recommends Enoch Humphrey as a cadet. States: "I was interrupted by Mr. Burke [4] great Vicar of Canada & a man perfectly acquainted with this Country, he observed To me during diner that he firmly believes the whole of the rumor among the Indians [5] To have arisen from the Secret Machinations of Some Individuals employed in that Department, because an Indian War would make their fortunes. . . ." Complains that James McHenry does nothing to investigate Captain James Bruff's charges [6] and states that he wishes to press charges against Bruff.

ALS, Hamilton Papers, Library of Congress.

1. A native of Switzerland, Rivardi was a major in the First Regiment of Artillerists and Engineers and was commanding officer at Fort Niagara.

2. The original of the plan, drawn by Rivardi and dated at Niagara, March 29, 1799, is in the William L. Clements Library of the University of Michigan.

3. Henry Burbeck, a resident of Massachusetts and a veteran of the American Revolution, was lieutenant colonel commandant of the First Regiment of Artillerists and Engineers and was stationed at Fort Michilimackinac.

4. Edmond Burke, a native of Ireland, was ordained a Roman Catholic priest in 1781. In 1787 he immigrated to Canada and held a variety of ecclesiastical posts before becoming Vicar General of Quebec in 1795. In 1799 he was also serving as chaplain to the British garrison at Fort George at Niagara.

5. For an explanation of these rumors, see Rivardi to H, March 21, 1799, notes 21 and 23.

6. In this letter Rivardi enclosed copies of James Bruff to Rivardi, January 15, 1799; Bruff to James McHenry, January 15, 1799 (copies, Hamilton Papers, Library of Congress). Rivardi noted on these copies: "I thought best to forward this Copy of Captn. Bruffs letter & charges, the Mail being on the Start I can not possibly Send my defense which is prepared long ago & in the Opinion of My friends More than Satisfactory. JJUR. I transmitted the Original to the Secretary of War." For Bruff's complaint, see Rivardi to H, March 21, 1799, note 13. See also Tobias Lear to H, March 30, 1799 (listed in the appendix to Volume XXII); McHenry to H, first letter of April 1, 1799 (listed in the appendix to this volume).

To Caleb Swan [1]

New York April 3rd. 1799

Sir

By Special direction of the Commander in Chief and in conformity with the views of the Secretary of War, I am to desire that you will as soon as may be repair to the Seat of the General Government, where when arrived, you will take the orders of the Secretary at War.[2]

Previous to your departure, you will constitute a Deputy, who must act as Paymaster to the Western Army, and with whom you will leave every necessary information and direction agreeably to the laws and your instructions from the Treasury and War Departments.

The 15th Section of an Act of the last Session entitled "An Act for the better organizing of the Troops of the United States & for other purposes," [3] directs that the Paymaster General of the Armies of United States shall always Quarter at or near the Head Quarters of the Main Army or at such place as the Commander in Chief shall deem proper, and that to the Army on the Western frontiers and to detachments from the Main Army intended to act separately for a time, he shall appoint Deputy Pay Masters, who shall account to him for the money advanced to them, and shall each *give a bond in the sum of 15000 dollars with sufficient sureties* for the faithful discharge of their duties respectively, and take an oath faithfully to execute the duties of their offices. The same Section provides also, that each Deputy shall receive in addition to his pay and other emoluments 30 dollars per month, in full compensation for his extra services and travelling expences—Whence it is to be inferred that the person is to be taken from the line of the Army.

Aware of the great importance of selecting a character fully competent to and worthy of the trust, it is not to be doubted that you will exercise peculiar care and circumspection in the choice.

This instruction would have been conveyed to you through the General commanding the Western army [4] had it not been for the very great distance between you. You will of course inform him of your departure and of the arrangement which you shall have made for a Substitute.

With great consideration   I am Sir   Your obed servt.

A Hamilton

You will of course bring with you your books and papers.

Pay Master Swan Esqr.
Pay Master General
Cincinnatus Ohio

Copy, in the handwriting of Philip Church, Hamilton Papers, Library of Congress.
   1. This letter was enclosed in H to James Wilkinson, April 3, 1799, which is listed in the appendix to this volume.
   2. See James McHenry to H, March 8, 1799; George Washington to H, March 25, 1799.
   3. 1 *Stat.* 749–55 (March 3, 1799).
   4. Wilkinson, who had been Swan's commanding officer, was at Loftus Heights (Fort Adams), Mississippi Territory.

To George Washington

Private   New York April 3. 1799

Dr. Sir

Agreeably to your letter of the 25th of March, which with its inclosures have come duly to hand, I have written to the Pay Master General to repair to the Seat of Government.[1] Your letter to Col Hamtranck [2] goes by the same opportunity.

The arrangements for beginning to recruit in the States of Connecticut, New York, Jersey, Pensylvania and Delaware, are so mature that it will be very extraordinary if the business does not actually commence in a week. Nothing in my power will be omitted to press it forward in the other States. The prospect of success in the middle and Northern States is not bad.

I get nothing very precise about the Insurrection.[3] But every thing continues to wear the character of feebleness, in respect to the measures for suppressing it. And though I hope it will not become very serious, yet it will not be astonishing, if from mismanagement, it should become more troublesome than it need to be.

With greatest respect & attachment   I remain Dr Sir   Your obed ser   A Hamilton

General Washington

ALS, George Washington Papers, Library of Congress; copy, in the handwriting of Philip Church, Hamilton Papers, Library of Congress.
    1. H to Caleb Swan, April 3, 1799.
    2. This letter was enclosed in Washington to H, March 25, 1799.
    3. Fries's Rebellion. See James McHenry to H, March 13, 15, 1799; William Macpherson to H, March 25, 1799; Oliver Wolcott, Jr., to H, April 1, 1799.

To Ezra L'Hommedieu [1]

New York April 4
1799

Sir

As the holder, I am to inform you that Mr. David Gelston has refused payment of his promissory note dated the first of August last for Eight thousand Dollars payable in Eight Months to you and indorsed by you, and consequently that I look to you for the payment of the same.

Mr. Gelston has however deposited with Mr. Wilkes [2] 4000 Dollars on account of the Note, which with your consent I will receive holding you responsible for the remainder.

Knowing that this engagement has been entered into to oblige Col Burr, I have every disposition to accomodate the parties which can be shewn without releasing either.

With esteem I am Sir   Your obed servt   A Hamilton

Ezra L'Hommedieu Esq [3]

ALS, Hamilton College Library, Clinton, New York; copy, MS Division, New York Public Library.
    1. The letter printed above concerns the efforts of L'Hommedieu and David Gelston to help Aaron Burr pay a debt which he owed to Louis Le Guen.
    L'Hommedieu represented New York in the Continental Congress from 1779 to 1782 and in 1788. He was a member of the New York Assembly from Suf-

folk County from 1777 to 1783, clerk of Suffolk County from 1784 to 1810, and a member of the state Senate from 1784 to 1792 and from 1794 to 1809.

Gelston, who was born in Bridgehampton, New York, was a New York City merchant, a Republican politician, and Burr's close friend and political associate. He had been a member of the New York Provincial Congress, the Continental Congress, the New York Assembly, the New York Senate, and the Council of Appointment. In 1799 he was surrogate of New York County and a member of the state Senate. For Gelston's role in the "Reynolds Affair," see "David Gelston's Account of an Interview between Alexander Hamilton and James Monroe," July 11, 1797.

Le Guen was a French citizen who arrived in the United States in 1794 and became a merchant in New York City. Both Burr and H had served as Le Guen's attorneys in the suits and counter-suits between Le Guen and Isaac Gouverneur and Peter Kemble. See Goebel, *Law Practice*, II, 48–164.

On August 1, 1798, Burr borrowed eight thousand dollars payable in eight months from Louis Le Guen. As security for this loan, Burr gave Le Guen a promissory note which Gelston had agreed to issue to L'Hommedieu for the same amount on the same terms. L'Hommedieu endorsed this note ("Aaron Burr's Account with Louis Le Guen," December 18, 1800 [AD, in Le Guen's handwriting, The Huntington Library, San Marino, California]). Burr assured Gelston and L'Hommedieu that they would not have to pay Le Guen in April, 1799, for he intended to pay him out of an additional twenty-five thousand dollars Le Guen had already agreed to advance him if satisfactory security could be provided. As security for this second loan, Burr offered Le Guen a mortgage on three hundred and sixty lots, exclusive of the buildings and garden, which formed his estate Richmond Hill. Although Burr valued each lot at from one hundred to three hundred pounds, the land was already encumbered (Burr to Le Guen, January 18, 1799 [ALS, The Huntington Library, San Marino, California]; Samuel H. Wandell and Meade Minnigerode, *Aaron Burr* [New York, 1925], I, 122). As the date for the payment of the Gelston-L'Hommedieu note approached, Le Guen had still not decided whether to lend Burr the twenty-five thousand dollars. On March 10, 1799, Burr wrote to Le Guen: "The note of Messieurs G. and L-H. will become due in a few Weeks; as that Note was given at my request, and I relied on your promise of a loan to enable me to take it up, I would now propose to give you a security on one hundred lotts adjoining Greenwich Street for the amount of that note and I could wish this negociation to take place immediately that those gentlemen may be discharged from their responsibility" (ALS, The Huntington Library, San Marino, California). See also Burr to Le Guen, March 12, 1799 (ALS, The Huntington Library, San Marino, California). After Le Guen had refused Burr's request, Burr on March 22 wrote to Le Guen: "Your answer surprized me much; but it would at this time be useless to enter into explanations.

"I have written to Genl. Hamilton [in a letter which has not been found] stating to him the purpose for which the Note of D[avid Gelston] & L-H. was given and the reliance which was placed on your assurances for taking it up, and I have proposed that it should be renewed for 60 Days, before the expiration of which time I shall be in N. York & may make other arrangements than those which have so unexpectedly failed." (ALS, The Huntington Library, San Marino, California.) Le Guen, however, changed his mind, and on April 1, 1799, he advanced Burr ten thousand dollars "Sur morgages" and credited Burr's account with eight thousand dollars in payment of L'Hommedieu's note ("Aaron Burr's Account with Louis Le Guen," December 18, 1800 [AD, in Le Guen's handwriting, The Huntington Library, San Marino, California]).

H was involved in the negotiations with Burr described above because he was serving as Le Guen's attorney. In addition, H, Richard Harison, and Aaron Ogden were trustees for a fund which Le Guen had established in an antenuptial agreement in February, 1799.

2. Charles Wilkes was cashier of the Bank of New York.

3. At the bottom of this letter Henry Brewerton, a New York City lawyer, wrote: "Two copies dld at the Post Office the day of the date, one for Albany the other for Southold. Hy Brewerton." L'Hommedieu's home was at Southold, New York.

Below Brewerton's note, William LeConte, H's law clerk, wrote: "Left a copy of the above letter at the house of Mr. Nathaniel G. Ingraham New York April 5th 1799. William LeConte." Ingraham was a New York City merchant.

From James McHenry

War Department 4th. April 1799.

Sir

I have been honored with your letter of the 2d. Inst.[1]

Inclosed is a copy of my letter to Mr. J. Huntington [2] of New London, to the purpose of entering into contracts, to supply rations &c. for the troops to be raised in Connecticut. Similar letters have been sent to J. Jackson Supervisor at Boston for Massachusetts, to Jacob Sheaff at Portsmouth for New Hampshire, and one inclosed to Mr. Elljah Paine, who is requested to direct it to a proper person to form Contracts for Vermont; also to   [3] of Wilmington for Delaware; to Colonel Carrington for Virginia, and to J. Mc.Rea [4] of Wilmington for North Carolina.

For the remaining states, contracts have been formed. The Contractors are as follow:

For New York	William Colefax,
For Pennsylvania	Michl. Gunkle and
	Henry Schriver,
For Maryland	James Baker,
For South Carolina	Dodridge Croker,
For Georgia	Solomon Ellis,
For Tenessee and Kentucky	James OHara.

If I comprehend your idea relative to the cloathing, whatever quantity is wanted for a Regiment or Regimental circle are to be deposited with the proper Officer of the Regimental Staff; which officer, you consider, should be the pay-master, and the articles to be distributed by him among the companies.[5]

It strikes me, that during the recruiting service, and before the Companies are brought to some one point, this mode you propose, might be attended with not only an increase of expence, but also of delay. The Regiment, for example, which Lieutenant Colonel Ogden is to command,[6] has ten recruiting rendezvouses, as follow, Hackinsack, Elizabeth Town, New Brunswick, Trenton, Burlington and Woodbury in Jersey, three others in Pennsylvania & Delaware. Should the whole of the cloathing for a Regiment be sent to any one place in Jersey for subsequent distribution by the pay-master, the requisite share of them must be brought back from thence, to supply the places of rendezvous in Pennsylvania and Delaware.

To prevent this expence, you will perhaps think it proper, that the pay-master of each Regiment, if charged with this duty, shall make requisitions for the Cloathing required for his Regiment or circle, and point out the parcels to be destined for each company or rendezvous, to be transported by the quarter master General, if drawn from Philadelphia, or agent of the War Department, as the case may be; the pay-master to take receipts from the companies officers for the quantity sent to them respectively.

It is not perceived, that this mode will break in upon the accountability of the pay-master, who will be charged with the cloathing, on the books of the Superintendent.

I have not been furnished with the names of any of the Regimental pay-masters.[7]

With great respect I have the Honor to be   Sir   Your Obedient and Huml. Servant   James McHenry [8]

Major General Hamilton

LS, Hamilton Papers, Library of Congress; Df, James McHenry Papers, Library of Congress.

1. Letter not found.

2. McHenry's letter to Jedediah Huntington, collector of customs at New London, Connecticut, is dated April 1, 1799 (copy, Hamilton Papers, Library of Congress).

3. Space left blank in MS. In the draft the space is filled in with "Mr. John Stockton." Stockton was commissioner of loans for Delaware.

4. Griffith John McRee was collector of customs for the District of Wilmington, North Carolina.

5. See H to McHenry, March 30, 1799.

6. Aaron Ogden, a resident of Elizabeth, New Jersey, was lieutenant colonel commandant of the Eleventh Regiment of Infantry.

7. For the selection of the regimental paymasters, see H to McHenry, March 10, 14, 19, 23, 29, 1799; McHenry to H, March 13, 21, 1799; "Circular to the Commandants of Regiments," March 23, 1799.

8. H endorsed this letter: "Mr. Brown will procure a Blank book & enter in one column the name of the Agents in another of the Contractors."

Ethan Brown, a Connecticut merchant, had become one of H's law clerks in 1797. On April 1, 1799, he was appointed assistant secretary to H in his capacity as inspector general. Admitted to the bar of New York in 1802, Brown later had a distinguished career as a Democratic governor of Ohio, United States Senator, and minister to Brazil.

To Timothy Pickering

New York April 4. 1799

Sir

I observe by the Boston papers, that some dispatches have been lately found on board a vessel from this port which was carried into Gibralter.[1] The late consul here, Mr. Rosier, has just been with me and suggested that the dispatches are probably from him and allude (but without naming me) to some conversations with me relating to his being received as Consul General some time last Winter. Being so much engaged as not to have been able conveniently to call upon you, I mentioned the subject while in Philadelphia to Mr Wolcott, and was informed by him that Mr Rosier could not then be received. In the interviews respecting this object some general conversation took place about the state of things between the two Countries. Mr Rosier will write to you offering the means of deciphering his dispatches, which he assures me with every appearance of candour will be found to contain nothing unfriendly to this Country. It is his wish in the meantime that no idea may circulate of his being a Conspirator.

With great regard Dr Sir   Your obed servt.   A Hamilton

Timothy Pickering Esqr.

Copy, in the handwriting of Philip Church, Hamilton Papers, Library of Congress.

1. On Friday, March 29, 1799, the [Boston] *Massachusetts Mercury* reported: "On Wednesday arrived from Alicans, via Gibraltar, the fast-sailing armed brig

Alers, Capt. Rich, only 29 days from the latter port, where he remained but 8 hours. The American Consul [John Gavino] confided to his care a package of Dispatches, written in cyphers, addressed to Citoyen TALLEYRAND, and found on board the ship Astrea, capt. Pearce, from New York, and professedly bound to Corunna in Spain. The ship was met with at sea by a British frigate—and capt. Pearce was desired to receive on board a few Spanish prisoners, which he refusing, with singular vehemence, suspicions were excited respecting her true designation, and the neutrality of her cargo. In consequence of which she was taken possession of. A few days afterwards, the Cabin Boy, in taking a bottle of porter from some straw in the stern locker, drew forth a letter, which the Captain, who was standing by, with confusion, instantly seized and pocketed. This being communicated to the Prize Master, induced him to search for other papers; and between the sealing and the quarter deck over the cabin was found the Dispatches in Cyphers. The nature of the letter from the locker, we have not heard. When the Prize arrived at Gibraltar the Captain and a Passenger were put into confinement. Soon after Capt. Rich arrived, on Wednesday. These papers were carried to the PRESIDENT at Quincy. Nothing has yet transpired of their contents."

A document, entitled "List of papers received . . . Samuel Cooper Esqr on Wednesday afternoon 27th March 1799," indicates that on that date Cooper presented these documents to President Adams at Quincy (copy, Adams Family Papers, deposited in the Massachusetts Historical Society, Boston). Two letters were given to Adams: Jean Antoine Bernard Rozier to Talleyrand, October 27, 1798, and Rozier to Talleyrand, November 22, 1798, which included an extract of a letter from Rozier to General Gabriel Marie Théodore Joseph, comte de Hédouville, November 20, 1798. Both letters are in code. Cooper also delivered to Adams a number of dispatches from John Gavino, United States consul at Gibraltar, including his letter of February 13, 1799, to Pickering explaining how the Rozier letters had come into his possession (AD, Adams Family Papers, deposited in the Massachusetts Historical Society, Boston; copies, Adams Family Papers, deposited in the Massachusetts Historical Society, Boston). Adams asked Cooper to have the Rozier letters deciphered. On March 28, 1799, Cooper wrote to Adams: "I find that Mr. [James] Lovell is the only Man in Boston capable of deciphering intricate papers. I have conversed with him upon the subject & shown him the method in which the figures are placed. He despairs of being able to find a Key to the papers, but will nevertheless wait upon your Excellency to see if there is a possibility of obtaining a Key by which he can decypher them" (ALS, Adams Family Papers, deposited in the Massachusetts Historical Society, Boston). On April 1, 1799, Adams wrote to Pickering: "Mr. Samuel Cooper came out with a packet from the consul at Gibraltar. My son [Thomas Boylston Adams] and Mr. [William] Shaw have taken the tedious pains to copy them. No man in Boston is found to undertake to decypher them. I hope you will find one in Philadelphia. Mr. Lovel the naval officer, who was much occupied in congress formerly in cyphering & decyphering, came out to see them; but despairs of being able to make a key. These numbers may contain much treason & they may be as empty as the tubs & bucketts at Charlestown. I thought it best to keep the copies from abroad for the present" (LC, Adams Family Papers, deposited in the Massachusetts Historical Society, Boston).

The letters in cipher were written by Rozier, former French vice consul at New York. On May 31, 1799, Pickering wrote to Joshua Sands, collector of customs at New York, that he had reason to think the letters in question were "harmless" (ALS, letterpress copy, Massachusetts Historical Society, Boston). For a summary of the contents of the letters in question, see Pickering to H, June 18, 1799.

From Ebenezer Stevens [1]

New York, April 4, 1799. "I have made out Mr Mangin acct of what I think he ought to be paid for his services [2] & I wish you to examine it, & if you approve of the Same, you will give me an order to pay him. . . . I have not made the price, it is what the military Committee [3] agreed to give him."

LS, Hamilton Papers, Library of Congress.
  1. For background to this letter, see Joseph F. Mangin to the Military Committee of New York City, June 18, 1798; Mangin to H, August 7, 1798, January 11, 1799; Stevens to H, November 29, 1798, February 29, 1799. See also the introductory note to H to James McHenry, June 1, 1798.
  2. Mangin's account reads:
"Military Committee

To Joseph F Mangin Dr:

1798
Novr. 15   For services rendered as Engineer from the 18th June last to this Day is 150 days at 5 Dollars pr. Day $750.

Ebenezer Stevens Esqr. Agent for the War department of the United States

To Joseph F. Mangin Dr:

1798
Augst. 10   For services rendered as Engineer employed in conjunction with Messrs Hill & fleming from the 18 June last 53 days @ 2 dollars pr. Day $106.
1799
Jany 1   For services as Engineer directing the Completion of the fortifications and Buildings erected in Fort Jay from the 15 Novemr to this day 46 days @ 5 dollrs pr Day   230.

Dollrs.   336"

(D, in the handwriting of Ebenezer Stevens, Hamilton Papers, Library of Congress).

  3. The Military Committee of New York City consisted of Aaron Burr, H, and Stevens. See "Call for a Meeting," June 4, 1798, note 2.

To James McHenry

New York, April 8, 1799. ". . . It has been suggested . . . that an advance of money to the officers on account of their pay is necessary.[1] All of them have to incur considerable expence for their equipment and many of them cannot afford it out of their own funds. I agree in the necessity of the measure. The advance ought not to be less than four Months pay and ought to extend to all the additional Regiments. The use of music is very conducive to the success of the recruiting service. It is therefore desireable that an adequate number of drums and fifes should accompany the Cloathing. Let me now urge that not a moment may be lost in furnishing the money cloathing and instruments of music—and that the measures for this purpose may embrace all the States from New Hampshire to Virginia inclusively. By the time it can be effected other preparatory steps will be matured in all of them. You have only sent me 90 copies of the recruiting instructions.[2] I ought to have at least 20 to a Regiment. I pray you to forward to me the residue without delay. It will be useful to put them in Packages of Twenty franked by you. . . ."

ADf, Hamilton Papers, Library of Congress.
    1. This suggestion was made in William S. Smith to H, March 11, 1799 (listed in the appendix to Volume XXII).
    2. See McHenry to H, March 21, 1799, note 10; H to McHenry, April 3, 1799.

To James McHenry

New York April 8 1799

Sir

Nothing can be more desireable than a well digested plan for connecting the different parts of our Military System, in regard to the procuring and issuing of supplies. I send you the outline of a scheme for that purpose. It is important that this, or a substitute more eligible, should be without delay established. It is particularly essential that the channels through which supplies are to pass to the troops and the modes of application for these should be designated and understood. The plan now transmitted embraces this among other objects. I beg leave to urge a speedy attention to the subject.

With great respect & consideration   I have the honor to be Sir Your Obed servant

The Secretary of War

ADf, Hamilton Papers, Library of Congress; copy, Connecticut Historical Society, Hartford; copy, Hamilton Papers, Library of Congress.

[ENCLOSURE]

Plan for the providing and issuing of Military Supplies [1]

The business of providing shall constitute one distinct branch of service that of issuing another.

The *Purveyor* shall be charged with the procuring of all supplies except those for which contracts are made directly by the Chiefs of the Treasury or War Departments.

The Superintendant of Military Stores shall superintend the issues of all supplies.

The Purveyor shall have near him three *Assistants*, by whatsoever Denomination, one in relation to the supplies which according to past practice fall within the department of Quarter Master General including the means of Transportation—another in relation to the supplies which according to past practice fall within the Department of Commissary of Provisions with the Addition of Medical & Hospital a third in relation to the supplies which according to past practice fall within the Department of Commissary of Military Stores with the addition of cloathing. The person who now resides at the seat of Government in quality of Qr. Master General may perform the duty of the first mentioned Assistant.

The Superintendant of Military Stores shall have near him *three* principal Clerks, each of whom particularly to superintend the issues in one of the abovementioned branches; aided by as many store keepers as may be necessary.

The Purveyor shall have with each army a Deputy to be charged with the procuring of all supplies necessary to be procured with the army.

The Superintendant shall have with each army a Deputy who shall have under him three Assistants, one to superintend the issues of Quarter Master's Stores another to superintend the issues of Provisions—a third to superintend the issue of other Military Stores & Cloathing.

The Purveyor & his Deputies shall deliver over all that they pro-

1. ADf, Hamilton Papers, Library of Congress; copy, Connecticut Historical Society, Hartford; copy, Hamilton Papers, Library of Congress; copy, Massachusetts Historical Society, Boston; copy, Adams Family Papers, deposited in the Massachusetts Historical Society, Boston.

vide to the Superintendant and his Deputies. The actual custody and issuing of articles to be with the Store Keepers pursuant to the written orders of the Superintendant and his deputies. The Quarter Master General with the Main Army & the Deputy Quarter Master General with each separate army shall have the superintendance of the Deputies of the Purveyor with the respective armies; to see that they do their duty according to their instructions from the heads of their respective Branches & the orders of the Commander of the Army.

The Inspector General with the main army & the Deputy Inspector General with each separate army shall have a like charge of the Deputies of the Superintendant of Military Stores.

These Officers to serve as checks upon the respective Deputies & points of Union between the Military & Civil authorities.

The Pay Master General shall reside at the seat of Government and be the fountain of all issues of money for the pay bounty &c. of the Troops.

He shall have a Deputy with each army who shall be charged with the issuing of all monies to the Regimental Pay Masters.

The Quarter Master of each *Division* shall be charged with the procuring of all supplies which may be occasionally necessary for such division in addition to the general Supplies.

The Quarter Master of each Brigade shall be charged with the like duty, when the brigade is detached only, and always with the superintendence of the issues for such brigade and consequently with the direction of all brigade Officers having the custody of supplies.

Each Brigade shall have a Commissary of Forage and another of Provisions to be charged respectively with the issues of those articles.

The Regimental Quarter Master shall receive and issue all supplies for the Regiment except of money or cloathing.

The Regimental Pay Master shall receive and issue all supplies of money and cloathing for the Regiment.

The Regimental Pay Master shall issue monies for the recruiting service to the Company Officers charged with that service, pursuant to Warrants from the commanding Officer of the Regiment or from the superintending officer of the recruiting service for such Regiment taking from each an Accountable receipt.

Whenever it is practicable, he will himself pay the Officers non Commissioned officers and privates of his Regiment individually. When by necess⟨ity⟩ of distant detachment, this cannot be done, ⟨he⟩ will deliver the money to the Officers commanding companies or to the officers commanding parts of companies at stations too distant for the agency of the commanders of Companies, taking from each an accountable Receipt. The money must in each case be paid and issued pursuant to pay rolls signed by such commanding Officers, and wherever it is practicable accompanied by warrants of the Commanding Officers of Regiments, or of batalions when detached.

For all monies which shall be issued to officers to be disbursed by them they shall account monthly with the Regimental Pay Master producing to him the requisite vouchers. Upon every such accounting he shall give a certificate of the substance thereof to the Officer with whom such accounting shall be specifying therein the vouchers which shall have been produced & left with him. This accounting shall be provisional only and liable to the revision and controul of the proper Officer of the War Department, to whom the accounts and vouchers must be forwarded.

The same regulations as nearly as the subject will admit shall be observed in respect to the issuing of Cloath⟨ing⟩ and other articles provisions excepted which shall be issued to the Non Commissioned officers & soldiers and in respect to the accounting for the same.

Every Receipt for pay bounty or other matter from a Non Commissioned officer or private who cannot write shall be certified by a commissioned Officer, who whenever it shall be practicable, shall be other than the person for whom it is to serve as a voucher.

All Documents or returns upon which issues of money or other articles are to be made must be countersigned by the Chief Officer of the Regiment or other particular corps for which the same is to be issued.

The Accounts of Regimental Pay Masters & Quarter Masters shall previous to their transmission to the War Department be presented to the commanders of Regiments or of Batalions when detached & to the persons from whom respectively they shall have received the objects for what they are accountable who shall summarily examine them and certify their opinion respectively.

The above regulation shall apply to all persons who may act as substitutes for the Officers to whom they relate.

All returns & requisitions for obtaining supplies from the Department of War shall go from the Deputy Superintendant of Military Stores with each army to the said Superintendant.

Estimates for supplies shall be reported by the Deputy Quarter Master General with each army to the Commander of such army and shall be by him transmitted to the Secretary of War with his opinion. Each Deputy shall send a duplicate of every estimate to the Quarter Master General, who shall report to the Commander in Chief general estimates for all the troops of the United States illustrated by the particular estimates; which general estimates shall be transmitted by the Commander in Chief to the Secretary of War with his opinion.

To James McHenry

New York, April 8, 1799. "The Commander in Chief having approved the idea of calling the Pay Master to the Seat of Government,[1] I send you inclosed by his direction an order for him to repair to the seat of Government. . . ."[2]

ADfS, Hamilton Papers, Library of Congress.
  1. George Washington to H, March 25, 1799.
  2. H to Caleb Swan, April 3, 1799.

From Timothy Pickering [1]

Philadelphia April 8 1799.

Dear Sir, (private)
You doubtless know General Eustace much better than I do. He mentions your name, as well as Mr. Jays, as of persons whom he respects. The inclosed extract from his news-paper publications of

ALS, Hamilton Papers, Library of Congress; ALS, letterpress copy, Massachusetts Historical Society, Boston.
  1. For background to this letter, see John Skey Eustace to H, October 27, November 3, 20, 1798.

last August give his picture of your friend Mr King.[2] In the same
series of papers he undertakes the vindication of Fulwar Skipwith,[3]
our late consul general at Paris, as an excellent patriot and an up-

2. The enclosure, which is in Pickering's handwriting, reads: "Extract from
the publications of General Eustace, (under the signature of 'An American
Soldier,') in the Gazette of [Archibald] Mc.Lean & [John] Lang of New-York,
in 1798, about the month of August:
"Having recited a letter from Mr. [William Vans] Murray, minister of the
U. S. at the Hague, relative to his (General E's) arrest in Holland, & the endeavours of Mr. M. to procure his enlargement, for which Genl. E. pays him
his tribute of gratitude, General Eustace adds—
" 'I shall not here contrast the dignified patronage, the cordial Sympathy,
the sedulous energy of this minister, with the pettifogging quirks, the *faithless*
profers of 'faithful service,' the treacherous negligence of another. I shall content myself with observing; that as our Constitution is virtually, if not expressly, Aristocratico-democratic, I could wish to see men of *native* respectability almost exclusively chosen to represent us *abroad*. There we can only be
known by the patterns we exhibit: the Man of birth and *early* education, will
do honour by doing Justice to the Man of our choice at home; the clod-bred
Rustic will ever prove the obsequious lackey of foreign Lords; for very few
exceptions will be found to the old rule of Horace:'
" ' "Quo semel est imbuta recens servabit adorem Testa dice." '
"In another place General E. says—'I promised, with due candour, to Mr. Mur-
ray, the prejudices long before excited *in France*, against the Chief of the
Union; enhanced by the perfidy of Mr. [Rufus] King [United States Minister
to Great Britain], in England; and then suspended by his' (Mr. Murray's) 'dig-
nified and unequivocal deportment.' " (Hamilton Papers, Library of Congress.)
These extracts are from an article by Eustace in *The New-York Gazette and
General Advertiser*, August 24, 1798.
Eustace arrived in England in February, 1797, from France. In explaining the
reasons for his exile, Eustace wrote: "To satisfy myself fully on the subject of
my Exile, I immediately waited on the Minister of Police [Charles Cochon de
Lapparent], with a Member of the Council of Ancients, to learn from him the
reasons assigned by the Directory for this act of extreme rigor. I urged that,
however recommendatory to me *in England*, the order, as it then appeared,
might affect my reputation in other parts of Europe; and particularly in the
United States. I added, that it would afflict me profoundly, should it create a
belief, *any where*, that I had violated the laws of hospitality or of amity during my residence under the protection of the French Government. I shall give
the reply he made me, in his own words. 'I am, said the Minister, as much in
the dark as yourself respecting the cause of your banishment; and it is for this
reason, that I omit to execute the order in its full extent. Were you so notori-
ously culpable as to merit such treatment, your crimes should not, and would
not, have escaped my vigilance. For some months past, not a single action, not
a single expression of yours, has remained unknown to my office. . . . I now
assure you . . . that every report of your conduct has evinced the most exemplary civic virtue. . . . A law exists, which authorizes the Directory to remove
even unoffending strangers at ten leagues from Paris, to this law alone you are
obnoxious; and by it alone shall I be governed in the present instance. . . .'
As I expressed a desire to embark for America, but to take England in my
route, he applauded my intention of removing *voluntarily* from France . . ."
(*The New-York Gazette and General Advertiser*, August 23, 1798). On February 22, 1797, Eustace wrote to King: "Having received a verbal order yesterday, said to be from the Duke of Portland [William Henry Cavendish-

Bentinck]—'*to leave this capital within twenty-four hours, and the Kingdom as expeditiously as possible,*' I have to request your passport for Lisbon. . . . having been asked whether I knew a certain book, on a leaf of which was my name in print, (the contents or title of which were not shewn me), I thought proper to reply—*That I did not feel it to consist either with my duty or my dignity to avow or deny it*—on which answer, the sentence of exile was politely pronounced. The fact is, that the letters comprising the book in question were written ten months previous to the signing of the Treaty of Amity *between the United States and Great Britain;* they were not printed or published by me, and were not published for sale; they were written, dated and printed and the blanks filled up by a friend of mine; and though I would not condescendingly submit to any sort of examination by the Secretary [Thomas Carter] of a *British* Secretary of State, on any book or pamphlet printed at Paris, yet I tell you, Sir, whilst I tribute to those personages the kind of respect they merit from me" (John Skey Eustace, *Exile of Major General Eustace, A Citizen of The United States of America, from the Kingdom of Great-Britain, by order of His Grace The Duke of Portland, Minister for the Home Department, &c. &c. &c.* [London: Printed for J. Parsons and J. Owen, 1797], 4–5). The book in question was *Letters on the Crimes of George III, addressed to Citizen Denis, by an American Officer in the Service of France* (Paris: H. Jansen et Comp., 1797). On March 7, 1797, King informed Eustace that ". . . no Foreign Minister possesses authority to resist the execution of the Resolutions of the Government where he resides—if the resolutions are in his opinion injurious to the rights of his country, he may make representations against them. . . . I have not been able to effect a change in the Resolution of this Government requiring you to leave the Country" (Eustace, *Exile*, 41). On the same day Eustace wrote to King: ". . . the reptile [King] who betrays his trust, and shrinks from the exercise of his highest duty (by a denial of protection to one of those fellow citizens from whose prowess and whose purses are drawn the entire profit and splendor of his present place and equipage) sinks beneath the dignity of personal reproach or revenge" (Eustace, *Exile*, 42). In late March, 1797, Eustace sailed from England to The Hague (*The New-York Gazette and General Advertiser*, August 23, 1798). King wrote to William Vans Murray on March 31, 1798: "P. S. Be cautious of Genl. Eustace; he is a very troublesome, but I do not think in any way a dangerous character. He was sent out of England, and his conduct towards me was rude and ungentlemanlike. He began his acquaintance with me with the Tale that I perceive he has related to you, respecting [James] Monroe, [Samuel] Fulton and others. By Monroe's Book I observe that Eustace was one of his addressers when he was replaced by General [Charles Cotesworth] Pinckney; Be assured that he is a more suitable acquaintance of Monroe than of you or me. He will be a Tale bearer between you and others, with whom he may seek an acquaintance, and is base enough for the office. In the end he will quarrel with you, either because you will not lend money, or countenance him in Pretensions that he will have no right to make" (King, *The Life and Correspondence of Rufus King*, II, 295).

While in the Netherlands Eustace was arrested, and in the "Embassy of Mr. Monroe" he wrote: ". . . I published, in August, 1797, a prediction of the subjugation of those Provinces by France, made as early as the year 1794. Having consummated this hellish purpose, in the seizure and exile of all the patriotic Members of the National Convention, by the partizans of the French Directory, on the 22d. January last, *only three days* were suffered to elapse before I was seized at my lodgings, and at midnight, by a party of eight or ten civil officers, headed by two Deputies of the *purified* Assembly! All the papers, public and private, found in my Apartment (my military and travelling

Diary, Correspondence, &c.) were carried in triumph to the Seat of Government, in three large trunks; escorted by three national Representatives—from an accident, not worth relating, my Biographical Journal escaped their inquisitorial scrutiny.

"I remained a State Prisoner, under a strong guard, without communication with any other person than the American Agent and my Physician, and this in the presence of a municipal officer, till the 16th February! The scarcely regenerated Batavian Convention had devoted the whole Day of the 13th to an investigation of my conduct. . . . the result was, that a solemn and sententious decree passed the Senate, requiring me TO LEAVE THE TERRITORY OF THE REPUBLIC IN THREE TIMES TWENTY-FOUR HOURS." (*The New-York Gazette and General Advertiser*, August 23, 1798.) See also Murray to John Quincy Adams, February 3, 20, 1798 (ALS, Adams Family Papers, deposited in the Massachusetts Historical Society, Boston).

Eustace is referring to the fact that in January, 1798, the "unitarist democrats" at The Hague effected a coup against the moderates. The leaders of the coup included Charles Delacroix de Constant, the French minister at The Hague, Herman Willem Daendals, the commander of the Dutch Army, and Barthélemy Catherine Joubert, the head of the French occupation forces. On January 22, 1798, the Batavian assembly convened. See *Réimpression de L'Ancien Moniteur*, January 31, 1798.

Murray, who secured Eustace's release, wrote to Pickering on March 8, 1798: "In a private letter I may venture to speak of individuals who may have *some* effect upon the public opinion. General Eustace who has been ordered to quit this nation in a few days sets off to America. He did not live at this place; and in consequence of expressions which I heard he was in the habit of using against the government of the United States I paid him not the smallest attention. He had expressed his intention of giving up his citizenship. I considered him as a weak enthusiast; very self-important.

"On his arrest I did not attend to him till I received a letter from him, acknowledging his errors, upon his determination respecting citizenship and his opinions respecting the French. On this he has completely satisfied me, that though his conviction is sincere, it was in a great degree forced. He assured me it was much owing to Mr. Harper's pamphlet.

"As I knew that he meant to go to America, and had to a certain degree attracted attention there; and would from his manners excite more, as well from a motive if possible of firing his mind with truth and genuine American zeal, I invited him to dine with me at Rotterdam because he was not suffered to come here. I knew also that he must possess much of the secrets of American Jacobins in Europe. I was not disappointed, particularly in my last object. As to the first, time only can show how far I was instrumental. The last was of most importance, & I think, sir, that if he be a little attended to, as he has a good deal of vanity, he will give some information of consequence respecting several dark particulars of the Southwestern and western plots of [Pierre Auguste] Adet, [Samuel] Fulton, [A. W.] Waldron and others. Of the second, he has a paper (a copy) of some importance as adding evidence to evidence. He can give much information respecting the public affairs and private incidents which gave to these a strange complexion at Paris from the Spring 1793 till 1795. Though I am sure that he cannot hurt the U States, yet I thought that such a convert might be extremely useful at this moment. It may be useful for obtaining all the intelligence that he   to mention that Mr. Vining is his old friend. Formerly he admired the leaders of opposition. It is right also, sir, to inform you that he keeps a journal of things and of conversation, and is apt to publish private correspondence.

right man. In his *reproaches* and in his *vindication* he is equally unfortunate.

These publications of Genl. Eustace he had cut out of the news-
papers, and pasted the columns on the leaves of two books—old
army lists of Great Britain. These he had lent me—one (containing
a long letter addressed to me) at my request [4]—the other he sent me
unasked. I have incautiously detained them too long—so that he intimated that he must come to Philaa. to demand them; suggesting at
the same time, that he presumed an officer of the government would
not refuse to return what had been lent him at his request.[5] I returned one volume by the mail of the 5th instant,[6] and the other by

---

"I shall give him a letter to Mr. Harper, to whom, if you please, you can
communicate anything in this letter. He published his correspondence with
Mr. King. A love of distinction through small means is the principal cause of
all his actions, and in such hands as you can put him will be a clue to all he
knows." (ALS, deciphered, Massachusetts Historical Society, Boston.) See also
Pickering to Murray, May 22, 1798 (ALS, Massachusetts Historical Society,
Boston). Robert Goodloe Harper's pamphlet is entitled *Observations on the
Dispute between the United States and France* (3rd ed., Philadelphia: Pub-
lished by William Cobbett, May, 1798).

John Vining, a lawyer from Delaware, was a member of the Continental
Congress from 1784 to 1786. He served in the House of Representatives from
1789 to 1793 and in the United States Senate from 1793 until his resignation
in 1798. For Eustace's praise of Murray, see *The New-York Gazette and General Advertiser*, August 24, 1798.

3. Skipwith was consul general of the United States in France from 1795 to
1799. For Eustace's "vindication" of Skipwith, see *The New-York Gazette and
General Advertiser*, September 11, 12, 1798.

4. See Eustace to H, November 3, 1798, note 3.

5. On April 1, 1799, Eustace wrote to Pickering: "As my former Letter may
probably have miscarried, or the object of a personal demand may have been
forgot amidst the public concerns of the session, I have now to request that
the two Selections from the N. Y. Gazette (which I forwarded in compliance
with the desire contained in your favor of the 30th. October) may be returned
to me.

"As General Hamilton was the bearer of one of these pamphlets, they can
be transmitted to this gentleman; or sent directly to my address. It is scarcely
necessary to add, Sir, that it would be a subject of serious consequence to my
health, and feelings, to make the journey to Philadelphia—in order to demand
them in person, and no act of my life can authorize a belief, that I would sit
down patiently under a privation of this sort, were it (as I <trust> *it is not*)
possible—that an officer of the Government should refuse to restore anything
confided to him at his particular and *written* request." (ALS, Massachusetts
Historical Society, Boston.) For Eustace's "former Letter," see Eustace to
Pickering, February 9, 1799 (ALS, Massachusetts Historical Society, Boston).
See also Eustace to H, November 3, 1798, note 2.

6. Pickering endorsed Eustace's letter of April 1, 1799: "April 5th. sent one
of his volumes."

this day's post addressed to him.[7] I trouble you with this information, because he desired me to send them either to himself or to you; and because he is of so singular a character there is no foreseeing what use he will make of facts and circumstances seemingly of little or no consequence.

If you have not already seen these publications, he will probably put them into your hands. I will therefore just remark that I was surprized to hear, while at Trenton last autumn,[8] that he had addressed a letter, or a series of letters, to me, on the affairs of France: this led me to request him to send them to me: for I did not take the newspapers of Mc.Lean & Lang.[9] But I was equally surprized to see his exordium—the motive or pretext for addressing me—or perhaps more properly the *introductory incident:* [10] That I had asked some questions & desired him to give me information, concerning the discipline & tactics of the French army, to great improvements in which, beyond any of their neighbours, I was disposed to ascribe in part their unexampled successes. His answers he says were very satisfactory to me: but proposed that I should commit my question to writing, that the information might be more full & accurate. This I have not done: for his verbal answers were so far from satisfactory, that I derived no information from him. His answer was substantially

7. On April 8, 1799, Pickering wrote to Eustace: "I send herewith your other volume of papers—the former I transmitted in the mail of last Friday" (ALS, Massachusetts Historical Society, Boston).

8. In mid-August, 1798, the United States Government moved to Trenton because of the yellow fever epidemic in Philadelphia. See Oliver Wolcott, Jr., to H, August 9, 1798, note 4.

9. Eustace's letter to Pickering, dated September 13, 1798, is printed in installments in *The New-York Gazette and General Advertiser*, October 10, 11, 12, 13, 20, 24, 25, 1798.

10. In his letter to Pickering, Eustace wrote: "You made me a long and friendly visit, at the moment of my departure from Philadelphia in July last, to solicit information on a subject which was considered of some importance to government, in the actual situation of our Country: my replies to your several questions were so apparently satisfactory, that I feel the less reluctance in now submitting *to you* a Project immediately connected with the Department of State.

"You will remember an observation of mine, *in our first conference,* that on so various and indefinite a topic as '*the Discipline of the French army,*' it would be more pleasing to me (and probably more serviceable to government) were the questions arranged at leisure, and with my answers, *detailed in writing*—as I could then present an equally prompt, though a more lasting testimony of my professional researches abroad; and of the very unreserved confidence, with which I made a tribute of them at home." (*The New-York Gazette and General Advertiser,* October 10, 1798.)

—That it was so long since he had served in the French army, and they had in the mean time made so many alterations in their military system, that he could tell me nothing about it!

I am dear sir,   truly & respectfully yours   T. Pickering.

General Hamilton.

To Oliver Wolcott, Junior

New York April 8. 1799

Dr. Sir

I send you in confidence the copy of a letter of this date to the Secretary of War and of the plan to which it refers. Consider it well. Make the Secretary of War talk to you about it, without letting him know that I have sent it to you—And urge the establishment of some plan which will effectually organise this important branch of our Military service. The proper course in the interior of the army is indicated by the plan I present. The connections between the Agents with the army and the Principal officers at the Seat of the Government admit of such modifications as may be deemed best. I think it desireable to separate the Quarter Master General from the business of procuring supplies and make him and his deputies in this respect checks. In addition to this duty he will have numerous military functions of great importance, which will give him abundant employment.

With great regard I am   Dr Sir   Your obed ser   A Hamilton

Oliver Wolcott Esq

ALS, Connecticut Historical Society, Hartford; copy, in the handwriting of Philip Church, Hamilton Papers, Library of Congress.

From James McHenry

War Department, April 9, 1799. Acknowledges receipt of Hamilton's letter of April 8, 1799. Has directed that "advanced pay" for officers be provided to the regimental paymasters.

LS, Hamilton Papers, Library of Congress.

To James McHenry

New York April 9. 1799

Sir

Your letter of the 4th. instant, informs me of the contracts, which have been already made, and of the measures, which are in train for forming others in the states where none at present exist. There is an omission of New Jersey. I request information concerning this State also.

You understand me rightly as to the issuing of Cloathing through the Regimental Pay Master. The execution will no doubt require to be accommodated in some such manner as you mention, to avoid inconvenient travelling of the Pay Masters and double transportation. It is only essential that the business shall always be managed in concert with the Pay Master. And it must be made the duty of the person, whose aid he may in any case require to obtain duplicate receipts from those to whom the cloathing shall be delivered and to transmit one of each to the Pay Master. Where he is very near that person he will himself take more immediately the management, using however his assistance in the transportation. For Pensylvania Delaware and New York The Quarter Master at Philadelphia naturally presents himself as the Auxiliary of the Pay Master. But it is necessary for you to fix and communicate to me a person and a station in each of the other states to whom and which you will cause to be forwarded the supplies of money and cloathing. I will then take care that the Regimental Pay Masters be instructed in conformity. The sooner, the better.

Let me urge you to send forward the cloathing and money to all the states, in which officers have been appointed as suggested in a former letter.[1] Other preparation will be mature as soon as this can be done.

Permit me also to remind you of the additional supply of recruiting instructions,[2] the prompt transmission of which is material.

With great respect

ADf, Hamilton Papers, Library of Congress.
1. H to McHenry, April 8, 1799.
2. See H to McHenry, April 3, 8, 1799.

To Richard Hunewell and Nathan Rice [1]

New York April 10th. 1799

Gentlemen

In consequence of a letter of which the inclosed is a copy,[2] the arrangement, of which a copy is also inclosed, was made by General Brooks.[3] But you will perceive that it is incomplete in respect to the delineation of the subdistricts and the fixing upon a place in each for a rendezvous. This place ought to be chosen with an eye to the accommodation of the recruits, to the convenient procuring of supplies on the spot, and to the easy conveyance of such as are to be sent there. I request that you will in concert with General Brooks complete the arrangement and transmit me the result.

Expecting a more rapid progress in the preliminary measures for

ADf, Hamilton Papers, Library of Congress.
1. During the American Revolution Hunewell served as a second lieutenant in the Third Continental Artillery Regiment. On March 3, 1799, he was appointed lieutenant colonel in command of the Fifteenth Regiment of Infantry (*Executive Journal*, I, 322, 323).

Rice served in the Continental Infantry during the American Revolution. He was an aide-de-camp to General Benjamin Lincoln and at the close of the war was a major in the Fourth Massachusetts Regiment. On March 3, 1799, Rice was appointed lieutenant colonel in command of the Fourteenth Regiment of Infantry (*Executive Journal*, I, 322, 323).

2. See "Circular on the Recruiting Service," February 18–19, 1799.

3. John Brooks of Massachusetts, who had served in the American Revolution from Lexington and Concord to the end of the war in 1783, was a brigadier general in the United States Army from April 11, 1792 to November 1, 1796. On July 19, 1798, he was again appointed brigadier general, but he declined the commission. See Heitman, *United States Army*, I, 249; *Executive Journal*, I, 117, 119, 292, 293; Godfrey, "Provisional Army," 133.

recruiting I had recourse to the Delegation of Massachusettes. Their ideas will be seen in the extract herewith sent of a letter from Mr. Sedgwick.[4] As the plan was digested in the close of the session, when there was little time for deliberation, I have supposed that it may be less perfect than it would otherwise have been. I therefore send it for consideration—to guide but not to govern.

It is now essential that all remaining measures preparatory to the commencement of the recruiting service should be executed with promptitude. I am anxious to receive the nominations of your Regimental Staff. If the consultation directed to be had with your officers towards the selection of a Pay Master should be likely to occasion further material delay,[5] I request, that you will yourself name to me provisionally the person, whom you think most likely to engage the suffrages of your officers.

One of you, to whose hands this letter shall first come, will be pleased to write immediately to the other on the subject of it, so as to effect a meeting without loss of time. Should absence or any other circumstance interfere with the speedy consultation of General Brooks you will together make the arrangement without his aid.

With consideration   I am Gentlemen   Yr Obed ser

Lt Colonels

[ENCLOSURE]

Proposed Arrangement of Recruiting Districts in Massachusetts [6]

[Medford, Massachusetts, March 5, 1799]

In forming the districts & sub-districts for the recruiting service it will be necessary to have recourse to the census taken, by order of the government of the United States, in the year 1790.[7] It will be

4. Theodore Sedgwick to H, February 22, 1799.
5. See "Circular to the Commandants of Regiments," March 23, 1799.
6. Copy, Hamilton Papers, Library of Congress. This document was originally enclosed in Simon Elliott to H, March 6, 1799 (listed in the appendix to Volume XXII).
7. The 1790 census was taken in accordance with the provisions of "An Act providing for the enumeration of the Inhabitants of the United States" (1 *Stat.* 101–03 [March 1, 1790]. For the census of Massachusetts, see *Heads of Families at the First Census of the United States Taken in the Year 1790, Massachusetts* (Washington, D.C., 1908).

found impossible to divide Massachusetts into four equal parts, without discarding many of the present boundaries of counties & towns, & substituting new & appropriate limits. Equality, however, in point of numbers, does not appear to be indicated by any circumstances connected with the recruiting service. Such a division of the state as shall nearly equalize the number of the people in the several districts—preserve as far as possible existing boundaries, & secure the greatest possible degree of compactness for each, will, it is conceived, fulfil the intentions of the Inspector General.

Upon these principles the following arrangement is suggested.

The *first District* to be formed of the counties of

Suffolk, containing 20877 inhabitants,	
Essex	57913
& Middlesex	42737
amounting to	121527

The *second District*, to be formed of the counties of

Hampshire	59681 inhabitants
Berkshire	30291
& ⅔ of Worcester	37872
amounting to	127844

The *third District*, to be formed of the counties of

Plymouth	29535
Bristol	31709
Barnstable	17354
Dukes county & Nantucket	7885
Norfolk	23998
& ⅓ of Worcester	18935
amounting to	129416

The *fourth District*, to be formed of the district of Maine, consisting of the counties of

York	28821
Cumberland	25450
Lincoln	29962
Hancock	9549
Washington	2758
amounting to	96540

It will be observed that the three first districts are formed of the territory of old Massachusetts, & the fourth of the province (as it [is] commonly called) of Maine. A considerable disparity in point of numbers will likewise be observed between the fourth, & the other districts. This disparity, however, it is apprehended may be less in fact than in appearance. But were it real, the inconveniencies attending it would be of less moment, than those which would probably result from uniting in one district parcels of territory seperated from each other by the territory of another state.

It is to be remembered that the district of maine, compared with old Massachusetts, is a new settled country; & it is a well known fact that the population of that district for many years past has increased in a ratio far exceeding the rate of increment ascribed to Massachusetts. It is, therefore, presumable that maine contains at the present moment a sufficient number of inhabitants to raise that district to an average with the other three. It may be observed besides, (& the observation may be applied to the second district with still greater force) that a less pressing demand has been made of late for seamen from that district, than from the first & third, within which are most of our old commercial towns, in which the demand has been very great.

Notwithstanding a wish to preserve the existing boundaries of the counties, it is found requisite to divide the county of Worcester. But the geographical situation & relations of that county render a division of it practicable & convenient. As, however, no correct map of the country is at hand, the line of division is not suggested. For the same reason it is not attempted to form at this moment the twenty subdistricts. With the aid of a correct map of Massachusetts, such as Mr. Carlton's [8] is supposed to be, this may be done at any future moment, without any material retardation of the recruiting service.

Medford March
5th 1799.

8. *An Accurate Map of the Commonwealth of Massachusetts Exclusive of the District of Maine Compiled Pursuant to an Act of the General Court from Actual Surveys of the Several Towns &c. Taken by their Order . . . by Osgood Carleton* (Boston: Published and Sold by O. Carleton and I. Norman; Sold also by W. Norman, No. 75 Newbury Street, 1795). For a listing of

Carleton's maps before 1800, see James C. Wheat and Christian F. Brun, *Maps and Charts Published in America before 1800: A Bibliography* (New Haven and London, 1969).

To James McHenry

New York April 10th. 1799

Sir

As it will require time to form contracts where there are none already existing, I submit that it will be expedient, in such cases, to advance money to some person, to procure them by purchases on account of the Government; Where there is no Agent preferred by you the Regimental Quarter Master Naturally presents himself, as the person to whom the service may be Committed. New Jersey and Connecticut claim in this respect immediate attention.

With great respect I have the honor   to be Sir   Yr most obt. Servt.

Secretary at War

Copy, in the handwriting of Ethan Brown, Hamilton Papers, Library of Congress.

From George Washington

Mount Vernon, April 10, 1799. "I have received your letter of the 27th. ulto., enclosing a design of dividing the State of Virginia into Divisions, & Subdivisions, for the head quarters of the Rendezvouses in each: asking my opinion of the proper distribution of them, for the convenience of the Recruiting Service. The Grand division of the State, I conceive to be well allotted and with . . . alterations, the sub division of it may be so likewise: but of the latter, I can speak with no precision, because of the number of new Counties which have been established, the situation of which I know not, and even the names of some were unknown to me before. . . . General Lee's absences from home, canvassing for the ensuing Election of Representatives to Congress, and an indisposition with which he has (as I have lately heard) been siesed, from it, has been, I presume, the cause of your not having received an answer to your letter. . . .[1] Not an officer in this State (that has come to my knowledge) has yet received his Commission; to the great dissatisfaction of *all*, & relinquishment of many; who would no longer remain in a state of suspence and idleness."

ALS, Hamilton Papers, Library of Congress; ALS, letterpress copy, George Washington Papers, Library of Congress.
1. H to Henry Lee, February 18, 1799.

From James McHenry

War Department
11th April 1799

Sir,

Governor St Clair [1] has made a representation to me in a letter dated the 18th of February of which I enclose you a copy,[2] by which it appears that much discontent, and uneasiness has been occasioned by the proclamation of Martial law at Detroit.[3] To give a full view of the subject, I have also enclosed extracts from a correspondence between the Secretary of War and Brigadier General Wilkinson relative to the same business.

By the first extract of a letter from the Secretary of War to Brigadier General Wilkinson dated 25 of July 1797 [4] you will perceive that it has been recommended to the commanding officer to suspend, or modify the military law, when no external danger was to be apprehended, so as only to suppress those practices, or sales of liquor to soldiers which incapacitates them from doing their duty, and render the Indians less manageable, and more burdensome.

The second extract from the Secretary of War to General Wilkinson states,[5] generally, the complaints made by the Inhabitants of Detroit, and the President's wish that, if circumstances will admit, the rigor of military law should not be exercised.

The third extract is from a letter of Brigadier General Wilkinson's to the Secretary of War dated Pittsburg March 8th 1798 [6] contains his reasons for proclaming martial law and the necessity there is for its continuance. This letter contains extracts from the general orders issued by the commandant of Detroit while under the British government; by these extracts it appears that the Inhabitants of Detroit have always been subject to martial law since the year 1785.

As this is a subject which requires particular and immediate attention, I request that as soon as you have given it the necessary consideration, you will cause such orders to be issued as the circumstances of the case may require.

I have the honor to be, with great respect, Sir, your most Obt Hb St   James McHenry

ALS, Hamilton Papers, Library of Congress; ALS, letterpress copy, Hamilton Papers, Library of Congress.
1. Arthur St. Clair was governor of the Territory Northwest of the River Ohio. A veteran of the American Revolution, he was a member of the Continental Congress from 1785 to 1787 and a major general and commander of the United States Army in 1791 and 1792.
2. Copy, Hamilton Papers, Library of Congress.
3. This proclamation, which James Wilkinson signed at Detroit on July 12, 1797, reads in part: "To guard the National Interests against the Machinations of its Enemies secret and overt, foreign or domestic, To baffle the arts of seduction which have led to numberless desertions from the public service and to restrain the licentiousness, and the infamous habits of drunkenness, encouraged among the Troops, by the disorderly conduct of the vendors of Ardent Spirits—The commander in chief considers it a duty . . . to declare martial Law, within the line of the Guards, and the limits of the Fortifications of the place and he hereby . . . declares that from and after the date of these presents, all persons resorting or residing within the limits aforesaid, shall be held and considered as followers of the Army, and will be treated accordingly without respect to persons or allegience. It is at the same time declared, that no hindrance will be opposed to the functions of the civil Magistrates, or to the due process of Laws of the Territory" (copy, Hamilton Papers, Library of Congress).
4. Copy, Hamilton Papers, Library of Congress.
5. Copy, Hamilton Papers, Library of Congress.
6. Copy, Hamilton Papers, Library of Congress.

From James McHenry

War Department
11th. April 1799

Sir

The Secretary of the Treasury, has represented to me, in a letter dated the 20th. March ulto.,[1] that a Party of Troops, heretofore ordered, to be detached, to assist the Surveyor General [2] in marking the Indian boundary line, conformably to the Treaty of Greenville,[3] had utterly failed to cooperate, and that in consequence, the Northern line has been marked in no other manner, than the boundaries of Townships. I therefore enclose you, a copy of a letter, from me, to Brigadier General Wilkinson dated the 18th March 1797 [4] advising him of a requisition by the Secretary of the Treasury, for a military escort, to cover the Surveyors while running the necessary lines, and requiring him, on the application of the Surveyor General, and information, when and where the Survey is to commence, to direct a suitable escort, instructed to assist, in marking the exterior line—also an extract from a letter, of General Wilkinson to me, dated the 25th April 1797 [5] which shews, that he had taken preparatory measures, to comply with my orders. You will be pleased, at a convenient time, to ascertain, why the cooperation of the military thus ordered, and intended, did not take place, and make report to me accordingly.

As the marking of the boundary line, is yet incomplete and the Secretary of the Treasury, still thinks military assistance, and protection necessary, to complete it, you will as soon as possible, give directions, that an adequate party of the troops in the North Western Territory, shall attend, at such time and place as shall be pointed out, by the Surveyor General, to cover him, and his workmen, and to assist in marking, such parts of the boundary line, as he may direct.

Mr. Wolcott has been requested, to inform you, of the place, where it is most probable, the Troops will be wanted, to enable you to determine, from what post or place, it will be most convenient and proper, to draw the necessary escort.

I am Sir   with great respect   Your obedient servant

James McHenry

Alexander Hamilton Esqr
Major General of the Armies
of the United States.

LS, Hamilton Papers, Library of Congress; LS, letterpress copy, Hamilton Papers, Library of Congress.
  1. ADf, Connecticut Historical Society, Hartford.

2. Rufus Putnam.

3. This treaty, which was signed on August 3, 1795, was submitted to the Senate on December 9, 1795, and approved on December 22, 1795 (*Executive Journal*, I, 193, 197). For the provisions of this treaty and the negotiations preceding its signing, see *ASP, Indian Affairs*, I, 562–82.

4. Copy, Hamilton Papers, Library of Congress.

5. Copy, Hamilton Papers, Library of Congress.

From James McHenry

War Department, April 11, 1799. Acknowledges receipt of Hamilton's letters of April 8 and 9, 1799, and notes that the contents of the letter of April 8 "will be duly weighed and attended to," but that until a "more perfect" system for supplying the troops is adopted, the existing system, as outlined in his letter to Hamilton of March 21, 1799, will remain in effect. States that he is ready to forward money but only when Hamilton furnishes the names of the particular paymasters who are to distribute it. States that the clothing supply for the New York and Connecticut regiments will be sent within a week and that the clothing for the Pennsylvania and New Jersey regiments will be sent as soon as he is informed of the names of the officers responsible. Suggests that each recruiting officer assemble his recruits at the district's general rendezvous so that they can be supplied with clothing.

LS, Hamilton Papers, Library of Congress; ADf, James McHenry Papers, Library of Congress; LS, letterpress copy, James McHenry Papers, Library of Congress.

From James McHenry

War department April 12. 1799

Sir,

By referring to a list of appointments to the old regiments of Infantry, sent you some time since,[1] you will find the names of the Captains to the respective Companies directed to be added to each of these regiments by the "Act to augment the army of the United States and for other purposes" passed 16. July 1798.[2]

I also transmitted to you the 8th. of March Ult.[3] a list of the names of all the Officers of the Army (old establishment) elapsed according to their respective regiments or Corps, with the dates of their Commissions. These two lists, taken together, will shew you the Officers belonging to each of these regiments.

Lieut Col. Butler,[4] who commands on the frontiers of Tenessee, is desirous to be enabled to recruit the two additional companies, and has requested money and instructions. I have informed him that he would receive his instructions from you and shall remit to his paymaster the necessary Money. I request you to give the orders proper upon this occasion, which may be forwarded to this Office for transmission.

It will also be proper that you should, as soon as possible, issue your orders and instructions for filling up the old regiments to their full complement.

I have the honor to be   with great respect   Your obedient servant
James McHenry

Major General Hamilton

LS, Hamilton Papers, Library of Congress; LS, letterpress copy, James Mc-Henry Papers, Library of Congress.
    1. In the margin opposite this sentence H wrote: "I do not find it." On the other hand, he must have seen the list at some time, for in the Hamilton Papers, Library of Congress, is a document which H endorsed: "List of Promotions in 4 Regiments of Infantry, shewing new Officers of Additional Comps."
    2. Section 1 of "An Act to augment the Army of the United States, and for other purposes" stipulated that "each regiment of infantry . . . shall consist of . . . ten captains . . ." (1 Stat. 604).
    3. See McHenry to H, March 21, 1799, note 9.
    4. A veteran of the American Revolution and a resident of Pennsylvania, Thomas Butler was lieutenant colonel commandant of the Fourth Regiment of Infantry and was stationed at South West Point, Tennessee, a post ". . . situate upon the south bank of the Clinch, within half a mile of its junction with the Tennessee, forty miles from . . . [Knoxville]" (Carter, Territorial Papers, IV, 366).

From James McHenry

War Department, April 13, 1799. "The enclosed copy of a letter from Lieutenant Colonel Strong[1] dated the 23rd: of January ultimo.[2] was intended to have accompanied the papers referred to you in my letter of the 11th. instant. . . ."

LS, Hamilton Papers, Library of Congress; LS, letterpress copy, James Mc-
Henry Papers, Library of Congress; ADf, James McHenry Papers, Library of
Congress.

1. David Strong was the commanding officer of the United States post at
Detroit. A veteran of the American Revolution, he had rejoined the Army in
1785 as a captain and at the time this letter was written he was lieutenant colonel commandant of the Second Regiment of Infantry.

2. In this letter Strong wrote: ". . . At the cession of the Posts on the North-
western frontier to the Government of the United States, they were held and
considered, as entirely subject to Martial Law (as they had antecedently been
done under the administration of Great Britain) for the most obvious reasons,
and more particularly this Post, situated on the margin of a powerful foreign
Nation, and the principal part of the Inhabitants of this place, and the adjacent
Country composed of indocile Canadians, and Subjects of a different Country;
under those circumstances it was found expedient to enforce (until Government had conceived it proper to introduce the operation of the laws of the
Territory) Military polity; and which was acquiesced in, until very recently
without a murmur.

"In order to arrive at a more certain opinion of my situation, I shall take
the liberty of giving you an imperfect description of the place.

"Encompassed on all sides with a stockade extended across the Esplanade,
so as to join the fortified Fort Lerault, the in and egress is by means of gates
where Centinels are placed to guard the Town from the introduction of a too
great number of Indians, and the Inhabitants from every kind of injury.

"Thus secure in their persons and property, they discover a great degree of
dissatisfaction, and complain of this security as an abridgement of their civil
immunities; but this is the least important part of their conduct which I wish
to represent. . . .

"In the execution of this task, altho' not openly opposed, a number of them
have attempted to contravene my orders; prohibiting the Soldiers from receiving credit from them, and anticipating their pay due from the United
States; to the manifest injury of service, and the introduction of a scene of
licentiousness and drunkenness among the Soldiery, subversive of every principle of discipline, and subordination, and a powerful inducement to desertion.

"Civil Officers have been appointed by the Governor of the Territory, and
acting in their several capacities as such, within the line of Centinels, conceiv-
ing that they have a right of exercising in its most unlimited sense, every privilege of a Citizen, however contrary to the interest of Government in a military
point of view.

"Thus circumstanced I confess the delicacy of my situation, and tenacious
of the rights of every person, I feel myself unable to act with that decision,
which my Country and Superiors may claim or look for.

"Perfectly aware of the invincible necessity of an entire subjection to, and
observation of civil law, I entreat you as early as possible, to prescribe the
principles upon which my future conduct can and must be founded." (Copy,
Hamilton Papers, Library of Congress.)

To James McHenry

New York April 13th. 1799

Sir

I have been yesterday & this morning honored with your several favours, three of the 11th and two of the 12th instant.[1]

The injunctions respecting the Indian boundary line will be carefully & promptly attended to. Speedy attention will also be paid to the affair of proclaiming Martial law at Detroit. At present I am not aware how the authority for it is found. But this as well as its expediency will be examined.

It did not appear to me that the measure of sending forward immediately money and cloathing to the several states could be attended with the inconvenience you mention—since it is exactly what has been done with regard to New York and what would naturally be done in the case of every distant State, with the difference only of the anticipation of the names of the Pay Masters. I presumed that these articles would always be sent to some Agents of the Department to deliver them over to the Pay Masters and take their receipts, and that the alternative would be to instruct those agents to deliver them to certain Pay Masters by name or to such persons as the respective Colonels of Regiments should designate to them as the Pay Masters.

It is true that none of my former communications indicates the names of the particular officers assigned to the several Subdistricts. This was a detail which I considered as properly to be referred to the Commandants of the Regiments, leaving it with them to instruct their respective Pay Masters and with these to concert with the agents of the War Department the distribution in detail. If matters so minute as these are to make the circuit of a previous communication through the Commanding General to the Secretary of War the obstacles to the execution of the service will be endless. In making this observation I have nothing in view but to present to consideration this important rule, that the efficient execution of any extensive branch of military service can only be attained by confining the principal actors to general arrangements, & by their employing competent organs and leaving to them the more minute details.

I write however this day to the Commanders of the Regiments of Pensylvania & New Jersey to effectuate the desired information.[2]

With very great respect & esteem   I have the honor to be   Sir Yr. Obed serv

The Secy of War

ADf, Hamilton Papers, Library of Congress.
   1. One of the letters dated April 12, 1799, is printed above. The second is listed in the appendix to this volume and concerns contracts for supplying rations and advances of pay to recruiting stations.
   2. See H to Thomas Lloyd Moore and Aaron Ogden, April 13, 1799.
   Moore, a resident of Philadelphia and a veteran of the American Revolution, was lieutenant colonel commandant of the Tenth Regiment of Infantry. For Ogden, see McHenry to H, April 4, 1799, note 6.

To Thomas Lloyd Moore and Aaron Ogden [1]

New York, April 13, 1799. "Relying that you will lose no time in assigning your Officers to the different subdistricts—I request that you will transmit me a list, showing the name of the *principal* Officer of *each* sub-district and the particular sub-district to which he is assigned. You will also . . . forward a duplicate to the Secy of War."

ADf, Hamilton Papers, Library of Congress.
   1. For background to this letter, see James McHenry to H, third letter of April 11, 1799; H to McHenry, April 13, 1799.

From Nathan Rice

Hingham [Massachusetts] April 13th. 1799

My dear General
   I have the honor to acknowledge the receipt of your favour of the 23rd ulto.;[1] inclosing a list of the officers who are to compose my Regiment, distributed into companies.

I delayed not to convene as many of my officers as could be assembled expeditiously for the purpose of electing a paymaster. A plurality of the votes were in favour of Lieutenant Robert Duncan.[2] The choice met my approbation, & I wish the nomination, if necessary, might meet the sanction of the President. You do not mention Sir, to whom his bonds are to be given, or who is to be the judge of the sufficiency of the sureties.

I have not as yet complied with your orders, in nominating *fit* Characters for Quarter Master & Adjutant not from a disposition to disobey, but from a want of due knowledge of the gentlemen of that grade, to designate the most deserving, & the best qualified among them, & I hope Sir you will admit my appology as sufficient, as those appointments are certainly very important in the organization of a regiment: An unnecessary delay shall not take place— should it be necessary a temporary appointment can be made.

Previous to the receipt of your favour, I had taken the liberty of expressing to you the high sense I entertained of the honor done me in being appointed to so distinguished & responsible a rank, under a General whose virtues, Talents, & bravery have placed him most deservedly second in command in the armies of the United States. I also took the liberty to suggest a query, whether in arranging the officers to each regiment it would not be promotive of harmony in the corps to permit the field officers to agree on their Captains & with them to arrange & assign the subalterns to the companies? As the arrangement is made, I wish to ask whether an exchange of any of the officers, if agreed to by all concerned is admissible, for I am informed some of the Gentlemen are unpleasantly arranged, owing to some private disputes.

The very small knowledge I have already acquired of the officers had convinced me of the propriety of your observations respecting the future adjustments of their rank, & that important alterations will be proper and necessary & that the reforms therefor should be kept silent.

On the subject of the recruiting service which you suggest will speedily commence [3]—permit me to observe that the winter the most promising season for the business being past, a further delay must very much injure it. Our young men will be engaging in husbandry & other employments, oweing to the superior encouragements which will be held out to them, beyond those held out by Government to their soldiers, & render it very difficult to obtain such men as I should wish to command. I hope Sir to have the honor of your particular instructions on this subject, as also on every other which will demand my attention, & beg you will do me the favour to believe I wait your orders therein: & that I am with the

highest esteem & respect Your obedient Servant   N Rice

ALS, Hamilton Papers, Library of Congress.
    1. "Circular to the Commandants of Regiments," March 23, 1799.
    2. Duncan was a lieutenant in the Fourteenth Regiment of Infantry.
    3. See "Circular to the Commandants of Regiments," March 31, 1799; H to Richard Hunewell and Rice, April 10, 1799.

From Arthur St. Clair

Cincinnati [Territory Northwest of the River Ohio]
14th. April 1799 [1]

Dear Sir,
    Under the same cover with this I have taken the liberty to enclose to you some observations of mine on a Letter from George Nicholas of Kentuckey to his friend in Virginia.[2] You will perceive that I have treated you very familiarly,[3] but I am under no apprehension that the purpose will be mistaken. It was a mortification that I could not get them out in proper time, when I had the vanity to suppose they might have done some good farther abroad than Kentucky. The severity of the Winter which disapointed the Printer in paper was the cause. It will not now miss entirely of effect in the Country for which it was chiefly intended.
    Be that as it may, it has afforded me an opportunity, which I embrace with great pleasure of assuring you of the great regard with which I ever am
    Dear Sir   Your obedient servant   Ar St. Clair

ALS, Hamilton Papers, Library of Congress.
    1. This letter is dated March 14, 1799, in *JCHW*, VI, 403–04.
    2. George Nicholas, a veteran of the American Revolution, was a prominent politician in Virginia and Kentucky. His brother, Wilson Cary Nicholas, helped to frame Thomas Jefferson's Kentucky resolutions of 1798. George Nicholas

wrote a defense of the Kentucky resolutions in a pamphlet entitled *A Letter from George Nicholas of Kentucky, to his Friend, in Virginia. Justifying the Conduct of the Citizens of Kentucky, as to some of the Late Invasions of the General Government; and Correcting Certain False Statements, which have been made in the Different States. Of the Views of Actions of the People of Kentucky* (Lexington: Printed by John Bradford, on Main-Street, 1798). St. Clair answered Nicholas in a pamphlet entitled *Observations on a Letter from George Nicholas; of Kentucky; to his Friend in Virginia; in which, Some of the Errors, Misstatements, and False Conclusions in that Letter are corrected, and the late measures of the Government, which have been complained of in Kentucky, are justified by an inhabitant of the North-Western Territory* (Cincinnati: Printed and Sold by Edmund Freeman, Front Street, February 14, 1799).

3. St. Clair mentions H twice in his *Observations*. The first reference reads: "But, there is danger in this army, discovered by mr. Nicholas which is truly alarming:—The *monarchy-loving Hamilton* is now so fixed as to be able, *with one step*, to fill the place of our present commander in chief. I am glad he is not the *democracy-loving Hamilton*, because, I respect that gentleman's character, and if I believed he had the least tincture of that love, I should despise him, notwithstanding the great services he has rendered to this country—greater than all the tribe of democrats, put together, would have been able to render had they been willing, and who would not have been willing had they been able. Then indeed, with an able democrat at their head, an army would be dangerous, and the historic page from whence mr. Nicholas has drawn his illustrations, give excellent instruction on the ambition, the cruelty, and the rapacity of democratic armies. But softly mr. Nicholas; if mr. Hamilton does really love a monarchy, which is not quite so clear, as he was with you, very early engaged in destroying the authority of one of this country, and *persevered in it until it was effected*, he is not within your one step of the command of the army. Were general Washington to resign tomorrow, the office of commander in chief would not devolve upon him, or upon any one else—and tho' a major general and the principal staff officer, he has not advanced a single step towards it. In no other country is that office ever filled but by the special appointment of the sovereign power, without regard to succession. It is too important to be left to a rule that might bring forward a man without talents, or any positive merit. In this country the appointment must be made in the constitutional way; and this has always been the case here: For since the resignation of general Washington, after the revolutionary war, tho' we have always had an army, we never had a commander in chief, until lately that he has been reappointed; so that mr. Hamilton, as to his being hereafter commander in chief, is just where he was before his appointment of major general and inspector" (St. Clair, *Observations*, 35–36).

The second reference reads: "That terrible fellow Hamilton, mr. Nicholas allows, argues well on the security of liberty from the constitution, and that he always argues as it is in the power of man to do, when he has truth on his side. One might be led to infer from that observation, that mr. Nicholas thinks a man may argue well when he has not truth on his side; but I differ from him:—ingeniously he may argue; and we have not a few specimens of it in the course of the letter we are considering . . ." (St. Clair, *Observations*, 39).

Circular to the Commandants of Regiments [1]

Circular   New York April 15. 1799

Sir

It is a question whether it will be most adviseable to distribute the Cloathing for your Regiment among the several *sub*districts to be furnished to the recruits as they shall be raised or to deposit the whole either at the Regimental Rendezvous or at the place which you shall fix as the rendezvous of each district. As the right decision of this question may depend in part upon circumstances of a local nature it is left with you. If it will equally comport with the success of the recruiting service, the last mentioned course is to be preferred; because among other reasons it will avoid expence in transportation and hazard of loss by distribution. In this case, the moment the necessary money shall have been received you may proceed in the recruiting service without waiting for the arrival of the Cloathing.[2]

I am with consideration Sir Yr. Obed servt.

ADf, Hamilton Papers, Library of Congress; LS, to Aaron Ogden, Lloyd W. Smith Collection, Morristown National Historical Park, Morristown, New Jersey.

1. For background to this circular, see James McHenry to H, March 21, April 4, 1799; H to McHenry, March 30, April 9, 13, 1799.

2. In the draft H enclosed this sentence in brackets and wrote: "omit."

From James McHenry

War Department, April 15, 1799. "I have received your favour of the 13th instant. The arrangement of sending the recruiting money, in the first instance to the Regimental Paymasters, instead of through an Agent to them, avoids a Commission of One per Cent generally to the Agent for paying the money to the Paymaster, and doubling the Accounts for the same object in the Accountants Books. Hence it is desirable . . . that the Paymaster should receive the money directly from this department. With respect to the transportation of

Cloathing, it has been suggested that the Cloathing for Pennsylvania, Jersey, and Delaware by being sent in parcels from this place to their respective districts would save double transportation. . . . Have you considered the idea of making an experiment of inlisting at the districts without Cloathing and transferring the Recruits in parcels as inlisted to the General rendezvous? Will not this mode save much transportation? . . ." [1]

LS, Hamilton Papers, Library of Congress; LS, letterpress copy, James McHenry Papers, Library of Congress.
   1. See McHenry to H, third letter of April 11, 1799.

To James McHenry

New York, April 15, 1799. ". . . A letter from General Washington of the 10th. instant has this passage 'Not an officer in this state has yet received his Commission to the great dissatisfaction of all and relinquishment of many, who would no longer remain in a state of suspense and idleness.' There is a strong impatience in the officers every where to have their commissions. It seems to me that it would be adviseable always to issue them as soon as appointments are made dated on the day of the confirmation by the Senate. Where any future alteration of relative rank may require it, the thing may be managed by endorsement or by recalling the former and issuing another Commission. . . . I will thank you, should you be able to procure Aidey's treatise on Court Martials [1] to send it to me." [2]

ADf, Hamilton Papers, Library of Congress.
   1. Stephen Payne Adye, *A Treatise on Courts Martial. Containing, I. Remarks on Martial Law, and Courts Martial in general. II. The Manner of Proceeding against Offenders. To which is added, An Essay, on Military Punishments and Rewards* (New York: Printed by H. Gaine, at the Bible and Crown, in Hanover-Square, 1769).
   2. This sentence is in the handwriting of Philip Church.

From James Wilkinson

Loftus' Heights [Mississippi Territory] Head Quarters
Western Army 15th. April 1799

Sir

It is in consequence of an order from the Minister of War received on the 4th. Inst., that I have now the Honor to begin my correspondence with you.[1]

Accustomed to the frankness of a Soldier, nothing less than the fear of incurring the imputation of adulation or of impertinence could prevent the expression of my feelings on the occasion, but altho I wave professions, I may express the high satisfaction I feel, at finding myself under the orders of a Gentleman, able to instruct me in all things.

I avail myself of the return of Lt. Hyde, of the 1st. Regt., who goes to the seat of Government, to adjust His public Accounts,[2] to send forward this Letter, (with a return of the Troops, stationed at Massac & on the Mississippi) to Cincinnati on the Ohio, from whence it will be transmitted to you, by the ordinary mail: I shall in the course of the Month, endeavour to make up returns from the several Departments to comprize every appertenance to the Service in this Quarter.

ALS, Hamilton Papers, Library of Congress; LS, Hamilton Papers, Library of Congress; Df (incomplete), Chicago Historical Society.

1. James McHenry's order has not been found, but see H to Wilkinson, February 12, 1799.

2. Charles Hyde, a resident of Vermont, was a captain in the first Regiment of Infantry.

On April 18, 1799, William Simmons, accountant of the War Department, wrote to McHenry: ". . . It may not be improper . . . to observe that Mr. Hyde, paymaster to the 1st United States Regiment has received very large sums of money part of which was intended for those soldiers who now claim their pay, and which remain to be accounted for, and if there was no other reason for directing an immediate settlement of his accounts, my being prevented from paying any balances to soldiers for which he has received the money and not yet produced his accounts is in my opinion a very cogent one and no time ought to be lost in directing an immediate settlement.

"I have repeatedly urged a settlement of those accounts and it is my opinion that no measure will be so effective in completing them as ordering Mr Hyde immediately . . . to this City with his vouchers. . . ." (Copy, Hamilton Papers, Library of Congress.)

Refering you for information to my communications, made to the Minister of War on the subject, I am now to report the sailing of the Detachment, destined to the mobile River, on the 10th Inst, under the Orders you will find copied within,[3] which may I hope meet your approbation.

Daily occurrences tend to evince the necessity of a Cordon of Posts, to extend from this point, along the national boundary, to the settlements of Georgia, in order to exclude foreign machinations, to lay the savages at our feet, & to repress the licentiousness of our erratic frontiers-Men. The Testimony enclosed [4] relative to a late robbery, commited on the trace leading from this Territory to Nashville, may be depended on, and it remains a matter of doubt, whether this party was purely savage, whether sent from Pensacola, or excited by one Duffy [5] a lawless Ruffian, not long since a Prisoner at Massac, for trespassing on the Indian Lands North West of the Ohio, from whence He made his Escape.

The Minister of War, in his Letter of the 31st. Jany.[6] having expressed some doubts, of the policy & expediency of taking Post at this place, it becomes my duty to state, in brief, the motives which governed my Conduct in this instance.

The distance of this Territory from National succour & its proximity to a foreign Power, exposes it more to dangers from invasion, than any other point of the Union.

The same causes will render the conquest more easy, & the recovery more difficult; and the occupancy would preserve a communication with the Southern Indians, & greatly facilitate foreign Intrigue & the acts of corruption among our wide extended western Settlements.

The People of this Territory, in general, have too often changed Masters, to foster any fixed principles of policy, or to cherish any permanent attachments to government, they are besides secured by

3. Wilkinson to Captain Bartholomew Shaumburgh, April 5, 1799 (copy, Hamilton Papers, Library of Congress).

4. This is a reference to a deposition, dated March 28–30, 1799, and signed by Joseph Sproull and Charles Conn, which described the Indian raid mentioned by Wilkinson (copy, Hamilton Papers, Library of Congress).

5. This is presumably a reference to Daniel Duffey who had been arrested in 1794 for his part in the Whiskey Insurrection. See Carter, *Territorial Papers*, III, 428–29.

6. McHenry to Wilkinson, January 21, 1799 (copy, Hamilton Papers, Library of Congress). This letter was enclosed in McHenry to H, February 4, 1799.

various causes: in this temper & with such dispositions, a position to controul as well as to protect appeared to me political.

The Spaniards are subordinate to the French, & the regular military of Louisiana is insufficient, to defend the Government for an Hour, against a general rising of the Inhabitants, who have been all armed, are almost exclusively French, & as frantic in their politicks, as the fish-women of Paris.

The heavy Artillery & portable Magazines of an invading Army, must move by Water, & the voyage from New Orleans, to the center of the population of the Territory, may be computed at twenty Days, tho it has been performed in fourteen.

The preceding reflections, which are in my judgment well founded, determined me to condense my small force, to take Post here, & fortify; a resolution which may I hope be justifiable on the following specifick grounds viz.

1st. Because it is the only spot on the Mississippi, below the Ohio, which is safe from the wash of the current, & effectually commands the pass of the River at all Seasons.

2ndly. Because the site is uncommonly strong, & the natural form of the ground, highly susceptible of defensive works, on œconomical terms.

3rdly. Because the position is approximate to the national boundary, & at the lower extremity of the Territorial settlements.

4thly. Because an insidious Enemy, such as we have to apprehend, meditating a stroke at this Territory, could masque his preparations behind Batton rouge, the frontier Port of Louisiana on the River & from thence, was no Barrier interposed, by an Energetic movement, might in eight or ten Days gain possession of the Country; a period too short for the transmittal of the Intelligence, to any Position we could take on the Mississippi, above the mouth of the Yazou.

5thly. Because this position properly fortified, will enable us to repel superior force, & to check an Host, until succours may be drawn from the upper Country—or should offence become necessary to carry a coup-de-maine against the Capital below. I forbear to remark on its vicinity, to the direct route into the mexican provinces of Texhas & St Afee [7] & St. Andero,[8] or to enlarge on the advantages

7. This is a reference to what is now Santa Fe, New Mexico.
8. Wilkinson is possibly referring to New Santander, a Mexican province on the Gulf of Mexico.

this circumstance might afford us, should Events compel us to attack, and

6thly. I proposed by condensing my force, to save the hazard of being beaten in detail, and by fortifying at this point to cover the Country, to give confidence to the Inhabitants, and to make demonstration of the power & decision of the Government.

I submit the case to you Sir, without further trespass on your time; in the belief, that should you find cause to condemn my judgment, you will not discredit my motives.

Anterior to the Death of Captain Demlar,[9] the senior Officer of Engineers, I had relied on Him for the Plan, elivation, & section of the ground to be occupied, but I have since discovered his measurements & calculations to be erroneous, and am now engaged in correcting his Errors; and by the next conveyance, I hope it may be in my power, to give you ample information, & in the meantime I send you, under cover, an accurate section of the Site, from high water mark to the summit of the Hill, which commands the circumjacent country.

Solicitous for the pleasure of an interview with you, I am preparing to meet the summons, which the minister of War, has notified me to expect from you,[10] with the utmost promptitude; I beg you to believe that the expectation interests not less my inclinations than my duty, but it will occur to you that the Arrangements indispensable to the preservation of due responsibility over such an extensive chain of Posts, separately commanded & instructed—To provide for the security of the public property, & the progression of the public service, every where within the Sphere of my Authority —and to guard the Health of the Troops against the ravages of this climate, on the Margin of the River, will require three or four Weeks; you may however rest assured, I shall not waste one moment, after the arrival of your mandate, which may I hope, for the sake of certainty, convenience, & expedition, allow me discretion as to the route, by which I may approach you.

I have just heard from unquestionable authority, that Mr. Gayoso [11] is soliciting a voluntary loan, at 10 ⅌ Ct. Interest, throughout

9. Captain George Demlar had died on March 11, 1799 (Heitman, *United States Army*, I, 366).

10. See H to Wilkinson, February 12, 1799.

11. Manuel Gayoso de Lemos, governor of Louisiana.

his jurisdiction, for the use of the Crown, & under the pretext that it is to support the War against Great Britain, but in reality I beleive to support his own immediate Government, as His treasury is empty, & the annual remittance from vera Cruz has failed; I have not ascertained his success, but think it will turn out a dull Business.

I have the pleasure to inform you, we have not had a single desertion, since Lt. Lovels [12] agreement with Governor Gayoso, was read at the Head of the Troops, and also that the Men in general now enjoy good Health, which I shall endeavour to preserve, by giving them a position in this vicinity, a few Miles removed from the River, excepting the necessary guards, which will be releived weekly.

I have taken measures to ascertain the party, which commited the outrage, on the trace leading to the State of Kentucky, & hope for success, as the offence should not be suffered to pass away un-noticed.

I have nothing material to add which may with propriety be com-mited to Paper.

With sincere admiration & great respect I am sir   Your Mo. Obedient Servant   Ja Wilkinson

Major General Hamilton

12. This is a reference to an agreement between Gayoso de Lemos and Lieu-tenant John M. Lovell, acting for Wilkinson, which was signed at New Or-leans, on March 1, 1799 (copy, Hamilton Papers, Library of Congress). On April 10, 1799, Wilkinson wrote to McHenry: "We have not had a Desertion since Mr. Lovell's agreemnt. with Governor Gayoso, was read at the Head of the Troops, but that Gentleman having given publicity to the engagement, and Governor [Winthrop] Sargent having expressed great apprehensions, of the effect it might produce, in the minds of the good people of this Territory, and threatened to bear public testimony against it, I have felt it my duty to dis-avow the Tenor of the instrument but have endeavoured so to qualify my language to Mr Gayoso, as not to relieve him from his obligations . . ." (copy, Hamilton Papers, Library of Congress). McHenry enclosed copies of both the agreement and Wilkinson's letter in his first letter to H, May 29, 1799 (listed in the appendix to this volume).

From James McHenry

War Department, April 16, 1799. "I have received this morning your two letters dated the 15. instant. . . ."[1] Several Officers appointed

to the new Regiments had expressed uneasiness upon the ground of
not receiving their Commissions. I know however the uneasiness
among some of them proceeded from another cause. They were
apprehensive they were to receive no pay 'till called into actual
service, while some of them would have hoped that the first commissioned would be intitled to priority of Rank. To quiet any
apprehensions on the first account and remove any expectations on
the second I issued a circular letter upon the first of April instant of
which the enclosed is a Copy.[2] I do not know whether you recollect that Commissions were not issued to the Officers of the Army
directed to be raised in 1792 [3] 'till a twelve month after their
appointment. . . . The field Officers for New Hampshire viz. One
Lieutenant Colonel and one Major and one Major for Vermont cannot possibly be appointed for some time. The Representation from
New Hampshire just before the rising of Congress [4] requested that
nominations to the President might be delayed till they could return home and have an opportunity to forward me the names of
qualified persons to fill these Offices. I have not yet heard from them
and after I do I must transmit my choice to the President for his
approbation before I can announce their being appointed. . . ."

LS, Hamilton Papers, Library of Congress; LS, letterpress copy, James
McHenry Papers, Library of Congress.
    1. One letter of April 15 is printed above. In the second letter, which is
listed in the appendix to this volume, H discusses a letter he received from
Lieutenant Nathaniel Leonard in command of soldiers from the Second Regiment of Artillerists and Engineers at Windsor, Vermont.
    2. This circular reads: "Major General Hamilton being charged with the
recruiting service, you will hold yourself in readiness to obey such orders or
instructions, relative thereto, as may be transmitted to you directly from him,
or through your commanding officer.
    "The materials for the appointment of officers to be drawn from North
Carolina, South Carolina, and Georgia, being yet incomplete, no final arrangement can be made respecting relative rank; it has therefore been thought adviseable to postpone any partial issue of commissions, until the officers from
these states shall be appointed.
    "Your pay and emoluments will comence from the date of your letter of
acceptance." (Copy, enclosed in McHenry to John Adams, April 8, 1799
[ALS, Adams Family Papers, deposited in the Massachusetts Historical Society,
Boston].)
    3. This is a reference to the force raised under the authority of "An Act for
making farther and more effectual Provision for the Protection of the Frontiers of the United States" (1 Stat. 241–43 [March 5, 1792]).
    4. The Third Session of the Fifth Congress had adjourned on March 3, 1799.

From James McHenry

War Department
17th. April 1799

Sir,

In my letter to you of the 4th February last, after intimating the disposition proposed, by the Commander in Chief, for the existing regiments of Artillerists, and Engineers, I added "You will therefore give effect, to the aforesaid disposition, and so arrange the Companies of Artillery, that those belonging to the same regiment or Corps, may form contiguous Garrisons."

I had written to Major General Pinckney to the same effect, in February last.[1]

It now appears to me proper, in order to give full effect, to the dispositions of the Companies of Artillerists &c in contiguous garrisons, at those points especially, where the respective spheres of your command, and that of General Pinckney,[2] meet, that a communication upon the subject should take place immediately between you, which I request you will commence without loss of time. I shall make the same request to General Pinckney.

I am Sir   With great respect   Your obedient servant

James McHenry

Major General
Alexander Hamilton

LS, Hamilton Papers, Library of Congress; Df, dated April 16, 1799, James McHenry Papers, Library of Congress.

1. McHenry to Charles Cotesworth Pinckney, February 11, 1799 (LS, letter-press copy, James McHenry Papers, Library of Congress).

2. For Pinckney's command, see the introductory note to H to James Gunn, December 22, 1798.

From James McHenry

War Department, April [*17*] *1799.* "I have occasionally thought of the plan for the providing and issuing military supplies, submitted in your letter of the 8th inst. It strikes me, that the additional assistants to the Purveyor and Superintendant of Military Stores which it proposes, will tend to facilitate both purchases and deliveries; and the powers assigned to the Inspector General and deputy Inspector Generals and Quarter Master & Deputy Quarter Master General with a separate army, over the Deputies of the Purveyors & Superintendants with the respective armies, to the discovery and correction of abuses. The details of the business enjoined upon these officers are similar to those under a former establishment. There was always with the main branch of the revolutionary army, the Qr Master General, Commissary General of issues and purchases of provisions, the field commissary of military stores and Deputy paymaster, whose duties were nearly the same as specified in the plan. So far therefore the plan is founded upon experience. The rest of the plan appears to correspond in general with present practice. . . . I shall request Mr Wolcott to consider the whole, when I shall take it up for a final determination. . . ."

ALS, Hamilton Papers, Library of Congress; ALS, letterpress copy, James McHenry Papers, Library of Congress.

To James McHenry

New York, April 17, 1799. "Your letters of the 15th. and 16th. are duly come to hand. . . . Tomorrow I shall leave this place for Philadelphia. Several things will best be settled by personal conference which in future will be mutually convenient & will promote the service."

Copy, in the handwriting of Ethan Brown, Hamilton Papers, Library of Congress.

From Ebenezer Stevens [1]

New York, April 17, 1799. "I will thank You to take the Statemt. of Mr Mangin's services,[2] with you, to the Secrety at War, there will be but little due him from Government, as the amount now Stands, he has been of essential Services in Conducting the Works of Fort Jay &c: and I am sincerely desirous to have a Settlement made with him. Respecting my Compensation for the Services I have rendered the UStates, the Secrety at War, has left it optional with me to Receive it by a Salary or Commission on Amount of Disbursements. I have preffer'd the latter, & will make out a Statement of the Disbursemts. charging 2½ ⅌ Cent Commissn on the Same—which will be for my Services up to the 5th. of Feby. last, And from that period, will accept of a Salary say of $2000 ⅌ Year, for my Services for the future. . . ."

ALS, Hamilton Papers, Library of Congress; copy, New-York Historical Society, New York City.
  1. For background to this letter, see Joseph F. Mangin to the Military Committee of New York City, June 18, 1798; Mangin to H, August 7, 1798, January 11, 1799; Stevens to H, November 29, 1798, February 28, April 4, 1799.
  2. For Mangin's account, see Stevens to H, April 4, 1799, note 2.

To John De Barth Walbach [1]

New York, April 17, 1799. "My object is to See exemplified the *elementary* evolutions of the Cavalry according to the Systems of Prussia,[2] France,[3] and Great Britain [4] in order to compare them with each other and Select the best. For this purpose I wished you to instruct in those different evolutions a troop of Volunteer horse. . . . You will readily understand that I do not wish to extend your attention to the more complicated movements—but to the simple formation into Columns and display in line."

Copy, in the handwriting of Ethan Brown, Hamilton Papers, Library of Congress.
  1. Walbach, a native of Germany, had been appointed a lieutenant in the Light Dragoons on January 8, 1799 (*Executive Journal*, I, 298, 303).

2. For the regulations of the Prussian cavalry, see Max Jähns, *Geschichte der Kriegswissenschaften vornehmlich in Deutschland* (Munich and Leipzig, 1891), 2607–38.

3. *Instruction provisoire arrêteé par le Roi concernant l'Exercice & les Manœuvres des Troupes à Cheval. Du 20 Mai 1788* (Paris: Imp. Royale, 1788) was amended by *Changemens faits à l'Ordonnance provisoire concernant les Manœuvres des Troupes à Cheval. Formation et Ecole d'Escadron* (Paris: Imp. Royale, 1789). Both documents were published in a single volume in several editions before being replaced in 1798 by *Instruction concernant l'Exercice et les Manœuvres des Troupes à Cheval, Rédigée sur les Ordonnances actuellement en activité, et suivie de Cent trente sept Planches* (Paris: Magimel, 1798), which was modeled on the 1788–1789 rules. A separate volume of plates entitled *Planches relatives à l'Instruction concernant l'Exercice et les Manœuvres des Troupes à Cheval* . . . (Paris: Magimel, 1798) was published as a supplement to the 1798 edition. Although the 1788 edition mentioned the volume of plates, that volume was not published until 1798.

4. [Sir David Dundas], *Instructions and Regulations for the Formation and Movements of the Cavalry* (London: Printed for the War Office by T. Egerton, n.d.). An order of June 17, 1796, made this work the official manual for the British cavalry.

To George Washington

New York, April 17, 1799. "I have the honor of your letter of the 10th. instant. . . . The alterations you suggest are adopted. . . ."

LS, in the handwriting of Ethan Brown, Hamilton Papers, Library of Congress; copy, in the handwriting of Ethan Brown, Hamilton Papers, Library of Congress.

From Robert Boyd [1]

New Windsor [New York] April 18, 1799. Seeks employment building the gun carriages for the "Arm'd Vessells now building" in New York.

ALS, Hamilton Papers, Library of Congress.
1. Boyd owned a gunsmith shop and operated a forge on Quassaick Creek in New Windsor.

To Elizabeth Hamilton

[*Philadelphia, April 19, 1799.* On April 20, 1799, Hamilton wrote to Elizabeth Hamilton: "I yesterday informed my beloved of my arrival here." *Letter not found.*]

From Rufus King

[*London, April 19, 1799.*[1] *Letter not found.*]

1. "List of Letters from . . . Mr. King" to H, Columbia University Libraries.

From Ebenezer Stevens

New York, April 19, 1799. "Since I had the pleasure of addressing you under date of the 17th: instant I have considered, that it will be better for me to accept a Salary of Two thousand Dollars pr. Year from the date of my appointment as agent to the War department than to have a Commission on my disbursements to the first of February last and afterward a salary at that rate pr. annum. . . ."

ALS, Hamilton Papers, Library of Congress; copy, New-York Historical Society, New York City.

To Elizabeth Hamilton

Philadelphia April 20
1799

I yesterday informed my beloved[1] of my arrival here. A very good night's rest has put me in as pleasant a state as I can be when absent from my dear and excellent Eliza. But the pressure of my engagements obliges me to confine myself to the information that

I am in good health; which I am glad to know is of more importance
than any thing else I could say. Kiss all my Children for me.

Adieu My Amiable   A H

Mrs. H

ALS, Mrs. John Church Hamilton, Elmsford, New York.
    1. Letter not found.

To James McHenry

Philadelphia, April 20, 1799. ". . . As I do not conceive the
United States to be now at War in the legal import of that term
(which I construe to be a state not of *partial* but of *general*, hostility) I consider it as beyond my power to approve or execute such
sentences as by the Articles of War are referred to the President in
time of peace.[1] But while I think it my duty on this ground to transmit the sentence without acting upon it,[2] I feel myself called upon
by a profound conviction of the necessity of some severe examples
to check a spirit of desertion which for want of them in time past,
has become too prevalent, respectfully to declare my opinion, that
the confirmation and execution of the sentence are of material
consequence to the prosperous course of the military service. The
crime of desertion is in this instance aggravated by the condition of
the Offender, who is a Serjeant, and by the breach of trust, in pur-
loining the money which was in his hands for the pay of his
company."

Copy, in the handwriting of Philip Church, Hamilton Papers, Library of Congress.
    1. Section 18 of "An Act to ascertain and fix the Military Establishment of
the United States" (1 *Stat.* 485 [May 30, 1796]) provided: "That the sentences
of general courts martial, in time of peace, extending to the loss of life, the
dismission of a commissioned officer; or which shall, either in time of peace or
war, respect a general officer, shall, with the whole of the proceedings in such
cases, respectively, be laid before the President of the United States; who is
hereby authorized to direct the same to be carried into execution, or otherwise,
as he shall judge proper." The articles of war were published in 1794. See H
to Jonathan Dayton, August 6, 1799, note 11.
    2. This is a reference to the case of Sergeant Richard Hunt of the Second
Regiment of Artillerists and Engineers, who was charged with desertion. He

was court-martialed on H's orders, tried in New York City on April 16, 1799, found guilty, and sentenced to death ("Proceedings of a General Court Martial . . . on the 16 day of April 1799" [copy, RG 59, Miscellaneous Letters, January 1, 1799–December 27, 1800, National Archives]).

From James Wilkinson

Head Quarters Western Army
Loftus' Heights [Mississippi Territory]20th. April 1799

Sir

It was not before the last Evening, I had the Honor to receive your Letter of the 12th. Febry: altho the messenger who brought it, delivered me philadelphia Papers, as late as the 8th: Ultimo. I regret the delay but cannot account for it.

I wrote you five Days since Fort Washington on the Ohio, & now enclose you a duplicate of that Dispatch, by a confidential half-bred Indian, who will bear this Letter direct to Knox Ville, from whence it will be forwarded by Mail. I have adopted this channel of prompt communication, to apprize you of my intentions, & to prevent any unpleasant interpretations, which might otherwise ensue unavoidable delays. I shall give the Troops I command, the best disposition without loss of time, & such substantial regulations will immediately follow, as may be best calculated to promote the service, secure the national Interests, & preserve tranquillity during my absence.

In the course of the ensuing Month, I shall certainly commence my Journey, but whether by Land or by Water, will depend on a variety of circumstances maturely examined; but anterior to my departure hence, I shall send orders to the Northern Posts, for the transmittal to philadelphia, of such documents as may, combined to those I shall cary with me, give you a clear comprehensive view, of the principles of Duty & of service which have obtained, of the Systems which prevail, & the Establishments which exist, from whence you may form precise conceptions, of the necessary modifications.

Believe me sir, I am sensibly affected by the expression of kindness in which you address me, and altho professions in general be vain & illusory, I will hazard the propriety of the assurance, that you shall find me, in all the relations of our profession, obedient, prompt, & zealous. Weded to the sword, I have no ambition but that of military Fame, fairly earned & soundly Established, & I am persuaded such views will find advocates in the Candor & the expansion of your Breast.

If I may judge from the exterior, our neighbours of Louisiana repose confidence in us, & are sincerely disposed to cultivate the Harmony which prevails. On my part to evidence my disposition to preserve a good understanding, & for other purposes which will occur to you, I continue to keep an Officer almost constantly in the City of New Orleans.

The route by Land to you will require two Months, by Water one only. To save time I shall adopt the last, provided the Governor of Louisiana,[1] will guarantee my free passage without search or hindrance.

With much consideration & respectful attachment   I am Sir   Your Obedt. Servant   Ja Wilkinson

Major General Hamilton

ALS, Hamilton Papers, Library of Congress; LS, marked "duplicate," Hamilton Papers, Library of Congress.
1. Manuel Gayoso de Lemos.

From James McHenry

War Department
22d. April 1799

Sir,

As the recruiting service, for the twelve regiments, immediately to be raised, for the service of the United States, is on the eve of its commencement and injurious delays to the same may be occasioned, from the difficulty or perhaps impracticability of procuring qualified musicians promptly by enlistment; I think it proper to advise you, that each Captain will be permitted, if he cannot enlist a

LS, Hamilton Papers, Library of Congress; LS, letterpress copy, James McHenry Papers, Library of Congress.

qualified drummer and fifer, or either of them, for his Company, to engage such musicians, during the period of recruiting, not to exceed two dollars, per month, over and above and in addition to the pay and emoluments (except cloathing) of a drummer or fifer regularly enlisted; of which I request you, to apprise the company officers.

I enclose copy of a set of regulations, adopted, by this department, respecting the extra-allowances to Officers, detached on service, so as to be obliged, to incur expences on the *road* and *at places*, where, there are *no military posts*, except, in the cases of Officers, for whose travelling expences, the Law,[1] has specifically provided.

The second article of these regulations provides, "That extraordinary cases only, for which greater allowances may be indispensible, be referred, to the special discretion of the Secretary of War, to be assisted by a Certificate, from the commanding officer, by whom the Officer claiming, was detached on the special service, stating the reasons and circumstances."

I have therefore to request, you will make known to the Officers of the Army generally, that the greater allowance in extraordinary cases, which is referred specially by the 2d article, to the discretion of the Secretary of War, cannot be made with propriety, until a certificate is produced, from the commanding officer, by whom the officer claiming was detached, stating particularly, the reasons, and circumstances, inducing extraordinary expence, and that in all cases the orders of the commanding officer, must be produced in writing, previous to any allowance being made.

I am Sir   with great respect   your obedient servant

James McHenry

Major General Alexander Hamilton

1. See Sections 12, 13, 18 of "An Act for the better organizing of the Troops of the United States; and for other purposes" (1 *Stat.* 749–55 [March 3, 1799]); "An Act making appropriations for the Military Establishment, for the year one thousand seven hundred and ninety-nine" (1 *Stat.* 741–42 [March 2, 1799]).

2. Two copies, Hamilton Papers, Library of Congress.

[ENCLOSURE]

Regulations Respecting Extra-allowances to Officers [2]

[Philadelphia, December 19, 1798]

In all cases where officers are detached on services, which oblige them to incur expences on the *road*, and *at places where there are no military posts*, except where the law has specifically provided for travelling expenses, the following regulations are to govern in the settlement of their accounts.

I. Every officer detached as aforesaid, besides his legal pay and emoluments shall receive a dollar and twenty-five cents per day for man and horse for each day that the officer must sleep at a place not a military post, and when the officer is of a rank to be entitled to a servant, then the addition of seventy-five cents per day for the servant and his horse. That the foregoing rule shall apply to all places but the Seat of Government, and the principal town in each state, at which places the allowance to be a dollar and a half for the officer and his horse.

II. That extraordinary cases only for which greater allowances may be indispensible be referred to the special discretion of the Secretary of War, to be assisted by a certificate from the commanding officer, by whom the officer claiming was detached on the special service, stating the reasons and circumstances.

III. That fifty cents, without reference to rank, be allowed to every officer detached from one military post to another, which he may reach the same night, not less than forty miles distant: In this case it is contemplated the servant can without inconvenience take his own provisions with him.

V. That the day's journey be regulated by the number of miles in the following proportions, viz. Forty miles to a day where the whole distance does not exceed two hundred miles: thirty to a day for all above two hundred and not exceeding three hundred and fifty; twenty-five to a day, for all above three hundred and fifty and not exceeding six hundred; and twenty to a day for all above six hundred.

V. That these rates do not retrospect but regard future allowances only. That all past and intervening cases, before a reasonable notice of the same, be settled on the former principle of reasonable expences according to circumstances, it being supposed that the application of a new rule may produce hardship and injustice where the service may have been performed in the expectation that practice on former occasions would prevail.

> Given at the Office of the War Department of the United States, in the City of Philadelphia by order of the President, this nineteenth day of December, 1798, and in the twenty-third year of Independence.
>
> James McHenry, Secretary of War.

Circular to the Commandants of Regiments

Circular
Philadelphia April 23d. [–24] 1799

Sir

The Secretary of War has assured me that a competent number of drums and fifes for your Regiment shall be forwarded with its Cloathing. And he has authorised me to instruct you to hire temporarily persons in the capacities of drummers and fifers to be employed in the Recruiting service till others can be enlisted, provided that they can be obtained for a compensation not exceeding eight dollars per Month and one ration per day and without cloathing.[1]

It appears to me expedient that the Recruits which shall be raised should not long remain at their company Rendezvousses but should speedily march to their District or Regimental Rendezvousses.

With great consideration   I am Sir   Your obed servt:

Df, in the handwriting of Philip Church, Hamilton Papers, Library of Congress; LS, to Aaron Ogden, dated April 24, 1799, Lloyd W. Smith Collection, Morristown National Historical Park, Morristown, New Jersey.

1. James McHenry to H, April 22, 1799.

From John Jay [1]

Albany 23 Ap. 1799

Dr Sir

Such was your Recommendation of Mr. Inglis [2] for the place of a notary, that it is proper to mention to you the Reasons why he was not appointed. I think the number of officers should be regulated in general by the occasion or necessity there may be for them.

In the City of New York there are at least Twenty public notaries; and that number being in my opinion more than sufficient, it does not appear to me advisable to increase it. There are many Candidates, and there are some among them whom it would give me particular pleasure to appoint—such as—Mr Malcom [3] who was recommended to me by the Presidt of the U. S.—Mr Lawrence,[4] the Son of our Senator—Mr. Inglis—& two or three more.

Exclusive of Mr. Inglis, I find no less than sixteen names on the List of candidates—some of them of more than three Years Standing.[5]

List of Notaries in the City of N York

John Wilkes	R. Van den Broeck	Ch. Adams	Wm. Bleecker
John Keese	Cadw. Colden	Fr. Lynch	Jams. Creighton
Jams. M. Hughes	Is. L. Kip	John S. Hunn	Ab. Skinner
Ed. Dunscomb	Th. Smith	Ch. Bridgen	Wm. Bache
Adrian Kissam	Ch. R. Richardson	John G. Bogart	Henry Remson

There were other notaries in the city (some of them I have heard are dead, and others removed—perhaps some of them may be still there)—vizt. Jams. De Haert—Paul R. Randall—J. F. Roorbach—Is. Van Vleck—Wm. Brodie—Teunis Wortman—Dan. Thew &c—

Since I have been in the Govt. I have appointed no more than three in the City—Ab. Skinner—Wm. Bache in whose favor Mr. Popham [6] resigned; and Henry Remson to succeed his Brother John.

These Details are prompted by the Respect due to your Recommendation and by the Esteem and Regard with which I am

Dr Sir   Your most Obt. Servt.

Maj. Genl. Hamilton

ADf, Columbia University Libraries.

1. Jay was governor of New York.
2. See H to Jay, September 17, December 18, 1798.
3. Samuel B. Malcolm, a New York lawyer, had been private secretary to John Adams in 1797 and 1798.
4. John McDougal Laurance.
5. At this point in the letter Jay wrote and then crossed out:

"George D. Cooper—1795   Gab. V. Ludlow ⎤
Ths. L. Ogden   ⎤   Peter Hawes   ⎥ 1796
Saml. Laurence   ⎥ 1796   James Wood—1797 ⎥
Wm. Paulding Jun   ⎦   Henry Sands—1798 ⎦

Ths. Ferdon   ⎤   John W. Mulligan ⎤
Wm Coleman   ⎥   Jonn. Pearsey   ⎥
Wm. Kettlelas   ⎥ 1798   S. B. Malcom   ⎥ 1798
Heny Brewerton   ⎦   John Lawrance"   ⎦

6. William Popham. See Philip Schuyler to H, August 31, 1795, note 7.

From James McHenry

private   War Department 23 Apl 1799

Dear Sir

I wish you ⟨to⟩ state to me 1st. The rule which in your opinion will be the least exceptionable, whereby to determine the relative rank of the Field Officers of the new regiments, and the reasons for prefering the rule. 2d. Whether any objections have occurred to you, which ought to induce any alteration in the general rules of promotion suggested by the General Officers in the Commander in Chiefs letter dated the 13 Decr. ulto [1] vz. "That all officers shall rise in the Regiments, to which they respectively belong up to the rank of Major inclusively; that afterwards they shall rise in the line of the army at large with the limitation, however, that the officers of Artillery cavalry and Infantry shall be confined to their respective corps, until they shall attain the rank of Colonel."

yours truly & affly   James McHenry

Gen. Hamilton

ALS, Hamilton Papers, Library of Congress; ADf, James McHenry Papers, Library of Congress.

1. See H's draft of George Washington to McHenry, third letter of December 13, 1798; McHenry to H, March 21, 1799.

To James McHenry

Philadelphia April 23
1799

Sir

Upon a careful inspection of the Articles of War I entertain doubts, whether I can *act* upon, by *approving* or *disapproving* sentences of Courts Martial referred to me from the Department of War, in cases in which the Courts have been instituted by that Department through organs other than myself.[1]

As there is peculiar delicacy in inflicting punishment upon questionable authority, I shall be glad to be exempted from the embarrassment which references of the above mentioned kind will occasion.

I have written provisionally to Col Strong[2] to abstain from the execution of Martial law at Detroit[3] till further order, as I desire maturely to reflect on the subject before a definitive Step.

With the greatest respect   I have the honor to be Sir   Yr. Obed ser

The Secy of War

ADf, Hamilton Papers, Library of Congress.
   1. In this paragraph H is replying to McHenry to H, first letter of April 4, 1799 (listed in the appendix to this volume), in which McHenry sent H copies of the proceedings of two courts-martial and asked H to issue the appropriate orders.
   In addition, on April 7, 1799, Thomas Lloyd Moore wrote to H (letter listed in the appendix to this volume) that a court-martial had been held at Fort Mifflin. He then wrote: ". . . they [the members of the court] ha⟨ve⟩ finished the Business, and have enclosed the Proceedings to me for my Opinion, but I am doubtful of my powers as to actin⟨g⟩ finally in this case and shall be glad to hear your sentimen⟨t⟩ on the subject."
   Article 2 of the appendix of the articles of war reads: "General Courts-Martial shall be ordered, as often as the cases may require, by the General or Officer commanding the troops. But no sentence of a Courts-Martial shall be carried into execution until after the whole proceedings shall have been laid before the said General or Officer commanding the troops for the time being; neither shall any sentence of a general Court-martial in time of peace, extending to the loss of life, the dismission of a Commissioned Officer, or which shall either in time of peace or war respect a General Officer, be carried into execution, until after the whole proceedings shall have been transmitted to the Secretary at War, to be laid before Congress for their confirmation, or disap-

proval, and their orders on the case. All other sentences may be confirmed and executed by the Officer ordering the Court to assemble, or the Commanding Officer for the time being, as the case may be" (*JCC*, XXX, 317). See also H to McHenry, February 23, 1799; H to Jonathan Dayton, August 6, 1798, note 11.

2. H's letter to David Strong has not been found.

3. See McHenry to H, first letter of April 11, April 13, 1799.

To Washington Morton [1]

Philadelphia April 23. 1799

Sir,

On revising the proceedings of the General Court Martial [2] received from you, I find that it does not appear by them whether two thirds of the members of the Court concurred on the Conviction of Sergeant Hunt. The articles of War (8th of Chapter Administration of Justice) [3] require that two thirds shall agree in cases where death is inflicted, and I am of opinion that this agreement ought to appear on the face of the proceedings. I presume there was a competent number to condemn. If so, I request you to insert a clause expressing it. This will properly be incorporated in the body of the sentence reading thus "The Court, *two thirds* (or *more than* two thirds if the fact be so) *of the members thereof having concurred therein*, find &c."

As this was not originally inserted, there must be a certificate at foot signed by the President and yourself declaring that the words &c (reciting them) were inserted after the first signature and that the fact is thereby stated.

When this is done, return the proceedings open under cover to the Secretary of War.

Washington Moreton

ADf, Hamilton Papers, Library of Congress.

1. Morton, who had been graduated from Princeton in 1792, was a New York City lawyer and the husband of Cornelia Schuyler, Elizabeth Hamilton's sister. He had served as acting judge advocate of the court-martial of Richard Hunt on April 16, 1799. See H to James McHenry, April 20, 1799, note 2.

2. Copy, RG 59, Miscellaneous Letters, January 1, 1799–December 27, 1800, National Archives.

3. *JCC*, XXX, 318. See H to Jonathan Dayton, August 6, 1798, note 11.

From Nathan Rice

Hingham [Massachusetts] April 23d. 1799

Sir,

I can only now, in answer to your favour of the 10th. instant,[1] do myself the honor, to acknowledge the receipt thereof, with its inclosures, consisting of General Brooks arrangement of this state, into districts & also some outlines of a similar nature by Mr. Sedgwick. I shall communicate to Colonel Hunnewell the contents of your Letter & sollicit a consultation with him; But as it may be attended with some delay shall immediately wait on General Brooks for his aid in perfecting the system in conformity to your ideas, & transmit the same to you with all possible dispatch.

I did myself the honor of writing to you on the 13th. inst. when I communicated the choice made by the officers of my Regt of a Paymaster. The same reasons which then prevented my nominating the other regimental staff, now exist. I am uninformed as to the late Report of the Secretary at War relative to the Military establishment, how far it was adopted, & is to be my guide.[2] It came inclosd to me from his office. Any information which you may think proper to make I shall be happy to receive.

I am Sir with the utmost consideration & esteem   Your most obt Servt.   N Rice

Major Genl Hamilton

ALS, Hamilton Papers, Library of Congress.
    1. H to Richard Hunewell and Rice, April 10, 1799.
    2. This is a reference to James McHenry's report to John Adams of December 24, 1798, which was communicated to Congress on December 31, 1798 (*ASP, Military Affairs*, I, 124–29). As a result of this report Congress enacted "An Act for the better organizing of the Troops of the United States; and for other purposes" (1 *Stat.* 749–55 [March 3, 1799]).

From James McHenry

War Department
April 24th: 1799.

Sir,

I have received your letter dated the 23rd: instant advising me, that you entertain doubts, whether you can act upon, (by approving or otherwise) Sentences of Courts Martial, referred to you, from the Department of War, in cases, in which the Court has been instituted by that Department, through other organs than yourself.

That there is a peculiar delicacy in inflicting punishment upon questionable authority, and you should therefore be glad, to be exempted from the embarrassment, which references of the above mentioned kind, will occasion.

The doubts which appear to have arisen in your mind, I should conceive apply more forcibly to those cases which were submitted to Courts, either by this Department or otherwise (and the Sentences of which, yet remain to be passed upon) before the period ⟨of⟩ your being called into Service—and of this kind I recollect but one or two, the irregularities in which either from want of authority in the Officer who ordered the Court, or other causes, seemed to render the Sentences void, or improper to be executed particularly when they affected Life, but left the party or parties as the first trial and Sentence, were considered nullities, subject to a new trial, or otherwise, as you should order.

Of those cases, in which the Court was instituted by this Department since your being positively in Service,[1] I recollect only the instance, of a Court directed to try some Mutineers from Fort Mifflin.

If you are of opinion, that in the latter case, you are not authorized to approve, disapprove or mitigate the Sentences, I pray you to transmit them to me, to enable me to judge of their nature, and put them in train of being decided upon by competent authority, and request you to do the same with the proceedings and Sentences, you doubt your competency respecting in all other cases.

I am Sir,   with great respect   Your obedt. servant

James McHenry

Major General Alexander Hamilton

LS, Hamilton Papers, Library of Congress; LS, letterpress copy, James McHenry Papers, Library of Congress; copy, James McHenry Papers, Library of Congress.

1. See H to McHenry, April 23, 1799, note 1.

From James Wilkinson

Head Quarters Loftus' Heights [Mississippi Territory]
25th. April 1799.

Sir

A confidential opportunity having offered to New Orleans, I avail myself of it, to give you the following extract from a Letter just recd. from Governor Gayoso & dated the 15th Inst.

"Your instructions to Captn Shaum Burgh,[1] are not only according to the strictest discipline, but they show your Genls. evident disposition, to cultivate the best understanding between our Nations.

"The party arrived yesterday within a League of this Capital, from whence Capt Shaum Burgh acquainted me with it, & we agreed that the Day ensuing at ten oClock in the Morning, the Troops should pass through this Town, to the place appointed for their Encampment which was executed.

"The movement was performed in the most military manner & seemed rather calculated to give a publick testimony of the cordiality & sincere Friend ship between our Nations, than with any other object. I assure you no attention shall be wanting to compleat this operation."

The remainder of the Letter, with several of a similar cast, I will reserve to make a smile, when I have the Honor to see you.

You have under cover a duplicate of my last;[2] which I hazard by Sea, under the necessary precautions for its safety again in proper Hands.

Should Gayoso furnish the Guaranty I have asked, I hope for the pleasure of presenting myself to you on the 20th. June.

And have the Honor to be most respectfully Sir Your Obedt Servant   Ja Wilkinson

Majr. General Hamilton

N. B. This Moment I learn by Letter from Mobile dated the 3rd. Inst: that a party of Creeks had called on the Commissioner of limits [3] at that place, & at first were insolent, but on finding they were treated with contempt, they changed their tone, & it is presumed no difficulty will be opposed to the progress of the Commissioner. The line crosses the Mobile River twenty one Miles above the Town of the same Name.   J W

ALS, Hamilton Papers, Library of Congress.
    1. See Wilkinson to H, April 15, 1799.
    2. Wilkinson to H, April 20, 1799.
    3. On May 24, 1796, Andrew Ellicott of Pennsylvania had been appointed United States commissioner to determine and mark "the southern boundary of the United States; which divides their territory from the Spanish colonies of East and West Florida; agreeably to the second and third articles . . ." of the Treaty of Friendship, Limits, and Navigation between the United States and Spain (Pinckney's Treaty), signed at San Lorenzo el Real on October 27, 1795 (*Executive Journal*, I, 210, 211; Miller, *Treaties*, II, 319–21).

From James McHenry

War Department 26 April 1799

Sir

A question has arisen, respecting appointments, to a part of the Army establishment,[1] on which I have to request your opinion, as soon as convenient, viz:

Is it within the authority of the President, to appoint, the Officers, to the additional batalion, to the second Regiment of Artillerists and Engineers, directed to be raised by "an act, for the better organizing of the troops of the United States and for other purposes," passed the 3d. March 1799?[2]

The Constitution of the United States, art. 2. Sect. 2. provides, that, "Congress may by law, vest the appointment of certain inferior officers, as they think proper, in the President alone, in the Courts of law, or in the heads of departments," and that, "the President shall have power to fill up all vacancies that may happen during the recess of the Senate, by granting commissions which shall expire at the end of their next Session."

It would seem, that under this Constitutional power, the President cannot alone make certain appointments or fill up vacancies that may happen during a session of the senate, without an express power derived from an act of Congress. The following acts are refered to viz:

1. "An Act for raising and adding another regiment to the military establishment of the United States, and for making further provision for the protection of the frontiers," passed the 3d. March 1791, which enacts, "that the President be, and he hereby is impowered to organize the said levies, and alone to appoint the Commissioned Officers thereof, in the manner he may judge proper." [3]

2. "An Act for making further and more effectual provision for the protection of the frontiers of the United States," passed the 5 March 1792: Which enacts "that the President alone be, and he hereby is authorized to appoint for the Cavalry so to be engaged, the proper commissioned Officers." [4]

3d. "An Act to augment the army of the United States, and for other purposes." passed the 16th. July 1798—which enacts, "and in recess of Senate, the President of the United States, is hereby authorized, to appoint all the regimental officers, proper to be appointed under this act, and likewise to make appointments, to fill any *vacancies* in the army, which may have *happened, during the present session of the senate.*" [5]

4th. "An Act, authorizing the President of the United States, to fill certain vacancies in the army and navy," passed the 3d. March 1799, which enacts "That the President of the United States shall be, and he is hereby authorized, to make appointments, to fill any vacancies in the army and navy, which may have happened during the present session of the Senate." [6]

See also an act authorizing the President of the United States, to raise a Provisional Army, passed the 28 May 1798,[7] and supplement to the aforesaid act, passed 25 June 1798.[8]

Is it not evident from the above acts, that it was the opinion of Congress, the Constitution did not authorize the President, to fill up any vacancies in the army, which might happen during a Session of the Senate, but that an express authority for the purpose was indispensibly necessary to be vested in him by law?

If such is the meaning of the Constitution with respect to actual vacancies, occuring during a Session of the Senate—another principle requires mature consideration, and a clear decision, before Officers can be appointed to the companies, intended to compose, the additional batalion of Artillerists in question—viz: Whether Offices, created, during the late session of the senate, and not then filled by appointments, by and with their advise and consent, can now be considered, as offering vacancies, happening during the said Session, to the filling of which the President is competent, independent of any act, by virtue of that part of the Constitution, which declares "The President shall have power to fill up all vacancies that may happen, during the recess of the Senate, by granting Commissions which shall expire at the end of their next Session."

I am Sir   With great Respect   Your Obedient Servant

James McHenry

Major General Alexander Hamilton

LS, Hamilton Papers, Library of Congress; LS, letterpress copy, James McHenry Papers, Library of Congress.

1. The question of the power of the President to make Army appointments during the recess of the Senate arose when John Adams wrote to McHenry on March 29, 1799, about appointing John Hastings, a resident of Newton, Massachusetts, to the Army (LC, Adams Family Papers, deposited in the Massachusetts Historical Society, Boston). On April 8, 1799, McHenry replied to Adams that he "entertained a doubt" whether "An Act authorizing the President of the United States to fill certain vacancies in the Army and Navy" (1 Stat. 749 [March 3, 1799]) "could be construed to intend appointments to offices which had never been filled" (ALS, Adams Family Papers, deposited in the Massachusetts Historical Society, Boston). Adams disagreed with McHenry and wrote to him on April 16, 1799: "It is not upon the Act of the 3d of March Ulto. that I ground the Claim of an Authority to appoint the Officer in question, but upon the Constitution itself. Whenever there is an office that is not full, there is a Vacancy as I have ever understood the Constitution. . . . All such Appointments to be sure must be nominated to the Senate at their next Session and subject to their ultimate decision. I have no doubt that it is my Right and my duty [to] make the Provisional Appointments" (LC, Adams Family Papers, deposited in the Massachusetts Historical Society, Boston). It was in order to answer Adams that McHenry consulted H in the letter printed above.

2. 1 Stat. 749–55.
3. 1 Stat. 222–24.
4. 1 Stat. 241–43.
5. 1 Stat. 604–05.
6. 1 Stat. 749.
7. 1 Stat. 558–61.

8. This is a reference to "An Act supplementary to, and to amend the act, intitled 'An Act authorizing the President of the United States to raise a provisional army'" (1 *Stat.* 569–70), which became law on June 22, 1798, not June 25 as McHenry states.

To James McHenry

Philadelphia April 26th.
1799

Sir

It being urgent that the Two Regiments of Artillery [1] should be organised into companies and disposed of to the several destinations which you have contemplated it results that a very inconvenient delay would attend the making of that arrangement in concert with General Pinckney as suggested in your late letter.[2] As, likewise, this arrangement is mere matter of organisation, the distribution of force having been previously determined upon, it is presumed there will not appear on further consideration any sufficient motive for incurring the delay of such a concert—and that you will think it preferrable by the intervention of your agency to settle the arrangement and communicate it for execution to the two Major Generals.[3]

In this expectation I beg leave to submit to you the plan of such an arrangement. The result will be seen in the paper herewith transmitted.

A preliminary basis, in conformity with the rule by which the

ADf, Hamilton Papers, Library of Congress.

1. There were two regiments of artillerists and engineers. What was to become the First Regiment of Artillerists and Engineers was organized as a corps under an act of May 9, 1794, entitled "An Act providing for raising and organizing a Corps of Artillerists and Engineers" (1 *Stat.* 366–67). The other regiment was provided for by an act of April 27, 1798, entitled "An Act to provide an additional regiment of Artillerists and Engineers" (1 *Stat.* 552–53) and expanded under an act of March 2, 1799, entitled "An Act giving eventual authority to the President of the United States to augment the Army" (1 *Stat.* 725–27). After the passage on March 3, 1799, of "An Act for the better organizing of the Troops of the United States; and for other purposes" (1 *Stat.* 749–55), the two were designated the "First Regiment of Artillerists and Engineers" and the "Second Regiment of Artillerists and Engineers."

2. See McHenry to H, first letter of April 17, 1799.

3. H and Charles Cotesworth Pinckney.

twelve Regiments have been numbered, is on the sea board, to give the right to the first Regiment, the left to the second. This, as it happens, will occasion the least possible dislocation of the companies from their present stations.

You will perceive that a Batalion of the first Regiment is left to the Western Army; and it so turns out, that the number of officers in that quarter corresponds.

Another Batalion of the same Regt is assigned to the posts in Georgia and South Carolina—And a third to the Posts in North Carolina Virginia & Maryland.

The fourth will remain for the troops in the field and may be annexed to the part of the army under General Pinckney.

One batalion of the second Regiment is assigned to the posts in Delaware Pensylvania New Jersey and New York.

Another to the States Eastward and Northward of New York.

The third is reserved for the field and will naturally form a part of my command.

The fourth batalion of this Regiment not being yet raised it of course cannot be comprehended in an immediate Disposition.

In the association of officers for the companies, I have availed myself of all the indications which I was able to discover of their actual relations. But it may happen when situations and characters are better ascertained, that some alterations may promote personal harmony and benefit the service. It is therefore desireable that the adoption by you may be qualified by a view to further information to be obtained through the field Officers and to eventual changes.

There were no indications to regulate the association of the Officers with the Western army. It is consequently proposed to refer this to Col Burbeck.[4]

When you shall have approved the plan now presented or with such alterations as you may judge adviseable, it will only remain to communicate your determination to the two Major Generals, who will concert its prompt execution.

It is extremely to be wished that a Commandant of the second Regiment may without delay be appointed.[5] You are sensible how

4. Lieutenant Colonel Henry Burbeck.
5. Lieutenant Colonel John Doughty was designated commanding officer of the Second Regiment of Artillerists and Engineers on June 1, 1798 (Heitman, *United States Army*, I, 51). Doughty declined the appointment on July 2, 1798

much, in the first stages of a military Corps, the want of the proper chief must impede the establishment of order and discipline.

With the greatest respect   I have the honor to be Sir   Your Obed ser

The Secretary of War

[ENCLOSURE][6]

Arrangement of the Artillery

[Philadelphia, April 25, 1799]
For the Western Army

NAMES	RANK	DATE OF COMMISSION	RESIDENCE
Henry Burbeck	Lieut. Colonel	7. May 1798	Michilimacinac
John J. Ulrich Rivardi	Major	26. February 1798	Niagara
Moses Porter	Captain	4 November 1791	Michilimacinac
Alexander Thompson	ditto	2. June 1794	Niagara
George Demlar	ditto	20. August 1795	said to be dead [7]
Piercy Pope	ditto	24. April 1798	Natchez
Theophilus Elmer	Lieutenant	17. July 1794	Detroit
Peter Talman	ditto	26. February 1795	ditto
Richard Whiley	ditto	19. December 1796	Michilimacinac
Andrew Marshall	ditto	1. November 1796	Mississippi
James Sterret	ditto	2. June 1794	ditto
Thos: Underwood	ditto	26. July 1795	Tenessee
Robert Parkison	ditto	19. December 1796	Massac
John Campbell	ditto	1. November 1796	Mississippi
John M Lovel Be: Major to General Wilkinson	ditto	26. February 1795	
Charles Brown	Surgeon	2 June 1794	Detroit
John G. Coffin	Surgeons Mate	" "	Niagara

(McHenry to John Adams, May 23, 1800 [ALS, Adams Family Papers, deposited in the Massachusetts Historical Society, Boston; copy, Hamilton Papers, Library of Congress]).

6. DS, Hamilton Papers, Library of Congress; Df, in the handwriting of Philip Church and H, Hamilton Papers, Library of Congress; ADf, Hamilton Papers, Library of Congress.

7. See James Wilkinson to H, April 15, 1799, note 9.

Georgia and South Carolina

Constant Freeman	Major	28. February 1795	Philadelphia
Michael Kaltieson	Captain	18. July 1794	Charleston
George Izard	Lieutenant	2. June 1794	"
Jonathan Robeson	ditto	"	"
Abimael Y Nicholl	Captain	29. November 1794	St. Mary's Georgia
William Morris	Lieutenant	29. July 1794	under Col: Gaither 8 Georgia
Howell Cobb		1. Novr: 1796	on the Mississippi
John Mc:Clellan	Captain	24. July 1798	wth. General Macpherson 9
Robert Rowan	Lieutenant	2. June 1794	sick near Wilmington
Staats Rutledge		22. February 1799	Litchfield Connecticut
Frederick Frye	Captain	2. June 1794	Governor's Island
Horatio Dayton	Lieutenant	17. July 1794	Governors Island
Samuel Fowles		22. February 1799	Massac

North Carolina, Virginia and Maryland

Machlon Ford	Major	7. May 1798	Reading
Richard S Blackburn	Captain	2 June 1794	Norfolk
John Saunders	Lieutenant	26. February 1795	
James Triplett		19. December 1796	
James Bruff	Captain	2. June 1794	Philadelphia
Henry Muhlenburg	Lieutenant		West Point
James P Heath		22. February 1799	Warwick Delaware
Ebenezer Massey	Captain	7. May 1798	Fort Mifflin
Peter A Dransy	Lieutenant	12. April 1795	West Point
Ebenezer Beebe		22. February 1799	Litchfield Connecticut
Staats Morris	Captain	26. February 1795	Baltimore
Philip Landais	Lieutenant	19. December 1796	
Samuel T Dyson			

8. Henry Gaither, a resident of Maryland and a veteran of the American Revolution, was lieutenant colonel commandant of the Third Regiment of Infantry and was stationed at Fort Fidius on the Oconee River in Georgia.
9. William Macpherson.

Delaware Pennsylvania New Jersey and New York

Benjamin Brooks	Major	4. June 1798	Upper Malbro Md
James Read	Captain		West Point
Theodore Memminger	Lieutenant		Northampton
Robert W Osburn			Fort Mifflin
Callender Irvine	Captain		Carlisle
George W Carmichael	Lieutenant		West point
Charles Wollstencraft			Northampton
James Stille	Captain		West Point
Philip Stewart	Lieutenant		
Patrick C Harris			North Carolina
Walter L Cochran	Captain		Northampton
William L Cooper	Lieutenant		Northampton
Richard Heaton Junr:		22 Feby: 1799	do

Connecticut. Rhode Island. Vermont. Massachusetts. New Hampshire

Daniel Jackson	Major	4 June 1798	Boston
Decius Wadsworth	Captain	4. June 1798	New London
Nathaniel Leonard	Lieutenant		Windsor ordd: to march
Francis Gibson			Northampton
John Henry	Captain	4. June 1798	Northampton P
John W Livingston	Lieutenant		New York
John Knight			Northampton
Lemuel Gates	Captain		Boston
George W Duncan	Lieutenant		
George Waterhouse		22. February 1799	Cambridge M
Amos Stoddard	Captain	4. June 1798	Portland
William Steele	Lieutenant		
Leonard Williams		22 February 1799	

For the Field

Lewis Toussard	Major	26. February 1795	New Port. R I
George Ingersoll	Captain	2. April 1798	West Point
Philip Rodrique	Lieutenant	19. December 1796	
William Littlefield	Captain	2. June 1794	Rhode Island
George Ross	Lieutenant	19. Decr: 1796	
Joseph Elliot	Captain	19 July 1796	with Genl: Macpherson

James House	Lieut	22. Feby: 1799	with Captn. Elliot
William Yates			Albany
Nathaniel Freeman	Captain	6 August 1798	West Point
Warham Shepard			Westfield
			Connecticut

For the Field

Adam Hoops	Major	4 June 1798	New York
William McRhea	Captain		Alexandria V
James White	Lieutenant		S Carolina
John Fergus			Wilmington
Samuel Eddins	Captain		Richmond
Alexander D Pope	Lieutenant		
John Leybourn			Savannah
Francis H Huger	Captain		Charleston S C
William Deveaux	Lieutenant		Savannah
James B Many			Charleston
John Bishop	Captain	4 June 1798	Winchester
John Hancock	Lieutenant		Kempsville V
David Evans Junr:		22 Feby: 1799	Fayetteville

Philadelphia April 25
1799
A Hamilton MG

To James McHenry

Philadelphia April 26th
1799

Dr. Sir

I have reflected, as you have desired,[1] on the most proper principles for regulating the relative rank of the field Officers of the twelve additional Regiments.

It is always prudent, when no special reasons dictate a deviation, to adopt for cases of this kind a rule which steers clear of comparison of personal merit and avoids the danger of wounding the pride of any of the parties concerned. With this view (since I am not aware of any special reasons that recommend a different course) I am of opinion that as to all such of the Field Officers, who have served in the army of the UStates, it will be adviseable, among those now of equal grade, to let their relative rank at the close of the War govern. This, according with military prepossessions, will be most likely to be satisfactory to all.

As to those who may not have served in the army, considerations of personal merit and weight of character can alone decide, except that where they may have served in the Levies or Militia, other things being equal, their relative rank there may guide.

As between those who have served in the army and those who have not, it appears to me expedient to prefer the men who have served in the army, except where very superior qualifications may manifestly claim a superiority.

With great esteem & regard   Dr Sir Yr Obed serv   A Hamilton

J McHenry Esq

ALS, Columbia University Libraries; ALS (photostat), James McHenry Papers, Library of Congress.
1. See McHenry to H, April 23, 1799.

To James McHenry

Philadelphia April 26. 1799

Dr. Sir

I have a second time maturely reflected on the proper rule for promotions in the army, and I continue to adhere to that which was adopted by the General Officers last Winter, & which is recapitulated in your letter.[1] I am persuaded that in the general course of things it will work well and satisfactorily.

A moment's hesitation as to its universal application arose from the situation of the four Regiments of the Old establishment. The understood rights of the older Captains, as resulting from past usage may appear to be infringed. But this inconvenience must be encountered, perhaps mitigated by a distribution of the oldest Captains among the four Regiments. There cannot with propriety or order be two Rules. That which is proposed will after a little time operate favourably every where & give equal chances.

    With great esteem & regard   I am Dr Sir   Yr Obed servt

                                      A Hamilton

Secy of War

The promotions to field Officers should be complete before the rule is applied.

ALS, Mr. Martin Weiner, Paterson, New Jersey; ALS (photostat), James Mc-Henry Papers, Library of Congress.
   1. McHenry to H, April 23, 1799.

To John F. Hamtramck [1]

New York April 27. 1799

Sir

    You will receive herewith duplicate of my letter to you of the 9th instant.[2]

    It appearing that discontent has arisen from the establishment of Martial Law at Detroit, and a representation having been made against its exercise by Governor St Clair, and there being a question of delicacy about the boundaries of the authority to establish and exercise Martial Law in time of peace, it has been judged expedient to instruct the Commanding Officer of Detroit to forbear the exercise of it, till a further order shall have been given as the result of mature reflection.[3]

    The Secy of War has forwarded to me a letter from you of the 21 of January last.[4] It contains among other things a suggestion respecting two companies of the first Regiment. I am not yet familiar enough with the arrangements of the Western army to be fond of giving directions at this distance concerning a detail of this kind, and it seems to me one appertaining naturally to the Commander of the Western Army, with whom in points of particular disposition I shall not incline to interfere. It is presumed you are now by the departure **of** General Wilkinson for Philadelphia, the temporary commander of that army and competent to the making of the change you suggest, if you continue to deem it eligible. But in general you will no doubt see it proper to be sparing in altering the permanent dispositions which may have been made by General Wilkinson. On the same supposition of your being the Commanding Officer you can take the measures you judge requisite with regard to Lt Webster.

It is proper to comply with the direction of General Wilkinson as to the building of houses for the *Turtle* and for the *Toad*. More carpenters if necessary must be employed. Soldiers so employed, if not regularly engaged as *Artificers* ought to receive extra compensation. You are at liberty to allow it—taking care to consult in every thing all reasonable œconomy.

You will not consider any observation in this letter as implying a censure on your report to the Secy of War. But merely as the manifestation of my desire to maintain principle. I am aware of the difficulty of communication which has arisen from the local situation of the Commanding General and I know well the strength of your attachment to military Order.

With great consideration   I am Sir   Your Obed serv

ADf, Hamilton Papers, Library of Congress.
1. A native of Canada and a veteran of the American Revolution, Hamtramck was lieutenant colonel commandant of the First Regiment of Infantry and was stationed at Pittsburgh.
2. In this letter, which is listed in the appendix to this volume, H informed Hamtramck that James Wilkinson had been ordered to Philadelphia and that in Wilkinson's absence Hamtramck would be the commanding officer of the Western Army.
3. See James McHenry to H, first letter of April 11, 1799; H to McHenry, April 13, 1799.
4. See McHenry to H, second letter of March 22, 1799, note 2.

From James McHenry

War Department, April 27, 1799. "I have considered the arrangement and distribution of the two Regiments of Artillerists and Engineers submitted to me . . .[1] and approve of the same. You will be pleased to cause the said arrangement and distribution so far as it relates to your command to be carried into immediate effect. . . ."

LS, Hamilton Papers, Library of Congress.
1. H to McHenry, first letter of April 26, 1799.

To James McHenry

New York, April 27, 1799. "I have reflected on the idea of furnishing the Regimental Quarter Masters with money to procure Quarters Transportation &c for the Recruits. It is a service which in an extensive State (New York for example) he cannot execute personally. If he employs substitutes at the different Stations, as the Contractor must do so likewise for his objects, it will either, by employing jointly the same Agent every where, come to the same thing as if the Contractor were authorised to perform the service, or there will be an inconvenient multiplication of Agents. If he confides a portion of the money for the purpose to the principal recruiting Officer in each sub district, this will extend and complicate the pecuniary agency and accountability of those officers. In general, I consider this as a thing to be avoided; and as there will be a contractor whose care will embrace every subdistrict I return to the opinion that it will be most expedient to instruct him to comprise in it the objects above mentioned. . . ."

ADf, Hamilton Papers, Library of Congress.

From Nathan Rice

Boston April 28 1799

Sir

In compliance with your directions,[1] I have proceeded to compleat the division of the State into subdistricts, at least that part of it which constitutes circle 14. I have not yet seen Colonel Hunnewell,

& that no further delay might take place I entered on the business without him.

It will be perceivd., that I have not exactly conformed to the division of the districts which was sketched by General Brooks: [2] But he approves the alterations. Conforming to the geographical rule, I began at the western extremity of the State to number the districts and subdistricts, the first of which is comprisd. of the Counties of Berkshire, Hampshire, & two thirds of Worcester. The 2d.—of Suffolk, Norfolk, Bristol, Plymouth, Barnstable, Dukes County & Nantucket. This Mode of division while it includes a pretty equal division of the Inhabitants, preserves also the greatest possible compactness of each circle. I have inclosed the distribution, with the names of the principal officers of each subdistrict, & place of rendezvous to which he is assignd. & hope it will meet with your approbation. I have not delineated the bounds of each subdistrict, not supposing it necessary, if however you think otherwise I shall do it.

In regard to the distribution of Cloathing to the Recruits,[3] I think œconomy in saving the expence of transportation, & the danger of loss in distribution would dictate a preference for a regimental deposite & issue. But I doubt whether the recruiting service would be so greatly promoted thereby; as by a prompt issue of the cloaths to the recruits as soon as they are inlisted. This will be attended with difficulty, as they will undoubtedly need alterations—but the commanding officer at each rendezvous must be made responsible to the pay master for the cloathing, & chargd. with the superintendance of the issues, & fiting them to the Soldiers, by the Taylors who can be procured undoubtedly, in each of those Towns.

Was it consistent with the Character of a soldier to enquire of his superior officers the reasons of his orders, I should be led to query why the regimental rendezvous was assignd to so uncentral a spot in the center. I myself happen to be entirely unacquainted with Sommerset,[4] & cannot send an opinion of the eligibility of that spot, for the accomodation of a regiment with Barracks or supplies of any kind.

I *presume* Sir, that the rank of the officers commanding regiments, is not designated, by the Geographical rule, which has determined the no. of their Regiments. *I shall be obligd by yr. ideas on this subject.*

No delay need be had in the recruiting service, by my not nominating my regimental Staff.[5] I hold myself responsible for the performance of the duties of those officers untill I make the appointments.

The plan of districting the state referd to in one of your favours of the 15th. instant [6] is not receivd. & I presume was not inclosd.

I have the Honor to be with great respect yr very humble Sevt

N Rice

[ENCLOSURE]

Distribution & Assignment of the 14th. Circle in the State of Massachusetts into SubDistricts, under the direction of Lieut. Colonel Commandant Rice [7]

NAMES OF THE OFFICERS SUPERINTENDING THE SUBDISTRICTS	NUMBERS OF THE SUB- DISTRICTS	THE PRINCIPAL TOWN OR THE RENDEZVOUS OF THE SUBDISTRICTS	OFFICERS SUPERIN- TENDING DISTRICTS	PLAN OF DISTRICT RENDEZVOUS
Captain Ashmun [8]	No. 1	Pittsfield		
Captain Phelps	No. 2	Great Barrington		
Captain Babbitt	No. 3	Springfield	Major Walker	Springfield
Lieutt. Cheney Captn. Lithgow not accepting }	No. 4	Northampton		
Captain Chandler	No. 5	Worcester		
Captain Tolman	No 6	Dedham		
Captain Thwing	No 7	Boston		
Captain Brown	No 8	Plymouth	Major Winslow	Taunton
Captain Emerry	No 9	Taunton		
Lieutt Rand } Captn Pierce not accepting }	No 10	West part of Bridgewater		

ALS, Hamilton Papers, Library of Congress.

1. H to Richard Hunewell and Rice, April 10, 1799.
2. See the enclosure to H to Hunewell and Rice, April 10, 1799.
3. See "Circular to the Commandants of Regiments," April 15, 1799.
4. See "Circular to the Commandants of Regiments," March 31, 1799.
5. See Rice to H, April 23, 1799.

6. See "Circular to the Commandants of Regiments," March 31, 1799.

7. D, Hamilton Papers, Library of Congress.

8. Phineas Ashmun had been appointed a lieutenant in the Fourteenth Regiment of Infantry on January 8, 1799 (*Executive Journal*, I, 300, 303). He declined the appointment (Godfrey, "Provisional Army," 171) and was appointed captain in the same regiment on March 3, 1799 (*Executive Journal*, I, 322, 323).

Solomon Phelps, Erasmus Babbet, Jr., Thomas Chandler, John Tolman, Nathaniel Thwing, James Brown, and Ephraim Emery were appointed captains in the Fourteenth Regiment of Infantry on January 8, 1799 (*Executive Journal*, I, 299, 303).

Arthur Lithgow and Joseph Peirce, Jr., were appointed captains in the Fourteenth Regiment of Infantry on March 3, 1799 (*Executive Journal*, I, 322, 323), but both declined appointment (Godfrey, "Provisional Army," 172).

Alpheus Cheney and Isaac Rand, Jr., were appointed lieutenants in the Fourteenth Regiment of Infantry on January 8, 1799 (*Executive Journal*, I, 300, 303).

John Walker and Isaac Winslow were appointed majors in the Fourteenth Regiment of Infantry on January 8, 1799 (*Executive Journal*, I, 299, 303).

From John J. U. Rivardi

Niagara [New York] April 28, 1799. Asks that soldiers employed in the quartermaster's department be given extra pay for extra work. States that Dr. John G. Coffin, surgeon's mate and acting quartermaster general, has had to assume responsibility for such payments and that he should be reimbursed.[1] Also states: ". . . the State of my health is Such as To induce me To sollicit To be relieved. . . . I am So reduced by the intermittent fever that I can hardly walk across my Room. The Climate of West Point would probably restore me Sufficient strength to make me fit for Service."

ALS, Hamilton Papers, Library of Congress.

1. Rivardi enclosed Coffin's bill, dated April 18, 1799 (ADS, Hamilton Papers, Library of Congress). Coffin stated that the United States owed $260 to merchants and $467.91 to soldiers employed in the quartermaster's department. See also Rivardi to H, March 21, 1799.

To John F. Hamtramck

New York, April 29, 1799. ". . . Are the Regimental Staff of the Regiments of the Western army complete? If not, let them be completed. I am not certain what has been the mode in time past of

appointing Officers in that army; but the mode intended to be pursued hereafter is this—The commander of each Regiment is to
nominate his Quarter Master & Adjutant, and the Pay Master so far
as may be practicable is to be nominated by the Regimental officers
by plurality of voices. Where the Regiment is so dispersed as to
prevent the assembly of the Officers generally for this purpose the
nomination must be made by the Commander and so many of his
Officers as can conveniently assemble. The nomination when made
must be reported to be submitted for Confirmation to The President.
But the persons nominated will in the mean time perform the duties.[1]
Communicate to me freely whatever may be in your opinion of
sufficient importance respecting the Western Army. I am particularly solicitous to be informed of its state, in point of organisation
and discipline. As you have formerly served under my immediate
command,[2] you are well apprised how essential is the latter in my
eyes. . . ."

ADf, Hamilton Papers, Library of Congress.
   1. See H to James McHenry, March 10, 14, 19, 1799; McHenry to H,
March 13, 21, 1799; "Circular to the Commandants of Regiments," March 23,
1799.
   2. See Hamtramck to H, January 25, 1799.

To John F. Hamtramck [1]

New York, April 29, 1799. ". . . a *Galley* lately built at Pittsburgh
called the *Senator Ross* has been . . . ordered to Massac there to
receive further orders. The Commander of the Western Army [2]
being from situation most competent to judge what will be the most
useful employment of this Galley, I leave it with you to dispose of
her as you shall think best; observing only that the lower posts on
the Mississippi would seem to me the most fit destination. . . . I
think it most expedient for the present that the Galley should be
officered and manned by officers and men to be detached from the
line. I presume it will not be difficult to find those who have sufficient marine knowlege to answer the purpose."

ADf, Hamilton Papers, Library of Congress; LS, The Indiana Historical Society Library, Indianapolis; LS (photostat), James McHenry Papers, Library of
Congress.

1. The copy of this letter which is in The Indiana Historical Society Library is enclosed in an envelope addressed to James McHenry. At the top of this copy H wrote: "General Hamilton respectfully transmits the Secy of War the copy of a letter to Col Hamtramck on the subject of the galley. It will shew what has been deemed by him the most eligible step."

2. In the absence of Brigadier General James Wilkinson, who was en route to Philadelphia, Hamtramck was the commanding officer of the Western Army.

To John F. Hamtramck

[*New York, April 29, 1799.* On July 17, 1799, Hamtramck wrote to Hamilton acknowledging receipt of "three letters of the 29th of April." *Third letter of April 29 not found.*]

From Rufus King

[*London, April 29, 1799.*[1] *Letter not found.*]

1. "List of Letters from . . . Mr. King" to H, Columbia University Libraries.

From James McHenry

private   [Philadelphia] 29 April 1799

Dear Sir

Has it struck you, that it will be proper, notwithstanding the Commander in chief of the army has formally declined taking any agency or responsibility in its affairs until a certain state of things shall occur,[1] for you to correspond with him, as the Chief, and give him such information from time to time relative to your comand as will enable him when he may enter upon actual service to exercise his functions with promptitude and a knowledge of previous arrangements and circumstances?

If you have not adverted to this idea, will you turn it in your mind and do what may be proper?

Yours affect.   James McHenry

Gen Hamilton.

ALS, Hamilton Papers, Library of Congress; ADf, dated April 28, 1799, James
McHenry Papers, Library of Congress.
  1. See H to George Washington, July 8, 1798, note 1.

From Nathan Rice

Boston April 29th 1799

My General

Mr Duncan, my Pay Master [1] was unable to compleat his bond in
season for this days mail, I enclose it now for tomorrows, to be submitted to the Secretary at war. I requested in a former letter [2] your
directions respecting the Person to whom his bond was to be given,
but have not had the honor of receiving your answer thereto.

In your favour of the 15th [3] you constitute me the judge of the
sufficiency of the sureties & wish my opinion of those named in his
bond. The first is his Father,[4] an officer in the customs, & a respectable Character. The other, Mr. West [5] is reputed a worthy man, of
handsome property, who keeps a large bookstore, & carries on the
bookbinding business very extensively. I should not hesitate, to receive them as sureties for that sum, in any private concern of my
own. The Bond is drawn in my favour, if it is improper, please to
let it be returned with your directions on the subject. A compliance
therewith, shall be instantly had by

Sir your very respectfull Servant   N: Rice

ALS, Hamilton Papers, Library of Congress; ALS (duplicate), dated April 19,
1799, Hamilton Papers, Library of Congress.
  1. See Rice to H, April 13, 1799.
  2. See Rice to H, April 13, 1799.
  3. "Circular to the Commandants of Regiments," March 31, 1799.
  4. Robert Duncan, Sr., was an inspector of customs at Boston.
  5. David West was a bookseller and auctioneer at 36 Marlborough Street,
Boston.

From James McHenry

War Department [*Philadelphia*] *April 30, 1799.* "The Governor
of the North Western Territory Arthur St. Clair Esquire being
ex-officio, Superintendant of Indian Affairs within the said Territory

he is to be respected as such by all military Officers within the sphere of his Jurisdiction, you will be pleased therefore to direct the said military Officers to respect him as such, and to cause to be issued at their respective posts such provisions to the Indians as he may think it adviseable should be issued to them from time to time, and to be executed his instructions relative to the safekeeping and delivery of the annual stipends promised to the Indians by the Treaty of Greenville. . . ." [1]

LS, Hamilton Papers, Library of Congress; LS, letterpress copy, James Mc-Henry Papers, Library of Congress; copy, State Library, Columbus, Ohio.
1. See McHenry to H, second letter of April 11, 1799, note 3.

To James McHenry

New York April 30. 1799

My Dear friend

I hear of no Cloathing arrived. The recruiting service is now actually begun here and elsewhere. I trust that the cloathing and other articles will certainly reach the Regimental rendezvousses before *any* of the men are there. It will be a discouraging omen if it proves otherwise. I beg you to appreciate the importance of having the articles forwarded as soon as they can be, even to those places where the business is not yet completely organised in the reliance that what remains to be done must be quickly completed.

Yrs. truly   A H

James Mc. Henry Esqr

ALS, Montague Collection, MS Division, New York Public Library; ALS (photostat), James McHenry Papers, Library of Congress; copy, in the hand-writing of Ethan Brown, Hamilton Papers, Library of Congress; copy, Duke University Library.

To William S. Smith [1]

New York May 1st. 1799

Sir

It is proper for you to be informed officially that I have appointed Capt. Church of your Regiment my Aid de Camp.[2] I am sensible that in strict propriety, this ought to have been done previous to his appointment—in order that you might have had an opportunity to state to me if any particular reasons, in respect to the interests of the Regiment stood in the way of the appointment. The Omission I trust will be considered as the mere effect of inadvertence. It will be my constant aim to pay due respect to every Officer and to no one more than to yourself.

Captain Church nevertheless has my permission to *commence* the recruiting services for his Company and is ready to obey your Commands for this purpose.

The Agent for the Contractor has informed me that he waits your particular instructions to make provision for the recruits at the respective Rendezvouses.

With great Consideration　I am Sir　Yr. Obedient servant

Lieut. Col: Smith

Copy, in the handwriting of Ethan Brown, Hamilton Papers, Library of Congress.

1. Smith, who was John Adams's son-in-law, held the rank of lieutenant colonel at the end of the American Revolution. After a brief tour of Europe with Francisco de Miranda, he returned to America and successively held the offices of United States marshal for New York and supervisor of the revenue for the District of New York. For his land speculations and financial difficulties, see Benjamin Walker to H, October 4, 1796, note 1. On January 8, 1799, Smith was appointed lieutenant colonel commandant of the Twelfth Regiment of Infantry (*Executive Journal*, I, 299, 303).

2. See H to Philip Church, January 12, 1799. Church was the son of John B. and Angelica Schuyler Church and was Elizabeth Hamilton's nephew.

Circular to the Commanding Officers of the Western Army

[*New York, May 2, 1799.* On May 30, 1799, John J. U. Rivardi wrote to Hamilton: "I do myself the honor of acknowledging your letter of the 2d. instant, respecting the Superintendent of Indian Affairs [1] & shall regulate my conduct accordingly." [2] *Letter not found.*]

1. See James McHenry to H, April 30, 1799; H to McHenry, second letter of May 2, 1799.
2. In addition to Rivardi's letter quoted above, the missing circular was acknowledged in Thomas Butler to H, June 5, 1799 (listed in the appendix to this volume), and in David Strong to H, July 2, 1799 (listed in the appendix to this volume).

To James McHenry

New York, May 2, 1799. "I have received yours of the 30 April. and your directions will be immediately complied with. . . ."

Df, in the handwriting of Philip Church, Hamilton Papers, Library of Congress.

To James McHenry

private   New York May 2d. 1799.

Dr Sir

Very much attached to the idea of leaving the commanding officer of a distinct & distant army to regulate himself his particular dispositions—I have referred the employment of the Galley to Col Hamtramck [1] on the supposition that by the departure of General Wilkinson the command has devolved upon him; with the *intima-*

tion only of my opinion that probably the lower posts on the Mississippi offer the most natural position.

It seemed to me, that this Galley would render more service as a kind of Sentinel and auxiliary defence to those posts than any other way. The *invasion* of the Western Country, by a Water expedition up the Mississippi, except the part immediately in the neighbourhood of the Spanish Territories, has never struck me as much to be apprehended—and if it shall happen it will doubtless be with means against which a single Galley will be of little consequence. Hence the keeping her unemployed at Massac to wait the possibility of such an event appears to me not likely to countervail in utility the expence of building and equipping her. As a protection to an offensive movement on our part, the position below will be as eligible as higher up.

But not being aware of the views which may have influenced the building of the Galley, I sent a copy of my letter to you [2] to enable you to do what you have done. And since you think it best that the Galley shall continue at Massac [3] till after a conference with General Wilkinson and as it is not important in my opinion that her destination be immediately fixed, I now send you another letter for Col Hamtramck, [4] directing him to permit her to remain at Massac till further order.

If General Wilkinson, as directed, [5] shall have left the Western army for the seat of Government, it is presumeable that Col Hamtramck will have changed his own position, so as to be in one more convenient for communication with this Quarter & with the different posts under his command. I have acted on this presumption, though my letter is addressed to him where he was known last to be. But at any rate especially in matters not urgent, I prefer delay to the breaking in upon the regular Military Order.

With great esteem & regard   Dr. Sir   Yr Obed ser

A Hamilton

P. S. I find by a return of Cloathing just received from Mr. Hodgsdon [6] that the progress in preparing the Cloathing continues to be very slow—proving more & more the expediency of changing the button No. 1 on the six hundred and odd suits. [7] I pray you to let such articles as are ready be forwarded to the several destinations, for it will dampen extremely the recruiting service which is now begun, if the supplies for the recruits are not ready to be delivered to them as fast as they may be raised.

James Mc.Henry Esq

ALS, The Indiana Historical Society Library, Indianapolis; ALS (photostat), James McHenry Papers, Library of Congress; copy, in the handwriting of Ethan Brown, Hamilton Papers, Library of Congress.
    1. H to John F. Hamtramck, second letter of April 29, 1799.
    2. See H to McHenry, April 29, 1799, note 1.
    3. McHenry to H, second letter of May 1, 1799 (listed in the appendix to this volume).
    4. H to Hamtramck, May 2, 1799 (listed in the appendix to this volume).
    5. See H to James Wilkinson, February 12, 1799.
    6. "Return of Clothing in the Public Store at Philadelphia (of the new Contract) on the 1st May 1799" (ADS, Hamilton Papers, Library of Congress). This return was enclosed in Timothy Banger to H, May 1, 1799 (listed in the appendix to this volume). Banger was Samuel Hodgdon's clerk, and Hodgdon was superintendent of military stores.
    7. The "Return of Clothing" contains the following entry: "Infantry Privates Coats. 624 . . . No 1 on the Button." The number on the coat button indicated the regiment to which the wearer belonged. H wished to have the number changed because the First Regiment of Infantry belonged to the Regular, as contrasted to the Additional, Army and the clothing in question was needed for recruits in the Additional Army. The First Regiment was stationed in the western United States and was commanded by Hamtramck.

From John J. U. Rivardi

Niagara [*New York*] *May 2, 1799.* Sends a plan of Michilimackinac. Defends his request for extra pay for extra duty.[1] Quotes from the following letter which he received from the Issuing Commissary: "By a letter which I received yesterday from the Contractor I am instructed (as this Garrison does not exceed 50 Men) To give up Stores under my charge To The Commanding Officer. . . . I hold myself in readiness To make the transfer whenever you think proper. . . ." States that he rejected this proposal on the grounds that the size of the garrison would soon be increased and that the proposal violated the "contract of 98." Complains that the contractor wishes him to accept "46000 lb of flour (the two thirds of which must be condemned when warm weather comes)." States: "The

Rumours respecting the Indians have greatly Subsided." [2] Complains
of shortage of clothing. Asks for leave for Captain Alexander
Thompson [3] "To fetch his family." States that Dr. John G. Coffin
has requested a leave, but that he cannot be spared "before an
other Surgeon takes his place."

ALS, Hamilton Papers, Library of Congress.
  1. See Rivardi to H, April 28, 1799.
  2. See Rivardi to H, March 21, notes 21 and 23, April 3, 1799.
  3. Thompson was a member of the First Regiment of Artillerists and Engineers.

To Oliver Wolcott, Junior

New York May 2nd. 1799

Sir,

When lately in Philadelphia,[1] I mention'd to you that the Secretary of War had given me to expect some Communication from
you previous to the Execution of an Order which he has given me
respecting a Military Escort to protect the marking of an Indian
boundary line.[2]

This is intended to remind you of the matter and to repeat to you
that I wait for this Communication.

With great respect   I have the honor &c

Oliver Wolcott Esqr
Secy. of the Treasury

Copy, in the handwriting of Ethan Brown, Hamilton Papers, Library of Congress.
  1. H had been in Philadelphia from April 19 to April 26, 1799.
  2. See James McHenry to H, second letter of April 11, 1799.

From James McHenry [1]

Philadelphia, May 3, 1799. ". . . The cloathing for New York,
New Haven & Trenton is packed up and will be immediately forwarded. . . . That for Pennsylvania is also ready to be delivered.

To guard against a failure in the quantity of coats wanted for Massachusetts, I have *obliged* the Purveyor . . .² to get made up in the most expeditious manner 640 Infantry coats . . . to be divided equally between the two Regiments. . . . I have taken the same step for half a Regiment from Maryland. . . ."

ALS, Hamilton Papers, Library of Congress; ADfS, James McHenry Papers, Library of Congress.
1. This letter was written in reply to H to McHenry, April 30, 1799.
2. Tench Francis.

To James McHenry

New York May 3d. 1799

Sir

After mature reflection on the subject of your letter of the 26th. of last month; I am clearly of opinion that the President has no power to make alone the appointment of Officers to the Batalion, which is to be added to the second Regiment of Artillerists and Engineers.

In my opinion *Vacancy* is a relative term, and presupposes that the Office has been once filled. If so, the power to fill the Vacancy is not the power to make an original appointment. The phrase "Which may have happened" ¹ serves to confirm this construction. It implies casualty—and denotes such Offices as having been once filled, have become vacant by accidental circumstances. This at least is the most familiar and obvious sense, and in a matter of this kind it could not be adviseable to exercise a doubtful authority.

It is clear, that independent of the authority of a special law, the President cannot fill a vacancy which happens during a session of the Senate.²

With great respect   I am Sir   Yr. Obedt. servt.   A Hamilton

The Secretary of War

LS, Stark Library, The University of Texas at Austin; LS (photostat), James McHenry Papers, Library of Congress; ADf, Hamilton Papers, Library of Congress.
1. H is quoting from Section 8 of "An Act to augment the Army of the United States, and for other purposes" (1 *Stat.* 604–05 [July 16, 1798]). This

section reads in part: ". . . And in recess of Senate, the President of the United States is hereby authorized to appoint all the regimental officers proper to be appointed under this act, and likewise to make appointments to fill any vacancies in the army, which may have happened during the present session of the Senate."

2. On May 7, 1799, McHenry wrote to John Adams that Attorney General Charles Lee believed that "An Act authorizing the President of the United States to fill certain vacancies in the Army and Navy" (1 *Stat.* 749 [March 3, 1799]) was "large enough to embrace old officers in the army and navy . . . and also to embrace new offices created during the session which had never been filled but remained vacant." But he also wrote: "After however all the consideration I have been able to give to the question, I cannot divest myself, of a certain force which I believe attached to my original conception" (ALS, Adams Family Papers, deposited in the Massachusetts Historical Society, Boston). McHenry then quoted the second paragraph of H's letter printed above. He did not, however, attribute the quotation to H, and he did not enclose it in quotation marks.

To Zebulon M. Pike [1]

New York, May 3, 1799. "The Secretary of War has transmitted me your letter of 23rd April.[2] The practice of drawing rations for the Sons of Soldiers cannot be sanctioned."

Df, in the handwriting of Philip Church, Hamilton Papers, Library of Congress.

1. Pike was a second lieutenant in the Second Regiment of Infantry.
2. In this letter Pike had written to James McHenry: ". . . I have with me a young lad whom I brought from the Mississippi whose father is in the service, it being customary in that Country to draw rations for the sons of soldiers. I had always drew his subsistence but a doubt arising after my joining the troops at this place [Reading, Pennsylvania] I omitted drawing till I should be better informed on the subject" (copy, Hamilton Papers, Library of Congress). On November 3, 1797, Brigadier General James Wilkinson, who was commanding the Western Army, had ordered: "The Children of the army are to be allowed a ration pr. day & a woman who suckles an infant half a ration extra but no allowance to the infant" (LC, RG 94, Adjutant General's Office, General Orders, General James Wilkinson, 1796–1808, National Archives).

To Nathan Rice

New York May 3rd. 1799

Sir

Your letter [1] with the ones therein mentioned have come to hand.

Inclosed is the Act for better organizing the army of the United States [2] which will give you all necessary information.

with true consideration   I am Sir   y ob S

⟨Nath⟩an Rice Esqr.

Df, in the handwriting of Philip Church, Hamilton Papers, Library of Congress.
    1. Rice to H, April 23, 1799.
    2. 1 *Stat.* 749–55 (March 3, 1799).

From William S. Smith

East Chester [*New York*] *May 3, 1799.* "I have been honoured with your Letter of the first of may; having always understood that Capt Church tho' honoured by the appointment of being your Aid De Camp, intended, with your permission to recruit his Company; I mentioned to him, when in Town last, that the money & recruiting instructions, were ready for him, when it was convenient for you to spare him, & for himself to proceed; I have however no particular wish that he should perform this duty, unless it should be pointedly agreable to you, as I conclude you cannot at present spare him, I take the liberty of requesting your influence with the war-office that the 6th. section of the act for the better organizing of the Troops of the United States,[1] be executed as promptly as possible. . . ."

ALS, Hamilton Papers, Library of Congress.
    1. Section 6 of "An Act for the better organizing of the Troops of the United States; and for other purposes" states in part: "That when any officer shall be detached from a regiment to serve as an aid to a general officer . . . the place of such officer in his regiment shall be supplied by promotion or new appointment, or both, as may be requisite . . ." (1 *Stat.* 752 [March 3, 1799]).

From Benjamin Stoddert [1]

Navy Department
3rd May 1799

Sir,
    I do myself the honor to enclose the copy of a letter I have written

to Capt Talb⟨ot.⟩ [2] I have proposed to the President that Nichol-
⟨son⟩ should be employed in superintending the building of one of
the 74 gun ships,[3] & I presume he will acquiesce.[4] Barry the brave,
seemed to be, and to think himself, too infirm for active service—
perhaps employment may be found for him also, on shore. It is
desireable the Frigates, whose Commanders will always have the
command of a number of inferior vessels, and generally separate
commands, should be commanded by active enterprising men. Truxtun may be the senior Officer in active service, Talbot next, & these
two men may not come in contact for years.

I trouble you with this view of the Navy prospects, in the hope
that you will influence Talbot to serve. He is a man of too much
merit to be lost to the service; & I see not how it is possible to retain
him on his own terms without losing Truxtun [5]—but what is of more
consequence, without violating principles, to do injustice to Truxtun.
As to Talbots legal right to be the senior officer, it stands upon the
same grounds which Knox contended for.[6] The Law reducing the
Frigates to three [7] terminated completely every thing done or authorized to be done, with respect to the other three—and the President, had he been so inclined, had no more right to continue Captains
in the service of the U States, for the three reduced Frigates, than he
had to continue the building of them. Captains Talbot, Dale and
Sever, therefore, returned to the mass of Citizens, just as Genl. Knox
did when the former army was reduced. Had the Letter written by
the Secretary at war, to these Gentlemen, contained the stipulation
that they should still retain their rank in the Navy of the United
States, it would have been nugatory. There was no power to make
such a stipulation.

But admitting I am wrong in this idea, as seemed to be your impression, when I had the pleasure of seeing you and as is at this time
the impression of the Attorney General: [8] still there is no getting
over, the second nomination in May 1798 of Capt Talbot to the
Senate.

I have the honor to be   with great esteem Sir   Yr Most Obed
Serv   Ben Stoddert

LS, Hamilton Papers, Library of Congress; LC, RG 45, Naval Records Collection of the Office of Naval Records and Library, Miscellaneous Letters Sent by
the Secretary of the Navy, National Archives.
    1. For background to this letter, see Silas Talbot to H, January 15, 1799;
Stoddert to H, February 6, 1799.

2. Stoddert to Talbot, May 2, 1799 (copy, Hamilton Papers, Library of Congress). In this letter Stoddert expressed his regrets that Talbot was outranked by Thomas Truxton and hoped that this fact would not prevent Talbot from remaining in the Navy and assuming the command of either the *United States* or *Constitution.* Stoddert also wrote that he would do his best to see that Talbot would never be "subjected to the command of Capt. Truxton."

3. Stoddert to John Adams, April 19, 1799 (ALS, Adams Family Papers, deposited in the Massachusetts Historical Society, Boston).

4. Adams agreed with Stoddert's proposal (Adams to Stoddert, April 27, 1799 [LC, Adams Family Papers, deposited in the Massachusetts Historical Society, Boston]).

5. On March 17, 1799, Truxton wrote to Stoddert that he did not think that Talbot was qualified to serve as a captain in the Navy (*Naval Documents, Quasi-War, November, 1798-March, 1799,* 516-17).

6. This is a reference to Henry Knox's insistence that he should outrank H in the Additional Army. See the introductory note to George Washington to H, July 14, 1798.

7. "An Act supplementary to an act entitled 'An Act to provide a Naval Armament'" (1 *Stat.* 453-54 [April 20, 1796]).

8. Charles Lee.

To George Washington

Private   New York May 3d. 1799.

Dr. Sir

At length the recruiting for the additional regiments has begun in *Connecticut New York New Jersey Pensylvania* and *Delaware.* The enclosed return of cloathing [1] will sufficiently explain to you that it has commenced at least as soon as the preparations by the Department of War would permit. It might now also proceed in Maryland and Massachusettes, and the next post will I trust enable me to add Virginia—but that I do not think it expedient to outgo our supply of Cloathing. It will have the worst possible effect—if the recruits are to wait a length of time for their cloathing.

I anticipate your mortification at such a state of things. Various causes are supposed to contribute to it.

It is said that the President has heretofore not thought it of importance to accelerate the raising of the army [2]—and it is well understood that the Secretary of the Treasury is not convinced of its utility.[3] Yet he affirms that for a long time past he has been ready & willing to give every aid depending on his department.

The Secretary of War imputes the deficiency in the article of

Cloathing to a failure of a contract which he had made and to the difficulty of suddenly finding a substitute by purchases in the market. It is however obvious that the means which have been since pursued have not been the best calculated for dispatch. The materials procured at distant places have been brought to Philadelphia to be made up. They are stated to be adequate in quantity.

You will observe that 6⟨oo suits⟩ [4] are numbered 1—This applies to a Regiment in the Western Country. I proposed to the Secretary to change the buttons.[5] It has not been done.

Yet if the Secretary's energies for execution were equal to his good dispositions, the public service under his care would prosper as much as could be desired. It is only to be regretted that good dispositions will not alone suffice, and that in the nature of things there can be no reliance that the future progress will be more satisfactory than the past.

Means, I trust sufficient, have been taken to procure from Europe a supply of Cloathing for the next year. And the Secy has assured me that he would immediately take measures for procuring a supply for the succeeding year.

As to other supplies I believe things are in tolerable train—and that there is a certainty of the most essential articles in due abundance.

The officers for North Carolina have been appointed.[6] No nomination has yet come forward from South Carolina.

Not a single field Officer has yet been appointed for the Regiment to be raised in New Hampshire Vermont & Rhode Island.[7] It seems the members of Congress dissuaded from the nomination of those who were proposed by the General Officers and promised to recommend preferable characters—but this promise has not yet been performed. This want of organisation is an obstacle to the progress of the affairs of this Regiment.

It is understood that the President has resolved to appoint the Officers to the provisional army [8] and that the Secretary has thought fit to charge the *Senators* of each state with the designation of characters.

With the truest respect & attachment I have the honor to be
Dr. Sir   Your Obed ser   A Hamilton

General Washington

ALS, George Washington Papers, Library of Congress; two copies, Hamilton Papers, Library of Congress.

1. See H to James McHenry, second letter of May 2, 1799, note 6.

2. As early as October 22, 1798, John Adams had written to McHenry: "As to the Recruiting service—I wonder whether there has been any Enthusiasm which would induce Men of common sense to enlist for five dollars a month who could have fifteen when they pleased by sea or for common work at Land? . . .

"There has been no national Plan, that I have seen, as yet formed for the Maintenance of the Army. One Thing I know, that Regiments are costly Articles, everywhere and more so in this Country than any other under the sun. If this Nation sees a great Army to maintain, without an Enemy to fight, there may arise an Enthusiasm that seems little to be foreseen. At present there is no more prospect of seeing a french Army here, than there is in Heaven." (ALS, Adams Family Papers, deposited in the Massachusetts Historical Society, Boston.)

3. Although no record has been found of the opinion of Oliver Wolcott, Jr., on the Army when H wrote the letter printed above, Wolcott subsequently revealed that he had consistently opposed plans for increasing the strength of the Army. On December 29, 1799, he wrote to Fisher Ames: "The only question which will arise respecting the army, will be whether it shall be disbanded, or the present establishment continued upon condition of suspending further enlistments. The subject is attended with vast difficulties in whatever light it is considered. The Generals, and I believe I may say the officers, with their connections and a great proportion of the wisest and best friends of the government, think the existing army ought to be preserved as a permanent establishment. Nothing, however, is more certain than that the army is unpopular, even in the Southern States, for whose defence it was raised. Who is to defend the army if the Southern members oppose the establishment, or even support it faintly? The Northern people fear no invasion, or if they did, they perceive no security in a handful of troops; nobody has thought it prudent to say that the army is kept on foot to suppress or prevent rebellions; for such a purpose, the troops are worse than nothing, especially as the state of idleness to which they are necessarily condemned, tends to corrupt their principles. . . .

"I anticipate your surprise at the perusal of these observations; candour requires me to say that my opinions are singular, and have been kept in my own breast as much as possible. A year since, the army was in the power of the government, and I then freely explained my sentiments to General Washington and General Hamilton, that it ought to be the immediate object of the government to form ample arsenals, and deposit therein arms and ammunition adequate to the supply of the whole force of the country; that but few officers ought to be appointed, and the expense of supporting idle men avoided as much as possible. I stated my doubts whether the best selection of officers could be made at that time, whether the best men could be enlisted, and whether it was probable that the establishment could be maintained. The reply was, that if money could be borrowed, the army ought to be raised; and that the delay which had happened was hardly to be excused. Finding the decision against my sentiments, the money was procured, and nothing has been omitted on my part to give success to the system of government. . . .

"I beg you to believe that my observations respecting the army are not dictated by a desire of being thought wiser, even on the point in question, than General Washington and General Hamilton. My self love, if I am not deceived, carries me no further than a desire that you may understand that I have been consistent, and have not adopted a new opinion in opposition to my friends at this critical period. My sentiments are but little known. I should not disclose them at this time, did not the plan of this letter require that I should open my whole heart." (Gibbs, *Wolcott*, II, 317–18.)

4. The material in broken brackets has been taken from a copy of this letter.

5. See H to McHenry, second letter of May 2, 1799.

6. See McHenry to H, April 10, 1799 (listed in the appendix to this volume). In this letter McHenry enclosed a list, which had been approved by John Adams, of officers for the troops to be raised in North Carolina.

7. See McHenry to H, April 16, 1799.

8. H is referring to the Eventual Army, which had been authorized by "An Act giving eventual authority to the President of the United States to augment the Army" (1 *Stat.* 725–27 [March 2, 1799]). See the introductory note to H to James Gunn, December 22, 1798.

To Nathan Rice

New York May 4 1799

Sir

I have received your letter of the 18. April,[1] and hope that as soon as convenient the nomination of Quarter master and Adjutant to your Regiment may take place. There is no objection to a change in the association of the company officers for good reasons; you will propose therefore such as you may deem proper. The bond of your Pay Master Mr Duncan did not accompany your letter of the 29 April: you must however have a new one executed made payable to the United States of America.[2]

I am particularly obliged by those of your observations which are personal to me. Whenever I see a deserving fellow Soldier resuming the Sword to cooperate with me it affords peculiar satisfaction.

with true regard   I am Sir   Your obed Servt.

Nathan Rice Esqr:

Df, in the handwriting of Philip Church, Hamilton Papers, Library of Congress.

1. H is mistaken. He is referring to Rice to H, April 13, 1799.

2. This bond was enclosed in Joseph Blake to H, April 30, 1799 (listed in the appendix to this volume).

To James McHenry

New York, May 7, 1799. ". . . Col Smith . . . recommends [1] as his Major . . . Theodosius Fowler Esqr. . . .[2] I do not find among the p⟨apers before⟩ me any list of the Officers of the Additional Troops of C⟨avalry⟩. Will you be pleased to have it transmitted? I promised Mr. Jones [3] your C⟨lerk⟩ a memorandum of the number of printed copies of oat⟨hs⟩ and weekly returns which it would be expedient to ⟨send⟩ to the several commandants of the Twelve Regiments. Wil⟨l⟩ you be so good as to direct him to forward to each Commandant 704 copies of oaths three hundred copies of weekly returns of recruits—and to add to these thirteen copies of the Articles of War? Col Stevens has renewed his inquiries of me as to his compensation.[4] I am anxious that this and the duties he is to perform, which is connected with the *general plan* you had under consideration, should be determined. The orderly and prosperous course of the service can only be the ⟨r⟩esult of a good organisation. And it is in every thing desireable to begin to lay the foundations well. . . . It has been well determined ⟨tha⟩t none but natives shall be enlisted for the ⟨ca⟩valry. I earnestly wish that this rule was adopted ⟨by⟩ the Artillery. It is extremely important that ⟨each⟩ corps shall be well composed and especially ⟨that⟩ there shall be every ground of reliance ⟨on⟩ its fidelity."

ADfS, Hamilton Papers, Library of Congress.
   1. Letter not found.
   2. A veteran of the American Revolution, Fowler was a New York City contractor and a speculator in securities and land. For H's earlier association with Fowler, see "Contract for Army Rations," October 28, 1790, note 2.
   3. Nathan Jones.
   4. See Ebenezer Stevens to H, April 17, 19, 1799. Stevens had asked for compensation on several previous occasions. See Stevens to H, December 18, 1798; February 23, March 14, 1799.

From David Strong

Detroit [Territory Northwest of the River Ohio] May 7, 1799. Calls attention to the "slender state of the Ammunition at this Post."

States that no supplies from the hospital department have arrived in two years. Complains that "his many Communications of a Public nature to the Secretary of War" are not acknowledged. Reports that "there is one uniform sentiment of discontent pervading the Indian Tribes, and it is said they are now collecting in a body and meditate some hostile operations against our Government, and in all probability against that of Great Britain." Denies the suggestion "from an Extract of a letter from . . . the Secretary of War of there having been issued a larger number of Rations . . . than the number of Troops."

LS, Hamilton Papers, Library of Congress.

Election by the Sixth Triennial General Meeting of the Society of the Cincinnati

Philadelphia, May 8, 1799. ". . . The members present then proceeded to the election of officers for the ensuing three years, when it appeared from the ballots that the following gentlemen were duly elected:

General George Washington, President General.

Major General Alexander Hamilton, Vice President General. . . ."

"Journals of the Cincinnati, 1784–1787, Vol. I," 93–94, Library of Congress.

From Oliver Wolcott, Junior [1]

Treasury Department
May 8 1799

Sir,

I have to acknowledge the receipt of your letter of the 2d instant.

The business to which you allude, relates to an application made to me by the Surveyor General, for a party of Men to assist in marking the Indian boundary line agreeably to General Waynes

Treaty; but, as the Surveyor General omitted to designate the time when and the place where the men would be required, I have written to him for the necessary information.[2] In the mean time I beg leave to suggest, whether it would not operate to prevent delay, if you were, to direct the Commanding Officer [3] in the North Western Territory, to confer with the Surveyor General on the subject—and to afford him such assistance as he may deem adequate to the object.

I have the honor to be very respectfully Sir, Your Obedtt. Servant   Oliv. Wolcott.

Major General Hamilton
New York

LS, Hamilton Papers, Library of Congress.
    1. For background to this letter, see James McHenry to H, second letter of April 11, 1799.
    2. Wolcott to Rufus Putnam, April 19, 1799 (Carter, *Territorial Papers*, III, 21).
    3. During the absence of Brigadier General James Wilkinson, Lieutenant Colonel John F. Hamtramck was in command of the Western Army.

To John F. Hamtramck [1]

New York May 9. 1799

Sir

It has been determined to make the following disposition of the first Regiment of Artillery. One batalion to be attached to the Western army, another to garrison the posts in Georgia & South Carolina, a third to garrison the posts in North Carolina Virginia and Maryland—the remaining one to be annexed to the troops in the field within the limits of Major General Pinckney's command. The inclosed shedule will exhibit the component parts of these several batalions. You will observe that the officers who are to compose the batalion assigned to the Western army are not distributed into Companies. This distribution is to be made by Col Burbeck.

You will therefore furnish him with the information contained in this letter and with a copy of the enclosed schedule—and you will direct him to arrange into companies the officers & men who are to compose the batalion attached to the Western Army.

With great consideration   I am sir   Your Obed. serv

Col. Hamtramck

ADf, Hamilton Papers, Library of Congress.
  1. For background to this letter, see H to James McHenry, April 26, 1799. See also "General Orders," May 16, 1799.

From James McHenry

War Department, May 9, 179[9].[1] "I have this morning received your letter dated the 7th. instant. . . . I shall direct a list of the Officers of the Regiment of Cavalry, to be made out, and sent to you. I desired Mr. Francis to inform Coll. Stevens,[2] that I intended he should be allowed at the rate of 1000 dollars per annum for his services. This is the Salary of the Storekeeper in this City,[3] who has more business to transact, and very much greater charge. The General plan for providing and delivering supplies, was returned to me the 26th. of April Ulto.[4] You may be assured, that it will not be laid asside, nor a decision delayed unnecessarily. I am too deeply impressed, with the utility of beginning our carier under the most perfect System not to feel sufficiently interested in the measure. You will find in my letter of this date, some further instructions respecting recruiting explanatory of those printed. The recruiting instructions which you inclosed in your letter to Captain Bruff,[5] are of the first impression: [6] not the revised instructions.[7] I have of course, transmitted to Bruff a sett of those revised. Lest similar mistakes should occur I request you will destroy all the old ones in your possession. The old are printed in a large type, and without my signature. All the revised which have been sent to you have my signature."

LS, Hamilton Papers, Library of Congress; LS, letterpress copy, James McHenry Papers, Library of Congress.
  1. This letter is incorrectly dated "1798."
  2. Tench Francis. See Ebenezer Stevens to H, April 17, 1799.
  3. Samuel Hodgdon.

4. McHenry had sent this plan to Oliver Wolcott, Jr. See McHenry to H, second letter of April 17, 1799.

5. H to James Bruff, May 2, 1799 (listed in the appendix to this volume), which was enclosed in H to McHenry, second letter of May 3, 1799 (listed in the appendix to this volume).

6. This is a reference to the 1798 edition of the War Department pamphlet *Rules and Regulations Respecting the Recruiting Service*. See H to Jonathan Dayton, August 6, 1798, note 6.

7. This is a reference to the March, 1799, edition of the War Department pamphlet *Rules and Regulations Respecting the Recruiting Service*. See H to Dayton, August 6, 1798, note 6; McHenry to H, March 21, 1799.

From James McHenry

War Department
9th. May. 1799

Sir,

A foriegner (an irishman) was lately enlisted at Lancaster, by Captain Matthew Henry of the tenth regiment of Infantry, and shortly after deserted. This occurrence has led me to reflect, that it will be well, to avoid as much as possible, the enlistment of foriegners.

The third article of the rules and regulations, for the recruiting service,[1] expressly gives a *preference* to natives, for soldiers, and only *admits* of the enlistment of foriegners of *good reputation*, for sobriety, and honesty. The ninth article, contemplating, that no foriegner is entitled in the army, to the full confidence, that may be reposed, in a native; provides, that at the foot of each return, which shall bear the name, or names, of any foriegner or foriegners, by birth, there shall be a note or notes, specifying that he is still an alien, or how, when, and where, each such foriegner, became a Citizen, if he shall have become one.

The articles cited, were intended to draw the attention of Officers, forcibly to the object, of attaining native soldiers. Foriegners of a class to enlist, are often profligate, and irregular in their habits; to introduce too many of them, into the army, would have a tendency, to corrupt the morals, of the native soldiers; and as they are bound by no principle of attachment to the country, their frequent desertions, might occasion, loss to the public, and fatal disappointments in the service.

Should you coincide with me, in opinion, you will instruct the different officers now recruiting, to attend strictly, to the preference, to be given to foriegners, to enlist none whose reputations are doubtful, and even to postpone enlisting those of the best characters, until the district of country, alotted them to recruit in, is exhausted of natives willing to enlist.

I am Sir   with great respect   your obedient servant

James McHenry

Major General Alexander Hamilton.

LS, Hamilton Papers, Library of Congress; LS, letterpress copy, James McHenry Papers, Library of Congress.

1. This is a reference to the March, 1799, edition of the War Department pamphlet *Rules and Regulations Respecting the Recruiting Service*. See H to Jonathan Dayton, August 6, 1798, note 6; McHenry to H, March 21, 1799.

To James McHenry

New York May 9. 1799

Sir

It is desireable as fast as possible to execute the arrangement which you have adopted for the Distribution of the Artillery.[1] The great distance of General Pinckney from the position of a large proportion of the companies allotted to his command seems to render the intervention of some other authority necessary in the first instance to cause them to be transported within the sphere of their destination. The company of Capt Frye[2] ought to proceed to Charles Town and the batalion of the first Regiment reserved for the Field ought to be collected on the Potowmack. As the removal of these troops from their present positions will require the concurring movement of those which are to replace them you will perhaps think it best to authorise me to give the requisite directions for the one purpose as well as for the other.

There are several considerations which induce me to think that it will be adviseable to annex the state of Maryland to the limits of General Pinckneys command. If on reflection you should be of the same opinion you will be pleased to signify it. This suggestion by a very obvious train of Ideas brings to my recollection a letter from

General Washington of the   [3] of which the following is an extract [4]—"When the disposition was contemplated of assigning to Major Genl. Pinckney and yourself your respective districts of superintendance, I was of opinion (as you will see by the inclosed copy of a letter which I wrote to the Secy. of War on my way from Philadelphia to this place) that the *whole* of General Wilkinson's Brigade should be considered as under your immediate direction; because, if a part of it which is, or may be stationed Within States Kentuckey and Tenassee, should be under the superintendance of Genl. Pinckney, and the other part under yours, it might occasion great inconvenience, and perhaps confusion, for General Wilkinson to have to communicate sometimes with one of the Major Generals and sometimes with the other. This I conceive, will still be the case, if the disposition which mention to have been communicated by the Secy. of War should continue. I am therefore yet decidedly of opinion, that the *whole* of Genl. Wilkinson's Brigade should be under your Superintendance."

ADf, Hamilton Papers, Library of Congress.

1. For background to this letter, see H to McHenry, first letter of April 26, 1799; McHenry to H, April 27, 1799.
2. Frederick Frye, a veteran of the American Revolution, was a captain in the First Regiment of Artillerists and Engineers.
3. Space left blank in MS. H is referring to George Washington to H, first letter of February 25, 1799.
4. The remainder of this letter is in the handwriting of Ethan Brown.

To Nathan Rice

New York May 9. 1799

Sir

Your letters of the 19 [1] & 28 of April have duly come to hand.

You have been informed that the Bond of your Pay Master must be to the UStates of America.[2] The orderly course of supplies to your Regiment requires the speedy appointment of your Quarter Master. That of your Adjutant may wait as long as you shall find expedient.

I am satisfied with the division you have made for the Circle within which your Regiment is to be raised. You have I presume communicated it to Col. Hunnewell as a guide in making the division of the residue of the State. If not, you will do it without delay. I am at a loss to imagine why it has happened that I have not as yet received a line from that officer.[3]

The disposition of the cloathing for your Regiment is left to your own judgment. Any alterations which they may require must be at the expence of the soldiers.

If there was no omission, in the copy of my letter, which was circular, you were invited to offer your opinion concerning the fitness of the place mentioned for your Regimental rendezvous.[4] The reasons for naming Somerset were   1   its vicinity to Rhode Island & to water Communication, which will facilitate the transmission of whatever supplies are to come from a distance   2   Its not being far distant from *Uxbrige* where it is contemplated that three Regiments will be stationed for a time.

But it is expected, that you will inform yourself of the local advantages and disadvantages of the place and if you judge it inexpedient will suggest a preferable substitute—bearing in mind that a great City is to be avoided & that facility of access for distant supplies is a consideration of weight.

The numbering of the Regiment has nothing to do with the relative ranks of the Commandants.

With great consideration   I am Sir   Yr obed

P.S. Money for the recruiting service of your Regiment has been forwarded to Jonathan Jackson Esq Boston who will deliver it to your Pay Master upon your order. It is hoped that cloathing and other articles will speedily be furnished likewise. If you judge it expedient to begin to recruit before their arrival you will do it—otherwise you will content yourself with having every thing prepared. I understand that Mr. Jackson has been instructed to form contracts for supplies.[5] Communicate with him & see that every necessary arrangement be mature.

Col Rice
Hingham

ADf, Hamilton Papers, Library of Congress.
1. H is referring to Rice to H, April 29, 1799.

2. See H to Rice, May 4, 1799.

3. On May 24, 1799, Richard Hunewell, commanding officer of the Fifteenth Regiment of Infantry, wrote to H that H's letters to him had been delayed because of "a long passage occationed by the breaking up of the Kennebic River & irregularity in the carriage of the mail." Hunewell's letter is listed in the appendix to this volume.

4. "Circular to the Commandants of Regiments," March 31, 1799.

5. See James McHenry to H, April 4, 1799.

From James McHenry [1]

War Department, May 10, 1799. Encloses a letter from William Macpherson [2] "relative to the positions proper to be maintained . . . by the regular troops, in the Country late the scene of insurrection and disaffection."

LS, Hamilton Papers, Library of Congress.

1. For background to this letter, see McHenry to H, March 13, 1799, note 12, March 15, 1799.

2. Macpherson to McHenry, May 3, 1799 (copy, Hamilton Papers, Library of Congress). In this letter Macpherson reviewed the movements of the forces under his command from March 19 to March 23, 1799. He stated that he had dismissed the volunteer companies and had left the regular troops under the command of Major Mahlon Ford at Reading. He recommended that the regular troops be garrisoned at Reading, Allentown, and Easton.

From James McHenry

War Department, May 10, 1799. ". . . I should prefer for the present, to continue the distribution of the command of the troops of the United States, as declared in your instructions dated the 4th. of February ultimo.[1] If hereafter, without reference merely to the Artillery, and upon general considerations, it should be found convenient to annex Maryland to General Pinckneys district it will be done. . . .[2] In all cases, in which persons have been requested to send forward recommendations, I have experienced complaints from them, if others than those they selected happened to be prefered. I shall however, be very well pleased, to possess the recommendations of the Commandants of Regiments, if to be obtained without my asking for it directly or indirectly; for altho these Gentlemen are

interested in having well qualifyed persons under them as Officers,
yet they cannot be considered exempt from the partialities but too
apt to intrude upon such occasions: I wish to be under as little
restraint as possible, for reasons which need not be enumerated. . . .
I do not recollect whether I have mentioned to you, that it will be
proper the Contractors should be early apprized of any change
which may be made in recruiting districts, and also of the districts
where provisions &c will be required: You will give the necessary
orders on this head. . . . Inclosed is the list of Officers in the Regiment of Cavalry."

[E N C L O S U R E] [3]

Cavalry

John Watts	Colonel	Virginia
Solomon Van Rensselaer	Major	New York
John Taylor	ditto	Virginia
James Taylor	Captain	
James V. Ball	ditto	
Richard Willing	ditto	Pennsylvania
Benjamin Williamson	ditto	New Jersey
John B. Armistead	ditto	Virginia
William Spencer	ditto	Maryland
James Burn	ditto	South Carolina
John Webb	Lieutenant	
Stephen G. Simmons	ditto	
William Tharp	ditto	
Robert Gray	ditto	Pennsylvania
John Walbach	ditto	ditto
George Washington Craik	ditto	Virginia
Laurence Washington	ditto	ditto
Richard Tilghman	ditto	Maryland
William C. Rogers	2. Lieut.	Pennsylvania
Alexander McComb Junr.	ditto	New York
Charles Tutt	ditto	Virginia
George W. P. Custus	ditto	ditto
Carter B. Fontaine	ditto	ditto
Richard Cooke	ditto	Maryland

LS, Hamilton Papers, Library of Congress; LS, letterpress copy, James McHenry
Papers, Library of Congress.
1. McHenry is presumably referring to McHenry to H, February 4, 1799.
2. See H to McHenry, May 9, 1799.
3. Copy, Hamilton Papers, Library of Congress.
In the Hamilton Papers, Library of Congress, is a second list of cavalry officers. This list, which is entitled "Officers of the Cavalry," gives the dates on
which the officers accepted their commissions.

From William Heth [1]

Petersburg [*Virginia*] *May 11, 1799.* ". . . I cant forego the
present oppy of congratulating you, and our Country, on the election of General Marshall,[2] as well as on the success which hath attended the federal cause throughout the State. I dont mean by this,
to say that we have obtained a majority in Congress,[3] or in the
State *Legislature* [4]—the members to the latter, not being yet all
known—but we have obtained such an accession of numbers as well
as of *talents*, that I think, we may consider Jacobinism, as completely
over thrown in this State. However—all this, you must have been
told by Carrington,[5] immediately after our triumphant election of
Marshall. . . ."

ALS, Hamilton Papers, Library of Congress.
1. Heth, a Federalist and a veteran of the American Revolution, was collector of customs at Bermuda Hundred, Virginia.
2. John Marshall had been elected in April, 1799, to the House of Representatives from Virginia.
3. In 1799 the Federalists won eight of Virginia's nineteen congressional seats.
This was an increase of four seats over their representation in the previous
session.
4. In the state contests Federalists were elected to more than one-third of
the seats in the Virginia legislature.
5. Edward Carrington was supervisor of the revenue for Virginia.

From James McHenry

War department May 11. 1799.

Sir,

If the new recruiting instructions have not been forwarded to the
several Officers who are inlisting men for the regiments of Artillery

and four old regiments of Infantry, whose names & places of rendezvous are contained in the list some time since sent you, I would
suggest the propriety of your transmitting them as early as possible [1]
together with the law making an alteration in the ration.[2]

Will it not be proper that the several Contractors should be
notified of the alteration that they may govern themselves accordingly?

I am Sir   with great respect   Your obed servant

James McHenry

Major General Hamilton

LS, Hamilton Papers, Library of Congress.
    1. See "Circular to the Commandants of Regiments," March 27–April 17,
1799.
    2. This is a reference to Sections 19 and 22 of "An Act for the better or-
ganizing of the Troops of the United States; and for other purposes" (1 *Stat.*
749–55 [March 3, 1799]). Section 19 reads: "That a ration of provisions shall
henceforth consist of eighteen ounces of bread or flour, or when neither can
be obtained, of one quart of rice or one and an half pound of sifted or bolted
Indian meal, one pound and a quarter of fresh beef, or one pound of salted
beef, or three quarters of a pound of salted pork, and when fresh meat is issued, salt at the rate of two quarts for every hundred rations, soap at the rate
of four pounds, and candles at the rate of a pound and a half for every hundred rations. . . ."
    Section 22 reads: "That it shall be lawful for the commander in chief of
the army, or the commanding officer of any separate detachment or garrison
thereof, at his discretion, to cause to be issued, from time to time to the troops
under his command out of such supplies as shall have been provided for the
purpose, rum, whiskey, or other ardent spirits in quantities not exceeding half
a gill to each man per day, excepting in cases of fatigue service, or other extraordinary occasions, and that whensoever supplies thereof shall be on hand,
there shall be issued to the troops vinegar at the rate of two quarts for every
hundred rations."

From James McHenry

War Department 11th. May 1799

Sir

Lieutenant General Washington in a letter dated the 28th. of
January ultimo [1] observes—

"In speaking of the Cavalry I must observe, that in specifying their
uniform it was intended that their breeches should be of leather and

consequently buff instead of white. This I doubt not will strike you as being most proper on every account, and in that case no time should be lost in correcting the error before the officers shall have provided their uniform."

This information having arrived after the regulations for the uniform for the army of the United States reported by the General Officers convened at Philadelphia [2] had received the approbation of the President, and been promulged, it was not conceived sufficiently important to demand a revision, especially as in its operation it could affect the officers only; and as leather breeches might be either white or buff, according to the manner of dressing the skins &c.

There have been some remonstrances made to me, respecting the change of buttons from yellow mettal to white in the artillery uniform. Yellow while it would serve as a mark of distinction between the Infantry and Artillery is considered less subject to be tarnished by powder and therefore thought to be preferable to white.

I have also been harrassed to make explanations to Officers relative to a more particular description of the regulations respecting their uniforms.

These circumstances have induced me, to refer the regulations to you, to request that you will carefully revise them; extend the descriptions of the several parts of the uniform of the Regimental and other Officers so as to relieve them from any ambiguity; correct whatever errors they may contain, and report the same as soon as convenient.

I have the honor to be   with great respect, Sir Your Obedient Servant   James McHenry

Major General Alexander Hamilton

LS, Hamilton Papers, Library of Congress.
    1. Copy, George Washington Papers, Library of Congress.
    2. See H's draft of George Washington to McHenry, third letter of December 13, 1798.

To John F. Hamtramck

New York May 12th. 1799

Sir

In the same expectation, which has dictated preceding letters to you;[1] namely that Brigadier General Wilkinson has left his station for the seat of Government & that the command in his absence has devolved upon you, I send you the copy of a letter from the Secy of War to me of the 11 of April last and of the inclosures to which it refers respecting the marking of the Indian Boundary line, also the copy of a letter from the Secy of The Treasury of the 8th instant on the same subject.

Agreeably to the intimation in the last letter it is my desire that you immediately communicate with the Surveyor General and afford him such assistance for effecting the object as he may deem adequate. In this you will fulfil the direction of the Secretary of War.

As this is a matter of great importance to the UStates, I shall rely that nothing on the part of the military will be wanting which can tend to a speedy and effectual execution.

With great consideration   I am Sir   Yr. Obed serv

If the cause of the past disappointments can be ascertained by you, I shall be glad that you will communicate it.

Col. Hamtramck
Fort Wayne.

ADf, Hamilton Papers, Library of Congress.

1. H to Hamtramck, April 27, two letters of April 29, May 9, 1799. H is also referring to two letters listed in the appendix to this volume: in a letter dated April 9, 1799, H discussed routine Army matters; on May 2, 1799, H requested Hamtramck to delay sending the galley from Massac.

To James O'Hara [1]

New York, May 12, 1799. Describes the provisions of Sections 19 and 22 of "An Act for the better organizing of the Troops of the United States; and for other purposes." [2]

Df, partially in H's handwriting, Hamilton Papers, Library of Congress.
  1. O'Hara was quartermaster general of the United States Army from 1792 until his resignation in 1796. From 1796 to 1802 he was a Government contractor in Tennessee and Kentucky.
  2. 1 *Stat.* 749–55 (March, 3, 1799). For these sections, see James McHenry to H, first letter of May 11, 1799, note 2.

From Silas Talbot [1]

New York 13th May 1799

Sir

Very soon after I Left your office Last week I wrote to the Secretary of the Navy [2] and Stated to him that I found it impossible for me to embrace the Service in the Station which it appear'd to be his intention to place me, and therefore I beged Leave to decline the Service altogether and added my request to him that he would be pleased to communicate such my desire to the President and the day following I Stated my account for pay up to the date of my resignation and Sent it on. In my Letter to Mr. Stoddert, I took the Liberty to suggest in pretty Strong terms my beleif that it was your Opinion that the Legal right of Seniority Over Captain Truxton was in my favor. Mr. Stoddert has been pleas'd to answer my address [3] Very fully, urges my continuance in the Service for the present, untill the President shall have made up his mind on the question of Seniority and adds that his Letter contains only his Opinion and not the Presidents, That perhaps he is wrong in regard to his Ideas on the Subject, and that he had not as yet been favor'd with your Opinion or answer thereon. As his Letter seem'd to be mark'd throughout with respect and a regret for my Situation which he

freely acknowledged I had just cause to complain of, and as he
declar'd that he would not communicate my Letter to the president
untill he should here from me again, It appear'd to be my duty to
resume my Station for the present and accordingly I wrote to
Mr. Stoddert yesterday,[4] that if it should be required I would take
such command as might be conferr'd on me, untill the President
should be pleas'd to Settle and make Known the relative rank I was
to hold in the Navy. But on the condition that I should not in the
meantime be subjected to the Orders or direction of any Officer
in the Navy Except Captains Barry and Nicholson.

Being thus Situated, I beg Leave to request the favor of you Sir,
to State your Opinion fully on the question alluded to which has
been submitted to you by Mr. Stoddert.[5] I am Sorry to trouble
you in this way, But I hope that you will have the goodness to
Excuse me, Since Matters have taken such a turn and have been so
conducted. If you should condescend to make the Statement in question, I shall be glad of an oportunity to take a Copy of it, If it is
agreable and perfectly proper that I should see it.

I have the honor to be with perfect respect   Sir   your Obedient
humble Servant   Silas Talbot

Major Genl. Hamilton Esqr.

ALS, Hamilton Papers, Library of Congress; ADfS, Manuscript Collection,
G. W. Blunt White Library, Mystic Seaport, Inc.
   1. For background to this letter, see Talbot to H, January 15, 1799; Benjamin Stoddert to H, February 6, May 3, 1799.
   2. In this letter, dated May 7, 1799, Talbot wrote: ". . . I find that General
Hamiltons Opinion, after all due consideration is perfectly in unison with my
Own, on the Subject of the legal right of Seniority, as he told me since my return home, that his Opinion in that respect was different from yours. When
you submitted the matter to Genl. Hamilton, I did conceive that his Opinion
was to have been in some measure conclusive, for you were pleased to observe
to me when Speaking on the Subject of referring the question to Genl. Hamilton, that if his Opinion should be different from my wish, you hop'd that I
would not consider the Situation in which I was placed as a Sufficient Cause to
decline the Service. Was it not then natural for me to infer, that Should his
Opinion be otherwise and comport with my own Ideas it would be respected?"
(ALS, enclosed in Stoddert to John Adams, July 12, 1799 [LS, Adams Family
Papers, deposited in the Massachusetts Historical Society, Boston]; copy, enclosed in Talbot to Adams, July 9, 1799 [ALS, Adams Family Papers, deposited
in the Massachusetts Historical Society, Boston]).
   3. Stoddert to Talbot, May 8, 1799 (copy, enclosed in Talbot to Adams,
July 9, 1799 [ALS, Adams Family Papers, deposited in the Massachusetts Historical Society, Boston] copy, enclosed in Stoddert to Adams, July 12, 1799

[LS, Adams Family Papers, deposited in the Massachusetts Historical Society, Boston]).

4. Talbot to Stoddert, May 11, 1799 (ALS, enclosed in Stoddert to Adams, July 12, 1799 [LS, Adams Family Papers, deposited in the Massachusetts Historical Society, Boston]; copy, enclosed in Talbot to Adams, July 9, 1799 [ALS, Adams Family Papers, deposited in the Massachusetts Historical Society, Boston]).

5. See Stoddert to H, May 3, 1799.

From Abraham Ellery [1]

Newport [Rhode Island] May 14, 1799. ". . . Adjutant General North,[2] in a letter, of the 30th. ult., did me the honor to offer me, the appointment of Assistant Adjutant Genl. and requests me to communicate to you, my answer, in case of acceptance. From a total inexperience of its duties, I felt a hesitation in making my determination, resulting from doubts of my adequacy to the employment, & it is with diffidence I now accept of it; but, I trust, no exertions on my part will be wanting to diminish my incompetence. . . ."

ALS, Hamilton Papers, Library of Congress.
    1. Ellery was a captain in the Sixteenth Regiment of Infantry.
    2. William North. North, who served throughout the American Revolution and was an aide-de-camp to Baron von Steuben, held the rank of major and inspector of the Army from 1784 to 1788. He was a member of the New York Assembly in 1792, 1794, 1795, and 1796, and was speaker in 1795 and 1796. From May 5, 1798, to August 17, 1798, he was United States Senator, filling the vacancy which had been created by the resignation of John Sloss Hobart. See John Jay to H, two letters of April 19, 1798. On July 19, 1798, North was appointed adjutant general of the United States Army with the rank of brigadier general (*Executive Journal*, I, 293).

Circular to the Artillery Field Officers [1]

Circular   New York May 15. 1799

Sir

    I send you for your information the arrangement which has been adopted for the organisation and disposition of the   Regt. of Artillerists.[2]

    You will perceive that the batalion which you are to command is to be stationed in

You will do well to apprise without delay the officers who are to compose this batalion of the arrangement—so that such of them who may not at present be with their companies may join them, and that the companies which are not now at their proper destinations may be getting into readiness to proceed thither when the order shall be given for that purpose.

With great consideration   I am Sir   Your Obed servt

ADf, Hamilton Papers, Library of Congress; copy, to Constant Freeman, Hamilton Papers, Library of Congress.
    1. H numbered the paragraphs of this letter, and on the back and at the bottom of the letter he wrote specific information which pertained to the individual to whom the circular was to be addressed. In the first and second paragraphs H left the spaces blank in the MS and put brackets around the blank spaces to alert the copyist to where he wished the material to be placed.
    2. See H to James McHenry, April 26, 1799; "General Orders," May 16, 1799.

General Orders [1]

New York, May 16, 1799. States: "The following disposition of the two Regiments of Artillerists and Engineers has been adopted. Of the first Regiment, one battalion commanded by Major Rivardi [2] is assigned to the Western Army, another Battalion commanded by Major Freeman [3] is to garrison the posts in Georgia and South Carolina, another Battalion commanded by Major Ford [4] is to garrison the posts in North Carolina Virginia and Maryland, and the remaining Battalion commanded by Major Toussard [5] is reserved for the service of the field. Of the Second Regiment, one Battalion commanded by Major Brooks [6] is to garrison the posts in Delaware Pennsylvania New Jersey and New York, another Battalion commanded by Major Jackson [7] is to garrison the posts in Connecticut Rhode Island Massachusetts and New Hampshire, and the remaining Battalion (one not having yet been raised) commanded by Major Hoops [8] is reserved for the service of the field. The definitive arrangement of Officers to the respective companies of the battalion of the first Regiment annexed to the Western Army is referred to Colonel Burbeck." [9] Lists the officers in the other battalions.[10]

Copy, in the handwriting of Philip Church, Hamilton Papers, Library of Congress.

1. For background to this document, see H to James McHenry, April 26, 1799.

In the Hamilton Papers, Library of Congress, is a list in H's handwriting entitled "Officers to whom orders are to be addressed." This list contains the names and location of thirteen lieutenant colonels commandant and eight majors.

2. John J. U. Rivardi. See Rivardi to H, April 3, 1799, note 1.

3. Constant Freeman, a resident of Massachusetts and a veteran of the American Revolution, was a major in the First Regiment of Artillerists and Engineers. Freeman's headquarters were at Charleston, South Carolina.

4. Mahlon Ford, a resident of New Jersey and a veteran of the American Revolution, re-enlisted in the Army in 1784 and held the rank of lieutenant when the Constitution went into effect. He was a major in the First Regiment of Artillerists and Engineers. Ford's headquarters were at Norfolk, Virginia, but because of illness he did not report for duty at Norfolk until September, 1799 (Ford to H, September 20, 1799 [listed in the appendix to this volume]).

5. Lewis Tousard, a native of France, had joined the Continental Army as a volunteer in 1777 and in the following year lost an arm in the fighting in Rhode Island. He was a major in the First Regiment of Artillerists and Engineers. Tousard, whose headquarters were at Newport, Rhode Island, had been assigned to that city by Secretary of War James McHenry (Tousard to H, March 10, 1799).

6. Benjamin Brookes, a resident of Maryland, was a major in the Second Regiment of Artillerists and Engineers. Brookes's headquarters were in New York City, but he was unable to report for duty because of poor health (Brookes to H, November 19, 1799 [listed in the appendix to this volume]).

7. Daniel Jackson, a resident of Massachusetts and a veteran of the American Revolution, was a major in the Second Regiment of Artillerists and Engineers. Jackson's headquarters were at Fort Castle William in Boston Harbor.

8. Adam Hoops, a resident of New Jersey and a veteran of the American Revolution, was a major in the Second Regiment of Artillerists and Engineers. His headquarters were at Fort Jay on Governors Island in New York Harbor.

9. Henry Burbeck. See Rivardi to H, April 3, 1799, note 3.

10. See the enclosure to H to McHenry, April 26, 1799.

From James McHenry

War Department, May 18, 1799. "The enclosed papers are, No 1 a copy of a letter from Major D. Bradley,[1] No 2 a copy of a letter from Colo Hamtramck,[2] No 3 a copy of a letter from Colo Strong [3] No 4 the Speech of Kesas, Nanqui, Okia, Abeeway & Machibas Kisegan, lately returned from Philada., and Cotowaso, pesoto, and peswas chiefs of the Chippiewa, Ottawa, and Potowatomie nations,[4] No 5 My answer to the Speech [5] delivered in Philada. by the above mentioned chiefs. . . . The information relative to the above mentioned Tribes of Indians, is given to assist you in forming your opinion, and it is left to you to decide, whether, as the garrison of Detroit consists of but about 160 Men, non commissioned officers and privates, it will be adviseable, and proper it should be reinforced. This garrison has been weakened by draughts for the Mississippi. The persons who have speculated illegally in Indian lands, and who have excited them to complain to government, will, no doubt, continue to practice upon them and even to stimulate them to acts of hostility, should they consider such a proceeding calculated, eventually to procure to them from the united States a title to their purchases."

LS, Hamilton Papers, Library of Congress; LS, letterpress copy, James McHenry Papers, Library of Congress.

1. On May 7, 1799, Daniel Bradley wrote to McHenry concerning the progress of his recruiting party (copy, Hamilton Papers, Library of Congress).

2. On April 1, 1799, John F. Hamtramck wrote to McHenry concerning his difficulties in dealing with the Indians in the vicinity of Fort Wayne (copy, Hamilton Papers, Library of Congress).

3. David Strong wrote to McHenry on March 22, 1799, that a saloon keeper in Detroit had sued him for trespass because he had placed a sentinel in front of the saloon to prevent soldiers from entering it (copy, Hamilton Papers, Library of Congress).

4. "Speech delivered [at Detroit] by Kesas, Nanqui, Okia, Abeeway & Machibas kisegan who have lately returned from philada: also Cotowaso (or black Chief) pesoto and peswas," February 23, 1799 (copy, Hamilton Papers, Library of Congress). This speech reads in part: "Father—Attend to us—Our former Chiefs and ourselves have given certain Tracts of Land to the Canadians, whom we conceive to be our Brothers and also to many Englishmen in this place, and are determined to make good their title to those Lands. What would you think of us should we sell our Lands, and take them back after disposing of the consideration which you had paid us? we again say we will protect them in their possession.

"Father—How would you like it? We are confident your feelings would be mortified, should we take the Lands on which we live, and drive you to the other side of the great water from whence you came.

"Father—But for you we should have been unacquainted with War. But for you we should never have felt its calamitous consequence. You have taught us the barbarous custom. In all disturbances your white people have been the Aggressors, and our Lands have been lost in the Contest.

"Father—Whatever may be your conceptions of the matter, We are of opinion, that you are under obligation to us for the Lands on which you dwell. When you first landed upon them their fertility created in you a desire to possess them.

"Father—do you get provisions from the other side of the great Water? No—the produce of our Lands supports you. You call us Children but might call us Fathers with greater propriety as we are the sources from whence your necessities are supplied.

"Father—Your Children have other complaints. You wish to reduce the quantity of their provisions—will this conciliate their affections? It should be augmented, for it is now too little.

"Father—When your Children arrived here from a great distance, they have no quarters prepared for them, the Inhabitants sometimes accommodate them, but as thro' us they sometimes sustain losses. We hope you will have a house built for us near the Town."

5. "Speech of the Secretary of War to the Chiefs and Warriors of the Potowatomies, Ottawa and Chippewa Nations," n.d. (copy, Hamilton Papers, Library of Congress). McHenry's speech reads in part: "Brothers. Your Father the President is convinced, and believes upon due reflection, you also will be convinced that it is much better for your respective nations, and for Indian nations in general, that all sales of their lands should be made at public open treaties in the presence of an agent specially authorized by the government of the United States. At public treaties all the Indians would be noticed, and could meet, be heard and would be secured by the public agent the impositions they must be liable to, at private meetings.

"With the same views, the security of the Indians against imposition, by designing purchasers, and to guard against the jealousies and animosities that might thereby be occasioned, we find that the British Government always exercised a power of superintending the sales of Indian lands within their limits."

To James McHenry

New York May 18. 1799

Sir

It is urgent that arms for the troops to be raised be at the respective Regimental rendezvouses as speedily as possible. Military pride is to be excited and kept up by military parade. No time ought to be lost in teaching the Recruits the use of arms. Guards are necessary as soon as there are soldiers and these require arms.

When I came to see the hats furnished for the Twelveth Regiment, I was disappointed and distressed. The Commander in Chief recommended cocked-hats.[1] This always means hats cocked on three sides. I was assured that cocked hats were provided. I repeated the assurance to the officers. But the hats received are only capable of being cocked on one side; and the brim is otherwise so narrow as to consult neither good appearance nor utility. They are also without cockades and loops.

Nothing is more necessary than to stimulate the vanity of soldiers. To this end a smart dress is essential. When not attended to, the soldier is exposed to ridicule and humiliation. If the articles promised to him are defective in quality or appearance, he becomes dissatisfied; and the necessity of excusing the public delinquency towards them is a serious bar to the enforcement of discipline. The Government of the Country is not now in the indigent situation in which it was during our Revolution War. It possesses amply the means of placing its military on ⟨a⟩ respectable footing; and its dignity and its interest equally requi⟨re⟩ that it shall act in conformity with this situati⟨on.⟩ This course is indeed indispensable if a faithful zealous and well regulated army is thought necessary to the security or defence of the Country.

With great respect   I have the honor to be Sir   Yr. Obed serv

Js. McHenry Esq

ADf, Hamilton Papers, Library of Congress.
1. See H's draft of George Washington to McHenry, third letter of December 13, 1799.

To Jeremiah Wadsworth [1]

New York May 18th. 1799

Dr Sir

I stand extremely in need of a capable prudent and trust worthy man to aid me in capacity of Secretary. He must possess a clear comprehension and a perspicuous correct and neat Style. I wish the emoluments which the law allows me to offer were a more adequate inducement to such a character. They are only the pay and emoluments of a Captain in the Army—in other words forty dollars per month and three rations per day or an equivalent in money. Perhaps it may hereafter be in my power to obtain an extension; but as this is casual the person must undertake upon the basis of the existing provision.

If you can find out & recommend to me such a person, willing to engage in the Station, you will do me a great favor. As I shall write to several Friends in different States on the same Subject, you must so manage the matter in sounding the disposition of the person as that no expectation is excited which in case of another appointment would embarrass you.

with very great esteem and regard   I remain Dr Sir   Your obed
Serv   Alexander Hamilton

Jeremiah Wadsworth Esqr:
Hartford Connecticut

LS, Connecticut State Library, Hartford; ADf, Hamilton Papers, Library of
Congress.
   1. Although the letter in the Connecticut State Library is addressed only to
Wadsworth, the draft lists as additional addressees Stephen Higginson of Boston, Aaron Ogden of Elizabeth, New Jersey, and Samuel Dexter of Charlestown, Massachusetts.
   Wadsworth, a resident of Hartford, Connecticut, had been deputy commissary general and commissary general of purchases during the American Revolution. From 1789 to 1795 he served in the House of Representatives as a Federalist.

To Richard Hunewell and Nathan Rice

New York May 21. 1799

Sir
   The following are the different contractors of the State of Massachusetts Joseph Ruggles Nathl: Ruggles Ralph Smith Aaron &
Charles Davis all of Roxbury.
   You will please as soon as be to make arrangements with them for
the supply of the troops at the several Recruiting Rendezvouses.
   with true consideration   A H

Col Rice & Hunnewell

Copy, in the handwriting of Philip Church, Hamilton Papers, Library of Congress.

From James McHenry [1]

War Department, May 21, 1799. "The house of Panton and Leslie,
of Pensacola, had several trading establishments, for supplying the
Indians with goods, within that part of the territory of the United

States, lately evacuated by Spain, agreeably to Treaty.[2] As these Gentlemen established, and carried on their trade with the Indians, under the protection of Spain, they expect their agents, will be permitted, to collect the debts, owing to them among the Indians, and to close their mercantile transactions, without interruption from our garrisons. Considering the expectation to be reasonable, I informed Brigadier General Wilkinson in a letter dated the 31st. January last [3] 'that it was proper the Agents of Panton and Leslie, be permitted, to proceed, in the course of winding up the business, and collecting the debts, owing to that house.' I have no doubt, if my letter has been recieved, by the General, that the necessary orders, have been issued, to the officers commanding on the Mississippi; Lest however my letter may not have been recieved, and to guard against any improper conduct of the Military officers in that quarter, you will be pleased, to issue such orders, as may secure to the agents of Panton and Leslie, all necessary and proper freedom, in the lawful prosecution of their business. I think it of some consequence, not to give offence to these Gentlemen, but to aid them, as far as it can be done with propriety. It has been too much a practice, with the commandants of Garrisons on the frontiers, to hold talks, with Indian tribes, and play parts, which belong exclusively, to the civil officers, employed to superintend the Indian affairs. This has consequently attracted to the Garrisons, numbers of Indians, and occasioned great and unnecessary expenditures of the public provisions. You will be pleased to issue such instructions on this subject, as will prevent as much as possible the continuance of such practices, and oblige the military officers, to refer the Indians in all matters, relating to their national affairs, or grievances, to the Governor of the North Western territory, and Governor of the Mississippi territory, or the temporary Indian agent, nearest to their post, as the case may require. It will also be proper, that you instruct the Commandants of Posts in the Mississippi territory, to furnish on the order of Governor Serjeant, when the same can be spared, such rations for the Indians, who may visit the said posts, as he may from time to time direct. . . ."

LS, Hamilton Papers, Library of Congress; LS, letterpress copy, James McHenry Papers, Library of Congress; extract, James McHenry Papers, Library of Congress.

1. For background to this letter, see H to McHenry, August 17, 1797; Mc-Henry to H, August 19, 1797.

2. This is a reference to Article II of the Treaty of Friendship, Limits, and Navigation (Pinckney's Treaty), signed at San Lorenzo el Real, October 27, 1795 (Miller, *Treaties*, II, 320).

3. Two copies, Hamilton Papers, Library of Congress.

To James McHenry

New York, May 21, 1799. ". . . It is . . . necessary that ⟨t⟩he officers generally should be possessed of 'The Rgulations for the Order and Discipline of ⟨t⟩he Troops of the UStates.'¹ I mean those which were instituted in our Revolution War. This system will of course obtain 'till there shall be a substitute. I pray that a competent number may be prepared & transmitted ⟨wi⟩thout delay."

ADf, Hamilton Papers, Library of Congress.

1. H is referring to *Regulations for the Order and Discipline of the Troops of the United States* (Philadelphia: Printed by Styner and Cist, in Second-street, 1779), which was written by Baron von Steuben and was repeatedly reprinted. For a list of the editions of this manual from 1781 to 1815, see Joseph R. Riling, *Baron von Steuben and His Regulations* (Philadelphia, 1966), 27–31.

Circular to the Commandants of Regiments

New York, May 22, 1799. "It has happened in one instance which has come to my knowledge that the hats sent on for the Recruits have been destitute of Cockades and Loops.¹ In a similar case I authorise you to procure the deficiencies to be supplied and I will take care that the expence be defrayed. Where there is an Agent of the war Department, you will first apply to him to have what is necessary done; but you will at all events have it done. I speak only as to Hats."

LS, to Aaron Ogden, Lloyd W. Smith Collection, Morristown National Historical Park, Morristown, New Jersey; ADf, Hamilton Papers, Library of Congress.

1. See H to James McHenry, May 18, 1799.

To David Strong

New York May 22. 1799

Sir

The Secretary of War has sent me your letter of the 22d. of March with the copy of a speech lately delivered by certain Indians.[1]

The pretension which they urge and the manner of urging it are alike to be discountenanced. It will be well to keep a watchful eye upon the affair and to endeavour to discover their instigators, who if discovered must be reported to Governor St Clair that he may pursue the proper methods to bring them to punishment.

But as they employ a strong style of menace it is proper to be well on your guard. I entertain at present an opinion that the advantages of a Post at Michilimacnac do not compensate for the disadvantages. It does not appear to me that a Post there will materially awe the Indians, and it is quite out of the reach of support. The troops there, if added to the garrison of Detroit, would render it more respectable, give greater security, and be in a better relative position for events which may arise: While both trouble and expence would be saved by the change of place.

Yet I have been unwilling to direct any material alteration in the disposition of the troops as made by General Wilkinson, till after a conference with that Officer, who has been directed to repair to the seat of Government with a view to a general arrangement of the affairs of the Western army.

But notwithstanding this desire of delay on my part, if appearances of hostility from any of the Indians shall appear to you to require a reinforcement of your post, you are at liberty to do it from the detachment at Michilimacnac. But in this matter I rely on your firmness and prudence that you will not take the step unnecessarily. It will however be satisfactory to me to know your ideas of the usefulness of the Post of Michilimacnac—& of the number of troops, if any, which you may deem indispensable to be stationed there.

You will before this gets to hand have received a letter from me [2] desiring you to forbear till further order the exercise of Martial law over the Inhabitants of Detroit. I have since reflected maturely on the subject, and so strong are my doubts of the authority to exercise Martial law in a similar case, in time of peace, that, I am obliged to confirm the suspension. I am aware of the inconveniences which it may occasion to the order of your post and the discipline of your men. But these inconveniences must be submitted to, rather than involve a contest with the civil power on a ground which may not be maintainable. You must only increase your vigilance and strictness towards your troops—and you will judge how far they can consistently with the general object for which they are stationed be kept within the *Fort*, where you can of course maintain martial law in exclusion of intruders.

Perhaps the feint of thus confining your men may, by alarming the inhabitants for their safety, lead to some arrangement which will bring the Magistracy to aid you in a reasonable plan of police. Sometimes that may be effected by address which cannot be accomplished by measures of direct authority. You will judge how you can go with propriety in improving this hint.

I observe with regret the unpleasant spirit which seems to have been displayed by the Court. According to your statement, I do not perceive that you were not intirely regular in placing your sentinel where you did for the purpose you mention.[3] But still, Sir, I recommend every effort to bring about an amicable concert with the Civil authority. Collision with it can produce no good and must be attended with much evil. I advise you to open a correspondence with Governor St Clair, to state to him calmly and frankly your difficulties & to request his influence and cooperation in obviating them in some mode which will not infringe civil rights.

You are already informed that Governor St Clair is *ex officio* Superintendant of Indians Affairs.[4] Nothing is more essential than that all shall act within their proper spheres. The political concerns of the UStates with regard to the Indians are committed to the management of the Superintendants and their deputies. The miliary officers are in this respect only to be auxiliary in the cases in which their agency is indispensable, and it is desireable that they avoid interfering except when their assistance is requested by the Superintendent or his representative or in conformity with some previous concert. In other cases, and especially in all matters relating to their national affairs or grievances, it is the duty of the Military Officers to refer the Indians to the Superintendant or his nearest Deputy. The contrary practice has many disadvantages & among others it is represented that it has a tendency to invite a frequent resort of the Indians to the several posts and to occasion great and unnecessary expenditures of provisions. But the chief objection is that it interferes with a regular system of conduct in the management of Indians Affairs.

The Secretary of War has particularly noticed the subject to me.[5] And I request that this view of the matter may strictly govern.

With great consideration I am Sir   Yr. Obed serv   A H

Col Strong

ADf, Hamilton Papers, Library of Congress.
    1. Both the letter and the speech were enclosed in James McHenry to H, May 18, 1799.
    2. Letter not found, but see H to McHenry, April 23, 1799.
    3. See McHenry to H, May 18, 1799, note 3.
    4. See "Circular to the Commanding Officers of the Western Army," May 2, 1799.
    5. See McHenry to H, May 21, 1799.

Circular to the Commandants of Regiments

Circular   New York May 23. 1799

Sir

It is important to the service in every way that vacancies which happen in the several Regiments should be as speedily as possible filled. As no persons can be more interested in this being done, and with a careful selection of character, than the Commandants of Regiments, it is desireable that they should from time to time propose to the General, under whose command they may be, candidates for filling those vacancies, in order that they may be by him offered to the consideration of the Executive.

In doing this, however, it must be recollected that there is no part of his functions in which it is upon principle more essential that the Executive should be perfectly free from extrinsic influence of every kind than that of the choice of officers. Hence it is proper, that no expectation should be entertained that the characters presented for consideration will be preferred: that no encouragement should be given to them which may occasion embarrassment or chagrin in case of their not being adopted, and that no inferences painful to the person recommending should be drawn from the failure of the recommendation. This failure will doubtless often happen. Information of more eligible candidates will frequently come through other channels. Collateral considerations will in no small number of instances occur, which between candidates of equal pretensions will naturally lead to a preference of persons who may have been presented through other channels.

In a word, the recommendation of the Commandant is only to be considered as *one mode* in which information of fit characters may be conveyed to the Executive.

It occasionally happens that experience leads to alterations in the subdistricts or their rendezvouses. It is expected that whenever this happens the Commandant within whose circle it occurs will give notice of the change to the Contractor of his circle in order that provision may be made for the requisite supply.

It is understood that some misapprehension has existed among some of the recruiting officers about the articles which the Contractors and their Agents are to supply. It will be proper to signify to them that these are only to embrace *Provisions Quarters, fuel straw*, stationary and, where there is no surgeon, medical aid and supply.

With great consideration   I am Sir   Yr Obed serv

Lt Cols Commandants

ADf, Hamilton Papers, Library of Congress; LS, to Aaron Ogden, Lloyd W. Smith Collection, Morristown National Historical Park, Morristown, New Jersey; LS, Hamilton Papers, Library of Congress; copy, Hamilton Papers, Library of Congress.

To John F. Hamtramck [1]

New York May 23. 1799

Sir

I send an extract of a letter from the Secy of War of the 21st instant on the subject of the house of *Panton* and *Leslie;* and I desire that you will as far as shall depend on the military give effect to his views. He will no doubt have made a similar communication to the Superintendants of Indian Affairs for their government. I know of no particular orders which the nature of the subject permits to be given on my part. The detail must be regulated by the occasion.

You are aware that the Governors of the North Western Territory and of the Mississippi Territory are severally *ex Officio* Superintendants of Indian Affairs. The management of those affairs under the direction of the Secretary of War appertain to them. The Military in this respect are only to be auxiliary to their plans and measures. In saying this, it mus⟨t⟩ not be understood that they are to direct milita⟨ry⟩ dispositions and operations. But they are to b⟨e⟩ the organs of all negotiations and communicatio⟨ns⟩ between the Indians and the Government. They are to determine when and where supplies ⟨are⟩ to be furnished to those people and what othe⟨r⟩ accommodations they are to have. The Military in regard to all such matters are only to a⟨ct⟩ as far as their cooperation may be required by the Superintenda⟨nts⟩ avoiding interferences without previous concert with them or otherwise than in conformity with their views. This will exempt the military from a responsibility which had better rest elsewhere and it will promote a regular and uniform system of conduct towards the Indians; which cannot exist if every commandant of a Post is to intermeddle seperately and independently in the management of the concerns which relate to them.[2]

This communication is made in conformity with an instruction from the Secretary of War;[3] who particularly desires that "The Military Officers may be required to refer the Indians in all matters relating to their national affairs or grievances to the Governor of the North Western Territory and the Governor of the Mississippi Territory or the temporary Indian Agent nearest to their post as the case may require; and that the Commandants of the Posts on the Mississippi Territory may be instructed to furnish on the order of Governor Serjeant when the same can be spared such rations for the Indians who may visit the said posts as he may from time to time direct."

This letter being addressed to you as the Temporary Commander in the presumed absence of General Wilkinson—you will act in it accordingly; recollecting that your attention is to extend to all the troops and posts from Pitsburgh Westward, to the Missi [ssi]ppi, on the Mississippi, on the Lakes and in Tenessee; in short to all which constitute the Western army and its dependencies. But in saying this as a guide to you, it is not my intention to contravene any arrangements of command which General Wilkinson may have made previous to his Departure.

With great consideration   I am Sir   Yr Obed serv

Col Hamtramck

ADf, Hamilton Papers, Library of Congress; LS (photostat), James McHenry Papers, Library of Congress; extract, RG 94, Adjutant General's Office, Letter Book of Major Thomas Cushing, National Archives; copy, Duke University Library.

1. This letter was enclosed in H to James McHenry, May 24, 1799 (listed in the appendix to this volume).

2. The contents of this paragraph are the same as those of "Circular to the Commanding Officers of the Western Army," May 2, 1799.

3. See McHenry to H, May 21, 1799.

From James McHenry

War department 23d. May 1799.

Sir

I received yesterday your two letters of the 18. and 21. instant. You will see by the enclosed schedule No. 1.[1] the quantity of Clothing Arms accoutrements &c. which has been ordered for the several regiments. Money for the recruiting service and pay and forage for the Officers has been forwarded as is mentioned in Schedule No. 2.[2]

It is to be understood that the whole Clothing for no one Regiment has been sent on, that a part only can or has been forwarded to each; and that the purveyor [3] is using every exertion to complete the reimainder in time to meet the wants of the several Regiments, which he will now be able to do a vessel having arrived from Liverpool supposed to have the articles he wanted.

I am extremely sorry at the misconception that has happened respecting the hats for the Infantry.[4] It could not however have been mentioned by me to you, that they were fashioned to be full cocked for the present year; because the Contract for them had been ordered before the General Officers decided on the Change,[5] and I understood the manufacturer of them had so far advanced as to admit of no change in their form, without a material loss to the public. I shall make enquiry of the Purveyor; who had the exclusive direction of this business, and at all events see that the Contract for the ensuing year shall produce hats of the proper form and dimensions. For this purpose I must request you to send me a pattern hat. The Purveyor expects also a Pattern Haversack.

Cockades and loops have always heretofore been furnished by the Soldier under the direction of his Officer. If you are of opinion the public ought to depart from this practice and furnish loops, cockades, and materials to cock the hats, I shall take measures accordingly.

I have directed sixty Copies of the Baron Steubens regulations for "the order and discipline of the Troops of the United States" [6] to be sent to Colonel Stevens, subject to your disposition.[7]

I received this morning the enclosed letter from Major Daniel Bradley.[8] You will take such order respecting its object as may be proper. I shall send him recruiting money and suspend forwarding Cloathing until I can learn your determination relative to the place he is to recruit at.

I am Sir   With great respect   Your obed servant   James McHenry

Major General Alexander Hamilton

LS, Hamilton Papers, Library of Congress; LS, letterpress copy, James McHenry Papers, Library of Congress.
    1. "No. 1, Articles ordered for the several Regts" (D, Hamilton Papers, Library of Congress).

2. D, untitled and undated, Hamilton Papers, Library of Congress.

3. Tench Francis.

4. See H to McHenry, May 18, 1799.

5. See H's draft to George Washington to McHenry, third letter of December 13, 1799.

6. See H to McHenry, May 21, 1799.

7. On the back of this letter H wrote: "Desire Col [Ebenezer] Stevens to forward six copies of the Regulations to each Commandant except [Thomas Lloyd] *Moore*. Send him the names & places. . . ." Philip Church sent this request to Stevens on May 24, 1799 (ALS, Hamilton Papers, Library of Congress).

8. Daniel Bradley to McHenry, May 15, 1799 (copy, Hamilton Papers, Library of Congress). In this letter Bradley discussed the assignment of recruiting officers in Virginia and requested a transfer to Connecticut.

Bradley, a resident of Virginia and a veteran of the American Revolution, was a major in the Fourth Regiment of Infantry.

From James McHenry

War Department
May 23nd 1799

Sir

The President thinks it highly expedient, that no time should be lost in selecting proper characters to officer the twenty four regiments of Infantry, the regiment and Battalion of Riflemen, the Battalion of Artillerists and Engineers and the three regiments of cavalry which may be raised in pursuance of the act giving eventual authority to the President of the United States to augment the army passed the 2nd of March last,[1] and contemplates, as soon as the selection is closed, to make the appointments.

The selection of officers for the eventual army appears to be an object of primary importance, requiring all imaginable circumspection and care: their characters for courage, talents, and conduct, ought, if possible, to be such as to inspire a general, and well grounded confidence that the fate of their country may be safely entrusted to them.

I have, therefore, to request you will accord your full attention to the subject, and furnish me, as soon as practicable, with a list of the names of such characters in your state to fill the annexed military grades, in the eventual army, as in your opinion, are best qualified, and willing to serve in case of an actual war, which will render it indispensable to recruit the men for the most extended army.

You will doubtless find a facility in forming the list from consulting and co-operating with proper persons in the different parts of your State who may be best calculated to give information of the requisite particulars, and upon whose patriotism and judgment a full confidence may be placed.

Every cautionary measure is necessary to guard against errors in appointments, which too frequently result from the case with which recommendations are generally obtained, the partialities of friends, and a delusive hope that men of bad habits, by being transplanted into the army, will become good officers and good men.

The officers proposed to be drawn from the State of New York are Viz

Two Colonels	One Major
Four Majors	Four Captains &
Twenty two Captns &	Eight Subalterns of Artillery
Forty four subalterns of Infty	

In making the selection it will be proper to allow, if fit characters present themselves for a choice, a due proportion of Captains and subalterns to the several counties, according to their respective population, as well with a view to facilitate the recruiting service as to give general satisfaction. This rule, however, is not meant to be invariably observed as to exclude great superiority of talents, by too strict an adherence to it.

As circumstances may exist at the time of the Presidents making the appointments which may render it proper to make some changes in the list with which I may be furnished, you are requested not to give the parties recommended such positive assurances as will render a change impracticable without wounding, too sensibly, their feelings.

With great respect, I have the honor to be, Sir, your most ob Hb ser   James McHenry

Major Genl A. Hamilton.

LS, Hamilton Papers, Library of Congress.
    1. 1 *Stat.* 725–27. See also the introductory note to H to James Gunn, December 22, 1798.

To James McHenry

New York May 23. 1799

Sir

In consequence of the information conveyed by your letter of the 21 instant, I have authorised Col Strong,[1] if from appearances he shall conceive there is well founded cause of alarm, to withdraw from Michilimacnac the whole or part of the Garrison for the reinforcement of his post. I did this for two reasons 1 because I did not perceive any other point from which he could be reinforced and 2 because I entertain a strong opinion, that considering the force likely to be kept on the Western & N Western frontier a corps at Michilimacnac is much less useful than it will be at several other places; while it is absolutely out of the reach of support and the supply of it is peculiarly difficult and expensive. Yet I have cautionned Col Strong to forbear to do it except under circumstances in his opinion urgent—being unwilling to change any of the dispositions of General Wilkinson until after an interview with him. By the way is it not high time to have heared from that Officer? Is there not danger that my letter directing him to repair to the seat of Government has miscarried [2] The inclosed [3] repeats the direction.

Embarrassment being likely to grow out of the question about the sales of the Indians to the Individuals alluded to,[4] Will it not be expedient for the public to hold a Treaty with them and make the acquisition of the lands to the use of the UStates? A small compensation to the Indians will satisfy all their scruples; and the UStates will be enabled to controul the intrusions of the irregular purchasers. Otherwise it is probable settlements will grow up under their titles hostile to government because originating in disobedience to law. It may also be a question whether if by the effect of their purchase the acquision can be made by the U States on easier terms, it may not be adviseable to extinguish their pretensions by the grant of a portion of the lands.

This probably may be accomplished without difficulty. Temporary measures on a distant frontier are often proper for a Government which does not choose to keep on foot a considerable force, effectually to awe sedition and hostility.

What do the Indians [5] mean when they say "You wish to reduce the quantity of provisions." Will this conciliate [6] their affections? They ask, it seems, a house to be built for them near the Town. Both these points will I presume, engage your attention in your communication with the Superintendant.

I submit that it is necessary that you should communicate to the respective Superintendants of Indian Affairs for their government the substance of that part of your letter, abovementioned, which respects the house of *Panton* & *Leslie*.

With great respect   I have the honor to be Sir   Your obed serv

The Secy of War

ADf, Hamilton Papers, Library of Congress.
  1. H to David Strong, May 22, 1799.
  2. H to James Wilkinson, February 12, 1799.
  3. H to Wilkinson, May 23, 1799.
  4. See McHenry to H, May 18, 1799.
  5. See McHenry to H, May 18, 1799, note 4.
  6. In MS, "conclitiate."

From Nathan Rice

Boston May 23d 1799

My General

In your favour of the 4th you have expressed your assent, that a change in the association of the Officers, might be made for good reasons. On a more mature consideration of the Division of my circle into subdistricts, from the information I have obtained, I am led to fix on Brookfield as the rendevous of a subdistrict; I am confident it will be more beneficial for the recruiting service, the young men within the limits of the 2d district have generally been in the habits of entering the sea service, have experienced the superior emoluments of that life & will very few of them I think enlist as Soldiers, & it so happens that not a single Officer who has received an appointment in the Army resides within three of those subdistricts.

I have therefore thought it adviseable to remove the One at Bridgewater, to Brookfield. The Exchange therefore I would propose, and I do it by the desire of Colo. Hunnewell [1] & full assent of the parties, is that Captain Draper who is an Inhabitant of Brookfield and his 2d Lieut Mr Durant,[2] might be assigned to my Regiment, in which case I shall station him at Brookfield where his influence is great, & that Captain Brown with his 2d Lieut. Mr. Harrington [3] who belong within the 15th. Circle, where he also is represented as a very influencial and popular man, may be transfered to the 15 Regt. each of which Officers if they continue as now arranged, must be removed to a considerable distance from the places of their abode and their influence in a great measure be lost. I have not other views in proposing these exchanges but the good of the service. Should you assent, Brookfield will be considered as subdistrict No 5. & belonging to the 1st: district under Major Walker Worcester No 6 Capt. Chandler, Boston No 7. Capn. Thwing, Dedham No 8 Capt. Tolman, Taunton No 9 Capt. Emery, Plymouth No 10 Lieut Rand, the 2d. District, under Major Winslow.[4] No reasons at present induce me to propose any other exchange of Officers. There are several vacancies in the Regiment. I am confident, with submission, that the good of the service require them to be filled. I have received a number of applications for my influence in obtaining appointments, I have written to the Secretary of War on the Subject, I could wish to be informed in what way & by whose recommendation the Surgeons and the mates are to be appointed to the Regiment.

I have the honor to be with the utmost respect yr. Humbl. Serv.

N: Rice

Genl Hamilton

LS, Hamilton Papers, Library of Congress.
1. Lieutenant Colonel Richard Hunewell, commanding officer of the Fifteenth Regiment of Infantry.
2. Simeon Draper and Thomas Durant were appointed to the Fourteenth Regiment of Infantry on January 8, 1799 (*Executive Journal*, I, 299, 303).
3. James Brown and Abijah Harrington were appointed to the Fifteenth Regiment of Infantry on January 8, 1799 (*Executive Journal*, I, 299, 303).
4. See Rice to H, April 28, 1799, note 8.

To James Wilkinson [1]

New York May 23d. 1799

Sir

I begin now to be anxious to learn that you had received my letter desiring you to repair to the seat of Government,[2] in conformity with an intimation from the Secretary of War, to the end that with the aid of your lights and experience, a general plan for the arrangement of the affairs of the Western army, with an eye to the existing posture of our political Concerns, might be digested and adopted. If by any Accident that letter should not have gotten to hand, I must urge you to lose no time in complying with its object. It left to your option to come by way of New Orleans, if you could obtain the needful consent there, and if you should think it the most convenient and a perfectly safe route.

You will of course previous to your departure leave the requisite instructions with the Officer who is to succeed in the command, making the proper reserves as to those discretionary powers which a confidence personal to you may have dictated.

On the presumption that you would have left the Western Army, several late letters from me have been addressed to Col: Hamtramck [3] as the Senior Officer of the Army.

With great consideration & Esteem   I have the honor to be   Sir
Yr. Obedient servt.   Alexander Hamilton

Brigadier Genl. Wilkinson

LS (photostat), James McHenry Papers, Library of Congress; ADf, Hamilton Papers, Library of Congress.
   1. This letter was enclosed in H to James McHenry, May 23, 1799.
   2. H to Wilkinson, February 12, 1799.
   3. H to John F. Hamtramck, April 27, two letters of April 29, May 9, 12, 23, 1799.

From James McHenry

War Department
24th May 1799

Sir

Letters similar to the enclosed [1] have been transmitted to the Senators of each State from New Hampshire to Maryland, and to Generals Washington Pinckney and Davie [2] for the States of Virginia, North and South Carolina and Georgia.

Messrs Watson and Lawrence [3] find it difficult, if not impracticable to co-operate in the object of this letter from the distance of their places of residence from each other, and have declined acting. You will perceive that this measure is purely precautionary, and that the officers who may be appointed are not to receive any pay or emoluments until called into actual service. [4]

I have the honor to be, with great respect, Sir, Your Most Obt Hb St   James McHenry

Major Genl A Hamilton

LS, Hamilton Papers, Library of Congress; LS letterpress copy, dated May 23, James McHenry Papers, Library of Congress.
   1. Enclosure not found, but see McHenry to H, second letter of May 23, 1799. McHenry enclosed a list of names of persons appointed from Virginia for the cavalry and infantry in McHenry to George Washington, May 21, 1799 (LS, George Washington Papers, Library of Congress).
   2. William Richardson Davie was a colonel and commissary general in the American Revolution. After the war he practiced law in North Carolina and was a member of the state legislature from Halifax County from 1786 to 1798. He was elected governor of North Carolina in 1798 and was appointed a brigadier general in the Provisional Army on July 19, 1798 (*Executive Journal*, I, 292–93). On June 1, 1799, he was appointed Envoy Extraordinary and Minister Plenipotentiary to France (*Executive Journal*, I, 326–27).
   3. James Watson and John Laurance were members of the United States Senate from New York.
   4. This is a reference to the appointment of officers under the authority of "An Act giving eventual authority to the President of the United States to augment the Army" (1 *Stat.* 725–27 [March 2, 1799]).

To James McHenry

New York, May 24, 1799. ". . . I shall confer with Col Smith on the subject of his Major [1] and communicate the result. . . . I am of opinion that the hat ought to be delivered with its furniture complete.[2] It will often be no easy matter for the Officers to supply a deficiency; and it is one of those instances in which œconomy will be likely to disgust by the air of excessive parsimony. Will it not be well to authorize the Commandants to make provision as to the hats already delivered? Patterns shall shortly be forwarded not only of the articles you mention but of cloathing and accoutrements generally. . . ."

ADf, Hamilton Papers, Library of Congress.
    1. On May 7, 1799, H wrote to McHenry that Lieutenant Colonel William S. Smith, commandant of the Twelfth Regiment of Infantry, had recommended that Theodosius Fowler be appointed a major in his regiment. On May 16, 1799, in a letter listed in the appendix to this volume, Smith wrote to H that he had changed his mind about Fowler's appointment and instead recommended Dowe J. Fondey. H sent Smith's new recommendation to McHenry on May 22, 1799 (in a letter listed in the appendix to this volume), and McHenry replied on the next day (in a letter listed in the appendix to this volume) that the President had already approved the appointment of Fowler but that he would wait for H's advice "whether to send Mr Fowler his letter of appointment, or to bring the person before the President who appears, upon an after thought, to be preferred by the Lt Colonel of the Regiment."
    2. See H to McHenry, May 18, 1799; McHenry to H, first letter of May 23, 1799.

From Nathan Rice

Boston May the 24th. 1799

My dear Generial

    By your favour of the 9th you have given me a latitude to exercise my judgment, in entering on the recruiting service or not, previous to the arrival of the cloathing, as I shall judge expedient. I have this day issued my orders for the officers to enter on that service, & I hope it will not be long before the cloathing arrives; I think a district deposit & issue thereof the best mode & the one I shall adopt, a part thereof will of course be wanted at Springfield & part at Taunton, it perhaps would be well as it would save expence of transportation, if that which is to be sent to Springfield, might be stoped there on its way from the war office, unless it is to come to Boston by water. I have applyed to Mr Jackson [1] who appears to have reced no information on the subject. He informs me that one quarter of the coats he was authorised to contract for will be rady for delivery by the last of this month, the remainder in three weeks after provided Buttons come in from Philadelphia, He can not determine by what mode they are to be sent to the districts. There is no Qr Master here & he is not impowered.

Pray Sir how are the troops to be serviced at the districts & regimental Rendezvous? & where are we to apply for Arms.

I have from the best information I can obtain thought proper to recommend Lieut Daniel Hastings [2] to be appointed Quarter Master of my Regiment & wish him confirmed as such.

I must beg Sir that some of the vacancies in the regiment may be fill[ed], as I have one or two companies which will have but one officer in each after the Staff appointments are made.

With the most perfect esteem   I am yr. very Humble Servant

N: Rice

P.S. It will I presume Sir be necessary for the officers to be possessd of the rules & Articles of War.[3] how are they to be supplyed therewith? and the troops with camp Utensils?   N: R

Honbl Majr Genl Hamilton

ALS, Hamilton Papers, Library of Congress.

1. Jonathan Jackson, who was supervisor of the revenue for the District of Massachusetts (*Executive Journal*, I, 216, 217), had been appointed to enter into contracts for supplying the troops in Massachusetts (James McHenry to H, April 4, 1799).

2. Hastings had been appointed an ensign in the Fourteenth Regiment of Infantry on January 8, 1799 (*Executive Journal*, I, 301, 303), and in accordance with Section 2 of "An Act for the better organizing of the Troops of the United States; and for other purposes" (1 *Stat.* 749–55 [March 3, 1799]) he became a second lieutenant on March 3, 1799 (Heitman, *United States Army*, I, 510).

3. See H to Jonathan Dayton, August 6, 1798, note 11.

To Ebenezer Stevens

New York May 24th. 1799

Sir

I understand from the Secretary of War, that in the capacity of Agent for the War Department I am to look to you for the Duties usually performed by the Quarter Master General, Clothier General and Commissary of Military Stores.[1] I shall look to you accordingly for these services, and therefore shall direct all returns relating to the proper objects to be made to you, in the Expectation that you will attend to the procuring and forwarding of such as are required with propriety. With this view you will open a Correspondence with the proper officers at the Seat of Government. The present system is that Tench Francis Esquire, as Purveyor of supplies, procures all Articles in the several Branches of supply which are placed by him in the disposition of Samuel Hodgdon Esqr, as superintendent of military stores, who is to oversee all the issues of those articles. I believe the Quarter Master General [2] is to take his station at the Seat of Government and is to be the auxiliary of those Officers.

It is expected that the great mass of supplies will be procured & furnished by the immediate Agency of the Officers abovementioned; and that you will only incidentally be called upon to provide. But you will have to make application for the supplies which will be wanted at the different stations and Posts of the Army, and to see that they are punctually and expeditiously furnished by those whose province it is to do so; for this purpose you will forward to them the returns which you shall receive, first taking such Abstracts from them as will enable you to judge how far they have been complied with. This points out the general line of the service expected from you. Explanations as occasions occur will be made for your more particular information.

I shall count fully upon your diligence and zeal, and if not in the first instance at least eventually, I shall confide that a compensation adequate to what shall appear to be the extent of your trouble and responsibility will be made.[3]

With great consideration   I am Sir   Your obedient servt

Alexander Hamilton

Col Ebenezer Stevens

LS, New-York Historical Society, New York City; ADf, Hamilton Papers, Library of Congress; copy, RG 217, Fourth Auditor's Office, Letters Received, 1799, National Archives.
    1. See James McHenry to H, May 9, 1799.
    2. John Wilkins, Jr.
    3. Stevens's endorsement reads: "Ansd." Letter not found.

From James Wilkinson

Natchez [Mississippi Territory] May 24, 1799. "Immediately after I received your Letter of the 12th: Feby: I dispatched an Express over land to Mobile, to gain intelligence of the Detachment, which had marched to take post on that River. . . .[1] The Night before the last, I had the satisfaction to receive assurances from the Commanding officer, that He had reached the point of his destination . . . and by the same conveyance, I received an accurate chart of the coast from New Orleans . . . to Mobile Bay, with a survey of the River. . . . An incident unworthy [of] record, & to be reserved for your presence, had suspended the agreement made with Governor Gayoso for the surrender of Deserters,[2] & in consequence of the suspension, the Scoundrels, in service began again to abandon their colours in such numbers, as to cause me serious alarm; but I have now the pleasure to inform you, that after a short discussion, Mr. Gayoso has been prevailed on to send back, two fugitives from the Corps of Artillerists & Engineers, who have been received at Loftus's Heights, tried, & sentenced. The papers under cover exhibit details. . . .[3] I . . . will commence my Voyage from this place the Day after Tomorrow. . . ."[4]

ALS, Hamilton Papers, Library of Congress.
1. See Wilkinson to H, April 15, 1799.
2. For this agreement and the reason for its failure, see Wilkinson to H, April 15, 1799, note 12.
3. Among the papers Wilkinson enclosed were Carlos de Grand Pré to Wilkinson, May 6, 16, 1799 (ALS, Hamilton Papers, Library of Congress); Wilkinson to Grand Pré, May 10, 1799 (copy, Hamilton Papers, Library of Congress). Grand Pré was the Spanish Intendant at Natchez. On the verso of Grand Pré's letter of May 16, 1799, Wilkinson wrote: "I send the originals because I realy have not time to copy them, & have no person near me who can do it intelligibly. Ja Wilkinson."
Wilkinson also enclosed in the letter printed above Isaac Guion to Wilkinson, May 20, 21, 1799; "Proceedings of a Court Martial" of John Wood and Thomas England, May 21, 1799; "Genl Orders" by Wilkinson approving the court's sentence, May 23, 1799 (copies, Hamilton Papers, Library of Congress).
4. Wilkinson did not leave Natchez until May 28, 1799. See the Inhabitants of Natchez to Wilkinson, May 28, 1799; Wilkinson to the Inhabitants of Natchez, May 28, 1799 (copies, Hamilton Papers, Library of Congress).

From Oliver Wolcott, Junior

Treasury Department
May 24th. 1799

Sir,

Enclosed I have the honor to transmit to you, the copy of a Letter from the Surveyor General of the United States [1] in Answer to my enquiries respecting the time when and the place where the troops required to assist in marking the Indian boundary line would be wanted. The opinion of the Surveyor General in relation to this business, confirms the expediency of directing the Commanding Officer in the North Western Territory to afford him the necessary assistance, as suggested in my Letter to you of the 8th. instant.[2]

I have the honour to be   Very respectfully   Sir   Your obedient Servant   Oliv Wolcott

Major General Hamilton

LS, Hamilton Papers, Library of Congress.

1. On May 9, 1799, Rufus Putnam wrote to Wolcott: "Your favor of the 19th ultimo came to hand last evening. The time proposed by Major [Israel] Ludlow to commence the survey of the Indian boundary was the first of June, as expressed in my Letter to you of the 15th of March: but as the Letter from the Secretary at War to Governor [Arthur] St Clair, which came under cover to me, could not reach Cincinnati untill after the 20th of April I doubted the practicability of collecting the Indians by the first of June, therefore in my letter to Governor St Clair of the 11th of April I informed him that Major Ludlow was instructed to wate on him respecting the business & prepare himself to commence the survey at any time the Governor Should agree to have the Indians notified to attend; it is not therefore in my power to fix upon the day when the Indians will be convened and the Surveys commence, but the Troops destined for that Servis ought to be drawn as Soon as may be to the Fort or Station near where Commences the portage from Lorimies Creek to St Mary's river & be there held in readiness; it being the nearest post or Station to the point of opperation of the commencing of the Survey" (ALS, RG 49, Records of the Bureau of Land Management, General Land Office, Letters Received from the Surveyor General, Vol. I, National Archives; copy, Hamilton Papers, Library of Congress; LC, RG 49, Records of the Bureau of Land Management, General Land Office, Letters Received from the Surveyor General, Vol. I, National Archives).

2. On the verso H wrote: "Rect. acknowledged. The order desired has been given to Colonel [John F.] Hamtramck as temporary Commander in the pre-

sumed absence of General [James] Wilkinson who has been ordered to the Seat of Government." See H to Hamtramck, May 12, 1799. H's acknowledgment to Wolcott has not been found.

To John F. Hamtramck

New York, May 25, 1799. "The Secretary of War has transmitted me a copy of your letter of 1st April.[1] Mine of the 24th [2] indicates the train in which it is desired that Indian Affairs may proceed. But I shall be glad to be regularly advised of every interesting matter respecting their movements & views. . . ."

Copy, in the handwriting of Philip Church, Hamilton Papers, Library of Congress.

1. James McHenry to H, May 18, 1799, note 2.
2. H is mistaken, for his letter to Hamtramck is dated May 23, 1799.

From James McHenry [1]

War Department, May 25, 1799. "I enclose you the Proceedings of two Garrison Courts Martial. . . . The rules and Articles of War,[2] do not it is supposed, require, a reference to the Secretary of War, or to the President in any instance, of the proceedings of a Garrison Court Martial, for approval or otherwise. It is only the Sentence of a General Court Martial, when capital, that is to be with the proceedings of the court transmitted for the Presidents approval or otherwise of the sentence, and the Proceedings of such higher Courts, in all cases, to be transmitted, and kept in the War Office, in order to the parties obtaining copies thereof, whether convicted, or acquitted. I wish Officers could be generally impressed with an opinion, that the business of my department is sufficiently extensive, without adding to it, what does not properly belong to it. As the Sentences of the Garrison courts, whose proceedings are enclosed, are understood not to have been executed, You will please, give such orders respecting them, as you may think proper."

LS, Hamilton Papers, Library of Congress; LS, letterpress copy, James McHenry Papers, Library of Congress.

1. For background to this letter, see McHenry to H, first letter of January 21, 1799; H to McHenry, February 23, 1799.
2. See *JCC*, V, 800–04; XXX, 316, 322. See also H to Jonathan Dayton, August 6, 1798, note 11.

From James McHenry [1]

War Department, May 25, 1799. ". . . I transmitted last Tuesday by a Mr: Jones [2] (lately appointed Consul at Orleans) a Duplicate of your letter to General Wilkinson. . . .[3] For the present I should not incline to give the Indians any encouragement on the subject of their illegal Sales, or respecting the possibility of a treaty to repurchase &c. Let us see a little more of the development of the plot of the Speculators, and the real intention of the Indians. When they say 'you wish to reduce the quantity of provisions—will this conciliate their affections?' This proceeds I imagine from what Col. Strong may have observed to them in consequence of a letter to him of mine dated the 29th: Decr: 1798, containing the following paragraph. 'The issues of provisions to the Indians appear to be so considerable as to make it proper that the strictest œconomy be observed and that none of them who are not entitled to consideration, should receive the public provision, and those only for as short a time as possible.' . . . I have heard no complaints relative to the Soldiery being obliged to find their Cockades and Loops. I shall however, as it is not an object of great expence, give orders to the purveyor [4] to procure the necessary furniture which will be forwarded to such of the Recruits as may not be provided. In the mean while you will be pleased to consider yourself authorized to direct the Commandants to make provision as to the Hats already, or that may be delivered without Cockades and Loops. The English Cartouch Box has been adopted. Of course you need not send a pattern for this article. . . ."

LS, Hamilton Papers, Library of Congress; LS, letterpress copy, James McHenry Papers, Library of Congress.
1. For background to this letter, see H to McHenry, May 23, 1799.
2. Evan Jones of Louisiana was appointed consul for the port of New Orleans on May 11, 1799, during the recess of the Senate. On December 10, 1799, the Senate confirmed his appointment (*Executive Journal*, I, 326, 327).
3. H to James Wilkinson, May 23, 1799.
4. Tench Francis.

To James McHenry

New York, May 25 [-27] 1799. "I recur to two of your letters of the 9th. & 10th. instant. The reflections in the first respecting the inlistment of foreigners intirely accord with my impressions, as you have heretofore seen. I adhere to the opinion, that none but natives or naturalised citizens ought to be engaged. Of the latter, residence in this Country anterior to our Revolution to be proved to the satisfaction of the recruiting Officer, or a certificate of naturalization ought to be the criterion, and none ought to be enlisted who have not resided in the County where they shall be inlisted at least one year immediately preceding the inlistment. It is true that contraventions of the rule, by imposition upon or connivance of the recruiting officers, will in some instances happen. But they will not be so numerous as to prevent the object being essentially at⟨tained.⟩ The idea is held out in your letter of *postponing* the inlistment of foreigners until after a district should be exhausted of natives willing to inlist. I should doubt the expediency of a distinction which is not to be permanent. The preference might create disgust and perhaps an injurious collision. I shall be glad to know speedily the result of your further consideration of the subject. In a scene so near the seat of Government as that in which the late insurrection [1] has existed and so perfectly within its command the policy of stationing for any length of time a small body of foot soldiers with the manifest intention to awe the spirit of insurrection appears to me questionable. . . ."

ADf, Hamilton Papers, Library of Congress.
1. This is a reference to Fries's Rebellion.

General Orders

[*New York, May 26, 1799.* Hamilton's general orders, March 13, 1800, refer to "the general order of May 26th. 1799." *General orders not found.*]

To William MacPherson

New York May 26. 1799

Dr Sir

The Secy of War has instructed me [1] to digest & propose a plan for the organization and arrangement of the volunteer corps [2] throughout the United States. As this subject has particularly occupied your attention,[3] I shall be glad to be assisted with your ideas at large concerning it. You will be sensible that it is necessary to order that every part of our military system should as nearly as may be correspond and that consequently the establishment of the army ought to form the basis of every plan: Yet so as to have due regard to any peculiarities which ought to discriminate corps of a distinct and particular nature.

With great esteem & regard   I am Dr. Sir   Yr. Obed serv   A H

Brigadier General McPherson

ADfS, Hamilton Papers, Library of Congress.
1. See James McHenry to H, February 4, 1799.
2. For the Volunteer Corps, see the introductory note to H to James Gunn, December 22, 1798.
3. See Macpherson to H, March 25, 1799.

Circular to the Battalion Commanders of the Second Regiment of Artillerists and Engineers [1]

New York May 27. [–June 1] [2] 1799

Circular

Sir

I have heretofore transmitted ⟨to⟩ you the arrangement of the second Regiment of ⟨Artillerists⟩ shewing the batalion which you are to command and its destination generally.[3] Measures are taking to bring the companies not already there within the sphere of that destination. But you will immediately assume the command of all the fortified posts in the vicinity of the sea board within the States of Connecticut Rhode Island Massachusettes including the Province of Maine & New Hampshire,[4] and you will cause all returns from them to be made to you. These, or abstracts of them, as the nature of each may require are to be forwarded by you in conformity with the General Order herewith transmitted of the 29th of last Month.[5]

If after returns have been duly made apparently unreasonable delays in forwarding supplies shall happen information is to be given to me by you.

I am to be regularly advised of all material occurrences or matters requiring my directions. Your correspondence ⟨on⟩ points of military duty will be with me—on the details usually connected with the office of the Adjutant General with him,[6] on the subject of supplies with Col Stevens.[7] Respecting pay you may correspond with the proper Officer in the Department of War till the Pay Master General [8] shall arrive at the seat of Government when communications on this subject will be to him. No other correspondence is to be had by you or any of the Officers under your command with that Department. It is as unnecessary as it would be irregular and it is essential that we shall as fast as possible get into a systematic course of acting.

You will consider any companies or detachments which are or shall be within your district of those that are to compose your batalion whether now in garrison or at other places as under your command and you will suggest to me such a disposition of your batalion to the several posts as you shall deem adviseable.[9]

With great consideration   I am Sir   Yr. Obed servt

ADf, Hamilton Papers, Library of Congress.
    1. A marginal note in H's handwriting on this draft, as well as the draft's contents, indicates that H intended to have this letter sent to Major Benjamin Brookes and Major Daniel Jackson.
    2. Although H dated this draft "May 27," his reference to the "General Order . . . of the 29th of last Month" indicates that the letters sent to Brookes and Jackson were dated sometime in June. See "General Orders," May 29, 1799.
    3. See H to James McHenry, April 26, 1799; "Circular to the Artillery Field Officers," May 15, 1799; General Orders," May 16, 1799.
    4. Above "The States of Connecticut . . . New Hampshire," H wrote: "Major Brooks, Maryland Delaware Pensylvania New Jersey & New York."
    5. See "General Orders," May 29, 1799.
    6. William North.

7. See H to Ebenezer Stevens, May 24, 1799.

8. Caleb Swan.

9. At the bottom of this draft H wrote: "(Jackson) The most proper general station for you appears to me to be Rhode Island. While Major [Lewis] Toussard is within the District of your Command on public service, you will be under his orders as your superior Officer. But as he is destined to command a batalion reserved for the field he will chiefly be employed in quality of Engineer while he remains within your district, he will of course leave to you the ordinary details of your command."

From James McHenry

[*Philadelphia*] *May 27, 1799.* "I have this moment recd. your letter of the 24th and several enclosures, among the latter a letter to Lt Col. Hamtramck[1] which I return for your reperusal. You will recollect, that the troops in Tenessee and on the Georgia Frontier are within Genl Pinckney's command. Your letter to Hamtramck extends his authority to the troops in Tenessee. Will you be pleased to have this corrected. . . ."

ALS, Hamilton Papers, Library of Congress; ADfS, James McHenry Papers, Library of Congress.

1. H to John F. Hamtramck, May 23, 1799.

To James McHenry

New York May 27th: 1799

Sir

The returns from every quarter shew that desertion prevails to a ruinous extent. For this the remedies are   1:   greater attention to discipline   2.   additional care in furnishing the Supplies due to the Soldiery of such quality and with such exactness as will leave no real cause of dissatisfaction   3,   the forbearance to inlist foreigners, and, lastly, energy in the punishment of Offenders.

To promote the first will be my peculiar care. The Second I doubt not, will have from you all the attention due to a matter of primary importance. The third I hope Soon to receive your instructions to put in execution. As to the fourth I must entreat that you will make

Such a representation to the President, as will convince him of the absolute necessity, where his Agency must intervene, of giving effect to the Sentences of the Courts. His determination upon one some time since reported to you [1] has not yet been received. I expect it with great Solicitude; there can not occur a more fit case for exemplary punishment. If this Culprit escapes, the example of his impunity will have a most malignant aspect towards the Service. I repeat it, Sir, this is a point of such essential consequence, that you can not bestow too much pains to Satisfy the President that Severity is indispensible. It is painful to urge a position of this Kind, especially where life is concerned, but a military institution must be worse than useless—it must be pernicious if a just Severity does not uphold and enforce discipline.

With great respect   I have the honor to be   Sir   Your Obt sert.

The Secy of War

LS, Hamilton Papers, Library of Congress; ADf, Hamilton Papers, Library of Congress.

1. This is a reference to the case of Richard Hunt. See H to McHenry, April 20, 1799, note 2.

From James McHenry

War Department, May 28, 1799. "I have received your letter dated 25th instant. The experiment of enlisting none but native citizens or naturalized foreigners at present in our army, I am much disposed to have fully made. The criterion of the latter to be either a residence in this country anterior to the revolution to be proved to the satisfaction of the recruiting officer, or a certificate of naturalization. You will, therefore, be pleased to cause an explanatory article on this subject to be duly promulgated to the recruiting officers. My own impressions would have inclined me to maintain a regular force in the Country, late the scene of insurrection,[1] for some time to come had it been compatible when the public service in other respects, but it is exclusively confided to your judgment to continue, or remove the whole, or any part of the regular force now stationed in that Country. I shall forward your letter to the Commanding officer at Reading,[2] directing him to order Captn Cochran[3] to march his company to Fort Mifflin. . . ."

LS, Hamilton Papers, Library of Congress; LS, letterpress copy, James McHenry Papers, Library of Congress.
1. Fries's Rebellion.
2. H to Mahlon Ford, May 26, 1799 (listed in the appendix to this volume).
3. Walter L. Cochran, a resident of New York, was a captain in the Second Regiment of Artillerists and Engineers. He was a son of Elizabeth Hamilton's aunt Gertrude Schuyler Cochran, the wife of Dr. John Cochran.

To Abraham Ellery [1]

New York May 29. 1799

Sir

You having been appointed Assistant to the Adjutant General and he being at this time absent,[2] I think it proper to indicate to you a general outline of the duties which you are to perform.

The duties of Adjutant General, who unites the capacity of Deputy Inspector General, are various and extensive. In the two characters he may be regarded as the Assistant of the Commander of the Army and of the Inspector General in whatever relates to the *police*, and *tactics* of the army.

He is to receive from the Commanding General and issue to the Army the general orders, for which purpose he is to attend the Commanding General dayly. He is to regulate the detail of officers and men for guards, fatigue service, commands &c. and to see that they are regularly furnished. All returns of the troops including those relating to the Inspectorship, and when the Pay Master General or his Deputy is not at head Quarters the Muster and Pay Rolls are to be made to him. From the returns of the troops which he receives he is from time to time to make out abstracts for the commander of the Army and the Secretary of War. For the present, a Monthly return for each will suffice. The returns relating to the Inspectorship are to be handed over to the Inspector-General with such remarks as may occur from an examination of them. The Muster and Pay Rolls must be transmitted to the accountant of the Department of War unless when the Pay Master General shall be at the seat of the Government in which case they must be sent to him.

Practice will point out better than a letter can define the modes of executing the duties of the Office.

To understand them perfectly it is essential to be well acquainted with the "Regulations for the Order and discipline of the army" [3] established under the auspices of the Baron De Steuben during our Revolution War, "The Articles of War" [4] and the "Rules and Regulations respecting the Recruiting service" [5]

With great consideration   I am Sir   Yr Obed serv

Capt Abraham R Ellery
Assistant to the Adjutant General

ADf, Hamilton Papers, Library of Congress; copy, Hamilton Papers, Library of Congress.
    1. For background to this letter, see Ellery to H, May 14, 1799.
    2. H is referring to William North.
    3. See H to James McHenry, May 21, 1799, note 1.
    4. This is a reference to the 1794 edition of *Rules and Articles for the Better Government of the Troops.* See H to Jonathan Dayton, August 6, 1798, note 11.
    5. This is a reference to the March, 1799, edition of the War Department pamphlet *Rules and Regulations Respecting the Recruiting Service.* See H to Dayton, August 6, 1798, note 6; McHenry to H, March 21, 1799.

General Orders

[New York] May 29th. 1799.

All Returns of the Troops, in Field and in Garrison, including Inspection Returns, and those relating to the Recruiting Service, and for the present, all Pay and Muster Rolls are to be sent addressed to Brigadier General North, Adjutant General, at New York, indorsed on Public Service.

All Returns of Ordnance, Arms, Accoutrements, Clothing, Forts, Camp Utensils, and in General, of all Public Stores, which are on hand, and those which are wanted, reporting the latter from the former in distinct Returns, are to be sent addressed to Colonel

Ebenezer Stevens, Agent for the War Department, at New York, indorsed as above.

Copy (incomplete), Hamilton Papers, Library of Congress.

From James McHenry

War Department
29th May 1799

Sir,

Complaints having been made, relative to the enlistment of apprentices, for the army of the United States, I have been led to reflect on the propriety, or even general policy of such enlistments.

Young men of respectable families, and handsome properties, are not infrequently bound apprentices, to learn a profession, or be initiated in some lucrative trade, art or mystery, it could only be in moments of indiscretion, that such would offer themselves as privates in the army; if enlisted prejudice would cast a stain on their characters, which would also extend to that of their families, and the act of enlisting them, would tend to make the recruiting service abhorred and unpopular.

A large class of Youths are constantly apprenticed, who are of less respectable connections, and smaller or no property, these are to learn agriculture, trafic, a mechanical trade, or some one of the inferior, and laborious occupations, such in the earlier stages of their apprenticeships, from want of strength, and skill, are a constant charge, altho' of little or no service to their masters, this charge is borne by the master, in expectation of being remunerated by the services of the apprentices when he acquires sufficient ability of body, and skill, which he does not acquire, untill he approaches, or perhaps arrives at an age, which would qualify him to become a Soldier, at this period to enlist him, would be a real injury to the master who had incurred a charge, for which he was about to be remunerated.

I have seen opinions of English Jurists which denied the capacity in an apprentice to enlist, being incompatible with his former contract, as well as the power or right to hold him to military service, in opposition to the masters claim.

The 14th Section of "An Act authorizing the President of the United States to raise a Provisional Army"[1] exempts private Soldiers who are, and who shall be enlisted, and employed in the service of the United States, during their time of service from all personal arrests, for any *debt* or *contract*. This Act appears to me to contemplate only persons, who have not engaged their personal labours, or services, but have the misfortune to be in debt. It is however under the 14th Section of this Act, that Officers have concieved themselves authorized to enlist, and detain apprentices from their masters.

Upon the whole as it appears to me, that the Act cited would not justify the detaining of apprentices if enlisted from their masters; that the detention of them, would do injustice in most cases to their masters; that an apprentice is perhaps disqualified, to enter into engagements for military service; and the enlistment only, altho' he should be afterwards discharged, would often occasion great affliction in families, I am induced to believe, that the practice of enlisting apprentices is improper, and as it would tend to make the recruiting service extremely unpopular, impolitic.

You will therefore, if you concur, with me in opinion, instruct the different recruiting officers, to avoid as much as possible the enlistment of apprentices, and in no case to do so knowingly, without the consent of their masters.

The enclosed purports to be the proceedings of a General Court Martial,[2] held at West Point, the 23d. May instant, by order of Captain George Ingersoll[3] commandant. You will recollect your opinion, formed after a deliberate perusal, and consideration of the rules an[d] articles of War, and transmitted to me, under date of the 23d February last,[4] "That no Officer commanding only a regiment or other corps (whether entire or consisting of detachments) which forms a command not superior to that of a regiment can appoint a General Court Martial; consequently that no Officer commanding either of the Garrisons on the Sea Board, has power to constitute such a Court. In other words, none but a General, or his representative, can do it."

Had no objections existed, to the authority of the Officer, who constituted this court, the want of a Judge Advocate (for one of the members is made to sign the Proceedings as Recorder) and neglect to set forth, that two thirds of the members of the court, concurred in a sentence of death, would have rendered it improper to execute the sentence.

You will be pleased to take such order, respecting the Prisoner implicated, as to you shall seem proper.

The Commandant, I have no doubt was induced to order the Court, in consequence of the late general error of opinion, that he in his capacity, had authority.

I am Sir   with great respect   your obedient servant

James McHenry

Major General Alexander Hamilton

LS, Hamilton Papers, Library of Congress; LS, letterpress copy, James Mc-Henry Papers, Library of Congress.
    1. 1 *Stat.* 560–61 (May 28, 1798).
    2. DS, Hamilton Papers, Library of Congress. This document concerned the "trial of Joseph Perkins . . . charged with deserting while on guard and taking with him two prisoners knowing them to be under sentence of a General Court-martial for desertion."
    3. A resident of Massachusetts and a veteran of the American Revolution, Ingersoll was a captain in the First Regiment of Artillerists and Engineers.
    4. See also McHenry to H, first letter of January 21, 1799.

To James McHenry [1]

New York May 29. 1799

The inclosed [2] my Dear Sir was written on the idea that though the Troops in Tennessee are annexed to the command of General Pinckney as far as a distinct supervision on the sea-board is concerned, yet they remain a part of the Western army and are subject to the general superintendance and direction of The Commander of that *Army*. This connection seems necessary to the due course of service in the Western Quarter. There appears to be an intimate relation of objects between the troops in Tenessee and the other troops in the Western Quarter—as to the Indians and as to military operations—and a necessity of mutual support, perhaps occasionally of detaching from the one to the other. If so the Troops in Tenessee can hardly be detached from the Western Commander and in matters of common concern he must extend his attention to all. If your idea be not radically different, if it extend not to a total separation of the Troops in Tenessee, the letter is proper. If it does extend to a total separation, then I will request you to expunge the words "in Tenessee" and to add after dependencies "except the troops in Tenessee" and thus to forward the letter. As to the troops on St Marys, I understand that they were never considered as forming a part of the Western army & so not included in the letter as it stands. Favour me with a line expressing what you shall have done.

Yrs. Affecly   A H

James McHenry Es

ADfS, Montague Collection, MS Division, New York Public Library; ADfS (photostat), James McHenry Papers, Library of Congress.
1. For background to this letter, see McHenry to H, May 27, 1799.
2. H to John F. Hamtramck, May 23, 1799.

From James McHenry [1]

[Philadelphia] 30 May 1799

My dear Sir

The Troops in Tenessee have never been considered as forming any part of the North Western army, or the Commander of the Western army as having any controul over them. It was necessary to the success of the objects to be accomplished in Tenessee, and the quick transmission of orders that this should be so.

There is no position, which it is possible for a general to assume in the North Western Country, or Mississippi Territory, which would enable him to correspond promptly with the troops in Tenessee and through you with the seat of Government. The delicate state of things in that quarter, will I am affraid long continue and forbid the intrusting to circuitous routes the orders that may be necessary.

The position to be taken by General Pinckney will lye directly on the shortest line of communication between Tenessee and the seat of Government.

I have made the alterations you propose vz. expunged the words "in Tenessee" and added after dependencies "except the troops in Tenessee" and shall forward the letter to-morrow.

Yours Affly   JMcH

ALS, Hamilton Papers, Library of Congress; ADf, James McHenry Papers, Library of Congress.

1. This letter was written in reply to H to McHenry, May 29, 1799.

To James McHenry

New York, May 30 [–31] 1799. ". . . I have this moment recd. your letter of the 29th. instant. I intirely agree with you on the subject of Apprentices & shall instruct accordingly. Indeed I ⟨th⟩ought it was universally to be understood that they were not to be enlisted. . . . The Court Martial at West Point being a *Nullity* it is my first impression that I can with propriety order another to try anew. This is not the case of a trial before a competent tribunal which would have rendered a second improper."

ADf, with a postscript dated May 31, 1799, in Ethan Brown's handwriting, Hamilton Papers, Library of Congress.

Receipt to the Trustees of the American Iron Company [1]

[*New York, May 30, 1799.* "I have receiv'd a deed from Peter Goelet & other Trustees of the American Iron Company. I certify that the fourth or last installment of the Purchase money with Interest remains to be paid, which will pay on demand. New York, May 30, 1799. Alexr Hambleton." *Receipt not found.*]

1. This receipt is quoted in, and has been taken from, Goelet to Robert Troup, August 19, 1799 (ALS, Miscellaneous Chancery Papers, American Iron Company, Clerk of the Court of Appeals, Albany, on deposit at Queens College, New York City).

Troup, a close friend of H since the time when they had been students at King's College, was a New York City and Albany lawyer. A veteran of the American Revolution, he served as secretary of the Board of War from 1778 to 1779 and secretary of the Board of Treasury from 1779 to 1780. He was a member of the New York Assembly in 1786. In 1796 he was appointed judge of the United States District Court for New York, and he served in that capacity for two years. When this letter was written, he was involved in land speculation in western New York and was associated with Charles Williamson in the development of the Pulteney Purchase in the Genesee country.

In describing this receipt in his letter to Troup, Goelet wrote: "on the 30. Inst May last Genl Hambleton called on me & requested I would give him Genl Schuylers deeds, the Genl. wanted to see them. When I delivered him the Deeds he gave me the following recpt."

For an explanation of the contents of this document, see the introductory note to Philip Schuyler to H, August 31, 1795. See also H to Phineas Bond, September 1, 1795; H to Robert Morris, September 1, 1795; H to Barent Bleecker, March 20, 1796, April 5, 1797; Goelet to H, June 25, 27, 1796; "Receipt from Peter Goelet," October 4, 1796; "Deed from Peter Goelet, Robert Morris, and William Popham," April 4, 1797; Goelet and Morris to H, December 12, 1798.

From John J. U. Rivardi

Niagara [*New York*] *May 30, 1799.* Acknowledges "your letter of the 2d. instant, respecting The Superintendant of Indian Affairs." [1] Describes repairs that have been made under his direction to Fort Niagara. States that among those individuals on boats passing the fort there was ". . . no body who could excite Suspicions—Most of those people being either Known traders from Schenectady or comon farmers going with their families To Settle in New Connecticut. [2] The number of the latter is considerable." Reports: "The British Fort advances rapidly—an additional Company is arrived from Quebec & they work even on Sundays." Complains that "There is Now Nine Months pay due To This Garrison & Contingent accounts of More than one years Standing." States that he has had "the Ague" and that it will "torment" him until he can "change Station."

ALS, Hamilton Papers, Library of Congress.
  1. This is a reference to "Circular to the Commanding Officers of the Western Army," May 2, 1799, which has not been found.
  2. This is a reference to the Western Reserve in the northeastern portion of the Northwest Territory.

To Nathan Rice

New York May 31. 1799

Sir

I have to reply to your two letters of the 23 and 24 instant.

The exchange of officers proposed by Col Hunewell & yourself [1] has been recommended to the Secy of War.[2] His sanction is expected, & as soon as obtained it will be made known.

I am content that Brookfield shall be come the rendezvous of a subdistrict & with the arrangement of Officers mentioned in your letter of the 23.

Persons as surgeons and mates may be recommended by you within the meaning of my circular of the 22 instant.[3]

Various articles of Cloathing have already been forwarded to Mr. Jackson. Some, as you are informed,[4] he is himself to procure. I have urged that the forwarding of the deficient ones be accelerated and I have mentioned that Springfield is a district Rendezvous to give an opportunity, if thought expedient, to send a proportion to that place.[5]

The Contractors for the supply of provisions are to furnish the means of transportation.

At the District and subdistrict rendezvouses the troops will be in houses, where there are not before hand public barracks, and tents will be sent on for the Regimental Rendezvous. You have not yet suggested a substitute for this Rendezvous.

Arms and accoutrements Tents and camp Utensils will be sent to the care of Mr. Jackson, unless a part of them should be ordered to Springfield in which case they will be addressed to some public agent there, accompanied no doubt with directions to deliver them to your order.

The name of Lt. Hastings as Qr. Master has been transmitted to the Secy. of War; [6] and I presume he will be confirmed.

I understand that a number of setts of the articles of War have

been forwarded from the War Department to the several commandants of Regiments.[7]

With great consideration   I am Sir   Your Obed ser

Colonel Rice

ADf, Hamilton Papers, Library of Congress.
    1. Rice to H, May 23, 1799.
    2. H to James McHenry, May 31, 1799 (listed in the appendix to this
volume).
    3. "Circular to the Commandants of Regiments," May 23, 1799.
    4. H to Rice, May 9, 1799.
    5. H to McHenry, May 31, 1791 (listed in the appendix to this volume).
    6. H to McHenry, May 31, 1799 (listed in the appendix to this volume).
    7. On May 31, 1799, in a letter listed in the appendix to this volume, H
wrote to McHenry: "It is very desireable that the 'articles of War' not less
than thirteen to a Regiment shall be transmitted."

General Orders [1]

New York June 1st 1799

Major General Hamilton announces to the officers, of the Troops
under his Command, the following regulations respecting Extra
allowances to officers established by an act of the War department
dated the 19th of December last.[2] In all cases Where officers are
detached on Services that oblige them to encur expences on the
road and at *places where* there are not Military posts, except where
the Law has Specifically provided for traveling Expences,[3] the
following regulations are to govern in their Accounts. 1st Every
Officer attached as a fore said, besides his legal pay and Emoluments
Shall receive a Dollar and twenty five Cents pr. day for man and
Horse, for each day that the Officer Must Sleep at a place not a
Military post and when the officer is of a rank to be entitled to a
Servent, then the addition of Seventy five Cents pr day for the
Servant and his Horse. That the foregoing rules shall apply to all
places, but the Seat of government, and the prinsible Towns in
each State, at which places the allowances to be a Dollar and a half
for the officer and his Horse. 2d   That, on extraordinary Cases only
for which greater Allowances may be indispensable be referd, to the

Special disgession of the Secretary of War to be assissted by a certificate from the Commang: Officer by whom the Officer claiming was detached on the Special Service Stating the reasons and circumstances. 3d   That fifty Cents without reference to rank be allowed to every Officer detached from one Military post to another which he may reach the same night not less than forty Miles distant, in this place it is contemplated the Servant cant without inconveniance take his own Provision with him. 4th   That the days Jurney be regulated by the number of Miles in the following proportion Viz forty Miles to a day when the whole distance does not exceed two Hundred Miles. Thirty to a day for all above two Hundred and not Exceeding three Hundred and fifty, twenty five to a day for all above three Hundred and fifty, and not exceeding Six Hundred— twenty to a day for all above Six Hundred. 5th. That these rates do not retrospect but reguard future allowances only, that all passed and Intervening cases before a reasonable notice of the Same be Settled on the former principle of reasonable expences according to circumstances it being Supposed that the application of a new rule may produce hardship and injustice where the Service may have been performed in the expectation of the practice on former Occation may prevail—respecting the greater allowances in extraordinary Cases which by the 2d Article is referd to the Special descristion of the Secretary of War it is understood that no application to that Effect Can be made with propriety until a Certificate is produced from the Commanding by whom the Officer claiming Such Extra allowance was detached Stating particularly the reasons and circumstances inducing Extraordinary Expences and that in all cases that the Orders of the Commanding Officer must be produced in writing previous to any allowance being made.

Abraham R. Ellery Asst.
Agt. Genl.

LC, RG 98, Post-Revolutionary Records, Orderly Book for the Company of John Steele, 3d Infantry, 1799, Volume 480, National Archives.

   1. For background to this document, see James McHenry to H, April 22, 1799.
   2. See the enclosure to McHenry to H, April 22, 1799.
   3. In the Hamilton Papers, Library of Congress, there is an undated draft in H's handwriting of a rule for the payment of officers. This draft reads: "The rule is that no officer ought to have any compensation, beyond the emoluments prescribed by law, for any services appertaining to his office—not any special

indemnification for expences, except when acting in situation out of or beyond the ordinary course of service relative to his grade or at places where he cannot avail himself of the accommodations to which he is intitled in Camps Quarters or Garrisons."

From James McHenry

[Philadelphia, June 4, 1799]

My dear Sir

I think the information contained in the inclosed letter from Mr Patterson[1] intitled to attention. The writer stands high in the opinion of Mr Sitgreaves,[2] and I have always heard him spoken of as a man of honour and veracity. He was a candidate for one of the Regiments. Be pleased to return me the letter.

Yours Affely   James McHenry

4 June 1799

Majr Gen Alex Hamilton

ALS, Hamilton Papers, Library of Congress; ADfS, James McHenry Papers, Library of Congress.

1. During the American Revolution, Alexander Patterson had been a captain in the Twelfth Pennsylvania Regiment. He retired from the Army in 1778.

Although Patterson's letter has not been found, it concerned the desirability of continuing to station troops in the region where Fries's Rebellion had occurred. See McHenry to H, June 6, 1799; H to McHenry, June 6, 1799.

2. Samuel Sitgreaves, an Easton, Pennsylvania, lawyer and a Federalist, had been a member of the House of Representatives from 1795 to 1798.

To John F. Hamtramck

New York June 5. 1799

Sir

I have received a letter from Col Strong dated at Detroit the 7th. of May last. You will judge from the information which you shall have when this reaches you how far it may be expedient to reinforce his post and from what quarter. The inclosed extract of a letter to him [1] may serve as a guide. I will only add that my view of the subject, probably imperfect at this distance, does not impress me with the probability of approaching Indian hostilities, or with the necessity of a further accumulation of force at Detroit.

With great consideration   I am Sir   Yr Obed serv

Hamtramck

ADf, Hamilton Papers, Library of Congress.
   1. H to David Strong, May 22, 1799.

To James McHenry

New York, June 5, 1799. ". . . As yet I have to regret that I am without the needful assistance to enable me to keep pace with the various objects of service—which occasions more delay in respect to the less urgent than is agreable to my plan. Measures are in train to obtain efficient aid [1] and I hope ere long the whole Machinery will be in complete operation. . . ."

Copy, in the handwriting of Ethan Brown, Hamilton Papers, Library of Congress.
   1. See H to Jeremiah Wadsworth, May 18, 1799.

To Staats Morris, George Ingersoll, and Ebenezer Massey

New York June 5. 1799

Sir

All the Garrison Posts within the Vicinity of the Sea Board in the States of Maryland Delaware Pensylvania New Jersey and New York are placed under the command of Major Brooks.[1] His general station will be at Fort Jay in the neighbourhood of this City.

You will communicate with him and obey his orders. Your returns of every kind are to be made directly to him.

But till he shall be at his station Major Hoops will command in his stead; and until you shall be advised of his being there you will address your letters to him to the care of Major Hoops at New York, whose orders in the interim you will obey.

With consideration   I am Sir   Yr Obed serv

Capt Staats Morris Commanding Officer Fort McHenry near Baltimore

    George Ingersoll &c. West Point

    The Commanding Officer at Fort Mifflin near Philadelphia

ADf, Hamilton Papers, Library of Congress; LS, to George Ingersoll, Harvard College Library.
    1. See "Circular to the Battalion Commanders of the Second Regiment of Artillerists and Engineers," May 27–June 1, 1799.
    On June 5, 1799, in a letter listed in the appendix to this volume, H wrote to Adam Hoops: "Inclosed are the copies of two letters of this date, one to Major Brooks, the other to Capt Staats Morris and others, as noted at foot. As in the absence of Major Brooks from his intended Station, at Fort Jay, the command within his district will be exercised by you. . . ." H's letter to Benjamin Brookes has not been found.

To Nathan Rice

New York June 5th 1799

Sir,

I have been informed by the Secretary of War [1] that all the articles for Arming clothing and equipping of your Regiment will be delivered to your order or that of your Pay & Quartermaster at your Regimental Rendezvous by Jonathan Jackson Esquire of Boston and Mr. Joseph Williams of Springfield six hundred and eighty stand of Arms and as many Gun worms to be furnished by the latter Gentleman and the rest by Mr. Jackson.

The Secy. of War has no objections to the exchanges proposed by yourself and Col: Hunnewell of Capt. Draper in the room of Capt. Brown & 2d. Lieut Durant in the place of 2d. Lieut Harrington.[2] They are therefore to take place.

Your nomination of your Regimental Staff is likewise approved. The Secy of War informs me [3] that the recruiting Money for your Regiment was transmitted on the 7th of May.

Df, in the handwriting of Ethan Brown, Hamilton Papers, Library of Congress.
    1. James McHenry to H, June 4, 1799 (listed in the appendix to this volume).
    2. For the proposed exchanges, see Rice to H, May 23, 1799. For the approval of the Secretary of War, see McHenry to H, June 4, 1799 (listed in the appendix to this volume).
    3. McHenry to H, June 4, 1799 (listed in the appendix to this volume).

To William S. Smith

[*New York, June 5, 1799*. On June 12, 1799, Smith wrote to Hamilton and acknowledged "the receipt of your Letter of the 5th. inst." *Letter not found.*]

To Decius Wadsworth, William Littlefield, Lemuel Gates, and Amos Stoddard

New York June 5, 1799

Sir

All the garrison posts within the vicinity of the Sea Board in the States of Connecticut Rhode Island Massachusettes including the Province of Maine and New Hampshire are placed under the command of Major Jackson.[1] His general station will be at or near New Port Rhode Island. You will consequently communicate with him and obey his orders. Your returns of every kind are to be made directly to him.

With consideration   I am Sir   Yr. Obed serv

Captains Decius Wadsworth Commanding Officer New London
        William Littlefield Fort Wolcott Rhode Island
        Lemuel Gates Castle William near Boston
        Amos Stoddard Portland Province of Maine
            To the care of Jackson Supervisor [2]

P.S. to Capt. Littlefield. You will understand that Major Toussard will exercise the same command as heretofore till Major Jackson assumes it; after which he will take care of all the ordinary details of service subject to the order of Major Toussard[3] as senior officer while the latter continues within his district.[4]

ADf, Hamilton Papers, Library of Congress.

1. H's letter to Daniel Jackson ordering him to assume this command, dated June 5, 1799, has not been found, but it was acknowledged in Jackson to H, June 25, 1799 (listed in the appendix to this volume).

2. Jonathan Jackson was supervisor of the revenue for the District of Massachusetts.

3. H notified Lewis Tousard of this arrangement on June 5, 1799, in a letter listed in the appendix to this volume.

4. The postscript is in the handwriting of Ethan Brown.

Circular to Four Captains in the Battalion Commanded by Adam Hoops[1]

New York June 6th. 1799

Sir

Your Company is to form part of a battalion under the command of Major Hoops.[2] You will, therefore, hereafter communicate with him and receive his orders; making all your returns to him. Your letters for the present will be addressed to him at New York indorsed on public service and with your name. I send you a sett of new recruiting instructions[3] to which you will strictly conform in whatsoever is relative to your situation.

With consideration   I am Sir   Yr Obedient servt.   A Hamilton

LS, Columbia University Libraries; ADf, Hamilton Papers, Library of Congress.

1. At the bottom of the draft H wrote the names and locations of the four captains to whom this letter was sent:

"Capt William Macrea of the 2 Regt. of Artillerists Alexandria Virginia
Capt Samuel Eddins   do.   Richmond   do.
Capt John Bishop   do.   Winchester   do
Capt Francis K Huger   do.   Charles Town *South Carolina.*"

2. On June 6, 1799, in a letter listed in the appendix to this volume, H wrote to Hoops: "Inclosed is a copy of a circular letter written to the four Captains who compose your batalion. You will see its object and you will attend to its execution. You are apprised that these officers are now on the recruiting service. It will be incumbent on you to see that it does not languish for want of exertion. . . ."

3. This is a reference to the March, 1799, edition of the War Department pamphlet *Rules and Regulations Respecting the Recruiting Service.* See H to Jonathan Dayton, August 6, 1798, note 6; James McHenry to H, March 21, 1799.

General Orders[1]

Pursuant to the instructions from the Secretary of War, the following additions to the "Rules and Regulations respecting the Recruiting Service," [2] are to be observed.

"None but *Citizens* of the United States shall be enlisted. Persons not born within the said States, who were within the same on the fourth day of July, 1776, shall be deemed Citizens for the purpose of enlistment. Every person, not born within the United States, who may have migrated hither since that day, must produce a certificate of naturalisation, from some competent Magistrate or Court before he can be enlisted; and every person whosoever, not born within the United States, before he can be enlisted, must produce proof by ye. affidavits of two reputable Inhabitants of the County, within which he shall offer himself to be enlisted, taken and certified by some Magistrate authorised to administer oaths, that he has resided within such County, for at least one year immediately preceding the time when he shall so offer him self to be enlisted: The said certificates & affidavits, when respectively necessary, shall be produced to the Officer who shall first muster any recruit, to whom they are applicable after he shall have joined his Regiment, towards the justification of the Officer by whom he shall have been enlisted.

"Apprentices shall on no pretext be enlisted. If any Apprentice shall be enlisted through ignorance of the Officer enlisting him, he shall be discharged; first refunding and returning any money, or other articles, which he may have received."

Major General Hamilton enjoins the strict observance of these regulations as points of material consequence to the Service. He equally enjoins a particular attention to those parts of the original rules and regulations, which forbid the inlistment of persons in a state of intoxication, and limit the ages, within which Recruits must be enlisted. It is learned with regret that in several instances they have not been sufficiently attended to. A faithful Army is to be preferred to a numerous one; and a regard to justice and propriety in the conduct of every part of the military service cannot fail ultimately to promote the honor and interest of those concerned in it, as well as the public good.

It is expected that the Commanders of Regiments will carefully attend to all wilful or negligent breaches of these Rules; and if any occur, will exert the means which the Articles of War provide for repressing disorders & neglects to the prejudice of good order and military discipline.

Copy, in the handwriting of Ethan Brown, Hamilton Papers, Library of Congress; printed copy, Hamilton Papers, Library of Congress; LC, RG 98, Post-Revolutionary Records, Orderly Book for Company of John Steele, 3d Infantry, 1799, Vol. 480, National Archives.

1. For background to this document, see H to James McHenry, March 15, May 25–27, 27, 1799; McHenry to H, second letter of May 9, May 28, second letter of May 29, 1799.

2. This is a reference to the March, 1799, edition of the War Department pamphlet *Rules and Regulations Respecting the Recruiting Service.* See H to Jonathan Dayton, August 6, 1798, note 6; McHenry to H, March 21, 1799.

To John F. Hamtramck [1]

New York [June 6, 1799]. ". . . Such of your remarks as are personal to me [2] are very gratifying. I hope your expectation will not finally be disappointed, though it will require time before a complete organisation, of what is now a very disjointed mass, will enable me to establish a perfect order. Zeal at least my friends know will not be wanting. The request you make with respect to yourself though unusual is very natural considering past experience. It will not fail to influence my Advice, unless I perceive that your *feelings* and your interest as a soldier can be mutually consulted. Communicate to me freely and confidentially on the subject of Western Affairs. You are sure of my discretion and honor."

Copy, in the handwriting of Ethan Brown, Hamilton Papers, Library of Congress.

1. H marked this letter "*Private.*"
2. See Hamtramck to H, January 25, 1799.

To William Heth

[*New York, June 6, 1799.* On June 20, 1799, Heth wrote to Hamilton and acknowledged "Your most obliging favor of the 6th." *Letter not found.*]

From Daniel Jackson

Castle William [*Boston*] *June 6, 1799.* ". . . I find Capt. Lemuel Gates Company has upwards twenty Men distitute of cloathing and some of them have been so about four months. Capt Gates informs me that he has wrote several times on the subject,[1] has had fair promises, but that those promises are not yet complied with. I find the Cloathing for the Infantry is ready, and in the mean time the Artillery is destitute. If the Officers here upon the recruiting service had complied with their instructions in taking from the recruits their Cloaths, the Men would now have been naked in Garrison, All these circumstances which I have mentioned prevent the Officers, from complying with their promises to the Men, and enforcing that strict discipline which the Service requires. . . ."

ALS, Hamilton Papers, Library of Congress.
1. On February 13, 1799, Gates wrote to James McHenry: "I have now seventy four men, enlisted, and have not received a sufficient supply of clothing and blankets . . ." (copy, Hamilton Papers, Library of Congress). This letter was enclosed in McHenry to H, first letter of February 22, 1799 (listed in the appendix to Volume XXII).

To James McHenry [1]

New York June 6. 1799

I return Mr. Patterson's letter. It is not my intention immediately to withdraw more than Cochran's & Henry's Companies.[2] The other troops may remain on the insurgents scene. I should prefer their remaining together. Perhaps the *vicinity* of Easton may be the best single station. But I am not without apprehension that the Troops may be corrupted by remaining long in a disaffected scene. Is there no well affected spot in the neighbourhood of Easton where they may answer the end?

Yrs. Affecly.   A H

J. McHenry Esq

ALS, Mr. Pierce W. Gaines, Fairfield, Connecticut; ALS (photostat), James McHenry Papers, Library of Congress.
   1. For background to this letter, see H to McHenry, May 25–27, 1799; McHenry to H, May 28, June 4, 6, 1799.
   2. Walter L. Cochran and John J. Henry were both captains in the Second Regiment of Artillerists and Engineers.

From James McHenry

private   [Philadelphia, June 6, 1799]

My dear Sir

Since my confidential letter to you,[1] inclosing one from Mr. Patterson, relative to stationing some troops at Easton, I have had verbal information, which shews, if not an absolute necessity for, yet that the stationing troops there would produce immediate salutary effects, upon the disorganizing inhabitants in that neighbourhood. I would advise therefore, if no important objection exists which ought to prevent it that the troops originally ordered to Easton be sent thither, or an equivalent force.

I had written the above when I reced. your letter returning Mr Patterson's.[2] Easton itself I have understood to be inhabited by people well disposed to the government. It is certain, the officers, who command the troops in the disaffected Country ought to be vigilant, and feel the necessity of keeping steadily with their men and constantly employing them in their exercises and discipline. If this is not the case, the consequences you suggest will be more or less experienced.

Yours Affly   J McHenry

Majr. Gen Alex Hamilton.

ALS, Hamilton Papers, Library of Congress; ADf, James McHenry Papers, Library of Congress.
1. McHenry to H, June 4, 1799.
2. H to McHenry, June 6, 1799.

From Philip Schuyler [1]

Albany Thursday June 6th 1799

My Dear Sir

We all arrived in good health at two O'Clock yesterday afternoon, the passage would have been perfectly agreable had It not been alloyed by the reflection that we had parted from friends so dear to us.

I hope My beloved Eliza is in better health than when we left her, perswaded that a change of air would benefit her we entreat her to come up as Speedily as possible, and to bring at least the two Youngest children with her, Johnny [2] will be Attended to by his Aunt [3] and myself, and from his own avidity to acquire information he will not suffer from his absence from School.

I shall transmit you the Cypher by Capt: Bogert. [4]

Accept our Love and Let My Dear Eliza and the Children participate in. Adieu My Dear Sir

Yours ever most affectionately   Ph: Schuyler

Hon: In: G. Hamilton

My son Philip [5] has procured a teacher for his children and they are now with him at Rhynbeck, so that the house will be perfectly quiet, and all our attention can be bestowed on my Eliza and the Children.

ALS, Lloyd W. Smith Collection, Morristown National Historical Park, Morristown, New Jersey.
1. Schuyler was H's father-in-law.
2. John Church Hamilton, H's fourth child, had been born in 1792.
3. Margarita Schuyler Van Rensselaer.
4. John Bogert was a New York City alderman and a member of the Military Committee of New York City.
The cipher referred to in this sentence had been requested by Rufus King. See King to H, October 20, 1798. For this cipher, see Schuyler to H, June 11, 1799.
5. Philip Jeremiah Schuyler.

From George Washington

Private   Mount Vernon June 6: 1799

Dear Sir,

I have duly received your letter of the 3d of May, and am glad to find that the recruiting service is likely to progress without further delay. To facilitate this, nothing will contribute more than Clothing.

It is certainly necessary to push on this business with proper energy, and to be provided with an ample and timely supply of every article wanted, if it is expected that such Troops as we have, should be, in any degree, respectable. This, I trust, will be done. And I should hope, ere this, that the field Officers for the Regiment to be raised in New Hampshire &c. have been appointed.

It is very desireable that the selection of Characters to Officer the Regiments, eventually to be raised,[1] should be such as will do credit to the service, if they should be called into the field. The Secretary of War has requested me to furnish him with a list of names for the quota from Virginia,[2] which I am taking measures to do; but, owing to my long absence from this State, I have so little personal knowledge of Characters, that I must rely very much on the information of others in whom I can confide.

With very sincere regard I am Dear Sir, Your Affecte Hbe. Servt.   Go: Washington

Major General Hamilton

LS, Hamilton Papers, Library of Congress; Df, in the handwriting of Tobias Lear, George Washington Papers, Library of Congress.

1. This is a reference to the Eventual Army. See the introductory note to H to James Gunn, December 22, 1798.

2. James McHenry to Washington, April 10, 1799 (LS, George Washington Papers, Library of Congress).

From James Wilkinson

New Orleans
June 6th: 1799

Sir

I arrived here on the 3rd Inst. & expect to Embark on the 10th. directly for the port of your residence.

I have Offered two & would have given four hundred do⟨l⟩lars for a passage in the Sloop which bears this as she is reputed a good sailer, but find myself excluded by a band of Kentuckeans, who anticipated my application.

Contrary to my expectations I do not find an armed Vessel in port, & that on which I am obliged to Embark is a clumsy Ship. The circumstance is a painful one, but it is unavoidable.

You have under cover a duplicate of my last,[1] the Original being transmitted agreably to Order.

With perfect consideration & respect I have the Honor to be Sir   Yr. Mo Obe St.

Majr. General Hamilton

ADf, Chicago Historical Society.
  1. Wilkinson to H, May 24, 1799.

To Aaron Ogden

New York June 7th. 1799

Sir

I do not recollect whether you have mentioned to me the points at which your majors will more particularly take their stations. It is in contemplation to order a detachment of Troops to Easton with a view to the insurgent spirit [1] in that quarter, and if it would not interfere with his duties in relation to the recruiting service, I should like very well to give the command of that detachment to Major Adlum.[2] Let me hear from you promptly on the subject.

With great consideration   I am Sir,   Yr. obedient Servt

A Hamilton

Col: A. Ogden
E Town N. Jersey

LS, Lloyd W. Smith Collection, Morristown National Historical Park, Morristown, New Jersey; ADf, Hamilton Papers, Library of Congress.
    1. This is a reference to Fries's Rebellion. See James McHenry to H, June 4, 6, 1799; H to McHenry, June 6, 1799.
    2. John Adlum was one of two majors in the Eleventh Regiment of Infantry.

From Aaron Ogden

Elizabeth Town [New Jersey] June 7. 1799

Sir.

In answer to yours of this day, I have to inform, that Reading was the more particular station, contemplated to have been taken by Major Adlum. Easton is within his district, and perhaps, nearly equally convenient. He has written to me that the spirit of disaffection, in the greater part of his district, will retard the recruiting very much, so that his aid in this service will be very important, and I should be really sorry if the nature of the Command of a detachment at Easton, should be such, as would necessarily confine him there, altogether, or otherwise very materially interfere with the service in which he is, at present, zealously engaged.

With the highest respect   I have the honor to be   Sir. your mo ob Servt.

Aaron Ogden

ALS, Hamilton Papers, Library of Congress.

To George Washington

New York June 7. 1799

Dr. Sir

I did myself the honor to write to you at some length on the 3 of May. I hope the letter got safe to hand.

The recruiting service is now in motion, in Maryland, Delaware Pensylvania New Jersey, New York, Connecticut and Massachusettes. I might perhaps add Virginia, from the assurances which I have received as to the transmission of supplies.[1] But I am not as yet informed of its actual commencement in that state. This cannot be much longer delayed.

The field Officers for the Regiment which embraces New Hampshire Vermont and Rhode Island have been lately appointed. They are Rufus Graves Lt Col Comdt Timothy Darling and Cornelius Lynde Majors.[2] The moment money and cloathing shall arrive the recruiting will begin there and in North Carolina. But I do not view this as *very* near.

I do not understand that the Officers for South Carolina and Georgia have yet been recommended.

The information I receive as to the progress and prospects of the recruiting service are sufficiently encouraging. Colonel Taylor, Commandant of the Regiment raising in Connecticut assures me that he is persuaded if no obstacle arises from supplies, that in two Months his Regiment will be filled by native Americans.[3] From other quarters the intelligence is very well. I permit myself to hope that in this summer and fall the army will be at its complement.

I send you a copy of the arrangement which has been made of the two Regiments of Artillerists.[4] Measures are taking to carry it into execution. The distribution of the Officers with the Western army is referred to Col Burbeck.[5]

There is nothing further in the military line worthy of your attention to communicate. When I shall have obtained more assistance I shall write more frequently.

A letter from Mr. King contains this unpleasant intelligence. The publication of the Treaty of *Campo Formio* by the Directory will injure the affairs of the Emperor.[6] It will increase the jealousy of the King of Prussia and of the Empire; whose safety and interests were too little in view in that Treaty. There is no end to the folly of the Potentates who are arrayed against France. We impatiently expect further accounts of the operations of the Arch Duke and entertain a strong hope that his genius and energy will turn to good account the advantage he has gained.

Most respectfully & Affecty   I have the honor to be Dr Sir   Yr very Obed   A Hamilton

General Washington

ALS, George Washington Papers, Library of Congress; copy, in the handwriting of Ethan Brown, Hamilton Papers, Library of Congress; copy, Hamilton Papers, Library of Congress.

1. See James McHenry to H, first letter of May 23, 1799, note 1.
2. Graves had been appointed lieutenant colonel commandant, and Lynde and Darling were appointed majors in the Sixteenth Regiment of Infantry on May 14, 1799 (Heitman, *United States Army*, I, 354, 471, 649). On May 14, 1800, the Senate confirmed the appointments of Graves and Lynde, but Darling had resigned his commission on December 20, 1799 (*Executive Journal*, I, 346, 355; Heitman, *United States Army*, I, 354).
3. See Timothy Taylor to H, May 27, 1799 (listed in the appendix to this volume). A veteran of the American Revolution, Taylor was lieutenant colonel commandant in the Thirteenth Regiment of Infantry.
4. "Arrangement of the 1st Regiment of Artillerists & Engineers," n.d. (D, Hamilton Papers, Library of Congress); "Arrangement of the 2d Regiment of Artillerists & Engineers," May 15, 1799 (D, in the handwriting of Philip Church and H, Hamilton Papers, Library of Congress). The arrangements of these regiments were fixed by "General Orders," May 16, 1799. See also H to McHenry, first letter of April 26, 1799; "Circular to the Artillery Field Officers," May 15, 1799.
5. See H to McHenry, first letter of April 26, 1799, note 4; McHenry to H, April 27, 1799; "General Orders," May 16, 1799.
6. Rufus King to H, March 22, 1799, note 7.

To John Adlum [1]

New York, June 8, 1799. "It is concurred to be expedient for some time to come to keep a body of troops in and near that district of Country in which the late insurrection existed. In this Service it is intended for the present to continue the troops now at Reading. . . . General McPherson recommended [2] the occupying of

three stations *Reading, Allentown,* & *Easton.* If the Corps of troops
was more considerable I should intirely approve this idea. But to
render them at all impressive there must not be too few at one
point. I have thought that a company at Easton and the remainder
at Reading might be the best disposition. It is my desire that you
assume the command of the whole body, as above described, and
that you make such a disposition of it, in reference to those points as
information on the spot shall induce you to prefer. . . . I confide
that you will be especially attentive to the discipline of the Troops
& to ⟨the⟩ prevention of injury or insult to the Inhabitants of
whatsoever description."

LS, Division of Public Records, Pennsylvania Historical and Museum Commission, Harrisburg, Pennsylvania; ADf, Hamilton Papers, Library of Congress.
    1. For background to this letter, see H to Aaron Ogden, June 7, 1799;
Ogden to H, June 7, 1799.
    This letter was enclosed in H to Ogden, June 8, 1799 (listed in the appendix
to this volume), in which H instructed Ogden to read his letter to Adlum
printed above and forward it with any observations he might think proper.
    2. William Macpherson to James McHenry, May 3, 1799, enclosed in
McHenry to H, May 10, 1799.

From Timothy Taylor

Danbury [*Connecticut*] *June 8, 1799.* "I have the Honor to inform you that upon my return from New York, I find it has become a Serious question wheather the recruiting Officers have a
right to enlist Minors after they arrive to the age of 18 Years, without the consent of their parents, Masters, or Guardians and repeated
application has been made for the releasment of some of those so
enlisted; it has been my opinion that the officers had a good right
to enlist them & that they ought not to be given up, but as I may
have errourd in Judgement, I beg the favour of your opinion upon
the subject as soon as convenient. . . ." [1]

ALS, Hamilton Papers, Library of Congress.
    1. Section II of the March, 1799, edition of the War Department pamphlet
Rules and Regulations Respecting the Recruiting Service stipulated that "Each
recruit must not be less than Eighteen." For an account of the editions of *Rules
and Regulations Respecting the Recruiting Service,* see H to Jonathan Dayton,
August 6, 1798, note 6; James McHenry to H, March 21, 1799.

From Josias Carvel Hall [1]

Havre de Grace [Maryland] June 10, 1799. Discusses details of recruiting and states: "The Clothing &c were so long in coming to Hand that the Officers were under the necessity of providing Blankets, Shoes, Potts &c. for the Recruits. . . ."

ALS, Hamilton Papers, Library of Congress.
1. A veteran of the American Revolution, Hall was lieutenant colonel commandant of the Ninth Regiment of Infantry.

From Charles Cotesworth Pinckney

Charleston, South Carolina, June 10, 1799. Discusses recruiting in Georgia and the Carolinas and the disposition of the Fourth Regiment. States: "Mrs. Pinckney (who has been very ill) unites with me in best respects to Mrs. Hamilton. I cannot imagine what gave rise to the Report, you mentioned [1] relative to the Review, as there was not the most distant cause for it. . . ."

ALS, Hamilton Papers, Library of Congress; ALS, letterpress copy, Hamilton Papers, Library of Congress.
1. H to Pinckney, first letter of March 7, 1799.

From Philip Schuyler [1]

Albany, June 11, 1799. "In the papers [2] which Accompany this I have pointed out three modes of wording in Cypher by aid of the copy of Entecks dictionary,[3] but as the copiest has not marked properly the directions for finding a word . . . It would be best to have two new copies. . . ."

ALS, MS Division, New York Public Library.
1. For background to this letter, see Rufus King to H, October 20, 1798; Schuyler to H, June 6, 1799.

2. Schuyler enclosed eight documents, some of which are in his handwriting. These documents explain how to prepare and use the cipher (MS Division, New York Public Library).

3. John Entick, *The New Spelling Dictionary, Teaching to Write & Pronounce the English Tongue with Ease and Propriety . . . with a List of Proper Names of Men and Women. The Whole Compiled and Digested in a Manner Entirely New, to Make it a Complete Pocket Companion . . . To Which is Prefixed a Grammatical Introduction to the English Tongue. A New ed., Carefully rev. and cor. To Which is Now first Added, a Catalogue of Words of Similar Sounds, but of Different Spellings and Significances* [By William Crobelt] (London: Printed for C. Dilly, 1783).

From Philip Church

Albany, June 12, 1799. ". . . My Second Lieutenant went yesterday at New Burgh to bring up my Cloathing, which is there, so that, I shall certainly commence recruiting the latter end of this Week. I have seen some Soldiers from Niagara who have been discharged having served their time; one of them stays with me intending to enlist when I shall have received the Cloathing. In my conversation with them I was astonished to find how lightly they talked of desertion assuring me that it was very common, but that the deserters when recovered were never punished. . . ."

ALS, Hamilton Papers, Library of Congress.

To James McHenry

New York June 12. 1799

Sir

A late letter from you [1] suggests some doubts whether in the case of the Serjeant, who was convicted of Destertion and Embezzlement, the form in which the proceedings were at first transmitted ought not to prevent the execution of the sentence.

My first impression was to defer a reply till the proceedings had been acted upon by the President; but on further reflection I have concluded to submit to you my ultimate ideas on the subject, in which I am supported by the opinion of Mr. Harrison,[2] Attorney of this District.

They are these—1 In strictness of law, it is not essential that it should appear on the face of the proceedings that two thirds of the members had concurred. When a certain proportion of a Court is required towards the rendering of a Judgment or sentence, and when a Court duly constituted does in fact give one, in a case in which the assent of that proportion is required, and the record of its proceedings, authenticated in the proper form, testifies that the Judgement or sentence was rendered, it is to be presumed, and need not be expressed, that there was a concurrence of the requisite number: Otherwise it could not be true in a legal sense that there was a sentence. Thus The law demands unanimity in the Verdict of a Jury—yet this unanimity is never declared on the Record. It is presumed, on the faith which is given to the Presiding & recording Officers, that the Verdict would not have been received, unless it had been unanimous, in other words unless it had been a *legal Verdict*. But

2dly. If this were not true, since the law intrusts the President and Judge Advocate with the duty of authenticating the proceedings, without the signature of any other member of the Court, it will consider them as competent to rectify an omission by an after act and to insert in the proceedings any circumstance, which may be necessary as evidence of their regularity, on the respo[n]sibility of those Officers that nothing shall be inserted which is not true. There can be no reason why as much Credit should not be given to their supplementary as to their original testimony.[3]

On either ground it is conceived that it will be legal and safe to approve and execute the sentence.

It is nevertheless conceived to be a good practice to insert in the proceedings the evidence that two thirds did concur. It will guard against the possibility of mistake through inattention, and will afford more complete satisfaction to the person, to whose approbation the sentence is to be referred, that all is right.

With great respect   I have the honor to be Sir   Yr Obed Serv

P. S. You will oblige me by causing the inclosed [4] to be immediately forwarded. It relates to a matter of urgency.

On recurring to your letter I find two points not noticed above. I am of Opinion that it is not necessary to specify the manner of the death, or to declare on what particular article the sentence is founded. Tis sufficient there is a warrant in the articles.

The Secy of War

ADf, Hamilton Papers, Library of Congress.
   1. McHenry to H, May 28, 1799 (listed in the appendix to this volume). In this letter McHenry discussed the case of Sergeant Richard Hunt who had been sentenced to death by a court-martial on April 16, 1799. On May 28, 1799, McHenry wrote to John Adams for his approval of the sentence (ALS, Adams Family Papers, deposited in the Massachusetts Historical Society, Boston). For information on this case, see H to McHenry, April 20, 1799, note 2; H to Washington Morton, April 23, 1799.
   2. Richard Harison.
   3. See H to Morton, April 23, 1799.
   4. H to Ebenezer Massey, June 12, 1799, enclosing H to Walter L. Cochran, June 12, 1799 (both listed in the appendix to this volume). In these letters H ordered Cochran to report to New York to serve as a witness at a court-martial.

To James McHenry

New York, June 12, 1799. Quotes from a "letter from Col: Hall of the 10th. instant" and states: ". . . In the commencement of similar operations, a good Zeal will occasion some wondering, which must be sanctionned as to the past and checked as to the future. I recommend that provisions be made for reimbursement. . . ."

Copy, in the handwriting of Ethan Brown, Hamilton Papers, Library of Congress.

From John J. U. Rivardi

Niagara [New York] June 12, 1799. Reports that "The British Garrison continues To Work with all Speed at Fort George. . . . Captn. Pilkington [1] who is the Engineer comunicated all the drawings relative To The execution of the place with a confidence extremely pleasing. It is him who constructed fort Miami & he has lent me all the papers in his possession by which I Shall be able To frame a Plan. . . ." States that progress is being made on the repair of Fort Niagara, but if the work is to be completed, the soldiers must receive extra pay for extra work.

ALS, Hamilton Papers, Library of Congress.
1. Robert Pilkington entered the British army in 1787, transferred to the Royal Engineers in 1789, and was ordered to Canada in 1790. He was promoted to first lieutenant in 1793 and to the rank of captain lieutenant and captain in 1797. He was the engineer in charge of the construction of Fort George, the British garrison across the Niagara River from Fort Niagara.

From William S. Smith

East Chester [*New York*] *June 12, 1799.* "I have the honor to acknowledge the receipt of your Letter of the 5th inst. . . .[1] we have neither tents nor the necessary Camp utensils. I will however endeavour to help them over these inconveniences, untill by your communications to the War office, the necessary supplies may be forwarded—each Company will at present require 4 good axes & 4 spades, and the earliest attention should be paid to the forwarding, the pelluses allowed—a further supply of Cloathing is necessary, and more money for the recruiting service. . . ."

ALS, Hamilton Papers, Library of Congress.
1. Letter not found.

From Timothy Taylor

Danbury [*Connecticut*] *June 12, 1799.* "From the progressive state of the recruiting service in the Circle under my Command, I have the Honor to inform you that a further supply of bounty Money will be wanted as soon as it can conveniently be sent forward. Thier has been but a small supply of Cloathing furnished for the recruits, and a number are now enlisted and drawn to thier rendizvous, almost naked, Arms are much wanted for some [of] them. . . ."

ALS, Hamilton Papers, Library of Congress.

From William Willcocks [1]

[*East Chester, New York*] *June 12, 1799*. ". . . I take the liberty . . . to report to you . . . that . . . it is probable that in a few days, the Recruiting Service, will be obstructed for the want of Bounty money, independent of all other occasions. . . ."

ALS, Hamilton Papers, Library of Congress.
1. Willcocks, a veteran of the American Revolution, was a New York City attorney. In 1794 he was a Federalist member of the New York Assembly. During the Quasi-War with France he was a major in the Twelfth Regiment of Infantry.

General Orders

New York June 13th 1799.

The Articles of War being obscore and unexplicit as to the power of appointing a General Court Martial,[1] and it being very meterial that there shall be no doubt about the legalaty of the Constitution of a Court which is intrusted with the power of inflicting the highest punishment known in our Military Code, Major General Hamilton thinks it proper to declear the constitution of those Articles upon this point which after careful examination and reflection he has adopted as that which is to govern within the Sphere of his command, it is this, every General of a department or of a Seperate army, Every General Commanding Troops a post or Station So detached from the army as that its ordinary police is of nec[e]ssity distinct every Officer inferior in rank to a General on whom the Command of a General may have devolved in one or other of the above cases may legally Constitute a General Court Martial, but no Officer who does not command as the immediate Representitive of a General especially no Officer mearly commanding a Regiment or other Corps Whether entire or composed of detachments not Superior to a Regiment can Constitute a General Court Martial Consequently no officer Commanding any of the Garrisons on a Sea Board and no Officer Commandg any tract of the Western amy except the Commander of that army for the time being can of his own authority direct the holding of such a court, it follows that all pending Sentences of any courts deno[mi]nated General Courts Martial which have not been appointed in Conformity with the foregoing Constructions are to be Null & Void. It is also considered essential to the regularity of a General Court Martial that there shall be a person who is not a member of the Court acting as Judge advocate. It is also for greater Caution directed that in the cases in which the consequence of two thirds of the members of the Court is required it shall be expressed in the body of the Sentence that two thirds or more than two thirds as the case may be did concur.

A deferrent practice having obtain at different posts in reguard to issuing Liquor to the Troops, it is thought proper to direct that the allowance of half Gill pr. day may be every whear issued when ever the Contractors can furnish the supply, this however is not to restrain the discresionary power of issuing for fatigue service or on Extraordinary Cases.

Abraham R. Ellery Asst. Adjt. Genl

LC, RG 98, Post-Revolutionary Records, Orderly Book for the Company of John Steele, 3d Infantry, 1799, Vol. 480, National Archives.

1. For the problems concerning general courts-martial, see James McHenry to H, first letter of January 21, May 29, 1799; H to McHenry, February 23, 1799.

To Timothy Pickering

[*New York, June 13, 1799.* On June 18, 1799, Pickering wrote to Hamilton and referred to "your letter of the 13th." *Letter not found.*]

To James McHenry

private & confidential   New York June 14. 1799

I use, my Dear Sir, the privilege of an old friend to write to you in language as explicit as the occasion requires. The fact is that the management of your Agents as to the affair of supplies is ridiculously bad. Besides the extreme delay, which attends every operation, articles go forward in the most incomplete manner. *Coats* without a corresponding number of *Vests*—Cartouch Boxes without belts &c &c nothing intire—nothing systematic. Tis the scene of the worst periods of our revolution war acted over again even with caricature.

Col *Stevens* tells me that lately materials for tents were purchased here and sent to Philadelphia. This is of a peice with what was done in regard to cloathing and it is truly farcical—proving that the microscopic eye of the purveyor [1] can see nothing beyond Philadelphia. It is idle to pretend that the materials in such cases cannot be made as well elsewhere as at Philadelphia and that double transportation and the accumulation of employment in a particular place beyond its means can tend to œconomy or any other good and—and the delay is so enormous as to overballance any minute advantage if any there be that attends the plan.

It is a truth My Dear Sir and a truth which you ought to weigh well that unless you immediately employ more competent Agents to procure and to forward supplies the service will deeply suffer and the head of the War Department will be completely discredited.

The object will very soon be much enlarged to an extent to which such men and such measures can never suffice.

You must immediately get a more efficient Purveyor & I believe a more efficient Superintendant,[2] or nothing can prosper.

My frankness & plain dealing are a new proof of the cordial friendship which I must always cherish for you. Adieu

Affecly yrs   A Hamilton

The Secy of War

ALS, Dr. Max Thorek, Chicago, Illinois; ALS (photostat), James McHenry Papers, Library of Congress; copy, in the handwriting of Ethan Brown, Hamilton Papers, Library of Congress.

1. Tench Francis.
2. Samuel Hodgdon.

To James McHenry

New York June 14. 1799

Sir

I send you copies and extracts of letters from Colonels Taylor [1] and Smith [2] and from Major Willcocks.[3] These shew that further advances of money will be speedily necessary and that there ought to be increased exertion in the business [of] the supplies.

It is my duty to observe that the dilatory and incomplete manner in which supplies are furnished, if not corrected, will quickly have an effect very disadvantageous and disreputable to the service. The Government will have the appearance in the eyes of the soldiery of want of means & of an indisposition to apply them. Either will lead to disrespect and discontent.[4]

The accounts which I received promise a more rapid progress in the inlistment of men than was anticipated. It is probable that in several states the complement will be raised in two or three months. It will never answer to raise the men and suffer them to remain without cloathing arms or any other necessary equipment or supply. It should be reduced to certainty what can be done & if the supply is not likely to keep pace, it is best to arrest the recruiting; a measure however which if unavoidable will be very unfortunate and which it is not easy to suppose will be unavoidable if proper measures are pursued with diligence and energy.

The Pay of the men raised must also begin to be thought of. Men newly enlisted will look for punctuality and it is important that they should not be disappointed.

With great respect & esteem I have the honor to be   Sir Yr Hbe Servt   A H

ADfS, Hamilton Papers, Library of Congress.
  1. Timothy Taylor to H, June 12, 1799.
  2. William S. Smith to H, June 12, 1799.
  3. William Willcocks to H, June 12, 1799.
  4. See H to McHenry, first letter of June 14, 1799.

From Thomas Parker [1]

Winchester [Virginia] June 14, 1799. ". . . on examining the Hats that have been sent on I find they are destitute of Cockades and loops. . . . The Recruiting money has been Received & distributed there was only a Sufficiency sent on to Recruit forty four men to a Company at eight dollars ℔ man. An additional Supply will be Immediately wanted as Several of the officers of my Regiment have been verry Successfull. . . . only a part of the Cloathing has yet arrived I coud wish the remainder to be forwarded as soon as possable as It woud give vigor to the Recruiting service. . . . I shall be glad to receive your Instructions with Respect to the propriety of Inlisting apprentices as It has occasioned Some uneasiness amongst the Inhabitants. . . ."

ALS, Hamilton Papers, Library of Congress.
    1. Parker, a resident of Virginia and a veteran of the American Revolution, was lieutenant colonel commandant of the Eighth Regiment of Infantry.

General Orders

New York June 15th 1799

A pretention having been raised by some of the Contractors, to issue either fresh or salt meat to the Troops at their discretion Major General Hamilton thinks it proper, to declear his Sence that this pretention is unfounded and without an Express declaration in the Contract that the option is reserved to the Contractor, it must be understood that it is reserved to the public, it is expected therefore except in situations which do not admit of it that fresh meat will be furnished five days in every week as the General rule, nevertheless the Commanding Officers of posts or Corps and Detacht are left at liberty to vary this propotion in such manner as may be most sattisfactory to those under their Command, and with reasonable accomodations to public Circumstances.

All letters either to Major General Hamilton or the Adjutant General or his assistant on matters relating to the service which pass though the post office are to be endorsed on public Service and with the name of the writer.

Abraham R. Ellery Asst Adgt Genl

Extract, RG 98, Post-Revolutionary War Records, Orderly Book for the Company of John Steele, 3d Infantry, 1799, Vol. 480, National Archives.

From James McHenry

Philadelphia, June 15, 1799. "Your observations relative to my agent for procuring supplies and the Superintendant are but too well founded.[1] The last has so strong a supporter,[2] that I cannot see when or how I am to get rid of him. As to the Purveyor, I have for some time been reconnoitring for an assistant[3] to him whose talents and activity joined to mercantile knowledge would supply his defects. Jonathan Williams[4] has appeared to me the best qualified, and I shall not lose a moment to induct him if he will accept of the appointment. The Quarter Master General[5] who is now at Pittsburg ought to be here: He was permitted to go thither to make the necessary dispositions for the western army, and adjust some private business. I shall unless you chuse to do it, write by next post to expedite his return. . . ."

ALS, Hamilton Papers, Library of Congress; ADf, James McHenry Papers, Library of Congress.

1. For H's "observations" on Tench Francis and Samuel Hodgdon, see H to McHenry, two letters of June 14, 1799.

2. This is a reference to Timothy Pickering, who was a close friend and former business partner of Samuel Hodgdon.

3. See the enclosure to H to McHenry, second letter of April 8, 1799.

4. Williams, a native of Boston and a great-nephew of Benjamin Franklin, had been prize agent and commercial agent for Congress at Nantes during the American Revolution. After the war he returned to the United States, settled in Philadelphia, and became an investor in various stock and land operations. In 1796 he was appointed associate judge of the Court of Common Pleas in Philadelphia.

5. John Wilkins, Jr.

From James McHenry

War Department, June 15, 1799. "I received by yesterdays mail, three letters of the 12,[1] and by the mail of this morning, two letters of June 14th instant. . . . The idea is undoubtedly correct respecting the keeping an extra supply of Clothing at the remote posts. It is not unknown to you, that from circumstances which I could not controul, even the quantity of Cloathing necessary for the old establishment, was not procured last year; that from an absolute deficiency of White Cloth (for Vests and overalls) within the United States the Contracts for these articles utterly failed, and that the utmost exertions may not possibly do more than enable us to keep pace with the demand for the recruiting service now that the spring arrivals have furnished the materials. I shall exert all the authority and power I possess to equalize the supplies to our wants. I think it right that the Commandants of Regiments should be made acquainted with the circumstances which have and may yet occasion some temporary delays. . . . Money will always be forwarded for the recruiting service when called for and the pay of the recruits immediately transmitted after their pay and Muster Rolls are received; or if you require it a Sum of money on account will be lodged in the hands of the respective regimental Paymasters for this purpose to be applied after the Musters."

LS, Hamilton Papers, Library of Congress.
 1. Actually H sent McHenry four letters on June 12, 1799. Two of these letters are listed in the appendix to this volume. In one of these letters H discusses clothing necessary for troops in a warm climate, and in the other he discusses gunpowder for the artillery.

To George Washington

Private   New York June 15. 1799

Dear Sir
  I wrote to you a few days since [1] chiefly to inform you of the

progress of the measures respecting the recruiting service & that the symptoms with regard to it were sufficiently promising. The accounts continue favourable.

I have just received a letter from General Wilkinson dated the 13 of April,[2] in which he assures me that he will set out in the ensuing month for the seat of Government. The interview with him will be useful.

It strikes me forcibly that it will be both right and expedient to advance this Gentleman to the grade of Major General.[3] He has been long steadily in service and long a Brigadier. This in so considerable an extension of the military establishment gives him a pretension to promotion.

I am aware that some doubts have been entertained of him and that his character on certain sides gives room for doubts. Yet he is at present in the service—is a man of more than ordinary talent—of courage and enterprise—has discovered upon various occasions a good zeal—has embraced military pursuits as a profession and will naturally find his interest as an ambitious man in deserving the favour of the Government; while he will be apt to become disgusted, if neglected and through disgust may be rendered really what he is now only suspected to be. Under such circumstances, it seems to me good policy to avoid all just ground of discontent and to make it the interest of the individual to pursue his duty.

If you should be also of this opinion, I submit to your consideration whether it would not be adviseable for you to express it in a private letter to the Secretary of War.

With great respect & Affection   I have the honor to be Dr Sir Your obed servt   A Hamilton

General Washington

ALS, George Washington Papers, Library of Congress; copy, in the handwriting of Ethan Brown, Hamilton Papers, Library of Congress; copy, Hamilton Papers, Library of Congress.
  1. H to Washington, June 7, 1799.
  2. H is mistaken, for Wilkinson's letter is dated April 15, 1799.
  3. "An Act to augment the Army of the United States, and for other purposes" (1 Stat. 604–05 [July 16, 1798]) had authorized the appointment of three major generals. The refusal of Henry Knox to serve under H (see the introductory note to Washington to H, July 14, 1798) had left a vacancy that was never filled. H is recommending Wilkinson for this vacancy.

To James McHenry

Private   New York June 16. 1799

Dr. Sir

Seeing the terrible delays which take place is it not adviseable immediately to authorise your Agents at New York & Boston to take prompt measures for increasing your supply of Cloathing tents and such other articles as are in Arrear? Considering past experience can you possibly depend on the present plan for the future supply? If blue Cloath *cannot* be found for the whole, better to take some other Colour by intire regiments for those which have not yet begun to recruit?

The brest fleet is out. Its destination is in all probability Ireland,[1] but ought we so intirely to rely upon this as to omit to take the precaution of having some fast sailing vessels on the look out before our principal ports—Charles Town, the entrances of the Chesapaek the Delaware New York, New Port Boston, with perhaps the establishment of signals?

It would be awkward to be intirely surprised & to have some of our banks fall into the hands of the *Philistines*. When we think of *Egypt* [2] we ought not to consider the attempt as impracticable. Announcing that it is a mere act of caution without intelligence no inconvenient alarm will be created. It may even be useful to bring home to the minds of our Citizens that our Government does not deem an invasion impossible.

Col Stevens [3] informs me that sometime since the UStates lent to New York a thousand stand of arms which are disposed in a situation to be lost and are not wanted by the State. There is no reason why their return should not be asked.

Adieu Yrs. Affecy   A Hamilton [4]

The Secy of War

ALS, Hamilton Papers, Library of Congress; copy, in the handwriting of Ethan Brown, Hamilton Papers, Library of Congress.

1. H is incorrect. On April 25, 1799, Admiral Eustache Bruix, French Minister of Marine, sailed from Brest with twenty-five ships of line and ten smaller

vessels. Avoiding the British blockading squadron under Alexander Hood, baron Bridport, Bruix sailed southward and passed the Strait of Gibraltar on May 5, 1799. He reached Toulon on May 14 and left on May 26 with twenty-two ships of line. From June 4 to June 8 he anchored in Vado Bay while part of the fleet reinforced the besieged garrison at Genoa. On June 22 he anchored at Cartagena, leaving there on June 29 with sixteen Spanish ships of line. On August 13 Bruix returned to Cadiz with the allied fleet.

2. This is a reference to Napoleon's invasion of Egypt on July 1, 1798, and his subsequent conquest of that country.

3. Ebenezer Stevens.

4. On the envelope McHenry wrote: "What clothing has Mr [Jonathan] Jackson been ordered to procure? Has [Timothy] Phelps & [Peleg] Sanford been engaged to furnish? [Caleb] Swan. has that order been enlarged?"

Jackson was the Army contractor in Massachusetts. Phelps and Sanford were New Haven, Connecticut, merchants and the Army contractors for that state. Swan was paymaster general of the Army.

To James McHenry

New York, June 16, 1799. States: ". . . the recruiting service . . . is . . . now in a course of execution in all the states from Massachusetts inclusively to Virginia inclusively. Thus the necessity of expedition in regard to the supplies becomes more & more urgent. . . ."

ADf, Hamilton Papers, Library of Congress.

To James McHenry

New York June 17. 1799

Sir

I have the honor of your letter of the 15 instant. The several points mentioned in it have been attended.

In the commencement of a new branch of service it is necessary for dispatch to wave the usual forms. Hence the omission of returns. But I shall speedily send you an exact statement of the various articles of supply requisite for each Regiment—and which from the accounts received it will be requisite to forward as speedily as shall be practicable.

I shall also mention what further supply of bounty money will be immediately requisite for certain Regiments, and I shall subjoin the result of my reflection on the subject of an advance of pay. The intention of my last was only to call your attention to this as an approaching object of expenditure.

With great respect etc.

The Secy of War

ADf, Hamilton Papers, Library of Congress.

From Jonathan Williams

Philadelphia, June 17, 1799. Encloses "a pamphlet on Fortification with six plates,[1] and 122 pages of a Treatise on Artillery with twenty four Tables." [2] States: "the remainder of the latter Work shall be forwarded as soon as it can be obtained from the Printer. . . ."

ALS, Hamilton Papers, Library of Congress.
  1. This is a reference to Williams's translation of Alexandre Pierre Julienne de Belair, *The Elements of Fortification, Translated From The French* (Philadelphia: Printed for the War Office by John Ward Fenno, 1799).
  2. This is a reference to Williams's translation of Henri Othon de Scheel, *Treatise of Artillery; containing a new system, or the alterations made in the French Artillery, since 1765, translated by Jonathan Williams* (2 vols., Philadelphia: Printed for the War Office by John Ward Fenno, 1800).

From Henry Burbeck

Michilimackinac [Territory Northwest of the River Ohio] June 18, 1799. "I had the Honour of receiving your letter of the 16th of February. . . .[1] The Fort is a very irregular work without Bastions or out works is situated on an eminence which completely commands the Harbour and Village its an extensive work and will require Five Hundred Men to completely man it. When I took possession, it was in a total state of ruin not defenceable even against small Arms. . . . I have repaired all the Stone Walls which were in a very shattered condition and have built new ones where it was necessary, on these Walls I have an excellent range of nine feet

Picketts which will be all completed in a short time. So that I can venture to say by the time this reaches you that this Garrison can be calculated on to be in a complete state of defence and repair. . . . The Indians who are numerous around this Post, by their Speeches and Actions appear perfectly friendly to the United States, and from every information I can obtain from the different Traders which have arrived from the Mississippi &c all is peaceable and friendly."

ALS, Hamilton Papers, Library of Congress.
    1. Burbeck is mistaken about the date of H's letter, for he is referring to H's "Circular to the Commanding Officers in Northern and Western United States," February 15, 1799.

Circular to the Commandants of Regiments

Circular   New York June 18. 1799
to Lt Col Comr

Sir

Intimations have been in some instances given that more bounty money will quickly be wanted.[1] The Secy of War will naturally expect that an application of this sort should be accompanied with some view of the progress of the recruiting. I am aware that it requires a little time to get into the train of exact returns—but it is necessary to require the transmission of information more or less correct and a summary of it must be communicated to me.[2]

The form of a monthly return will soon be transmitted & then it will be expected that it will be regularly made.

With great consideration   I am Sir   Yr Obed ser.

ADf, Hamilton Papers, Library of Congress; LS, to Aaron Ogden, Lloyd W. Smith Collection, Morristown National Historical Park, Morristown, New Jersey.
    1. See Timothy Taylor to H, June 12, 1799; William S. Smith to H, June 12, 1799; William Willcocks to H, June 12, 1799; Thomas Parker to H, June 14, 1799. See also H to James McHenry, June 14, 17, 1799; McHenry to H, second letter of June 15, 1799.
    2. See McHenry to H, second letter of June 15, 1799; H to McHenry, June 17, 1799.

From James McHenry

War Department
18th June 1799

Sir,

Officers have been appointed for six additional companies of cavalry.[1] It is not however deemed expedient, at present, to enlist for, or mount the Cavalry.

I submit it, to your consideration, whether these Officers, may not be usefully, and properly employed, untill called into their appropriate service, by being attached to the Infantry companies, as well to assist in recruiting, as in training the men.

This measure would initiate the Cavalry officers, in the general principles of service, and prepare them to execute their duties, with facility, and correctness, with their own companies.

It will be recollected, that the twelve regiments of Infantry, and the six companies of Cavalry, authorized to be raised,[2] and the former now raising, are additional to the existing military establishments—and that "An Act to ascertain, and fix, the military establishment of the United States" passed the 30th. May 1796[3] provides that the two companies of Light Dragoons, retained in service, shall do duty on horse or foot, at the discretion of the President of the United States.

If you approve of this measure, you will please to issue your orders to the Officers of Cavalry accordingly, and cause so many of them, and at such time as you may think proper, to be employed in the service of the Infantry.

I know objections may be made, but are they of sufficient importance, to prevent these officers, from being usefully employed and instructed, at present? and they are now recieving the pay and emoluments of their respective grades, without rendering any service whatever.

I am Sir   with great respect   Your obedient servant

James McHenry

Major General Alexander Hamilton.

LS, Hamilton Papers, Library of Congress.
1. See the enclosure to McHenry to H, May 10, 1799.
2. "An Act to augment the Army of the United States, and for other purposes" (1 *Stat.* 604–05 [July 16, 1798]).
3. 1 *Stat.* 483–86.

To James McHenry

New York, June 18, 1799. Quotes an extract from Major Daniel Jackson's letter of June 6, 1799, concerning the shortage of clothing and lack of money to pay recruits.

Copy, in the handwriting of Ethan Brown, Hamilton Papers, Library of Congress.

To James McHenry

New York June 18. 1799

Sir

You will be pleased to receive herewith a statement of the articles of supply requisite for a Regiment of Infantry.[1] It is necessary that the full quantity, including what has been heretofore forwarded, should be transmitted as fast as possible. With all the diligence that can be made, it is not probable that they will arrive too soon.

After the proportion, which was indicated in the first instance, shall have been furnished to the several Regiments of which the Officers have been appointed, the additional supply had best be forwarded first to the 10th. 11th. 12th. and 13th. Regiments, next to the 8th. 9th. and 14th then to the 7th and 15th & lastly to the 6th and sixteenth.

An additional supply of bounty money, sufficient with what has been already sent for the raising of three fourths of each Regiment, ought immediately to be furnished to the 10th. 11th. 12 & 13th Regiments. And it will be well to forward to the pay Master of each of these Regiments One Months pay, with the addition of the retained bounty for One third of a Regiment, exclusive of Officers. If this is determined upon, I shall be glad to be advised of the Determination.

The inclosed Copy of a general order of the 6th instant [2] is conformable to your instructions by letter. You will judge whether any farther or more formal sanction is requisite.

With great respect   I have the honor to be   Sir Yr. Obed. S

The Secy of War

ADf, Hamilton Papers, Library of Congress.
   1. "Articles of Military Supply for each Regiment of Infantry," June 20, 1799 (AD, New-York Historical Society, New York City; copy, Hamilton Papers, Library of Congress).
   2. In addition to this general order, see McHenry to H, May 28, second letter of May 29, 1799.

From Timothy Pickering [1]

Department of State
Philada June 18th 1799

Dear Sir,

Mr. Rozier presented yesterday, your letter of the 13th; [2] and, agreeably to my appointment, he called this morning and exhibited his cypher, and comparing with it his cyphered letters to Mr. Talleyrand which were taken in the Astrea and transmitted to me from Gibralter, I found in every passage examined, an exact correspondence with those letters written in words, copies whereof he gave me to *read*. Their contents justify his assurances to you, that they exhibited nothing which could be construed into a design to injure the United States. The opinions he expressed of the state of parties and of the then recent elections to Congress, are such as might be expected from a French agent to his government, willing to please it with a representation of American affairs in relation to France as favourable to the latter as the information to be derived from French partisans, in news-papers, letters and conversations, would warrant; but the whole without any symptoms of acrimony or ill-will. I took the occasion to remark, That the French Government was encouraged to persevere in its hostile and pernicious designs against the United States by representations importing that they had numerous friends in this country, and perhaps a majority in the ensuing Congress, or if not, that the federal majority would be feeble, and consequently little efficient: adding that he could obtain from you more correct information.

I am with great respect &c   Timothy Pickering.

LC, RG 59, Domestic Letters of the Department of State, Vol. 11, June 30, 1798–June 29, 1799, National Archives; copy, Massachusetts Historical Society, Boston.
    1. For background to this letter, see H to Pickering, April 4, 1799.
    On April 12, 1799, Pickering wrote to Jean Antoine Bernard Rozier: "I have received your letter of the 3d. instant; but suspended an answer until I should receive the letters found on board the ship Astrea, and sent to America by the American Consul at Gibraltar [John Gavino]. The letters are now come to hand. Among them are two from you to the Minister of Foreign Relations, numbered 1 & 2 dated the 6th. Brumaire & 2d Frimaire, 7th. year of the French era, with a postscript to the last dated 3d. Frimaire. As a proof that these letters contain nothing contrary to the interests of the United States, you offer to let me know their contents, by communicating your cypher to some person at New York, whom I shall judge worthy of that confidence. The length of the letters will render the decyphering a work of more labour than I wish to give to any gentleman there; and propose, therefore, that you should transmit a copy of your cypher to me. I trust you will not think this an improper step: because no French citizen who wishes to enjoy here the rights of hospitality, can be entitled to them while he maintains a *secret correspondence* with the *French Government;* and it is for a *secret correspondence* only that a *cypher* can be wanted.
    "I am led, by the frankness of your offer and the favourable opinion of General Hamilton to assure you of my respect." (LC, RG 59, Domestic Letters of the Department of State, Vol. 11, June 30, 1798–June 29, 1799, National Archives.)
    2. Letter not found.

Circular to the Commandants of Regiments

Circular to Commanders   New York June 19. 1799

Sir

Inclosed is the form of a monthly return [1] which you are to make to me pursuant to the XXXV of the "Rules and Regulations respecting the Recruiting Service." [2] It now becomes urgent that these returns shall be regularly made. They will govern my application to the Secy of War for provisions of money.

You will, consequently, enforce punctually in the returns which according to those Rules & Regulations must be the basis of that now prescribed. And you will be particularly attentive to procuring the regular transmission of all those Documents which are to regulate the accountability for money and other supplies.

As soon as Recruits shall reach the Regimental rendezvous they must be definitively mustered. This duty for the present must devolve upon you with the aid of Your Regimental surgeon. If none has been appointed, You must with the cooperation of the Contractor employ a capable Medical Man in his stead. And it is relied upon that this service will be executed with exemplary strictness. The disability of Rupture is found in experience to occur frequently. The Surgeon must inspect without ceremony wherever there may be latent defects. And all disqualified men, from whatever cause, must be instantly discharged; first taking fro⟨m⟩ them as far as practicable whatever they may have obtained fro⟨m⟩ the public by imposing themselves up⟨on⟩ its service.

No money after the arrival at the Regimental Rendezvou⟨s⟩ must be paid to a soldier till he shall have been there carefully examined & mustered.

With great consider⟨ation⟩   I am Sir Yr. obedient servt.

ADf, Hamilton Papers, Library of Congress.
    1. Copy, Hamilton Papers, Library of Congress.
    2. Section XXXV of the March, 1799, War Department pamphlet *Rules and Regulations Respecting the Recruiting Service* reads: "The officers commanding circles or districts, will on the first Monday of each month, make a return, according to a form to be prescribed by the Inspector General, to the said Inspector General, of the recruits enlisted within the preceding month."

From James McHenry [1]

private   [Philadelphia, June 19, 1799]

My dear Sir
    I wrote a letter yesterday to the Secy. of the Navy respecting the propriety of being alert at our port, knowing that the French fleet is at sea, and the expediency of the measure suggested. Something will be done; but not much partly through want of means.

All these things help forward the army, and the army and the expences attending it, are not to all views equally desirable. The Secy. of the Navy has no objection to a few regts. but thinks the rest of the revenue would be better applied on the marine. I go on.
    Yours

AL, Hamilton Papers, Library of Congress.
    1. This letter was written in reply to H to McHenry, first letter of June 16, 1799.

From James McHenry

Philadelphia, June 19, 1799. "I received this morning your letter of the 17th instant. I have ordered two thousand dollars to be forwarded to the Paymaster of the 12 [1] and an equal sum to the Paymaster of the 13th Regiment. . . .[2] There has been also delivered to the Paymaster of the Tenth Regiment [3] One thousand five hundred and forty four dollars and fifty cents. . . ."

LS, Hamilton Papers, Library of Congress.
    1. Lieutenant James Smith, Jr., of the Twelfth Regiment of Infantry was appointed paymaster of the regiment on April 5, 1799 (Godfrey, "Provisional Army," 166).
    2. Lieutenant Trueman Mosely of the Thirteenth Regiment of Infantry was appointed paymaster of the regiment on April 10, 1799 (Godfrey, "Provisional Army," 169).
    3. Lieutenant John Sharp of the Tenth Regiment of Infantry was appointed regimental paymaster on April 26, 1799 (Godfrey, "Provisional Army," 157).

From George Washington

Mount Vernon, June 19th: 1799

Dear Sir,

Your favour of the 7th instant, with its inclosures, has been duly received.

I am very glad to learn that the recruiting business, so far as it has been put in operation, succeeds agreeably to your wishes. It has commenced in Virginia, and I am informed that, in this vicinity (and I have no intelligence from the more distant parts of the State) its progress is very flattering. A supply of Cloathing would, however, promote this service even hereabouts; and unless it be furnished soon I am apprehensive it will languish, if not stop entirely.

I understand, by a letter which I received a few days since from General Pinckney,[1] that the selection of Officers from No. & So.

Carolina and Georgia, has been transmitted to the War Office.[2] I hope, on every account, there will be no delay in completing this arrangement.

The disposition you have made of the Artillery Regiments is, I have no doubt, just and proper, and calculated to promote the good of the Service.

I thank you for the information from Mr. King. I have long believed that France owes the facility of her Conquests more to the Jealousy and want of cordial cooperation among the powers of Europe, whose interest it is to check her desolating Ravages, than to any exertions of her own, great as they may have been. It appears from every account (altho' there is none so full and distinct as I could wish) that her Armies have not only been checked; but obliged to retreat. And her internal affairs do not seem to be in the best situation. Should these advantages be properly improved, I think the happiest effects may result from them.

With very sincere regard   I am, Dear Sir,   Your affecte & Obedt. Servt   Go: Washington

General Hamilton.

LS, Hamilton Papers, Library of Congress; Df, in the handwriting of Tobias Lear, George Washington Papers, Library of Congress.

1. Charles Cotesworth Pinckney to Washington, June 4, 1799 (ALS, George Washington Papers, Library of Congress).

2. Pinckney to James McHenry, May 29, 1799 (copy, George Washington Papers, Library of Congress).

General Orders

[*New York, June 20, 1799.* On July 11, 1799, John J. U. Rivardi wrote to Hamilton: [1] "I received also General orders of the 6th, 15th, & 20th. of June." *General orders of June 20, 1799, not found.*]

1. This letter is listed in the appendix to this volume.

From William Heth

Petersburg [*Virginia*] *June 20, 1799.* "Your most obliging favor of the 6th [1] found me a day or two ago at the commencement of my spring harvest, the crop of which, I fear will not be very abundant. This kind answer, Tho has settled all my Jealousies, and made me happy. But you must really drop me a line *now and then,* merely to prove that you some times think of a man, who scarce lets a day pass without giving a glass to Alexander Hamilton. Yes, I ask this—notwithstanding I well know, how fully your time is occupied. . . . You must have heard ere this, of the death of our great HENRY.[2] In the loss of this wonderful man, AMERICA itself, hath received a deep wound. But, Virginia, unfortunate, distracted Virginia! hath received a blow, which she will long feel. The good, the virtuous, and the liberal minded of all classes, seem truly sensible of the severe stroke & shew much, & deep affliction; while some few of the Jacobin tribe, are found so lost to every sense of decency & humanity, as openly to express their pleasure at an event, melancholy in the extreme, & which at this crisis of American affairs, may truly be calld a *national misfortune.* But, what are not such degenerate, & contemptible wretches capable of? You have our last paper, to show how this misfortune has been mentioned here & in Richmond. . . . I should like to see this published in one of your papers *embellished* by you—in order to get into ours. If you approve of this, send me yr paper. . . ."

ALS, Hamilton Papers, Library of Congress.
  1. Letter not found.
  2. Patrick Henry had died on June 6, 1799.

From Richard Hunewell

[*Portland, District of Maine, June 20, 1799.* On July 10, 1799, Hamilton sent to James McHenry "an Extract of a letter of the 20th June from Col: Hunewell." *Letter not found.*]

From James McHenry

[Philadelphia] 20 June 1799

Dear Sir

I received this morning from on board a vessel from London 4 set of military figures for the practice of tacticks one of which I send you for your amusement. It may be made a substitute for the game of chess.

There is a book which I would advise you to send to England for intitled the Officers manual in the field [1] with 10 copper plates price in boards 15/Sg. It displays a series of military plans, representing the principal operations of a campaign, is a translation from a german work which was published at Berlin, under the auspices of General Czettiritz,[2] & supposed to have been written a few years subsequent to the peace of 1763 in the reign of Frederick the 2d.

I shall order in a few copies and should you decline procuring one, send you one of them.

Yours truly   J McHenry

ADfS, James McHenry Papers, Library of Congress.
    1. *The Officer's Manual in the Field; or a series of military plans, representing the principal operations of a campaign,* trans. from the German (London: Printed by Egerton, 1798).
    2. Ernest-Henri, baron de Czettritz-Neuhass, who was born in 1713, served as a cavalry officer in the Prussian army. He became a major general on December 2, 1757, and was promoted to lieutenant general on April 10, 1761.

To Jonathan Williams

[*New York, June 20, 1799.* "I have to thank you for your obliging attention to my request in transmitting the translations mentioned in your letter of the 17th. I shall peruse them with an eye to the claim of indulgence, which you prefer, though I am persuaded that you might safely have left them to pursue their fortune upon their intrinsic capital. The army is certainly indebted to you for the trouble you have taken." [1] *Letter not found.*]

ALS, sold at Parke-Bernet Galleries, Inc., November 16–17, 1943, Lot 137.
  1. Extract taken from dealer's catalogue.

From Rufus King

[London, June 21, 1799.¹ Letter not found.]

1. "List of Letters from . . . Mr. King" to H, Columbia University Libraries.

From James McHenry

War Department, June 21, 1799. ". . . I wish you . . . to direct
. . . the Quarter Master of the 13th. 14th: and 15th: Regiments to
send his order to Mr: Williams Storekeeper at Springfield for the
articles to be drawn from thence for these Regiments. . . .¹ It is
expected that Muster Rolls will be made out and precede any disbursement of money to the recruits for their pay. If this is not done
I apprehend considerable difficulties in settling the accounts of the
Officers, in cases of desertion before Muster. If also the whole of the
Bounty should be paid to the Recruit before joining his Regimental
Rendezvous, it may occasion like difficulties. I pray you to attend
to the 5th: Section of the Act for the better organizing of the Troops
of the United States and for other purposes passed the 3rd March
ulto: ² before issuing your orders relative to payments under these
two heads.³ Agreeably to this Section the Officer who enlists a
Recruit is not entitled to the compensation of two Dollars unless he
stands muster, nor the Recruit to four dollars of the Bounty until
he shall have joined the Army. . . ."

LS, Hamilton Papers, Library of Congress.
  1. On May 22, 1799, McHenry wrote to Joseph Williams and ordered him
to deliver to each of these regiments "Six Hundred and eighty Stands of Arms,
and Six hundred and eighty Gun-worms, and have the same transported to
their respective Regimental Rendezvous" (copy, Hamilton Papers, Library of
Congress).
  2. 1 *Stat.* 751.
  3. See H to McHenry, second letter of June 18, 1799.

To James McHenry

[New York] June 21. 1799

I thank you My Dear Sir for the military figures you have sent me.[1] *Tactics* you know are literally or figuratively of very comprehensive signification. As people grow old they decline in some arts though they may improve in others. I will try to get Mrs. Hamilton to accompany in games of Tactics new to her. Perhaps she may get a taste for them & become better reconciled to my connection with the *Trade-Militant*.

I will endeavour to get the Book you mention.

Adieu Yr   A H

In answer to a private letter long since received from you[2] I ought to tell you that I am in the *habit* of writing to *General Washington*.

Secy of War

ALS, Mr. Cyril Clemens, Kirkwood, Missouri; ALS (photostat), James McHenry Papers, Library of Congress.
    1. See McHenry to H, June 20, 1799.
    2. McHenry to H, April 29, 1799.

To James McHenry

New York, June 21, 1799. "The suggestion respecting the Cavalry in your letter of the 18th. instant leads to the supposition that the actual raising of the additional troops will be postponed for a considerable time. Though I have no doubt that powerful motives will have influenced this intention; yet I cannot but regret their existence; as well because the body of Cavalry provided for would promise signal utility in various ways, as because it is a corps which requires more time for instruction and preparation than the Infantry. It appears reasonable that the Officers of the Cavalry should render services for the emoluments they receive; but the plan of employing them out of their proper line is attended with very great difficulties. Nothing is more delicate than to contravene established prepossessions in an army; and there is none more fixed than the dislike of Officers of Cavalry to serve as Officers of Infantry except in extraordinary & temporary emergencies. Give me leave to offer to your consideration a middle course. Let one Troop be raised and mounted and the non commissioned Officers of the remainder be inlisted. Let these be stationed at some eligible point and let all the officers be collected there for instruction & exercise. In this situation it will be more manageable, if desireable, to detach them from time to time on Infantry service. The Tactics of both corps can be taught them together. . . ."

ADf, Hamilton Papers, Library of Congress.

From William Macpherson [1]

Philadelphia, June 21, 1799. ". . . With respect to the Volunteers it is certainly necessary some arrangement of them shou'd be made, and I suppose the proper mode is, to take the whole of the Troops of that description in the United States, and form them into Battns. Regiments, Brigades, and Divisions agreeably to their numbers. It would also perhaps be proper to make three or more districts, and appoint in each district some proper Character to whom the officers commanding the particular Corps shou'd be accountable. It is to be observed that in some instances it will be impossible without many great inconveniences, indeed injury, to collect the companies together owing to the remoteness of their situation. It will however still have a good effect their being formed into Corps, even if they shou'd never be collected—as the Officers will feel a degree of responsibility they perhaps might not—were they independent. . . ." [2]

ALS, Hamilton Papers, Library of Congress.
  1. For background to this letter, see H to Macpherson, May 26, 1799.
  2. H endorsed this letter: "Answered with thanks." Letter not found.

From Ebenezer Stevens [1]

New York, June 21, 1799. Encloses the "extract of a letter" from James McHenry concerning Joseph F. Mangin's accounts, which reads: "When General Hamilton was here, we examined my letter to you, respecting the pay of the Engineer which you employed. He found it sufficiently explicit. You will receive from him an explanation which I hope will enable you to settle finally his Account." Asks Hamilton to "give orders to make a settlement with" Mangin.

LS, Hamilton Papers, Library of Congress.
    1. For background to this letter, see Joseph F. Mangin to the Military Committee of New York City, June 18, 1798; Mangin to H, August 7, 1798, January 11, 1799; Stevens to H, November 29, 1798, February 28, April 4, April 17, 1799. See also the introductory note to H to James McHenry, June 1, 1798.

To David Strong

New York, June 21, 1799. "Yr. letter of the 7th of May I have received. There are several points in it which will be attended to in the conferences which will speedily be had with Genl. Wilkinson; in conjunction with whom the disposition of the Western Army will be revised. . . . The paragraphs of your letter respecting the supposed excessive issues of provisions have been communicated to the Secy. of War.[1] As he has made no observation in reply, I presume he is satisfied. I cannot persuade myself that there exists at this time any serious disposition of hostility in the Indians; hence I have contented myself with communicating the information in your letter to Col: Hamtramck [2] & leaving to his discretion to act upon it. My letter of the 22d. of May enables you to derive a reinforcemt. from Michilimacinac if indispensable."

Copy, in the handwriting of Ethan Brown, Hamilton Papers, Library of Congress.
    1. Letter not found.
    2. H to John F. Hamtramck, June 5, 1799.

To Timothy Taylor

New York, June 21, 1799. ". . . In answer to your letter of the 8th Inst. There is no doubt that minors who have arrived at the age of eighteen and who are *not Apprentices* may and ought to be inlisted and retained in the service without the consent of any other persons. . . ."

Copy, in the handwriting of Ethan Brown, Hamilton Papers, Library of Congress.

To James McHenry [1]

New York, June 22, 1799. Encloses a letter from William S. Smith [2] and suggests that it be forwarded to President Adams for his decision. States: "Let me recall to your mind the establishment of rules of promotion & especially the principle that when the field officers of the new Regiments are once appointed the *Routine* begins."

ALS (photostat), James McHenry Papers, Library of Congress; copy, in the handwriting of Ethan Brown, Hamilton Papers, Library of Congress.
   1. For background to this letter, see H to McHenry, May 7, 24, 1799.
   2. Smith to H, June 18, 1799 (listed in the appendix to this volume). In this letter Smith again proposed promoting Captain Dowe J. Fondey to second major in his regiment rather than appointing Theodosius Fowler to that position. See H to McHenry, May 24, 1799, note 1.

From Richard Stockton [1]

Princeton [New Jersey] June 22, 1799. "The cause of Samuel & Miers Fisher agt Walter Rutherfurd and others is set down for Argument in the Circuit Court of the U S. for this district on the first day of October next. I am desired by the Complainants to inquire of you whether they may place dependence on your being at the Court to argue this important cause for them. . . ."

ALS, Hamilton Papers, Library of Congress.
1. For background to this letter, see Miers and Samuel Fisher to H, March 30, 1795.
Stockton, a lawyer and Federalist from Princeton, New Jersey, was a member of the United States Senate from 1796 to 1799.

From Aaron Ogden

Elizabeth Town [New Jersey] June 23, 1799. ". . . The success in recruiting in the several sub-districts, hes been exceedingly various, which may be ascribed in part to the different degrees of address or talent in that way, and of activity, in the recruiting Officers, in part to the good or ill disposition of the inhebitents toward the government and in part, to a went of Officers occesioned by vacancies and sickness—(the former cause has been removed, but we still have two officers who are invalid). In some instences all these causes have unhappily co-operated."

ALS, Hamilton Papers, Library of Congress.

From Nathan Rice

Hingham [Massachusetts] June 23d 1799

Sir

I have visited Taunton, Dighton, & Sommerset for the purpose of selecting the most eligible spot for a regimental rendezvous; I am decidedly in favour of Sommerset: [1] It not only embraces the objects which induced you to fix on that spot, but is besides a most healthy situation, in the neighbourhood of a fertile country, abounding with provisions and sufficiently retired, to afford ample opportunity, for training and disciplining a young regiment.

I have not yet received returns from the officers superintending districts, but I have reason to believe there are about one hundred recruits engaged. The service most certainly suffers for the want of officers, there are I believe ten or twelve vacances now in my regiment. I have directed my Quarter master to apply to Mr. Williams for the arms,[2] & as soon as the Cloathing is compleated shall order the recruits to the district rendezvous, & from thence, when Tents arrive to the rendezvous of the regiment.

With the highest respect I am your obt Servt   N: Rice

Major Genl Hamilton

LS, Hamilton Papers, Library of Congress.
   1. See Rice to H, April 28, 1799.
   2. See H to Rice, June 5, 1799.

From Callender Irvine

Carlisle [Pennsylvania] June 24, 1799. "I have received your letter of the 6th instant,[1] covering a new set of Recruiting instructions. . . . I repeatedly reported to the Secretary of War last fall, that I could have enlisted many more men, indeed treble the number, if furnished with money & advice for that purpose. I never was informed what the establishment, was or is to be, nor how many men I should inlist."

ALS, Hamilton Papers, Library of Congress; copy, in Irvine's handwriting, Dickinson College Library, Carlisle, Pennsylvania.
   1. See "Circular to Certain Recruiting Officers," June 6, 1799 (listed in the appendix to this volume).

From James McHenry

War Department,
June 24. 1799.

Sir,

Inclosed are certain regulations respecting the delivery of Fuel, Straw and Stationery, and Horses furnished to Officers.[1] I wish you to consider them, and to offer such additional ones to, or alterations in those proposed as in your opinion may be proper. The last has been conceived necessary to check an evil which may grow to magnitude.

I request you particularly to determine how many Horses to the different Grades entitled to receive Forage from the public shall be allowed to each respectively. If this is not determined, a Lieutenant Colonel or Major may keep Six Horses, and draw forage for them all.

I have the honor to be, with great respect, Sir, Your obedt. servant,   James McHenry

Major General
Alexander Hamilton

LS, Hamilton Papers, Library of Congress.
  1. "Regulations to be observed in the delivery and distribution, of fuel, straw, and stationary, to the army, the Garrisons on the Sea-coast, and recruiting parties; and respecting horses furnished to Officers" (copy, Hamilton Papers, Library of Congress).

From James McHenry

War Department, June 24, 1799. "I received this morning your letter of the 21st: Instant. The remarks you have offered relative to the Cavalry are deserving of attention, and the course you propose which combines a temporary saving, with immediate employment for the Officers in a mode conformable to the constitution of this kind of Troops will be considered. I shall inform you of the result. I observe however that my present opinion is it will be best to adopt the mode you propose. . . ."

LS, Hamilton Papers, Library of Congress.

To James McHenry

New York, June 24, 1799. Discusses duties and salary of Ebenezer Stevens.[1] States: "The necessity of a more adequate organisation of our Departments of Military supplies (to which adequate compensation is an essential idea) presses more and more upon my conviction. The details of execution are extremely defective." Gives examples of defects in supply system and concludes: "These are small

samples of the continual succession of irregularities of which almost
every new occurrence furnishes evidence."

Copy, in the handwriting of Ethan Brown, Hamilton Papers, Library of Congress.
 1. See Stevens to H, April 17, 19, 1799; McHenry to H, first letter of May 9, 1799.

To Nathan Rice

New York June 24th. 1799

Sir

I am advised by the Secy. of War [1] that Mr. Williams Storekeeper
at Springfield has been instructed to furnish to the Quarter master
of your Regiment upon your order 680 stands of Arms and as many
Gun worms. Mr. Williams is to have them transported to your Regimental Rendezvous if they have not been received, you will take
measures to obtain them.

With great consideration   I am &cc

Copy, in the handwriting of Ethan Brown, Hamilton Papers, Library of Congress.
 1. James McHenry to H, June 21, 1799.

From Josias Carvel Hall

Havre de Grace [Maryland] June 25, 1799. ". . . Your order of
the 15th [1] explanatory of the Contractor's agreement with the Secretary at War is very timely. . . . There are Complaints that the
small Parts of Rations are not regularly supplied. . . . I was . . .
much disappointed, when I arrived at Balt:, to find there was not an
article of Quarter Master Stores, except Drums & Fifes & but a
very partial Supply of Clothing. Tents & Kittles are much wanted.
The Troops are generally but badly Quartered. . . ."

ALS, Hamilton Papers, Library of Congress.
 1. "General Order," June 15, 1799.

To James McHenry

Private   New York June 25. 1799

My Dear Sir

I conclude from your letter by todays post,[1] that your own opinion in regard to the raising of a Troop of horse is made up and that you only delay a determination from the necessity of a reference elsewhere. This is a point, which I have so much at heart that I should be sorry any thing should be risked about it. If you think there is the least danger of disappointment, I will write to the Commander in Chief to obtain for you the support of his ideas.

It is of very material consequence to have a Troop raised as a Stock on which to engraft a system of Tactics for the Cavalry. Hitherto it may be said we have had none. Improvements are going on in Europe; this particular *arm* is not brought to perfection even there—opinions are somewhat unsettled. It is very desireable to have an organ by which we can essay the various plans and upon which we can establish the model of a good system.

As to the two troops already raised, they ought to remain where they are. Another subject—

General Wilkinson is soon expected. I am strongly inclined to see him made a Major General.[2] He has now had a great deal of experience—he possesses considerable military information—he has activity courage and Talents. His pretensions to promotion in every view are strong. If he should become disgusted without it, it would not be extraordinary.

Half-confidence is always bad. This officer has adopted Military life as a profession. What can his ambition do better than be faithful to the Government if it gives him fair play?

Yrs. Affecly   A Hamilton

Jas. McHenry

ALS, Mr. Herbert R. Strauss, Chicago; ALS (photostat), James McHenry Papers, Library of Congress; copy, in the handwriting of Ethan Brown, Hamilton Papers, Library of Congress.
    1. McHenry to H, second letter of June 24, 1799.
    2. See H to George Washington, June 15, 1799, note 3.

To James McHenry

New York, June 25 [–July 1] 1799. Summarizes the contents of "letters . . . from Major Rivardi, at Niagara," which "contain very unpleasant representations of the state of things at that post." [1] Describes steps taken to meet some of Rivardi's complaints.[2] States: "It appears by the statement of which a copy is enclosed that debts have been contracted for purposes of the garrison to the amount of 727 Dollars & 91 Cents. I would advise that besides money for the pay of the troops 1200 Dollars be sent to discharge the debts & the surplus to form a small military chest, which at such very remote points is peculiarly requisite. This fund may among other things be usefully employed as bounties in the reinlistment of soldiers whose time of service shall have expired & in the recovery of Deserters, which must always occasion expence. You will observe that part of the debt now due is for extra pay to soldiers who have performed services in the Quarter Master Department." Also states: "Major Rivardi strongly recommends Enoch Hunt [3] for the place of Cadet. On the credit of the character he has given of this person I shall be glad to see a confirmation."

ADf, Hamilton Papers, Library of Congress.
  1. John J. U. Rivardi to H, March 21, April 3, 28, May 2, 30, June 12, 1799.
  2. For H's reply to Rivardi's complaints, see H to Rivardi, June 25, 1799.
  3. H is mistaken, for the name was Humphrey rather than Hunt. See Rivardi to H, April 3, May 30, 1799.

To John J. U. Rivardi

New York June 25. 1799

Sir

I embrace the first moment which I am able to spare from objects of greater urgency and more extensive concern to reply to your several letters of the 21 of March the 3 & 28 of April the 2 and 30th of May; which with the documents mentioned in them have been duely received.

ADf, Hamilton Papers, Library of Congress.

It is matter of regret to me that I have not been able to pay an earlier attention to them; but the various and weighty occupations in which I have been engaged, the want of organisation heretofore in the several branches of our Military service, and the want of competent aid near my person (which it requires time to select) [1] have conspired to render unavoidable a silence, which may have appeared to you extraordinary.

I yielded the more readily in the outset to the obstacles which stood in the way, from the belief that your difficulties as to money and supplies had been obviated. I am sorry to find that the relief has been partial and insufficient. Further and adequate supplies have been strongly urged,[2] and may I take it for granted be shortly expected.

The expedience of an additional allowance to the person performing the duties of Qr. Master has been pressed.[3]

The cloathing and equipments of the army are undergoing a systematic revision. Your suggestion as to the coats of the Artillerists will not be forgotten.[4]

Nothing has been altered or established in regard to the Apparatus or Exercise of this Corps. The practice at different posts is various. I have directed part of the Troops now at Fort Jay to be instructed in the French method,[5] to enable me to compare that with our former method, and to decide which is preferable. Any ideas, which you shall communicate respecting the establishment and instruction of the corps, will be very acceptable. In relation to this, I will just observe that my present conviction is, that a separation between the Engineering & Artillery branches is necessary to the perfection of each.

I can assure you, with certainty, from a knowlege of circumstances, that the remark in the report of the Secy of War, with regard to the difficulty of avoiding imposition in the employment of

1. See H to Jeremiah Wadsworth, May 18, 1799; H to James McHenry, June 5, 1799.
2. On May 23, 1799, H wrote to Samuel Hodgdon: "I enclose you the return of military stores &c at Fort Niagara and request you will immediately forward a competent supply of the Articles . . . wanted." This letter is listed in the appendix to this volume.
3. See Rivardi to H, April 28, 1799; H to James McHenry, June 25–July 1, 1799.
4. See Rivardi to H, March 21, 1799.
5. These instructions were given in H to Adam Hoops, June 10, 1799 (listed in the appendix to this volume).

foreigners, originated in motives which ought not to have occasionned to you a moments uneasiness. It certainly had not the remotest allusion to your case; but was dictated essentially by the experience of our Revolution War. Though in that war, we derived much benefit from the services of several foreigners of merit; yet it is certain that we were encumbered with many ignorant pretenders, whose credentials were in a variety of instances fair, in some strong. Hence the observation that it was difficult to avoid imposition. This explanation while it is due to the Secretary, will I trust be grateful to your feelings. I may add with truth that previous to the charges of Capt Bruff, every thing which I had heared of your character and conduct was favourable.

On this point of Capt Bruffs accusations it appears to me, as it has done to you, necessary that there should be a Court of Inquiry.[6] In the pursuit of this Inquiry, Capt Bruffs presence at Niagara is indispensable. It was thought adviseable, in the first instance, to permit him to enter upon a course of recruiting for his company,[7] which has delayed the ordering of the Court. But this end has now been answered, and he has been directed to repair to Niagara.[8] The court will be composed of the Commanding officer at Presquile,[9] Lt. Vischer [10] who is at Oswego, and a third officer to be detached from Detroit by Colonel Strong. The inclosed copies of my letters to these officers [11] will apprise you of the instructions which have been given. You may do whatever you think proper to accelerate the assembling of the Court. You are sensible that the institution of a Court properly composed was not free from embarrassment. I shall be glad if the mode which has been adopted shall be satisfactory to you.

The intelligent & perspicuous view which you have given of the several posts, mentioned in your letters and exhibited in your drafts claims my acknowlegement.

6. The Court of Inquiry was to hear charges brought against Rivardi by Captain James Bruff. For these charges, see Rivardi to H, March 21, 1799, note 13; April 3, 1799, note 6.

7. H to Bruff, April 25, 1799 (listed in the appendix to this volume).

8. These instructions are contained in H to Bruff, June 25, 1799 (listed in the appendix to this volume).

9. Cornelius Lyman, a veteran of the American Revolution and a resident of Massachusetts, was a captain in the Second Regiment of Infantry and the commanding officer at Presque Isle, Pennsylvania.

10. Nanning J. Visscher was an ensign in the Second Regiment of Infantry.

11. Letters not found.

Very soon after my being called into service, I wrote to General Wilkinson desiring his attendance at the seat of Governt.[12] in order to a careful review of the system of our Military affairs in the Western Quarter. He is now every moment expected to arrive. I have thought it proper to defer to the event of this conference any alterations in that system. In judging if such as may be adviseable I shall carefully bear in mind your suggestions the propriety of which appears extremely obvious.

No measures have been taken which admit of the immediate rein-forcement of your post. Some are in train which will produce it in the course of the temperate season. Among these I have recom-mended the sending a small sum of bounty money to be disposed of under your direction in making occasional inlistments.[13]

Let me add that you are at liberty to call from Oswego to Niagara Lt. Vischer and all of his men who may remain after leaving a Discreet non Commissioned officer and four trusty privates as a guard. Considering the force which we are likely for some time to come to keep up on the Lakes—it has struck me that perhaps nothing more was expedient at Oswego than a small guard to take care of any stores, which in their progress Westward might make a stage at that place. It has also appeared to me questionable whether the station of Michilimacnac was comparitively speaking an eligible military point.[14] *Detroit Niagara* and *Presque Isle* seem to deserve peculiar attention, and it was my wish to have had a careful examina-tion of the Military points in the vicinity of the junction of the Miamia and Lake Erie. To secure well this *Lake* and the *streights* which connect it with the *Ontario* and the *Huron* are in my present conception cardinal objects. The better to effect this, I am not very fond of the dissipation of our force to other and distant positions.

I regret not a little that the state of your health and your situation in other respects have interrfered with the mission I had chosen for you. I hoped to derive from it better lights towards an eventual plan than have been hitherto acquired. But after weighing all the cir-cumstances which are brought into view I have concluded not to press the execution at this time. You will allow me however to re-mark to you with frankness that there is in my opinion something

12. H to James Wilkinson, February 12, 1799.
13. See H to McHenry, June 25–July 1, 1799.
14. See H to David Strong, May 22, 1799; H to McHenry, May 23, 1799.

too absolute in your manner of declining this service, and that I cannot give my sanction to the sentiment in your letter contained in these words "I cannot *possibly*, except in actual war, separate myself from her (your wife) and my Children &c." You have too much discernment and too well know too the principles of service not to be sensible that in peace as in war an officer shall be ready to execute the trusts, relatively to his station, to which he may be designated—That the peremptory claim of an exemption from this rule cannot be advanced whatever may be the hope of indulgence towards a very peculiar situation. Doubtless therefore you will see it proper to correct the latitude and force of the expressions which you have used, as transcending your real meaning.

The payment of the debts contracted in relation to the Quarter Masters Department has been urged.[15]

The affair of extra pay to the soldiers is nevertheless attended with some difficulty. The nature of the services rendered by them not having been specified, it is not easy for me to judge of the propriety of the allowance. But as a guide in future cases, I ought to say that the general rule of our service is against the allowance of extra pay, except to those who not having been enlisted as Artisans or Ar[ti]-ficers, are employed in those capacities—or those who are devoted to some *constant* employment different from the ordinary duties of soldiers. As to occasional employment in procuring wood fuel straw or in other services, by rotation, relative to the accommodation of the troops and their officers, this is considered as incident to the duty of soldiers without giving any claim to extra compensation. A small additional allowance of Rum is the usual douceur in such cases.

But considering that you had precedent for what you did—that there seems to have been an implied sanction from the Secretary of War—that the strength of your garrison was greatly disproportioned to the labours probably necessary for keeping the works in some degree of preservation—and finally that it is of importance to maintain the faith of a commanding officer acting with good intentions—I have given my opinion explicitly that the expence which has been incurred in this particular should be defrayed.

If the principles which I have stated have not governed in time

15. See H to McHenry, June 25–July 1, 1799.

past, you will endeavour to conform to them in future, or you will mention to me with precision and detail what deviations are in your judgment indispensable.

The appointment of Cadets is made through the War Department [16] which is ready to receive recommendations for the purpose. Enoch Hunt has been proposed to the Secy of War [17] upon the credit of your nomination.

If you shall continue to desire to be removed from your present situation you will renew the expression of your wish hereafter. The desire of an advance of pay in the event of a removal will not be unattended to.

The letter of the issuing Commissary to you is I understand agreeable to an arrangement made with the Secretary of War. Its object is to enable the Public to make better terms with Contractors by saving to them the expence of keeping an Agent at every post however small. And in the cases for which it was intended it appears to be not an unreasonable regulation. But the permanent situation of Niagara ought to be and must be such as to render it inapplicable there. Your declining the transfer does not therefore contravene the spirit of the rule.

If you draw Lt. Vischer to your post, it will enable you to give a furlough to Capt Thompson [18] which you are at liberty to do even before any other officer shall join you. You have already been written to on the subject of Doctor Coffin.[19] How far a substitute for him could be spared from any other post of the Western army is unknown to me. The number of surgeons who have been ap-

16. Article XXXVI of the March, 1799, edition of the War Department pamphlet *Rules and Regulations Respecting the Recruiting Service* provides in part: "Commandants of regiments, corps, or companies, cannot appoint cadets. They may be recommended through the commander in chief, the inspector general, or general commanding a separate army, to the Secretary of War, and if approved of, warrants of appointment will issue in due form." For an account of editions of *Rules and Regulations Respecting the Recruiting Service*, see H to Jonathan Dayton, August 6, 1798, note 6.

17. H to McHenry, June 25–July 1, 1799. H meant to refer to Enoch Humphrey. See Rivardi to H, April 3, 1799.

18. See H to John F. Hamtramck, May 2, 1799 (listed in the appendix to this volume).

19. On June 21, 1799, H wrote to Rivardi that he could grant John G. Coffin a furlough "on condition that an Arrangement, satisfactory to you, be made for the care of the sick in his absence." This letter is listed in the appendix to this volume.

pointed being as yet very insufficient, none can immediately be spared from this Quarter. To engage a person for the special service would either be impracticable or would occasion an expence extravagant compared with the object. This could not be justified for the mere personal accommodation of the individual. Indeed no extraordinary expence to the public ought to accrue unless the absence is demanded by ill health. A copy of my letter on this subject is enclosed.

I shall now conclude with an assurance to you that I shall apply a particular attention to the affairs of your post and I cannot doubt that I shall procure to be promptly done whatever is necessary to justice comfort order and respectability; I participate with [you] in the mortifications of the past period. They must not continue.

With great consideration   I am Sir   Yr. Obed ser

Finding on examination that I cannot conveniently constitute the Court as mentioned above, I have concluded to send two Officers from this Quarter.

From George Washington

Private   Mount Vernon 25 June 1799

Dear Sir,

Your private letter of the 15th instant came duly to hand.

So far as my information extends (which by the bye is very limited) the Recruiting Service in this State progresses beyond my expectations, But is retarded very considerably from the want of cloathing, the ragged appearance of the Recruits having a tendency to disgust, rather than to excite enlistments.

I think with you, that policy dictates the expediency of promoting Brigadier Wilkinson to the Rank of Majr General, and will suggest the measure to the Secretary of War in a private communication.[1] It would feed his ambition, sooth his vanity, and by arresting discontent, produce the good effect you contemplate. But in the appointment of this Gentleman, regard must be had to time, circumstances, and dates; otherwise by endeavouring to avoid Charibdas we might run upon Scylla.

What I mean by this is, that the President may deem it expedient to take ye next Majr General from the Eastern States; again, may recur to the former appointments of that Gra⟨de in⟩ the Provisional army; and further (if services in the Revolutionary army are to be regarded) to relative Rank also in dating the Commissions of the Major Generals yet to be appointed.

If Genl Wilkinson should be promoted, it will be expected, no doubt, that the oldest Lieut. Coll. Commandant should step into his shoes as Brigadier; of course, the oldest Major of the old line, would succeed to the vacancy occasioned thereby. Who & what the character of these Gentlemen are, I know not. The measure deserves consideration. I am always

Yr. Affecte   Go: Washington

Majr. Genl Hamilton

ALS, Hamilton Papers, Library of Congress; ALS, letterpress copy, George Washington Papers, Library of Congress.
    1. On June 25, 1799, Washington sent H's letter to him of June 15, 1799, and a copy of the letter printed above to James McHenry (ALS, letterpress copy, George Washington Papers, Library of Congress).

From James McHenry

private & confidential   [Philadelphia] 26 June 1799

My dear Sir.

I find from frequent and repeated conversations that we have not been able to remove any one of the prejudices entertained by the Secretary of the treasury against the augmentation of the army: [1] that he thinks, or seems to think, that the means of resources of the U. S. which *can be called forth* without annual loans, are inadequate to the expenditures required for the support of the army and navy, consequently that some part of the one or the other must soon be suspended or dropped; and that he even contemplates a statement of facts relative to our means to the President. I regret all this from the bottom of my soul, feeling as I do how much, our peace, honour & respect at home and abroad depends upon the permanency of our little army. I continue in the course which I had prescribed to myself, determined to intermit or suspend indispensible measures only, when officially informed of its being no longer in the competency of the treasury means to support them, or answer the requisite demands. The Secy tells me, that notwithstanding his opinion about the army, he will not do any thing to prejudice his friends or the public against it. I reason in all forms I can think of, and have thought it proper to keep throwing into Fenno [2] paragraphs tending to shew the necessity of an army.

I know not how all this is to end. It will be mortifying if we have to retrograde altho under an act of Congress. I considered it necessary to apprise you of the state of opinions here, and to request your aid to the Eastward to keep up a due sense of the propriety of the measure among our friends in that quarter. The Secy of State thinks right, at least I have seen no indications to the contrary.

Mr Goodrich [3] has the following paragraph in a letter I recd. from him this morning: "The recruiting service is proceeding successfully in this State; The sooner the troops can be withdrawn from Towns, embo[d]yed, disciplined and employed, the less speculation will be excited about the army."

I think the plan heretofore recommended ought to be attended to. I mean to hasten the recruits to their respective regimental rendesvouses.

Your affectionate   J McH

ALS, Hamilton Papers, Library of Congress; ADfS, James McHenry Papers, Library of Congress; copy, Hamilton Papers, Library of Congress.
    1. See H to George Washington, May 3, 1799, note 3.
    2. John Ward Fenno had succeeded his father, John Fenno, in 1798 as editor of the *Gazette of the United States, and Philadelphia Daily Advertiser.*
    3. Chauncey Goodrich to McHenry, June 23, 1799 (ALS [photostat], James McHenry Papers, Library of Congress).
    Goodrich, a Connecticut Federalist and a brother-in-law of Oliver Wolcott, Jr., was a member of the House of Representatives from 1795 to 1801.

To Ebenezer Stevens

New York, June 26, 1799. "In consequence of the reference to me by the Secy. of War in the letter which you shewed me,[1] respecting Mr. Mangin's compensation, I give it as my opinion that you pay him the four Dollars per day for the times of his employment which you have heretofore stated to me. . . . You have informed me [2] that at the time of employing Mr. Mangin [3] you promised him compensation at the above rate. I consider the public faith as engaged to comply with the promise, and the good of the service as interested in the compliance."

ALS, New-York Historical Society, New York City.
  1. Stevens to H, June 21, 1799.
  2. Stevens to H, April 4, 1799.
  3. Stevens to H, February 28, 1799.

From James McHenry

War Department
27th June. 1799

Sir,

I enclose a copy of a Letter to me, from John King,[1] the Contractor for District No. 2 including the Counties of Essex, and Morris, in the State of New Jersey, relative to an order issued by you, on the 15th. instant, directing the Contractors, to issue fresh meat to the military. five days in each week; together with a Copy of my answer,[2] and an extract from the particular contract with Mr. King.[3]

You will perceive, that I consider the alternative, or kind of ration permitted by Law, to form the ration for the troops, to be at the discretion, and choice of the Superior or Commanding Officer only, who may issue his orders accordingly, and this for very substantial reasons, as I conceive. A meaning can certainly, niether be given to the Law, nor the Contracts, which will subject the soldiers, to be fed with the most unwholsome provisions, of the kind permitted, in the different seasons.

I am Sir   with great respect   your obedt servant

James McHenry

Major General Alexander Hamilton

LS, Hamilton Papers, Library of Congress.
  1. King to McHenry, June 22, 1799 (copy, Hamilton Papers, Library of Congress).

2. McHenry to King, June 26, 1799 (LS, letterpress copy, Hamilton Papers, Library of Congress).

3. "Extract from the Contract, with John King . . . dated the 6th day of April 1799" (copy, Hamilton Papers, Library of Congress).

From James McHenry

Private & Confidl.   June 27th 1799

My dear Sir. I answer to yours (just rcd.) of the 25th inst.

It will be agreeable to me to see a troop of horse completely organised, that we may ascertain, as far as it is practicable, with so small a model, the improvements of which cavalry are yet susceptible. You may write therefore an official letter on the subject proposing it, and request my final directions. I shall give them.

General W.[1] has certainly claims to promotion, and so far as it respects myself I shall not oppose it. It will be proper however, that General Washington be consulted[2] before the least step be taken in the business. Your maxim is in general a good one: Half confidence is bad. Of this however be assured that until the commercial pursuits of this gentleman with, and expectations from Spain are annihilated, he will not deserve the confidence of government. Further I recommend it to you most earnestly to avoid saying any thing to him which would induce him to imagine government had in view any hostile project, however remote or dependent on events, against any of the possessions of Spain. I require this caution on good grounds.

Your affecy   J McHenry

Gen Hamilton

ALS, Hamilton Papers, Library of Congress; ALS, two letterpress copies, James McHenry Papers, Library of Congress; copy, Hamilton Papers, Library of Congress.

1. Brigadier General James Wilkinson.

2. See H to George Washington, June 15, 1799; Washington to H, June 25, 1799.

To James McHenry

New York June 27. 1799

It is a pity, My Dear Sir, and a reproach, that our administration have no general plan. Certainly there ought to be one formed without delay. If the Chief is too desultory, his Ministers ought to be the more united and steady and well settled in some reasonable system of measures.

Among other things—It should be agreed what precise force should be created *naval* and *land,* and this proportioned to the state of our finances.[1] It will be ridiculous to raise troops and immediately after to disband them. *Six* ships of the line & *twenty* frigates and sloops of war are desireable—more would not now be comparatively expedient. It is desireable to complete and prepare the land force which has been provided for by law.[2] Besides eventual security against invasion, we ought certainly to look to the possession of the Floridas & Louisiana—and we ought to squint at South America.[3]

Is it possible that the accomplishment of these objects can be attended with financial difficulty? I deny the possibility. Our Revenue can be considerably reinforced. The progress of the Country will quickly supply small deficiencies, and these can be temporarily satisfied by loans—provided our loans are made on the principle that we require the aliment of European Capital & that lenders are to gain and their gains to be facilitated not obstructed.

If all this is not true our situation is much worse than I had any idea of. But I have no doubt that it is easy to devise the means of execution.

And if there was every where a disposition without prejudice and nonsense to concert a rational plan I would chearfully come to Philadelphia and assist in it. Nor can I doubt that success may be ensured.

Break this subject seriously to our friend *Pickering.* His views are sound and energetic; and try together to bring the other Gentlemen⁴ to a consultation. If there is every where a proper temper & it is wished send for me & I will come.

Yrs truly   A H

Js. McHenry Es

ALS, Columbia University Libraries; ALS (photostat), James McHenry Papers, Library of Congress; copy, in the handwriting of Ethan Brown, Hamilton Papers, Library of Congress.
    1. See McHenry to H, June 26, 1799.
    2. H is referring to the authorized increases in the Regular Army as well as in the Additional Army and Eventual Army. See the introductory note to H to James Gunn, December 22, 1798.
    3. H is referring to Francisco de Miranda's plans for the liberation of Spanish America. See Miranda to H, April 1, 1797, February 7, April 6–June 7, August 17, October 19–November 10, 1798; H to Miranda, August 22, 1798; King to H, May 12, July 31, October 20, 1798, January 21, March 4, 9, 1799; H to King, August 22, 1798; Timothy Pickering to H, August 21–22, 1798.
    4. Attorney General Charles Lee, Secretary of the Navy Benjamin Stoddert, and Secretary of the Treasury Oliver Wolcott, Jr.

From John J. U. Rivardi

Niagara [*New York*] *June 27, 1799.* Encloses "a Map of river Miami, also a plan of The Fort of the Same Name."¹ States: "My health is I hope perfectly restored & as the fever has left me I trust soon to recover my usual Strength."² States that he is willing to remain at Niagara throughout the winter. Maintains that "a public Vessel on this lake . . . would I am Sure prove œconomical in the end."

ALS, Hamilton Papers, Library of Congress.
    1. Rivardi had prepared these maps from copies supplied by Robert Pilkington, a captain in the British army. See Rivardi to H, June 12, 1799.
    2. This is a reference to Rivardi's previous requests to be transferred to the East because of poor health. See Rivardi to H, March 21, April 28, May 30, 1799; H to Rivardi, June 25, 1799.

From Aaron Ogden

Elizabeth Town [*New Jersey*] *June 28, 1799.* "In order to fulfill your request,¹ I have been casting about, for a character, to be recommended to you, as suitable for your secretary, and, now, beg leave to mention to you Mr Thomas Y. How[2] of Trenton, as a Candidate well-worthy of your consideration. . . . Mr How has received a liberal education, at Princeton college, and has been lately admitted to the practice of the Law in New-Jersey. . . ."

ALS, Hamilton Papers, Library of Congress.
   1. See H to Jeremiah Wadsworth, May 18, 1799, note 1.
   2. Thomas Yardley How was appointed H's secretary on July 11, 1799. See H to Caleb Swan, October 14, 1799. On July 17, 1799, he was appointed a second lieutenant in the Eleventh Regiment of Infantry. See H to James McHenry, first letter of July 17, 1799.

From Thomas Parker

Winchester [Virginia] June 30, 1799. ". . . We have enlisted nearly Two hundred men for the 8th Regt many of whome are almost naked & extreamly dissatisfied with their Situations, as we were taught to believe that the cloathing would be ready to dress them as soon as they were enlisted. only a small Supply of Hats Shirts & Shoes have yet come to hand. I Beg Sir that you will exert your Influence to have the Residue sent on without delay as I fear the withholding of them much longer will put a Total Stop to the Recruiting service & Create great uneasiness amongst those men who are already enlisted. . . . I have been obliged to Borrow money for the Recruiting Service. . . ."

ALS, Hamilton Papers, Library of Congress.

From Thomas Pasteur[1]

[Fort Massac, Territory Northwest of the River Ohio, June 30, 1799. In a letter to James McHenry on August 22, 1799, Hamilton referred to a "letter of the 30 of June from Massac from Capt Pasteur." *Letter not found.*]

   1. A veteran of the American Revolution, Pasteur was a captain in the First Regiment of Infantry and the commanding officer at Fort Massac.

From John F. Hamtramck

Duplicate.   Fort Wayne [Territory Northwest of the
                             River Ohio], July 1st [Detroit, July 18], 1799.

Sir

I have to acknowledge your Letters, of the 9th, 12'th and 23'rd of May, with their several inclosures, to which, I shall devote my particular attention, they all came to hand on the 27th Ultimo. The Object of the Indian boundary line,[1] is so much forwarded that Mr Ludlow, Deputy Surveyor will be at Lormies on the 10th Instant.[2] I have this information from the Governor;[3] in consequence of which, I have directed an Escort of an Officer, One Serjeant, One Corporal, and fifteen Men from Fort Washington. I cannot for the present inform you, why there was nothing done last Year, Mr. Ludlow who has been the Executive Officer in this business, can possibly give the reason; I have wrote to him on the Subject, as also to the Surveyor General, but I am induced to believe that no defect will be found on the part of the Military as I never heard that any application has been made for an Escort, since the first Year, at which time, One was furnished.

The Orders respecting the Indian Department are sent to all the Posts,[4] and will relieve the Military from a great deal of trouble.

The extent of the Command of the Western Country, which perhaps comprehends not less than Sixteen or Seventeen Degrees of Latitude, is so extensive, that it is almost impossible for the Commanding Officer to Ascertain a correct State of the different Garrisons, without the Assistance of an Agent. Due credit should no doubt be given to Monthly Reports and to the different Statements made, but, I conceive, that an Officer Visiting himself the extent of his Command, is always conducive to the Interest of the Nation, and to the promotion of Discipline, and on that fixed principle, and as there is no immediate cause that claims my presence to any particular point, I have determined to Visit in Person as many of the Northern Garrisons, as the Season, and the Circumstances will Admit; and have commissioned Major Hunt,[5] to Visit those of the Southward, as far as the Chickasaw Bluff: The Reason why I have not ordered the Major, to go farther down, is, that General Wilkinson having lately left the other Posts, Superceeds the Necessity of an inspection on my part.[6] The Major has Orders to examine into the State of the different Fortifications, to see with his own Eyes all Public property appertaining to the different Departments, and whether the Quantity and Quality agrees with the Returns, and to examine strictly into the Quality of the Ammunition, Arms, and any other Ordnance Stores. To inculcate the principles of rigid economy, in all Issues and Expenditures, by observing to every Commandant of Posts that the Nation will probably be under the Necessity of entering into an Expensive War, to examine into the State of Magazines or other Stores, the kind of Provision whether good or bad, the State of the Barracks and what Reparations are wanted, to Inspect and Exercise the Troops, and strictly to examine into their Police, and to see that all duties are done with precision, to examine strictly, if General Wilkinson's standing Orders are attended to, to correct all unmilitary conduct, or irregularities, that may have crept into Service, and to receive any cause of complaint if any existed: The whole of which to be faithfully Reported to me; I have been led to take this step, the more so, as I had received good information that a certain Garrison was far from being in Order, but this communication was made me at a time when I had no Authority to interfere; the Posts being independent of each other.

I shall immediately go to Detroit, Visit Michilimacanac, and be back to Detroit by the middle of next Month, and if on my return to Detroit, (to which I shall direct any letters for me to come,) I find no Official communication, which will induce me to counteract my present intention, I shall then proceed to Presque Isle and Pittsburgh.[7]

Inclosed are the Returns of the Garrison, a Copy of my first Order to the Western Army,[8] and also of my last Letter to Governor St. Clair,[9] by which you will see, that some Indians have been killing, and that the Turtle a Miami Chief, who is the Oracle of the Indians is much dissatisfied with the White People.

It is a painful task Sir, that in my first Official Letter I should trouble you with Grievances, but as the Parent and the first Agent of the Regiment I have the honor to Command, I am bound to represent its lawful Claim. The case is this, when the Commission of Commissary General of Issues ceased, the Officers and Soldiers of my Regiment were in possession of a large Number of Due bills, for Rations and Component parts of Rations; all the Regiments were then settled with except the first, this injustice has fallen particularly heavy on me, who in the undoubted expectation, that the first Regt. would be paid as well as the others, Order'd my Quarter Master to purchase half Gaiters for the Men on my Credit, and to have me secur'd by the Mens Due Bills; I once wrote to Mr. Day [10] the Depty Coms'y Genl., who had settled with the other Troops, and his Answer was that if he had any Public Money or Property on hand, that he would settle with the Regiment, but had nothing left. I once laid the matter before General Wilkinson, who I know laid it before the Secretary at War, but I believe Received no Answer, or if he did was the Unsatisfactory, this is humbly laid before you for consideration.)

I have the honor to be, With every Sentiment of Respect, Sir, Your Most Obedt., and Very Humble Servt.   J F Hamtramck

Major Genl. Hamilton.

P. S. We are told, that some Laws and Regulations Relative to the Army, took place last Session of Congress; but nothing Official has yet come to hand. I shall also be Oblig'd to you to inform me, whether the Provisions issued to the Indians by the Governor or Superintendent, is to be taken into the Monthly Abstracts of the Garrison, by its Commanding Officer.   J F H

Detroit July 18th. 1799.
NB. The Returns of the Garrison are not inclosed the Copy of them being left at Fort Wayne, and this Duplicate being sent from Detroit.

LS, marked "Duplicate," Hamilton Papers, Library of Congress; LS, Hamilton Papers, Library of Congress.

1. See James McHenry to H, second letter of April 11, 1799; H to Oliver Wolcott, Jr., May 2, 1799; Wolcott to H, May 8, 24, 1799.
2. Loramie Creek, which is in western Ohio, flows into the Grand Miami River.

On March 15, 1799, Rufus Putnam, the Surveyor General, wrote to Oliver Wolcott, Jr.: "by a letter recived last evening from Major [Israel] Ludlow I am informed that the Surveys on the Westerly Side of the great Miami River are So far advanced that he will be ready by the first of June to commence runing the Indian boundary line (agreably to the Treaty made by General [Anthony] Wayne) from the Fork of Lorremies Creek to Fort Recovery & from thence to the ohio opposit Kentucky River" (ALS, RG 49, Records of the Bureau of Land Management, General Land Office: Letters Received from the Surveyor General, Vol. I, National Archives).

On July 20, 1799, Ludlow wrote to Putnam: "The 10th of this month was appointed to meet the chiefs of the different nations of Indian parties to the treaty of Greenville—no Indians have yet appeared—in consequence of their delay I sent an express to the Ottawa towns to acquaint them I was waiting for them,—after a long council they sent me a letter a true copy of which I enclose you. I very much suspect their fears they express about the Chickasaws are not real; that some kind of policy dictates the substance of their letter. I am only 24 miles from them & none of them have visited me" (ALS, RG 49, Records of the Bureau of Land Management, General Land Office: Letters Received from the Surveyor General, Vol. I, National Archives).

3. Arthur St. Clair.

4. See "Circular to the Commanding Officers of the Western Army," May 2, 1799.

5. Thomas Hunt, a veteran of the American Revolution, was a major in the First Regiment of Infantry.

6. See James Wilkinson to H, April 20, June 6, 1799.

7. This paragraph appears only in the copy marked "Duplicate."

8. "Colonel Hamtramcks Orders to the Western Army," June 28, 1799 (two copies, Hamilton Papers, Library of Congress).

9. Hamtramck to St. Clair, June 27, 1799 (copy, Hamilton Papers, Library of Congress).

10. Edward Day.

From Timothy Pickering

Philadelphia July 1. 1799

Dear Sir,

The original of the inclosed letter to Genl. Pinckney was written by Major Mountflorence,[1] whose character and situation I presume you know. Last Saturday I recd. a copy from the Genl. which he desired me to communicate to you.

I am very sincerely yours   T. Pickering.

I have sent another copy to Genl. Washington.[2]

General Hamilton.

[ENCLOSURE]

John Cole Mountflorence to Charles Cotesworth Pinckney [3]

The Hague March 12th 1799

Sir,

In my letter to the Secry of State of the 9th instant, I communicated the *positive* intelligence, I had from Paris, that the Consul there [4] & Mr. Barlow,[5] had individually written to the French Directory,[6] praising their wise & prudent conduct towards the U States, & recommending that a Minister be immediately sent to America to adjust matters, & thereby to be beforehand with the President. They recommend particularly, that this person should have manifested even before the French Revolution, if possible, Republican principles, & done some great service to America.

I smell in this, a double intrigue of crafty Talleyrand, & I believe you will be of my opinion, when I inform you, that La Fayette, has been in this country for some weeks, with an intention of going to America [7]—That he has letters from Talleyrand advising him strongly to it, and buoying him up with his canting flattery; that a man of his talent respectability &c. could be of infinite service in settling matters between the two Nations; & sounding his disposition to that effect.

Now the two Letter writers may, possibly, not be informed of the views of Talleyrand, as to the Person, he wishes to be intrusted by the Directory, but it appears evident that he did insinuate to the Writers the manner in which they should word their Addresses which corresponds exactly with the person in question. Another difficulty occurs however, respecting the predicament, this gentleman stands in, as to the laws of France. This can only be remedied by making use of him as an unqualified Agent, & assuring him, should he accomplish in America, what he would be recommended to do, he would be restored to his former situation, in *part only*, in his own country. Trusting to what popularity, & influence this character may still retain in the U States, especially among the people, Talleyrand expects that on his arrival, he would be courted, flattered & cherished, by the Democrats & Antis, & as he has always been made a tool of by designing & tricky men who knew how to play on his *foibles*, Talleyrand may have strong reasons to think, that the presence of such a man among us, if properly made use of, would add great strength to the declining party, & bring about events, which would embarrass our Government. Pains will be taken by all the friends of Administration, on this side of the Water, previous to his sailing to enquire into his dispositions, & to be further informed of what may still pass between him & Talleyrand, & every effort will be made to open his eyes to the danger of the character he is sollicited to act in America, which if he accepts it will undoubtedly terminate in the loss of his credit, reputation, & influence together with the loss of the friendship & esteem of the worthy persons, who, took his misfortunes, so much at heart. I have had myself, some conversations with his intimates, on the subject, & you will be duly informed of the Result of our endeavors, & of what further will be done in that business.

Young Dupont [8] will certainly sail soon for Philadelphia, as also Dupuzy,[9] who with his family is looking out for a passage.

with great respect & e——

The Hon'ble Genl Pinckney

ALS, Hamilton Papers, Library of Congress; copy, Massachusetts Historical Society, Boston.

1. James Cole Mountflorence of North Carolina was a veteran of the American Revolution. After the war he practiced law in Nashville. He went to France in 1791, and he subsequently served as secretary to Fulwar Skipwith, the United States consul general. From September, 1798, to January, 1799, he was secretary pro tem to William Vans Murray, and he agreed to act as Murray's honorary secretary after that date. In 1801 he became commercial agent for the United States at Paris (*Executive Journal*, I, 384-85).

2. Pickering to George Washington, July 1, 1799 (ALS, letterpress copy, Massachusetts Historical Society, Boston). Charles Cotesworth Pinckney had also sent Washington a copy in a letter dated June 25, 1799 (ALS, George Washington Papers, Library of Congress). See also Washington to Pickering, July 14, 1799 (ALS, Massachusetts Historical Society, Boston).

3. Copy, George Washington Papers, Library of Congress; copy, Hamilton Papers, Library of Congress; two copies, Massachusetts Historical Society, Boston.

4. Fulwar Skipwith had been appointed consul general of the United States in France on June 25, 1795 (*Executive Journal*, I, 189, 191).

5. Joel Barlow, an American poet and diplomat, arrived in Europe in 1788 as European agent for the Scioto Company. David Humphreys appointed him United States consul in Algiers on September 7, 1795. He arrived in Algiers on March 6, 1796, and left on July 18, 1797. He returned to Paris in September, 1797, and was a private citizen in the spring of 1799.

6. See Skipwith and Barlow to Philippe Antoine Merlin (of Douai), February 11, 1799; Skipwith to Talleyrand, March 11, 1799 (*Arch. des Aff. Etr., Corr. Pol., Etats-Unis*, LI, 36–37, 94–95).

7. For the suggestion that the Marquis de Lafayette be appointed French Minister to the United States, see H to Lafayette, January 6, 1799, note 4.

8. Victor Marie Du Pont de Nemours, son of Pierre Samuel Du Pont de Nemours, was appointed French consul general in Philadelphia to replace Philippe Joseph Létombe in June, 1798, when Létombe's exequatur was revoked. See Pickering to Létombe, July 13, 1798 (LC, RG 59, Domestic Letters of the Department of State, Vol. 11, June 30, 1798–June 29, 1799, National Archives). Soon after his arrival in Philadelphia, Létombe returned to France because the Adams Administration refused to recognize officially his mission. See Rufus King to H, July 3, 1798, note 1. In France he suffered from the hostility of the Directory to his father. Abandoning his career in the French diplomatic service, he returned to the United States in 1799 and became a merchant in New York.

9. Jean Xavier Bureaux de Pusy, a French army officer, had been a member of the Estates General in 1789. He was elected president of the Constituent Assembly three times. With the overthrow of the French monarchy, he abandoned his support of the revolution and attempted to escape to America, but he was captured by the Austrians and imprisoned in Olmütz prison with other Frenchmen including Lafayette. He was released from prison during the winter of 1796–1797 and sailed from Hamburg to the United States. He married a daughter of Marie Françoise Robin Poivre, a widow who had married Pierre Samuel Du Pont de Nemours in 1794.

From John Adlum [1]

Reading [*Pennsylvania*] *July 2, 1799.* "I arrived here on the 29th. Ult. and assumed the Command of the detachment at this place. . . . Since my arrival at this place I have been at some pains to get information from persons of trust Citizens of this place, and it is very generally their opinion that to take away a part of the troops from this place would have a bad effect, that they ought rather to be augmented to make them have that impression necessary to keep the Country in order. In consequence of the above opinions I have determined to decline sending a detachment for the present to Easton, untill I hear further from you, being of opinion myself it would have a bad tendency, to send off a part of the force from this. And if I understand your letter right, you give me a discretionary power to that effect. . . ."

ALS, Hamilton Papers, Library of Congress.
1. This letter was written in reply to H to Adlum, June 8, 1799.

From James McHenry

War Department 2nd July 1799

Sir

You will find by copies of the several contracts for the garrisons under your command (with which you have been furnished),[1] compared with the returns of troops in garrison, at which of them it will be proper to provide for the issues of the provisions by an officer appointed and paid by government.

The late Major General Wayne was instructed by me, by letter dated 25th June 1796,[2] as follows "As Mr O Hara[3] is only to deliver to the army in the quantities and at such posts as you may direct, it will be necessary that a qualified person should be appointed at each post, to receive the rations and issue them to the troops."

"The business of issuing, it is thought, may be conducted by subaltern officers; you will therefore appoint one for each post (where the Contractor is not bound to issue) with an extra monthly pay graduated from *8 to 20* Dollars according to the number of troops to be supplied."

I expect this arrangement has been regularly carried into effect. You will, however, now, and from time to time, make all appointments, in conformity with the said instructions whereever necessary.

It will, perhaps appear to you, that as each Garrison has an officer, who is charged with the Quarter Masters stores and cloathing, the same person may also be charged with the issuing of the provisions. I mean such Garrisons as are without a regiment Quarter Master.

I am Sir   with respect   your obedient Servant   James McHenry

Major General Alexander Hamilton

LS, Hamilton Papers, Library of Congress.

1. Contract with John Bray, New Brunswick, New Jersey, April 6, 1799, enclosed in Jonathan Rhea to H, April 6, 1799; contract with Joseph Hugg, Woodbury, New Jersey, April 13, 1799, enclosed in McHenry to H, April 15, 1799; contract with Joseph Ruggles, Nathaniel Ruggles, Ralph Smith, Aaron Davis, and Charles Davis, Roxbury, Massachusetts, May 7, 1799, enclosed in Jonathan Jackson to H, May 10, 1799; contract with John Elliot, Wilmington,

Delaware, May 11, 1799, enclosed in John Stockton to H, May 11, 1799; contract with Asa Freeman, Dover, Delaware, May 14, 1799, enclosed in Stockton to H, May 22, 1799; contract with James Caldwell, New Castle, Delaware, May 20, 1799, enclosed in Stockton to H, May 22, 1799; contract with John L. Boss, Newport, Rhode Island, May 21, 1799, enclosed in Archibald Crary to H, May 21, 1799; contract with Robert Ball, Wilmington, North Carolina, June 21, 1799, enclosed in Griffith John McRee to H, July 10, 1799. The letters in which these contracts are enclosed are listed in the appendix to this volume.

2. For McHenry's letter to Anthony Wayne, see Knopf, *Wayne*, 488.
3. James O'Hara.

From James McHenry [1]

War Department, July 2, 1799. "If you find any thing to alter or propose which will make the enclosed regulations [2] more perspicuous or perfect, I wish you to mention it and return them as soon as possible."

[ENCLOSURE]

The following Rules have been adopted by the president of the United States relative to Rank and promotion in the Army.[3]

RANK

The Field Officers of the Twelve Regiments of Infantry raised in pursuance of the Act of the 16th. July 1798 [4] who served in the Regular Army during the late War and continued therein to the end thereof shall take rank of all others of the same Grade who were not in Service or who were deranged in pursuance of any Resolution of Congress—their relative rank with each other to be the same as at the end of the War.

Those Officers who have been deranged in pursuance of any Resolution of Congress to take rank next after those who continued to the expiration of the War—their relative Rank with each other to be agreeably to their respective Grades and dates of Commission.

Provided always that Colonels who were deranged shall take rank of Lieutenant Colonels who served to the end of the War—Lieutenant Colonels of Majors—Majors of Captains &ca. Officers who have served in the Army or Levies since the peace and have been disbanded shall take Rank next after the Officers deranged during the late War.

Resignations shall preclude all claim to Rank.

The Rank of those Officers who have not been in Service shall be determined by the Commander in Chief.

PROMOTIONS

The Captains and Subalterns in the Cavalry, Artillery and Infantry shall rise regimentally to the rank of Major inclusive. Promotions from the Rank of Major to that of Lieutenant Colonel shall be in the line of the Army—provided however that the said promotions in the Cavalry, Artillery and Infantry shall be confined to their respective lines.

On a Vacancy happening the Senior Officer of the next inferior Grade in ordinary cases shall be considered as the most proper person to fill the same. But in cases of extraordinary merit, Officers altho' not senior in rank may be appointed to fill vacancies.

LS, Hamilton Papers, Library of Congress.
1. McHenry sent the same letter on the same day to George Washington (LS, George Washington Papers, Library of Congress).
2. On the back of this letter H wrote: "Rule of promotion." H had discussed the rules of promotion with the general officers in Philadelphia in November-December, 1798 (H's draft of Washington to McHenry, third letter of December 13, 1798; McHenry to H, March 21, April 23, 1799; H to McHenry, second and third letters of April 26, 1799). McHenry had consulted Washington regarding the proposed rules on March 31, 1799 (ALS, letterpress copy, James McHenry Papers, Library of Congress). On April 29, 1799, McHenry sent a copy of the proposed rules to John Adams (ALS, Adams Family Papers, deposited in the Massachusetts Historical Society, Boston), and on the same day he also wrote to Washington (ALS, George Washington Papers, Library of Congress) and enclosed copies of his letter to Adams and of the proposed rules. Washington agreed to them on May 5, 1799 (ALS, letterpress copy, George Washington Papers, Library of Congress), and Adams sent his approval of the rules to McHenry on May 7, 1799 (LC, Adams Family Papers, deposited in the Massachusetts Historical Society, Boston). On July 2, 1799, McHenry sent a copy of the approved rules to Washington and to H (see note 1). Washington accepted them on July 7, 1799 (Df, in the handwriting of Tobias Lear, George Washington Papers, Library of Congress). H sent McHenry suggestions for revising the rules on July 8, 1799. McHenry adopted one of these changes and sent a final copy of the rules to H on September 3, 1799.
3. Copy, Hamilton Papers, Library of Congress; copy, George Washington Papers, Library of Congress. The copy in the Hamilton Papers, which is incorrectly filed under the date of September 3, 1799, is endorsed: "Relative to Rank in the army."
4. "An Act to augment the Army of the United States, and for other purposes" (1 Stat. 604–05).

To James McHenry [1]

New York July 2d. 1799

Sir

I beg leave to recall your attention to the suggestion contained in my letter of the 21st. of June, respecting the raising mounting and equipping of one of the Six additional troops of Horse together with the Non commissioned Officers of the other Troops—and to request your final direction on the subject.

The service of the Cavalry in this Country has never been but imperfectly understood. Even in Europe ideas about the formation and tactics of that species of troops appear to be less well settled than about the other branches of Military Service. It is in my opinion very important to possess the means of making an experiment of the different principles in order to the formation of a good system adapted to the Geographical circumstances of the Country. For this purpose alone a Small body of Cavalry is indispensable.

With great respect &c.

Secy. of War

Copy, in the handwriting of Ethan Brown, Hamilton Papers, Library of Congress.
1. For background to this letter, see McHenry to H, June 18, 1799; H to McHenry, second letter of June 21, 1799.

To Thomas Y. How [1]

New York July 3. 1799

Sir

It gave me pleasure to learn from Col Ogden [2] that it would probably not be incompatible with your views or inclination to accept the appointment of Secy to the Inspector General. I regret that this place will at present offer to you only the pay & emoluments without the rank of Captain. It will be my endeavour to render it more advantageous but of the success of that endeavour I cannot be certain.

In saying this to you, which I think necessary by way of information, I do not forget that the motives which may induce your acceptance will have a character far more laudable than can arise from considerations of recompence. I trust they will not miss their aim; while on my part I anticipate real advantages from your talents & work.

With great esteem   I am sir   Yr Obed Ser

Thomas Y Howe Es

ADf, Hamilton Papers, Library of Congress.
1. This letter was enclosed in H to Aaron Ogden, July 3 1799.
2. Ogden to H, June 28, 1799.

To James McHenry

New York July 3d. 1799

Sir

I transmit you the proceedings of a Court Martial in the case of Joseph Perkins, who is sentenced to death for desertion aggravated by very atrocious circumstances.[1]

I see nothing to occasion a doubt as to the regularity of the proceedings or the propriety of the sentence.

I observe indeed that in this as in a former instance [2] the articles on which the sentence is founded are not specified. But neither principle nor usage requires that they should be. It is enough that the Military Code does authorise such a punishment for such a crime. The Court need not lay its finger upon the particular clauses. To require a nice detail of this sort would be to fetter and clog the operation of Military Justice by the subtil forms of special pleading.

I will only add that every day brings fresh proof of the necessity of severe examples to check a wanton spirit of desertion, which if not checked will render the inlistments of soldiers a mere waste of the public Treasure.

I entreat that a prompt decision may be obtained.

With great respect   I have the honor to be   Sir   Your Obed ser

The Secy of War

ADf, Hamilton Papers, Library of Congress.
  1. Perkins had been tried twice. For the first court-martial, which both H and McHenry believed was illegal, see McHenry to H, May 29, 1799, note 2. See also H to McHenry, May 30, 1799; "General Orders," June 13, 1799. On June 25, 1799, a second court-martial ordered by H (H to George Ingersoll, May 29, 1799 [listed in the appendix to this volume]) tried Perkins and found him guilty. The proceedings of this court-martial were published in *The New-York Gazette and General Advertiser*, July 26, 1799. On July 19, 1799, McHenry wrote to H that the President had confirmed the sentence (letter listed in the appendix to this volume), and on July 20, 1799, H ordered that the sentence be carried out ("General Orders," July 20, 1799). For an account of the execution, see *The New-York Gazette and General Advertiser*, July 26, 1799.
  2. See H to McHenry, first letter of June 12, 1799.

To Aaron Ogden

New York July 3. 1799

Dr. Sir

I thank you very much for your attention to my request respecting a Secretary.[1] The testimony of Mr Stockdon [2] & yourself would be decisive as to Mr Howe had not information from other quarters prepossessed me extremely in his favour. The enclosed letter [3] offers him the place; have the goodness to forward it without delay.

How would the idea suit you and him of an appointment to a second Lieutenancy in your Regiment? It would increase his advantages among the rest & put him in a course of military promotion. I am aware it is not within the system & would so far mutilate your regiment. But perhaps I may surmount the obstacle from the first consideration & I thought that your friendship for Mr. Howe might dispose you to some sacrifice for his benefit.

Yrs. truly

A H

Col Ogden

ALS, The Andre deCoppet Collection, Princeton University Library.
1. Ogden to H, June 28, 1799.
2. Richard Stockton.
3. H to Thomas Y. How, July 3, 1799.

From Thomas Parker

Winchester [Virginia] July 3, 1799. ". . . Our Cloathing has not yet arrived which appears unaccountable as I am credably informed that the officers in maryland have received their proportions. My Duty has prevented me from making application in any other way than By letter. I trusted however that no preference would be given to personal applications that might be made by those who were nearer the seat of Government & I hope that a stop will be put to the dissatisfaction that prevails among officers and Soldiers by a Speedy arrival of the Cloathing. . . ."

ALS, Hamilton Papers, Library of Congress.

From James Wilkinson

Balise, Mouth of the Mississippi, July 3, 1799. "I reached this place the 30th. Ultimo where we are detained for a Wind to pass the Bar. . . . Immediately after my Arrival At New Orleans, I droped you a line [1] by a Sloop, bound directly to New York, and I send this by the Schooner two Brothers bound to Baltimore. I am on Board the Willm. of Charlestown bound to London, to touch at the Port of your residence. . . ."

ALS, Hamilton Papers, Library of Congress.
1. Wilkinson to H, June 6, 1799.

To Benjamin Stoddert

New York July 4
1799

Dr Sir

Mr. Hudson [1] who will deliver you this is desirous of the place of Midshipman on board of our Navy. This Gentleman completed his Studies in the law with me. He possesses talents and animation and I have no doubt will succeed in the naval career. An active temper joined to the pressure of pecuniary circumstances has determined him to embrace this course. I interest myself in his success as far as it may be compatible with your general arrangements. [2]

With great respect I have the honor to be Dr Sir   Yr Obedt ser
A Hamilton

B Stoddert Esquire

ALS, Adams Family Papers, deposited in the Massachusetts Historical Society, Boston.
  1. Frederick N. Hudson. See H to James McHenry, August 19, 1798, note 1.
  2. Stoddert accepted H's recommendation and appointed Hudson a midshipman when Hudson presented the letter printed above to Stoddert on July 5, 1799 (D, RG 24, Bureau of Naval Personnel, Register of Officers' Services, National Archives). Stoddert assigned Hudson to the *Constitution*, which was then outfitting at Boston under Captain Silas Talbot, and forwarded Hudson's warrant to the President for his signature. See Stoddert to John Adams, July 5, 1799 (ALS, Adams Family Papers, deposited in the Massachusetts Historical Society, Boston).

Statement by Aaron Burr and Alexander Hamilton [1]

[New York, July 5, 1799]

We the Subscribers do certify that Col Ebenezer Stevens was together with ourselves appointed by the Citizens of this City a Committee to devise and cause to be erected fortifications for its immediate Defence—that Col Stevens in the course of the execution of this trust was charged with a particular superintendence of the execution of the works and with a variety of details which occasioned to him extraordinary trouble occupying a great portion of his time for which he is well intitled to an adequate compensation.

New York July 5, 1799
Alexander Hamilton
A. Burr

DS, in the handwriting of H, The H. and A. S. W. Rosenbach Foundation, Philadelphia.

1. For background to this document, see the introductory note to H to James McHenry, June 1, 1798. See also "Call for a Meeting," June 4, 1798, note 2.

To James McHenry

New York, July 6, 1799. Quotes from Colonel Thomas Parker's letter of June 30 concerning lack of clothing for recruits and states: "If any thing remains to be done to accelerate the arrival of the Cloathing I pray that it may be done and that inferior considerations may give way to the necessity of preserving contentment among the troops and maintaining in their eyes the justice and *respectability* of the Government. This circumstance leads me to observe that if there be not an absolute certainty that the supply of cloathing will henceforth keep pace with the progress of recruiting it is better to suspend it than to suffer a number of men to be brought together to contract disgust & discredit the public operation. . . ."

ADf, Hamilton Papers, Library of Congress.

From Aaron Ogden

Elizabeth Town [New Jersey] July 6 1799

Sir.

The intervention of the 4th. of July and the Affairs of the Society of Cincinnati [1] having occupied the day succeeding, have delayed my answering yours [2] respecting the appointment of Mr. How to a second Lieutenancy in the 11th. regiment. I beg you to be assured that the measure proposed, will be to me perfectly agreeble, and I have accordingly in my letter to Mr Howe enquired of him whether such an appointment as you have proposed for him in the line would be acceptable.

With the most respectful attachment   I am Dr Sir.   your mo. ob. servt   Aaron Ogden

Major General Alexander Hamilton

ALS, Hamilton Papers, Library of Congress.
1. Ogden was a charter member of the New Jersey chapter of the Society of the Cincinnati, which was founded in 1783. Its annual meeting was scheduled for July 4, 1799 (*The Institution of the Society of the Cincinnati in the State of New Jersey from 1783 to 1866* [Albany, 1866], 41).
2. H to Ogden, July 3, 1799.

From Thomas Parker

Winchester [Virginia] July 6, 1799. ". . . Some of the officers wish to take their own Slaves as Servants & wish to be Informed whether any & what Compensation will be made for their Services. . . ."

ALS, Hamilton Papers, Library of Congress.

From Staats Morris

[*Fort McHenry, Maryland, July 7, 1799.* In a letter to James McHenry on July 9, 1799, Hamilton quoted from "A letter from Capt S Morris of the 7 instant." *Letter not found.*]

From James McHenry

[*Philadelphia, July 8, 1799.* On July 9, 1799, Hamilton wrote to McHenry: "I have the honor to acknowlege the Receipt of your letter of yesterday with the list of some new appointments, in the 7th 8 & 9 Regts." *Letter not found.*]

From James McHenry [1]

War Department, July 8, 1799. Discusses Major John J. U. Rivardi's account of conditions at Fort Niagara. Refers to McHenry's letter of July 2, 1799, concerning former quartermasters.[2] States that Rivardi disbursed extra pay for extra work and points out that such payments should not be given "for procuring supplies or performing work in the ordinary line of a soldiers duty. . . ." Encloses quotations from a British work on military finance [3] that present new ideas for "establishing a scale of extra allowance for extra service. . . ." Promises to attend to Enoch Humphrey's application for an appointment as a cadet.[4] Notes that measures are in progress for establishing a military academy.[5]

LS, Hamilton Papers, Library of Congress.
  1. This letter was written in reply to H to McHenry, June 25–July 2, 1799.
  2. See McHenry's second letter to H of this date.
  3. John Williamson, *A Treatise on Military Finance; containing the Pay, Subsistence, Deductions, and Arrears of the Forces on the British and Irish Establishments . . . With an enquiry into the method of Cloathing and Recruiting the Army etc.* (London: T. Egerton, 1782).
  4. See Rivardi to H, April 3, May 30, 1799.
  5. See Charles C. Pinckney to H, January 17, 1799; H to Pinckney, March 7, 1799; H to Louis Le Bègue Du Portail, July 23, 1798; Du Portail to H, December 9, 1798; H to McHenry, December 26, 1798, note 2; McHenry to H, December 28, 1798, note 4.

To James McHenry

New York July 8. 1799

Sir

I have considered the rules transmitted in your letter of the 2d. instant relative to rank & promotion.[1]

They appear to me founded on just principles nor do I know that they can be improved. I will however present to your consideration some observations on two or three points.

It seems to me questionable whether the preference given to full Colonels of the deranged Officers over Lt Col Comts., who served to the end of the War be expedient. It is making that a matter of substance of which was purely nominal. The grade of Lt Col Commandant was in our system to all purposes of service & promotion equal to that of Colonel. And the general principle of preserving officers who served to the end of the War seems to be as applicable to this particular as to any other.

It is desireable to exempt a military commander from the exercise of a discretion in personal matters which may expose him to the supposition of favouritism. It is possible the Commander in chief may not like to be charged with that which is proposed to be conferred upon him; though he could have no objection to aid the determination of the President with all requisite information.

Perhaps the clause may with advantage be altered to stand thus:

"The relative Rank of officers who have not been in service will be determined by the President. The commander in Chief will report to him their names with such information as he may deem proper."

The last clause will I think be more accurate, if altered into this form.

"On the happening of a vacancy, the officer next in rank will in ordinary cases be considered as the most proper person to fill the same. But this rule is considered as subject to exceptions in extraordinary cases." [2]

It will be useful also in my opinion to add a clause to this effect—

In promotions to the several ranks of generals, The officers of Cavalry Artillery & Infantry will be considered as eligible indiscriminately or without distinction of one Corps from another.

To confine the Officers of Artillery and Cavalry to their particular corps with appointments of General Officers is to render the chance of promotion unequal, and to discourage in the several classes of Officers the study of all the branches of Tactics. The contrary principle will have a contrary effect; and though it is rarely to be expected that an officer of Cavalry or infantry will be competent to the service of the Artillery, yet nothing is more easy than for the officers of those corps to be acquainted with the tactics of each, and an officer of Artillery can without difficulty make himself Master of the Tactics of the Cavalry & Infantry. The plan of an indiscriminate choice will also increase the chances of having qualified Generals.

And if the idea itself be approved it is expedient to prepare the army to expect its application by ingrafting it in the system of Promotion.

With great respect   I have the honor to be sir

The Secy of War

ADf, Hamilton Papers, Library of Congress.
1. See the enclosure to McHenry's second letter to H of this date.
2. McHenry adopted this suggestion. On September 3, 1799, McHenry sent a copy of the final rules concerning rank and promotion to George Washington (LS, George Washington Papers, Library of Congress) and to H. Washington approved of the final version of the rules on September 15, 1799 (Df, in the handwriting of Tobias Lear, George Washington Papers, Library of Congress).

From Nathan Rice

Hingham [Massachusetts] July 8th 1799

My dear General

Your several favours of the 18th. 19th.[1] & 24th. ulto. I have received. I have sent my Quarter Master[2] to Springfield for the arms & have directed him to distribute them to the several companies at their rendesvous, many of which are in the vicinity of Springfield, & will save thereby considerable expence to the public for transportation to the regimental rendesvous. I do not yet find that any provision is made in this quarter for cartridge boxes, pray Sir how shall I obtain them? Knapsacks must be immediately necessary for the soldiers, if such could be had as would keep out the rain, being covered by some kind of skin dressd with the hair in, they would be very much preferable to painted canvass; I think in the end, by their durability they would be cheapest to the public. Canteens will be also wanted, if they are not provided already I think I can procure them cheaper where I live, than they can be obtained in any other place, as that kind of business employs most of its inhabitants. Would it not be best to have a set of Tent poles, provided, made of such wood as would be light for transportation, & in such a manner, as would prevent them injuring the Tents by pitching.

Perhaps Sir there may be an impropriety in addressing these enquiries to you, a conviction of which very forcibly impresses my mind—but Mr Jackson the Supervisor who appears in some instances to be acting, in the department to which these things belong,[3] is destitute of authority & Instructions in many points, & will not act without them. I knew not therefore to whom I am to make application, & pray you to excuse my addressing them to you.

The Hats, as you suggested might, have arrived without cockades;[4] I applied to the Supervisor, he had no instructions, & could not supply them—agreeable to your directions, I have contracted for a sufficient number for the regiment at eight Cents each, a sample of which I have seen. they are well made. The Tin Eagles I have also engaged, for a Cent & half each.

I have received the form of the monthly return,[5] a copy of which I have put into the hands of the commanding officer of each company. I expect to be able to transmit you my monthly return in the course of next week.

You may be assured Sir, the most exemplary strictness shall be had in scrutinising into the state of the recruits on the definitive Muster of them, at the regimental rendezvous. As a caution to my officers I have informed them, that every disqualification for the service which shall be discovered, in a recruit, at this scrutiny, which existed at the time of his inlistment, & which it was in the power of the officer inlisting him to have known—He will be held responsible for; & for all monies he shall have paid him.

General Lincoln has inform'd me that a Mr. Francis Barker who has received letters recomendatory of him, for an appointment,[6] needed an expression of my wishes & approbation only, in order to his meeting with success in his application.[7] I had written at his desire to the Secretary of War in his favour & I can only now say that I believe him to be a deserving young man & would make a good Subaltern officer.

With every expression of esteem   I have the honor to be   Your Most obt Servant   N: Rice

ALS, Hamilton Papers, Library of Congress.
    1. See "Circular to the Commandants of Regiments," June 18, 19, 1799.
    2. Daniel Hastings. See Rice to H, May 24, 1799.
    3. See "Circular to the Commandants of Regiments," May 22, 1799.
    4. See "Circular to the Commandants of Regiments," May 22, 1799.
    5. See "Circular to the Commandants of Regiments," June 19, 1799.
    6. Benjamin Lincoln to H, May 18, 1799 (listed in the appendix to this volume).

7. Barker became a second lieutenant in the Fourteenth Regiment of Infantry on July 22, 1799 (Heitman, *United States Army,* I, 190). On May 14, 1800, the Senate confirmed his appointment as first lieutenant in place of Nathaniel Soley (*Executive Journal,* I, 345, 355). Soley, who had been nominated on December 31, 1798, had declined his appointment (*Executive Journal,* I, 300).

To James McHenry

New York, July 9, 1799. "I have the honor to acknowlege the Receipt of your letter of yesterday [1] with the list of some new appointments, in the 7th, 8 & 9 Regts which will be communicated to the respective commandants. . . .[2] On this subject of Cadets it may be proper to fix some rule. I doubt the present expediency of appointing more than two to each Regiment of Infantry. But it is believed to be expedient to appoint the full number allowed in the corps of Artillerists. . . .[3] A letter from Capt S Morris of the 7 instant [4] has the following paragraph 'I must take the liberty of repeating to you the necessity of a supply of Cloathing to this Garrison. Some of the men of the infantry are *actually almost naked.*' This passage speaks itself the urgency of the demand. I think Col Stevens [5] informed last Evening that he had written ⟨for⟩ a supply of cloathing for the garrisons in this vicinity ⟨and⟩ received for answer that there were none in store. These deficiencies in a time of peace with such a hand⟨ful⟩ of troops to be supplied are greatly to be *lamented.*"

ADf, Hamilton Papers, Library of Congress.
1. McHenry wrote two letters to H on July 8, 1799. Only one of these letters has been found, and it is not the one mentioned in the letter printed above.
2. "List of Persons to fill vacancies in the regiments hereinafter mentioned" (copy, Hamilton Papers, Library of Congress). This list is endorsed by H: "List of Additional Appointments in the 7. 8 & 9 Reg."
3. Section 1 of "An Act for the better organizing of the Troops of the United States; and for other purposes" (1 *Stat.* 749–50 [March 3, 1799]) provided for thirty-two cadets in each regiment of the Corps of Artillerists and Engineers.
4. Letter from Staats Morris not found.
5. Ebenezer Stevens.

To Philip Schuyler

[*New York, July 9, 1799.* On July 15, 1799, Schuyler wrote to Hamilton and referred to "Your letter of the 9th Instant." *Letter not found.*]

To William C. Bentley [1]

[*New York, July 10, 1799.* On August 17, 1799, Bentley wrote to Hamilton: "Yours of the 10 Ultimo . . . was received in proper time." *Letter not found.*]

1. Bentley, a Virginian and a veteran of the American Revolution, was lieutenant colonel commandant of the Seventh Regiment of Infantry. He was stationed in Richmond, Virginia.

From James McHenry

War Department
10th July 1799

Sir,

I enclose you Copies of a letter from J Jackson [1] Esqr. Supervisor at Boston, with my indorsement of reference, to the accountant of this Department, and of the Accountants answer,[2] or report, dated the 6th instant.

The difficulties you will percieve, are almost daily occurring in the Accountants Office, relative to settlements for quarter Master's supplies, by Contractors, or agents, and for repairs of barracks &c, ordered by Commandants of Posts, induce me, to request, you will report, as soon as convenient, on the regulations, submitted to you, in my letter of the 24t June ultimo.

You will be pleased to add, whatever may appear necessary, to make the regulations apply as much as possible, to all Quarter

Masters supplies and to extend them, if proper, so as to give a suitable latitude to, but define the extent of authority in Commandants of Posts, on the subject of repairs for barracks, hospitals, the building of expensive barges &c.

I wish also to call your attention to two subjects which have been presented for decision, one in a letter from Major General Pinckney of the 22d June ulto relative to allowances, to the Servants of Officers, who are entitled to servants, but which servants are not soldiers. The General had been applied to, by Major Freeman,[3] now commanding at Fort Johnson in South Carolina, who stated that his *two* servants are not taken from the line, that he had not drawn provisions from the Contractors for them for fourteen months, and requested to be permitted to receive the same allowance for them, from the United States as he should have received had he taken them from the line. The General cites a resolve of Congress of the 11th March 1780,[4] which allows clothing, pay, and rations to any Officer entitled to a servant, who shall bring into the field with him a servant of his own: the Officer in such case, not to be allowed a servant out of the line; observes that he does not know accurately, whether this resolve is acted upon at present, but adds that General Wilkinson in his orders of the 3d. June 1797,[5] allows Officers, who provide themselves private servants and do not take them from the line, to draw subsistence for them. Under the impression that such an allowance would be beneficial to the service Major Freeman has been permitted to draw subsistence for his servants, from the 19th June ulto until my decision is known. Since this Subject has presented itself it may require a general regulation, or order. Before however such regulation or order can be formed, it is necessary to settle what officers are or shall be entitled to servants, and whether any officer shall be entitled to more than one.

The other respects, the drawing of provision for the Children of the Army, which Colonel Hamtramck[6] informs me, is authorised by a General Order,[7] and greatly encreases the issues.

On both these subjects of reference, I request your deliberate opinion.

I had omitted to mention that Lieutenant Leonard, for undertaking to order repairs to the Hospital and Officers Quarters on Bedloe's Island, and more especially to expend Public monies, without your authority, and when an Agent of the war Department was present, whose duty it is to superintend such civil operations, must be considered as highly *reprehensible*.[8]

I am Sir   with great respect   your obedient servant

James McHenry

Major General Hamilton

LS, Hamilton Papers, Library of Congress.

1. On June 29, 1799, Jonathan Jackson wrote to McHenry that the Department of War had refused to approve the payment of several bills submitted by Army contractors at Boston (copy, Hamilton Papers, Library of Congress).

2. On July 6, 1799, William Simmons wrote to McHenry and reviewed in detail the accounts and contracts of the individual Army contractors at Boston (copy, Hamilton Papers, Library of Congress).

3. Constant Freeman.

4. *JCC*, XVI, 250.

5. On May 22, 1797, James Wilkinson issued the following order: "Servants to be taken by voluntary consent from the Regiment, Corps or detachment to which the officer served may belong . . . otherwise they must employ domestics to be paid and clothed from their privy purses, as no further indulgence on the part of the Public can be admitted" (LC, RG 95, Adjutant General's Office, General Orders, General James Wilkinson, 1796–1808, National Archives). On June 3, 1797, Wilkinson issued a new order, which reads: "It is to be understood, that when Officers provide themselves private Servants, in Conformity to the orders of the 22d Ultimo, and do not take them from the line, they are to draw Subsistence on the returns of their masters, countersigned by the commanding Officer of the detachment, Post district or department, to which they belong" (LC, RG 94, Adjutant General's Office, General Orders, General James Wilkinson, 1796–1808, National Archives).

6. John F. Hamtramck.

7. See H to Zebulon M. Pike, May 3, 1799, note 2.

8. On July 12, 1799, H wrote to Adam Hoops: "I request information relative to the following Extract of a letter from the Accountant's Of the Dept of War dated July 6th 1799.

"'I will mention two circumstances now before me in which I am really at a loss how to act. Lieut. [Nathaniel] Leonard has had the Hospital and Officers Quarters repaired at Bedlow's Island to the amount of 257 Dollars for which he has obtained payment by an Order on the Contractor; this was done within the vicinity of Colonel Stevens agency for the War Department without any directions from him although he is daily making disbursements of like nature at Fort Jay.'" This letter is listed in the appendix to this volume.

From James McHenry

War department 10 July 1799

Sir,

I received your letter of the 6. of July containing a paragraph from a letter from Colonel Parker, by which it appears that his supply of Clothing had not then arrived except some hats and shoes.

The articles in the annexed list No. 1.[1] which comprehends the whole of your requisition left this City as appears by a note made on it by the Assistant Quarter Master General[2] on the 29. May and June 22d. and 29. The distance from hence to Winchester is 192 miles the last parcel therefore ought to have got to hand yesterday. A Warrant has issued for the money required for Col. Parker and will be transmitted by the first mail.

I think with you that if the supply of Cloathing will not henceforth keep pace with the progress of recruiting, it is better to suspend it, than to suffer a number of men to be brought together to contract disgust and discredit the public operations.

It may be proper in reviewing this subject to attend to the following circumstances

1. That the Contract for supplying cloathing for the last year failed in consequence of there not being in the United States a sufficiency of white Kersey for vests and overalls.

2d. That no person could be found to contract to furnish the Cloathing for the present year (to include the additional army) from a well founded belief that a sufficiency of white and blue Cloths for the purpose could not be procured within the United States in season to have enabled them to have completed their Contract before late in the Autumn or beginning of Winter.

3. That a considerable proportion of the Cloth was not obtained till after the arrival of the spring vessels, it not being previous thereto within the United States.

It is presumed these causes will account satisfactorily, and without calling in any others, for the seeming delay that has occurred in furnishing the cloathing required to commence the recruiting service, and must when known to the Officers specially concerned, as well as the persons who may have ascribed these delays to neglects, exculpate the parties that may have been censured. I request these circumstances may be freely communicated to the Officers.

The enclosed schedule No. 2 [3] furnished by the Assistant Quarter Master exhibits the articles of Cloathing &c. and the dates when they left this City for their respective places of destination. It appears that your several requisitions for the twelve regiments of Infantry have been nearly complied with and those for North and South Carolina anticipated.

It will further be seen from the paper No. 3 [4] that Mr Billington expects to be able to deliver into the public Store every Week about four hundred Suits until the whole complement for the Sixteen regiments of Infantry shall be completed.

As I have not received any returns stating the number of recruits inlisted and not being in possession of any facts to enable me to ascertain our future progress, I must with these facts submit it exclusively to you to determine whether (a sufficiency of Cloth being on hand) the weekly supply of four hundred Suits promised by Billington will be sufficient to justify you to continue the recruiting business, or whether it will be proper to suspend it until such time as the whole of the Cloathing required is actually in store.

I have the honor to be with great respect Your obedient servant   James McHenry

Major Genl Hamilton

This letter has been delayed waiting for returns.[5]

LS, Hamilton Papers, Library of Congress; extract, Lloyd W. Smith Collection, Morristown National Historical Park, Morristown, New Jersey.
1. "List of Articles delivered the Quarter Master General for Transportation, and forwarded to Joseph Tidball Esqr Winchester Virginia 8th Regiment" (copy, Hamilton Papers, Library of Congress).
2. James Miller.
3. "Return of Clothing forwarded the twelve additional regiments, from the 27th April 1799 to the 10th July following," July 11, 1799 (DS, signed by Samuel Hodgdon, Hamilton Papers, Library of Congress).
4. This document, which is signed by Thomas Billington, an Army contractor in Philadelphia, has no title and is dated July 10, 1799. The document lists the number of Army uniforms under the headings "Quantity cut," "De-

livered in War Stores," and "In the hands of the worker & in house" (copy, Hamilton Papers, Library of Congress).

5. The postscript is in McHenry's handwriting.

To James McHenry

New York, July 10, 1799. Quotes from Josias Carvel Hall's letter of June 25, 1799, concerning the shortage of clothing and states: "I trust that . . . the deficiencies complained of have been obviated. The continually increasing catalogue is very embarrassing."

LS, Hamilton Papers, Library of Congress.

To James McHenry

New York, July 10, 1799. "I send you an Extract of a letter of the 20th June from Col: Hunewell,[1] recommending Eli Forbes[2] Esqr. for Captain in place of Capt. Philips.[3] It was an idea talked of between us though not settled, that the routine of promotion should take effect in ⟨ea⟩ch regiment as soon as the places of field Officers were ⟨ac⟩tually filled. If this rule is to govern it would be an obstacle to the success of the present recommenda⟨tion⟩. If on the contrary the routine is not to begin ⟨until⟩ the rules of promotion[4] have been finally adopted ⟨and p⟩romulged, then I think it most probable that it ⟨wou⟩ld consist with the good of the Service to make the appointment recommended. . . ."

Copy, in the handwriting of Ethan Brown, Hamilton Papers, Library of Congress.

1. Richard Hunewell. Letter not found.

2. Eli Forbes was appointed a captain in the Fifteenth Regiment of Infantry on July 12, 1799, during the recess of the Senate, and the Senate confirmed the appointment on May 14, 1800 (*Executive Journal*, I, 346, 355).

3. Thomas Philips, who had been appointed a captain on January 8, 1799 (*Executive Journal*, I, 299, 303), had declined the appointment.

4. For information on the rules of promotion, see the enclosure to McHenry to H, second letter of July 2, 1799. See also H to McHenry, July 8, 1799; McHenry to H, September 3, 1799.

To James McHenry

Private   New York July 10 1799

Why, My Dear friend, do you suffer the business of providing to go on as it does. Every moment proves the insufficiency of the existing plan & the necessity of auxiliaries. I have no doubt that at Baltimore N York Providence & Boston additional supplies of Cloathing may promptly be procured & prepared by your Agents & it ought to be done though it should enhance the expence. Tis terrible at this juncture that there should be wants any where.

So of Tents—Calls for them are repeated from Massachusettes where better and cheaper than any where else they can certainly be provided.[1]

Pray take a resolution adequate to the exigency & rescue the credit of your Department.

Yrs. Affecly   A H

J McHenry Es

ALS, Mr. Pierce Gaines, Fairfield, Connecticut; ALS (photostat), James Mc-Henry Papers, Library of Congress; copy, in the handwriting of Ethan Brown, Hamilton Papers, Library of Congress.
1. On May 24 and June 4, 1799, Richard Hunewell informed H that his troops had no tents (letters listed in the appendix to this volume).

To James McHenry

New York, July 11, 1799. Quotes from Lieutenant Colonel Thomas Parker's "letter of the 3d Inst." concerning the shortage of clothing and states: "You see how the delay works & how necessary it is to apply an instant remedy."

Copy, in the handwriting of Ethan Brown, Hamilton Papers, Library of Congress.

To Nathan Rice

N. York July 11th. 1799

Sir

Agreably to your own ideas communicated in your letter of the 23. Ulto. you will consider Somerset as established for your regimental Rendezvous. I urge constantly the completion of the appointment of Officers. I am not sure whether a competent number of proper candidates are as yet before the Secy. of War. If not it is to be wished other fit characters may be presented.

With great considr. &c

Col Rice

Copy, in the handwriting of Ethan Brown, Hamilton Papers, Library of Congress.

From Jonathan Williams

Perth Amboy [New Jersey] July 11 1799

Dear sir

As your favour of the 20th June did not require an immediate reply, I have defered it till I could send the enclosed sheets of my translation: [1] The tables are not yet all printed, but if the plates could be ready, the whole might appear in a fortnight.

The Essay on military fireworks, which does not require plates, will soon be published in a separate Pamphlet.

Nothing could be more gratifying to me, than the kind sentiments with which you close your Letter, although the object hinted it is still in suspense from a cause that would very much wound my feelings, if my conscience did not inform me that I deserve, and must obtain a compleat triumph. You, Sir, are no stranger to such sensations. You have heard the hissings of Calumny and have indignantly crushed the Viper. To your inspection, therefore, should

I be happy to unfold the Conduct of my whole life, and expose all its motives; and were it not for the fear of trespassing upon your patience, I would request you to peruse the Papers I have lately submitted to the secretary of War.[2]

My family being here with a view to pass the summer, I shall remain untill I am ordered by the secretary of War, to enter on the duties that may be assigned me. I understand that the office of Purveyor is to be divided into military & maritime, the former of which divisions would be most agreeable to me for many reasons, of which the Opportunity I should have of receiving orders from you is, to my mind, among the greatest.

With perfect Respect and real Esteem   I have the honor to be Sir   Your obliged & most obedient Servant   Jonn. Williams

Inclosed are some crude conjectures in pursuance of the Idea you communicated when I last had the honor of seeing you.

Major General Hamilton

ALS, Hamilton Papers, Library of Congress.
    1. See Williams to H, June 17, 1799, note 2.
    2. See McHenry to H, first letter of June 15, July 20, 1799.

To James M. Hughes [1]

[New York, July 12, 1799]

D Sir

Let me know whether you have received the money from Astor. Having informed Mr L [2] that the affair was arranged, I am in momentary expectation of his drawing upon me which makes me anxious to have the business closed.

Yrs. truly   A H

July 12th.

ALS, MS Division, New York Public Library.
    1. Hughes was one of the masters of the New York Court of Chancery.
    This is a reference to the case of *William Laight, John Jacob Astor, and Peter Smith, Appellants, against John Morgan, (who was impleaded with Jona-*

than Danforth, and thirty-three others,) Respondent. The suit concerned eighteen thousand acres in Albany County that George III had granted to Michael Byrn and seventeen others in 1768, and twenty-five thousand acres in the same county that the king granted two years later to Sir William Johnson and twenty-five others. In 1770 the patentees deeded their interests in both tracts to Johnson because he had paid all the expenses involved in securing the patents. The appellants had received their title to the two tracts from the executors of Johnson's estate. During the American Revolution Johnson's papers were damaged, and the defendants, who had settled on the tracts to which Johnson then held title, claimed title to part of the land (William Johnson, *Reports of Cases Adjudged in the Supreme Court of Judicature of the State of New York, From January Term 1799, to January Term 1803, both inclusive: Together with Cases Determined in the Court for the Correction of Errors, During That Period* [New York, 1846], 429–30). On December 18, 1797, the Court of Chancery dismissed the bill of complaint (MS Minutes, New York Court of Chancery, 1793–1797 [Hall of Records, New York City]). In February, 1799, the Court of Errors reversed the decision of the Chancery Court (Johnson, *Reports,* 429–35).

2. Brockholst Livingston was one of the attorneys for the complainants.

To James McHenry

New York July 12, 1799

Sir

The contracts which have been made for the supply of the troops on the sea board have contemplated a small scale of issues, where to be worth the undertaking, the price must be high. Accordingly in most of the States the price is much greater than it ought to be. It has occurred to me as possible to reduce it.

It is in the option of the Government to station its troops where it will. It is not very material while unemployed whether a station be on the North or on the South of a line which divides two states, as at *Uxbrige* in Massachusetts or *Gloucester* in Rhode Island or *Norwich* in Connecticut—at East Chester in New York Brunswick or Trenton in New Jersey—the North or the South side of the Potomack &c.

On this basis it may be made known to the several Contractors in States in the vicinity of the contemplated stations that it is the intention to assemble as soon as may be at one point *three* Regiments [1]—That for the present it is thought indifferent where the precise point may be within a certain extent to be in each case defined—That the election would be materially influenced by the cheapness of the Rations—that the Contracts heretofore had been predicated upon a different view of the force to be supplied—that consequently it has been judged expedient to invite a competition upon this basis of the concentration of a considerable body at one point—and that eventually the disposition of the force would be in a great degree regulated by the result of the Offers which should be made toward forming new Contracts. This accordingly would be to be done.

And I shall be much disappointed if the experiment does not produce a great saving. Should you approve the idea no time is to be lost in giving it effect in order that early measures may be taken for Winter Quarters.

In your proposals for future contracts will it not be adviseable to invite offers upon different alternatives? 1. the supply of all the troops except those composing the Western army. 2 the supply of all the troops within any one of three great Districts. Georgia South & North Carolina & Virginia forming one—Maryland Pensylvania Delaware New Jersey & New York forming another—The four Eastern states & Vermont forming a third. 3 The supply of the troops within any one of five great districts Georgia South & N Carolina forming one Virginia & Maryland another Pensylvania Delaware & New Jersey a third New York Connecticut & Vermont a fourth Rhode Island Massachusettes & New Hampshire a fifth. Lastly the supply of the troops within each state.

I think it very likely that the combinations of Individual Interest on this plan would enable you to make a much better bargain than upon any other. Tis certain the Government pays much too dear now for its supplies of provisions.

With great respect   I have the honor to be   Sir   Yr Obed ser

The Secy of War

ADf, Hamilton Papers, Library of Congress.
    1. This is a reference to the plan to concentrate the regiments in winter quarters. See H's draft of George Washington to McHenry, first letter of December 13, 1798; McHenry to H, February 4, 1799.

From Charles Cotesworth Pinckney

Charleston [South Carolina] July 12, 1799. ". . . I have found many officers in my division very fond of throwing off their uniform & appearing in frocks. I have directed them always to wear their uniforms; we discussed, & I think agreed on the propriety of that measure at Philadelphia,[1] but I do not see it in the regulations. I wish some general rule was made on the subject, and particularly that the same system in every respect should be adhered to in my division which you establish in yours. Our artillery Corps here are very thin, I will be obliged to you to give them directions to recruit."

ALS, Hamilton Papers, Library of Congress.
    1. This question was discussed at the conferences which H, George Washington, Pinckney, and James McHenry held in Philadelphia in November and December, 1798. See "Queries propounded by the Commander in Chief to Majors Genl. Hamilton & Pinckney," November 10, 1798, printed as the second enclosure to Washington to H, November 12, 1798.

From Louis Le Guen [1]

Morris Ville [Pennsylvania] 13. Juillet 1799.

Cher Général

J'ai Eu L'honneur de vous Ecrire,[2] Et plus depuis faire prïer par Mr. Stoughton,[3] de M'envoyer Les Observations de Monsieur Tilghman,[4] Les reponsès de Mrs. fitzimon [5] Et Morris,[6] et Votre Avis Sur Ce que Jaurait à faire. Voilla, cher Géneral, 19-Jours que Je les attand, pour me rendre a philadelphia. Jatribue Ce retard a vos fortes Occupations, et Néamoins Vous Suplie de me renvoyer Ses papiers et Vos Observations, pour de Suitte Me rendre a philadelphia.

Veuillés bien San retard avoir Eguard à ma Priere.

Jay L'honneu D'Estre Bien Sincerment   Votre tres Obet. Serviteur
                                                    L. Le Guen

Alexander Hamilton Esqr:

ALS, Hamilton Papers, Library of Congress.

1. Although it cannot be stated with certainty, it seems likely that this letter reflects the concern of Le Guen, a New York City merchant, over the effect of his status as an alien on the ownership of land in the United States, for he was both a French citizen and the owner of property in Morrisville, Bucks County, Pennsylvania. In any event, before the letter printed above had been written, he had applied for citizenship, and on June 18, 1799, the United States District Court for the District of New York ruled: ". . . And the Court nevertheless entertaining a doubt whether the said Louis Le Guen can be admitted to become a Citizen of the United States by reason of the proviso to the first section of the act entitled 'An Act supplementary to and to amend the act entitled "An act to establish an uniform Rule of Naturalization and to repeal the act heretofore passed on that subject."' For that in the said section of the said Act it is declared 'that no alien who shall be a native, Citizen, Denizen or subject of any Nation or State with whom the united States shall be at War at the time of his Application shall be then admitted to become a Citizen of the United States.' And the Court therefore not thinking fit to proceed farther in the naturalization of the said Louis Le Guen unless by the Direction of some Competent Superior Tribunal" (RG 21, Minutes of the United States District Court for the Southern District of New York, 1789–1801, National Archives). For the texts of the relevant statutes, see "An Act supplementary to and to amend the act, intituled 'An act to establish an uniform rule of naturalization; and to repeal the act heretofore passed on that subject'" (1 Stat. 566–69 [June 18, 1798]); "An Act to establish an uniform rule of Naturalization; and to repeal the act heretofore passed on that subject" (1 Stat. 414–15 [January 29, 1795]); and "An Act to establish an uniform Rule of Naturalization" (1 Stat. 103–04 [March 26, 1790]).

The refusal of the Court to grant Le Guen citizenship created a possible threat to his right to own land in Pennsylvania. From 1789 to 1797, Pennsylvania had placed no restrictions on alien ownership of land, except in times of war. For the appropriate statutes, see Tench Coxe to H, May 10, 1795, note 3. Then, in 1797, the state legislature allowed the existing statute to expire. Although legislation enacted on April 11, 1799, recognized all existing contracts, patents, or deeds of conveyance involving aliens, Section 1 of this act provided for the following restriction on all future purchases: "That any foreigner or foreigners, alien or aliens, shall previously to such purchase or purchases, declare his or their intention to become a citizen or citizens, agreeably to the act of Congress, entituled 'An Act supplementary to and to amend the act, entituled An Act to establish an uniform rule of naturalization, and to repeal the act heretofore passed on the subject,' passed the eighteenth day of June, one thousand seven hundred and ninety-eight" ("An Act to enable aliens, in certain cases, to purchase and hold real estate in this commonwealth" [Pennsylvania Laws, 1798–1799 Sess., Ch. CCXXII]).

Le Guen may have been going to Philadelphia in July, 1799, to apply for citizenship in the United States Courts in Pennsylvania or to secure his title to his property in Morrisville. No evidence has been found that Le Guen ever received citizenship, but he did retain his land until his death. On May 11, 1835, his heirs, Louisa, Emily, and Josephine Le Guen, sold more than fourteen acres in Morrisville through their attorney, George W. Richards, to Joseph Wood of Trenton, New Jersey, for two thousand dollars (copy of the deed, Bucks County Historical Society Library, Doylestown, Pennsylvania). H was involved in these matters because he was Le Guen's legal adviser.

2. Letter not found.

3. Thomas Stoughton was a New York City merchant. For his role in Le Guen's protracted dispute with Isaac Gouverneur and Peter Kemble, see Goebel, Law Practice, II, 77, note 126.

4. Either Edward or William Tilghman, both of whom were Philadelphia lawyers. For William Tilghman's opinion on the cases involving Le Guen, Gouverneur, and Kemble, see Gouverneur to H, January 7, 1798, and Goebel, *Law Practice*, II, 74–75.

5. Thomas FitzSimons, a native of Ireland, was a Philadelphia merchant. He was a Federalist member of the House of Representatives from 1789 to 1795.

6. Either Robert Morris or Gouverneur Morris. Robert Morris, the financier, had owned land in Morrisville, but in 1799 he was in debtors' prison. If Le Guen's property in Morrisville was part of Morris's original holdings, then the financier may have been helping Le Guen secure his title to the land. Gouverneur Morris had remained in Europe for four years after James Monroe had succeeded him in 1794 as United States Minister Plenipotentiary to France. He arrived in New York on December 23, 1798. Le Guen may have requested Gouverneur Morris's assistance in securing acceptance of his application for citizenship, as Morris had helped other foreigners with their applications in 1799 (Anne Cary Morris, ed., *The Diary and Letters of Gouverneur Morris, Minister of the United States to France; Member of the Constitutional Convention, etc.* [New York, 1888], II, 377, 378).

From Aaron Ogden [1]

Elizabeth Town [New Jersey] July 13. 1799

Sir.

Mr. Thomas Y How in answer to my enquiry whether a second Lieutenancy, in the 11th regiment, in addition to his appointment, as Secretary to the Inspector General, would suit his ideas, says, "As the measure has been proposed by General Hamilton, he will accept with pleasure."

I have the honor to be   with the most perfect respect   your mo: ob. servt   Aaron Ogden

Major General Alexander Hamilton.

ALS, Hamilton Papers, Library of Congress.
   1. For background to this letter, see H to Thomas Y. How, July 3, 1799; H to Ogden, July 3, 1799.

From Rufus King

London July 15, 1799

Dear sir

The french still maintain themselves in switzerland tho' unless soon and strongly reinforced they will be driven out of it. The success of the Allies has been almost uninterupted in Italy, from whence according to present appearances the Enemy must be in a short time be totally expelled. Thus far the Coalition has performed Prodigies—but the confederates are not without mutual Jealousies, which will increase with their success, and which already has had the Effect of preventing an agreement upon a precise and ultimate object. Between Eng. and Russia the greatest union and confidence exist, and these Powers do not disagree in what ought to be the End to be aimed at and avowed. An uncommon coldness and even more than coldness exists between Austria & England, and between the former & Russia there is less cordiality than could be wished, & expected. The issue of the campaign for these Reasons is less certain than it would be, were the Allies heartily & disinterestdly engaged in the only species of war that can give Peace and security to the different nations of Europe.

It is extremely difficult yet to understand the late changes at Paris; [1] there are Persons who see in them the death Blow of french Republicanism, I doubt very much this Opinion, & am inclined to consider the last in the same light as I have done the former Revolutions. I did expect that the changes wd. be followed by measures of more Energy than have been adopted. There seems to be no reason, to suppose that we are likely to be benefited by the Revolution; Seiyes opinions concerning America are no secret, and they give us no room to expect a Treatment different from that we have so long and so patiently endured. [2]

The inclosure relates to a subject that I cease to write or talk of, for reasons that you will be at no loss to conjecture. [3]

Adieu

K.

ALS, Hamilton Papers, Library of Congress.

1. This is a reference to the *coup d'état* of June 18, 1799. On June 29, 1799, *The* [London] *Times* reported: "Late last night we received complete sets of PARIS Journals to the 23d inst. *inclusive,* which confirm the reports that have been for some days past in circulation respecting the accusation and dismissal of three of the Members of the Executive Directory, and the impeachment of [Barthélemy Louis Joseph] SCHERER. These accusations originated in the Council of Five Hundred, where the debates have been conducted with a boldness of expression that has not been remarked since the period which preceded the expulsion of the Deputies in September 1797, and their deportation to *Cayenne.* . . .

"The following are the names of the new Directors:

"[Louis Antoine] GOHIER is chosen Director in the room of [Jean Baptiste, compte] TREILHARD; [Pierre] Roger DUCOS in the room of [Philippe Antoine] MERLIN [of Douai]; and General [Jean François] MOULINS, (commanding *per interim* the Army of England!!!) in the room of [Louis Marie La] REVEILLERE LEPAUX. [Emmanuel Joseph] SYEYES is chosen President of the Directory."

2. On July 15, 1799, King wrote to Timothy Pickering: "I find very little in the late french Papers respecting America, nor do I hear any thing from Paris concerning the opinion of the new government. Perhaps nothing can be inferred from the silence that seems to be observed upon our affairs. . . ." In the same letter he stated: ". . . but not a word in reference to America has escaped any member of either of the Councils." He concluded his discussion of France with the statement: "One of the last french papers states as an article of intelligence, that all the Commissions granted to American Consuls in the different french Ports were repealed—but I am uncertain whether this paragraph inaccurately refers to the act of our own government, or announces the withdrawal of the Exequaturs of our Consuls, by the Directory" (LS, RG 59, Despatches from United States Ministers to Great Britain, 1791–1906, Vol. 8, January 3, 1799–December 18, 1800, National Archives).

3. Enclosure not found. This is, however, a reference to plans for the independence of the Spanish-American colonies. See Francisco de Miranda to H, April 1, 1797, February 7, April 6–June 7, August 17, October 19–November 10, 1798; H to Miranda, August 22, 1798; King to H, May 12, July 31, October 20, 1798, January 21, March 4, 9, 1799; H to King, August 22, 1798; Timothy Pickering to H, August 21–22, 1798.

From Philip Schuyler

Albany, July 15, 1799. Acknowledges Hamilton's letter of "the 9th Instant." [1] Lists the amounts of fuel and other supplies "for which a compensation, in money was allowed, to the British troops, in the barracks, and when quartered on the Inhabitants in this city, Schenectady, and the vicinity." Recommends Joseph Herkimer and Jacob Mancius [2] as subalterns.

ALS, Hamilton Papers, Library of Congress.
1. Letter not found. See James McHenry to H, first letter of June 24, 1799.
2. Herkimer and Mancius were appointed second lieutenants in the Twelfth Regiment of Infantry on September 13, 1799. Their names were submitted for confirmation on April 1, 1800, and confirmed on May 14, 1800 (*Executive Journal*, I, 345, 355).

From James McHenry

War Department 16th. July 1799

Sir

I received this morning your letter of the 12th July instant on the subject of a modification of the invitations to supply rations for the troops of the United States on the Sea board.

You will recollect that the advertisement, calling for proposals for the year 1799, is dated the 21st March ulto., and that the time within which proposals may be received is limited to the 25th July instant.[1] Altho' I could have wished for your ideas sooner, it may not be too late to make some use of them. I shall attempt it. You will also by adverting to the copies of the Contracts with which you have been furnished[2] for the supplies for the Troops, and my letter of instructions[3] upon which these have or ought to have been founded, perceive, that the object you have in view for the ensuing year, has been substantially effected for the present year, in the articles which provide for a diminution of the price of the ration, as the issues at any one place shall be encreased.

There is nothing, you will also see, to prevent one or more persons from offering to supply for the whole troops within the United States, or the troops in any combination of the States.

Whatever may be the result of this measure I shall take respecting this subject, with those who have sent or may yet send in proposals before the 26th July, it need not delay any arrangements, which you contemplate, or any orders it may be necessary for me to issue relative to the Winter Quarters of the Troops especially as nothing has occured to me to induce an opinion that any change ought to be made in the places fixed on in my letter of instructions.

Should more eligible places have occured to you, I shall be obliged to you to mention them.

An answer to your letter of the 6th inst. is still delayed for want of a return which I expect from the Q M Genl.

I have the honor to be   Sir, your obedient Servant

James McHenry

Major General Alexander Hamilton

LS, Hamilton Papers, Library of Congress.

1. McHenry's advertisement, which is dated March 21, 1799, reads in part: "*Notice is hereby given,* that separate proposals will be received at the office of the Secretary of the Department of War, until the expiration of the 25th of July next ensuing, for the supply of all rations, which may be required for the use of the United States from the first day of October, 1799, to the thirtieth day of September, 1800, both days inclusive, at the places and within the two districts herein after first mentioned; and also the separate proposals will be received at the said office upon the expiration of the 25th day of July next ensuing for the supply of all rations which may be required as aforesaid, from the first day of January in the year 1800, to the thirty-first day of December in the same year, both days inclusive, at the place and within the several states herein after mentioned, viz . . . The Ration to be supplied, is to consist of the following articles, viz. eighteen ounces of bread or flour, or when neither can be obtained, of one quart of rice, or one and a half pound of sifted or boulted indian meal, one pound and a quarter of fresh beef, or one pound of salted beef, or three quarters of a pound of salted pork, and when fresh meat is issued salt at the rate of two quarts for every hundred rations, soap at the rate of four pounds, and candles at the rate of a pound and a half for every hundred rations.

"It is expected the proposals will also extend to the supply of rice, whiskey, or other ardent spirits at the rate of half a gill per ration, and Vinegar at the rate of two quarts for every hundred rations. The proposals will specify the price of the several component parts of the ration, as well as those of substitutes or alternatives for parts thereof.

"The rations are to be furnished in such quantities that there shall at all times, during the term of the proposed contracts, be sufficient for the consumption of the troops at Michilimackinac, Detroit, Niagara and Oswego for six months in advances, and at each of the other posts on the western waters, for at least three months in advance of good and wholesome provisions, if the same shall be required. It is also to be permitted to all and every of the commandants of fortified places, or posts, to call for at seasons when the same can be transported or at any time in case of urgency, such supplies of like provisions in advance, as in the discretion of the commandant shall be deemed proper. It is to be understood that the contractor is to be at the expence and risk of issuing the supplies to the troops, and that all losses sustained by the depredations of an enemy, or by means of the troops of the United States, shall be paid for at the price of the article captured or destroyed, on the depositions of two or more persons of creditable character, and the certificate of a commissioned officer, ascertaining the circumstances of the loss, and the amount of the articles, for which compensation shall be claimed.

"The privilege is to be understood to be referred to the United States of requiring that none of the supplies which may be furnished under any of the proposed contracts shall be issued, until the supplies which have or may be furnished under contracts now in force have been consumed, and that a supply in advance may be always required at any of the fixed posts on the Sea board or Indian frontiers not exceeding three months." ([Philadelphia] *Gazette of the United States,* March 29, 30, April 1, 1799.)

2. See McHenry to H, first letter of July 2, 1799.
3. See McHenry to H, February 4, 1799.

From Richard Kidder Meade [1]

Frederick [Virginia] July 16, 1799. Recommends Edmund Taylor [2] as a brigade inspector and adds: ". . . I have often delighted myself with the pleasing idea of seeing you before our long farewell, & it now appears as if we were approaching each other—the nature of your office may lead you here, but if not into this Valley, a few score miles will be no bar to my carrying my heart & hand to you. I am engaged in the harvesting business my friend and will only add that you may be assured that I am yours with the purest regard esteem & affection. How does your Wife & Family? Present my love to them all & tell them they are often in my mind. My Wife adds hers. I wish I could say her health was good. The six children with us enjoy a large share. Our eldest Daughter is married [3] & settled in the neighbourhood. I hope well married, the present prospect furnishes bliss, he is a good man of a good family with a good Virginia estate."

ALS, Hamilton Papers, Library of Congress.
  1. Meade and H had become friends when each served as an aide-de-camp to George Washington during the American Revolution. After the war Meade purchased and operated a thousand-acre farm in Frederick County, Virginia.
  2. Taylor was a captain in the Eighth Regiment of Infantry.
  3. Ann Randolph Meade married Matthew Page of Clark County, Virginia.

From Thomas Morris [1]

Albany, July 16, 1799. "I am compelled by the impossibility of converting landed property into cash to make an offer to my Creditors [2] of all my property and to seek from them a discharge of my debts. I need not enter into a detail of the Circumstances that have led me into this unpleasant Situation. suffice it to say that I was seized with the Mania of the times and have incurred debts in the purchase of property which is at the present Moment perfectly unsaleable. . . . My first object at present is to get a discharge from my debts without taking the benefit of the Insolvent Act.[3] If in this

Attempt I should fail, however painful the Step may be I shall be compelled to resort to the other. . . ."

ALS, Hamilton Papers, Library of Congress.

1. Morris, the son of Robert Morris, had been his father's principal agent and representative in the Genesee country in western New York. See the introductory note to H to Robert Morris, March 18, 1795. Thomas Morris practiced law in Canandaigua, New York, and was a member of the New York Assembly from 1794 to 1796.

2. Morris's creditors included Richard Harison, a New York City attorney; Peter R. Livingston, the brother-in-law of Chancellor Robert R. Livingston; Charles Williamson, the agent of the Pulteney Associates in the Genesee country; and Oliver Phelps, a member of the Massachusetts Assembly and Senate, who owned land in the Genesee country. See the introductory note to H to Robert Morris, March 18, 1795, note 29.

3. "An Act to amend the Act entitled an Act for the relief of Debtors with respect to the Imprisonment of their Persons" (*New York Laws*, 22nd Sess., Ch. LXXXV [April 2, 1799]).

From John F. Hamtramck

Detroit [*Territory Northwest of the River Ohio*] *July 17* [*–18*], *1799.* "On the 7 Inst I left Fort Wayne, and on the 14 in the evening arrived at this place. . . . Not finding an opportunity of Sailing immediately for Michelemakinac as I had the honour of informing you in my letter of the 1st. and the uncertainty of returning in time to execute any Command you might charge me with, I have concluded that, after having examined in to the State of this Garrison, to repair to Pittsburg, its proximity to New York, and the Posts on the lakes, with the facility of Communicating with those on the Mississippi and others; renders that post the most eligible for me to be Stationary at during the Summer. . . ."

ALS, Hamilton Papers, Library of Congress; LS, marked "Duplicate," Hamilton Papers, Library of Congress.

To James McHenry [1]

New York, July 17, 1799. "Power has been given to the Inspector General to appoint a Secretary.[2] For some time I have employed in this Capacity a person, who is a mere copyist,[3] with an allowance less than the law authorises to be given to the Secretary. But I have now appointed as permanent Secretary, Thomas Y How of Trenton in New Jersey. The Kind of person required for this station, and who has actually been obtained, is such, that a Captain's emoluments afford a very inadequate compensation. Hence I am led to request for Mr. Howe the appointment of second Lieutenant in the *Eleventh* Regiment, a circumstance which will be perfectly agreeable to its Commandant. . . ."

Df, Hamilton Papers, Library of Congress.

1. For background to this letter, see H to Thomas Y. How, July 3, 1799; H to Aaron Ogden, July 3, 1799; Ogden to H, July 13, 1799.
2. See Section 26 of "An Act for the better organizing of the Troops of the United States; and for other purposes" (1 *Stat.* 755 [March 3, 1799]).
3. Ethan Brown.

To James McHenry

[New York, July 17, 1799]

My Dear Sir

I perceive by your letter of the 16th. that mine of the 12th has not been rightly understood. Its principal object was the supply of the present year. This it aimed at cheapening by exciting a competition among the *actual Contractors*, on the ground that the troops, while not required for actual service, might be stationed collectively where the supply was cheapest, as at Brunswick *or* Trenton in New Jersey, or East Chester or New York or Bristol in Pensylvania, it being immaterial whether *three* Regiments are at one or the other of those places and the Government having its option to station them at either. Thus the Contractors in Pensylvania New Jersey & New York might be induced to bid against each other. So the Contractors in Maryland & Virginia it being indifferent whither the three Regiments shall be on one or the other side of the Potowmack.

In Massachusettes the ration is Eleven Cents & five Mills. This is reasonable & shews how it may be afforded. In the state of Rhode Island it is fourteen Cents. No reason for this difference. In Connecticut it is still higher with still less reason. The three Regiments for the Northern Quarter will of course be stationed in Massachusettes in the vicinity of Uxbrige.[1]

The Price in New York when issues exceed 400 is 16 cents & 5 Milles. This is much too high though predicated on the old ration. At Brunswick in Jersey, it is 16 Cents & 2½ Milles predicated on the New Ration. This is higher still. At Trenton it is 16. This is still too high. But the difference ought in my opinion to give a preference to Trenton over Brunswick. I think however upon my plan a reduction may be obtained at both places. And tis by care in operations of this kind that œconomy on a large scale will be attained.

I hope I have now explained my self sufficiently. If your views vary in consequence of the explanation you will inform me officially —if not privately. And I shall govern my self accordingly. It was my intention to have written my self to the Contractors respecting Winter Quarters after having settled with you the General Principles. But if you think proper to do it yourself it will be equally agreeable to me. But I shall be glad previously to know your intention & submit to you some ideas.

Yrs. Affecly.   A Hamilton

P.S My suggestions as to the Contract for next year were merely incidental. I had not seen your advertisement [2] as I recollect.

Js. McHenry Esq

ALS, Montague Collection, MS Division, New York Public Library; ALS (photostat), James McHenry Papers, Library of Congress; copy, in the handwriting of Ethan Brown, Hamilton Papers, Library of Congress.
1. Uxbridge had been recommended as the site for the permanent camp for two regiments in H's draft of George Washington to McHenry, first letter of December 13, 1798. H's official instructions had repeated this recommendation. See McHenry to H, February 4, 1799.
2. See McHenry to H, July 16, 1799, note 1.

From Thomas Parker

Winchester [Virginia] July 17, 1799. ". . . A partial Supply of Cloathing has at last arrived. . . . I Cannot help however Complaining of the Waistcoats that have been sent on one part of which—I mean the Backs—is absolutely Composed of Indifferent negro Cotton which is peculiarly disgusting to the Soldiery in this part of the Country. . . ."

ALS, Hamilton Papers, Library of Congress.

From Thomas Y. How

Trenton July 18th 1799

Since the receipt of your letter of the 3rd inst., which did not come into my hands untill the 11th, I have been making the necessary preparations. I have now the honor to inform you that I am in readiness, and wait your orders.

With the highest respect   I am yr. obt. servant   Thos: Y: How

ALS, Hamilton Papers, Library of Congress.

From Benjamin Stoddert

Navy Dept. 19 July 1799.

Dr sir

I have directed the commanding officer of the Constellation, to conform strictly to the health regulations of the City.[1] I shall deem it unpardonable conduct if he has not already done so.

I very much fear, that Talbot after all, will not go out in the Constitution—or if he Should, that Truxton will quit the Service.[2] This avarice of rank, in the infancy of our Service, is the Devil. What think you of an early introduction of this principle in the Navy Service—I presume not to meddle with the land—that the Prest may appoint if he pleases, a Lt. to command the oldest Captains on any particular enterprize? I ask not this in levity, but for your serious opinion. I have thought for sometime, of getting Truxton, & some other Capts. of more understanding, to go on a cruise under the command of a younger officer. Something like this, or the

British practice of laying by indifferent men on half pay, must be adopted—or the best concerted plans will be ruined in the execution.

I have the honor to be   with very great esteem D sir   Yr most Obed Sevt   Ben Stoddert

ALS, Hamilton Papers, Library of Congress; LC, RG 45, Naval Records Collection of the Office of Naval Records and Library, Miscellaneous Letters Sent by the Secretary of the Navy, National Archives.

1. On July 19, 1799, Stoddert wrote to *"The Officer Commanding* the Frigate *Constellation* in the absence of Captain [Thomas] Truxton" that he had received from New York a letter "of which the following is an Extract": "Our Health Physician represented to me that an infectious disease brought from the West Indies has existed and still exists on board the Frigate *Constellation*—that the Lieut. who commands in the absence of Captain Truxton disregards all the Quarantine Laws and keeps open a free communication with his Vessel, thereby exposing the health of the Citizens. He is a man of warm temper & may colour strongly but his statement is probably not without foundation. The intention is not that this go to you as Complaint but as ground of some Instructions to the Commander to acquiesce in the Necessary precautions" (*Naval Documents, Quasi-War, April 1799–July, 1799,* 515–16).

2. For an explanation of the contents of this sentence and the remainder of this paragraph, see Silas Talbot to H, January 15, May 13, 1799; Stoddert to H, February 6, May 3, 1799.

General Orders [1]

New York, July 20th. 1799.

The general court martial of which Major Willcock [2] was president, having convicted Joseph Perkins, a private soldier of the 1st regiment of artillerists and engineers of the crime of desertion, aggravated by that of liberating and taking off with him two prisoners confined under the sentence of a court martial for desertion, over whom he was sentinel, and having condemned him to suffer death: The President of the United States, in pursuance of the authority vested in him, and considering the flagrancy and complication of the crime of the said Joseph Perkins, and not only the beneficial influence, but the absolute necessity of well placed examples in military service, has thought fit by warrant under his hand and the seal of the War Office, to order and direct that the said sentence shall be put into execution.

Accordingly Major General Hamilton appoints wednesday the 24th Inst. between the hours of eight and ten in the forenoon for the execution of said sentence at Fort Jay, at which time and place the said Joseph Perkins is to be shot to death.

The Reverend Mr Mason [3] will visit the prisoner in his confinement. The garrison under arms will be present at the execution. Major Hoops [4] will make the necessary arrangements.

Examples of capital punishment in the army of the United States are as rare as they are painful. It were to be wished that the crime for which it is now to be inflicted, was equally rare; a crime which disgraces the offender by the double character of perfidy and cowardice; abandoned must the man be who takes the rewards of his country, pledges himself by oath to its service, and meanly deserts its defence amidst prospects of foreign dangers. May the character of the American soldiery cease to be stained by examples of such baseness; but, if a sense of faith and duty, under a mild treatment, shall continue insufficient to restrain from the commission of a crime so pernicious, the severity of punishment must do it; while the past forbearance of the President demonstrates his reluctance to exert capital punishment, his decision in the present case ought to be received by the Army, as a full proof of his firm determination, to repress, by adequate means, offences destructive to the service.

Abraham R. Ellery
Assistant Adjutant General.

LC, RG 98, Post-Revolutionary War Commands, Castle Island Records, National Archives.

1. For background to this document, see H to James McHenry, July 3, 1799.
2. William Willcocks.
3. The Reverend John M. Mason was the minister of the Scotch (Associate Reformed) Presbyterian Church in New York City.
4. Adam Hoops.

From James McHenry

Philadelphia, July 20, 1799. "Mr Jonathan Williams the gentleman I had intended for an assistant to Mr. Francis [1] has suggested to me that he would be glad you should read certain papers explanatory of his conduct in a transaction relative to his Father in law Mr Alexander,[2] which Mr Francis, on a representation by Mr Morris

had viewed in a criminal light, and objected to the proposed association on that account. The inclosed papers [3] are those alluded to with
my letter which accompanied them. From the vague manner Mr.
Francis expressed himself when he returned them, neither wholly
acquitting nor blaming him I do not think the appointment can take
place with his consent. Can I make it without his consent? Your
regulations for supplying the army [4] contemplates assistants to the
Purveyor and as Mr Francis is also Purveyor for the Navy Department can I give him an assistant without the concurrence of the
Secry. of the Navy? These questions require some attention. I proposed to the Secy. of the Navy a joint letter to Mr. Francis on the
subject of his resigning absolutely the office. . . . So the matter
rests at present. Nothing is suffering in the mean time. . . ." [5]

ADfS, James McHenry Papers, Library of Congress.
    1. See McHenry to H, first letter of June 15, 1799.
    2. William Alexander was the son of an Edinburgh, Scotland, banker. He
lived in Saint-Germain, France, until 1783, when he moved to Virginia.
    Throughout the seventeen-eighties, Alexander and Robert Morris were in-
volved in several schemes to monopolize the tobacco trade between the United
States and France. In September, 1783, Alexander and Williams contracted to
supply the French Farmers-General with fifteen thousand hogsheads of tobacco
from the United States annually for three years at thirty livres tournois per
quintal. Williams, who at that time was living at Nantes, managed the business
in France, while Alexander went to Virginia to purchase the tobacco. Because
of a shortage of funds and in an effort to establish their credit, they secretly
offered Morris a one-third interest in the contract.
    Because Alexander had been unable to live up to the terms of the contract,
Morris was able to secure a new agreement with the Farmers-General early in
1785. Under the terms of this new contract, Morris supplied twenty thousand
hogsheads of United States tobacco annually for three years at thirty-six livres
tournois per quintal. In July, 1786, Alexander, originally Morris's silent partner,
decided to accept a commission on each hogshead instead of a share of the
business.
    The tobacco monopoly met with so much opposition from French and
American merchants that the Farmers-General and members of the French
government met at Berni and on May 24, 1786, modified their plans. Although
the terms of Morris's contract would be fulfilled, the Farmers-General agreed
to purchase an additional twelve thousand to fifteen thousand hogsheads of tobacco annually from other merchants in the United States.
    Because of problems concerning the quality of tobacco Morris provided and
the failure of London banking houses to honor his drafts, he faced financial
difficulties when his tobacco contract ended late in 1787. Alexander, on the
other hand, had profited from their partnership, for he had purchased public
securities with the funds Morris had advanced for the purchase of tobacco. In
July, 1787, he owed Morris more than fifty-four thousand pounds, Virginia
currency, which Morris had provided for advances to subagents and individual
merchants. After Morris and Alexander dissolved their business connections in
1787, both men brought suit in the Virginia Court of Chancery in an effort to
settle their accounts. In 1800 the Court decided in Morris's favor.

During the legal controversy Williams served as a mediator between Alexander and John T. Griffin, a Virginia merchant. Alexander had advanced money to Griffin on his tobacco contract, and Griffin pledged bonds and other certificates as security. When Griffin failed to meet his payments, he sold his title to these securities to Morris, who tried to collect from Alexander.

For information on the tobacco trade, see Jacob M. Price, *France and the Chesapeake: A History of the French Tobacco Monopoly, 1674–1791, and of Its Relationship to the British and American Tobacco Trades*, II (Ann Arbor, 1973). See also the undated opinion of the Court of Chancery; Morris's undated answer to the bill of complaint filed against him and Griffin in Chancery by Alexander and his company; Morris's answers in Chancery to Alexander's bills of complaint, October 8, 1789, June 15, 1796, June 4, 1798; affidavits of Griffin, June 2, 1791, January 16, 1792 (Arents Tobacco Collection, New York Public Library).

3. On July 3, 1799, McHenry wrote to Tench Francis, purveyor of public supplies: "I communicated to Mr Jonathan Williams, the Gentleman I informed you I contemplated with the approbation of the Secretary of the Navy [Benjamin Stoddert], as a suitable Character for the appointment of assistant purveyor, the unfavourable allegations you intimated to me against his Character, founded on certain conduct of Mr. Williams in the Course of a legal controversy, to which Mr Robt Morris was a party.

"Mr Williams in consequence lodged in my hands the enclosed papers. I have read and attentively considered them, and must suppose that after doing the same, you will agree with me in Opinion that they refute the allegations. You will please to return the papers to me after you have perused them." (Copy, Hamilton Papers, Library of Congress.)

On August 6, 1799, McHenry wrote to Williams: "I inclose a copy of my letter dated July 3d. ulto. to Tench Francis, the Purveyor of public supplies, relative to certain allegations he had intimated to me, unfavourable to your character and communicating to him, certain papers, you had deposited in my hands, to prevent the allegations from making an undue impression on my mind.

"The opinion I therein expressed I have not for a moment doubted of. I still think that your letters, and the papers mentioned, completely refute the allegations made.

"If I should not for the present, have it in my power, to derive the facilities, in the business of my Department, I expected from your services, and abilities, in the station of an assistant Purveyor, you may be assured I shall take a sincere pleasure in recommending you, when proper, to an appointment, in which your industry, intelligence, and integrity will qualify you to render good service to your country." (ALS, James McHenry Papers, Library of Congress; copy, Hamilton Papers, Library of Congress.)

On August 8, 1799, Williams wrote to McHenry: "I have been honored with your interesting Favour of the 6 Inst.

"Nothing is so valuable to my mind as the good Opinion of respectable Characters, and nothing so detestable as the calumnious whispers of interested & designing men.

"Your conduct towards me claims my sincere and gratefull acknowledgments; you have sir, three times endeavoured to attach me to your department without my having even a knowledge of the object at the time you were taking measures to obtain it, and when you found my reputation attacked, you immediately communicated the subject yourself, and gave me the Opportunity of making an effectual defence: This was as honorable as it was friendly.

"Let me beg of you sir, to act in the same manner on any future occasions resting assured that there can be no attack I am either ashamed or afraid to meet." (Copy, in Williams's handwriting, Hamilton Papers, Library of Congress.)

4. See enclosure to H to McHenry, second letter of April 8, 1799.

5. In discussing his proposed appointment as assistant purveyor, Williams wrote to John Adams on May 18, 1800: "In the beginning of last summer he [McHenry] represented to me the advanced age of Mr Francis & the want of activity in his department, offering me (should you approve of it) the appointment of assistant purveyor & suggesting at the same time that, being once introduced as an assistant, I had a reasonable chance, in the natural course of things, to become a principal by survivorship. To this, I answered, that I was ready to perform any thing that could be acceptable to the Government. In the Secretarys mind this arrangement required only your approbation to make it conclusive; and of that I could not for a moment doubt.

"In this stage of the Business, a strange objection was raised by Mr Francis, which proceeded from a prejudice he had imbibed through the partial medium of Mr Morris, in consequence of the long legal warfare that has subsisted between him and my father in law, by which an act, to my conscience highly meritorious, was viewed with a jaundiced eye, & placed under false colours. The details of this matter would be tedious, but the Secretary of War has all the papers, and it would give me great satisfaction if this, and every wound, that has been, or may be, given to my reputation, could be probed to the bottom by your just & accurate investigation. The result of the Secretarys examination of the subject, is contained in the following extract of a Letter he wrote to me on the 6th of August last. . . .

"Thus satisfied on the score of Reputation I retired without a murmur, assuring the Secretary that I would hold myself ready to obey any orders he might give me. . . ." (ALS, Adams Family Papers, deposited in the Massachusetts Historical Society, Boston.)

From Thomas Parker

Winchester [*Virginia*] *July 20, 1799.* "One Quere in my last letter [1] you did not answer (to wit) whether an officer had permission to take his Slave into service and whether any or what Compensation would be allowed him. I observe in the Regulations for Straw & fuel; [2] *servants & Batmen* not soldiers, are mentioned But I have seen no law that allows them either pay Cloathing or provisions. You will oblige me by Enabling me to give an answer to my officers on the Subject. . . ."

ALS, Hamilton Papers, Library of Congress.

1. Parker to H, July 6, 1799. See also James McHenry to H, first letter of July 10, 1799.

2. For these regulations, see McHenry to H, first letter of June 24, 1799.

From John Adlum

Reading [Pennsylvania] July 22st. 1799

Sir

In not having an answer to my letter of the 2nd inst. I take it for granted, you aquiece in my opinion, with respect to dividing the troops at this place. I am yet of opinion it will be improper, to divide so small a force, it will make us appear little in the eyes of the disaffected part of the Country, and lose that effect, a military force ought to have.

Persons of trust of this place, say it is their opinion that if any troops are removed the whole ought, for the Democrats as they call them, will crow over them, as they express it, if too small a force was left here, and it would only have the same effect if they were all gone.

But from information I have from Easton it appears that there ought to be a force there. Capt. Faulkner [1] informs me that they prevent his recruiting, by dissuading persons from enlisting, and that a few days since they attemped to take two deserters that he had apprehended from him.

In this place we have little or no communication with the disaffected; upon meeting them they take no notice but pass us in sullen silence, and do not at all associate with the military here, neither do they attempt to disturb us, although we suspect them very much for having persuaded a number of the troops to desert.

I do not believe they are hardy enough to attempt anything. But after all I think some troops stationed at Easton, Allentown & Cootstown [2] in addition to those we have would have a very good effect in this Country, all those places as well as the intermediate Country being disaffected to our Government.

This and Northampton County is a very strong Country there are a great many passes which can easily be defended, and if it would not give the disaffected an opportunity of making an improper use of it among the people, I think it would be prudent to have a *Military Survey* made of this Country from the Delaware to the

Susquehanna for from the present disposition of the people, I have no doubt but that numbers would join the French were they to invade our Country.

I inclose you a morning report that you may see our present State and force. The principal disease among the men is the flux. Doctor Diemer [3] of this place attends the Sick.

I am With great respect   Your most Obedt. Hble. Servt.

John Adlum

ALS, Hamilton Papers, Library of Congress.
  1. Peter Faulkner was a captain in the Eleventh Regiment of Infantry.
  2. Kutztown, Pennsylvania.
  3. James Diemer.

Circular to the Commandants of Regiments

Circular   New York July 22
                                             1799

Sir

Agreeably to the intimation of the Secy of War I transmit you an extract of a letter from him of the tenth instant by which you will perceive the causes which have hitherto interfered with a supply of cloathing adequate to the demand. If the assurance of the Contractor can in any degree be relied upon, the supply in future will more than keep pace with it.

With great consideration   I am Sir   Yr Obed ser

ADf, The Sol Feinstone Collection, Library of the American Philosophical Society, Philadelphia; LS, to Aaron Ogden, Hamilton Papers, Library of Congress.

From James McHenry

War Department, July 22, 1799. "I recd. this morning your letter of the 17th July inst. and have submitted Mr. Ths. Y. How to the President to fill the office of 2d Lieutenant, and recommended the appointment. . . ." [1]

ALS, Hamilton Papers, Library of Congress.
1. McHenry to John Adams, July 22, 1799 (ALS, Adams Family Papers, deposited in the Massachusetts Historical Society, Boston).
On July 27, 1799, Adams wrote to McHenry: "I see no material or reasonable objection against the appointment of Mr. Thomas Y How to be a second lieutenant in the eleventh regiment" (LC, Adams Family Papers, deposited in the Massachusetts Historical Society, Boston). The Senate confirmed How's appointment on May 14, 1800 (*Executive Journal*, I, 345, 355).

To James McHenry

New York July 22d. 1799

Sir

The information respecting the causes which have interfered with the supply of Cloathing contained in your letter of the 10th. instant received on Saturday is in train to be communicated by a circular letter.[1] I am glad to find that so much progress has been made.

If the Contractor delivers in two thirds of the daily quantity he promises, and the articles are expeditiously forwarded, it will suffice. The recruiting service will consequently be permitted to proceed without interruption. An abstract of the returns of recruits is in preparation for you.

With great respect   I have the honor to be Sir   Yr Obed ser

The Secy of War

ADf, Hamilton Papers, Library of Congress.
1. "Circular to the Commandants of Regiments," July 22, 1799.

To James McHenry

New York July 22d. 1799

Sir

I have the honor to send you an abstract of the returns of the Troops under my command so far as they have been received. They are not complete & from the imperfection of the forms very far from satisfactory. In some instances it is not possible to distinguish with certainty to what regiments the men belong which has prevented the abstract being digested regimentally. This will be remedied as soon as it shall be practicable.

The superintendant of military stores has heretofore requested an abstract of this kind in order to the transmission of Cloathing & other supplies. I presume the one now Sent will be communicated to him. But it is not complete enough to serve as an exclusive guide. Additional sources of information probably exist in your department, & it is proper that extra quantities be forwarded to convenient deposits, to be issued to such as may not appear in the present return, and to the augmentations of force which are contemplated.

With great respect &c &c &c   A Hamilton

Copy, Hamilton Papers, Library of Congress.

To James McHenry

New York July 22. 1799

Dr Sir

The return lately sent me [1] shews strongly the want of system of your Agents. Instead of an equal apportionment, while some Regiments are altogether without certain articles, others have a full or very ample supply of them. This appears particularly as to Muskets, Cartouch boxes, *Knapsacks* & *Canteens*. With regard to some of these articles, indeed, I know that orders have been given for supplies which do not appear in the return. But as to others I am not informed of any similar circumstances. I call your attention to these particulars that the inaccuracy may not in the pressure of your business escape your observation.

An apportionment, where all cannot be fully supplied, tends to distribute accommodation & to prevent discontent.[2]

Yrs. truly   A Hamilton

Js McHenry Es

ALS, St. Croix Museum, St. Croix, Virgin Islands; ALS (photostat), James McHenry Papers, Library of Congress; copy, in the handwriting of Ethan Brown, Hamilton Papers, Library of Congress.
1. See McHenry to H, second letter of July 10, 1799.
2. In the margin McHenry wrote: "This not so. His error arises from the articles being forwarded at different times."

To David Strong

[*New York, July 22, 1799.* On September 7, 1799, Strong wrote to Hamilton: "I received your favour of the 22d. July." *Letter not found.*]

From Thomas Lloyd Moore [1]

Bristol [Pennsylvania] July 24, 1799. ". . . I made a trip to the Westward some time ago in order to visit some of my recruiting Posts, and am happy to inform You that the Officers conduct themselves with great propriety, and they have met with considerable success, but they all agree in opinion that the late General Orders [2] will put almost an entire stop to the recruiting business in Pennsylvania. . . . I can inform you that I have 200 to 250 Recruits on their march to Head Qrs. where they will arrive about the last of this month. . . ."

ALS, Hamilton Papers, Library of Congress.
1. A resident of Pennsylvania and a veteran of the American Revolution, Moore was lieutenant colonel commandant of the Tenth Regiment of Infantry.
2. "General Orders," June 6, 1799.

From Thomas Parker

Winchester [Virginia] July 24, 1799. "I have received your letter of the 12th Instant.[1] Since the date of my last letter [2] the Residue of the cloathing mentioned in yours have come to hand. we are much in want of the Horsemans Tents for the officers & I will thank you to Request of the S of war to order a Marque for my use as the one

sent from Shepherds Town is not fit for Service. . . . Majr Campbell [3] writes me that his officers are greatly in want of money & hopes
that at all Events their Subsistence money may be sent to them. Be
pleased to answer my Quere with Respect to Off Servants not
Soldiers. . . ." [4]

ALS, Hamilton Papers, Library of Congress.
    1. In this letter, which is listed in the appendix to this volume, H states that
"clothing supplies" were being forwarded to Parker's regiment.
    2. Parker to H, July 20, 1799.
    3. A veteran of the American Revolution, William Campbell was a major in
the Eighth Regiment of Infantry.
    4. See Parker to H, July 6, 20, 1799.

From James McHenry

[Philadelphia, July 25, 1799]

My dear Sir.
    I request your opinion, upon the inclosed circular, to the different
contractors &c for supplies of rations for the ensuing and the present
year, predicated upon the ideas, communicated to me, by your
letter of the 12th inst. and that you will return it to me and your
opinion without delay if it, or any thing like it is to be acted upon.
    Some doubts have rested on my mind, whether such a step, might
not injure the business of procuring contracts in future, as a few
of the existing contracts for the present year embrace whole States.
Believing however, the issues contemplated by the contractors generally were upon a smaller scale than that for three collective Regiments, and that neither their means nor arrangements may reach the
capacity of the intended supplies, and a disappointment from their
failure might be experienced, I have concluded if your opinion continues the same, to send a circular to each contractor, and to each
person from whom I have received proposals under the advertisement of the 21st of March ulto.[1]
    This, the 25th is the last day for receiving proposals for rations
&c agreeably to that advertisement. I have before observed it admits
of a contract for the purpose of any extent, from particular posts
to whole States, and any number of the latter on the sea board—the
same with respect to the western army.

I mean that you should direct yourself, whatever respects winter quarters, general principles being settled.

Yours affecy

James McHenry

25 July 1799

Gen Alex Hamilton

ALS, Hamilton Papers, Library of Congress; ADf, James McHenry Papers, Library of Congress.
1. For this advertisement, see McHenry to H, July 16, 1799, note 1.

From James McHenry

War Department

25th July 1799

Sir,

I enclose a Warrant, under the signature of the President, and the seal of the War office of the United States, for the execution of Richard Hunt, a Serjeant in a Company of the Second regiment of Artillerists, and Engineers, commanded by Captain James Stille, who was tried on a charge of desertion, and also of carrying away the money for their pay entrusted to him, by the men of his company, and sentenced to suffer death, by a General Court Martial, held at the City Hall, of the City of New York on the 16t day of April last, by your order.[1]

The President in his letter [2] enclosing the Warrant to me, expresses a wish "that Courts Martial may be advised, to be as cautious, and as regular as possible, in all their proceedings, especially in cases of life, because the discipline of the army, will depend much on this habit," and adds "Yet if you and General Hamilton, think that one example, may suffice, for the purposes of public justice, the execution of Hunt or Perkins,[3] may yet be respited."

You will issue such orders, as in your judgment may be proper, and return the Warrant for deposit in this office.

I am with great respect   your obedt. servant   James McHenry

Major Genl Hamilton

LS, Hamilton Papers, Library of Congress.

1. Hunt had been convicted of desertion. For information on this case, see
H to McHenry, April 20, note 2, May 27, first letter of June 12, 1799; H to
Washington Morton, April 23, 1799. On May 27, 1799, McHenry sent the
court-martial proceedings to John Adams for his approval (ALS, Adams Family Papers, deposited in the Massachusetts Historical Society, Boston). Adams,
who was reluctant to approve the death penalty in a case of desertion, also
questioned whether Hunt's trial had been legal in that none of the members of
the board trying him had at that time received their commissions in the Army.
He was, moreover, displeased by the fact that the court-martial board had not
attempted to dissuade Hunt from pleading guilty (Adams to McHenry, June 5,
19, July 19, 1799 [LC, Adams Family Papers, deposited in the Massachusetts
Historical Society, Boston]). At Adams's request McHenry submitted the proceedings of the court-martial to the other members of the cabinet (McHenry
to Timothy Pickering, Benjamin Stoddert, and Oliver Wolcott, Jr., June 29,
1799 [LS, RG 59, Miscellaneous Letters, January 1, 1799–December 27, 1800,
National Archives; LS, letterpress copy, Adams Family Papers, deposited in the
Massachusetts Historical Society, Boston], enclosed in McHenry to Adams,
July 12, 1799 [ALS, Adams Family Papers, deposited in the Massachusetts His-
torocal Society, Boston]). McHenry's fellow cabinet members unanimously
approved the sentence (Wolcott to McHenry, July 3, 1799; Stoddert to Mc-
Henry, July 6, 1799; Pickering to McHenry, July 6, 1799 [copies, Adams Family Papers, deposited in the Massachusetts Historical Society, Boston], enclosed
in McHenry to Adams, July 12, 1799 [ALS, Adams Family Papers, deposited
in the Massachusetts Historical Society, Boston]).

2. Adams to McHenry, July 19, 1799 (LC, Adams Family Papers, deposited
in the Massachusetts Historical Society, Boston).

3. Joseph Perkins. See McHenry to H, May 29, note 2, May 30, 1799; H to
McHenry, July 3, 1799; "General Orders," July 20, 1799.

From John J. U. Rivardi

Niagara [New York] July 25th 1799

Sir,

I had the honor of receiving last Evening your letter of the 25th.
Ulto. which claims my warmest acknowledgments not only for the
attention paid to my different requests, but also for the very delicate
Manner in which you Notice an expression of my letter of the 21st.
of March. The impropriety of it Struck me after the Post was gone.
I Shall not endeavour to apologize for it by any other way than by
confessing that it was the momentary effect of the impatience &
disgust created on a mind debilitated by Sickness & Soured by cir-

ALS, Hamilton Papers, Library of Congress.

cumstances. Permit me to assure you Sir, that my conduct will convince you that I am as anxious as any Officer in the Army to discharge in their fullest extent the duties of my Station.

Receive also my Sincere thanks for your explanation of the expressions contained in the Secretary's report—it is perfectly Satisfactory & I have to lament that I wrote with perhaps Too much heat on the Subject.

I am perfectly of your opinion that a Separation between the Engineering & Artillery branches would be necessary to the perfection of each. The Officers belonging to the former ought of course to be well acquainted with both—but their number need not be large. The Officers belonging to the latter may render great Services to their country & Justice to their comissions without being Skilled in the former. The Mode of forming Brigades of Engineers as adopted by the Brittish Seems to me to be a very good one.

As you will See on the ground the difference between the English & French exercise of Field pieces,[1] I Shall Say Nothing concerning the facility with which the latter is performed—only I beg to observe that the first Mates being within the wheels in the Brittish method they are always maimed if the piece is dismounted by a Shot or if it bursts. They are also frequently in the way of the guner who directs the piece & who ought to See not only before him but to his right & left—The dragrope requires a great Space of ground—four pieces with Slings can be manœuvered where two would hardly find room if they had to be moved by dragropes.[2]

A Single Ball in the latter Method may also Sweep away the half of the men when marching & the whole when dressed in parade. Encouraged by your condescension in receiving my observations I shall beg leave to remark that too little has been done in the Artillery establishment for Sappers & Miners—Separate companies of which

1. The French deployed field artillery as an independent arm, massing all the guns together as a unit. The British divided the artillery pieces among the infantry units. During the course of the French Revolutionary Wars, the British increasingly used the French method.

2. For information on the material in this and the following paragraph, see *The Little Bombardier and Pocket Gunner* (London, 1801); Théodore Bernard Simon Durtubisse ou Dhurtebize, dit Le Chevalier d'Urtubie de Rogicourt, *Manuel de l'artilleur, ou Traité des différents objets d'artillerie practique dont la connaissance est nécessaire aux officers du corps royal* (2nd ed., Paris: Didot fils aîné, 1787); MS manual entitled "Instructions for firing Ordnance," 1796 (National Army Museum, London).

were deemed the best plan both in Germany & in France. It is a Service which requires much Knowledge on the part of the Officers & great practice on that of the men—who generally are better paid than any other Kind of Troops—in Austria they are educated from their infancy in Military School & are anexed but never incorporated with the Artillery. I do not Know if it would not be advisable also to have a proportion of bombardiers—in fact the division of the branches always brings nearer to perfection than attempts to encompass the whole.

I Shall in consequence of your instructions Call imediately Lieutt. Visher with his garrison & Military Stores leaving enough of the latter to make the Small detachment which will be left behind Comfortable. I return you, Sir, my warmest thanks for the arrangements which you have made for a Court of *Inquiry*.[3] The Officers being Selected by you [4]—there is no possibility of the choice Not being perfectly Satisfactory. I regret the departure of Doctor Coffin [5] who was my most important Evidence,[6] however I hope to have a Sufficient number of others.

You will have received Since plans of the river Miamy [7] &a. I hope they will prove Satisfactory. I Shall endeavour after the Court is over to procure of the Brittish Engineers a Correct Map of the lakes & if I Succeed I may perhaps transmit Copies before Winter. I must only request to have Some large Velum Paper forwarded as well as brushes & a box of Reeves's Colours.[8] Mine are exhausted

3. The Court of Inquiry was to hear charges brought against Rivardi by Captain James Bruff. For those charges, see Rivardi to H, March 21, 1799, note 13; April 3, 1799, note 6.
4. For the officers selected for the Court of Inquiry, see H to Rivardi, June 25, 1799.
5. On May 30, 1799, Doctor John G. Coffin wrote to H requesting a furlough. On June 21, 1799, H wrote to Rivardi authorizing the furlough "on condition that an Arrangement satisfactory to you, be made for the care of the Sick in his absence." Both letters are listed in the appendix to this volume.
6. On July 11, 1799, Rivardi wrote to H: "By the departure of Doct. Coffin I shall loose a valuable Officer. . . . He was one of my most necessary evidences had Captn. Bruffs charges been examined." This letter is listed in the appendix to this volume.
7. See Rivardi to H, June 27, 1799.
8. In 1766 William J. and Thomas Reeves, who were brothers, established Reeves and Sons, Limited, a company manufacturing supplies for artists, at Little Britain in London. The company, which is at present located in Enfield, Middlesex, received a special award in 1781 from the Royal Society of Arts for the invention of the water-color cake.

indeed for the last plans which I sent you I had to borrow those Articles which can not be procured here, of Captain Pilkington.[9] I conceive also that there is little Necessity of keeping a Garrison at Mackinac.[10] That Post is out of the reach of assistance in case of a War & its chief object which was to Secure the Indian Trade is done away Since the Brittish have formed an Establishment at St. Joseph [11] where by dint of large presents they attract the furr traders the more easily as we do not enter in competition with them. Doctor Coffin will before the arrival of this letter be at New York. Our Sick are visited regularly by the Surgeons of the Brittish Garrison. pleasing as this act of Kindness is To me, I wish Sincerely that it may not be put to Too long a Trial. it was well understood at Doctor Coffin's departure that if any charges were made they would fall on him. With regard To The procuring wood &a. by rotation I beg leave To State that there are few Posts labouring under greater disadvantages. We procure Wood from a greater distance than five miles. The Season for Cutting is Short considering the length of the Winter & the impracticability of the roads in the Spring & fall it becomes therefore Necessary To Station a Party of four or five men who by the Small allowance of five dollars extra are in my opinion paid little enough for their labour, the wearing off of their clothes & the torture arising from the Musketoes. I procured Several thousands of Pickets which will not cost Sixty dollars To The U. States. In fact I hope that when men are indispensably & constantly employed in works which they did not contemplate when they enlisted, that Small allowance will not be refused. I have the pleasure To inform you that the whole Fort is fraised new. I am Now making new Platforms where they were wanted. I Must further observe that at West Point Norfolk, Baltimore Detroit &c. wood is bought or procured by contract—here no contract can be made. Before I finish this letter I Shall State concerning Mr. Hodgdon that he had forwarded To me in the same letter two Invoices of the Same Tenor. I Supposed that it was a Mistake & that An other Invoice was left behind. I was confirmed in that opinion when I received two Tierces More than expressed in the Invoice & as they were without direction I had them opened & an Inventory for-

9. Robert Pilkington. See Rivardi to H, June 12, 1799, note 1.

10. See H to David Strong, May 22, 1799; H to James McHenry, May 23, 1799; H to Rivardi, June 25, 1799.

11. St. Joseph is located on an island in the northwestern part of Lake Huron.

warded. Finally I had letters which explained the business & Law that we had received all what was destined To This Post & Some Articles above which it Seems ought to have been directed To Oswego where I imediately dispatched them. It is a fact however that no Hogshead contained what was mentioned in the Invoices —but it is merely want of attention in those who packed up the clothing which otherwise arrived in very good condition. We issued yesterday the last infantry Coat.

I have the honor To be with most respectfull consideration Sir Your Most Obedient & Very humble Servant   J J U. Rivardi
Majr. 1st Regt. A & E.

Major General Ar. Hamilton

P. S. Captain Thompson who begs To be gratefully & respectfully remembered will set off in order To fetch his family [12] as Soon as Lieutenant Visher arrives.[13] I shall endeavour To engage here a Vessel To Send To Oswego—otherwise the Military Stores could not come on as boats there are very Scarce. Enoch Humphrey is here yet. I persuaded him To Stay as he will be an usefull evidence To me—besides that motive I am in hopes his nomination as Cadet will arrive Soon [14]—he will be a most usefull person here as he can act as quarter Master. I am very happy To hear that there is a prospect of Some emoluments being granted To The persons acting in that capacity.

12. Rivardi had requested a leave for Alexander Thompson in Rivardi to H, May 2, 1799.
13. H had suggested that Rivardi transfer Nanning J. Visscher and most of the garrison at Oswego to Fort Niagara in H to Rivardi, June 25, 1799.
14. H had recommended Humphrey's appointment to James McHenry in H to McHenry, June 25–July 1, 1799. McHenry had promised to attend to the appointment in McHenry to H, July 8, 1799.

To John Jay [1]

New York July 29. 1799

My Dear Sir
The completion of the works in the vicinity of our City proceeds heavily. Some embarrassment is understood to arise in the

War Department from the Question of Appropriations. I beg to be informed whether the sum appropriated by the Legislature of this State will come in aid of the Operation.[2] Limited as that sum is, nothing upon a large scale can be undertaken in reference to it. Its Agency in fortifications on the Islands, at Powles Hook, and on the projection from Long Island opposite Governors Island (I forget at this moment its name) is the only one which can be useful.

With great respect & esteem   I have the honor to be Sir   Yr Obed serv   A Hamilton

His Excellency
Governor Jay

ALS, Columbia University Libraries; copy, in the handwriting of Ethan Brown, Hamilton Papers, Library of Congress.
    1. For background to this letter, see the introductory note to H to James McHenry, June 1, 1798.
    2. This is a reference to "An Act for the payment of certain Officers of Government, and other contingent expences" (*New York Laws*, 22nd Sess., Ch. XCIV [April 3, 1799]). The last clause of this act reads: "*And be it further enacted*, That the comptroller shall and he is hereby directed, as soon as conveniently may be, to collect and liquidate the expences incurred by the fortifications in this state, for the defence of the United States; and shall also liquidate with the secretary of the treasury of the United States, the specie value of the funded debt of the United States assumed by the said states of the debt of this state, on the principles contained in the act of Congress passed the fifteenth day of February last, relative to the balances reported by the commissioners for settling the accounts between the United States and the several states."

To James McHenry

Private   New York July [29] 1799

Dear Sir

I return you enclosed your draft of a letter dated the 25 instant [1] to the several contractors &c with a paragraph at foot which is submitted to be added for reasons that itself will announce.

The doubts you mention are natural. They had occurred to my mind. But considering that the Public is entirely free as to the stationing of the troops, I think that both in candour and good policy the measure may be pursued.

I hesitate whether the invitation ought to extend to the Contractors for Massachusettes.[2] Their price is as low as it can well be. The position heretofore intended for three Regiments is in Massachusettes, and it seems just that the *moderation* of the contractors there should be rewarded by the enjoyment of the advantage. The competition of Connecticut New York & New Jersey may be excited with a view to the three regiments, which were intended to be placed in the vicinity of Brunswick.[3]

With great regard   Yrs. truly   A H

Js McHenry Es

ALS, The Sol Feinstone Collection, Library of the American Philosophical Society, Philadelphia; ALS (photostat), James McHenry Papers, Library of Congress.
  1. See McHenry to H, first letter of July 25, 1799.
  2. For these contractors, see McHenry to H, July 2, 1799, note 1.
  3. See H's draft to George Washington to McHenry, first letter of December 13, 1798; McHenry to H, February 4, 1799; H to McHenry, July 12, 1799.

To James McHenry

New York July 29. 1799

Sir

I have the honor to acknowlege the receipt of your letter of the 25 instant inclosing a warrant for the execution of Serjeant Hunt.

I have reflected carefully on the point submitted to our joint consideration, and upon the whole I incline to the side of Forbearance.

The temper of our country is not a little opposed to the frequency of Capital punishment. Public opinion, in this respect, though it must not have too much influence, is not wholly to be disregarded. There must be some caution not to render our military system odious by giving it the appearance of being sanguinary.

Considering too the extreme lenity in time past, there may be danger of shocking even the opinion of the army by too violent a change. The idea of cruelty inspires disgust, and ultimately is not much more favourable to authority than the excess of lenity.

Neither is it clear that one example so quickly following upon the heels of another, in the same corps, will materially increase the impression intended to be made or answer any valuable purpose.

If for any or all of these reasons the utility of the measure be doubtful in favour of life it ought to be foresworn. It is the true policy of the Government to maintain an attitude which shall express a reluctance to strike united with a firm determination to do it whenever ⟨it⟩ shall be essential.

It is but too certain, that it will not be long before other instances will occur in which the same punishment will be decried for the same offence. To disseminate the examples of executions, so far as they shall be indispensable, will serve to render them more efficacious.

Under these impressions if I hear nothing to the contrary from you by the return of the Post I shall issue an order to the following effect "That though the President has fully approved the sentence of Serjeant Hunt and from the heinous nature of his conduct considers him as a very fit subject for punishment—yet being unwilling to multiply examples of severity, however just, beyond what experience may shew to be indispensable and hoping that the good faith and patriotism of the Soldiery will spare him the painful necessity of frequently resorting to them, he has thought fit to authorise a remission of the punishment; directing nevertheless that Serjeant Hunt be degraded from his Station."

I request to be speedily instructed.

With great respect &c

The Secy of War

ADf, Hamilton Papers, Library of Congress.

To Ebenezer Stevens

New York July 29. 1799

Sir

Inclosed is a ⟨plan⟩ [1] for the uniforms &c of the army [2] prepared at my request by Col Smith, with the aid of Col Fish [3] and Capt Armstrong.[4] I am desirous of seeing some models of Cloathing made agreeably to this plan—be⟨ginning wi⟩th those of the privates. It is my ⟨wish that⟩ the models may be framed as well with a view to the quality of the materials as to the fashions and ornaments of the Cloathing. The sooner they can be prepared, the better.

But to be the more certain that we meet the ideas of the framers of the plan—you will be pleased to have recourse to the assistance of Capt Armstrong who has been very obliging on the occasion and who I doubt not will with pleasure lend his further aid.

With great consideration   I am Sir   Your obed ser   A Hamliton

General Stevens

ALS, New-York Historical Society, New York City; copy, in the handwriting of Ethan Brown, Hamilton Papers, Library of Congress.
  1. The material within brackets has been taken from the copy of this letter.
  2. This is an untitled document which concludes: "all which is respectfully Submitted—With the approbation of Capt. Armstrong. Eastchester May 3d 1799. William S. Smith" (ADS, Hamilton Papers, Library of Congress). In the margins of this document H wrote comments and made additions.
  In the Hamilton Papers, Library of Congress, there is another version of this document which is undated and entitled "General Principles of the uniform of the Troops of the United States."
  3. Nicholas Fish, a veteran of the American Revolution and a close friend of H, was supervisor of the revenue for the District of New York.
  4. William Armstrong was a New York City merchant.

To Benjamin Stoddert

N. York July 29th. 1799

Dr Sir

A pressure of various business has delayed a reply to your favor of the 19th. instant.

The principle you suggest for my consideration, though if it could be introduced it would work well, cannot in my opinion be put into practice. It would contravene too much, pretensions rooted as well in the human heart as in unconquerable prejudices of the military State, by which expression I include the naval Department. Carrying in the very fact, an avowed preference, humiliating to the pride of the Superior Officer and reversing the order of antecedent relations, a chearful submission could never be obtained.

The alternative you mention is the proper expedient, & a very necessary one it is. It will be happy if Congress can be induced to adopt it.

With very great esteem   I have the honor &c

Copy, in the handwriting of Ethan Brown, Hamilton Papers, Library of Congress.

To James McHenry

New York July 30, 1799

Sir

In the list of additional appointments, which you lately transmitted to me,[1] I find the names of several persons as Captains and first Lieutenants in the 9th. 14th & 15 Regiments who were not before officers of those Regiments. Whether I have been in any instance accessory to a circumstance of this nature, I do not now recollect, but be this as it may, I am sorry that it has happened. For as it contravenes the reasonable expectations of the officers previously appointed it cannot fail to produce discontent, and it will be unfortunate to mingle this ingredient into the mass, at our first outset.

I must entreat that henceforth the routine of promotion may govern as to all the Regiments which have their *field officers* and even as to any one which has not its complement, that it may govern to the rank of Capt inclusively. And that I may be authorised to declare that this is the intention, saving cases of extraordinary preferment for extraordinary service. It is a point on which I am anxious.

Col Hall [2] writes me that some of the late appointments have been dissatisfactory to his Regiment.

It is very desireable that the rules which are to regulate promotions should be fixed and promulged. This is a point which can no longer with convenience be left afloat. It is very important as fast as possible to ascertain and fix every part of our system.

I have the honor to be   Sir   yr obed ⟨ser⟩

The Secy of War

ADf, Hamilton Papers, Library of Congress.
1. Letter not found.
2. Josias Carvel Hall to H, July 22, 1799 (listed in the appendix to this volume).

To James McHenry

New York July 30th 1799

Sir

On a subject, not very familiar to my experience I thot it well to consult others (one at a distance) [1] which has occasioned a delay in fulfilling the object of your letter of the 24th of June respecting regulations for issuing straw, fuel &.

I send you herewith the result of my enquiries and reflections.[2] In regard to fuel, the late improvements in the construction of chimneys by Count Rumford,[3] which may be adopted in quarters and garrisons, has had influence in diminishing the quantity, which independant of this circumstance is conceived to be too liberal in your plan. This being in the view of œconomy a matter of great importance, I would advise that an abstract be made of those chapters of Court Rumford's treatise which are applicable to chimnies in order that a printed copy be furnished to each commanding Officer of a Garrison &c. Mr Jonathan Williams would execute this in an eligible manner.[4] The more *Simple* and *concise* the abstract, the better.

The Scheme of regulation now Submitted contemplates, likewise that the officers will be arranged in Messes of six to a Mess.

Give me leave to ask whether in the future construction of barracks it will not be expedient to have the rooms large enough to contain each twelve men. It has been found that messes of this number conduce to the comfort of the Tr⟨oops⟩ preventing waste & consequently rendering ⟨the⟩ Supply more ample. The effect of the arran⟨gement⟩ in relation to fuel is very obvious.

In the field it is usual for the ⟨troops⟩ to provide themselves with fuel; & straw is fur⟨nished⟩ as it can be had. The regulations are there⟨fore confin⟩ed to Troops in Garrisons & Quarters.

With great respect I ⟨have⟩ the honor to be, sir   yr. ob. Ser.

A. Hamilton

The Secy of War

Copy, Hamilton Papers, Library of Congress.
    1. See Philip Schuyler to H, July 15, 1799.
    2. "Regulations to be observed in the delivery and distribution of fuel, straw and stationary to the Army respecting horses furnished to Officers & respecting those which they may keep themselves" (Df, in the handwriting of William LeConte with additions and corrections in H's handwriting, Hamilton Papers, Library of Congress; copy, in the handwriting of Ethan Brown, Hamilton Papers, Library of Congress).
    3. Sir Benjamin Thompson, Count Rumford, *Of Chimney fireplaces, with proposals for improving them, to save fuel; render dwelling-houses more comfortable and salubrious, and effectually to prevent chimnies from smoking* (3rd ed., London: Printed for T. Cadell Jun. and W. Davies, 1797).
    4. Williams had performed similar tasks for H in the past. See Williams to H, June 17, July 11, 1799.

To James McHenry

N. York July 31st. 1799

Sir

I have the honor to transmit the proceedings of two General Courts Martial in the cases of Capt. Frye & Doctor Osborne [1] with transcripts of general Orders containing my opinion concerning them.[2]

You will observe the ill use which has been made by Capt. Frye of a correspondence with you, and my remark on that point.[3] It is understood that this circumstance had weight with the Court.[4]

With great respect &c

Secy. of War

Copy, in the handwriting of Ethan Brown, Hamilton Papers, Library of Congress.
    1. Although these proceedings have not been found, McHenry sent transcripts of the records of the courts-martial of Frederick Frye and Samuel Osborne to H on August 14, 1799 (in a letter listed in the appendix to this volume). These transcripts are in the Hamilton Papers, Library of Congress.

2. These general orders have not been found.

3. Although some of the relevant documents have not been found, it is possible to reconstruct the events which caused H to rebuke McHenry.

On October 8, 1799, Major Adam Hoops, commanding officer at Fort Jay, New York, charged that Captain Frye had been guilty of, among other things, "mustering early in the month of February last the detachment or company of the first regiment of artillerists and Engineers in garrison at Fort Jay *Himself*" (copy, Hamilton Papers, Library of Congress, enclosed in McHenry to H, March 14, 1799 [listed in the appendix to this volume]). During the court-martial proceedings, Frye maintained that he had acted under the authority granted to him by McHenry in a letter dated January 10, 1799. McHenry's letter to Frye has not been found, but see McHenry to H, August 2, 1799. For Osborne's court-martial and an earlier court-martial of Frye on different charges, see McHenry to H, January 29, 1799; H to McHenry, second letter of March 18, 1799, notes 4 and 5.

4. This letter was enclosed in the letter to McHenry of the same date printed below.

To James McHenry

N Y July 31 1799

You will see my Dear friend in the case of Capt. Frey the evil tendency of correspondence by the head of the War Department with inferior officers, when there is a superior.[1] For a thousand good reasons it cannot be too carefully avoided. Perhaps a sudden emergency where the superior officer is in a situation that recourse to him might defeat the object is the only exception.

Yrs. truly   A H

ALS, Montague Collection, MS Division, New York Public Library; ALS (photostat), James McHenry Papers, Library of Congress; copy, in the handwriting of Ethan Brown, Hamilton Papers, Library of Congress.

1. See H to McHenry, first letter of July 31, 1799.

From James McHenry

Augt. 2d 1799

I always receive from my friend, his intimations, with at least a disposition to benefit by them. Your private note of the 31st ulto.

ALS, Hamilton Papers, Library of Congress; ADf, James McHenry Papers, Library of Congress.

recd yesterday morning with the proceedings of the general Court martial on Capn. Frye, suggests to me, either that the Court ought not to have suffered, my letter of the 10th of Jany to have weighed in their decision, or if it ought to have had influence, that they should have required from my office, the circumstance which occasioned it.

Could the Court have been ignorant, that I have nothing to do with receiving muster & pay rolls; that these are received and acknowledged by the accountant, and always without my privity or participation, unless, when through ignorance in the officer sending them, they are addressed to me, in which case, they are immediately and without examination as to who had mustered, referred to the accountant; or when some peculiarity accompanies them, requiring their communication from the accountant; that I act upon the accountants report only; issue warrants for the monies, and cause the same to be transmitted. If they knew all this, why not have inquired before suffering it to influence an opinion, into the circumstance which produced the letter in question. Why suppose, what was not the fact, that a correspondence existed between Cap Frye and the Secry. of war, after the appointment of Major Hoops to the command. It is not pleasant to have such ideas entertained and countenanced, especially when no such correspondence had been kept up or taken place.

But the letter in question is merely to transmit discharges for certain men of Cap Fryes company resulting from the muster roll. If any error has been fallen into, it was in directing these discharges to the Capn instead of passing them through Major Hoops to the Capn. I cannot at this moment recollect, the circumstance which induced to this mode of transmitting the discharges. I rather think it was at the instance of the accountant, or from information that Major Hoops was or would be absent from the garrison, or it might be from mere *inattention*. Be this however as it may, certainly infinitely more importance has been attached to this solitary letter, than it merits, and this has given me some pain.

I find upon inquiry, that the muster and pay roll acted upon by the accountant, was that made by Capn Frye, and for this reason. The muster and pay roll made out by Col. Stevens was for a *part* of the month of February only. vz. from the 1st. to the 18th. and not for the whole month which is required. Thus the accountant could not act upon, in consequence that sent by Frye for the whole of the same month was adopted.

You observe, in your general orders [1] upon Fry's having exercised this power. "The exercise of it, after such information, was consequently irregular and disorderly, nor can the seeming countenance which was subsequently given to his acts by the department of war vary their real nature. The circumstances which had intervened were probably unknown, and a disposition to give facility to the service must be presumed to have caused the Secretary to have overlooked the incompatibility of the proceedings with his instructions."

The last part especially of this stricture does not appear to me, to have been necessary, and therefore ought to have been avoided, as implicating misconduct or want of consistency in the Secretary.

As to a correspondence with Frye, I informed Cap Frye on the 4th of Octbr. 1798, as follows. "Sir. on the 10th of Sept. Major Hoops was directed to repair to New York and assume the command of the troops in garrison in that harbour, and the general superintendance of the works and repairs to the fortifications ordered by the U.S. for the defence of that City. He is therefore, to be considered as Commandant of the harbour and of course, your reports to me will be made through him."

This and the letter quoted by Cap Frye are the only letters which I find on record since the appointment of Major Hoops to his command. Is this a correspondence between the Secy. of War and Capn Frye?

These points, perhaps ought to have been more inquired into than to me, they appear to have been. At any rate it strikes me, that any supposed correspondence with an inferior officer, his superior being presumed present, has been too slightly examined and admitted.

I make these observations more freely to you, because I think the head of the department of war, ought not to be held up in *a general order* as having been ignorant of, or having been inattentive to, his

1. H's general orders have not been found. See H to McHenry, first letter of July 31, 1799.

duties; and because I perceive you entertain an opinion, that I have wantonly or ignorantly given orders to inferior officers within the command of their superior. This is not the case whatever may have been insinuated to you to the contrary.

Your truly & affecy   James McHenry

Gen Hamilton

From John Jay

Albany 3 Augt. 1799

Dear Sir

I was this morning favored with yours of the 29 ulto. requesting to be informed, whether the Sum appropriated by the Legislature of this State, will come in aid of the completion of the works in the vicinity of New York?

The act passed the 3d. of april last,[1] for the paymt. of certain officers of governmt. and other contingent Expences, contains the following clause—it is the *third* from the End of the act—

"And be it further enacted, that until further legislative Provision be made, all *further* Expenditures under the act, entitlled 'an act for the further Defence of this State, and for other purposes'[2] shall cease, so far forth as respects the Erection of new fortifications, or the completion of such as have been erected or constructed."

I presume that the Reason of this Clause may be inferred from the last Clause in the Act, whereby the Comptroller is directed to liquidate the Expences encurred by the fortifications in this State; and also to liquidate with the Secy. of the Treasury, the specie Value of the *assumed* Debt &c.

I have the honor to be with great Esteem & Regard   Dear Sir Your most obt. Servt   John Jay

Majr. General Hamilton

ALS, Hamilton Papers, Library of Congress; ADf, Columbia University Libraries.
1. *New York Laws*, 22nd Sess., Ch. XCIV.
2. *New York Laws*, 22nd Sess., Ch. V (August 9, 1798).

To James Wilkinson [1]

[New York, August 3, 1799] [2]

General Hamilton presents his Compliments to General Wilkinson [3] & sends him at foot heads for conversations which it is proposed to have; in order to call the attention of G W to the several points. Most of them have no doubt been topics of communication with the War Department but the freedom & particularity of conversation will yield additional lights & lead perhaps to a correct system for the management of our Western Affairs in their various relations.

Objects

1. The disposition of our Western Inhabits. towards the UStates & foreign powers.
2. The disposition of the Indians in the same aspect.
3. The disposition of the Spaniards in our Vicinity. Their strength in numbers & fortifications.
4 The best expedients for correcting or controuling hostile propensities in any or all these quarters including.
5 The best defensive disposition of the Western army; embracing the Country of Tenessee & the Northern & N Western Lakes and having an eye to œconomy & discipline.
6 The best mode (in the event of Rupture with Spain) of attacking the two *floridas*. The troops Artillery &c. requisite.
7 The best plan for supplying the Western army with provisions transportation forage &c.
8 The best arrangement of Command so as to unite facility of Communication with the sea board & the proper combination of all the parts under the General commanding the Western Army.

ADf, Hamilton Papers, Library of Congress.
    1. At the head of this letter H wrote: "April 15. 1799
                                                April 20
                                                April 25
                                                May 24. 1799."
This list contains the dates on which Wilkinson had written to H.
    2. In *JCHW*, V, 247, and *HCLW*, VII, 75, this letter is dated April 15, 1799.
    3. Wilkinson had left New Orleans en route to New York City on June 25, 1799 (Wilkinson to H, July 3, 1799), and arrived in New York on August 2,

1799 (Wilkinson to Timothy Pickering, August 2, 1799 [ALS, RG 59, Miscellaneous Letters, January 1, 1799–December 27, 1800, National Archives]).

During the two days after his arrival in New York, Wilkinson met twice with H. In his memoirs Wilkinson gave the following account of their conversations: "I immediately called on the General and left my card: he returned my visit the next morning, and at our meeting shewed some sensibility, for which I respected his heart, and remunerated him without loss of time, by observing to him, 'that considering my superior rank during the revolution, and my subsequent military services, it might be presumed there would be some opposition to his command in my mind; but that however tenacious of rank, whatever might be my professional pride, and I acknowledged an ample share of it, I should be vain and weak indeed, did I oppose my pretensions or my talents to his, that I believed the course he had run, and the services he had rendered, gave him a title to the appointment he had received, and that I should take his orders with satisfaction;' he was affected, and laying his right hand on his breast replied, 'upon my word, General Wilkinson, I admire this frankness, and shall not shew myself unworthy of the example; I have not experienced the same obliging concession from other quarters;' he was proceeding, when a messenger required his presence in court, which was then sitting; and having appointed the next afternoon for an interview, we parted.

"I waited on the General agreeably to appointment, and opened the conversation by observing, 'that in obedience to his order of the 12th February, I presented myself to receive his commands, but before entering on business, I considered it a matter of propriety towards him and of duty to myself, to remark, that my ignorance of his personal sentiments, and my knowledge of the secret slanders by which, I had been assailed during his administration of the treasury department, enjoined the utmost circumspection on my part; I therefore begged leave to premise, that should the objects for which I had been recalled from the Mississippi require formal reports, I hoped he would apprise me, whether I should confine myself to strict official forms, or might add such political facts and reflections as appeared to me essential to his information. That in the last case relying on his confidence, I should bare my bosom to him, and than in the first he would find me dumb to all but specific objects of professional duty;' he answered, 'I have no objection General Wilkinson to indulge your desire, nor will I hesitate to tell you, Sir, that I sent for you, to borrow the information which I have in vain sought for elsewhere; estranged from military pursuits, since the revolution, my faculties have been directed to different objects; you know how easy it is for a soldier to forget the mechanical parts of his profession, which is my case; I have grown rusty in military affairs, and have in reality forgotten much of what I learnt in the war of the revolution, and wish to avail myself of your knowledge; you therefore cannot be too diffuse in your communications; I am not a man of professions, but on a further acquaintance, I think, you will find something here, (laying his hand on his breast) trustworthy; in the mean time, I will barely say, that whenever you desire confidence you have only to intimate it.' A long desultory conversation ensued, chiefly respecting our south-western country, of which he appeared to have formed a just estimate, remarking it was 'a treasure worth cherishing;' at taking leave, I observed to him, 'well, Sir, having fatigued you with my prattle, I now propose to visit an old friend whom I have not seen for several years, I know you are twain in politics, but I hope there is no disagreement between you, which might render the renewal of my acquaintance with him indecorous to my superior officer;' he asked me if it was 'Lamb,' meaning Colonel [John] Lamb, I replied in the negative, and named Colonel [Aaron] Burr. 'Little Burr,' said he, 'Oh no, we have always been opposed in politics but always on good terms, we sat out in the practice of the law at the same time, and took opposite political directions, Burr beckoned me to follow him, and I advised him to come with me; we could not agree, but I fancy he now begins to think he was wrong and I was right.'" (Wilkinson, *Memoirs of My Own Times* [Philadelphia, 1816], I, 437–39.)

To James McHenry [1]

New York Aug 5th. 1799

If there be any thing in my general order lately sent you, which imputes to the Secretary of War ignorance or inattention, I agree with you, my Dear friend, that it ought not to have been there. I add that if done with design it would be a *very culpable* indecorum. But if it does bear this construction, I have very clumsily executed my own intention. And I give you my honor that so far from being sensible of it, my aim was quite the reverse.

I have already told you my opinion, that the letter from you to Capt Frye was in the view of Military Etiquette irregular. It ought to have been addressed to Major Hoops. If my memory serves me right it refers to the muster by Capt Frye & thus gives him the pretext of your sanction. It was necessary to do away this inference and at the same time to obviate in the mind of the army the idea of irregularity on your part. My object was to reconcile these two things.

The means, I employed, were these two suggestions—1 That the intermediate circumstances were unknown to you. In this you see nothing amiss. 2 That from a disposition to give *facility* to the service you *overlooked* the inconsistency of what was done with your *instructions*. Does this imply ignorance or inattention? I think not. Every superior sometimes *overlooks*, that is *forbears to take notice of*, the incompatibility of the conduct of an inferior with his instructions, though he clearly perceives (and consequently acts neither from ignorance nor inattention) that incompatibility—but willing to give facility to the service in the particular instance he thinks it best to wave any objection to what has been done & even to give effect to it. In civil & military life this has happened to myself; and yet to hear it stated would not in my opinion charge me with ignorance or inattention. There may often be good reasons for *overlooking* a fault which we *perceive*. To *overlook* is very different from *not to see* or not to attend to. It is in one sense to excuse, to forbear to punish or animadvert upon. And it seems to me that it is plainly in this sense that it is used in the general order. Most certainly it was intended so to be.

Now let me rebuke you in turn. How could you imagine that I entertain an opinion that you have *wantonly* or ignorantly given orders to inferior officers within the command of their superior? It is to injure my friendship for you to suppose that I could think you had *wantonly* done so. That you may have done so through want of a *strict habit* on the subject or perhaps from some incorrectness of ideas with regard to military Etiquette, I have indeed believed but nothing worse. And I cannot think that this belief ought to give you pain. It only implies that you have not been long enough called by situation to contemplate or practice upon that etiquette, to have formed exact notions of it and a habit of conforming to it. I do not myself pretend to be an adept in this species of knowlege; though I have endeavoured to systematise my ideas on the subject. They are these in brief that the Departt. of War may regularly correspond with the *Civil Staff* or officers charged with the business of *expenditure* & *supply in its various branches* without passing through the medium of the Chief Military Officer. But that in all other matters the correspondence ought to be with him exclusively—saving the cases of sudden emergency in which the object would suffer by using him as the medium.

Yrs. Affecy   A H

Js McHenry E

ALS, The Sol Feinstone Collection, Library of the American Philosophical Society, Philadelphia; ALS (photostat), James McHenry Papers, Library of Congress; copy, in the handwriting of Ethan Brown, Hamilton Papers, Library of Congress.
    1. This letter was written in reply to McHenry to H, August 2, 1799.

From Thomas Parker

Winchester [*Virginia*] *August* 7, *1799*. ". . . I must Beg pardon for . . . urging a Remittance of money for the pay & Subsistence of the officers many of them are Really distressed for the want of It. I shall be obliged to you also to Inform me how they are to be paid for money advanced for postage of Letters Travelling expences and Stationary; the *latter we are now supplied with by the Contractor.* Expecting that the whole of the Cloathing woud be Immediately on I sent forward to the most distant Rendezvous too large a proportion of the Cloaths that did arrive so that at some of the Stations we are in want of Coats & Vests. I coud wish that a Supply of these articles may be sent on as soon as possable. I trust that we shall suc⟨ceed⟩ well in the Recruiting Busine⟨ss. We have⟩ now upwards at Two hundred ⟨recruits⟩ & are going on verry well. . . ."

ALS, Hamilton Papers, Library of Congress.

From Theodore Meminger

Philadelphia, August 8, 1799. ". . . I beg leave to remark that the Company are in a ragged state many of them being destitute of Overalls of Linen & those of Clothes past repair. Blankets & Woolen Overalls I have not included in the return as it will be some time before they are wanted & would be an incumberance."

ALS, Hamilton Papers, Library of Congress.

From John J. U. Rivardi

Niagara [New York] August 8, 1799. Again requests extra pay for soldiers doing extra work.[1] Reports that he has hired a boat "to remove the Garrison of Öswego."[2] States that "Several of our men are unwell." Discusses the repair of Fort Niagara.

ALS, Hamilton Papers, Library of Congress.
  1. See Rivardi to H, July 25, 1799.
  2. See Rivardi to H, July 25, 1799.

From Daniel Bradley

Staunton [*Virginia*] *August 9, 1799*. ". . . Captain Brock . . .[1]
informs me he has no Arms, Clothing, or public Stores of any kind,
these men of Capt. Gibsons,[2] & Lieut. Lewisis[3] at this place are in
much want of clothing. I have received a suit of clothing per. Man,
for two complete Companies but dont know whether I ought to
give any part of it to these men who have drew before, or keep it
for the recruits, I wish for information on the subject. Sir I take the
liberty to remind you that I feel very anxious to visit my family,
from which I have been absent near four years." [4]

ALS, Hamilton Papers, Library of Congress.
    1. Joseph Brock was a captain in the Fourth Regiment of Infantry.
    2. Alexander Gibson was a captain in the Fourth Regiment of Infantry.
    3. Meriwether Lewis was a lieutenant in the First Regiment of Infantry.
    4. Bradley had earlier requested a leave in Bradley to H, July 5, 1799 (listed
in the appendix to this volume).

Circular to the Commandants of Regiments

Circular   New York Aug 9th 1799

Sir
    Our political situation renders it very urgent that not a moment
shall be lost in disciplining our troops as fast as they shall be raised.
To this end it is essential that every officer shall personally exert
himself to the utmost and that a very faulty practice which has occasionally prevailed in our armies as well as others shall be carefully
avoided; namely Commanders of Regiments leaving too much to
their Majors, these to the Adjutants and the Company Officers to
their sergeants.
    It is expected that each commandant of a Regiment will himself
industriously exercise his Regiment in the manual & evolutions; that
each Major will do the like in his batalion and the company officers
in their several companies. These last must charge themselves with

the detail of instructing their men from the beginning—using their non commissioned Officers as auxiliaries not as their representatives or substitutes; and the field officers must carefully superintend the company Officers in relation to this detail.

This course will have the double advantage of ensuring the rapid improvement of the soldiers and of giving every Officer practical expertness within his sphere; without which an army is nothing but a mass of disorderly elements.

In the visits which I expect to make to the several corps I hope for the gratification of observing the proficiency of officers and men that the instruction contained in this letter has been carefully & zealously executed.

With great consideration &c

ADf, Hamilton Papers, Library of Congress.

From James McHenry [1]

Philad. 10 Augt. 1799

I am fully satisfied my dear Hamilton from what you say, that you had no intention to insinuate in the general order, any thing that could affect my character in the eye of the public or army, and I am no longer uneasy.

Upon the other point, let me assure you, that the military rule of correspondence, which I have departed from, in some instances, as relative to General Wilkinson, did not take place without substantial cause. I am in possession of my justification were it necessary to stir the subject. There may be however, particular cases, independent of these, when I have erred through inattention. And who is it will not, with so much business to attend to as I have?

I recommended to you some time since to send to England for the officers manual in the field, or a series of military plans, representing the principal operations of a campaign.[2] I now transmit you a copy, for which you will be pleased to return me a receipt.

The book has merit. But as Aristotles rules never produced a good tragedy, neither in my opinion will the best military book produce a great general. Both characters are the result of the energies of genius.

Your sincere & affec   James McHenry

ALS, Hamilton Papers, Library of Congress; ADfS, James McHenry Papers, Library of Congress.
1. This letter was written in reply to H to McHenry, August 5, 1799.
2. See McHenry to H, June 20, 1799, note 1.

From Thomas Parker

Winchester [Virginia] August 11, 1799. ". . . Some of my officers are so distressed for money that I have been Obliged to procure a loan to enable them to go on with the Recruiting service.[1] Their expences in continually Removing from post to post has entirely exhausted their Resources & I trust It will be Convenient at all events to send on at least their Subsistance & allowance for Recruiting."

ALS, Hamilton Papers, Library of Congress.
1. See Parker to H, August 7, 1799.

From George Washington

[*Mount Vernon, August 11, 1799.*[1] *Letter not found.*]

1. "List of Letters from G—— Washington to General Hamilton," Columbia University Libraries.

General Orders

[*New York, August 12, 1799.* On August 14, 1799, William S. Smith wrote to Hamilton: "Agreeably to General Orders of the 12th. inst. I attend here as President of a General Court Martial. . . ."[1] *General orders not found.*]

1. This letter is listed in the appendix to this volume.

From James McHenry

War Department August 12, 1799. "I transmit under cover to you for each of the Officers named in the enclosed list [1] a Copy of the elements of fortification,[2] and request that you would have the same forwarded to them respectively. . . ."

LS, Hamilton Papers, Library of Congress.
  1. "Names of the Officers for whom the Elements of fortification have been transmitted to Major General Hamilton" (copy, Hamilton Papers, Library of Congress).
  2. For Jonathan Williams's translation of this work, see Williams to H, June 17, 1799, note 1. See also Williams to H, July 11, 1799; H to Williams, June 20, 1799.

To James McHenry

New York Aug. 13. 1799

Sir

It is now time to take measures for the establishment of the additional Regiments in Winter Quarters. It has been already determined to dispose of them in four bodies and the positions generally have been designated.[1] These positions will of course be adhered to, unless alterations shall become expedient from considerations relative to the comparitive prices of rations at different places. It is necessary speedily to understand whether any deviations will result from this source which has been heretofore a subject of correspondence between us.

As to mode, I incline to that of Hutts. Every thing in our military establishment is too unsettled to justify the expence of permanent barracks and the hiring of quarters in Towns will be adverse to the health and discipline of the Troops and may lead to disorders unfriendly to harmony between the citizens and the soldiery. The experience of last war has proved that troops cannot be more comfortable in any way than in hutts; and these they can build themselves. Perhaps as those in question are quite raw it may be expedient, where they do not happen to have carpenters among themselves to indulge each Regiment with the aid of a few to be procured here; who may direct the mode of construction and lend a helping hand to the hutts of the officers.

The ground will be to be hired. The material for building must be found upon each spot. If you approve and as soon as I shall receive from you the information which is to guide as to the prices of rations, I will give direction to the respective Contractors to procure the ground with the cooperation, when it can conveniently be had, of the Agent for the War Department, and of the Commandant of a Regiment nearest to the intended site.

Any suggestions which you shall think fit to make with regard to the detail will receive careful attention.

Applications have been made to me to authorise the providing a waggon and four horses for the use of each Regiment.[2] It is suggested that for transporting of fuel & straw and for a variety of current services many difficulties attend the continual depending on the Contractor, which would be obviated by a waggon attached to the Regiment.[3] I am of opinion that the measure is right and would direct it to be put in execution but that it is my rule to enter into no new arrangement involving expence without previous recourse to you when there is no pressure of circumstances to require immediate decision.

With great respect

The Secy of War

ADf, Hamilton Papers, Library of Congress.

1. See H's draft of George Washington to McHenry, first letter of December 13, 1798; McHenry to H, February 4, 1799. See also H to McHenry, July 12, first letter of July 29, 1799.

2. On July 30, 1799, William S. Smith wrote to H: "Enclosed is a Letter from the Quarter Master of the Regt. stating the inconvenience he is exposed to, and the expence arising to the public, for the want of a Waggon and Horses attached to the Regt. . . . Will you do me the favour to point out a mode, by which the Regt. can obtain a Waggon & Horses" (letter listed in the appendix to this volume). The enclosure which Smith mentions is Henry Ludlow to Smith, July 29, 1799 (ALS, Hamilton Papers, Library of Congress).

3. In the Hamilton Papers, Library of Congress, there is an undated document entitled "Conjectures in the form of Queries," which reads in part: "Might not a stage waggon be so constructed as to answer the purpose of a

Limber to a field piece, an ammunition waggon, & a vehicle for the transportation of 12 Men? Might not a pintle be fixed behind, of sufficient strength to receive the trail upon it, and draw the Carriage after it? Might not the seats of the Carriage be converted into ammunition Boxes to the extent of 50 or 60 rounds? . . ."

To James McHenry

N. York Augt. 13th. 1799

My dear Sir

Every day must prove more and more to every body that it is impossible to serve two masters. I cannot be a general and a Practicer of the law at the same time without doing injustice to this Government and myself. Hence I am anxious to disentangle myself more completely than I have yet done from forensic pursuits. But to be able to do this I must call to my succour all the emoluments which I have a right to claim. Hitherto I have had neither Quarters nor fuel nor servants. The two last I shall take measures for myself. But the former I have some scruples about, and wish an instruction concerning it from you, which may be addressed as well to General Pinckney as to myself. On this article too I have no doubt of my right to order the person acting as Quarter Master to provide Quarters for me and my suite. Every commanding general has this right, and situated as I am, in a time of no active operations, with the force under my command dispersed to various points, I have no doubt that the strictest propriety accords with my personal station being where it is, and that in this station it is in every view fit that I should have provided at public expence for myself and suite a house as quarters suited to my rank and command. The procuring of a better one than I now occupy would be Strictly justifiable but it is not my wish to do it.[1]

How do you construe the 4th. Section of the Act of March 3d. 1797,[2] respecting double rations, in reference to the Officers appointed under the act for augmenting the army? [3] This Question has in cases foreign to the spirit of the provision come up from some of the Officers of the 12 additional regiments, and it will probably soon come up in others. It is important to the two major Generals as well as others and it ought to apply to them. Yet the law must not be strained but future provision made where the existing one is deficient.

You must not think me rapacious. I have not changed my character. But my Situation as commanding General exposes me to much additional expence in entertaining Officers occasionally in the City of N. York and citizens and foreigners who come to pay their respects to the commanding general and adding this consideration to the circumstance of a wife and 6 Children whose maintenance and education are to be taken care of.[4]

Adieu

Secy. of War

Copy, in the handwriting of Ethan Brown, Hamilton Papers, Library of Congress.

1. H lived at 26 Broadway, and his law office was at 69 Stone Street.
2. Section 4 of "An Act to amend and repeal, in part, the Act intituled 'An Act to ascertain and fix the Military Establishment of the United States'" (1 Stat. 507–08) reads in part: "*And be it further enacted*, That from and after the thirtieth day of June next, . . . That to the brigadier, while commander in chief, and to each officer, while commanding a separate post, there shall be allowed twice the number of rations to which they would otherwise be entitled."
3. Section 3 of "An Act giving eventual authority to the President of the United States to augment the Army" (1 Stat. 725–27 [March 2, 1799]) provided "That the officers, non-commissioned officers and privates of the troops, which may be organized and raised pursuant to this act, shall be entitled to the like pay, clothing, rations, forage and other emoluments, . . . as the officers, non-commissioned officers and privates of other troops of correspondent denominations, composing the army of the United States . . . *Provided*, that no officer . . . shall be entitled to any pay or other emolument until he shall be called into actual service."
4. An additional sentence to this letter, which has been crossed out, reads: "I shall stand in need of all I can fairly get from the public if I am essentially to renounce my profession."

To James McHenry

New York August 13th. 1799

Sir

I have considered the drafts of the proposed contracts sent me through Mr. O Hara,[1] and have had some conversation with him concerning them. There are a few points some of which appear to me to require to be differently arranged, others to stand in need of explanation for the avoiding of Disputes.

1. In the proposed contract for the supply of the Western army, it is put in the option of the Contractor to furnish either beef pork or Bacon; but it is not said to whom the option shall belong as between *fresh* and *salt* meat. In the contract proposed for Virginia &c. the instrument is wholly silent on this point. In this case, you are apprised that I should hold the option to rest with the public. But in the other, the Contractor would find colour to contend that a different construction is implied.

It is in my opinion proper that the right of election throughout should be reserved to the public and that, to avoid controversy, this should be declared, on the opposite principle, the contentment & health of the army are placed in the discretion of the Contractor which is inadmissible. Though there may be on the one side danger of oppression, as on the other of abuse; yet it is more reasonable that confidence should be reposed in the Agents of the Government than in the Contractors whose private interest may lead to an improper use of discretion; and that these should run the hazard of a diminution of profit rather than the public that of a derangement of the service.

Mr. O Hara accordingly consents that the option shall be reserved to the Government, provided the exercise of it be confined to the General or officer commanding *an army* or within a *great military district* to be regulated by general orders promulged a reasonable time before hand. This certainly is a proper modification of the thing.

2 It is submitted that whenever due Bills are issued, for parts of rations retained they be payable absolutely in money. Otherwise a double supply of particular articles may take place at certain periods; occasioning at times an intire deficiency at another times an excess. This plan will also have the advantage of simplicity, which is always conducive to exactness to good faith and to the satisfaction of those concerned.

3 The regulation for cases in which the dayly issues may not exceed 50 rations is conceived to be inexpedient. It serves to destroy that reciprocal check between the military officers and contractors which is requisite to the security of the Government—and implicates

the former in duties not very congenial with the spirit of their stations. Without extra compensations the service would be disgusting to them, and if these are to be made they had better be given to the Contractors as an indemnification for procuring agents distinct from the military. General Wilkinson whom I have consulted is strongly of the same opinion.

3 The option as to the issuing of flour or bread ought likewise to be settled in the contract. Unless proportions are defined this option also ought to belong to the Government to be exercised through the Chief Military Officer. It is believed that it may be restricted to three days in the week leaving the choice for the rest of the time to the Contractor. A proportion of flour is very necessary as an ingredient in the soup of the Troops and for the purpose of dressing their hair.

4 Provision should be made for a deposit of Nine Months at Michilimacnac. The very remote situation of that place recommends this provision.

There is one point more upon which I shall offer to your consideration some thoughts. The small parts of the ration as they are called are rated so low in these contracts that it is clearly the interest of the Contractor never to furnish them but to pay the stipulated equivalent in money. This is a real evil. Candles and soap are at all times extremely necessary & Vinegar especially in Southern Climates is very important to health. The furnishing of the two first mentioned articles ought to be ensured by an adequate equivalent; and as to vinegar it seems to me that it ought not to be the subject of Contract at a fixed price. It should be among the articles to be provided by the Contractor upon Commission. The Troops will then have it when stationary; and in other cases it must be dispensed with.

It will deserve the attention of the Department of War, in the adjustment of subsistence money, to indemnify the Officers for the parts of Rations which are contingent, whenever they are not included in the contract price.

With very great respect   I have the honor to be   Sir   Yr. Obed ser

The Secy of War

ADf, Hamilton Papers, Library of Congress.

1. A printed copy of this contract, dated August 1, 1799, and signed by James O'Hara and McHenry, was enclosed in McHenry to H, September 11, 1799 (listed in the appendix to this volume).

To Charles Cotesworth Pinckney

New York, August 13, 1799. "Your several favours of the 10th. of June 12. and 29 [1] of July have been received. . . . The course is for money and other supplies for the recruiting service to go immediately from the department of War upon application from me. As yet no regular military chest has been established nor have the proper organs of the Staff been appointed. . . . A more perfect organisation is indispensable. The Secretary of War has been and will continue to be urged on the subject. I presumed he had made an arrangement for your command similar to that which has provisionally obtained in this quarter. . . . You are right in your recollection that it was the joint idea at Philadelphia to require the Officers always to appear in public in their Uniforms. But it was referred to future regulation in a code which must be devised and to which I shall seriously devote my attention this Winter. . . . Difficulties arise from the separation of command . . . in cases in which there is something to be done affecting both districts. The Secy of War is the natural organ in these cases—but resort to him . . . must sometimes occasion delay. The mutual confidence which I am happy to know subsists between us must relieve the embarrassment and any agency which either may occasionally take in a matter that may concern the command of the other must be deemed as it must be intended the effect of a desire to aid each other. . . . On the subject of the Recruiting service. . . . Hitherto I have addressed myself directly to the Colonels . . . who are recruiting within your district. . . . The course has been conducive to dispatch though less agreeable to my ideas of regulation than to have resorted in the first instance to your agency. . . . If you think that the course begun ought, for the reasons which dictated, to be continued—I submit whether it may not be adviseable for you to drop a line to those officers. . . ."

ADf, Hamilton Papers, Library of Congress.
  1. Pinckney's letter of July 29, 1799, is listed in the appendix to this volume. In this letter Pinckney discussed the distribution of the troops under his command.

From Josias Carvel Hall

Havre de Grace [Maryland] August 14, 1799. ". . . The men begin to be urgent for their Pay. To some there is three months due. I had much rather the proper Officer was appointed to this Duty. It is not agreeable to me to tell an Officer, who perhaps can not well afford it, he must lose the Bounty advanced. . . . Our recruiting money is nearly expended. The Paymaster,[1] of the money appropriated to that Purpose, has but $1070 in Hand. Some of the Officers who have not had Success have still some remaining; tho' very little in the hands of any Individual; Others will require more in a few Days. . . ."

ALS, Hamilton Papers, Library of Congress.
  1. Ninian Pinkney, a first lieutenant in the Ninth Regiment of Infantry, was appointed paymaster of that regiment on April 23, 1799 (Godfrey, "Provisional Army," 153).

From James McHenry

War Department, August 14, 1799. "Governor Davie of North Carolina, lately transmitted to me, three copies of the inclosed work, entitled 'Instructions, to be observed for the formations, and movements of the Cavalry,'[1] published agreeably to a resolution of the Legislature of North Carolina.[2] One of these copies, the Governor requested I would present to you. . . ."

LS, Hamilton Papers, Library of Congress.
  1. William Richardson Davie, *Instructions to be Observed for the Formations and Movements of the Cavalry, Published Agreeably to a Resolution of the Legislature of North Carolina* (Halifax: Abraham Hodge, 1799).
  2. On December 22, 1798, the House of Commons of North Carolina resolved: "That the Governor of this state be and he is hereby authorised and requested to contract with the Printer, for one hundred and fifty copies of the regulations for disciplining the cavalry, as laid down by General Davie:

and when the pamphlet shall be so completed, the Governor is further requested to distribute them in equal proportion among the several officers commanding the different regiments of cavalry in the state, in such manner as he shall judge most convenient" (*Journal of the House of Commons of North Carolina. At a General Assembly begun and held at the City of Raleigh, on Monday the nineteenth day of November, in the year of our Lord one thousand seven hundred and ninety-eight, and of the Independence of the United States of America the twenty-third. It being the First Session of this Assembly* [n.p., n.d.], 71). The Senate had approved the same resolution on December 21 (*Journal of the Senate of North Carolina. At a General Assembly begun and held at the City of Raleigh, on Monday the nineteenth day of November, in the year of our Lord one thousand seven hundred and ninety-eight, and of the Independence of the United States of America the twenty-third: It being the First Session of this Assembly* [n.p., n.d.], 74).

To Nathan Rice

New York August 14th 1799

Sir

Your letter of the eighth of July has been delivered to me. The articles of which you speak have arrived, I presume, before this. However the Secretary of war shall be informed of the deficiency of which you complain. All applications of the kind you will please, in future, to direct to Ebenezer Stevens Esqr. who is the Agent of the War Department in matters of this nature. The applications should be accompanied with returns of the articles wanted. Knapsacks have already been provided for the current year—your suggestion will be considered [1] in the arrangements for the year following. Mr. Francis Barker will receive my interest with the Secretary of war.

I enclose to you a letter which I have received from Cat. Ashmun.[2] This would have been directed, with more propriety, to you; altho addressed to me, doubtless from good motives. Some of the questions contained in Capn Ashmun's letter you will be able to answer without any information from me. With respect to the exchange of soldiers I would observe that no soldier can be exchanged after he has been regularly enlisted without my consent. When any circumstances occur which may render an exchange advisable they should be reported to me for my consideration & direction.

The fourth section of the Act of Congress passed the third of

March ninety seven[3] does not apply to officers in the situation of Captain Ashmun. The contract price within the state is, I understand, the rule which governs on the subject of rations.

With great consideration   I am, Sir &c. &c.

Df, in the handwriting of Thomas Y. How and H, Hamilton Papers, Library of Congress.

1. The words "be considered" are in H's handwriting.
2. Letter from Phineas Ashmun not found.
3. For Section 4 of "An Act to amend and repeal, in part, the Act intituled 'An Act to ascertain and fix the Military Establishment of the United States'" (1 *Stat.* 507–08), see H to James McHenry, second letter of August 13, 1799, note 2.

From William Willcocks

Head Quarters, Broncks [*New York*], *August 14, 1799.* States that in the absence of Colonel William S. Smith[1] he commands the regiment. Asks what procedures to use in filling out payrolls. States that the officers "complain heavily" of the delay in receiving their pay. Adds that the men, who are "next to a state of mutiny," are stealing vegetables, and because of a lack of "platters or trenchers, bowls and dishes," they either "eat their provisions like dogs, on the ground" or hire utensils. Complains that the regiment, though entitled to "three Marquis," has only one. Believes that "some Arrangements are universally known to be so dilitory—erronious—or deficient, that the confidence of application is lost, in any other channel than 'thro' you."

ALS, Hamilton Papers, Library of Congress.

1. On August 14, 1799, Smith wrote to H from Fort Jay, New York: "Agreeably to General Orders of the 12th inst. I attend here as President of a General Court Martial . . ." (listed in the appendix to this volume). H's general orders of August 12, 1799, have not been found.

Receipt from John C. Hummel

[Trenton, August 15, 1799]

Recd. Trenton August 15th. 1799 of General Hamilton by the hands of Abraham Hunt [1] One Hundred and Twenty Dollars in full for my Bay Horse [2] Peacock—Warranted sound.

$120   John C. Hummel

ADS, Hamilton Papers, Library of Congress.
  1. A resident of Trenton and a veteran of the American Revolution, Hunt had been an agent for purchasing horses for the Army in 1792. In 1794 he became contractor for Army supplies at Trenton, a position he still held in 1799.
  2. An entry in H's Cash Book, 1795–1804, under the date of September 1, 1799, reads: "paid for a horse & 125" (AD, Hamilton Papers, Library of Congress).

To William Willcocks

New York Aug 15. 1799

Sir

I have received your letter of yesterday as the actual commander of the 12th Regiment.

The delay of money for the troops is owing to the want of muster and pay rolls. It is well understood that the permanent forms cannot in the present state of the Regiment be exactly complied with. But it will be with reason expected at the public offices that they shall be approached as nearly as possible. This has not been done. I have personally explained to Lt. Smith [1] Pay Master how it may be done. Any officer of a company may represent his Captain & the Regimental Pay Master by special order of the Commandant may act for those Companies which have no officers present. It is at least essential that the names as well as the numbers of officers and men should appear.

If the Officers are already discouraged by the difficulties they have experienced—it is an unlucky presage of what may be expected in relation to the far greater difficulties incident to their military career. It is hoped for their reputation that you have expressed yourself too strongly. As far as their complaints respect the delay of pay, it is to be ascribed to the want of proper documents from the Regiment. This observation is not intended as censure; for it is not doubted that the best intentions have existed and that any defect in this particular which may exist has arisen from misapprehension of what might and could be done. But circumstances like these ought to inspire a spirit of accommodation.

With regard to platters &c the public stores when they were called for by me were found empty, because it had not been the practice to furnish them. It is known to the Officers who served regimentally during our revolution war, that these articles were seldom supplied, and that various contrivances were made for substitutes. And I am told that the furnishing of such articles has been for a long time discontinued. When furnished, in the course of active operations they are very apt to be lost or destroyed and then they are of necessity dispensed with.

I mention these things to shew that these articles are not deemed indispensable and that a delay in obtaining them ought to be met with good humour. It has not been usual in our service to furnish Marquees to any officer of a grade below the commandant of a Regiment. This explains that point.

You will not I trust misconceive me. I am not displeased with your giving me the information which is contained in your letter. It is right I should know the discontents which prevail whether well or ill founded, proportionate or exaggerated. But it is also right and necessary that I should frankly disclose the impression I have of them.

I shall only add that it is essential to cultivate a spirit of accommodation and that it is expected that every officer will in his station do so as a duty of the first importance.

With great consideration & esteem I am Sir   Yr Obed ser

Major Wilcocks

ADf, Hamilton Papers, Library of Congress.
    1. Lieutenant James Smith, Jr., of New York City was elected paymaster of the Twelfth Infantry Regiment on April 5, 1799 (Godfrey, "Provisional Army," 165–66).

From James McHenry

[*Philadelphia, August 16, 1799.* On August 21, 1799, Hamilton wrote to McHenry: "Your letter of the 16 instant respecting Cloathing for the Western Army did not reach me till yesterday." *Letter not found.*]

From James Wilkinson

N: York August 16th: 1799

Sir

I send you the only Letter Book I have with me—unfortunately the most material one has been left behind.

The inaccuracies of the copiest may be readily excused, but the frivolity & fallibility of Intellect, too current in my correspondence with the Minister,[1] will require an exertion of your indulgence. My humiliation has been profound, my sufferings exquisite, whether justly or unjustly you can best determine; but the Issue is I flatter myself closed forever, & I now look forward to better & to brighter Days, content to forget the irritations, which have ensued the conflicts of principle & power.

I am sensible the perusal is hardly worth your time, yet you may, perhaps, pick out of my observations respecting Cox's machinations,[2] the dispositions of the Western People generally, & the defence of our Mississippi Possession in particular, some Ideas which may not again occur to me. Would you remark in the course of my communications to the Minister, any circumstance worthy explanation, you have only to note it to me.

I must express my regret for not being able to find the Letter wrote Mr. McHenry in Decr. or Jany: 97.8. in which while conjuring Him not to urge the presidential sanction to his Essay, for the government of the Troops, I add "in the mean time permit me to refer you to Col Hamilton, for his Opinion on the subject, as I consider Him the ablest military Judge of our Country; this opinion is not founded on any personal Intimacy with Col. H but is the result of informations on which I can rely." This Letter was I believe marked *private* & therefore has not been copied into the Book, yet I made reference to it, in my Letter to the Minister of the 10th April last,[3] wherein I observe "It is with singular pleasure I receive orders to address myself to Major General Hamilton; you possess strong testimony of my high respect for his Military Talents, and it will be my study to merit his confidence & his approbation." I am ashamed to tresspass this detail on you, but anterior conversations held in the fullness of my Heart makes it necessary.

I send you also for your amusement, Loyds Campaigns,[4] with Lindsays miscellany, containing his own & Tempelhoffes strictures on the Works of the first.[5] Neither are exempt from Errors & prejudices, but I think much useful information may [be] culled from them. I am better this morning, under my antiphlogistic regimen, yet the sensorium continues deranged, tho not insensible of the report & the attachment due to you from

Your obliged & affectionate   Ja Wilkinson

Majr Genl Hamilton

ALS, Hamilton Papers, Library of Congress.
1. James McHenry.
2. For Zachariah Cox's activities, see McHenry to H, March 19, 1799, note 2; April 2, 1799, note 4.
3. Copy, Hamilton Papers, Library of Congress. McHenry sent this copy of Wilkinson's letter to H on May 29, 1799 (letter listed in the appendix to this volume).
4. [Henry Humphrey Evans Lloyd], *The History of the Late War in Germany, between the King of Prussia and the Empress of Germany and her allies . . . By a General Officer, who served several campaigns in the Austrian Army* (London, 1766). There are several editions of this work with similar, but not identical, titles.
5. Colin Lindsay, *Extracts from Colonel Tempelhoffe's History of the Seven Year's War. A Military Miscellany. Also a treatise on winter posts. To which is added a narrative of events at St. Lucie and Gibraltar, and of John Duke of Marlborough's march to the Danube, etc.* (2 Vols., London, 1793).
Georg Friedrich von Tempelhof's work was originally published as *Geschichte des siebenjahrigen Krieges in Deutschland, zwischen dem Könige von Preussen und der Kaiserin Königin mit ihren Alliirten, vom General Lloyd, aus dem Englischen aufs neue übersetzt, mit verbesserten Planen und Ammerkungen* (2 Vols., Berlin: J. F. Unger, 1783–1785).

From William C. Bentley

Richmond [Virginia] August 17, 1799. "Yours of the 10 Ultimo [1] notifying the appointments of the Medical Staff and the Com: officers to fill vacancies within my Regiment was received in proper time. The manner in which the vacancies were filled was unexpected to me, as well as to those who received the appointments; They all excepted to have been the junior officers of the regiment, and that those who had been in service, would have been promoted. The arrangement of relative rank of my Regiment as reported by me on the 15th Ultimo,[2] was made under that Idea, and yours of the 31st [3] establishes the rank, agreeably to the report, and authorizes me to act upon it accordingly; which makes those two letters irreconcilable. I will be obliged to you to have a reference to them and if they appear to you in the same light, to reconcile the differences and transmit a compleat list, agreeably to the rank as now fixed. . . ."

LS, Hamilton Papers, Library of Congress.
  1. Letter not found.
  2. Letter listed in the appendix to this volume.
  3. Letter listed in the appendix to this volume.

To James McHenry

New York Aug 19, *1799*

Dear Sir

I return you the papers of Mr. Williams which you sent me [1] at his desire for perusal. The explanation and your final opinion of the affair have given me pleasure, as I should be sorry that any circumstance of improper conduct should have stood in the way of the employment of Mr. Williams.

I regret extremely that obstacles should exist to the requiring of the resignation of Mr. Francis. You are apprized of the good opinion I entertain of the probity of this Gentleman and of his talents for business within a sphere of action which will admit of an immediate personal attention to every thing which is to be done. But you are no less apprised of my perfect conviction of his incompetency, at his present time of life, to execute an office which embraces extensive and complicated objects; in which system and arrangement and various combinations are necessary. It is a satire upon our Government that he cannot for whatever cause be removed. The number of powerful connections which he has [2] is I trust not the obstacle. If it has any weight, I think it may be relied upon that the most inflential of them would from conviction acquiese in the propriety of the measure. But if he must remain, certainly there ought to be no ceremony about giving him good assistants whether of his own choice or not. In this it is most regular that the two departments should concur. But if they cannot, as Secy of War I should not hesitate to insist that he should employ such organs as I deemed requisite for executing well the business of my department.

You observe that no present inconvenience attends the suspension of such a measure. Believe me the service every where is suffering for the want of proper organisation. It is one thing for business to drag on—another for it to go well. The business of supply in all its branches (except as to provisions) proceeds heavily and without order or punctuality—in a manner equally ill adapted to œconomy on a large scale as to efficiency and the contentment of the army. It is painful to observe how disjointed and peace-meal a business it is. Among other evils is this that the head of the War Department and the Chief of the several divisions of the army exhaust their time in details, which, beyond a general superintendence are foreign to them. And plans for giving perfection to our military system are unavoidably neglected.

Let me repeat, my Dear friend, my earnest advice, that you proceed to organise without delay the several branches of the Department of supply, that is to fix the plan and appoint the agents. You will experience great relief and many advantages from it. The saving from better management will infinitely overpay the expence of salaries.

The Contractors who feel little responsibility execute very carelessly every thing in which they are merely agents. The increase of numbers will make this a very important consideration.

Supplies in general are neither duly procured nor duly forwarded, frequently not of good quality nor agreeing in kind—and the system of accountability for issues, excellent in its theory, I venture to say intirely fails in execution. The inevitable consequence is that there must be great waste of property. It is in vain to have good plans if there are not proper organs of execution. Every new step to be taken is attended with embarrassment for want of organisation.

It is much to be regretted that *Carrington* was not appointed Qr Master General [3] according to the new arrangement before the last session of the Senate ended—so that every thing in that branch of service might be now in complete train. If his appointment is determined upon, will it not be well to notify the intention to him & to prevail upon him to come to the Seat of Government to the end that you may concert with him the proper arrangement. Till the Commander in Chief shall take the field his residence would very naturally be at or near the seat of Government & you would find his assistance in every view very valuable.

I have heretofore requested Mr. Hodgsdon [4] to send me *from time to time* a return of the supplies which he forwards. This may save you the trouble of reading applications for things which have been done. The request has not been complied with. I do not mention this by way of complaint but for information to induce you to give him a specific direction. Once a week such a return ought to be made to you & a duplicate might be sent to me. Adieu

Yrs. very truly   A Hamilton

Secy of War

ALS, Columbia University Libraries; ALS (photostat), James McHenry Papers, Library of Congress; copy, in the handwriting of Ethan Brown, Hamilton Papers, Library of Congress.

1. McHenry to H, July 20, 1799.

2. Tench Francis, purveyor of public supplies, was the son-in-law of Charles Willing, the brother-in-law of Thomas Willing and William Coxe, and the uncle of Anne Willing Bingham, the wife of William Bingham.

Charles Willing, the founder of the American branch of the family, had been born in England. He moved to Philadelphia, where he became a prosperous merchant and mayor of that city. He died in 1754.

Thomas Willing, the son of Charles Willing, joined his father's counting-house in 1751 and subsequently served as a partner in such firms as Willing, Morris, and Company; Willing, Morris, and Inglis; and Willing, Morris, and Swanwick. He held several governmental positions in colonial Pennsylvania, and he was a neutral during the American Revolution. He became president of the Bank of North America in 1781 and president of the first Bank of the United States in 1791. His fortune was estimated to be approximately one million dollars.

Anne Willing Bingham was the daughter of Thomas Willing and the niece of Anne Willing Francis. In 1780, at sixteen, she married William Bingham, a Philadelphia merchant and one of the wealthiest men in North America. Bingham was a member of the Continental Congress from 1786 to 1789 and of the Pennsylvania Assembly from 1790 to 1795, and was a United States Senator from 1795 to 1801. He had extensive landholdings in Pennsylvania, New York, and New England, and was among the first promoters of internal improvements in the United States.

William Coxe, Tench Coxe's father, was a Philadelphia merchant.

3. George Washington had asked Edward Carrington to serve as quartermaster general (Washington to Carrington, July 15, August 5, 1798 [ALS, letterpress copies, George Washington Papers, Library of Congress]). Carrington had agreed to serve only if Washington took field command of the Army in the event of a war (Carrington to Washington, August 14, 1798 [ALS, George Washington Papers, Library of Congress]).

4. H to Samuel Hodgdon, April 15, 1799 (listed in the appendix to this volume).

To James McHenry

New York, August 19, 1799. Asks what "the rate of allowance to which officers are entitled for their retained rations" is and how the allowance is obtained.[1] Agrees with McHenry's decision to defer the appointment of cadets,[2] but thinks that "in the meantime . . . it will be well to appoint two Cadets to each regiment . . . to act as ensigns." States that he has received "Pressing applications" for money from different regiments. Believes that as officers are dispersed among the recruiting stations, the forwarding of muster and pay rolls should be dispensed with [3] and money should be forwarded "upon estimate so as to complete the payment of arrearages of the officers up to the first of this month, of the non Commissioned Officers and privates up to the first of July." States that several regimental commandants have asked for an extra supply of clothing [4] and adds that recruiting in some districts has been so successful that the allotted clothing supplies are low. Recommends that the clothing supply be "as speedily as possible extended to three fourths of the complement of each Regiment." States that the number of recruits in each of the twelve additional regiments is as follows:

"11th Regiment	300
13 do	300
8 do	250
9 do	200
10	200
12	200
7	150
14	150
15	150
16	100
6	100
5	– ."

Df, in the handwriting of H and Thomas Y. How, Hamilton Papers, Library of Congress.

1. See William S. Smith to H, June 12, 1799; H to McHenry, June 25, 1799; Thomas Parker to H, June 14, August 7, 1799; William Willcocks to H, August 14, 1799.
2. See McHenry to H, July 8, 1799.
3. See McHenry to H, June 15, August 2, 1799; H to Willcocks, August 15, 1799.
4. See H to McHenry, June 14, July 9, 1799; Josias Carvel Hall to H, June 25, 1799; Parker to H, June 30, August 7, 1799; Theodore Meminger to H, August 8, 1799; Daniel Bradley to H, August 9, 1799.

From Thomas Butler

South West Point, Tennessee, August 20, 1799. "Permit me to inform you, that Capn. Jonathan Taylor[1] of my Regt. has been recruiting in the town of Lexington (State of Kentucky) for some time past, his last return dated the 26th July ulto. reported forty Six Recruits, all destitute of Cloathing, Capn. Taylor observes, that if he had a supply of Cloathing, he could soon compleat his company. . . . I have thought it my duty to State to you Capn. Taylor wants, not doubting but that you will give such orders as may be necessary, to enable Capn. Taylor to compleat his Compy."

ALS, Hamilton Papers, Library of Congress.
1. Taylor was a captain in the Fourth Regiment of Infantry.

From John Wilkins, Junior

Philadelphia 20th. August 1799

Sir

I expected when the law of March last was passed "for the better organizing of the Troops of the United States, & for other purposes" [1] that the Quarter Master department would be immediatly arranged according to it, & that a Quarter Master Genl. would be appointed with high military rank; but I have been ordered to this place to take charge, for the present, of the Department. All that I have done, as yet, is to establish an office at this place, to examine & settle the accounts of the different persons employed, & to distribute stores to them to their different places of destination. It is now most certainly time, that the department was organized, & that Deputies were appointed for the different armies; and that its duties were distinctly separated, & reduced to system. Should I proceed in this organization, making the appointments of Deputies, together with Division & Brigade Quarter Masters, & establishing a system under my instruction, when soon after another head must be appointed to the department, who may dislike my appointments & the arrangement I have made and desire to change them, which would be the source of great confusion & embarrassment. The sooner therefore, a Quarter Master General is appointed under the law, the sooner will order & system be introduced into the Department.

I have had the appointment of Quarter master General for the Western army upwards of three years. The dispersed situation of the troops, the extent of country they embrace, the number of posts, the variety of transportation used, & to keep up the accounts for the disbursements of cash, & the expenditure of different stores, require constant attention & controul. Being ordered to remain here has occasioned considerable embarrassment in my accounts & abuses have been made, which from my remote situation I have not been able to correct.

The following order is pursued in the distribution of publick stores—Indian goods, Ordnance stores, Hospital stores & clothing are transported from Philadelphia to Pittsburgh, from whence, they are distributed to the different post they are intended. Those destined for the Lakes, are sent up the Allegheny river to the mouth of French Creek & from thence to Le Boeuf, which is at the head of the navigation of French Creek; at both those posts there are excellent store houses, built on publick ground, & surrounded by good pickets. From Le Boeuf the stores are transported in waggons to Presq'Isle, & shipped from thence to the posts on the Lakes. At Presq'Isle there are good store houses & a saw mill belonging to the United states on publick ground. The Stores for the posts on the Ohio and Mississippi are ship'd at Pittsburgh for the places of their destination. The store keepers at the different posts, under the title of assistant Quarter Masters, are charged with all the stores sent to the post under their direction, together with all the Quarter Master stores purchased, & delivered them, & are to account for the same by regular orders & receipts.

The principal objects of disbursement of cash for the western army, are the purchase of Quarter Master stores & means of transport; Transportation; building & repairs to Forts & Barracks; building & repairs to their vessels on the Lakes & payment of their captains & crews; the captain & crews of two Gallies on the Mississippi; store keepers; &c. which when extended into detail occasion a great Variety & complication of accounts.

I have been particular respecting the Quarter Master department for the western army, to explain its situation, & the necessity of being with it. My services can be best rendered in that country, & my wish is to remain in the same situation I have been with respect to it. The law of March last states, "but the provisions of this act are not to affect the present Quarter Master General of the army of the United States, who in case a Quarter Master General is appointed by virtue of this act, is to act as Deputy Quarter Master Genl." [2] My services as Deputy will probably be required, where I am most capable of performing the duty, with the western army.

In the plan you propose "for providing & issuing the military supplies" [3] in the part respecting the Purveyor, it directs his having three assistants, & that "the person who now resides at the seat of Government in Quality of Quarter Master General may perform the duty of first mentioned assistant." When I was appointed Quarter Master Genl my sphere of Duty was confined to the western army, with which I still wish to serve. I have been long with it, & during the time, I hope, I have not been inattentive to acquire a knoledge of the Military & civil duties relative to the department of which I had the direction. Abstracted from every other consideration, which under the circumstances of this arrangement would be among the least, the compensation allowed to me would not enable me to reside at the seat of government.

I submit these observations to your candor & better judgement with pleasure.

I have the honour to be   Sir   with the greatest respect your obt. Sr   Jno. Wilkins Jr

The Honble Major Genl. Hamilton

ALS, Hamilton Papers, Library of Congress.
   1. 1 *Stat.* 749–55 (March 3, 1799).
   2. The portion of Section 12 of "An Act for the better organizing of the Troops of the United States; and for other purposes" which Wilkins is quoting concludes: ". . . and shall hereafter have the rank of lieutenant-colonel . . ." (1 *Stat.* 752). Wilkins had served as quartermaster general of the Army since June 1, 1796 (*Executive Journal*, I, 214). On June 1, 1799, he became quartermaster general with the rank of major general (Raphael P. Thian, ed., *History of the General Staff of the Army of the United States* [Washington, 1901], 140). See James McHenry to H, March 8, 1799.
   3. See the enclosure to H to James McHenry, April 8, 1799.

From John Wilkins, Junior

Philadelphia, August 20, 1799. ". . . There ought to be a plan adopted such as you propose for the providing & issuing of Military supplies; [1] or that the Quarter Master General & his deputies should procure the articles appertaining to their department; and that there should be a Commissary of Military stores, who should have the providing of all supplies relating to the Ordnance Department, & whose Deputies within the army should have the safe keeping & issuing of them, & have the direction of the Armourers & artillery artificers. This plan would have one advantage, that the Quarter Master General and the Commissary of Military stores, from their knowledge & experience, would be the best judges of the quality & kind of articles requisite to their respective Departments. I am afraid the supply of wood in the "Regulations" [2] will be found too small. At Detroit a general order was issued in Septr. 1797 [3] fixing the allowance of wood, which was much greater than that now proposed, yet below what had been allowed by the British & it was found little enough. . . ."

ALS, Hamilton Papers, Library of Congress.
1. H's "Plan for the providing and issuing of Military Supplies" is enclosed in H to James McHenry, second letter of April 8, 1799.
2. For these regulations, see H to McHenry, second letter of July 30, 1799, note 2.
3. This general order is dated September 23, 1797 (LC, RG 94, Adjutant General's Office, General Orders, General James Wilkinson, 1796–1808, National Archives).

From Peter Goelet [1]

Major General Hamilton   New York August 21, 1799.

Sir

Enclosed is a statement of the balance due on the Lands bought by General Schuyler of the Trustees of the American Iron Company with Interest to this day. When Mr. Morris comes to Town his stay is generally very Short. And as I wish to have the whole of the Company's business in a train so as to make a final settlement of it before Mr Morris leaves the City I shall be exceedingly happy if You could now make it convenient to settle the balance.

With Respect I am   Sir   Your Most Humble Serv.   Peter Goelet

Major General Hamilton

[ENCLOSURE]²

[New York, August 21, 1799]

To the Trustees of the American Iron Company Dr
To the last Installment in Lands in Crosbies Patent   £605,13.5
Interest to 4 April 1797 on £605.13.5 is 1 Y.   4 M   56.10.7
   do   20 Decr. 1798   do   1 Y.   8 M 16 D 72.10.10
   do   7 June 1799   do   5 M 18 D 19.15.8
   do   21 Aug 1799   do   2 M 14 d 8.14.4

                                   157.11.5
                              £763.4.10
                       is Dols 1808 10/100

Copy, Miscellaneous Chancery Papers, American Iron Company, Clerk of the Court of Appeals, Albany, on deposit at Queens College, New York City.
  1. For an explanation of the contents of this letter, see the introductory note to Philip Schuyler to H, August 31, 1795. See also H to Phineas Bond, September 1, 1795; H to Robert Morris, September 1, 1795; H to Barent Bleecker, March 20, 1796, April 5, 1797; Goelet to H, June 25, 27, 1796; "Receipt from Peter Goelet," October 4, 1796; "Deed from Peter Goelet, Robert Morris, and William Popham," April 4, 1797; Goelet and Morris to H, December 12, 1798; "Receipt to the Trustees of the American Iron Company," May 30, 1799.
  Before sending this letter to H, Goelet showed a draft of it to Robert Troup, one of the attorneys for the American Iron Company, and asked for his opinion (Goelet to Troup, August 19, 1799 [ALS, Miscellaneous Chancery Papers, American Iron Company, Clerk of the Court of Appeals, Albany, on deposit at Queens College, New York City]). On August 20, 1799, Troup wrote to Goelet: "I have perused the letter you propose to send to Genl Hamilton; and have made a trifling alteration or two in it. I think it would be proper to send the letter" (ALS, Miscellaneous Chancery Papers, American Iron Company, Clerk of the Court of Appeals, Albany, on deposit at Queens College, New York City).
  2. Copy, Miscellaneous Chancery Papers, American Iron Company, Clerk of the Court of Appeals, Albany, on deposit at Queens College, New York City.

To James McHenry

New York Aug 21. 1799

Sir

Your letter of the 16 instant¹ respecting Cloathing for the Western army did not reach me till yesterday. It has been referred to General Wilkinson² and no time will be lost in complying with its object.

I have maturely considered the proposition in your letter of the

17th[3] for stationing three Regiments at Carlisle in Pensylvania and
I am of opinion that the measure is not expedient.

Considering the difference in the price of the ration and how
common it is for repairs of barracks to exceed the previous estimate
of their amounts, and adding the difference in the expence of transportation to so remote a point, I am convinced that experience
would prove th⟨at⟩ nothing is to be gained by sendi⟨ng⟩ the troops
to Carlisle instead of kee⟨ping⟩ them in New Jersey.

In other respects New Jersey is far preferable. Besides being a
situation more relative to our military point⟨s⟩ it is a country w⟨ell⟩
affected to the Government an⟨d⟩ in which the principles of the
tro⟨ops⟩ will run no risk of being perverte⟨d.⟩ On the contrary
though the boro⟨ugh⟩ of Carlisle may in this view be li⟨able⟩ to no
objection the surrounding country contains a great mass of dissaffec-
tion and many individual⟨s⟩ who would be glad to tak⟨e⟩ pains to
poison the minds ⟨of⟩ the soldiery. The station of Carlisle would be
viewed as a stage to the Western Country and the going to that
place would consequently be likely to injure the recruiting service.
The remoteness of this station, by placing the troops at a greater
distance from the eye and influence of the commanding General
will of course be less favourable to their progress in discipline than
if they are nearer to him. Indeed it is easy to foresee that at Carlisle
they will be left very much to their own will, and will become a
disorderly horde whereas in N Jersey I will be answerable for the
contrary.

I conclude therefore that it is infinitely more adviseable to adhere
in this particular to the plan of the Commander in Chief than to
depart so widely from it.

I am now anxious to be authorised to take the preparatory measures for Winter Quarters.

With great respect   I have the honor to be   Sir   yr Obed ser

The Secy of War

ADf, Hamilton Papers, Library of Congress.
    1. Letter not found.
    2. See H to James Wilkinson, August 21, 1799.
    3. McHenry's first letter to H of August 17, 1799, is listed in the appendix
to this volume. In this letter McHenry suggested repairing the ". . . Barracks,
and other public Buildings . . . near the Borough of Carlisle . . ." for the use
of three regiments.

To George Washington

New York August 21st. 1799

Sir

I was yesterday honored with your letter of the 14th. instant.[1]

The recommendations of Captains Taylor and Blue will not fail to be considered when the situation of things is mature for the appointment of Brigade Inspectors.

Inclosed you will find a general abstract of the recruiting Returns,[2] which at its date were received at the Office of the Adjutant General. Other Information induces me to estimate that the number now actually inlisted for *Eleven* of the *Twelve* additional Regiments exceeds Two thousand. The *other* is not yet in activity.

I ought to have informed you before this that General Wilkinson had arrived at this place. I have delivered to him heads of inquiry and conference, which embrace all the material points of consideration in our Western affairs.[3] He is busily engaged in reporting upon them; written rather than verbal communication being by him preferred. The result of our Consultations will be transmitted to you for any direction which you may think fit to give.

With the truest respect & attachment   I have the honor to be   Sir yr. obed. servant   Alex Hamilton

Lt. General Washington

LS, George Washington Papers, Library of Congress; ADf, Hamilton Papers, Library of Congress.

1. In this letter, which is listed in the appendix to this volume, Washington stated that he had received several letters "recommending Captain Edmund Taylor and Captain William K. Blue for the Office of Brigade Inspector." Richard K. Meade had recommended Taylor as brigade inspector in Meade to H, July 16, 1799.
A resident of Virginia, Blue was appointed a captain in the Seventh Regiment of Infantry on July 12, 1799 (Heitman, *United States Army*, I, 226), and the Senate consented to the appointment on May 14, 1800 (*Executive Journal*, I, 343, 355).
2. "General Abstract of Monthly Recruiting Returns of Troops Under the Command of Major General Hamilton," August 17, 1799, signed by Abraham Ellery, assistant adjutant general (DS, George Washington Papers, Library of Congress).
3. See H to James Wilkinson, August 3, 1799.

To James Wilkinson

New York Aug. 21. 1799

Sir

I have received from the secretary of War a letter of which the inclosed is a copy.[1] I will thank you to enable me without delay to present him with the requisition he desires. To assist you in the distribution as to places the Adjutant General will furnish you with any materials which he may possess and which you do not. The requisition must refer to the Present Position of the Troops; but I should be glad you would indicate such intermediate points to which the Cloathing may be sent, as may suit the disposition you contemplate, there to be met with orders for its final destination.

With great consideration & esteem   I am Sir   Yr. Obed ser

A Hamilton

Brigadier General Wilkinson

ADfS, Hamilton Papers, Library of Congress.
  1. Letter not found, but see H to James McHenry, August 21, 1799.

To James McHenry

New York Aug 22. 1799

Sir

You will find herewith the copy of a letter from General Wilkinson[1] relating to a supply of Cloathing for the troops on the Northern and South western frontiers. The return designates itself the quantity requisite for the present numbers of the troops and the portions for each post. I have no data for judging whether any additional quantity ought to be sent forward for arrearages.

I agree in the suggestion, that it is expedient to send a surplus of 100 suits to the Natchez and of three hundred to Pittsburgh. Independent of the idea of recruiting, within the scene in question, it appears to me very important, that there should always be a surplus on hand in so remote a region to meet contingent demands, and to serve as a substitute, when accidents prevent the regular transmission of the stated supply to a particular post. The deficiency of cloathing mentioned in the inclosed letter of the 30 of June from Massac from Capt Pasteur [2] (which it were to be wished was the only instance that had occurred) is a lamentable fact; which places in a strong light the necessity of having an extra quantity of Cloathing always in disposal at some one of the Western Posts.

A new disposition of the Western army is one of the points in consultation between General Wilkinson and myself. It will probably be our joint opinion that some of the present posts ought to be relinquished and others reinforced. An eye has been had to this in the routes suggested for the Cloathing. You are, I believe, already informed that the garrison of Oswego (except a Corporals guard) has been removed to Niagara.[3]

If an armed vessel can be spared for the purpose, the way by New Orleans is evidently the best channel of conveyance to the troops on the lowest parts of the Mississippi. I have thought that such a vessel might perhaps be assigned to this object coupled with that of a convoy for some of our Merchant vessels trading towards the same quarter. It is feared that casualties incident at the approaching season to the interior navigation may possibly prevent the timely transmission of this part of the Cloathing by the route of the *Ohio*.

It would be a great facility and saving if it could become a rule of practice to forward the various articles of supply together. To combine them in one transportation, at one time and under one superintendence, would be attended with many advantages.

The letter from Massac presents also the idea of a very disagreeable procrastination of pay. It is extremely to be wished that there could be greater exactness in this particular. The disadvantages of witholding the pay for a length of time & accumulating into a mass are obvious and numerous.

In relation to the subjects of supply and pay, I must be permitted to observe generally that it is essential to the prosperity of our military affairs that there shall be much more system and punctuality than have heretofore obtained. No one knows better than myself the obstacles which stood in the way of both, when we were without an efficient government, and even in the first stages of a new though

more adequate political establishment; but happily the progress of
our affairs (as I trust and believe) puts it in the power of our ad-
min[i]stration to remedy former defects and to give vigour and
consistence to the institutions which respect the defence and
security of our country. Satisfied of the dispositions of those who
are charged with that administration to attain such desireable ends,
I the more freely indulge observations which have for object a
course of proceeding better adopted to their accomplishment.

I send you a monthly abstract of recruiting returns.[4] Later advices
assure one that the numbers of recruits is materially greater than it
there appears. A rapid increase may now be expected, requiring a
prompt augmentation of the means.

You have said nothing to me respecting the propriety of furnishing each Regiment with a waggon & four horses.[5] The thing is
more & more pressed upon. If I hear nothing to the contrary speedily
I shall direct the measure.

With very great respect   I have the honor to be &c

The Secy of War

ADf, Hamilton Papers, Library of Congress.
  1. Letter not found.
  2. Letter from Thomas Pasteur not found.
  3. See H to John J. U. Rivardi, June 25, 1799; Rivardi to H, July 25, August 8, 1799.
  4. See H to George Washington, August 21, 1799, note 2.
  5. See H to McHenry, August 13, 1799.

To James McHenry

New York, August 22, 1799. ". . . I send you . . . some extracts
from Col. Hall's letter of the fourteenth of this month. He . . . requests a supply of money for recruiting purposes. I must revive my
request on this subject.[1] I should wish a supply to be sent on sufficiently large to make up the complement of three fourths of the
several regiments. . . ."

Df, in the handwriting of Thomas Y. How, Hamilton Papers, Library of Congress.
  1. See H to McHenry, second letter of August 19, 1799.

To Aaron Ogden

New York Augt. 22d.
1799

Sir

An early preparation for Winter Quarters will conduce to the comfortable accommodation of the Troops, and is the more necessary as sufficient Barracks no where exist in which they may be quartered in entire Corps; a circumstance extremely desirable.

It is therefore conceived that it may be found most eligible to hut the Troops during the ensuing Winter.

Some point in the vicinity of the *Raritan* in the State of New-Jersey has been thought of as a fit station for three Regiments, (the 10th. 11th. 12th.).[1] I request that you will, without delay, cause a careful examination to be made in that Quarter whether a fit situation can be found for the purpose. It must of course have upon it Wood sufficient and proper for the construction of the huts and for fuel; a convenient and adequate supply of good Water; a healthful site and a plentiful surrounding Country are also indispensable requisites. It is most desirable to procure the ground upon hire, as it may never be wanted but for the special occasion, and it might not be easy afterwards to dispose of it. But if this should prove intirely impracticable, inquiry must be made as to the price for which it can be purchased.

Though the vicinity of the Raritan be mentioned, yet, if there be no fit position there, it must be sought for at some other point in the State of New Jersey; preferring a Station as nearly intermediate as maybe to Philadelphia and New York.

It being part of the Duty of the several Contractors to provide Quarters for the Troops you may as far as you think adviseable avail yourself of their aid.

But it is my desire that you will devote your personal attention to the subject; Nor is any time to be lost. When the necessary examination shall have been made you will report the result with all the particulars including the terms of hire or purchase to me for final Direction.

If I recollect rightly there are Barracks at Amboy. Will you make enquiry as to their present State, the number they will accommodate and the repairs they may require.

With great consideration I am Sir Yr. obedt. servant

A Hamilton

Col: Ogden

LS, Lloyd W. Smith Collection, Morristown National Historical Park, Morristown, New Jersey; Df, in the handwriting of Ethan Brown, Hamilton Papers, Library of Congress.

1. New Brunswick had been recommended as the site for the permanent camp for two regiments in H's draft of George Washington to James McHenry, first letter of December 13, 1798. H's official instructions had repeated this recommendation. See McHenry to H, February 4, 1799.

To Nathan Rice

New York Aug 22. 1799

Sir

An early preparation for winter Quarters will conduce to the comfortable accommodation of the troops and is the more necessary as sufficient barracks no where exist in which they may be quartered in entire corps;[1] a circumstance *extremely* desireable.

It is therefore conceived that it may be found most eligible to hut the troops during the ensuing winter.

The vicinity of Uxbridge in the state of Massachusettes has been thought of as a station for three Regiments (the 14th. 15 & 16).[2] I request that you will without delay cause a careful examination to be made in that quarter whether a fit situation can be found for the purpose. It must of course have upon it wood sufficient and proper for the construction of the huts and for fuel—A convenient and adequate supply of good water—a healthful scite and a plentiful surrounding Country are also indispensable requisites.

It is most desireable to procure the ground upon hire, as it may never be wanted but for the special occasion and it might not be easy afterwards to dispose of it. But if this should prove intirely impracticable enquiry must then be made as to the price for which it can be purchased. Though Uxbridge is particularly mentioned, yet if there be no fit position in the neighbourhood of that place, it must [be] sought for somewhere else. But a preference is to be given to some position intermediate to Boston and New Port.

It being a part of the duty of the contractors for Massachusettes to provide quarters for the troops you will have recourse to their aid— and you will consult Jonathan Jackson Esquire Agent for the War Department upon the subject.

But it is my desire that you will devote your personal attention to the subject. Nor is any time to be lost. When the necessary examination shall have been made you will report the result with all the particulars including the terms of hire or purchase to me for final direction.

I begin to be anxious to know the progress which has been made in recruiting for your regiment.

With great consideration & esteem   I am Sir   Yr. Obed ser

Col. Rice

ADf, Hamilton Papers, Library of Congress.
1. See H to James McHenry, first letter of August 13, 1799.
2. See H to McHenry, July 17, 1799, note 1.

To Nathan Rice

New York August 22 1799

Sir

I have just received a letter from the Secretary of war [1] in which he informs me that the resignation of Lieutenant Samuel W. Church [2] of your regiment is accepted. You will please to signify the same to Lieutenant Church, and inform me when he actually receives the notice.

With great consideration   I am &c. &c.

Df, in the handwriting of Thomas Y. How, Hamilton Papers, Library of Congress.
1. James McHenry to H, August 21, 1799 (listed in the appendix to this volume).
2. Church was appointed an ensign in the Fourteenth Regiment of Infantry on March 3, 1799 (*Executive Journal*, I, 323), and on the same day, in ac-

cordance with Section 2 of "An Act for the better organizing of the Troops of the United States; and for other purposes" (1 *Stat.* 749–55 [March 3, 1799]), he became a second lieutenant (Heitman, *United States Army*, I, 301).

To Nathan Rice

New York Augt. 22. 99.

Sir

I have received a letter from Cn. Ashmun [1] of your regiment in which he informs me that he has sent Samuel Woolcott, a deserter from the first regiment of Artillerists to the commanding officer of the district at Springfield. You will immediately send this deserter under the guard of a corporal and file of men to Major Tousarde [2] at Rhode Island.

With great consideration

Df, in the handwriting of Thomas Y. How, Hamilton Papers, Library of Congress.
    1. Phineas Ashmun to H, August 16, 1799 (listed in the appendix to this volume).
    2. Lewis Tousard.

To John Adlum [1]

New York, August 23, 1799. ". . . I am not anxious that any part of your force should be stationed at Easton if you think it of importance to keep the whole united. It would however be a strong motive to the stationing of a small party at Easton if the recruiting service could be benefited by the measure. It is not convenient at present to reinforce your detachment, but as I am not apprehensive of an attack on your troops from the disaffected of ⟨the⟩ country,[2] I should have no objection on that score to your sending a company to Easton, if on other accounts you should deem it advisable. . . ."

LS, in the handwriting of Thomas Y. How, Hamilton Papers, Library of Congress; Df, in the handwriting of Thomas Y. How, Hamilton Papers, Library of Congress.
    1. This letter was written in reply to Adlum to H, July 22, 1799.
    2. This is a reference to Fries's Rebellion. See James McHenry to H, March 13, 1799, note 12.

To Richard Harison [1]

New York August 24. 1799

Sir

Attempts are making in different parts of the country to procure the enlargement of soldiers on writs of Habeas Corpus issued by and returnable before state Judges.[2] As this practice will probably involve serious consequences it becomes necessary for me to avail myself of the information of those officers of the United States who are particularly charged with the consideration of legal questions. I wish therefore for your deliberate opinion, distinguishing between Courts and individual judges, on the legality of this practice, and especially on the effect of a return to the writ that the person demanded had been duly enlisted by an officer of the United States in conformity with the laws, and with his instructions. You will also be pleased to consider whether upon such a return it is necessary to produce the person who is the object of the Habeas Corpus. The charge for this opinion you will make against the department of War.

With great considn &c. &c.   A Hamilton

Richard Harison Esqr

Df, in the handwriting of Thomas Y. How, Hamilton Papers, Library of Congress.
    1. Harison was United States attorney for the District of New York.
    2. H wrote this letter because of a case in Virginia involving one Edward Walker. Following Walker's enlistment in July, 1799, in the Seventh Infantry Regiment, his father appeared before Hugh Nelson, justice of the peace, York County, Virginia, to secure his son's release from the Army on the ground that the son was twenty years old and therefore a minor. Nelson ruled: ". . . The Father hath the Legal Custody of the said Infant, and hath a Right to his Services untill he shall arrive at the Age of Twenty One years" (undated and untitled copy of proceedings, Hamilton Papers, Library of Congress). This case is discussed in James Baytop to H, July 10, 1799; H to Baytop, August 15, 1799; H to William C. Bentley, August 15, 1799; Bentley to H, August 15, 1799 (all listed in the appendix to this volume).

To James McHenry

New York, August 24, 1799. "On the subject of Winter Quarters [1] my attention will of course be confined to my own district.[2] Doubtless attention is paying by others to the troops which will be stationed within General Pinckney's district."

ADfS, Hamilton Papers, Library of Congress.
1. For H's views on winter quarters, see H to McHenry, first letter of August 13, 1799.
2. See H to Aaron Ogden, August 22, 1799; H to Nathan Rice, first letter of August 22, 1799.

To James McHenry

New York, August 24, 1799. "I send you an extract from Col. Parker's letter of the Fifteenth of this month.[1] By this you will see the extremities to which the officers of his regiment are put from the want of money for recruiting purposes. I enclose likewise an extract from Major Rivardi's letter of the twenty fifth of July. It would appear to be proper that the officers of the corps to which Major Rivardi belongs should be furnished with the enumerated articles, but not being acquainted with the arrangements which you may have made, I have declined taking any measure in the case."

Df, in the handwriting of Thomas Y. How, Hamilton Papers, Library of Congress.
1. In a letter listed in the appendix to this volume, Thomas Parker wrote to H: "I have procured loans of money for several of my Officers whose situations woud not permit them to continue the Recruiting Service without assistance & I shall be obliged to advance the money out of my own private funds unless it is shortly sent forward."

From Thomas Parker

Winchester [Virginia] August 24, 1799. ". . . The want of Coats & Vests for the Soldiers & *Subsistance* money for the officers are

Verry Great Bars to the Success of the Recruiting Service. Many of
the officers who are upwards of one hundred & fifty miles from
their friends & Connections are entirely destitute of money & have
no means of Procuring any. . . . The arms that we have Received
are so Rusted for the want of attention in the Store Keeper that it
is almost Impossable to make them appear Tolerably decent. . . .
The Cartridge Boxes are extreamly unwealdy & indifferent some of
them are fixed with Shoulder & some with waist Belts. . . . I am of
opinion that the appointment of Cadets would conduce to the Success of the Recruiting Service. I enclose you a list of Such as I have
Recommended. . . ."

ALS, Hamilton Papers, Library of Congress.

To James McHenry

New York, August 25, 1799. States that the lack of a rule regarding "compensation to the members of Courts Martial and to persons
acting as Judge Advocates" causes "some embarrassment." Believes
that an officer should be indemnified when "employed in objects or
at places, not military posts, which oblige him to incur extra expence." [1] Requests "information in a particular case [2] respecting the
extra expences of recruiting officers." Asks if "two Dollars per head"
is considered "as the equivalent, or is there a further allowance &
how adjusted?" Encloses one extract from Major John J. U. Rivardi's
letter of July 25 "which explains and corrects the information before given by him" and a second extract which describes how wood
is procured at Fort Niagara. Inquires if there is a "standing regulation of the Qr Ms Departt. countenancing the allowance of *five
Dollars* ℔ Month to men permanently employed in any such service" and if "it is applicable to such a case."

ADf, Hamilton Papers, Library of Congress.
    1. See the enclosure to McHenry to H, April 22, 1799; "General Orders,"
June 1, 1799.
    2. See Thomas Parker to H, August 11, 1799.

To James McHenry

New York Aug 25. 1799

Sir

Inclosed is a letter which I have just received from Col Bentley.[1] In transmitting him the list of new appointments for his Regiment I did not advert to what they were; but took it for granted that all was in conformity with what had been before established and with the recommendations of the commanding Officer of the Regiment. I find that the reverse has happened in this case as well as in that of the Eight Regiment.[2] And whether I am to charge myself with any omission or not in the matter I am extremely sorry for the event.

It is certain that if this course of proceeding is to obtain the Regiments will never be organised and there will be in all the Officers a just and deep rooted dissatisfaction.[3]

You will probably remember that it has been long since communicated [4] as my idea that the routine of promotion among the company Officers should commence when the places of the field officers of a Regiment were once filled by persons accepting. It has been my wish that this rule should govern except in the cases in which the Commandants of the Regiments, before a formal and definitive arrangement was made, should recommend deviations. Some of the appointments in question appear to have been made with the greatest latitude and without reference to any principle.

It may be requisite to explain in relation to the observation of Col Bentley about the arrangement of relative rank reported by him and approved by me.

You recollect that in the Lists of appointments originally sent me [5] there was a provisional arrangement of relative rank distinguished numerically. In your letter of instruction of the 21 of March last you give me authority to fix the relative rank of the Company Officers in each Regiment. As a guide to myself I directed the Commandant of each Regiment in conjunction with his Majors to report for my consideration such an arrangement as they should think adviseable.[6] This has been done in four instances including the seventh Regiment and my sanction has been given.[7] These arrangements have been directed by me to be transmitted to you as they were made and approved.[8] Duplicates are now inclosed lest there should have been any omission.

The lat⟨est a⟩ppointments for the 7th Regiment ⟨made in⟩ contravention of the scale of relative rank settled ⟨by⟩ me are attended with proportionably greater difficulty.

I owe it to the service to the officers and to myself to recommend and urge that except as to Capt Blue[9] all these new appointments may be reversed the first lieutenants brought down to second lieutenants and all the lieutenants considered as junior to all the others before appointed. I except Capt Blue because this alteration would as to him be equivalent to a dismission & as he has served with reputation there will probably be an acquiescence in his case. But he ought to rank as the youngest Captain.

And I earnestly entreat that no future appointment in any of the Regiments may be made of any but as second lieutenants & junior to those previously in service.

I must again press for the settlement of a Rule of promotion. It is essential to fix principles and the conditions and expectations of officers as fast as possible. The army never will be organised and in order, unless points are successively established as they occurr to consideration and when established strictly adhered to. The total defect of organisation in the western Army (the extent of which I did not know till very lately) has increased my solicitude for another course of things; lest we get every where into an inextricable chaos.

I send you an arrangement of the 7 Regiment[10] in conformity with my ideas, which I hope may be adopted.

With great respect   I have the honor to be &c

ADf, Hamilton Papers, Library of Congress.

1. William C. Bentley to H, August 17, 1799.

2. Thomas Parker to H, July 24, 1799 (listed in the appendix to this volume). In this letter Parker complained that two newly appointed lieutenants in his regiment outranked all other lieutenants and that this arrangement was contrary to his understanding of the rules governing relative rank.

3. H had received other complaints concerning the discontent caused by new appointments. See Josias Carvel Hall to H, July 22, 1799; Parker to H, August 15, 1799; H to Parker, August 16, 1799 (all listed in the appendix to this volume).

4. See H to McHenry, May 5 (listed in the appendix to this volume), June 22, July 10, 30, 1799.

5. See McHenry to H, March 21, 1799, note 1.

6. See "Circular to the Commandants of the Regiments," March 23, 1799. See also McHenry to H, April 23, 1799; H to McHenry, April 26, 1799. Further discussion on this subject may be found in H to Richard Hunewell, August 14, 1799 (listed in the appendix to this volume). The Fifth Regiment was exempted from this procedure. See H to John Smith, August 16, 1799 (listed in the appendix to this volume).

7. In his letter to H of September 3, 1799, McHenry acknowledged receipt of the arrangements for the Seventh, Tenth, Eleventh, and Twelfth Regiments, which H sent in the letter printed above. For earlier correspondence concerning the relative rank in several regiments, see the following letters listed in the appendix to this volume: (for the Seventh Regiment) Bentley to H, May 17, July 15, 1799; H to Bentley, June 1, July 31, 1799; (for the Tenth Regiment) Thomas Lloyd Moore to H, June 6, 1799; H to Moore, June 7, 1799; (for the Twelfth Regiment) H to William S. Smith, August 16, 1799; Smith to H, August 22, 1799; (for the Sixteenth Regiment) Rufus Graves to H, July 26, 1799; H to Graves, August 13, 1799.

8. H sent a list of the relative ranks of the officers of the Tenth Regiment to McHenry in his first letter of June 8, 1799 (listed in the appendix to this volume).

9. William K. Blue.

10. AD, Hamilton Papers, Library of Congress.

From Thomas Parker

Winchester [*Virginia*] *August 25, 1799.* "Since I had the honor of writing to you yesterday a Supply of Cloathing & Horsemans Tents have come to hand which I am much pleased with. I am sorry however to find that there are *no Jackets* amongst them and only Eighty Coats. An additional Supply will be wanting verry soon as we are Tolerably Successfull in Recruiting. . . ."

ALS, Hamilton Papers, Library of Congress.

To John J. U. Rivardi

New York, August 26, 1799. Has ordered Major Adam Hoops and Captain James Stille to Fort Niagara to investigate Captain James Bruff's charges against Rivardi.[1] States that although most men had enlisted when "the allowance" of spirits "was but half a gill per day. . . Those who entered the Service whilst the act of Congress which allowes a gill pr. day was in force . . . have some colour to contend that the withholding from them of any part of that allowance would be a breach of contract." [2] States that he has "for some time considered as important to the United States to have a vessel in the lake." Reports that "The Secretary of war has determined to postpone the appointment of Cadets to a future day." [3]

Df, in the handwriting of Thomas Y. How and H, Hamilton Papers, Library of Congress.
    1. On August 27, 1799, H wrote to Adam Hoops: "You will forthwith proceed together with Captain Stille of the Second Regiment of Artillerists & Engineers to the Post of Niagara. When there you will associate yourselves with some other officer . . . sufficient to serve. Together you will constitute a Court of Inquiry . . . & . . . examine into certain charges . . . by Captain Bruff . . . against Major Rivardi. . . ." This letter is listed in the appendix to this volume.
    For Bruff's charges, see Rivardi to H, March 21, 1799, note 13.
    2. Rivardi had raised a question about the allowance of spirits in Rivardi to H, July 11, 1799 (listed in the appendix to this volume), as a result of H's "General Orders," June 13, 1799.
    Section 6 of "An Act to augment the Army of the United States, and for other purposes" provided that ". . . every non-commissioned officer, private and musician shall receive daily . . . a gill of rum, brandy or whiskey" (1 *Stat.* 604–05 [July 16, 1798]). Section 22 of "An Act for the better organizing of the Troops of the United States; and for other purposes" (1 *Stat.* 749–55 [March 3, 1799]) provided: "That it shall be lawful for the commander in chief of the army, or the commanding officer of any separate detachment or garrison thereof, at his discretion, to cause to be issued, from time to time to the troops under his command . . . rum, whiskey, and other ardent spirits in quantities not exceeding half a gill to each man per day. . . ."
    3. This is a reference to Rivardi's request to have Enoch Humphrey appointed a cadet. See Rivardi to H, April 3, July 25, 1799. For James McHenry's decision concerning the appointment of cadets, see McHenry to H, second letter of July 8, 1799.

From James Wilkinson

[New York, August 26, 1799]

Brigr. Gen. Wilkinson has the Honor to transmit Majr. Genl Hamilton, an original communication from the Officer commanding Fort Massac,[1] near the Mouth of the Ohio River, which appears to Him to merit some attention. He sends the Original, because the retention of it, is important to the Brigadier, & may be most properly deposited with the Majr. General. The debauch & consequent absence of the Brigrs. Clerk, since Saturday, prevents his offering a short report to Majr. General Hamilton this morning, which He regrets. No condition shall be omited to accomplish the object in the course of Tomorrow.

Monday Morning

The Brigr. has to take shame to Himself for his idle delusion, respecting the *legitimate* mode of electing Regimental Paymasters. It is not less singular than absurd.

AL, Hamilton Papers, Library of Congress.
1. Thomas Pasteur.

Circular to the Commandants of Regiments [1]

New York Aug 27. 1799

Sir

In military service, it is essential that each individual should move within his proper sphere—according to a just gradation and to the relations which subsist between him and others. It is a consequence of this principle that a regular chain of communication should be preserved, and that *in all matters relating to service* each person should address himself for information or direction to his immediate superior and should not step beyond him to a higher authority. This observation, of course, excepts the case where an individual having received an injury from his immediate superior is disposed to such redress from the superior of both. But in other cases the principle ought to be rigidly observed.

It is not so in practice. I have received communications from Captains of companies which in propriety ought to have been addressed to the Commandants of their Regiments or of the districts within which they were stationed. And I know that communications have in some instances been made by particular Officers to the Secy of War which ought to have been addressed to me.

These things are not regular and must be avoided. The good of the service and the dignity of every officer from the highest to the lowest require that they should not prevail.

The Officers & persons attached to the army who are charged with the expenditure of money and with the providing or issuing of supplies will properly correspond with the Department of War on those subjects. But every other officer ought to address himself to his immediate military chief and the Chiefs of corps or distinct commands must make their communications immediately to me except in the cases in which particular regulations direct otherwise.

To apply the rule [2]—The officers of your Regiment *within the district of your command* must not go beyond you with their verbal or written communications. You must addr⟨ess⟩ [3] yours to me except 1 Returns and applications respecting ordnance, arm⟨y⟩ accoutrements ammunition and other military stores, cloathing articles of Quarter Master's supply, Hospital Stores including Medicines which for the present must be add⟨ressed⟩ to Ebenezer Stevens Esquire Agent for the War ⟨Department⟩ in New York (the proper officers in respect to ⟨these objects⟩ not being yet appointed); 2 Monthly and ⟨other⟩ returns respecting the numbers & State of corps & detach⟨ments,⟩ including inspection and recruiting Returns wh⟨ich⟩ must be addressed to Brigadier General North Adjutant General; 3 Muster and Pay Rolls to Caleb Swan Esquire Pay Master General at the seat of Government. These last had best be forwarded by the respective Pay Masters of Regiments and detachments where any exist. The Pay Master General has been advised to confine his communications to Pay Masters & to such others as have received public money for which they are accountable *directly* to the War Department.

It is expected that other officers will shortly be appointed and annexed to *Head Quarters,* to whom the objects under the first and third head will properly belong. This when it takes place will be announced in General Orders.

You will take care to make these instructions known within the limits of your Command. [4]

With great consideration

ADf, Hamilton Papers, Library of Congress; two copies, in the handwriting of Ethan Brown, Hamilton Papers, Library of Congress.
    1. For background to this document, see H to James McHenry, July 31, August 5, 1799; McHenry to H, August 2, 10, 1799.
    2. For this rule, see "Circular to the Batallion Commanders of the Second Regiment of Artillerists and Engineers," May 27–June 1, 1799.

3. The material within broken brackets has been taken from the copies of this letter.

4. H's endorsement reads: "Circular seven Copies."

To James McHenry

New York Aug 27, 1799

Sir

A letter from Major Toussard of the 19 instant has the following paragraph "The commissioners [1] at Fort Wolcott and Fort Adams have received by the last mail the copy of your general Order, transmitted to them from Boston by Major Jackson which lessens the allowance fixed by the regulation to be observed in the delivery & Distribution of fuel and Straw to the Garrisons on the Sea Coast. The regulations I allude to, signed by the Secretary of War were transmitted to me a fortnight ago from the War Office and with order to conform myself to them. Your last order on the subject shall be complied with." [2]

I have never heared from you whether the proposed Regulations as to Fuel and straw [3] or any modification of them have been adopted or not. It would seem from Major Toussard's letter that they have been adopted & even forwarded to officers under my command.

It became necessary to give directions about laying in supplies of these articles, to avoid the increased expence which has heretofore attended the laying them in at late periods and occasionally through the Winter. I therefore directed the Officers commanding within particular districts to call upon the contractors to lay in adequate stores for the ensuing Winter, and merely as a scale for this operation transmitted the regulations as reported by me. I sent them to Major Jackson because the batali[o]n which garrisons the posts from Connecticut Northward, & the *ordinary command* within the district are his; subject to the occasional interposition of Major Toussard for special reasons; to preserve to the latter the authority due to his rank and avoid collision where he might happen to be in the course of the execution of your orders.

This instance is only to illustrate the necessity of some settled plan of communication between your Department and the army; to avoid inconsistent dispositions; to preserve to superior officers the due respectability of their stations; to prevent the ideas, unfavourable to subordination, which are apt to grow up in inferior officers from the habit of immediate intercourse with the chief of the War Department, to save that chief from a multiplication of correspondence & detail improper for him, and on the results of these different considerations to promote and secure order harmony and efficiency in the service.

In my conception the true rule is this—The Secretary of War and his subordinate Agents may correspond immediately on the business of expenditure & supply in its various branches with all those officers who are charged with it such as Quarter Masters Commissaries Pay Masters and other descriptions of persons forming what is commonly called the civil staff; but they ought to hold no communication with any merely military Officer (that is any officer not *attached* to the business of expenditure or supply) other than the principal officer of an army or within a military district or command. This rule would confine the communications of the Secy of War to General Washington and the two Major Generals.

It is true that there are special cases in which it may be proper to depart from the rule; such as sudden and unforeseen emergencies when the public interest or service might suffer by a delay incident to a communication with the chief; geographical [4] circumstances which may require exceptions but these ought to be previously settled with the chief, defining the extent and the objects; complaints by inferiors of injuries received or supposed to have been received from the Chief. But the cases are few and must always be supported by some important reason of a special nature. Little conveniences or inconveniences are not proper grounds of exception.

Even in the case of communicating with the Officers in the branches of Expenditure and Supply, great care ought to be observed to address the Chief & not his Subalterns.

If these ideas appear to you well founded you will no doubt adopt them as a rule of practice; if not it is desireable that some other rule more agreeable may be fixed upon and understood. This will tend to prevent misapprehension & dissatisfaction.

I present the subject without reserve because it is better to avoid difficulties, by settling principles beforehand, than to find remedies after they shall have occurred.

With great respect & esteem &c

ADf, Hamilton Papers, Library of Congress; copy, Hamilton Papers, Library of Congress.

1. H misquoted Lewis Tousard's letter, which is listed in the appendix to this volume, for Tousard actually wrote "Commandants." William Littlefield was the commandant at Fort Wolcott at Newport, Rhode Island, and Lemuel Gates was the commandant at Fort Adams (Castle William) in Boston Harbor.

The general order to which Tousard referred is H to Adam Hoops and Daniel Jackson, August 5, 1799 (listed in the appendix to this volume). In this letter H wrote that "for want of beginning early to lay up a supply of fuel for the use of our garrisons, a very great addition of expence has been incurred. . . . To prevent a repetition of this the ensuing winter, you will take care that a proper supply be immediately laid in, to serve till the first of April next. . . ." To aid in regulating the proper quantity of fuel to be purchased for each post under the command of Hoops and Jackson, H added as a guide "the scale at foot applied to the number of officers & men."

2. The quotation is in the handwriting of Ethan Brown.
3. See H to McHenry, second letter of July 30, 1799, note 1.
4. In MS, "geophaphical."

General Orders

New York, August 28th 1799.

As some difficulties have risen, and may hereafter arise, in consequence of its not being known, whether the general orders and forms issued from the Adjutant General's office have been regularly received, it is in future directed, that the receipts of all general orders, all letters inclosing forms, or the alteration of forms, all letters containing new arrangements in material directions, shall be acknowledged by the return of the post, or where there is no post, by the first proper conveyance.

Abraham R. Ellery
Assistant Adjutant General

LS, RG 98, Post-Revolutionary War Commands, Castle Island Record, National Archives.

To James McHenry

New York Aug 28 1799

Sir

It would appear from the representations of G Wilkinson that the number of officers of the four old Regiments [1] who have reported themselves to me pursuant to your notification [2] bear no comparison to the number actually absent. The case seems to require some more decisive measure.

I submit whether it will not be expedient for you to signify in the public papers throughout the States that all Officers of the first second third and fourth Regiments of Infantry and of the first Regiment of Artillery who are absent from their corps from whatever cause are as soon as possible to report themselves to the Secy of War liable to render an account for any unnecessary delay and that all such of them who do not so report themselves within 4 months from the date of the notification will be presumed to have resigned their commissions.

The measure is a strong one but the protracted absence of these officers is intolerable. A remedy is essential & to be effectual it must be strong.

With great respect &

Js McHenry Esq

ADf, Hamilton Papers, Library of Congress.

1. This is a reference to the infantry regiments composing the Regular Army. See the introductory note to H to James Gunn, December 22, 1798.

2. This "notification," dated April 15, 1799, reads: "All Officers within the States of New-Hampshire, Massachusetts, Rhode-Island, Connecticut, Vermont, New-York, New-Jersey, Pennsylvania, Delaware and Maryland, belonging to the first, second, third and fourth regiments of Infantry, and the first and second regiments of Artillery, now upon furlough, or absent from their commands will, without delay, report themselves to Major General Hamilton, and obey his orders. James M'Henry Secy of War" (*Gazette of the United States, and Philadelphia Daily Advertiser*, April 16, 1799). In accordance with this order H received the following letters: Isaac Smith for his son, Charles Smith, to H, April 16, 1799; Jonathan Cass to H, April 30, 1799; Yelverton Peyton to H, April 30, June 1, 1799; Benjamin Brookes to H, May 8, 1799; Joshua Rogers to H, May 18, 1799; Thomas Underwood to H, August 26, 1799 (all listed in the appendix to this volume).

From James McHenry

War Department
August 29th. 1799

Sir,

I received at Trenton on the 27th: instant,[1] your letter dated the 22nd: enclosing a Return and letter from General Wilkinson, relative to Supplies of Cloathing for the Troops on the Northern and Southwestern Frontier, and designating the quantity requisite for the present numbers of the Troops as well as the portions for each post, also a letter from Captain pasteur dated Massac the 30th: June last,[2] exhibiting long arrearages of Cloathing and pay due at that post.

The letter from Massac occasions your observing "The deficiency of Clothing mentioned (which it were to be wished was the only instance had occurred) is a lamentable fact, which places in a strong light the necessity of having an extra quantity of Clothing always in deposit at some one of the Western posts."

I now recollect but one place on the Northwestern frontier, which has been represented to me, to have been incompetently supplied with Clothing. You will remember that upon an investigation, Major Rivardi's representation of facts appeared incorrect,[3] and that at the time of making his statement to you, there was Clothing at Niagara and Oswego, sufficient for their respective Garrisons, and a surplus, the return for these posts having been fully complied with.[4]

Respecting the deficiency at Massac, I think it proper to inform you that the requisition or return made by General Wilkinson for Cloathing for the frontier Army was duly attended to, and that I ad-

---

LS, Hamilton Papers, Library of Congress; LS, letterpress copy, James McHenry Papers, Library of Congress.

1. The Government offices had moved to Trenton because of an outbreak of yellow fever in Philadelphia.

2. Thomas Pasteur.

3. See John J. U. Rivardi to H, May 2, 1799; H to McHenry, June 24, June 25–July 2, 1799; McHenry to H, June 29, 1799 [listed in the appendix to this volume].

4. See Rivardi to H, July 25, 1799.

vised him on the 31st: of January last "Cloathing has been forwarded to the extent of our means for all the troops on the frontiers, including the Mississippi, it is however to be regretted that from a failure of the Contract, the Supplies have in some instances fallen short of the complement, and in others have been so long delayed, as to produce without doubt, serious sufferings and complaints."

The failure of the Contract, was occasioned by circumstances not to be controuled or avoided—there was an actual want in the United States of some of the Articles necessary for Soldiers' Cloathing, and some importations orders of Kerseys and other articles by the Contractor, were captured on their passage at Sea.

I take the occasion also to observe, that I consider it the duty of a Commanding General, not only to make Returns of all Articles, among these Clothing wanted for his troops, but to make them in such Season, as to allow of making up, and transporting them to their destinations.

That I consider it to be my duty to direct as far as practicable, and as promptly as may be, a compliance with the requisitions made, by causing the delivery of the Articles called for, to the Quarter Master General for transportation. I suppose my duty is completed by such delivery to the Quarter Master—and that all ulterior orders, respecting the destination and distribution of the Articles proportionally at different posts, should exclusively emanate from the Commanding General.

If indeed any of the chain of Officers, concerned in the putting up, labelling, transportation or delivery of the Articles, shall neglect or err in their duties, and can no otherwise be legally punished, than by a reference to the Department of War, it is proper the Secretary should be informed of the circumstances and facts, that the competent authority may judge what is right to be done on every such occasion that may occur.

The letter from Captain Pasteur you say presents also the idea of a very disagreeable procrastination of pay, that "it is extremely to be wished there could be greater exactness in this particular" and that, "the disadvantages of with-holding the pay for a length of time and accumulating the arrears into a mass are obvious and numerous"— and add, "in relation to the subjects of supply and pay, I must be permitted to observe generally, that it is essential to the prosperity of our Military affairs, that there shall be much more system and punctuality, than have heretofore obtained."

On the subject of the pay of the troops, it is proper there should be a clear understanding. "An Act making alterations in the Treasury and War Department" passed the 8th: of May 1792 [5] Section 3rd: provides, "that there be a paymaster to reside near the Head Quarters of the Troops of the United States—that it shall be the duty of the said paymaster to receive from the Treasurer all the monies which shall be entrusted to him, for the purpose of paying the pay, arrears of pay, Subsistence or Forage, due to the Troops of the United States. That *he* shall receive the pay Abstracts of the paymasters of the several Regiments or Corps, and compare the same with the returns or Muster Rolls which shall accompany the said pay Abstracts. That *he* shall certify accurately to the Commanding Officer the Sums due to the respective Corps, who shall thereon issue his Warrant on the said paymaster for the payment accordingly. That copies of all reports to the Commanding Officer, and the Warrants thereon, shall be duly transmitted to the Office of the Accountant of the War Department in order to be there examined and finally adjusted at the Treasury."

The 15th: Section of "An Act for the better organizing of the Troops of the United States and for other purposes" past the 3rd: of March last,[6] does not appear to modify or change the duties of the paymaster General, altho' it may substitute his Deputies for certain purposes. The prescriptions of the former Act are definitive and directory, and make it the duty of the Treasurer by Section 2nd: to disburse all such monies, as shall have been previously ordered for the use of the Department of War, by Warrants from the Treasury, which disbursements shall be made, pursuant to Warrants from the Secretary of War countersigned by the Accountant."

Under the Act cited consider the requisition on the War Department for the pay of the Army to rest with the paymaster General, that when this is made, it is the duty of the Secretary of War to make a demand on the Treasury, to deposit the amount with the Treasurer to be drawn out on his Warrants countersigned by the Accountant in favor of the paymaster General for the purpose of

5. 1 *Stat.* 279–81.
6. 1 *Stat.* 749–55.

actual payments to the Military by himself or through his Deputies on Warrants drawn by the Commanding General or Officer, the General or paymaster I suppose competent to, and the proper persons, to devise facilities, with a due attention to œconomy and security for the payment of the Army.

Monies for the recruiting Service, Bounties, Subsistence and forage of the Army, it is understood are to take the same course. In a word the Secretary 'tis supposed, has only to sanction the disbursement of monies required for all the said purposes, by his Warrants on the Treasurer, in favor of the paymaster, who will apply the same according to the Warrants and orders of the Commanding General.

I have the honor to be, with great respect, Sir Your obedt: servant   James McHenry

Major General Alexander Hamilton.

From James McHenry

War Department, August 29, 1799. Writes in reply to Hamilton's letter of August 25 and states: "It is understood to have been the general custom in the Army to act, pro hac vice, as Judge Advocate on General Courts Martial, whenever the Judge Advocate to the Army, could not be present, or that Office, as is now the case, was vacant; it is not known that any established pay or compensation was allowed to the person thus acting." Adds that for "expences on the road and for boarding and lodging" an allowance is granted and that it is "the duty of the Accountant to settle the quantum." Discusses the question of Charles W. Hare's [1] compensation as judge advocate at two courts-martial. States that payment for Lieutenant William W. Wands's [2] service as a member of the court that tried Captain Samuel C. Vance [3] will be determined by the regulations of December 19, 1798,[4] which established "the allowance to be made to officers detached on Service so as to be obliged to incur expences on the road, and at places not Military posts." Declares "that the allowance to Recruiting officers of two dollars for every Recruit they enlist was designed to cover the whole expences of the Services,

and that it precluded a further allowance." Concludes that it would
be "dangerous and inexpedient" to increase the allowance.

LS, Hamilton Papers, Library of Congress; LS, letterpress copy, James Mc-
Henry Papers, Library of Congress.
1. Charles Willing Hare, a resident of Philadelphia, was twenty years old in
1799. On December 7, 1799, he was admitted to the Philadelphia bar (*The
Philadelphia Bar. A Complete Catalogue of Members from 1776 to 1868* [Phila-
delphia: Review Printing House, 1868], 12).
2. Wands was a second lieutenant in the Twelfth Regiment of Infantry.
3. Vance was a captain in the Third Regiment of Infantry. On July 25, 1799,
Caleb Swan appointed Vance deputy paymaster for the Western Army (Swan
to H, June 14, 1799 [listed in the appendix to this volume]). Vance was accused of insulting William Simmons, the accountant of the War Department
(McHenry to H, February 22, 1799 [listed in the appendix to Volume XXII]).
4. See the enclosure to McHenry to H, April 22, 1799.

From James McHenry

War Department
Trenton 30th: August 1799

Sir,

I received yesterday evening your two letters dated the 25th: and
27th: instant.

On the subject of late Military appointments, presented by a letter
from Lieutenant Colonel Bently dated the 17th: copy of which you
enclose [1]—I have to observe, First—That it was the established practice of the Department of War, previous to my coming into it, to
fill vacancies in newly created Regiments or Corps with new Men,
and to continue to do so, until the Regiment, Legion, or Corps was
recruited, or nearly so, and had marched to Head Quarters, after
which and not before, the relative Rank was settled, and the rise of
Officers took place, according to the known principle of succession.
Second—That most of the Regimental Officers lately appointed,
were recommended by the Lieutenant Colonels, and it was understood to fill the vacancies to which they have been appointed. Third
—That no appointments are recollected to have been made lately,
except to vacancies occasioned by non-acceptances or selections for

LS, Hamilton Papers, Library of Congress; LS, letterpress copy, James Mc-
Henry Papers, Library of Congress.
1. H to McHenry, August 25, 1799.

the Regimental Staff, and never in cases of resignation after acceptance, a few instances of which have occurred. Fourth—That the Regiments were to be considered on every principle open to new appointments, without cause for sensibility in those previously appointed, until the relative Rank was settled, and that I had no information either from you or any other Officer, through you, that the relative Rank for the Regiments mentioned, or any other, had been settled in consequence of my letter to you dated the 31st: March last, [2] until I received your letter of the 25th: instant. Fifth— That the provisional designation to Grades and Ranks in the Twelve Regiments now raising, made by the Board of General Officers last winter at the Seat of Government could only be considered as an adapting of Office from the information before them, to the pretensions and abilities of the Candidates, and not in any measure as giving a right to preferment in consequence of non-acceptances by those placed above them. Sixth—That Vacancies in Regiments, other than those you contemplate, have been filled, generally by the recommendations of the Lieutenant Colonels without respect to Officers, who would have been next in succession, if promotion had commenced, and this without occasioning any complaint, that has come to my knowlege. Seventh. That it was natural hence to conclude that it was almost universally understood by the officers themselves that vacancies occasioned by non-acceptance, or Staff regimental appointments were open, and might be filled by persons, not hitherto selected to office without derogation to their respective pretensions, or characters, or injury to their feelings.

The Commander in Chief in a letter to me dated the 25th March last,[3] expressed himself in the words following: "I would not be understood to mean that if a Captain, (and so of any other Grade) declines his appointment that *during the act of formation*, the vacancy is to be filled by the next in seniority *necessarily;* so far from this I maintain, that where a vacancy is occasioned by non-acceptance, that it may without injustice, be filled by a *new character* as in the first instance; but it is my opinion at the same time, that if you have

2. McHenry is mistaken. He is referring to McHenry to H, March 21, 1799.
3. George Washington to McHenry, March 25, 1799 (ALS, letterpress copy, George Washington Papers, Library of Congress).

recourse to *promotion,* that the arrangement which was made by the Board of General Officers (in all its posts) who had regard to all the combinations and qualifications, that have been enumerated in settling the relative rank, is the safest guide you could have resorted to." The occasion of the observations just quoted, was the annunciation in the public prints of the appointment of Mr. Mercer [4] of Virginia to a Captaincy in the Cavalry and on the supposition, that it was a promotion, as this Gentleman had been originally arranged a Lieutenant. The fact however is, that Mr. Mercer had declined the Lieutenancy and was afterwards appointed as a new man to a vacant Captaincy.

I have presented the opinion of General Washington to shew it coincides with that I have uniformly held, viz: That all vacancies occasioned by non-acceptances during the formation of a Regiment or Corps, are to be considered open to new appointments, and that new characters, not heretofore selected (and Mr: Mercer's was a stronger case) may be placed in them without injustice to those already appointed. The new character to stand precisely on the ground he would have occupied, if appointed originally, and to have the same pretensions respecting relative Rank. Acting from such impressions, the General has recommended to vacancies in Grades superior to Lieutenants occasioned by non-acceptances.

Proceeding upon this principle, the Senate were apprized by the president, when the first nominations were made to them that the relative Rank of the Candidates would be in abeyance until the ap-

4. In his letter of March 25, 1799, Washington wrote to McHenry: "I find by the Gazettes (I have *no other* information of these matters) that Lieutt [Charles Fenton] Mercer, of the Light Dragoons, is promoted to the Rank of Captn. in that Corps. In the arrangement of Officers, where every attention was paid (that personal knowledge or information could reach) to *merit, age, respectability & standing* in the Community, he was not even placed (if my memory serves me) high up among the Lieutenants. What then will those Lieutenants who were his *Seniors* in that arrangement, greatly his *Seniors* in age, of at *least* as much *respectability—better known,* and of *equal merit* think, of having him placed over *them?* Mercer, compared to some of them, is a boy; and in such an Army as it was our wish to form, it will have an odd appearance to place a young man of 20 or 21 years of age over a Lieutent. of 30, in *every other respect his equal*" (ALS, letterpress copy, George Washington Papers, Library of Congress). Mercer had been appointed a lieutenant in the cavalry on January 8, 1799. He declined the appointment, and he was then appointed a captain on March 3, 1799, in place of Lawrence Lewis who had declined (*Executive Journal,* I, 298, 303, 323).

pointments for the whole Twelve Regiments were filled,[5] and Commissions have not yet been issued to the Officers, but wait the final and full adjustment of relative Rank throughout the Army, of which the Officers have been informed individually by circular letters from this Department.[6]

From the considerations and for the reasons detailed, it will be perceived I do not think it proper, to revise, the late appointments which have been made, upon the ground that the rule of succession had been established, this cannot be supposed previous to the settlement of relative Rank and a promulgation accordingly of such rank.

If however Colonel Bentley will signify to me (what it was impossible to collect from a general recommendation) that when he recommended certain characters lately appointed to fill vacancies to his Regiment, he meant and intended they should only be appointed Junior Second Lieutenants, and did not so express himself, or particularize, from a presumption that his arrangement was before me, and also represent that the measure will now have no inconveniencies, nor occasion discontent, I shall have no objection to act upon such information, and correct an error produced by his general recommendation.

Rules of promotion have been delayed until the appointments for the whole Twelve Regiments were completed. I shall however transmit them as soon as the derangement consequent upon a removal of the Office will permit.

You observe, "the total defect of organization in the Western Army (the extent of which I did not know till very lately) has encreased my solicitude for another course of things, lest we get every where, into an inextricable chaos." I must request to be informed

5. On December 31, 1798, John Adams sent the following message to the Senate along with a list of nominations for officers to the Additional Army: "A want of materials alone, has prevented a complete nomination for the whole of the troops directed to be raised. Care will be taken that this necessary postponement shall in no manner affect the relative rank of the officers to be yet appointed. Nor is it intended that the order of nomination in this list shall have any influence in the ultimate settlement of the rank of these officers. They will only be directed to obey in the order in which they here stand, until an ulterior arrangement shall be made" (*Executive Journal*, I, 302).

6. For the rules concerning rank and promotion, see the enclosure to H to McHenry, July 2, 1799. See also H to McHenry, July 8, 1799; McHenry to H, September 3, 1799.

on this subject of particulars in order, that if the defect of organization mentioned, has been occasioned by error or inattention on my part, I may in future avoid it.

The existing regulations respecting fuel and Straw, and Stationery,[7] I have supposed were not so exceptionable, or important, as to make it necessary, to lay aside more important business to take up the revised regulations,[8] so far as they relate to these Articles, for consideration. A cursory view of the same, as extended to the number of Horses, to be allowed to certain Grades of Officers, also left an impression upon my mind, that upon this subject of them, a mature deliberation is requisite, previous to their being transmitted to the president for his Sanction, especially as in this part of them, you appeared to have trusted more to others than to yourself. The whole of the revised regulations (which were not received by me, before the first of this month) will be taken as soon as practicable, into consideration, and when sanctioned by the president, they will be immediately transmitted to you.

The existing regulations respecting fuel, Straw &c: must be considered in force, until the revised and extended ones supercede them by their adoption. It is therefore presumeable that Major Tousard may have received them in the course of the correspondence relative to his accounts, from the Accountant of the Department.[9] It is certain I have lately neither transmitted, nor given any orders on the subject to this Officer. The occurrence is regretted, but you must permit me to observe, that it will always be the safest course, and most effectual to prevent Embarrassments, and apparent clashing of dispositions to forbear acting upon regulations, which are to emanate from the president, until they have been confirmed by him, and regularly communicated.

With the greatest respect, I have the honor to be, Sir, Your most obedt: servant,   James McHenry

Major General Alexander Hamilton

7. See McHenry to H, June 24, 1799.
8. For the revised regulations, see H to McHenry, second letter of July 30, 1799.
9. See H to McHenry, August 27, 1799.

To James McHenry

New York, August 31, 1799. "I have lately received pressing applications from various quarters . . . for a supply of Horsemens Tents.[1] On this subject I can only renew the urgent requests which I have so frequently made to you. . . ."[2]

Df, in the handwriting of Thomas Y. How, Hamilton Papers, Library of Congress.
    1. These requests are in William S. Smith to H, August 15, 1799; Thomas Parker to H, August 15, 17, 1799 (both letters listed in the appendix to this volume).
    2. See H to McHenry, third letter of July 10, 1799.

From Nathan Rice

Hingham [Massachusetts] August 31st 1799

My General

Your several favours of the 14th, and the 22d instant I have recvd. Severe indisposition of body and deep affliction for the loss of my eldest Son prevented my acknowledging the receipt of the former untill now. I communicated to Capt. Ashmun your ideas, and my opinion on the several subjects of his letter. I have advised Lieut Samuel W. Church this day of the acceptance of his resignation by the Secretary of War, and have directed him to inform me the precise time of his receiving the Notice.

The deserter shall be forwarded to Rode Island and with as little delay as possible I will devote my personal attention to reconnoitreing the country for a situation, for winter quarters, which shall embrace the several advantages you propose.

I presume Sir, you have by this, received my two monthly recruiting returns. Altho our success, has not equaled my wishes, it has exceeded my expectations. A more favorable season for the service is approaching, when I hope the regiment will be soon compleated.

Pray Sir are the officers on the recruiting service, to be allowed their premium out of the money which they receive of the pay master for that service? and are they to appropriate a part of the same to pay the Musick which they hire (this I find has been done by most of them). If this is the case there may be a propriety in the application which they are making for a further supply of money. I have required of them, the expenditure of the whole of the payment of the *bounty to the recruits.* I think it a hardship on them.

The present System of discipline contemplates a regiment to consist of eight companies & points out the manner in which those companies & the officers commanding them are posted in the formation of a regiment.[1] Our present Establishment making a regiment consists of Ten companies and no disposition being made for the two additions leaves the officers at a loss. Uniformity ought to prevail throughout the army in the minutia of discipline. Will therefore thank you for some directions on the subject.

The recommendation of Mr. Boyle which I have enclosed,[2] coming from so respectable a sourse, induces me altho ignorant of the character to sollicit your support thereof and likewise of a Gentleman I lately recommended to the Secretary of War, by the name of Wilson,[3] an Englishman, not naturalised, has resided in this country three years, & means to remain here, is a genteel well informed man, & his zeal for our service gives him a strong claim on my friendship he asks but for a Lieutenancy.

Should a vacancy of a first Lieutenancy be made in my Regt. by the appointment of an adjutant from that Grade whom I shall very soon nominate—I must intreat in justice, to as much merit as I have known in any officer of his grade, that it might be filled by the promotion of Mr. Roulstone,[4] who was (altho recommended as I am informd for a company) appointed & stands a 2d Lieutenant, his abilities attention & exertions will I am sure justify my request.

With the highest respect   I am Sir yr Obt Servt   N: Rice

Maj Genl Hamilton

ALS, Hamilton Papers, Library of Congress.
    1. See H to James McHenry, May 21, 1799, note 1.
    2. The enclosure, which has not been found, was enclosed in H to McHenry, September 9, 1799 (listed in the appendix to this volume).

3. Edward LeBritton Wilson.

4. John Roulstone had been appointed an ensign in the Fourteenth Regiment of Infantry on January 8, 1799 (*Executive Journal*, I, 301, 303). In accordance with Section 2 of "An Act for the better organizing of the Troops of the United States; and for other purposes" (1 *Stat.* 749–55 [March 3, 1799]) he became a second lieutenant on March 3, 1799 (Heitman, *United States Army*, I, 848).

From James Wilkinson

[New York, August, 1799]

Genl. Hamilton will find in the "Reglemens pour L'infanterie Prussienne" [1] many substantial principles of duty & of service, inapplicable perhaps to our Modes of thinking & acting, but susceptible of modification. Brig Genl. W. begs leave to refer to the Chapter on "Subordination" in the second Volume particularly—and will be obliged by General Hamiltons attention to the Letter for Lt. Boote. [2]

Saturday Morning

Maj Genl Hamilton

AL, Hamilton Papers, Library of Congress.

1. *Reglemens Pour L'Infanterie Prussienne. Traduit de l'Allemand Par M. Gourlay de Keralio* (2 Vols., Imprimé a Berlin. Et se Trouve à Paris, Chez les freres Estienne, rue S. Jacques, 1757).

2. William R. Boote was a lieutenant in the Third Regiment of Infantry.

From James McHenry

Trenton, War Department, September 2, 1799. "I have received your letter of the 28th August ulto representing that the number of Officers of the four old Regiments, who have reported themselves to you in pursuance of my notification, bear no comparison to the number actually absent, and requiring some more decisive measure. I shall issue, in conformity with your suggestion, the inclosed notification [1] to all the Officers of the 1st Regiment of Artillerists and Engineers and the four old Regiments absent from their commands. . . ."

LS, Hamilton Papers, Library of Congress; LS, letterpress copy, James Mc-
Henry Papers, Library of Congress.

1. Copy, Hamilton Papers, Library of Congress.

This notice, which is dated September 2, 1799, first appeared in the *Gazette
of the United States, and Philadelphia Daily Advertiser* on September 3, 1799,
and was then reprinted in other newspapers. The notice reads: "All officers of
the first regiment of Artillerists and Engineers, and of the first, second, third
and fourth regiments of Infantry in the service of the United States, who are,
from whatever cause, absent from their command, are required with all possible expedition to report themselves by letter to Major General Alexander
Hamilton. The officers thus called upon, will be held amenable for any avoid-
able delay in reporting themselves, and those who do not report in four months
from the date of this notification, will be presumed to have resigned their commissions."

McHenry had issued a similar notice on April 15, 1799. See H to McHenry,
August 28, 1799, note 2.

To James McHenry

New York September 2nd. 99

Sir,

A rule respecting the allowance of Barracks and Quarters is wanting. I submit to your consideration the following scale. To a Major
General for himself four rooms, for each Aid one room, and a
Kitchen. To a Brigadier General for himself four rooms, for his Aid
one room, and a Kitchen. To the Inspector General in addition to
his allowance as Major General two rooms for officers, and one for
his secretary. To the Quarter Master General in addition to his
allowance as Major General two rooms for offices and one for each
Assistant or Clerk. To the Adjutant General and each principal
Deputy with a separate army the additional allowance of two rooms
for Offices. To each field officer two rooms. To each Captain one,
to each of the regimental staff one, to two Subalterns one, to every
mess of eight officers two. To every Inspector or Quarter Master of
a Division or Brigade one additional room for an office. To every
twelve persons other than commissioned and staff officers a room of
the dimensions of   .¹ And so in proportion when rooms shall be
greater or smaller.

To the Commander in Chief or General Commanding in a separate department or District the allowance may be exceeded accord-

ing to circumstances of which he must judge upon his responsibility for any abuse of the discretion.

The allowance of fuel to General Officers requires also to be regulated. The following scale is submitted. From the first of October to the first of April in every year—To a Major General two Cords and a half cord per month. To a Brigadier General the same quantity. To the Inspector General the additional allowance of a Cord per month. To the Adjutant General and each principal Deputy with a separate army the additional allowance of a Cord per month. To the Quarter Master General the additional allowance of one Cord per month or such quantity as the commanding general shall approve. To each Inspector or Quarter Master of a Division or Brigade the additional allowance of half a Cord per Month. From the first of April to the first of october in every year one third of the foregoing allowances. The Commanding General under special circumstances may by orders in writing enlarge or diminish the foregoing allowances & may by the like orders direct allowances in cases not provided for.

No compensation in money to be paid or received in lieu of allowances of fuel.

With great respect   I am, Sir   Yr. obt sert.

Df, in the handwriting of H and Thomas Y. How, Hamilton Papers, Library of Congress; ADf, Hamilton Papers, Library of Congress.
  1. Space left blank in MS.

To James McHenry

New York Sepr. 2nd 1799

Sir

Your letter of the 29 instant [1] is received.

I shall conform to what I understand to be the spirit of the practice of which it gives examples. It is right not to make an extra allowance to *officers* for performing a military duty at a place where they are *stationed* or where they *actually* are resident, or where there is a *military post* at which they can be accommodated as usual except for travelling from another place to that post. But I submit that this is not applicable to a person, not a member of the army, who may be specially designated to such a duty. Nor do I think that it consists with the dignity or policy of the government to desire the service of such a person *gratis*. A person not of the army acting as Judge Advocate ought in my opinion to be compensated. Trials in some instances exhaust too large a portion of time to be employed for a public purpose without an equivalent. It will be agreeable to me in the three instances in which I have been the Agent to announce that an allowance is to be received. I have thought of three dollars per day. The persons are Mr. *Hare* in the trial of Capt. Vance [2] Mr. *Morton* in the Trials of captains Freye and Doctor Osborne [3] and Mr Malcom in those of Major Hoops & Captain cochran.[4] The state of the military hereafter will obviate the necessity of incurring a similar expence.

In the case of the Court Martial of which Major Wilcocks [5] was President, I applied the regulations of December 1798,[6] though from the wording of them I thought there might be some doubt of their applicability; but your construction will solve the doubt: It is the convenient one.

I shall announce to the several commandants that law and usage consider the two dollars per head as the equivalent for the extra expences of recruiting officers and that no further allowance can be made.

Nothing is more just than your observation that "officers instead of encouraging the complaints of their men on the occasions to which you refer ought to endeavour to satisfy them that the articles complained of for some good reason could not be otherwise." I have inculcated this doctrine in different instances and shall make it the subject of a circular instruction.

You add that nothing is more common among officers than complaints about every thing furnished by the public. I am inclined to believe with you that the spirit of complaint is apt to be carried to an excess. But it is important, when it is observed to prevail, to inquire with candour and calmness whether it has not been produced in whole or in part from real causes of complaint. If it has, it is then essential that any defects in the public plan which may have occasionned these should be corrected. This is essential for two reasons, one that justice the success of the service and the public good require that right should be done to the troops, the other that the doing of it will most certainly and effectually remedy the evil. In a new army especially, the force of discipline can hardly be expected to stifle complaint if material grounds for it truly exist.

To be frank on this point is a duty. Viewing the matter from a variety of positions in which I have stood, it is an opinion of some standing with me that the supply of the army, except in the article of provisions, has been most commonly so defective as to render a considerable degree of discontent a natural consequence. In some instances, the quality of articles, in others their form or workmanship have been faulty. In others they have been supplied too irregularly and too much by retail. These things amidst a revolution will be acquiesced in—in the first essays of a new government they will be tolerated; but in a more mature state of its affairs, as that of ours at present, a government should not stand in need of indulgence from its armies. In strict justice to them it should lay the foundation of an absolute claim to their strict obedience and rigid compliance with every duty.

In recurring to ideas of this sort I only embrace an occasion which seems to call for the expression of them. I well know your disposition to ameliorate our plan. I count upon the success of your efforts but till the amelioration has been exemplified you are not to wonder if murmurs continue. It will not be my fault if they are not as moderate as possible.

With great respect   I have the honor to be   Sir   Yr. Obed ser

The Scy of War

ADf, Hamilton Papers, Library of Congress.
    1. This is a reference to McHenry to H, second letter of August 29, 1799.
    2. Charles W. Hare was the judge advocate at the court-martial of Samuel C. Vance. For the charges against Vance, see McHenry to H, second letter of August 29, 1799, note 3.
    3. Washington Morton, a New York lawyer, was the judge advocate at the courts-martial of Frederick Frye and Samuel Osborne. For the charges against Frye, see H to McHenry, two letters of July 31, 1799. Doctor Samuel Osborne, a surgeon's mate with the First Regiment of Artillerists and Engineers, was charged with disobeying his commanding officer (Hare to H, March 12, 1799; Morton to H, March 14, 1799 [listed in the appendix to Volume XXII]). For earlier plans to try Osborne by court-martial on the same charge, see McHenry to H, January 29, 1799; H to McHenry, March 18, 1799.
    4. William Malcom, a New York merchant, was the judge advocate at the courts-martial of Major Adam Hoops and Captain Walter L. Cochran. Frye

had accused Hoops of "insulting and provoking lanuguage" and of striking him with a cane; he had accused Cochran of threatening to strike him (Frye to H, August 7, 1799 [listed in the appendix to this volume]).

The court-martial acquitted Hoops of "any *scandalous,* or *infamous Conduct,* such as is *unbecoming an Officer, and a Gentleman*" and "of any *disorderly Conduct,* unbecoming an Officer" (D, undated and signed by William S. Smith' Hamilton Papers, Library of Congress). Although H stated in an undated memorandum that he agreed with the acquittal of Hoops on the first charge, in the same document he also stated that he believed Hoops was guilty of the second charge because his actions were "incompatible with the relative situation of officers, with the respect which every officer owes to the military character in the abstract, and with the decorum of behavior which every Gentleman bearing a commission ought to deem the inseparable attribute of his station. . . . In manifesting his sense of an injury received from another officer he ought to shew by the manner of doing it, that contempt for the person of his adversary has not caused him to lose sight of the consideration which is appropriate to the station" (ADf, Hamilton Papers, Library of Congress).

5. Major William Willcocks presided over the courts-martial of Frye and Osborne (H to Morton, March 14, 1799 [listed in the appendix to Volume XXII]).

6. For these regulations, see the enclosure to McHenry to H, April 22, 1799.

From James Wilkinson

[New York] 2nd. Sept. 1799.

Indisposition Sir has prevented my seeing you, since the day before the last. I have a terible Cold, caught I know not how. If the Ministers report [1] be correct, & it accords with my own information, & that of the adjutant Generals Office—the 1st. and 2d. Regiments want each two Mates, and the 3d. and 4th. each one, to compleat the Establishment, which should I humbly conceive be appointed, & ordered to join their respective Corps, but whether taken from those in Service, or out of it, cannot be very material. When I left the Mississippi Territory—for the Posts of Massac, Pickering, McHenry, Sargent, Loftus's Heights & Stoddert on the Mobile, we had a single surgeon only—of the appointment, or the Movement of the Gentlemen, directed to that Quarter I was unadvised. We have neither mate nor Surgeon, at the secluded *post of Macanac,*[2] and my Camp of two hundred & odd men near Natchez, depends entirely on the Surgeon to Fort Sargent. Two additional Mates are Certainly necessary on the Mississippi & Tombigby, whether we increase our force in that Quarter or not.

I am at this moment in a profuse Sweat, but will see you in the afternoon, if I may go out with propriety.

What can be the policy of appointing temporary Mates, while the Regimental Staff is incompleat? I cannot comprehend it.

With respectful & true Attachment   I am sir   Yr. Obdt & Hbl sert   Ja. Wilkinson

Maj. General Hamilton

LS, Hamilton Papers, Library of Congress.
   1. This is a reference to James McHenry to H, August 30, 1799 (listed in the appendix to this volume). In this letter McHenry listed the vacancies in the officer corps of the Western Army.
   2. Michilimackinac.

From James McHenry [1]

Trenton War Department 3d. Septr. 1799

Sir

Inclosed are regulations adopted by the President of the United States, relative to military rank and promotion. The Commander in chief, to whom they were submitted, made no objection to take upon himself, to determine the relative rank of those officers who had not been in service. I have therefore prefered leaving this point as it stood originally. I shall transmit to the Commander in Chief all the information I have obtained from the Lieutenant Colonels and Majors respecting their claims, together with such information as the office affords, that as little delay as possible may take place in the assignment to the field officers of their relative rank and its due promulgation accordingly. In the mean while you will hasten to fix the relative rank of the Company Officers of such Regiments as you have not yet reported to me. I have only received your arrangement for the 7, 10, 11, & 12, transmitted in your letter of the 25th Ultimo.

I think the rule a good one, that in promotions to the rank of General, the officers of Cavalry, Artillery, & Infantry, should be considered as eligible indiscriminately, or without distinction of one Corps from another. The probability is that this rule will generally govern. I have not however found a fit opportuny to submit it to the President; it has not therefore been incorporated with the regulations. Is there no danger, if established and published, that the latter rule will induce in the Army, an idea, that all appointments of Generals must be made from the Officers of the Army, and in a regular ro[u]tine of promotion, which is by no means intended?

I have the honor to be, with great respect, Sir, Your Most Obedient Servant   James McHenry

Major General Alexander Hamilton

LS, Hamilton Papers, Library of Congress; LS, letterpress copy, James McHenry Papers, Library of Congress; copy, George Washington Papers, Library of Congress.
   1. For background to this letter, see McHenry to H, second letter of July 2, 1799; H to McHenry, July 8, 1799.

From John J. U. Rivardi [1]

Niagara [New York] September 5, 1799. ". . . I hope Captain Thompson will by the time this letter comes to hand, have had the honor of Seeing you & as I requested him To lay the different wants of this Garrison &a. before you." [2]

ALS, Hamilton Papers, Library of Congress.
   1. For background to this letter, see Rivardi to H, July 25, 1799.
   2. Thompson and H did not meet, but in a letter dated September 23, 1799, which is listed in the appendix to this volume, Thompson wrote from Albany to H stating that he was about to return to Niagara. In this letter he enclosed a document entitled "Memorandums delivered to me by Major Rivardi" (ADS, Hamilton Papers, Library of Congress). This document consists of a list of Rivardi's requests for supplies and equipment for Fort Niagara.

From Nathan Rice

Hingham [Massachusetts] Sepr. 6th. 1799

My General

I am sorry to be under the necessity (in conformity with the directions given in the 34th article, in the recruiting instructions),[1] to report to you the desertion of Six recruits, from the district rendezvous at Taunton. I enclose the list forwarded me by Major Winslow who commands there.[2] He writes me, they had expressed some uneasiness at not receiving the remaining four dollars of their bounty, which they said was promised by Captain Chandler[3] who inlisted them, should be paid them immediately on their arrival at the district rendezvous. Every step is taking in order to apprehend them.

A man in Captain Chandlers Company by the name of Sewall Moore, has applyed for a discharge or an exchange of him for another man, he pleads I am informd, among other reasons therefor, intoxication at the time of inlistment. I have inclosed the Statement of Lieutenant Flagg[4]—please to communicate directions for a guide to me herein.

With the utmost respect   I am Sir your Obt Servant

Nathan Rice

N:B   In case of the apprehention of all, or any of the deserters, how shall they be tryed & punished?   N Rice

Major Genl Hamilton

ALS, Hamilton Papers, Library of Congress.
    1. Article XXXIV of the March, 1799, War Department pamphlet *Rules and Regulations Respecting the Recruiting Service* reads: "On the desertion of a recruit, besides the usual exertions and means to be employed on such occasions, the recruiting officer will transmit, as soon as possible, a description of the deserter to the field officer of the district, and will cause all descriptions of deserters that may be sent to him, to be entered in a book kept for that purpose, and will use his endeavors to discover and apprehend all deserters. The commander of the district will immediately report the same to the commander of the circle; and he to the Inspector General at his quarters, and to the commanders of all the circles, who shall be nearer to his post, than the quarters of the Inspector General, to the end, that measures may every where be taken for the apprehension of deserters, and the prevention of impositions by them." See also H to Jonathan Dayton, August 6, 1798, note 6; James McHenry to H, March 21, 1799.
    2. See the enclosure to Rice to H, April 28, 1799.
    3. Thomas Chandler.
    4. Samuel Flagg, Jr., to Rice, September 2, 1799 (ALS, Hamilton Papers, Library of Congress).
    Flagg was appointed a lieutenant in the Fourteenth Regiment of Infantry on January 8, 1799 (*Executive Journal*, I, 300, 303).

From James Wilkinson

New York September 6, 1799 [1]

Sir

I have the Honor to submit to your Consideration, a rough delineation of the Maritime Coast of the United States, and those parts of the interior of our Country, which lay contiguous to the Dominions of Great Britain and Spain, as far North as the "Saut de St. Marie," with the intention to exhibit to you, at one View, the Military posts occupied at this time by the several Powers, and such as have been heretofore occupied & abandoned by us, to which I have added projections of other Posts, recommended to our occupancy by sound policy—with this sketch you will also receive sundry Documents, numbered progressively from 1. to 9, to which I shall, in the Course of this report, find it necessary to have reference.

In the exposition of the Ideas, the opinions, & the facts which I am about to render you, I shall avail myself of the Lattitude you have allowed me, & banishing reserve, will repose on your magnanimity, for indulgence to my Errors & a liberal interpretation of my motives. Should my Language appear either Confident or dictatorial, I pray you impute it to my desire to avoid verbosity, on a Subject necessarily too prolix, & to acquit me of any indecorous propensity. Pardon this exordium perhaps too formal.

When we survey the Geographical position, investigate the local properties, and cast an Eye to the Agricultural improvements of the United States; the extent & the Direction of the St. Lawrence & Mississippi Rivers will not escape the attention of the intelligent, nor fail to excite the Sollicitudes of every sound American Breast, for future Consequences.

These immense Rivers, together with the infinity of their Ramifications, traverse almost every Clime, circumscribe our most valuable Domains, embrace our whole interior population, and open Avenues

LS, Hamilton Papers, Library of Congress.
1. This letter is dated September 4, 1799, in James Wilkinson, *Memoirs of My Own Time* (Philadelphia 1816), I, 440–58.

to the Heart of our Country, by which in the present State of National incaution, we are liable to be successfully attacked by an inconsiderable force.

The attempt to dispossess a respectable Enemy, once in possession of our Western or Northern Frontier, will be found expensive, (beyond Calculation) difficult in the extreme, and at best of doubtful issue. For while He may derive powerful Aids, from the unconquerable animosities of the Savages, and the versatility of our own Erratics, we shall be exposed to the solid obstructions and impediments, which arise from the distance of our resources, and the Difficulties of the route. To wait for events, will put it out of our power to guard against them. We should therefore, anticipate probabilities at least, & determine to erect substantial Barriers, against those dangerous Portals, which open the way directly to our most vulnerable Parts. To this end, we should augment our force on the Mississippi & the Lakes, we should condense that which is now there, and occupy the most Critical and commanding passes, by durable Works judiciously constructed.

We at present hold several useless Posts on the North-western Frontier, merely to awe to conciliate & to watch the Indians, or to aid the transition of Public Stores in their progress—such are Oswego, Presque Isle, Fort Fayette,[2] Fort Washington,[3] Fort Wayne [4] & Fort Knox,[5] these should be broken up and the Troops incorporated, for by such fritterings we destroy both Officer and Soldier, & expose ourselves always to be beaten in Detail. Should the disposition & the clamours of our transmontane Settlers, be offered in opposition to this proposition, I answer that while We command the House, we shall be able to govern the Inhabitants, and therefore the Hostility of the Indians within our Cordon, who are dependent on us for the implements of War, cannot eventuate in any thing serious, and as to the clamour of the Inhabitants it is desireable, because a State of Alarm or "le petite Guerre" will find employ for our Frontier discontents, will silence their political misrepresenta-

2. Fort Fayette was located at Pittsburgh, Pennsylvania.
3. Fort Washington was located at Cincinnati in the Territory Northwest of the River Ohio.
4. Fort Wayne was located at the confluence of the St. Joseph and St. Marys rivers in the Territory Northwest of the River Ohio.
5. Fort Knox was located at Vincennes in the Territory Northwest of the River Ohio.

tions, & bring home to the Heart their dependence on Government. As to those posts which protect the Transport of the Public p[r]operty, they are surrounded by strong settlements and embosomed by the Civil Authority, which can certainly effect the same Security of the National Interest as those of Individuals; it is therefore presumed, that suitable Agents in charge for the Public, will suffice for every object of Utility at such points.

The Notes attached to the Garrisons, enumerated in the proposed disposition No. 1, will exhibit in brief, the motives which have directed the Distribution & Station of the Troops therein refered to, but as I deem it highly necessary, strong Works should be erected near the Head of the Straits, which lead from Lake Huron and from Lake Erie, it is proper I should assign my reasons for this opinion.

It is presumed, the British Government will never again attempt, the Strength of our Country on the Atlantic Quarter, by an invasion from the Northward, but it is possible a state of things may occur to invite a repossession, and even the extention, of their former occupancies to the North and Westward; in such case, she must commence Her operation from Montreal, and may approach us by the direct route of Cataraqui, or by what is called the Back route, of Grand River and French River into Lake Huron—or by both at the same time.

The Scite which I recommend for a Post at the Bottom of Lake Ærie, was pointed out to me by one McNiff,[6] formerly an Engineer in the British Service, who represented the Ground to be well adapted to fortification, with the advantage of a good Harbour & safe Anchorage, which is not I understand to be found elsewhere in that neighbourhood. He added, that immediately Anterior to Mr. Jay's Treaty, Lord Dorchester had determined to Erect a fortification on that spot.[7] A post there, I am informed, will overlook Fort

6. Patrick Macniff, a deputy surveyor for the British in Upper Canada, had been dismissed as incompetent. On September 29, 1796, he was appointed surveyor and justice of the peace in Wayne County in the Territory Northwest of the River Ohio.

7. As Governor in Chief and Captain General of the British Provinces in North America, Dorchester ordered Lieutenant Governor John G. Simcoe to establish Fort Miamis at the rapids of the Maumee River, approximately twenty miles south of Lake Erie. See Dorchester to Simcoe, February 14, 1794 (E. A. Cruickshank, ed., *The Correspondence of Lieut. Governor John Graves Simcoe, with Allied Documents Relating to His Administration of the Government of Upper Canada* [Toronto, 1923–1931], II, 154).

Ærie, and command the Mouth of the Strait, in case of Hostility it will leave no Harbour in that Vicinity, for the Vessels of the Enemy on Lake Ærie; & at the same time will afford protection to our own, it will form a second Barrier, & preserve the Communication with Pennsylvania, & it will oppose additional obstacles to the advance of an Enemy, by the route of the Cataraqui & Lake Ontario; considered in these Views, merely to the defence of the Country, I conceive the Subject worthy examination, but viewed irrelativly to Military purpose, it will not I believe be found undeserving attention. For at the present time, the want of a road within our own Limits, & a place of "Depot" near Lake Ærie, oblige us to carry our Stores & Merchandize, public & private, through the British Territory, from New Ark to Chepawa Creek by Land, and from the last place to Fort Ærie in Batteaux, which involves much delay and expence, and exposes our Citizens to undue Constraints & partialities. The Scite of Old Ft. Schlosser, erected anterior to the Revolution & long since Destroyed, was occupied under my orders in 1797, but the rapidity of the Current at that point, forbiding the approach of Vessels of Burthen, & the ascent of the Stream being found difficult to Batteaux, the Small garrison was withdrawn. These difficulties and disadvantages will all be removed, by the establishment proposed at the Head of the strait, as the Ground from thence to Niagara is, I am assured, susceptible of a good road.

If in our course we examine the position of Presque Isle, it will be found, that it can have no controul over the Navigation of Lake Ærie. The present Work is injudiciously posted, and consists merely of Block houses connected by ranges of pickets. The scite presents no Critical Spot for occupancy, the surface being towards the Country every where flat. Six & an half feet water only, can be carried into the Harbour. The settlements around it are considerable, & are progressing rapidly—it cannot be possessed by an Enemy, before the Posts in advance are carried—and on an exigency, in twelve Days notice, four Thousand Men may be assembled there with Arms, from the State of Pensylvania. Under these Circumstances, I have recommended the removal of the Garrison.

From this point, passing Detroit, we will proceed to the Head of the Strait, leading from Lake Huron, where a post, in case of hostility, will be found indispensable, to cut off the communication to &

from that Lake, with the British settlements below. The Nature of
the Ground, & the narrowness of the pass, will enable us to do this
effectually, and by such Establishment, we guard against a Coup de
main by French River, which is very practicable in Birch Canoes.
No. 2 covers a particular Sketch of the Spot taken by me in 1797,
and the Post becomes the more indispensable, because Detroit, altho'
proper for a place of Arms & of General "Depot" and necessary to
keep the Indians in Check, & to cover the settlements in that Quarter, does not command the Strait, which opposite to the Fort is a
mile Wide, and the main Channel running close under the British
Shore. Whenever it may be found expedient, to shut out the British
from Lake Superior, a Post must be established at the "Saut de
St. Marie," which may be conveniently done from Macanac,[8] in
Vessels drawing 7 feet water or by Batteaux & Birch Canoes.

As this Chain of Posts may Effectually exclude all foreign intercourse (from the Northward) with our Citizens & our Savages,
which we are not disposed to permit, as it may effectually bar all
communication between Canada & Louisiana, at our will, and cannot
be forced but by a regular attack, (which with tolerable Vigilance
in the Government we shall always be able to anticipate by a Superior force) I consider the positions well adapted, and the force
assigned, in our present relation with Great Britain, competent to
every object of national security; it is however my decided opinion,
that the height which looks into the present Works of Macanac,
should be occupied by a small but strong regular Work, and the
Garrison transfered to it. This precaution & proper endowments,
will enable 250 Men to defend the place, against any force which
can be brought against it; such are the obstacles in the approach to
it, the difficulty of finding Subsistence there, & the shortness of
the season for operations—combined to these preparations, we must
have a Navy for Lake Ærie, to bear some proportion to that of the
Enemy.

In addition to the motives assigned for maintaining & reinforcing
Fort Massac, it may be observed, that this post, constituting the
immediate portal of the Ohio, in the Face of the whole Western
Country, is viewed with exultation by the Friends of Government, &
with infinite disgust by its Enemies; it should therefore be made to

8. Michilimackinac.

take a respectable aspect, in order to give confidence to the well disposed, to appal the Turbulent & to convert the wavering. The works, at present a mere stockade, should be strengthened, and then it may be employed to coerce obedience by the occlusion of the River, should the step become necessary, or in case of exigency, an hundred men may be spared from thence to the Service below.

In this place perhaps it may be most proper, to call your attention to the State of our Ordnance at the several frontier Posts. The Return under Cover No. 3 will exhibit our whole Artillery with their appertinents at every Post except Macanac & Niagara, & in No. 4 you have a brief Abstract of the Cannon & Howitz at each post, to which I have annexed an Estimate of the pieces indispensable, to the Safety of our Fortifications and the Honor of our Arms; on this Subject it would be presumptuous in me, to adress you in detail, as your peculiar intimacy with this branch of service, will best enable you to form the proper Conclusions; it may however be proper for me to inform you, that altho' I have no Return from Macanac, I believe the heaviest metal there, are Brass 6 pounders & 5½ inch Howitz. Look Sir at the Endowments of Fort Lernoult, (at Detroit) a work of some Regularity, & you will find our field Artillery sadly misapplied. It may be material also to add, that Shot and Shells of any Diameter & in any Quantity, can be had from the furnaces on the Monongahela, well executed under the direction of Major Craig[9] of Pittsburgh, for less than 6 Cents per Lb. The Mass which you will find reported on the Mississippi, was cast there in the spring 1798 by my Orders. On this subject I have written urged and intreated again & again, and for fear it should be forgotten, I send you under Cover No. 5 the transcript of a requisition, made in February or March 1798, which has not been attended to in any respect. The Artillery for the Lakes, may I presume be most promptly & Œconomically transported, from this place by the Mohawk River & Fort Schuyler, in the proper season, and that for the Mississippi may, in the present moment, with facility & very light expence, be safely sent forward by the City of New Orleans. With Submission I will ask should this moment be lost?

The quantum and disposition of our force, on the Mississippi and

9. Isaac Craig, a Pittsburgh shopkeeper, was deputy quartermaster general at Pittsburgh.

the Southern Frontier, are subjects, which in the present State of things, have claim to prompt deliberation & decisive Action; the present calm in that Quarter, may prove a deceitful one, and if the Storm should take us unprepared sad scenes may ensue. The handful of Men now on that Station, could make but feeble resistance, even against the enthusiastic yoemanry of Louisiana once put in motion. It appears rational and necessary, that we should determine either to Defend the Country, or to abandon it; in the first case, the means should be correspondent, and in the last case, the Troops now there should be withdrawn, for in the present State of Hands the Game on our part may soon become a desperate one. The imbecility of the Spanish Government on the Mississippi is as manifest, as the ardor of the French fanatics of Louisiana is obvious. A Single Individual of hardy enterprize, presenting himself with directorial Credentials, and hoisting the National Standard at New Orleans, might depose the Spanish administration in one hour, and have the population of the Country at His disposal, for whatever desperate Enterprize—under such circumstances will it be indecorous, should I express my apprehensions, that we repose in false Security & that if we are not seasonably aroused, the dismemberment of the Union may be put to hazard.

Whoever consults the passions and interests of the human Breast, and is acquainted with the Geography of the Country, will discover, that the Nation which holds the arbitrary controul of the Navigation of the Mississippi, must eventually direct the policies of the Western Americans, and it is equally obvious, to all who are acquainted with the habits & relative Interests, of the Citizens and the Indians of the United States, that the latter can never cease to be the enemies of the former, and will continue ever ready to strike for Vengeance, when opportunity may favor. The savages who inhabit the tract of Country, bounded by the Tombigby on the East, The Tennessee on the North, The Mississippi on the West, and the Mexican Gulph on the South, can muster at least 6,000 fighting Men. I speak from good information; we will suppose their force armed against us, and 1,000 regular Troops & 500 Chassieurs, posted at the Walnut Hills (the first spot below the Chickasaw Bluffs which is not inundated during the Winter & Spring) with ten Stout Gallies, bearing 6s. 12s. & 24 pounders, well built and well manned, at a point so remote, with the impediments which intervene, the Casualties to which we shall be subject, the delays which are unavoidable, and the disaffection we may have to encounter, among our own people, who can calculate the time, the toil, the Blood, and Treasure which may be found necessary, to drive the Usurpers out of the National Territory? or if the power in possession, be hardy & enterprizing, who can ascertain the practicability of the attempt? In my own Judgement, the event would, at best, be problematical, because the resources of the usurpers would be more convenient, & their inter-courses, more prompt & facile than our own could be. Before we dismiss the Subject, it may be necessary to take into View, that we dare not move out of the Ohio, until we have built a River Navy of decided Superiority, for it may be received as a truth, that an expedition, after four days sail down the Mississippi, must succeed, surrender, or perish, as we can find no retreat to an army, through deep, difficult, extensive, & trackless wilds—for instance an Army driven on Shore near the River St. Francois, with an Enemy in front, will find itself at least four hundred Miles removed from Succour, & without Transport must fall a pray to hostile Savages or Starve. Reverting to the question of abandonment or Defence, which has been suggested for the sake of Argument & Elucidation, let us contemplate the boundless range of the Mississippi, let us view its countless tributaries, which bathe the most extensive tract of Luxuri-ant soil in the Universe, let us reflect that the most valuable portion of this soil is ours of right, and that on the Maintainance of this right, must depend the National Unison; under such well founded reflexions & the impressions Consequent, I flatter myself we shall not hesitate, and that a Determination may ensue, no longer to hazard such precious and important Interests.

For the safety, the subordination, & prosperity of our Western possessions, the most Cheap and conclusive plan, would be the Cap-ture of New Orleans, but as this Step is at present unwarranted, we must turn our thoughts to the defensive protection of our Settle-ments in that Quarter, and in this View it will naturally occur, as a general principle, that the means to be opposed, must bear due pro-portion to the force which may be employed against us, but in the present State of things, I deem three Regiments of Infantry, three Companies of Artillery, Two Troops of Cavalry, and our two Gal-lies, competent to the Defence of the Country, against any Force which could have been brought into Action from Louisiana, when I left that province in June last, provided we receive a seasonable supply of Artillery & Ordnance Stores.

The particular disposition which I should prefer for this force, under the Circumstances in which I left the Country, may be briefly comprized in the following Detail Vizt. A Subaltern's Command at Fort Pickering (say Chickasaw Bluffs) as a "locum tenens" to preserve our (exclusive) intercourses with the Chickasaw Indians, and for their accommodation. A Garrison at Fort Adams, competent to command the pass of the River & to protract a Siege for three months, and to this service, I consider 500 Infantry & two Companies of Artillery adequate, the Works being finished and properly armed & endowed. From Fort Adams along the Line of National Demarkation, at the critical passes, I propose a Chain of small Posts, to prevent foreign intrigues with our Indians, & to detect any desultory movements, which might be attempted by our left, & towards our rear. The Garrisons of these Posts may be calculated to repel the attacks of small Arms, & to retire without loss before the approach of Cannon. With my main Body, I would select a healthy position, to cover our settlements, favour a Co-operation with Fort Adams, should it become necessary, & enable me to give Battle to an invading force, or to deny it at my discretion. In this situation I would make soldiers, & wait Events & Orders.

Having thus Sir run over our whole frontier, from Canada to East Florida, permit me to call your attention to the sources, from whence we are to derive the force requisite to carry into Effect, the propositions which I have the Honor to offer to your Consideration.

The Regimental Returns No. 6 are calculated to expose to you, the paucity & terrible derangement of those Corps.

The Battallions of Artillery, necessarily acting in Detachment, we find deficient seventy one privates (more than one fourth of the Establishment) we perceive also one Captain deficient, one Subaltern absent, & another about to resign his Commission.

The first Regiment we find scattered from one extreme of the Nation to the other, we find two Companies mustered to the same Officer (Captain Tinsley),[10] & six Companies furnishing 232 privates only instead of 360, & it is painful to remark, that in this number

10. Samuel Tinsley was a captain in the Third Regiment of Infantry.

consists the Strength of the Regiment. We find also four Captains & four Subalterns only present with those six Companies, (which leaves two Captains and eight Subalterns to be accounted for) and we see a Deficiency of four Lieutenants & two Surgeons mates to complete this Corps.

The second Regiment is more compact, but it is also much dispersed; we perceive a great deficiency in the Ranks of this Corps likewise, eight Companies furnishing 301 privates in place of 480, the Establishment. We find four Captains and sixteen Lieutenants absent, and One Lieutenant & two surgeons Mates wanting to compleat.

Of the Third Regiment, we find five Companies on the Mississippi, and one in the State of Tennessee, of the last I have no Return, the five Companies return only 216 privates instead of 300, and we find in this Corps also, a great dispersion of the Officers, The Lieutenant Colonel [11] being in Georgia, the 1st. Major in New Hampshire,[12] a plurality of the Company Officers, the Surgeon, & Mate absent, and six Lieutenants and one Surgeon's Mate wanting to compleat.

The Fourth Regiment was taken from my Command in 1797 [13] & I have no Return of it.

To Compleat the three first Regiments to the Establishment, the summary annexed to the Regimental Returns, exhibits a deficiency of eleven Lieutenants, five Surgeons mates, thirty Cadets, three Serjeants Major, five Quarter Master Serjeants, five Senior Musicians, Sixty Serjeants, fifty one Corporals, ten Drummers, Sixteen Fifers, & one thousand and fifty one privates, and Eighteen Captains & forty four Lieutenants are reported absent.

This great deficiency, of nearly three fifths of the Establishment, is an affecting circumstance, but the derangements & distraction of the Corps, and the Seperation of the men from the Officers, and the Officers from the men, tear up the fundamental principles of Mili-

11. Henry Gaither was lieutenant colonel commandant of the Third Regiment of Infantry.

12. Jonathan Cass, a resident of New Hampshire and a veteran of the American Revolution, was a major in the Third Regiment of Infantry.

13. The Fourth Regiment of Infantry under the command of Lieutenant Colonel Thomas Butler had been detached to Tennessee in 1796 to prevent speculators and adventurers such as William Blount and Zachariah Cox from complicating American relations with the Indians, Spaniards, and British in that area. See James McHenry to H, May 27, 30, 1799; H to McHenry, May 29, 1799.

tary institutions—they extinguish the Pride of Corps, that power-fully operative impulse—They prevent Emulation—they perpetuate ignorance—they produce insubordination & indiscipline—and they destroy responsibility, without which all multitudes become Mobs, and an Army the worst of all.

It is irksome to retrace lost ground—it is difficult to combat suc-cessfully the prejudices of the ignorant & the indolent—it is some-times odious to correct abuses—and it is always laborious to extract order out of Confusion, but I and all within the sphere of my Com-mand, look up to you Sir (in full confidence) for such radical re-forms, as may rescue the profession from Disgrace, And the Army from utter ruin; we languish to behold innovation & presumption, yield to principle & subordination—we wish to see rightful preroga-tives and just distinctions maintained, against partial innovations & capricious whims. And we thirst for the restoration of responsibility, throughout the various Grades. To the accomplishment of these desirable objects, we deem it important, that an immediate Organiza-tion of the Companies ensue, that the Officers be ordered to join without delay, and that they be not hereafter seperated from their Companies, but by permission of the Commanding General—That the Regiments be incorporated when practicable, and when imprac-ticable, that the parts be approximated, as nearly as the service may permit. That the Field Officers be attached to, and act with their several Corps, & that in the Gradations of Rank & the relations of Duty, no authority may intervene between a Superior and an in-ferior.

In the present Situation of the Troops under consideration, I find some difficulty in devising a plan for their incorporation, & to bring the several Garrisons to the Posts proposed for them, but to delay the Corrective, will be to foster the disorder which menaces our dissolution, & with great Objects before us, we must step over small impediments.

With due deference then, and pursuant to the Ideas before ex-pressed, I will propose that the first Regiment & two Companies of Artillery, be assigned to the posts of the Lakes & the Garrison of Massac on the Ohio, and that the 2d, 3d, & 4th. Regiments be or-dered to the Mississippi.

Should this proposition be adopted, it seems adviseable that the whole of the Infantry in Georgia, be transfered to some one of the

New Corps, and the Officers be ordered to your Head Quarters for instructions; by this arrangement we save the expence of double transport, we prevent delay, and avail ourselves of the services of men, who are Seasoned to an unhealthy Country.

The troops now at Oswego & Niagara, with Whistlers [14] Company from Fort Wayne, will complete the Garrison proposed for the second place, to one Lieutenant of Artillery, & three Lieutenants, one Serjeant, and four privates of Infantry, and will leave us one Serjeant, two Corporals, one Drummer, one Fifer, two Artificers & sixteen privates of Artillery, with three fifers & one Corporal of Infantry, to be carried forward to Detroit, and transfered to the first Regiment & Captain Thompsons [15] Artillery, to which place also, the Residue of the Garrison of Fort Wayne should be ordered, & that Post left in Charge of the Indian Agent there; we shall then find at Detroit of Artillery 1 Captain, 1 Lieutenant 3 Serjeants 4 Corporals 2 Fifers 1 Drummer 2 Artificers & 33 Matrosses, and of the Infantry of the 1st. Regiment One Lieutenant Colonel 1 Major 1 Captain 1 Lieutenant 1 Surgeon 3 Serjts. 5 Corporals 3 Fifes 1 Drum & 36 privates, to which I propose to add by transfer, from the Men of the Second Regiment now there, in exchange for the same Number of the first Regiment on the Mississippi, 6 Serjts. 7 Corporals, 2 Drums, 2 fifes, & 75 privates, which will give us a Total of 9 Serjeants, 12 Corporals, 3 Drums, 5 Fifes, & 111 privates, Infantry, & these I would form into two Companies and Officer compleatly. And of the Supernumerary Non Commissioned Officers, Drums & fifes, One Serjeant, one Corporal, one Drum, and one Fife, may be assigned to Captain Prior,[16] who wants them, and the residue may be either reduced to the Ranks, or employed in the Recruiting Service. Thompson's Artillery should be compleated without delay, and in the mean time a Detachment sent to relieve Porter [17] at Macanac, who with his Company should be ordered to Massac, via Chicago & the Illinois River, a safe easy & expeditious

14. John Whistler, an Englishman who had served under General John Burgoyne in the American Revolution, was a captain in the First Regiment of Infantry. Whistler was the grandfather of the painter.

15. Alexander Thompson was a captain in the First Regiment of Artillerists and Engineers.

16. A veteran of the American Revolution, Abner Prior served during the Quasi-War with France as a captain in the First Regiment of Infantry.

17. Moses Porter was a captain in the First Regiment of Artillerists and Engineers.

Posts	Species of Troops	Lieut. Colonel	Majors	Captains	Subalterns	Surgeons	" Mates	Serjeants	Corporals	Drummers	Fifers	Artificers	Privates & Mattrosses	Total Non Commissd. officers Rank & file	Companies
Niagara	Artillery	=	1	=	=	=	1	1	1	=	=	2	16	20	Thompsons
	Infantry	=	=	=	=	=	=	3	4	=	1	=	56	65	Whistlers
Detroit	Artillery	=	=	1	=	=	=	3	4	1	2	2	20	32	Thompsons
	Infantry	1	1	1	1	1	=	8	12	2	4	=	111	137	Britts [18] &
Macanac	Artillery	=	=	1	1	=	=	1	1	=	=	=	13	15	Thompsons
	Infantry	=	=	1	=	=	=	4	4	1	1	=	32	42	Priors
Massac	Artillery	=	=	=	1	1	=	3	4	1	1	7	26	42	Porters
	Infantry	=	=	1	=	=	=	3	4	1	1	=	49	58	Pasteurs [19]

18. Daniel Britt was a captain in the First Regiment of Infantry. He died on October 23, 1799 (Heitman, *United States Army*, I, 246).
19. Thomas Pasteur, captain in the First Regiment of Infantry.

Route, during Spring or Autumn, in Perogues Or Birch Canoes & for the sake of Responsibility & Œconomy, the Detachment of Thompsons Company now at Massac, should be transfered to Porter. The following will then be found, the Actual Strength of the 1st. Regimt. & the force of those Garrisons respectively.

A Comparison of this Return, with the Garrisons proposed for the Posts it Comprehends, will exhibit a great deficiency of men and Officers, to repair these defects, the due Complement of Officers for the five Companies, should be ordered immediately to Join, and the residue should be actively employed in the recruiting service, and it is presumed that fifteen Officers, which will be left for that Duty, may with industry, compleat the Regiment by the next Spring, before which period we have little to apprehend, as the frost will soon lock up that Country.

Of the second Regiment, we have eight Companies returned, which gives us 301 privates, these should be organized into Six Companies compleatly Officered, and the residue of the Gentlemen in Commission, the surplus Non Commissioned Officers Drums & Fifers, Should be ordered to the recruiting service. The detachments of this Corps may with facility, with expedition, & Œconomy, reach the destination proposed for it, by the Miamis of the Lakes, the Wabash, & the Ohio Rivers, and should the proposition be adopted, Orders ought to be immediately issued for the movement, as the Autumnal floods are at Hand, and it is important to the Health of Troops destined to the South, that they should reach their Stations in autumn.

The Third Regiment Returns five weak Companies in the Mississippi Territory, & we are assured of one Company in the State of Tennessee, this last should be ordered to join the main Body. The whole should be officered to the Establishment, & the Recruiting Service should be pushed by the Supernumeraries. The Colonel, who has never seen his Regiment in seven Years service,[20] should be ordered to Join it, & the first Major,[21] who has been more than three years absent, should be ordered to do Duty, either with his Corps or at a recruiting Rendezvous.

With respect to the 4th Regiment, Stationed in the State of Tennessee, I have no report on which to found Details, but as it appears

20. See note 11.
21. See note 12.

that Peace & Content have been restored in that Quarter, The objects of the Command there have ceased and the Corps may with Facility & without expence, be readily transfered to the Mississippi. The fragment of an Artillery Company, & a troop of Dragoons attached to this Regiment, may also be ordered by the same Route, to the most feeble, exposed, & succourless frontier of the Nation—but Special Care should be had, in the removal of this Corps, that the due Complement of Officers march with it.

Under the Cover No. 7, you will find (respectfully submitted) a plan for the Organization of the four old Regiments,[22] which by the late Augmentation [23] & change of establishment, have been entirely disorganized; in the distribution of the Officers, I have consulted Talents, Qualifications, & Merits, as far as my knowledge extends, & when this failed me, I have cast lotts. I beg to call the Generals attention to my preference of Captains, as I have seen most of them tried, and have made the selection with a View to Combat.

In examining the Ordnance Return for Fort Wayne, you will perceive a handsome stock of small Arms and a small Quantity of Powder; should the Garrison be removed, it will become a matter worthy Consideration, whether these articles should be carried to Detroit or forwarded to the Mississippi, the expence will be nothing in either Case, and the reflexion which should determine us, will rest on the greater or less Safety and Utility of those Articles, at the respective posts. To account to you for the small Quantity of our fixed ammunition, at the Barrier on the Mississippi, I must observe, that we sat down in the Woods, & had our Buildings to form from the Stump, which prevented the completion of an Elaboratory, until within a few days of my departure; and I may add with great truth, (I do it with sensible pain) that I have not an Officer there who knows how to drive a fuze or fix a Shell. This is a point of too much magnitude to escape your attention, & I trust some Officers of skill & Experience, may be forthwith Ordered to that Quarter, & among them a Field Officer is indispensable. Pope [24] is now Senior

22. Although this list was enclosed in the letter printed above, it was subsequently forwarded in H to McHenry, October 31, 1799, and is printed as an enclosure to that letter.

23. This is a reference to the Additional Army. See the introductory note to H to James Gunn, December 22, 1798.

24. Piercy Smith Pope, who had been a captain in the First Regiment of Artillerists and Engineers, had died on July 12, 1799 (Heitman, *United States Army*, I, 798).

on that Station, and he is not only ignorant, but at intervals his Conduct actually approaches to insanity. It appears essential, that some person should be Employed for that Station, capable of instructing our Officers in the inferior Branches of the Mathematics (to comprehend the Doctrine of projectiles) & in the use of the necessary instruments, as I know not an Individual in service there, who can take either height or Distance, or who understands the application of Hadleys Quadrant.[25] on this subject it is necessary to add, that Books & Instruments should be furnished, as I have never received either from the public. A Theodolite, a Sextant, a circumferenter with a Chain, and three setts of packets Instruments would I apprehend suffice.[26]

Under the Cover No. 8. I take leave to offer you a Variety of information relative to the interior communications of our Country from Michilimacanac to "le prarie des Chiens" by the West Shore of Lake Michigan, Green Bay Fox River & the Ouisconson, & by the East Coast of the same Lake, to the River St. Joseph & Chicago, and from thence across into the Illinois River, & by that Stream into the Mississippi, & down to Cahokia. Also the route from Cahokia up the Mississippi, to "le prarie des Chiens," where we have annually, the most numerous assemblage of Savages, & the most considerable mart for Indian Traffic, within our Limits, or within one Thousand miles of the same point. Under the same Cover, you will find reports touching the Tombigby, and the Country intervening from thence, to our lowest Establishments on the Mississippi, which will be accompanied by a General (tho' incorrect) Map of the Country, & a Sea Coast Chart from New Orleans to Mobile Bay, with a pretty exact projection of the Mobile River up to Fort Stoddart & a Sketch of Lake Michigan from Macanac to Chicago, for which I must refer you to Lieutenant Heton.[27]

25. In 1731 John Hadley, an English mathematician, invented the quadrant, which was used at sea to measure the altitude of a celestial body in order to ascertain the position of a vessel.

26. On June 30, 1800, Ebenezer Stevens received one hundred and forty-three dollars for the purchase of "1 theodolite, 1 surveyor's chain, 3 cases mathematical instruments, 1 sextant and circumferentor" (*A Statement of Expenditures*, 309).

27. Robert Heaton, Jr., of New York had been a lieutenant in the Second Regiment of Artillerists and Engineers. He died on September 9, 1799 (Heitman, *United States Army*, I, 519).

Under No. 9 I take the Liberty to offer you certain Manuscripts from my Orderly Book, which taken with my Order of the 22nd. May 1797.[28] before submitted to you, have constituted Standing Rules of Service which it may be necessary for the Commanding General to Change, modify or sanction in order to prevent the quibbles & controversies of the impatient & Litigious.

The moral, physical & political principles, ⟨pro⟩perties, & relations of several Subjects, which we have glanced at in this detail will be examined in another report, which I Shall digest during my Journey to the Eastward, and may be conveniently suspended, as it can have no influence on any immediate Operation.

I am conscious Sir that you will find in these Sheets much useless prattle, but in ballancing between precision & prolixity, I decided that it was safer to tresspass on your time, than to suppress information however frivolous. In matters of Speculation your Intelligence will correct my Errors, But in Matters of Fact, you may repose confidently on this report, which is most respectfully submited to you

By Sir   Your Obliged, faithful & Affectionate Servant

Ja Wilkinson

Major General Hamilton

28. LC, RG 94, Adjutant General's Office, General Orders, General James Wilkinson, 1796–1808, National Archives.

To John Adams

New York Sepr 7. 1799

Sir

General Wilkinson, who has been some weeks in the City, in consequence of an invitation having for object the readjustment of our Western Military affairs, is about to make a journey to Bra[i]ntree to pay his respects to you. On such an occasion, I hope it will not be thought improper that I should address you on the subject of this officer; since what I shall say will accord with what I know to be the views of General Washington and with what I have reason to believe has been already suggested to you, with his support, by the Secretary of War.[1]

You are apprised, Sir, that General Wilkinson served with distinction in our revolutionary war, and acquired in it the rank of Brigadier General—that for many years since that war he has been in the military service of the Government with the same rank, in which rank he for some time had the chief command of the army—That he has also served with distinction, in this latter period, General Wayne,[2] who was not his friend, has, in one instance within my knowlege, very amply testified.

The decided impression on my mind as the result of all that I have heard or known of this Officer, is that he is eminently qualified as to talents, is brave enterprising active and diligent, warmly animated by the genuine spirit of his profession and devoted to it. The recent communications between us have satisfied me more than ever that he is well intitled to the character I have just given of him.

So circumstanced and so qualified, all military usage and analogy give the General a very strong claim to promotion. His sensibility would suffer with reason, if he has it not, and it would require more than usual patriotism and magnanimity to preserve him from discontent and disgust.

I, as well as others, have heard hard things said of the General, but I have never seen the shadow of proof, and I have been myself too much the victim of obloquy, to listen to detraction unsupported by facts.

Permit me to add, that I hold nothing so unsafe in public affairs as *half confidence*—that in my opinion to imploy a man in delicate and important stations, and to act towards him so as to convince him that he is not trusted and is not to receive the common share of public reward, is the most effectual way that can be adopted to make him unfaithful: while, if we only allow him a well-informed ambition, his fidelity may be assured by letting him see that it will best advance the interest of his ambition.

In hazarding these remarks, I do not mean to present to you observations which could possibly excape your own reflections; but merely to indicate the manner of viewing the subject which determines my judgment that it is both right and expedient to promote General Wilkinson to the rank of Major General in the present army.

Should the matter appear to you, in the same light, I submit whether it will not be proper previously to understand [3] with General Wilkinson, that it may happen in the event that General Knox may be called into the army with a priority to him.[4] For this there are many reasons which will occur to you without being mentioned, and I may without impropriety add that it will meet the ideas of General Washington.

In the course of his conversations with me General Wilkinson has stated that important advantages might result from the appointment of leading characters at the Natches and elsewhere on the Western Waters as officers in the *Evenutal* army;[5] calling them immediately into service with a title to the emoluments of their grades.

I have not had time to reflect so maturely on the proposition as to have formed a definitive opinion of its expediency—But it strikes me in a very agreeable manner & accordingly I offer it to your consideration. The arguments in its favour will not require to be specified in order to be appreciated by you. It is obviously a powerful mean of conciliating the inhabitants, in the quarter to which it applies, and of rend[er]ing them auxiliary in case of need to our military operations. It is presumed they may be provisionally embodied under the leader who may be selected.

I will make no apology for the liberty I take by this letter. The solitariness of the example will I trust evince that it is not my wish to travel out of the regular and ordinary road of communication.

With high respect and true esteem   I have the honor to be   Sir Your obedient serv   Alex Hamilton

The President of the U States

ALS, Adams Family Papers, deposited in the Massachusetts Historical Society, Boston.

1. See H to George Washington, June 15, 1799; Washington to H, June 25, 1799; H to James McHenry, June 25, 1799; McHenry to H, June 27, 1799. See also Washington to McHenry, June 25, 1799 (ALS, letterpress copy, George Washington Papers, Library of Congress).

2. See Anthony Wayne to Henry Knox, May 9, 1793; Knox to Wayne, June 28, 1793 (Knopf, *Wayne*, 234-35, 248).

3. In MS, "unsterdand."

4. See H to Knox, March 14, 1799.

5. For the Eventual Army, see the introductory note to H to James Gunn, December 22, 1798.

Circular to the Commandants of Regiments [1]

Circular   New York Sepr. 7th [–17] 1799 [2]

Sir

It has been suggested to me that particular officers in some instances have incautiously indulged remarks in the presence of their men respecting the bad qualities of articles furnished, which were of a nature to foster discontent in the minds of the soldiery. Instances of this sort, I am persuaded, must have been very rare, as the impropriety of the thing is too glaring to escape an officer of the least reflection; and I am convinced it is only necessary to mention the matter to you to engage your endeavours to prevent the repetition of a similar imprudence. If any articles of supply are exceptionable, the proper course is to represent it to me, in order that the remedy if in my power may be applied, if not that it may be sought through the Secy of War. Of my constant exertions to place the army on a comfortable and respectable footing no doubt need be entertained.

Desultory observations have from time to time been made to me respecting particular articles. I am desirous of having a special & very accurate report from the commandant of each Regiment of the quantity and quality of all the articles which have been received for its use (viz) arms accoutrements cloathing tents and camp utensils. You will as soon as possible transmit one. Any suggestions [for] improvements in the articles which are supplied will be acceptable.

With great consideration   I am Sir   Yr. obed serv

The several Colonels

ADf, Hamilton Papers, Library of Congress.
    1. For background to this document, see James McHenry to H, August 29, 1799; H to McHenry, second letter of September 2, 1799.
    2. On October 4, 1799, Nathan Rice acknowledged receipt of this "Circular of 17th Sept."

From James McHenry

Trenton War Department
7th September 1799

Sir

Inclosed is copy of a letter from Colonel Stevens to me dated the 6th inst [1] and of one to him from Major Jackson dated the 29th Ulto. [2]

You will perceive that Major Jackson conceives Colonel Stevens to be the proper person to apply to for authority to procure a Boat for the use of the Garrison on castle Island, to make carriages for Cannon, and for the erection of Barracks, or other buildings at Fort Independence.

If inferior Officers are to be permitted to consider themselves empowered to demand the acquiescence of Agents in such cases as are presented in Major Jacksons letter, an immence portion of the time of the Secretary of War must be employed in a correspondence with the commanding General, and the accountant of the War Department before the expenditures incurred can be admitted to a course of settlement. This consideration added to the total irregularity of the acts, the confusion they lead to and increased expence they necessarily involve, renders it indispensible that a stop be put to such attempts in future.

For the present and untill an Inspector of Fortifications is appointed under the 18th Section of the "Act for the better organizing of the Troops of the United States and for other purposes," passed the 3rd March 1799,[3] the following course may be observed.

1st   When a Boat or Seine is wanted for a Garrison, let the kind required, and an estimate of what it will probably cost be reported by the Commandant of the Garrison to the artillery officer who commands over the District. If he considers the estimate and requisition proper, let him so certify and transmit it to the Commanding General, who will decide upon the propriety of the requisition and estimate, and if approved of transmit the same with his approbation entered thereon to the agent of the Department of War in the vicinity of the Garrison where there is one, or to the Secretary of War, when there is none.

2d Let the same mode of ascertaining the expence and necessity for Gun Carriages, additional Barracks or other buildings appertaining to the Fortifications, be observed, and the estimates and approvals as aforesaid transmitted to the Secretary of War for his final orders, except in cases, when in the opinion of the Commanding General the service would materially suffer by the time which must elapse by a strict observance of this procedure. In such cases the Commanding General, upon the estimate and requisition of the Commandant of the Garrison, approved of by the Commandant of the District, will certify his approbation and will transmit the whole to the agent of the War Department, where there is one, with his orders to execute the requisition, and where there is no agent, will direct a proper person accordingly, giving immediate information of the proceeding to the Secretary of War, and of the circumstances which rendered the measure necessary.

These estimates ought to be formed with care, and the approvals unequivocal, being authorities which the Agents must lodge with the Accountant to justify him in admitting their Accounts. These points will deserve your attention.

It is proper to inform you that I have directed a quantity of suitable timber to be procured and stored at Fort Mifflin with a view of constructing Gun Carriages, from approved models, under the direction of an intelligent officer, and that I contemplate to supply from that place a number for the use of other Garrisons, particularly in the Southern quarter of the Union.

With great respect I have the honor to be, Sir, Your obedient Servt   James McHenry

Major General Hamilton

LS, Hamilton Papers, Library of Congress; LS, letterpress copy, James McHenry Papers, Library of Congress.
    1. Ebenezer Stevens to McHenry, September 6, 1799 (copy, Hamilton Papers, Library of Congress).
    2. Daniel Jackson to Stevens, August 29, 1799 (copy, Hamilton Papers, Library of Congress).
    3. 1 *Stat.* 749–55.

From William S. Smith

Camp, 12th Regiment [Bronx, New York] September 7, 1799.
". . . Upon a close inspection of the Regiments arms at present issued It pains me to observe, that they too generally appear to be old furbished up barrels, many of them full of flaws, new stocked & dressed perhaps to fulfil a contract, certainly not render essential service; of one hundred and ninety men inspected, including music, I have marked fifty three musquets unfit for service, some fused, some without touch hole & some touch holes covered by the lock, my duty to the public obliges me to be thus particular, & my duty to you as Inspector General, forces me to make the communication that you may guard the public hereafter from similar imposition. In short Sir I protest against the arms, and solicit that they may be proved, for the Regiment would feel no confidence in entering upon actual service, with the arms at present furnished. . . . Duty further obliges me to state, that the Horseman's tents Supplyed the Regt. are not fit for service, they are old & worn out & many of them in a filthy condition. . . ."

ALS, Hamilton Papers, Library of Congress.

From David Strong

Detroit [Territory Northwest of the River Ohio] September 7, 1799. "I received your favour of the 22d. July,[1] and am pleased with the hopes of greater Uniformity in the Clothing in future. The Indians in this quarter seem much dissatisfied at the promises made them by the Secretary of War, that the Governor of the Territory should be at D'Etroit in the course of the present summer to redres any Complaints (many of which they have) which might be laid before him, and attend to the equal and Just distribution of their annual Presents. . . ."

LS, Hamilton Papers, Library of Congress.
  1. Letter not found.

To Nathan Rice

New York Sept. 9. 1799

Sir

I have received your letter of the thirty first of August.

You will recollect that it has been referred to you in conjunction with your majors to prepare an arrangement of relative rank for your regiment.[1] This has not yet been done. Should Mr. Roulstone be placed first on the list of second Lieutenants he will have the place which you request for him in the regular course of military promotions & this is the most proper way of affecting your object.

The recommendation of Mr. Boyle has been transmitted to the Secretary of War,[2] and has received the usual support. I recollect nothing in the recruiting instructions[3] which prevents the officers from retaining out of the Money they receive for the recruiting service the premium[4] to which they are entitled. There is a particular provision, you will remember, on the subject of music—[5] within the limits of this provision the expence for music may be defrayed out of the money received for the recruiting service. The officers will state the money employed for the purpose as applied to that particular object.

It is my intention, in the course of the ensuing winter, to review a system of tactics and discipline, and to propose such alterations as shall appear to me to be advisable. I shall however give immediate attention to the formation of a regiment, and transmit circularly to the several commandants such instruction as may appear necessary. The monthly recruiting returns of which you speak have, I believe, been received.

With great consideration   I am Sir &c

Df, in the handwriting of Thomas Y. How and H, Hamilton Papers, Library of Congress.

1. See "Circular to the Commandants of Regiments," March 23, 1799.

2. H to James McHenry, September 9, 1799 (listed in the appendix to this volume).

3. This is a reference to the March, 1799, War Department pamphlet *Rules and Regulations Respecting the Recruiting Service*. See H to Jonathan Dayton, August 6, 1798, note 6; McHenry to H, March 21, 1799.

4. H is referring to Section 5 of "An Act for the better organizing of the Troops of the United States; and for other purposes" (1 *Stat.* 749–55 [March 3, 1799]). This section provided in part: ". . . each commissioned officer, who shall be employed in the recruiting service, shall be entitled to receive, for each . . . non-commissioned officer and private and artificer, and for each sufficient musician duly enlisted and mustered, the sum of two dollars, the same being in full compensation for his extra expenses in the execution of this service."

5. See McHenry to H, April 22, 1799.

From Caleb Swan

Trenton September 9th 1799

Sir.

I have the honor to inform you that in obedience to your letter of the 3d April last, I arrived at Philadelphia on the 1st July following and reported myself to the secretary of war. On Commencing business at the seat of government it was understood that payment might be made under the usual forms with the exception of the warrant from the commanding officer, and payment has been made by me accordingly in twenty five instances to the amount of 13.599 $21/100$ dollars.

I was apprehensive of impropriety in dispensing with this part of my original instructions,[1] and wrote a letter to the comptroller of the treasury on the 3rd instant,[2] in which I stated the difficulties that had occurred under present circumstances, in the execution of the system laid down for the payment of the troops, and on the 7th instant received his answer,[3] copies of which are herewith enclosed.

In this situation I do not feel myself at liberty to proceed in making further payment, until I receive your direction as to the mode to be adopted. In the meantime it is respectfully suggested, whether if I were removed to your head quarters it would not in a great degree facilitate the business of paying the troops and remove the inconveniencies now attending it. The secretary of war has authorized me to make this suggestion, and to say that if you approve of the measure he will concur in it.

My letter to the comptroller, and his answer will explain to you minutely the existing difficulties so far that it is unnecessary to be more particular.

As it is decided that your warrants are indispensible to my payments, I hope there will be no difficulty in obtaining them for those I have already made?

I have the honor to be with the greatest Consideration and respect, Sir Your most obedient Humble Servant

C. Swan P. m. genl.

Major General Alexander Hamilton
New York.

ALS, Hamilton Papers, Library of Congress.
1. Swan's "original instructions" are dated July 26, 1792, and are from Oliver Wolcott, Jr., who was then comptroller of the Treasury. The instructions read in part: ". . . One sett of the Pay rolls will . . . be transmitted to the Commanding Officer, who will grant his warrant on you for the amount. . . . When a warrant has been obtained payment is to be made" (Df, partly in Wolcott's handwriting, Connecticut Historical Society, Hartford; copy, Hamilton Papers, Library of Congress).
2. Swan to John Steele, September 3, 1799 (copy, Hamilton Papers, Library of Congress).
3. In his answer to Swan, dated September 7, 1799, Steele wrote: ". . . I have concluded that it would not be proper to modify your instructions in such manner as to dispense with the Warrant of the commanding officer in relation to the pay of the troops" (copy, Hamilton Papers, Library of Congress).

To George Washington

Private   New York Sepr. 9. 1799

Dr. Sir,

Two days since, I received from General Wilkinson a Report [1] of which I now send you the original. You will find it intelligent and interesting. Perhaps on the score of intrinsic propriety it deserves to be adopted to a larger extent than some collateral and extraneous considerations may permit.

I had previously thought of the subject but had purposely limited myself to a few very general ideas, that I might examine with the less prepossession the plan of an officer, who possessing talents to judge has for years had his mind occupied with the scene to which he refers. Since the receipt of his plan, I have assiduously contemplated it with the aid of a full personal explanation, and my judgment has formed a result, though not definitive but liable to revision. I adopt several of the leading ideas of the General but I vary in

ALS, George Washington Papers, Library of Congress.
1. James Wilkinson to H, September 6, 1799.

some particulars; as well because I think the change might be too strong with reference to its influence on public opinion and the feelings of the parts of the country immediately concerned as because it seems to me that motives of real weight dictate a modification of his plan.

Premising that one complete Regiment of Infantry should be left for *Tennessee* and the Frontiers of Georgia I would propose the following Disposition for the Remaining three of the old Regiments & for the batalion of Artillerists and the two troops of Dragoons allotted for the Western Army. It is taken for granted that the plan must contemplate only the four old Regiments of Infantry (with those portions of Artillerists and dragoons) inasmuch as these are the only infantry regarded by our system as permanent. The twelve additional Regiments will dissolve of course, as to the non commissioned officers and privates, by the simple fact of the settlement of our dispute with France.

Let these Troops be disposed as follows (viz)

Totals		
	Niagara	Two (2) companies of infantry & a half company of Artillery
A batalion of Infantry & a company & a half of Artillery	Detroit	Three (3) companies of Infantry & one company to Artillery to furnish a Detachment for
	Michilimacnac of	A subaltern two serjeants and Twenty four rank & file Infantry and a serjeant and twelve Artillerists
A batalion of Infantry & a company of Artillery	Fort Fayette } Pittsburgh	One company of Infantry & a quarter of a Company of Artillery
	Fort Wayne	One Company of Infantry & a quarter of a Company of Artillery
	Fort Massac	Three Companies of Infantry half a company of Artillery to furnish detachments for
	Fort Knox	A serjeant and Eight rank & file
	Fort Pickering } Chickesaw Bluffs	A subaltern two serjeants & Twenty four rank & file
A batalion of Infantry & a Company of Artillery	Fort Adams } Loftus Heights	A batalion of Infantry and a company of Artillery to furnish for
	Fort Stoddard Junction of Alabama & Tombegbee Rivers Mobille	not exceeding a company of Infantry & a quarter of a company of Artillery

There will then remain A Regiment and a batalion of Infantry half a company of Artillery and Two troops of Dragoons: Let these be stationed at some convenient point at or near the *Rapids of the Ohio* to form an army of observation and act as exigencies may require.

The other posts now occupied to be relinquished.

A few remarks will illustrate the reasons of this plan.

As a general principle it is desireable to concentrate the force as much as possible. This tends to efficiency for action to the preservation of order and discipline & to the promoting of œconomy. It is conceived that the occupying a small number of critical points with a reserve of force to support or attack will be more impressive on the Indians than the dissipation of the whole force among a great number of small posts. This reserve ought to be so placed as to look to all the principal objects, and it may as an incidental one with propriety look to that of preventing or suppressing insurrection. The concentration of force with a proper disposition will render the maintenance of it far less expensive than if subdivided into small and scattered portions.

These more particular considerations cooperate.

As to *Niagara* and *Detroit.* The effectual possession of the streights which connect Lake Erie on the one side with the Ontario on the other with the *Huron* appears to me very material as a security against British Attack and as a mean of controuling the Northern and North Western Indians by enabling us to obstruct communication. These points are mentioned because they now exist as posts but the streights ought to be reviewed by a skilful Engineer and such point selected as will be most defensible & will best command the streights. The force proposed for these stations at present is inadequate in a *perspective* view, but as there is a probability of a continuance of good understanding with Great Britain for some time, it is conceived that it may now suffice for the sake of obtaining a respectable corps de reserve to be augmented as our military means may increase.

When the proper points shall have been definitively selected it would be my plan to have at each station a *regular fortification* requiring a garrison of from 500 to 1000 men as the nature of the ground to be occupied may indicate; with a citadel in each defensive by from two to three hundred men. These in times of complete harmony with G Britain may suffice but on the appearance of approaching differences to be increased to the complement. The posts at all times to be supplied for a seige. The progress of settlement will speedily furnish the means of prompt reinforcement.

As to *Michilimacnac*. The only motive to retaining this post is to preserve the occupancy of an old communication in some sort calculated to influence the Indians. As to Trade it is now only useful to the British and likely to continue so for some years; except so far as they find it their interest to turn their Trade into our Channels. There are here a few White families supposed to be able to furnish about sixty arms bearing men who are said to be well disposed to our Government & who certainly in a controversy merely with the Indians would cooperate with the garrison. A small one is deemed sufficient for the present purposes of the post. For this an additional reason is that the maintenance of troops there is excessively costly. Any greater force, which with our present total could be thought of for that station must be considered as a *corps perdue* in case of war with Britain, as it would be intirely out of the reach of succour. Consequently the smaller the force there if sufficient for the other objects the better. It is to be observed as to this place that the Indians whose situations are relative to it are in no view formidable. The insular situation is a further security.

As to *Fort Fayette*. It may be doubtful whether any force here is really essential and whether as being a mere depot it may not be left as at other places to the safeguard of the Inhabitants. But considering that it is a portal to the Western Country & that disaffection to the Government has been shewn by the inhabitants of the neighbouring country,[2] the force proposed is deemed expedient as a guard and as a rallying point to the well affected.

As to Fort Wayne. The critical situation of this place with regard to a number of different waters and the influence of its immediate aspect upon the most warlike of the Indians in that quarter make it in my view a post to be maintained contrary to the idea of General Wilkinson.

As to *Fort Massac*. This being another portal & the great outlet for the commodities of the North Western Territory Kentucke &c.

2. This a reference to the Whiskey Insurrection in 1794.

it appears to me that for obvious reasons it ought to be secured by a strong regular fortification & a respectable garrison.

As to *Fort Knox*. There has been for some time no more force than is now proposed which is only necessary as a guard. The settlement is of itself an overmatch for the feeble indians in the vicinity; who besides will be within the speedy stroke of the main body.

As to Fort Pickering. The considerations mentioned by General Wilkinson are referred.

As to *Fort Adams*. I make the like reference. This is an essential point. It is on a height which completely commands the River and the surrounding Country and according to General Wilkinson can easily be put in a state to defy every thing but famine with a garrison of about Two (2) hundred men. The force allowed will always afford this garrison.

As to *Fort Stoddard*. This is now occupied with a Company. It is critical as to an important River. The Indians are in the habit of seeing it occupied by the Spaniards. It commands an important communication with the powerful nations of Savages in the neighbourhood, and is calculated to have an influence upon them. It is in the bosom of a white settlement. These are reasons for keeping it as a post. But an objection to it is that at present it can with difficulty be supplied otherwise than through the Spanish Territory. To make it proper as a permanent an easy communication through our own territory must be established. General Wilkinson says this is practicable.

I take no notice of the other posts suggested by General Wilkinson to be established along our Southern line; because in his own view they are eventual. The Indians must be first reconciled there. And leaving a Regiment for Georgia & Tennessee there is no present force for the purpose. It is also liable to the objection of an extreme frittering of our force.

I do not coincide with General Wilkinson in the disposition of the Corps De Reserve. He would have it in the neighbourhood of *Fort Adams* (say Natches). I propose for it the vicinity of the rapids of the *Ohio*.

On G Wilkinson's plan its great utility would be narrowed to a point, the making in the first instance an invasion from below and in case of rupture of a prompt attack upon New Orleans.

But the strength of the reserve alone could not be relied upon as adequate to either object. If a superior force from below should attack, the principal body of our regular force might in the outset be defeated dissipated & lost. This depriving the Militia of a necessary support might lead to greater misfortunes. If an attack is to be made as little as possible should be left to chance & consequently the force ought to be greater than this plan would admit.

The stationing of a large body below would give jealousy to the Spaniards & lead to the measure of augmenting their regular force by drawing reinforcements from some other quarter.

Stationed above no jealousy will be excited. For attack or defence the regular force can descend with the addition of the force of the Country. Concerted and combined operations may insure efficacy.

In this situation, the force will look to various points; to the Northern Indians to the disaffected of the neighbouring country &c &c. Enough is said. Your reflections will supply the rest.

I send this letter without a copy that I may not lose a post as time & the season urge. Favour me as soon as possible with your observations and directions for which I wait.

With the greatest respect & affection I have the honor to be Sir Yr Obed ser   A Hamilton

P.S. Presque Isle is a very unhealthy situation & incapable of much defence. The neighbouring Country is growing fast powerful so as to take care of itself.

General Washington

To James McHenry

New York Sepr. 10th. 1799

Sir

I have been lately honored with several letters from you down to the ninth inst. inclusively to all which due attention will be paid.

I am on the point of setting out to accompany Mrs. Hamilton a

part of her way on a visit to her father; with the expectation of
being back in five days. My return shall be immediately communicated. The model of a Coat and vest for the Dragoons will be sent
addressed to you for your decision. If approved you will cause it
to be sent to the Contractor.[1] The Specimens only aim at colour
and fashion. The quality you will prescribe. There is also the model
of a Helmet for the Officers.

I have the honor to be, Sir yr. obt

Secy of War

Df, in the handwriting of Thomas Y. How, Hamilton Papers, Library of Congress.
1. In his letter to H of September 9, 1799, which is listed in the appendix to
this volume, McHenry enclosed "a Copy of the orders that have been given for
forwarding the Clothing to the posts on the lakes and on the Mississippi."

From Josiah Ogden Hoffman [1]

[Albany, September 11, 1799]

D Sir

I mentioned to you some time since, a request by the G.—— for
my opinion, on the subject of appointment of Auctioneers under the
Laws of Congress in this State. On my return to this City, I sent him
my sentiments, a Copy of which, I now inclose you.[2] He yesterday
returned them to me—and at the same time observed, that I had
no[t] fairly met the question—that Auctioneers perhaps were to be
considered merely, as *municipal Officers*—(his own phrasing) not in
any way to be appointed by Congress—that in Counties, where we
had not appointed, they had—and if we could agree in judgment, he
was determined to lay the business before the Legislature, that an
Act might be passed, making it penal for any one to sell at Auction,
without being first appointed by this State. I only replied, I meant
to be explicit, for my Mind was very decided on this question. He
wished me however to reconsider my opinion—adding, he had no
doubt, of the power of the U.S. to appoint Collectors of Excise
Taxes &c but, repeating the Idea, Auctioneers were our municipal
Officers, and meaning, as I judged, the duty could be collected from

them, without any of the Checks contained in the Act of Congress. I foresee a difference in opinion between the G. & myself and it is not improbable, my opinion may be submitted to the Legislature. The subject therefore perhaps ought to be gone into, more thoroughly, than my Information will enable me to do—indeed, I barely know how to express myself in stronger Terms, than I have already done. Will you have the goodness to devote some Consideration to the business, and to favour me with your ideas, in the shape of an Argument, or otherwise, as you shall find convenient. It is of importance, that no delay take place in my receiving your Communications. I would wish to meet fairly the question, although I must confess myself wholly at a Loss for the Necessity of making any question about it.

I can only offer my *federal* Motives, as the best Apology for giving you this trouble; and the same Motive I flatter myself will ensure your aid & assistance.

I need not remind you, that this Letter is perfectly confidential— it might perhaps do me an injury to have it known, that its Contents were imparted *even* to you. Had you not therefore for fear of accident better destroy it, after perusal.

Pray let me hear from you by the first Mail, as I may be called upon for an Answer to his last Request, and permit me to assure of the great Esteem and Attachment of, D Sir

Your respectful hl ser   Jos: Ogden Hoffman
                                               Albany. Sepr 11. 1799

ALS, Hamilton Papers, Library of Congress.

1. Hoffman, a Federalist lawyer who served as attorney general of the State of New York from 1798 to 1801, had represented New York City in the state legislature from 1791 to 1795 and again from 1796 to 1797. For his speculations in land and his arrest for debt, see Stephen Van Rensselaer to H, November 6, 1797.

2. On August 15, 1799, Hoffman wrote to John Jay: ". . . the question submitted to my consideration in your Letter of the 2d July last 'Whether the Constitution and Constitutional Laws of the United States, Authorize their Government to appoint or license Auctioneers in this State' have been considered, and in my Judgment, the Constitution of the United States Authorizes Congress to pass Laws for the Appointment and regulation of Auctioneers in this State *so far only*, as may be necessary to secure the regular payment of such duties, as may be imposed by their Government, on Sales of property at Auction.

"By the 8th. Section of the 1st. Article of the Constitution of the United States, it is declared That 'Congress shall have Power to lay and collect Taxes,

Duties, Imposts and excises.' This power is general, and certainly includes the right of laying a Tax or duty on property sold at Auction. If so, it results, that Congress are competent to prescribe the means, calculated to ensure the punctual payment of such Tax. A contrary principle might render the Constitution in this respect, a Nullity. If Auctioneers were *exclusively* subject to the State Governments, it might be in *their* power by a non-Appointment, wholly to defeat the Laws of the Union, or by regulations concerning the Appointment and Conduct of Auctioneers, the payment of the Tax might be liable to evasion. The Government of the United States and the State Government possess a concurrent Jurisdiction, in this Article of Taxation, as they do in ma[n]y other Instances and each Government may prescribe its own regulations, for the Collection of whatever Tax may be thus imposed, and their Agents in this respect although the same persons, will be equally amenable, as well to the Laws of the Union, as of the several States, and liable to Punishment for a violation of such Laws in the Courts of the United States, or in the State Courts as the case may require.

"In the Act of Congress for laying duties on property sold at Auction passed 9th. June 1794, great Attention is manifested to obviate any Inconvenience to the State Governments on this subject. The 2nd. Section Enacts, That no person shall exercise the Trade or business of an Auctioneer, unless such person shall have a license or special Authority, continuing in force, pursuant to some law of a State, or issued pursuant to the directions of said Act. The 3rd. Section declares that it shall be the duty of Auctioneers holding a License under any State, to give notice thereof to the Office of Inspection and to give a bond in the Penalty of $1500 to the United States, that he will truly Account for and pay the duties imposed by the said Act in the manner therein directed. If any sale is made without such bond he forfeits $400. No license or permit in such case is granted.

"By the 4th. Section the Supervisors are authorised to grant Licenses from year to year, but no such License is to be granted to carry on the said Trade or business, in any City, Town or County of any State in respect to which provision hath been made by any Law of such State, for the allowing and regulating of the said Trade and business therein.

". . . Upon the whole I am of opinion that the Law of Congress is a Constitutional Law. . . ." (Copy, Hamilton Papers, Library of Congress.)

For "An Act laying duties on property sold at Auction," see 1 *Stat.* 397–400.

From John J. U. Rivardi

Niagara [New York] September 12 [–16] 1799. Encloses "a New Ark paper containing an anonymous paragraph against me—also my letter on the Subject to the Magistrates of New Ark together with their answer." [1] Has employed Dr. James Muirhead to attend the sick at the fort during Dr. John G. Coffin's absence and at Coffin's expense. [2]

ALS, Hamilton Papers, Library of Congress.
1. On September 7, 1799, Rivardi wrote to William Dickson: "An Anonymous paragraph in the New Ark paper of yesterday (which this morning only

fell into my hands) forces me To apply To you as To a Magistrate, not only To State the facts alluded To in Said Paragraph, But also to request your advice with regard To The conduct which I ought to follow against the writer of false reports, as well as against the printer who gives them currency. On Saturday last at half after Ten, The Night being very dark, a boat was discovered close To The garrison Wharf & hailed; I heard myself the Sentry call out distinctly three times with a Speaking Trumpet, after which he fired *twice* before The Boat came To. That Same Night, about one hour before This circumstance Took place a Soldier of this Garrison deserted & Took with him a boat from the Same Wharf. I lamented the fright of the Ladies, but they did not *Sleep on the beach* nor were they detained till ten the Next Morning. The owner of the boat being informed by myself that he could proceed To New Ark either the Same Night or early in the Morning. I acquainted him with the Standing orders of the Fort which direct that no boat Shall Set off from this Shore after Tatoo before it is examined & reported. . . . I waited on The Ladies in The Morning at the house where They put up, apologized for the fear they had undergone . . ." (copy, in Rivardi's handwriting, Hamilton Papers, Library of Congress).

On September 8, 1798, Dickson wrote to Rivardi: ". . . Allow me To Say I am flattered by The Condescension in your application To my advice. Your dispising The Printer & Publisher, and consigning both To Their own reflections would be The line of conduct I Should pursue in which opinion I am Sanctioned by the Most intelligent Part of this Com[m]unity" (copy, in Rivardi's handwriting, Hamilton Papers, Library of Congress).

2. While Coffin was on leave, no substitute had been found for him at Fort Niagara (Rivardi to H, July 25, August 8, 1799). Muirhead was a physician who lived on the British side of the Niagara River opposite Fort Niagara.

From James McHenry

War Department, Trenton, September 13, 1799. "I herewith transmit you a Copy of a letter from the Secretary of the Navy of this date [1] requesting that the Marine Guard at Norris Town [2] may be relieved by a competent number of Infantry of the Army. You will be pleased to take such order thereon as to you may appear proper." [3]

LS, Hamilton Papers, Library of Congress; LS, letterpress copy, James McHenry Papers, Library of Congress.

1. Benjamin Stoddert to McHenry, September 13, 1799 (copy, Hamilton Papers, Library of Congress), enclosing Major William Ward Burrows to Stoddert, September 11, 1799 (copy, Hamilton Papers, Library of Congress).

Burrows was appointed major of Marines on July 16, 1798 (*Executive Journal*, I, 286, 290).

2. Because of the yellow fever epidemic in Philadelphia, John Fries and the other prisoners who had been taken during Fries's Rebellion had been moved in early September from a prison in Philadelphia to one in Norristown. Stoddert had written to Burrows on September 6, 1799, ordering Burrows "to furnish a Marine Officer, and a sufficient Guard" to conduct the prisoners to

Norristown (*Naval Documents, Quasi-War, August, 1799–December, 1799,* 165). On September 11, 1799, William Nichols, United States marshal for the District of Pennsylvania, wrote to Richard Peters, who as United States judge for the District of Pennsylvania had interrogated Fries shortly after his capture and had presided over Fries's trial: ". . . a military guard from the temper of the people & the situation of the jail is absolutely necessary. . . . unless a guard is kept here the prisoners cannot be kept secure . . ." (copy, enclosed in Peters to Timothy Pickering, September 12, 1799 [ALS, Massachusetts Historical Society, Boston]). Peters on September 12, 1799, wrote to Burrows: ". . . At the instance of the Marshall I . . . request you to station the Guard there. . . . I think there ought to be a prudent Officer to command the Guard, who would do his duty with Firmness, without getting into any disputes with the People of the Country; many of whom in that Quarter would be glad to pro- voke a Quarrel not only from a Jacobinical seditious disposition—but perhaps for a worse purpose, if worse there can be . . ." (copy, enclosed in Peters to Pickering, September 12, 1799 [ALS, Massachusetts Historical Society, Bos- ton]). On September 12, 1799, Burrows wrote to Peters: "The Detachment sent off can stay till relieved by other Troops. I will immediately send 8 or 9 Men more, which are all I can spare. The Men I sent were all picked; and the officer I can depend on. I lament I have it not in my power to send a full Comple- ment of Men. The Reinforcement I mean to send, shall be at Norris-Town this Eveng. . . . I think it will be adviseable, that you write to the Secretary of State to procure a Guard of Infantry to relieve the Marines, for I do not think they are sufficiently strong" (copy, enclosed in Peters to Pickering, Sep- tember 12, 1799 [ALS, Massachusetts Historical Society, Boston]).

3. On the envelope H wrote: "Guard at *Norris Town* Col. Moore to furnish it." H wrote to Thomas Lloyd Moore on September 16, 1799, to "take mea- sures that an adequate number of the Soldiers under your command be sta- tioned there to complete the guard wanted . . ." (letter listed in the appendix to this volume).

To Nathan Rice

New York Sepr. 13. 1799

Sir

I enclose to you the copy of a letter from Captain Draper [1] of your regiment. I am of opinion, from the circumstances which are stated, that it will be proper to discharge the person to whom the letter relates. You will therefore discharge him accordingly.

Df, in the handwriting of Thomas Y. How, Hamilton Papers, Library of Con- gress.

1. Simeon Draper to H, August 16, 1799 (listed in the appendix to this vol- ume). Draper wrote: "At the special request of William Richardson 2d. of Brookfield . . . and his friends the following statement of facts are made and humbly submitted. On the 18th of June last, said Richardson, having been pre- viously arrested by, & escaped from a Sheriff, on mesne process, came to me and inlisted in the service of the United States. The same day the sheriff re- took him and committed him to Goal. On application of Richardsons Friends

for his discharge, I told them if a good man was produced to inlist in his stead I would endeavour that he should be discharged in consequence. The friends of Richardson did produce a good soldier in his stead who inlisted & recd. his bounty, and now does duty. . . . But several Hours previous to his inlistment I had made my Weekly return . . . and the name of Richardson was on the return. I then told his Friends I would write & use my influence that he should be discharged. . . ."

From Philip Schuyler

Albany Friday Sept. 13th 1799

My Dear Son

I had the pleasure at Seven this morning to embrace my Dear Grand Children who with the Maids arrived in good health.

A young woman was taken Ill on board supposed occasioned by being frightened, at seeing a coffin which passed the Sloop in a boat, the captain had the precaution immediately to put her on shore, a few Miles below this, and she is come to town, and has *not* the yellow fever.

Such Accounts as we can rely on, give us the distressing intelligence that the contagion is spread over every part of the City of N York.[1] Angelica[2] informs me that you did not intend to remain in New York. I hope so, and most earnestly intreat you, on no Account to enter that City, pray give me assurances that you will comply with my request, and If possible to come here.

Margret[3] is much better, Altho Still very weak. Mr Rensselaer returned Last evening from Niagara.

Adieu My Dear Sir,   Your ever most affectionate   Ph Schuyler

I suppose Eliza will be here on Sunday or Monday next.

ALS, Hamilton Papers, Library of Congress.
   1. Yellow fever broke out in New York City at the end of July, 1799. On September 9 the Common Council "Ordered that the Street Commissioners be appointed to aid the Health Commissioner during the prevailing Sickness to administer Relief to the indigent Sick and to open one of the Wards at Belle Vue Hospital for the Reception of the Sick until the further Order of the Board" (*Minutes of the Common Council*, II, 570). See also *The* [New York] *Spectator*, July 24, August 1, 1799.
   2. This is a reference to H's daughter Angelica, who was born on September 25, 1784.
   3. Elizabeth Hamilton's sister, Margarita (Mrs. Stephen Van Rensselaer).

To James McHenry

New York, September 14, 1799. ". . . Information from different Regiments [1] gives me to understand that my recommendations as to an advance of pay [2] have not succeeded. As the troops are much discontented at the delay, it is my duty to renew the subject. And I must take the liberty to urge that by your interposition forms may be dispensed with so at least as to effectuate an advance of two months pay upon account. The peculiarity of the situation of troops in the act of being raised is a good reason for departing from ordinary forms."

Df, in the handwriting of H and Thomas Y. How, Hamilton Papers, Library of Congress.

1. Thomas Parker to H, August 15, 1799; H to Parker, August 16, 22, 1799; William C. Bentley to H, August 18, 1799; Rufus Graves to H, August 18, 1799 (all listed in the appendix to this volume).

2. See H to McHenry, June 17, 1799, note 1. H repeated this request in his third letter to McHenry, August 28, 1799, which is listed in the appendix to this volume.

To Nathan Rice

New York Sepr. 14. 1799

Sir

Your letter of the Sixth of this month has been delivered to me. I have no objection to the discharge of Sewal Moore if he will procure a good and substantial person in his place. With regard to the pay to which he supposes himself to be entitled I would observe that it can not be advanced to him because altho' he has served three months yet that service must be considered as merely a preparation for future and more important service. This last, in consequence of the discharge, will never be rendered to the US. You will take care that the business be so conducted as to involve no loss to the public.

With great consn   I am, Sir

Col. Rice

Df, in the handwriting of Thomas Y. How, Hamilton Papers, Library of Congress.

To Caleb Swan

N. York Sept. 14th. 1799

Sir

I perceive by your letter of the 9th inst. that a difficulty has occurred in the paymt. of the troops, in respect to the provision which requires the warrant of the command. Genl.

It is my opinion that it is upon the whole expedient that the chief of each Branch of the departt. of Supply and Pay should be stationed at the Seat of Governmt., and that he should have a Deputy with each Army or Separate military District to perform the requisite duties there. This Dep. ought always to be attached to the head Quarters—which will obviate the Difficulty in question. When temporarily he is separated by peculiar Situations and any advance of money is indispensable, it may be understood between the commandg. General and him that the money is to be furnish'd in the expectation of an after Sanction.

In every general plan accommodations of this Kind are occasionally necessary and it is by them that the main end of salutary general regulations can be effected, with due regard to extraordinary cases which do not admit of a rigid and literal conformity.

In this spirit I am ready retrospectively to give my Sanction by warrant to the past payments you mention, and to such future ones as exigencies may require, till you shall have appointed a Deputy to reside near me.

But I advise you to do this without loss of time; and also to appoint another Deputy to act with the Army under General Pinckney. You perhaps possess or may easily obtain information of a fit character among the Regiments raised in the States within my district. If General Pinckney were not so far Distant it might be adviseable for you to request him to make the Selection in the Southern Quarter. But circumstanced as he is, it will perhaps be expedt. for you instead of this, to ask the assistance of Colonel Carrington,[1] in whose Judgement, knowledge of Characters, and caution you may safely place entire confidence. You will receive these suggestions as to the mode of making your choice, not as directions (for it does not belong to me to give them) but as Advice dictated by a desire to promote the service in a manner consistent with the Satisfactory discharge of your functions.

It is however proper for me to observe to you, on this point that while the law vests you the right of selecting your Deputy it is a rule of military etiquette not to appoint definitively till you have reported to the Commandg. General & understood from him whether he has any valid objection to the measure. On My part I engage beforehand a concurrence in your choice. As to the person whom you may select for the Southern District he may act in the mean time, in expectation of the Sanction of General Pinckney which will, no doubt, be given.

It is very essential that obstacles of form shall be without delay surmounted or waived. New troops must not be disgusted by delays in giving them their dues. Much discontent on the Article of pay already exists in the new regiments and it is the cause or pretext of Desertion. I am extremely anxious that the arrear of bounty money and two months pay be sent to each of these regiments. Nor should the want of Muster or Pay rolls be an impediment in the progress of raising troops, it is Difficult to comply with forms which are calculated for established Corps: temporary deviations are right and indispensable.

If your own views of the subject render your presence near me requisite to the course of the payments called for previous to the appointment of Deputies—I request you, after obtaining permission of the Secy. of War, to come to this Island. You need not be absolutely in the City.

With great consideration &c

Caleb Swan Esr
P. Mr. General

Copy, in the handwriting of Ethan Brown, Hamilton Papers, Library of Congress.
    1. Edward Carrington was supervisor of the revenue for Virginia.

From George Washington [1]

Mount Vernon, September 15th: 1799.

Dear Sir,

Mrs. Washington's indisposition (being confined eight or ten days) and other circumstances, would not allow me to give your letter of the 9th instant, and the Reports, Journals &c. &c. which accompanied it, an earlier consideration.

Having done this, however, with as much thought as I have been able to bestow, under the circumstances mentioned, I can see no cause (with the limited force which has been enumerated, and which, I presume, is all that can be calculated upon) to differ from you in the disposition of it. Although, at the same time, I shall make some observations thereupon for consideration.

It may be remembered, that, at the time the Secretary of War laid before the General Officers in Philadelphia, the letters of General Wilkinson respecting the propriety (in his Judgment) of placing a considerable force at the Natches, I gave it my decided disapprobation.[2] Inasmuch as it would excite, in the Spaniards, distrust and jealousy of our pacific disposition, would cause an augmentation of force on their part; and so on with both, if our Government would go into the measure, until the *thing* which was *intended* to be *avoided* would, more than probable, be produced—i.e.—hostility. Whereas, keeping that force in the upper Country, besides its looking to *all* points, and exciting no alarm in *any*, might, if occasion should require it, either for defence or Offence, descend the stream like lightening, with all its munitions and equipments; which could be accumulated with ease, and without noise, at the upper Posts, and make the surprise more complete.

Although I have said (in effect) that the Corps de reserve, or

LS, Hamilton Papers, Library of Congress; Df, in the handwriting of Tobias Lear and Washington, George Washington Papers, Library of Congress.

1. For background to this letter, see James Wilkinson to H, September 6, 1799; H to Washington, September 9, 1799.

2. Washington is referring to the conference of the general officers which was held in Philadelphia in mid-December, 1798. See H's drafts of the three letters which Washington sent to James McHenry on December 13, 1798.

Army of Observation, should take post at the place you have mentioned—namely—in the vicinity of the Rapids of the Ohio (Louis-
ville);—yet I can see but two reasons which entitle it to be prefered
to the *present Post* above, i.e. Fort Washington, in a geographical
point of view:—And these are—that there is no water above the
former, that can float large Vessels at all seasons,—And that, by
being so much lower down, the passage of the Ohio would be facilitated if an Expedition should descend the Mississippi. In other respects the latter, in my Opinion, has the advantage. 1st. Because it is
a Post *already* established, and would incur no additional expense.
2dly. Because it is *more* contiguous to Fort Wayne, Detroit, Michilimacanac, and all the Indians on the Lakes, from whom, in that
quarter, we have most danger to apprehend. 3dly. Because communications with it (and for the most part by water) are already established. And 4thly. In case of Insurrections above or below, it is
equally as well, if not better situated.

Were it not that the Mouth of the Wabash empties itself into the
Ohio so low down, and yet above its confluence with Cumberland
and Tennessee, I should be inclined to give a position thereabouts
the preference of either the Rapids or Fort Washington; because
it would command a greater water Inlet towards the Lakes.

But, whether the position for the Corps de reserve be chosen at
the Rapids of the Ohio—above—or below—it had better, I conceive,
be on the North side of the Ohio than within the State of Kentucky
—Thereby impeding more the intercourse between the Army and
the Citizens, and guarding against the evils which result from that
mixture, and too much familiarity.

I am so far from agreeing with General Wilkinson that Fort
Wayne ought to be abolished, that, if I mistake not the place
(central between the heads of the Miamis of Lake Erie and the
Ohio;—the St. Joseph and the Wabash;) affording good water
transportation, with small portages, in every direction, I would
pronounce it (were it not for the expence of subsisting Troops
there) the most eligible position for the Army of observation of
any in that Country. It would be an effectual security against all the
Indians who could annoy us in that Region; it would cover our
Barrier Posts, on the line between the British and us; and Troops
from thence might descend rapidly into the Mississippi by the
Wabash.

General Wilkinson, in speaking of Posts along our Southern Frontier, is general; and you only notice Fort Stoddart. But, on an inspection of the Maps, a place presents itself, to my view, as very eligible to occupy; provided the Creek Indians would consent to it. I mean the Apalachicoli—at its confluence with Flint River,[3] where the line of demarkation strikes it.

But, in my opinion, if we had, or could obtain an Engineer of *real* skill, and attached to the true policy and interest of the United States, he ought to devote his whole time to the investigation of our interior Country; and mark and erect its proper defences; for these, hitherto, have been more the work of chance and local consideration, than national design.

If the harbour of Presque Isle is good, I should think a small Garrison ought to be retained there. It certainly is the *best* on the American side of Lake Erie; and one there is important; but I see very little use of a Sergeant and 8 privates at Fort Knox. It is either unnecessary, or too small; and Sergeants at a distance rarely conduct well, when they have not the eye of an Officer to inspect their conduct.

There are several references in General Wilkinson's Report[4] which were not sent. No. 1 appears to have been essential. They are all returned.

By his statement of the mutilated condition of the Troops, and present disposition of them, there must have been most horrible mismanagement somewhere. A corrective is, indeed, highly necessary. The practise of furloughing Officers, and then renewing the furloughs from time to time, is extremely injurious to the Service, and ought to be discontinued on ordinary occasions.

And that of frittering the Army into small Garrisons, is, if possible, worse. It will never be respectable where these evils exist; and until it can be more concentrated, and Garrisons frequently releived by detachments from the main body, discipline will always be lax, and impositions on the public will prevail.

If the British are resolved to keep up armed Vessels on the lakes, I presume it will be expedient for us to do the same; but in time of peace a better way, in my opinion, is, for neither to have any. In

3. The Apalachicola River is formed by the junction of the Flint and Chattahoochie rivers.
4. See Wilkinson to H, September 6, 1799.

case of a rupture, or the appearance of one, with that nation, there can be no doubt of our arming on those waters much more expeditiously than they would be able to do.

I have now gone over the material points in your letter and General Wilkinson's Report; but, as I mentioned before, it has been done under circumstances unfavorable to minute investigation or mature deliberation, and my sentiments, where differing from you, given more for consideration than decision. Should anything of importance on this subject, not noticed here, occur to me, I shall not fail to communicate it to you; for the measures now taken with respect to guarding our Frontiers and interior Country ought to be such as will be permanent and respectable.

With very great regard, I am, Dear Sir, Your most Obedt. Servant   Go: Washington

Major General Alexander Hamilton

From William C. Bentley

Richmond [Virginia] September 16, 1799. "I have this day forwarded to the proper officer A return of my Regiment up to the 1st day of this month—the number returnd is only 133. I lament that our success has not been greater, but you may be assured that no blame ought to be ascrib'd to the Recruiting officers, they have been incessant in their labors. It is not easily to conceive the Democratic rage that we have had to encounter. But appearances are now more flattering; the approaching Season will facilitate the business. . . ."

LS, Hamilton Papers, Library of Congress.

From James McHenry

War Department
Trenton 16 September 1799

Sir

In answer to the last paragraph of your letter of the 13~ instant,[1] just received—I observe—That I have already informed you,[2] Law and express instructions from the Treasury Department, to the Pay Master General, have opposed obstacles to making advances of pay to the troops. After a mature deliberation on the subject, by the Comptroller,[3] he appears indisposed to alter the instructions to the Pay Master General, and strongly bears, against the expediency of advances.

It is certain, that advances involve many inconveniencies; they promote irregularity in accounts, favour indolence in officers, by dispencing with forms, that ought to precede receipts, and may, in cases of premature deaths occasion losses to the public. Persuaded of these truths, I have no hesitation to avow, that I am desirous of avoiding responsibility on the score of advances myself, and to compel Officers to produce their returns and rolls in due form and in proper time, to the appropriate offices.

Would I be justified, in acting contrary to a course specifically prescribed by a law, and deemed indispensible by the Treasury Department, unless indeed circumstances exist, of such a nature, and urgency, as to render a strict compliance, manifestly prejudicial to the Public interests?

It will ever be proper, that the Commanding General of the Army, should represent, the circumstances of urgency, which impose a necessity for a departure from established forms, to the Secretary of war—military operations in all countries, do frequently impose such necessities, but contemplating the existing law of the United States, will it not be proper to endeavour in all possible cases in this Country, to make the usage of armies, bend as much as possible to the law—and considering the intimate connection, the lat-[t]er has created, between the General and the Pay Master of an army, will it not always be most congenial with the existing law, while it continues in force, that the General direct his order or warrant to the Pay Master General, when advances are required—that he make his requisition of the secretary, who previously informed of circumstances imposing the necessity of a call, and approving thereof, can give every facility to the attainment of the object.

Permit me to intimate that Colonel Ogden [4] was lately with me, and proposed an advance, under a full impression, that the present circumstances of his regiment required established forms should be dispenced with. I thought otherwise and succeeded in convincing him, that no difficulty attended a due compliance with the law.

Nothing more seems to me to be required, than 1st, That the Inspector General shall name persons to muster the troops monthly at every regimental rendezvous Sub rendezvous or in whatever situation they may be. 2d. That where there is no muster master the officer commanding each troop or company or parts thereof, with one other officer provided there is one, shall sign the usual certificate. This regulation which dispences with a muster master is agreeable to instructions from the Comptroller to the Pay master General.[5]

This course being pursued the pay of the troops may immediately assume its legal channel. I pray you therefore to give it your early attention, that we may be respectively relieved from embarrassment and responsibility, and preserve an attitude superior to insinuation.

I shall direct the Pay master General to report to me the advance required as far as he has any information on the subject, and will for this time sanction it.

I inclose the instructions to the Pay Master General by the Comptroller, for your more particular information.

I have the honor to be, with great respect, Sir,   Your Most Obedient and Huml. Servant   James McHenry

Major General Alexander Hamilton

LS, Hamilton Papers, Library of Congress; LS, letterpress copy, James McHenry Papers, Library of Congress.
   1. McHenry is mistaken, for he is referring to H's letter of September 14, 1799.
   2. McHenry to H, June 21, 1799.
   3. John Steele. See Caleb Swan to H, September 9, 1799, note 3.

4. Lieutenant Colonel Aaron Ogden, commandant of the Eleventh Regiment of Infantry.

5. See Swan to H, September 9, 1799.

The instructions from Oliver Wolcott, Jr., to Swan, dated July 26, 1792, read in part: "In case an Inspector shall be present, the muster rolls are to be certified by him according to the form presecribed, but in case no Inspector shall be present, the muster rolls are to be certified by the two senior Officers of the Company or Corps, in case so many shall be present" (Df, partly in Wolcott's handwriting, Connecticut Historical Society, Hartford; copy, Hamilton Papers, Library of Congress).

To James McHenry

New York Sepr. 16 1799

Sir

In recurring to your letter of the 29th of August, I observe there are some points which for a clearer understanding require from me some observations.

I shall make this preliminary remark, that in presenting with emphasis, as I am accustomed to do, deficiencies which appear to have existed—I am actuated by the sole and exclusive motive of shewing by particular instances that the past plan has been productive of imperfect results and that more comprehensive and adequate measures are necessary for the future. Our provisions have been made too much on the spur of the occasion, have been too generally confined to the absolutely necessary for the moment; rejecting the idea of a surplus for future casualties and exigencies. This defect in our plan is not imputable to any one individual; it may be traced partly to the immaturity of our institutions and affairs and partly to errors of opinion which embrace persons in various situations.

I am sensible that important steps both legislative and administrative have been taken towards a more provident and efficacious system; but a frequent contemplation of the imperfections of the past plan ought to have the effect of increasing the tendency towards improvement.

I must at the same time be permitted to add that in my opinion the want of a proper organisation of agents in the various branches

ADf, Hamilton Papers, Library of Congress.

of the public service and of a correct and systematic delineation of their relative duties have been a material cause of the imperfect results which have been experienced—that it continues to embarrass every operation and that while it lasts—it can not fail to enfeeble and disorder every part of the service.

To exemplify this present defect of organisation—it is sufficient to refer to the situation of the Quarter Master Generals Department, of the Medical establishment and of that of the Pay-Office. The Pay Master General [1] with propriety is stationed at the seat of Government; but he has no deputy either at my head Quarters or at that of General Pinckney.[2]

I am sensible that where the appointment of the Chiefs requires the consent of the Senate, it must now be deferred to the future meeting of that body, and that the subordinate persons whom the law places in the choice of those Chiefs cannot be constituted without them—but temporary arrangements may still be made as a substitute; and I confess my anxiety that this may be done, either immediately by you or by your direction to General Pinckney and myself each to regulate the matter within the sphere of his command.

Permit me earnestly to request that this business of organisation in all its branches may engage a prompt and decisive attention. Till this shall have been the case no Commanding Officer can perform well his peculiar duties; as his time and attention must be engrossed in details which are foreign to his station. And the consequence must be inefficiency and disorder.

I proceed to some particulars of your letter.

"You observe that you consider it as the Duty of the Commanding General not only to make returns of *all articles*, among these Cloathing wanted for his troops, but to make them in such season as to allow of making up and transporting them to their destinations."

If this idea shall be adhered to I shall be very ready to perform my part; but I should wish a more precise definition of the objects. What are the articles to be embraced? There are some objects, as Artillery Muskets &c. of which it is always to be presumed there

1. Caleb Swan.
2. See H to Swan, September 14, 1799.

are sufficient quantities constantly ready in the public Arsenals and Magazines. What time or times will be deemed proper for the transmission of the returns? Are the destinations in detail to be pointed out or not?

But I beg leave to recommend the point to a serious reconsideration; and I take the liberty to offer some reflections in relation to it, which seem to me to deserve attention.

The total force which is to compose the Military establishment is regulated by law.[3] That force as presented by law is itself the standard of all ordinary supplies *to be provided,* which ought always rather to exceed than fall short of the Complement. The Secretary of War consequently possesses *ipso facto* the rule which is to govern as to providing all the fixed and stated supplies.

If this force is to be divided into different armies still the aggregate of supply must be the same. Besides, that distribution will be arranged by the Secretary of War in Concert with the Commander in Chief. If left to the discretion of the latter he only is competent to furnish the Criterion.

It follows that the principal articles of supply, all those which are not dependent on the particular nature of military movements, will always depend on the establishment and will not be to be regulated by returns from particular Generals.

The temporary strength of corps, at one time increased by the accession of recruits at another diminished by the casualties of service ought never to be a guide in *providing;* because such a standard is fluctuating and uncertain, and because the supply ought to be commensurate with the full complement of the establishment.

The Commanding General who should have to present an estimate to the head of the War Department (and whose agency as to the ordinary and stated supplies is rendered unnecessary by the circumstance of there being other data previously in the possession of the Department) would be bound to govern himself in his estimate by the scale of the establishment and not by the temporary state of things.

Requisitions *from time to time* for the *issuing* of supplies may fall under a different consideration. These would have reference to the actual state of the forces; but these do not answer to the import of

3. For the laws fixing the permissible strength of the Army, see the introductory note to H to James Gunn, December 22, 1798.

the terms you employ, which appear to aim at some annual or other periodical estimate to govern the *providing* as well as the *issuing* of the articles.

Premising these things as objections to the idea you have suggested in its full latitude, it remains to examine what is the proper course.

The head of the War Department must no doubt be aided by Agents who are conversant in the various branches of supply and competent Judges of what may be wanted.

These Agents ought to be certain officers or Boards established at the seat of Government more permanently fixed in their stations than the precarious commander of a particular army; such as the Purveyor of Supplies, a Board or Master of Ordnance or instead of these the Inspector of Artillery, the Superintendant of Military Stores; which officers ought to be aided by information from the Chiefs of the *branches of supply connected with the army*, as in our present system the Quarter Master General &c &c.

These latter officers being under the direction of the Military commanders would be obliged to communicate with them to receive their instructions and to inform them of what is done or intended so that they may be apprised of the competency of the provision made or to be made and may be able to direct calls or to represent to the Head of the War Department such further provisions as they may judge expedient.

As to the supplies to be from time to time issued, requisitions ought to come from *the chiefs of the several branches of supply* acting with the armies *to those officers who at the seat of Government are charged with providing and furnishing the respective articles.*

As on the one hand the complement of the establishment will be the guide in providing so on the other the returns of actual force to the Secretary of War from the Commander of each army will in the first instance be a collateral guide to the issues and a check upon extravagant demands and the accounts afterwards to be rendered will shew the application.

The forming of the permanent Arsenals and Magazines of a Country which ought to be always prepared to furnish the principal articles of supply is naturally a work of administration predicated upon an entire view of the political and military relations and

the forces & resources of the Country. When these are thus formed
—how few are the objects which the estimate of a particular General can apply? How are the partial & detached estimates of several
particular Generals to reach the full extent of the supplies aggregately necessary? How is each to make his estimate of what may be
requisite unless each has under his eye the entire state of all the
national arsenals and magazines and enters into a minute examination
of all the issues which may have been made? If he is [to] do all this
upon his own responsibility—what time will he have for his purely
military duties? Is it proper in theory that each General having a
separate command should possess a complete view of the State of
all the public Arsenals & Magazines?

I conclude that from the nature of the thing the *business* of procuring and of *issuing* supplies ought in a general view to be unconnected with the particular Commander of a particular army;
that it is properly a business of administration in which the head of
the War Department is to be aided by the subordinate organs of his
department stationed at the seat of Government and by the heads of
the several branches of Supply who act with the armies.

The Agency of the Commander in Chief and the Commanders of
particular armies where requisite ought to be collateral and auxiliary
not direct and primary.

It is true that there is a class of supplies which being governed by
the actual operations contemplated such as transportation forage &c
must be regulated by estimates and returns to come from the armies.
But even in these cases the responsible persons to make the estimates
and returns ought to be the chief or Chiefs of the Departments of
Supply with the armies; who ought previously to submit their estimates and returns to the military commanders in order that they
may be transmitted with their opinion and observations. Thus far
it is conceived the Agency of the commanding General may be
useful and proper. But the scheme of it as now indicated supposes
as a preliminary the appointment of the proper heads of the several
branches of supply.

Indeed this preliminary is essential to every form of agency in
this respect which may be assigned to a commanding General. It is
not presumable in principle and would never be found true in fact
that the General of an Army is so minutely acquainted with all the

details of supply as to be qualified to present a correct view of all the objects which may be requisite without the intervention of those officers whose peculiar province it is to manage the business of supply.

As to the subject of Pay, it would seem from your manner of expression to be your idea, that the Warrants of a Commanding General must be founded on certificates of the *Pay Master General*. But I must conclude, that this cannot be your meaning; as a very natural and fair construction of the laws will for this service substitute to him his deputy with each army; and as it is essential, in practise, that the interpretation shall admit of this substitution. How else are the troops remote from the Pay Master General to be paid at all? Consider especially the position of the Western army.

When the law of the 8 of May 1792 [4] which charges the duty on the Pay Master General was passed, there was but one army—hence that act designates him singly.

But the act of the 3 of March last,[5] contemplating that there may be several different armies, provides that there shall be a Deputy Pay Master General to each of them—without particularly defining his duties. It is evident that he must be intended to perform duties and important ones. What are they? The law being silent, they are of course all such as the Pay Master General is to perform where he may be; except as to any particular one, which from the nature of the thing ought to be confined to the chief. On any other principle, the Deputy will be as much excluded from one duty as from another which was before performed by his chief, and the appointment will become nugatory.

4. This is a reference to Section 3 of "An Act making alterations in the Treasury and War Departments" (1 *Stat.* 280). See McHenry to H, August 29, 1799.

5. This is a reference to Section 15 of "An Act for the better organizing of the Troops of the United States; and for other purposes" (1 *Stat.* 753). This section reads in part: "That the paymaster-general of the armies of the United States, shall always quarter at or near the headquarters of the main army, or at such place as the commander in chief shall deem proper; and that to the army on the western frontiers and to detachments from the main army intended to act separately for a time, he shall appoint deputy paymasters, who shall account to him for the money advanced to them, and shall each give a bond in the sum of fifteen thousand dollars, with sufficient sureties for the faithful discharge of their duties respectively, and take an oath faithfully to execute the duties of their offices, and the several regimental paymasters shall also give bond in the sum of five thousand dollars with one or more sufficient sureties, and take an oath as aforesaid. . . ."

I infer, that all monies for the purpose of paying the pay subsistence and forage of the troops must still be delivered in the first instance by the Treasurer to the Pay Master General because this is conducive to union and to a regular chain of accountability: But that the Pay Master is to deliver over to each Deputy in mass a sum sufficient to answer all these purposes with the army to which he is attached and the Deputy is to disburse it in detail, and to execute all the services preparatory to that disbursement which by the first law were charged upon the Pay Master General including that of certifying the sums due to the Commanding General.

Principles of law no less than those of convenience warrant this construction, beyond the possibility of doubt after mature reflection.

Accordingly, in consequence of a representation of difficulty, on the point of Warrants, by the Pay Master General, I have advised him as the legal and proper remedy to appoint without delay one Deputy to the troops under the command of G Pinckney another to those under my command.[6] I confidently trust that you will approve and if necessary enforce this advice. The ground of it is unquestionably solid.

The course which you indicate in the last paragraph but one of your letter appears to me perfectly correct and convenient.

With great respect   I have the honor to be sir   Yr. Obed se

The Secy of War

6. H to Swan, September 14, 1799.

From Thomas Parker

Winchester [*Virginia*] *September 16, 1799.* ". . . I Really think that a Supply of money for the Troops is absolutely Essential. Many of the Soldiers are Becomeing Verry uneasy & Restless having been informed by the enemies to Government that they are to Receive no pay, and the Report Rediculous as It may appear gains Credit; especially as the officers have no money to advance them to Remove their Uneasiness & Reason without money has But little effect on such Characters. . . . Be pleased to Inform me how we are to be

Supplied with Ammunition we have not a Supply at present even for the use of the Guards. We are not furnished with Bayonet Belts Scabbards or oil Rags & the Cartridge Boxes are Verry Clumsy & Indifferent. we have Received no further Supply of Coats or Vests Both which are much wanted. If the Information woud not be Improper I Should be pleased to be informed where It is probable we Shall be ordered to winter. . . ."

ALS, Hamilton Papers, Library of Congress.

To Nathan Rice

N. York Sept. 16th. 1799

Sir

The season advances so fast that I am extremely anxious to have the result of your enquiry after winter Quarters. After you shall have made the examination heretofore directed,[1] and reported to me, I request that you will direct your enquiry for the same object towards the upper parts of Connecticut River, from Springfield westward. It has been suggested that eligible positions may be obtained in that Quarter, with great advantages in the view of Œconomy. But let no time be lost.

With great consideration   Sir

Col N. Rice

Df, in the handwriting of Ethan Brown, Hamilton Papers, Library of Congress.
1. H to Rice, first letter of August 22, 1799.

From Lewis Tousard

Portsmouth [New Hampshire] September 16, 1799. States that "In general the Fortifications of the New England States are in the most Shabby condition," that they have been incorrectly constructed by unqualified personnel, and that the mounted guns are altogether inadequate. Also states: "I may tell you, dear Sir, that as long as an Inspector of Artillery is not appointed [1] and charged alone with that department—a great deal of money will be Spent to no advantage to the United States and rather to the disadvantage of the Service in the moment of danger. . . . The President I think is much divested of his antient prejudices against me. I think a new application for that inspectorship as Soon as the Senate is assembled would prove effectual. . . ."[2]

ALS, Hamilton Papers, Library of Congress.
  1. Section 9 of "An Act to augment the Army of the United States, and for other purposes" (1 *Stat.* 705 [July 16, 1798]) provided for the appointment of "an inspector of the artillery, taken from the line of artillerists and engineers. . . ."
  2. Tousard had applied for this position in Tousard to H, August 7, 1798; H proposed the appointment in H to John Adams, August 22, 1798; and Adams rejected the proposal in Adams to H, September 4, 1798 (all listed in the appendix to Volume XXII).

To James McHenry

New York Sepr. 17. 1799

Sir

Part of the contents of your letter of the 10 of July last (which has happened to escape a definitive attention) being connected with the subject of that the 7 of Sepr., I shall reply to them together.

Previous to the receipt of the last I had drafted rules relating to extra expences which after careful revision I send for your determination. They contemplate, it will be seen, a discretion to make exceptions in special cases. The rule in such matters, cannot be entirely absolute, without involving too much embarrasst. As the establishment of a general rule will attach a particular responsibility to each deviation from it, it will in the main prevent unnecessary deviations.

The Regulations do not include the restrictions which may be thought fit to be laid on the commanding Generals. These it is supposed had better be the subject of particular communications by letter to those officers.

The two other points mentioned in your letter of the 10th. of July shall now be attended to.

ADf, Hamilton Papers, Library of Congress.

First as to compensations or Allowances to servants not Soldiers.

It appears to me a clear point that the resolution of Congress of March 1780 [1] is not in force and consequently cannot be an authority for such allowances. There being no other it is not seen how any general practice of the sort could be now supported.

With regard to the expediency of the practice, in principle, I have strong doubts. I fear that it might lead to the abuse of compensations for nominal servants while soldiers would still be the real ones. Pretexts of sickness &c. in the hurry of a campaign might disguise the abuse. I question too whether in times of peace it would be adviseable to augment the public expences by the addition of persons of this description.

I incline most to the plan of the Great Frederick; which was to let the Officers in time of peace be served by the ordinary soldiers, in time of war by supernumeraries specially inlisted for the purpose and discriminated by a distinct uniform or livery, forbidding the soldiers of the ranks on any pretence to [be] employed in this capacity. This practice procured all the advantages without the dangers of the other plan.

The number of servants which it is conceived proper to allow to the respective grades of Officers are

To the Commander in Chief or General having a separate Command three without arms to attend him on horseback.

To the Inspector General, Quarter Master General, each Major General not having a separate command and to the Adjutant General two of the like description.

To the Brigadier General, Pay Master General or Deputy Quarter Master General Deputy Inspector General one of the above description and one with arms.

To each field officer and every other officer who ordinarily serves on horse back one of the firstmentioned description.

To every officer who usually serves on foot one with arms.

The servants required to have arms in all general exercises marches and movements are to be found in the ranks. When annexed to officers detached from corps they must join the guards connected with such Officers or their baggage. In the cases in which they

1. JCC, XVI, 250.

would be otherwise without arms, if they are attached to Officers of Dragoons they will retain their arms.

The drawing of provisions for Children appears to me inadmissible and as far as I know unusual.[2] They are, without this, incumbrance enough, when in Camp or Quartered especially in the course of a Campaign.

I remark incidentally that it is to be wished that a corps of Invalids and an Establishment for the maintenance and Education of the Children of persons in the army and navy were provided for by law. Policy Justice and humanity forbid the abandoning to want and misery men who have spent their best years in the military service of a country or who in that service have contracted infirmities which disqualify them to earn their bread in other modes. Employment might be found for such a corps which would indemnify the Public for the mere maintenance of its members in *cloathing lodging* and *food*. The UStates are perhaps the only country in which an Institution of this nature is not to be found; a circumstance which if continued will be discreditable. The Establishment as to Children is recommended by similar motives with the additional consideration that they may be rendered by it useful members of Society and acquisitions to the army & Navy as Musicians &c.

I shall wait for your opinion as to the abolition of issues to Children.

You will observe what articles are supposed by me to be proper to be furnished by the Contractors. Those are the only ones which I recollect as of ordinary and stated supply that will not naturally come from the Superintendant of Military Stores. Contingent or extra articles had better be under the management of the Agents. As to the scale of allowance in each case this has either been regulated by your Department or has already been the subject of some former communication from me—except in the instance of forage. I forbear to offer any scale for this article because I take it for granted that one is already established on the basis of long Experience. If you are desirous of a Revision of it by me I shall be ready to obey your orders for the purpose.

One point occurs in connection with the general subject of this letter. It appears to be the practice of the accounting Offices to re-

2. See H to Zebulon M. Pike, May 3, 1799; McHenry to H, July 10, 1799.

ject items in the accounts of Contractors, which have been furnished upon the orders of particular military commanders even in cases in which no rule has been prescribed to the contractors. This in my opinion is neither just nor regular. The disbursement if vouched by such an order ought to be admitted to the Credit of the Contractor & charged to the Officer till a satisfactory explanation shall satisfy the Department that it ought to be a public charge. In most cases when not strictly proper in the abstract it will be expedient that the expence shall be defrayed by the Public, and a repetition prevented by more precise instructions, or where these have not been deficient, by the reprehension or punishment of the Officer. One bad consequence of embarrassing the adjustment of the Contractors accounts may be, that they will refuse in cases of the least doubt to comply with orders which are dictated by necessary and emergent services. Besides that on principle *two discretions* in *undefined* cases are an absurdity; and if but one it is properly with the commanding officer upon his responsibility; and the contractor who ought not to exercise a discretion ought in no event to suffer.

With great respect   I have the honor to be   Sir   Yr Obe

The Secy of War

[ENCLOSURE]

Regulations respecting certain supplies and respecting objects of special and extra Expence [3]

The several contractors besides rations including ardent spirits and vinegar shall only provide & furnish *Quarters transportation forage, fuel straw stationary*, and where there shall be no other provision for the purpose, medical assistance. The Quarters intended are those of a temporary kind. The power to provide them shall not extend to the building or repairing of barracks. In what they furnish they shall govern themselves exclusively by the regulations which shall have been established by law or by the war Department, and where none exist, by the orders of the particular Commanding Officer.

No barrack or other building shall be erected but by the order of

3. ADf, Hamilton Papers, Library of Congress.

the Quarter Master General the Deputy Qr Mr G in a separate Command, the Commander of an army or the Commander within a separate military district or department, or of the Secretary of War. No repairs shall be made to any barrack or building which shall incur a disbursement of money exceeding fifty Dollars but by the like order. Where there are several distinct forts or posts in a subdivision of a great military district united under the command of an intermediate superior, the particular commandant of either of those posts shall not cause any such repairs to be made though occasioning no greater expence than fifty Dollars without a previous report to such superior and his approbation. No extra expence for any special object or purpose shall be incurred by such particular commandant without a previous report to the said superior; who when such expence may exceed fifty Dollars shall not authorise it without first obtaining the sanction of his superior. The Commandant of a particular fort or post having no intermediate superior shall incur no expence for repairs nor any extra expence for any special object or purpose, which may require a disbursement exceeding fifty Dollars without the permission of the Commander of the army or district or of the Secy of War.

As often as any matter which may require any special or extra expence can wait without material injury to the service for a communication to and the direction of the Commander of an Army or District, it is not to be undertaken till after such communication and direction shall have been had.

These regulations admit of exceptions in cases of extraordinary emergency and of peculiar urgency, when the service would be likely to suffer material injury from the delay which might attend the observance of them. Every such exception will be on the special responsibility of the Officer by whom it may be made, who must *immediately* report to his superior the occasion and the expence *probable* or *actual*.

The Commander of an army or within a great district may by instruction in writing to be forthwith communicated to the Secy of War make exceptions in such cases where the remoteness of a fort or post shall render the application of these regulations manifestly inconvenient; entrusting a large discretion to the Commandant of such fort or Post.

The Quarter Master General, his Deputies and Assistants are primarily charged with the making of the disbursements in the cases abovementioned. Where there is no such officer, the Agent of the War Department in the vicinity shall do it. All orders for such disbursements must be definite & in writing to be transmitted with the accounts of them to the Accountant of the War Depart.

From James McHenry

War Department Trenton 18~ Septr. 1799

Sir

I received this morning your letter of the 16~ instant inclosing extracts from Lieutt. Coll. Smiths letter to you of 7~ instant.[1]

I cannot doubt the correctness of the Colonels representation relative to the state of the muskets. It is probable the old stock, long since provided, from which the delivery to his regiment may have been made is generally as he has represented. The muskets which have been fabricated under my administration, will be found, I expect, less exceptionable and next year, or when the soldiers shall have become acquainted with the use of their arms and acquired habits of attention to the care of them, it may be proper to put our best into their hands. Such of these they are now in possession of, which the Inspectors shall report unfit for service or *to train with*, will be exchanged.

The sacks I must presume conform to pattern and have been passed by sworn inspectors. They may however be illy calculated for hard service.

The appointments to the Regiments which are defective in their complement of regular mates will be made next session of Congress. No inconvenience I apprehend can possibly result to the service from this delay, the temporary surgeons mates supplying their places.

Having determined to appoint two Cadets to each of the new Regiments you will be pleased to require a recommendation from the Lieutenant Colonels of two young gentlemen whom they would respectively prefer. Cadets should be informed they are to expect promotion, from merit only, and by no means on the principle of succession. This ought to be clearly understood.

Inclosed is a copy of a letter from John Bray, dated Brunswick the 17~ instant.[2] Mr. Bray will be informed, that the business his letter relates to, is exclusively with you.

I have the honor to be, with great Respect, Sir, Your most Obedient and Huml. Servt.   James McHenry

Major General Alexander Hamilton

LS, Hamilton Papers, Library of Congress; LS, letterpress copy, James Mc-Henry Papers, Library of Congress.
  1. H's letter to McHenry of September 16, 1799, is listed in the appendix to this volume.
  2. In this letter, Bray, the Army contractor at New Brunswick, New Jersey, discussed proposed sites in New Jersey for winter quarters for the Eleventh, Twelfth, and Thirteenth Regiments of Infantry (copy, Morristown National Historical Park, Morristown, New Jersey).

From William North

Albany Sept 18th. 1799

Dr Sir,

Having heard that you were at Ball Town Springs [1] & to return to Albany on Monday last, I came here to pay my respects to you & ask your directions with regard to my entré upon the duties of my Office.[2] When here, the Family informed me that you were on your way from New York—On tuesday, that you, with Mrs Hamilton & Mrs Church [3] were at Claverac.[4] The arrival of Mrs Church last evening, left me no hope of seeing you here at present. It is my intention of being at, or in the vicinity of New York on the first of October, should you still think it proper,—if however, owing to the sickness [5] or any other cause, you should think fit to lengthen my leave of absence, or alter my destination, I shall receive your commands with pleasure, not only because they are your commands, but because they will coincide with my own & the wishes of my friends.

With the greatest respect I have the honor to be Sir Your Ob Servt   W North

ALS, Hamilton Papers, Library of Congress.
    1. Ballston Spa, Saratoga County, New York.
    2. On July 16, 1799, in a letter which is listed in the appendix to this volume, North had asked H for leave of absence until October 1, 1799.
    3. Angelica Church was Elizabeth Hamilton's sister and the wife of John B. Church.
    4. Claverack, Columbia County, New York.
    5. This is a reference to the yellow fever epidemic in New York City. See Philip Schuyler to H, September 13, 1799.

From William C. Bentley

Richmond [*Virginia*] *September 19, 1799.* ". . . Our recruiting instructions forbids recruiting Mulatto's.[1] As Batmen are allowed to officers, may not recruits of that description be taken for that purpose alone? They are better Calculated than the White natives of this Country for menial Service. Will an Officer who shall take a Servant with him, be intitled to draw rations for him? If this indulgence should be granted, It will only be accepted by the Field Officers. By an Act of Congress intitled 'An Act to amend and repeal, in part, the Act intitled, "An Act to ascertain and fix the Military establishment of the United States"'[2] Says the 4th Sec., That to each Officer commanding a Seperate post, there shall be allowed twice the number of rations to which they would otherwise be intitled. I shall be glad to be informed whether this allowance extends to any Officer commanding a recruiting Station, and how far it does extend. . . ."

ALS, Hamilton Papers, Library of Congress.
    1. Article III of the March, 1799, edition of the War Department pamphlet *Rules and Regulations Respecting the Recruiting Service* reads: "Natives, of good character, are always to be preferred for soldiers. Foreigners of good reputation for sobriety and honesty, may be enlisted; but Negroes, Mulatoes, or Indians are not to be enlisted." H's "General Orders," June 6, 1799, amended the section respecting foreigners and specifically banned the enlistment of apprentices.
    2. 1 *Stat.* 507–08 (March 3, 1797).

Circular to the Commandants of Regiments

Private & confidential   New York Sepr 19. [–20] 1799

Sir

I request the favour of your opinion as to such of the Majors captains & Lieutenants of your Regiment as may be best qualified for service in the department of the Inspectorship or of the Quarter Master. This is an inquiry for information which will be extended to the several Regiments. It is hoped that the opinion will be given with freedom & frankness as it may be relied upon that it will be received in perfect confidence. It will be understood that it is altogether eventual and uncertain whether any appointment of either sort will be made from the Regiment.

With great consideration & estm   I am Sir   Yr Obed ser

ADf, Hamilton Papers, Library of Congress; LS, to Aaron Ogden and dated September 19, 1799, Lloyd W. Smith Collection, Morristown National Historical Park, Morristown, New Jersey.

Circular to the Commandants of Regiments

Circular.   New York Sepr. 19th. 99

Sir

The Secretary of War has Determined to appoint immediately two Cadets to each regiment, and he has directed me [1] to request from the several Commandants a special recommendation of two young gentlemen for the purpose.

You have nominated different persons, from time to time, as cadets severally: [2] but [it is now wished that you should make a selection of two whom you prefer.] [3]

The Secretary of War observes in his letters that the Cadets are to expect promotion from merit only, and not on the principle of

succession. You will be pleased to [take care that this be well understood by the parties.]

With great consn   I am Sir

The Several Coms.

Df, in the handwriting of H and Thomas Y. How, Hamilton Papers, Library
of Congress.
  1. James McHenry to H, September 18, 1799.
  2. For recommendations by commanders of appointments to the rank of
cadet, see Aaron Ogden to H, August 5, 1799; William S. Smith to H, August 11,
1799; William C. Bentley to H, August 17, 1799; Richard Hunewell to H, August 22, 1799; Thomas Parker to H, August 24, 1799. All these letters, except
the one from Parker, are listed in the appendix to this volume.
  3. The words within brackets in this letter are in the handwriting of H.

From John F. Hamtramck

Pittsburgh September 19, 1799. Acknowledges Hamilton's letters
of June 5, July 2, 22, 31, 1799.[1] States that at Detroit the officers
and men need practice in maneuvers, that the non-commissioned officers do not command the respect of the men, and that the problems with the police have been corrected. Adds that all the garrisons
need copies of "the Baron[2] and the Articles of War."[3] Complains
of the drunkenness of the Indians at Detroit. Supports the passage
of a law for the Northwest Territory similar to the Canadian act of
March 29, 1777,[4] prohibiting the sale of liquor to the Indians without written permission from the Governor General of the province,
the Superintendent of Indian Affairs, or the commanding officer of
a post. Encloses a copy of a letter from the chief of the Kaskaskias,
which has been forwarded to Governor Arthur St. Clair.[5] States that
Detroit should not be reinforced, for Colonel David Strong's information concerning Indian hostility[6] was unfounded and was originated by land speculators.

LS, Hamilton Papers, Library of Congress.
  1. H's letters of July 2, 31, 1799, are listed in the appendix to this volume.
For his letter of July 22, see "Circular to the Commandants of Regiments,"
July 22, 1799.
  2. For the manual written by Baron von Steuben, see H to James McHenry,
May 21, 1799, note 1.

3. *Rules and Articles for the better Government of the Troops Raised, or to be raised and kept in pay by and at the expense of the United States of America* (Philadelphia: Printed by Steiner and Kammerer, 1794). See H to Jonathan Dayton, August 6, 1798, note 11.

4. "An Ordinance To prevent the selling of strong liquors to the Indians in the province of Quebec, as also to deter persons from buying their arms or cloathing, and for other purposes relative to the trade and intercourse with the said Indians" (Lower Canada. *Ordinances made and passed by the Governor and Legislative Council of the Province of Quebec*, 17 Geo. III, C. 7).

5. See Daniel Strong to H, July 12, 1799 (listed in the appendix to this volume). In this letter Strong stated: "Governor St. Clair has not yet arrived but I have much solicitude to see him, that some definite arrangement be concerted for the government of the Indians."

6. See Strong to H, May 7, September 7, 1799; H to Strong, June 21, 1799.

To James McHenry

New York Sep. 19th 1799

Sir

I have communicated to Col Bentley your resolution as expressed in your letter of the 30th of Augt in respect to the late appointments for his Regiment.[1]

But the occasion claims from me some remarks, as due to my own opinion of propriety and the good of the service.

I cannot doubt that the practice of your Department, as to the filling of vacancies in new corps, previous to your coming into it, was such as you state; but in the latitude in which it is stated, I cannot easily be persuaded, that it is such a practice as ought to be continued, or that it is not of a nature to sow the seeds of permanent discontent in the infancy of every corps.

I can nevertheless agree in the position of the Commander in Chief, that when, in the case of a newly created Corps, an officer *declines his appointment, during the act of formation,* the vacancy is not *necessarily* to be filled by the next in seniority.

But this is a rule rather to be narrowed than extended in its application; because it clashes with expectations that will inevitably grow up in the minds of Officers and in which their pride and self-love will always take a very active part. It is, in my opinion, to carry it to an impolitic extreme, to say, that it shall operate, until the *"Regiment Legion or Corps has been recruited or nearly so and has marched to Head Quarters":* And to apply it to a single case of *promotion* is to mistake its principle; as from the subsequent expressions of the Commander in Chief may be inferred to be his idea. The rule is naturally confined to the case of an officer, in the original creation, who *declines* his appointment; in other words who refuses to accept. The moment a station has been filled by acceptance though but for a day the right of promotion attaches to it, and if becoming afterwards vacant it is filled by a new person, this is a violation of the principles of service and of the just expectations of subordinate Officers.

It is not a correct answer to this to say that a Corps "is open to new appointments" or as I understand the phrase, that the right of promotion does not commence till after the relative rank of the officers who have been appointed has been settled.

The want of a settlement of relative rank among them only leaves it doubtful what individual of their number shall succeed; but it does not involve any doubt whether aggregately they do not exclude a stranger. There is a still a clear right of *some one* of them to succeed, to be effectuated as soon as the relative rank is established, and new persons ought to come in junior to them all.

The appointment therefore of a new person in the place of one designated to an office in the Regimental Staff to take precedence of others before appointed is irregular, and not warranted by the rule, if taken within just limits or within the definition of the Commander in Chief.

Even the practice of introducing new men to vacancies occasionned by the non acceptance of officers in the original appointment ought not in my judgment to be continued till the Corps should have been *recruited or nearly so and marched to head quarters,* as you state to have been the case. This may be so long protracted as to postpone inconveniently the routine of promotion and produce dissatisfaction. A reasonable period should be fixed within which acceptances may with due diligence be ascertained—suppose three months from the first appointment of Officers. To keep the thing open for a year or more, which is likely to be the case in the present instance if completion of the regiments should be the criterion, could not fail to beget discontent—even in men of moderate and subordinate tempers.

The recommendation of persons as officers by the Commandants of Regiments ought I think, where the contrary is not expressed, to be understood to mean that they shall come in as junior second Lieutenants.

If I recollect rightly, in one or two instances of an early date, they have expressed the contrary, and relying upon their judgment of the probable effect on their Regiments, I have countenanced the recommendation. But I am clearly of opinion that this ought not to be the case in future; and that considering the length of time, which has elapsed since the organisation of the Regiments, it is indispensable that the routine of promotion shall henceforth prevail; with the exception perhaps of the fifth Regiment in consideration of the recency of the appointments for it.[2]

Military prejudices are not only inseparable from but they are essential to the Military Profession. The Government which desires to have a satisfied and useful army must consult them. They cannot be moulded at its pleasure. It is vain to aim at it.

I must entreat, Sir, that the observations which I have offered in this letter may be attentively weighed. They are urged upon mature reflection; and are believed to be material to your satisfaction and that of the officers principal in command, to the satisfaction of all the officers, present and future, to whom they are applicable & to the harmonious course of our Military Affairs.

With great respect & esteem   I have the honor to be

ADf, Hamilton Papers, Library of Congress.
    1. H to William C. Bentley, September 18, 1799 (listed in the appendix to this volume).
    2. Of the thirty-six officers in the Fifth Regiment of Infantry, twenty-nine had been appointed in April, May, and July, 1799 (Godfrey, "Provisional Army," 137–40).

From Caleb Swan

Trenton September 19th. 1799.

Sir.

I have been honored with your letter of the 14th instant.

I have been so long absent in the western country that I am entirely unacquainted with the officers of the new Regiments, and therefore shall be obliged if you will please point out one whom you may consider as a suitable character to act as deputy paymaster to your district, and reside at your head quarters.

Although the law vests me with the right of selecting the deputies,[1] yet from the high respect I owe to your superior knowledge and judgment, and my desire to appoint such an one as may be satisfactory to you, I shall not for a moment hesitate in appointing the officer you may please to nominate for that duty.

I am sensible the business of paying the troops has been in a languid State for want of some more efficacious mode of conducting it, and am extremely anxious, that every obstacle may be removed as soon as possible.

The secretary of war informs me that general Pinckney is now at Rhode Island [2] to which place I shall address him on the subject as recommended in your letter, and therefore suppose it will be unnecessary at present to write to Colonel Carrington. But it appears to me that a deputy to reside in Virginia will be found necessary and useful, that being also a distant and extensive circle and should it appear to you in the same light, I can then avail myself of Colonel Carringtons information and advice.

The deputy appointed for the northwestern frontier [3] cannot extend his payments below Massac on account of the great distance & uncertain communication hence I have constantly been of opinion that a deputy for the Mississippi district to reside at Natchez is indispensible, and have waited some time expecting to see general Wilkinson, and obtain his advice particularly on that head.

Perhaps it may not be improper for me to observe that at present there is no Regimental paymaster, to either the first or second Regiment of artillerists and Engineers. The payments have hitherto been made in detail by the accountant to officers, commanding companies and detachments. It is respectfully submitted to your consideration that if paymasters were appointed to those Regiments, it would facilitate payment by lessening the details, and enable me to procure the bonds required by law and fix the accountability on the proper officer.

The enclosed extract of a letter I wrote from Cincinnati to the secretary of war,[4] will Shew that I have been aware of the propriety of consulting the commanding General as to the selection of deputies, as well from motives of respect, as from a desire to avail myself of advice in a transaction of Such importance.

I have the honor to be with the greatest respect   Sir your very obedient Humble Servant   C. Swan P m. genl

Honble Major General Hamilton

ALS, Hamilton Papers, Library of Congress.
    1. This is a reference to Section 15 of "An Act for the better organizing of the Troops of the United States; and for other purposes" (1 *Stat.* 749–55 [March 3, 1799]). See H to James McHenry, September 16, 1799, note 5.
    2. An item in the *Newport Mercury*, September 17, 1799, reads: "In the Brig Hermes, Capt. Earle, which arrived on Friday [September 13], came Passengers Major-General Charles C. Pinckney and Family. We are informed, that the State of Mrs. Pinckney's Health has brought the General to the Northward at this late Season of the Year. . . ." The Pinckneys had left Charleston, South Carolina on September 1, 1799 (Pinckney to H, October 5, 1799).
    3. Swan had appointed Captain Samuel C. Vance of the Third Infantry Regiment deputy paymaster for the Western Army on July 25, 1799. Swan had informed H of this appointment in his letter of June 14, 1799 (listed in the appendix to this volume).
    4. Swan to McHenry, April 15, 1799 (extract, Hamilton Papers, Library of Congress).

From James McHenry [1]

War Department, Trenton,
September 20th: 1799.

Sir,

Upon the repeated representation of Judge peters to the Secretary of State for a Guard of Regular Soldiers to be stationed over certain State prisoners confined in Norristown Goal, and his request for an immediate order to Major Adlum for the purpose, I directed a letter to that Officer of which the enclosed is a copy.[2] I return your letter to Colonel Moore [3] received yesterday, that it may undergo a modification should you think it proper to relieve the Guard which may have been ordered by Major Adlum from the Troops at Reading.

With great respect,   I have the honor to be,   Sir, your obedt: servant,   James McHenry

Major General Alexander Hamilton

LS, Hamilton Papers, Library of Congress; LS, letterpress copy, James Mc-Henry Papers, Library of Congress.
1. For background to this letter, see McHenry to H, September 13, 1799.
2. On September 14, 1799, Timothy Pickering wrote to Judge Richard Peters that John Adlum would send the troops requested (ALS, letterpress copy, Massachusetts Historical Society, Boston). On September 15, 1799, McHenry directed Adlum to provide a guard for the Norristown prison (copy, Hamilton Papers, Library of Congress).
3. H to Thomas Lloyd Moore, September 16, 1799 (listed in the appendix to this volume). For the contents of this letter, see McHenry to H, September 13, 1799, note 3.

From James McHenry

War Department Trenton 20 Septr. 1799

Sir

The ill state of Mrs. Pinckney's health, has been such as to induce a permission to be granted to the general, to accompany her to New Port Rhode Island, where I expect he now is or soon will be.[1]

It is not impossible that the alarming indisposition of Mrs. Pinckney may have engaged for a considerable time past much of the generals solicitude and attention, and his removal with her to Rhode Island has also abstracted him from the business of his command. Lest these circumstances, may occasion a postponement to too late a period, of such measures as are requisite to insure the best winter-quarters for the three Regiments, destined to be cantonned at or near Harpers Ferry,[2] I must request you to take such steps as you may think necessary, to ascertain the fittest ground for their quarters; and to gain such information, relative to the price or rent of land and wood in that quarter, and other circumstances essential to a good choice.

I have the honor to be, with great Respect, Sir,   Your Obedient Humble Servant   James McHenry

Major General Alexander Hamilton

LS, Hamilton Papers, Library of Congress; LS, letterpress copy, James Mc-Henry Papers, Library of Congress.
1. See Caleb Swan to H, September 19, 1799, note 2.
2. See H's draft of George Washington to McHenry, first letter of December 13, 1798; McHenry to H, February 4, 1799.

From James McHenry

War Department
Trention 20~ September 1799

Sir

I have received your letter of the 16~ instant containing very important, and detailed observations, on a system of military supplies, for the armies of the United States.

Altho' I fully agree with you, that the old and existing system, is defective in particulars, too weakly manned in some of its branches, and susceptible of amelioration [1]—I must recollect, that it is yet the existing system, and that every thing now done, to facilitate our army supplies must have reference to its parts, and intents, and indulge a hope, it will enable us to go on, (as we must) under it, for some time longer.

I lost no time, in laying the system proposed by you, before the President for his sanction.[2] He has returned it, with a request, that it should be submitted to the Heads of Departments, as (he expresses it) involving a great expence, and suggested a doubt, whether it can be adopted without Legislative aid. The System has accordingly

LS, Hamilton Papers, Library of Congress; copy (incomplete), RG 45, Naval Records Collection, Entry 464 (Subject File), XA File, "Records of Naval Stores Kept by the Army," National Archives.

1. See McHenry to H, March 21, 1799.
2. McHenry is referring to H's "Plan for the providing and issuing of Military Supplies," which H had enclosed in H to McHenry, April 8, 1799. H had also written to Oliver Wolcott, Jr., on the same day asking him to discuss the plan with McHenry. McHenry wrote to H on April 11, 1799, and acknowledged receipt of H's plan, and on April 17 he wrote to H that he was going to ask Wolcott to consider the plan. In a letter to H on May 9, 1799, McHenry stated that Wolcott had returned the plan on April 26. McHenry is less than truthful when he states: "I lost no time, in laying the system . . . before the President for his sanction." Not until he had received H's letter of June 24, 1799, which prodded him to do something about the supply system, did McHenry write to John Adams. On June 29, 1799, McHenry sent a copy of the plan to Adams and told him that Wolcott had approved it (ALS, Adams Family Papers, deposited in the Massachusetts Historical Society, Boston). In his letter to Adams McHenry wrote: ". . . The plan appears to me a good one. It comprises such of the regulations as were found useful and necessary during the revolutionary war, with some additions to our present system."

448 SEPTEMBER 1799

with them.[3]

In our present situation then, it is still necessary, that the existing
system for supplies, be our rule, and this, until an improved one,
which certain difficulties now oppose, can be established.

What this system is; the course to be pursued under it; where it
imposes duty; and attaches responsibility; I shall endeavour to exemplify, under distinct heads.

1st, CLOATHING. It was recently the duty of the Secretary of the
Treasury, and is at present that of the Secretary of War, to provide
annually, by Contract, or otherwise, the full complement of cloathing for all the men required by the military establishment.[4] This, as

3. On July 7, 1799, Adams wrote: ". . . I have read the plan for providing &
issuing of military supplies inclosed in your favor of the 29 of June. I suppose
I may keep it in order to recur to it upon occasion. I wish to be informed
whether this is proposed to be adopted by Congress into a law? I presume the
presidents authority alone is not adequate to the establishment of it. I wish it
to be considered by the Secretary of the Treasury, and by yourself as closely
as possible, before it is recommended. The discipline of the army & the national oeconomy are deeply interested in it. The Secretary of State has had
experience which ought to be consulted upon the occasion" (LC, Adams Family Papers, deposited in the Massachusetts Historical Society, Boston). On
July 12, 1799, McHenry replied: "According to the lights, in which I have
received the plan for supplying the Army, it does not appear to me to require
the sanction of any act of Congress. It is only a system, to execute powers
actually given, or incidental to given powers. If it is otherwise, this department, and the Navy department ever since their existence have been offending
against law. I shall however consider the question, and as closely as possible
the plan, and submit it formally to the Secretary of the treasury and secretary
of State for their mature opinions" (ALS, Adams Family Papers, deposited in
the Massachusetts Historical Society, Boston). On July 19, Adams wrote to
McHenry: ". . . It appears to me, that officers were created & salaries made
necessary in the plan for supplying the army, which would require the interposition of Congress. But if the powers already given to administration are
sufficient, I am satisfied. I wish only that the heads of department may be satisfied & that no embarrassments may be brought upon them which they are not
previously apprized of" (LC, Adams Family Papers, deposited in the Massachusetts Historical Society, Boston). McHenry, in the meantime, had delayed
consulting Secretary of State Timothy Pickering until July 21, 1799 (ALS,
Massachusetts Historical Society, Boston).
4. Section 1 of "An Act to establish the Office of Purveyor of Public Supplies" (1 Stat. 419 [February 23, 1795]) reads in part: "That there shall be in
the department of the treasury, an officer to be denominated, 'Purveyor of Public Supplies,' whose duty it shall be, under the direction and supervision of the
Secretary of the Treasury, to conduct the procuring and providing of all arms,
military and naval stores, provisions, clothing, Indian goods, and generally all
articles of supply requisite for the service of the United States. . . ."
Section 3 of "An Act to alter and amend the several acts for the establishment and regulation of the Treasury, War and Navy Departments" (1 Stat. 610

the army can never exceed the establishment, and from casualties will always be below it, implies a surpluss, but there is also, an additional quantity always ordered, to meet contingencies.

This cloathing when provided is deposited in the Public Stores. It is drawn out of stores and its transportation, and distribution is effected, in the following manner. The General Commanding in chief, or the General commanding a seperate army, or the General or other officer commanding a district, or detachment only, acting separate from the army, causes returns, to be made to him, by the proper officers, exhibiting all the cloathing required by, and due to, the troops under his command, taking care, whenever his command is divided into posts, and comprises different regiments, or different species of troops, that the returns shall exhibit with precision, the quantities required, for each particular regiment, corps, or post. These returns are to be transmitted to the Secretary of War, by the commanding General or officer. The Secretary is then to transmit them, to the Superintendant of military stores, whose duty it becomes, to see, that the cloathing is carefully made up, or packed up and labelled or directed, conformably to the returns and directions of the General or officer making the same. The Superintendant next, charges on his books, the officers respectively, to whom each parcell is directed, considering them as the persons who are to receive, and distribute the articles directed in their names. The Superintendant afterwards, is to deliver the whole of the Packages to the Quarter Master General, or his Deputy, as the case may be, who immediately becomes accountable, for their transportation, to the respective places of destination, for which they are labelled and invoiced—and their delivery at such places, to the persons charged to receive and distribute the cloathing. The Quarter Master General discharges his responsibility, by taking and producing to the Superintendant, the receipts of the officers respectively, charged on his books, with

<hr>

[July 16, 1798]) provided: "That all purchases and contracts for supplies or services for the military and naval service of the United States, shall be made by or under the direction of the chief officers of the departments of war and the navy. . . ." Section 4 of the same act stated: "That it shall be the duty of the purveyor of public supplies, to execute all such orders as he may, from time to time, receive from the Secretary of War or Secretary of the Navy, relative to the procuring and providing of all kinds of stores and supplies . . ." (1 *Stat.* 610).

the different parcells, these officers in their turn exonerate themselves from accountability, by receipts from each soldier, for the cloathing he has received, which aggregately shew the final application of every article so delivered.

2d. Ordnance, and arms, Military Stores, and Camp Equipage.

It is the duty of the Secretary of War, to cause ordnance &c and military stores of every description, to be procured, and to an extent commensurate with appropriations made for the purpose. The appropriation is sometimes particular or specific, as a given sum of money, for small arms cannon &c and nothing is left to discretion. It is generally aggregate, as for military stores in the mass. In the latter case, much is left in the discretion, and to the responsibility of the Head of the War Department. He is to determine on the proportions of the various kinds of articles, comprised under the term Military stores—to be procured with a limitted appropriation. Whence shall he draw accurate information, to enable him to form a solid Judgment? In this case he considers it to be, the usage of all armies, to require information from the commanding General, and to be his duty, to give it with much deliberation and under a high sanction.

When the articles now contemplated are provided, and deposited in the Public arsenals or stores, the same course of requisition on the Secretary, must be observed, with like specifications and the articles must go thro a similar rotine, in the subordinate departments, be transported and delivered to the distributing officers or agents, for use or application under the same responsibility, and equal regard to exoneration of trust, as in the cases of cloathing.

3d. Medicines, Surgical Instruments, and Hospital Stores.

The Arrangement contemplated, by "An Act to regulate the Medical Establishment" passed the 2d. March last,[5] not being acted upon—It becomes necessary, to proceed on the existing or old system;[6] with respect to this Department at least for some months. Complaints of inattention to the safe keeping, and due distribution, or wanton waste, of medicines and hospital stores, especially the

5. 1 *Stat.* 721–22.
6. See Sections 3 and 4 of "An Act to alter and amend the several acts for the establishment and regulation of the Treasury, War and Navy Departments" quoted in note 4 above.

latter have of late been indistinctly heard, to mention this, may occasion some means of correction.

In the old system, no provision has ever existed for an Apothecary, to prepare medicines to be sent to the different quarters of the Army, nor for a distinct Purveyor, to purchase medicines, instruments, and Hospital Stores. The course has been for the senior surgeon of an Hospital, or attached to a Garrison, Regiment or permanent Detachment, to make returns to the commanding General or other officer exhibitting the medical articles and stores, necessary for a given time, for the sick of the troops, placed under his individual superintendance and care. These returns are transmitted by the Commanding General or other officer to the Secretary of war, who (sometimes submitting them, to experienced Physicians) considers it to be his duty, to direct the ordinary Purveyor of his Department, who is furnished with the returns, to purchase their contents. When purchased the articles are turned into the Public Store. The requisition is thus made, for medicine, instruments and stores, before the articles are procured, and is the guide for procuring them. The returns should be explicit as to destination—and the articles must go through the same rotine, under the same responsibility, and necessity of exoneration of trust as before mentioned.

4th. Quarter Master Stores, and means of transportation.

All things necessary for the transportation of troops, are to be procured by and from the Quarter Master General (or his Deputies or agents) who take orders for this purpose from the Commanding General or other officer. The same Department is to provide transportation for all military articles of every description and disburse the expence.

Quarter Master Stores are in part of a kind, that must be procured on the spot, and promptly, to answer immediate necessity. These it is the duty of the Quarter Master General or his Deputies to provide. A large proportion of them are however of a nature, to, either require time to prepare in any quantities, or, afford an opportunity to purchase more economically by means of the Purveyor of the War Department.

Requisitions for the latter, are expected to come in season to the Secretary of War, specifying quantities and kinds, either from the

Commanding General or directly from the Quarter Master General, as circumstances may require. When procured by the Purveyor, these articles, are placed in the Public Stores, are charged to the Quarter Masters Department, deliverable for application to use, on other returns, from the Quarter Master General or (when he is too distant to be used as the medium) from the Commanding General, or other superior officer, and pass through the same rotine, under like responsibility, and necessity of exoneration as before.

It is proper to observe, that all articles, when put in packages, are directed by the Store-keeper, in the name of the Commandant of the Post they are destined for, and that he is charged with them; that it is understood, he delivers them over, to the custody of a Quarter Master where there is one, if none, to an officer acting in that capacity to a garrison, or if the post is a small one, to a confidential serjeant also acting in the same capacity—who can issue the articles composing the packages, only on the orders of a commandant or superior officer.

6th. Pay of the Army.

Having already explained my conceptions respecting the manner in which this is to be effected,[7] and the injunctions of Law, and instructions to the Pay-master-general, intended to be conformable to law, from the Department of the Treasury on the subject; I must at present repeat, that it is required, muster and pay rolls in due form shall be made out and presented previous to payments in any case to the troops. That the rolls shall be examined, checked, and the sums due, thereon certified by the Pay Master General (or when he has appointed them) by his Deputies, if the Comptroller shall, (as I do explicitly concur in your opinion) to the Commanding General or other superior officer, who shall thereupon issue his warrant upon the Paymaster for payment accordingly. That it is considered to be the duty of the Secretary of War, to place such sums of money in the hands of the Pay Master general, from time to time, as he shall require, either upon his own estimate, or conformably to requisitions upon him, by the Commanding General, for the aforesaid purposes.

Heretofore the Law had made no provision for Deputy-paymasters, and it would appear that the 2d. Section of "An Act in

7. McHenry to H, August 29, September 16, 1799.

addition to the Act for making further and more effectual provision for the protection of the frontiers of the United States" [8] by providing "that the army be in future paid in such manner, that the arrears shall at no time exceed two months" had imposed a course, I shall immediately mention—but muster and pay rolls, I have never understood to have been dispensed with. They must necessarily have been required, previous to actual payments to the troops, for no credits have ever been allowed at the Treasury without rolls in due form as exhibits or vouchers.

To facilitate payments, and make them conform as much as possible, to the short periods prescribed by the law just cited, at the most remote or detached military points of the western army from communication with the Pay master, necessity obliged a recourse to the appointment of agents, such was Capt. Guion [9] at the Natchez, Colo. Henley [10] at Knoxville and Major Freeman [11] in Georgia, and on the Seaboard to the substitution of the Accountant for Pay master, who certified the pay due in the latter quarter, to the different Garrisons, recruiting parties, or detachments, directly to the Secretary, always on muster and pay rolls in due form, forwarded or presented by the proper officers. The rolls were never dispensed with, and in no instance, that has come to my knowledge, has advances been made to troops, these were sometimes made to officers only, under peculiar circumstances, as when they were ordered to a distant command requiring an equipment, and involving extra expence.

I have not only mentioned to the Pay Master General my approbation of the appointment of distant Deputies, for the commands of General Pinckney and yourself, but urged his taking measures for the appointments without delay.

With respect to Deputy Quarter Masters General for the separate armies—I [re]collect that your opinion accords with mine, that until the Principal is appointed there can be no regular Deputy—and I am sorry to intimate that if my recollection is correct, the Gentleman

---

8. 1 *Stat.* 390 (June 7, 1794).

9. Isaac Guion, a resident of New York and a veteran of the American Revolution, was a captain in the Third Regiment of Infantry.

10. David Henley. See H to Henley, August 27, 1793.

11. Major Constant Freeman of the First Regiment of Artillerists and Engineers.

contemplated for Quarter Master General, made his acceptance of the office depend upon the events of General Washingtons taking the field, and an actual state of War.[12] I shall look into my information on this head, and at all events write to him to know, whether if appointed next session of the Senate, he will accept and enter immediately into service. Should this (which is to be desired) not be the case, necessity may compel to have recourse to agents—and it will be well to consider who may be suited to the appointments.

The existing system of supplies, executed as I have delineated, will bring the wants of the service in a great degree, if not completely, before the Commanding General—consequently will enable him to exercise the superintendance expected from him with much effect; It would seem too, that the general superintendence of all military concerns, peculiarly belongs to him as he can exercise it to most advantage. The observation applies to every Commander of a seperate army or great military District.

I must therefore request you will (until it can be ameliorated or a better substituted) that you will give to the existing system all possible efficacy, within your command. I shall enjoin the same upon General Pinckney—and rely implicitly upon both Generals for compelling the officers whose duty it shall be, to furnish estimates and returns, to make them in proper form and in due season. It must be evident, that if estimates of quantities when necessary, and returns for supplies, are not made in season, I may fail in making my provisions in due proportions, and delay in, or want of, transportation will often be unavoidable.

Permit me more particularly to expect, that you will revise the returns, or if necessary devise new ones, relative to cloathing—in order that they may exhibit, at stated periods, not only the articles actually delivered to the soldiery but the quantities remaining on hand at each post or encampment—and that you will explicitly enjoin it on the proper Officers to take receipts from each soldier, for the articles of cloathing delivered to him.

I have the Honour to be, with great Respect Sir Your Most Obedient & Most Huml. Serv.   James McHenry

Major General Alexander Hamilton

12. This is a reference to Edward Carrington. See H to McHenry, August 19, 1799, note 3.

From Peter Goelet [1]

Major General Hamilton   New York Sepr. 21st. 1799.

Sir

On the 21st. Augt: last I Enclosed You a Statement of the Ballance due on the Lands bought by General Schuyler, of the Trustees of the American Iron Company, with Interest to that day, Wishing to have that buseness in a Train so as to make a final Settlement when Mr Morris comes to Town, as his Stay generally is very short, but have not been favord with Your Answer, And shall be very Happy if You could now make it Convenient to Sittle the Ballance, I am with Respect

Sir Your Very Humble Servant   Peter Goelet

Major General Hamilton

To the Trustees of the American Iron Company D

1799 Aug' 21. To Balle. due this Day	£763.4.10	Doll	1808^{10}/$_{100}$
To Interest on ditto up to 21 Sepr. 1 Month	4.1.1		10^{13}/$_{100}$
	£767.5.11	Dole	1818^{23}/$_{100}$

Copy, Miscellaneous Chancery Papers, American Iron Company, Clerk of the Court of Appeals, Albany, on deposit at Queens College, New York City.

1. For an explanation of the contents of this letter, see the introductory note to Philip Schuyler to H, August 31, 1795. See also H to Phineas Bond, September 1, 1795; H to Robert Morris, September 1, 1795; H to Barent Bleecker, March 20, 1796, April 5, 1797; Goelet to H, June 25, 27, 1796, August 21, 1799; "Receipt from Peter Goelet," October 4, 1796; "Deed from Peter Goelet, Robert Morris, and William Popham," April 4, 1797; Goelet and Morris to H, December 12, 1798; "Receipt to the Trustees of the American Iron Company," May 30, 1799.

To James McHenry

New York Sepr. 21. 1799

Sir

I feel it as a mark of consideration for my recommendation, that notwithstanding the force of the difficulties, which in your view operate against further advances not founded upon the prescribed forms, you are pleased to declare that you will once more give your sanction to the measure.[1]

I must entreat you even to go a step further and to order that it be without fail done. For Symptoms bordering on mutiny for the want of pay have been reported to me as having appeared in the twelveth and thirteenth Regiments.[2] And discontents less turbulent have been communicated from several other quarters. An explosion any where would injure and discredit the service, and wherever the blame might really be would be shared by all.

No one can be more deeply impressed than I am with the necessity of a strict adherence to general rules and to established forms. But there will occur circumstances in which these ought to be dispensed with. And it is equally important, to judge rightly when exceptions ought to be admitted as when the general rule ought to be maintained.

The creation of a new army, in which every officer from the highest to the lowest is of new appointment, & in respect to which in and out of the administration there is a deficiency of some essential organs, presents a case which with the utmost diligence and care will require and justify relaxations.

For instance, the law and the instructions of the Treasury Department require that the Pay of the troops shall be founded upon warrants of the Commanding General regulated, by the reports of the Pay Master General or, as I maintain the construction of the late law [3] to be, of his Deputy with a separate command. How was that practicable when the Pay Master General was at Cincinnati and he had no deputy any where? How can it now be done with reasonable convenience and expedition, when he resides at Philadelphia and he has no deputy attached either to my command or to that of General Pinckney?

Again Muster and Pay Rolls are to be in certain precise forms prescribed by the Treasury. These forms were received by me only four days since, and consequently could not hitherto be in the possession of the commandants of Regiments. It will not be said that I ought to have called for them; because certainly it lies with the department to communicate its own regulations uncalled for. Are the soldiery to suffer a privation of pay for several months, because these forms never prescribed, have not been fulfilled?

It is true that when I was at the head of the Treasury Department these forms passed under my eye; but it is no less true that I had forgotten the circumstance, and that considering it as an attribute of the Inspector General to devise forms, where none were before established by higher authority, I had caused to be prepared forms of Muster and Pay Rolls to answer the present exigency. Surely as the matter is situated, these forms ought provisionally at least to serve as substitutes for the established ones.

Various other particulars might be added to prove that dispensations with the ordinary forms ought to take place in relation to the new Regiments. But the foregoing are sufficient for illustration.

Every effort no doubt ought to be made and on my part will be made as fast as possible to put this and every other matter in its proper and regular train. But time is requisite and the organs which depend on administrative authority must first be instituted.

The Treasury as well as the war department, has too often experienced the necessity of accommodating relaxations in special cases not readily to admit upon reflexion that they are right in the existing position of our new army.

As to the persons, who are to muster the twelve regiments they are by my direction the Commandant of the Regiment and the surgeon or person officiating in that capacity.[4] It seems to me that till inspectors are appointed—nothing would be done which would promise greater security to the public. I did not like to multiply Agents. I conceive that this is substantially conformable to the instruction from the Treasury and will be so understood. If not you be pleased to inform me.

With great respect   I have the honor to be Sir   Yr. Obed Ser

The Secy of War

ADf, Hamilton Papers, Library of Congress.

1. See Caleb Swan to H, September 9, 1799; H to Swan, September 12, 1799; McHenry to H, September 16, 1799. See also H to McHenry, September 14, 16, 1799.

2. For the Twelfth Regiment, see William Willcocks to H, August 14, 1799. Willcocks had written this letter in his capacity as acting commanding officer in the absence of William S. Smith. But see also Smith to H, September 21, 1799 (listed in the appendix to this volume), in which Smith denied the existence of any mutinous spirit in his regiment. For the Thirteenth Regiment, see Timothy Taylor to H, September 6, 1799 (listed in the appendix to this volume), in which Taylor reported that "a Soldier . . . an old and hardened villain . . . was endeavouring to excite the Soldiers to Mutanize and to rise in opposition to the officers and march off. . . ."

3. See H to McHenry, September 16, 1799, note 5.

4. See "Circular to the Commandants of Regiments," June 19, 1799.

From Nathan Rice

Springfield [Massachusetts] Sepr. 22d. 1799

My dear General

I have devoted my personal service during the last week intirely to the object of winter quarters for the troops.[1] I had not considered it so difficult to find & obtain a proper position, as on tryal it appeared to be. Many were eligible, as embracing partial advantages, some which comprehended all could not be obtained of the owners at any price, others at so exorbitant ones, that I at once gave them up.

I consulted Mr Jackson agreeable to your request who could not offer me the least aid.[2] I calld on Mr Ruggles[3] the Contractor who accompanyed me to Uxbridge—whither I turned my first attention, and after examining it & reconnoitreing the adjoining Towns for two or three days, I contracted for a situation which appears to imbrace the indispensable requisites. It is an elevated, healthfull, plesant, Situation; near the centre of the Town of Uxbridge, containing twenty one acres of oak & chesnut Timber, estimated to contain 20 Cords of wood p Acre. It has in its ⟨–⟩ at 150 yards an excellent Spring reported amply sufficient for the Troops—in front of which at a small distance, is grounds for encamping while the hutts are erecting, & which will answer for discipline. The Use of which for the purpose, may be had for a small consideration. In my agreement Government have the election of purchasing the Soil for twenty one dollars pr acre—or the Wood, & use of the ground, for eighteen dollars p. acre, which were the best Terms I could obtain of the owner. Saw mills are in the neighbourhood, where as many boards as will be necessary, (of which some for the officers will be requisite) can be had at about Six Dollars pr M. Slabs also to cover the hutts, can be had for a trifle, which will be convenient & as cheap to Government as any thing which can be used. Uxbridge is twenty three miles from Providence thirty seven from Boston & nineteen from Worcester. It has a pretty fruitfull surrounding country & will well accommodate the Contractors, as Rum Whiskey, Leyder brandy, are distilld. in the place.

Mr. Ruggles returned to Boston as soon as I had agreed for the spot. I then proceeded to *Oxford* distant fourteen miles west of Uxbridge here I met with an eligible Spot for hutting. In some respects this Town is preferable to Uxbridge. It has a more compact settlement an extensive plain for a Parade and a fertile surrounding country—within half a mile of the centre of the Town & One hundred yards of a large Stream & pond of water I found a grove of excellent oak Timber, standing on a sufficiently elevated ground, with a southern aspect, estimated to afford at least forty cords of wood to the acre, which can be purchased, with the use of the grounds for twenty five dollars pr. acre. A Saw mill stands very near it. Boards & Slabs may here also be had & springs of good water. If the advantages of being near Providence are not important Oxford I conceive would be the most eligible Spot which I saw of that Sir you can better judge than myself.

Thus I have to the best of my ability executed your commission— it has been an unplesant one, as it attachd to it so great responsibility. You ought not to be deceived and our discipline has not arrived to that perfection—but every officer & Soldiers, will take the liberty to judge of the propriety of my representation & choice, & decide agreeably to their own wishes.

I conceive Sir whatever may be your determination, as to situations no time ought to be lost in having the troops on the spot—that the hutts may be erected previous to the setting in of cold weather.

With the highest respect   I am Sir your most Obt Servant

N: Rice

General Hamilton

ALS, Hamilton Papers, Library of Congress.
1. See H to Rice, September 16, 1799.
2. H to Rice, first letter of August 22, 1799.
3. Either Joseph or Nathaniel Ruggles. See H to Richard Hunewell and Rice, May 21, 1799.

To Caleb Swan

New York Septr: 22. 1799

Sir

Having forgotten the circumstance, known to me when at the head of the Treasury Department, that forms of Muster and Pay Rolls had been prescribed by the Comptroller of the Treasury, I instructed the Assistant Adjutant General [1] to devise forms of those documents and to transmit them to the several commanders. You will find herewith the forms thus prescribed with a letter from the Adjutant General [2] explaining the differences and the reasons of the alterations. Brevity was the principal motive of them. In all military documents it is peculiarly desireable to consult conciseness as far as it may comport with perspicuity and accuracy. Military men in the midst of active operations have very little leisure for writing.

Having observed this much, I shall only further say on this point that I have no predilection for the new forms and am perfectly content, that the old shall continue with or without modifications to meet such of the alterations as may be deemed improvements.

But the essential point is to have the Officers without delay furnished with those forms which it is expected shall be observed accompanied with the requisite instructions for carrying them into Execution.

To this end I have issued the order of which the enclosed is a copy [3] and I expect that you will without delay send the several Pay Masters and persons acting as such the forms and instructions. Till you have a deputy it appears to me regular that your communications ought to be with this description of persons. Where you have or shall have a Deputy it is and will be proper for you to communicate with him and he with the Officers in Question. I may add that wherever a particular officer receives money from your Department for which he is accountable You or your deputy may with propriety hold a direct communication with him whatever be his station.

But it is proper that correspondence and communication between your office and the military should be restricted to persons of this description, except where for any special reason you find occasion to communicate with the Commanding General or other commander of an army or within a great military District.

The pointing out at an early period this course of proceeding is dictated by a love of regularity to which nothing is more conducive than great strictness in the modes of communication between Officers. It will be necessary to furnish each Commanding General with all the forms and *general* instructions which may be sent from your office for his information and government.

You may learn the names of the several Pay Masters from the Secy of War to whom they have been reported.

With great consideration   I am Sir   Yr. Obed ser

Caleb Swan Esq

ADf, Hamilton Papers, Library of Congress.
  1. Abraham Ellery. Letter not found.
  2. William North. Letter not found.
  3. "General Orders," September 24, 1799.

From James McHenry

War Department, Trenton,
September 23rd. 1799.

Sir,

I have received your letter of the 19th: instant.

On the 30th: ultimo I detailed my conceptions on the subject of late appointments to the new Regiments, these were grounded on former usage, on principles suggested by the Commander in Chief, as I thought on expedience and utility, and on calculations to ensure to the different Grades in a small establishment, the best selection of Officers.

I had supposed that the opinion of the Board of General Officers respecting relative Rank among the Officers they had selected, was explicitly declared, by the measure they adopted of numbering them provisionally, leaving it to a future time, and future indications to settle the Stations of those of the same Grade relatively and definitively. I had however considered, what they did by the list they formed, a definitive adaptation of office from the information before them, to the pretensions and abilities of the Candidates, in the last view, and during the formation or creation of the Corps of Officers.[1] I could not but suppose, that declinations, left open the precise Ranks they happened in, to be filled from former or subsequent applicants, whose pretensions suited them to the vacancy; the former appointed being measured and fitted, and no experience intervening to enhance their merits. The same views would also induce the same opinion, respecting vacancies occasioned, (a few instances of which have occurred) by the resignation of Officers, who resigned immediately after appointment—from unsteadiness, intervening inducements, or a change in their private affairs, incompatible with Military Service.

I cannot but suppose that the ideas I have expressed were entertained by all persons in any manner concerned in army appointments—as vacancies occurred in the different Regiments, recommendations were forwarded to fill the precise Grades, by the Commandants themselves, and in some instances by General Pinckney and yourself, and this altho' it might not have been attended to indiscriminately in cases of resignation and declension of acceptance. I will only refer to the case of Eli Forbes recommended by you in the place of Captain Philips, after the resignation of the latter on the 10th: July last.[2]

The prospect of a better selection seemed to attend, a practice grounded on these ideas, which appeared too strictly sanctioned by former precedents in the creating of new Corps, to be of course, and to create no uneasiness. The first intimation of discontent, was conveyed by your letter,[3] enclosing a copy of a letter to you from Lieut: Colonel Bentley, dated the 17th: ulto:

Permit me to observe that military etiquette, on the subject of succession, is the production of Rank once settled, and at least in our Armies, has not shewn itself heretofore, until that period arrived, altho' afterwards it has been tenaciously adhered to, most probably with beneficial effects.

Having no inclination to protract the date at which the rule of succession should commence but expecting useful results from it, when it was proper it should take place—I contemplated a mode of determining its commencement in a way that was compatible with securing all the Military Talents probably attainable for the different regimental Grades, and therefore preferable to a prefixed, and declared day. The mode was, to refer to the Commanding General the declaration of relative rank definitively for the Majors and Company Officers of each Regiment. This reserved to the General, perfectly acquainted from his correspondence, with the internal state of each Regiment, the advantage in his discretion, of acquiring talent for the different company Grades, in case of vacancies, as long as any chance remained of such acquisition. In a word this mode was intended to give to the General the full power of declaring relative Rank, and commencing the rule of succession in each Regiment, at such time as the organization of its Officers, and the good and harmony of the Service might in his judgement appear to require.

I have the honor to be, with great respect, Sir, Your obedt. servant   James McHenry

Major General Alexander Hamilton

LS, Hamilton Papers, Library of Congress.
  1. McHenry is referring to the final list of nominations for officers in the Army. George Washington, Charles Cotesworth Pinckney, and H had prepared this list at their conferences in Philadelphia in November and December, 1798. For this list, see McHenry to H, December 28, 1798, notes 1 and 2.
  2. See H to McHenry, July 10, 1799.
  3. H to McHenry, August 25, 1799.

From Staats Morris [1]

Fort McHenry [Baltimore, Maryland] September 23, 1799. ". . . I am extremely sorry to inform you Sir, that an epidemic is raging to an alarming degree in my Garrison, and on that account it is very fortunate that so many men have been sent out of the way of it. My nephew Lieut. Lawrence [2] fell a victim to it yesterday, after only four days ilness. I shall this day give orders to have the men encamped at a distance from the barracks and shall remove my family immediately. . . ."

ALS, Hamilton Papers, Library of Congress.
1. A resident of New York, Morris was a captain in the First Regiment of Artillerists and Engineers.
2. Thomas John Lawrence.

To Thomas Parker

New York Sepr. 2[3].[1] 1799

Sir

It is contemplated to establish the Eighth Ninth and Tenth Regiments in Winter Quarters somewhere in the Vicinity of the Potowmack and near Harpurs Ferry.[2] As this station is within the territorial limits of General Pinckneys Command,[3] the providing of quarters there did not fall within my province. But very urgent circumstances having suddenly induced General Pinckney to proceed to Rhode Island,[4] which has deranged the natural course of the business, The Secretary of War has just directed me to take the requisite measures for effecting the object.[5] The Quarter Masters Department not being yet organised I have concluded to confide the matter to your management.

The plan is to hut the troops during the present Winter which method the experience of the last war shewed to be extremely conducive to comfort as well as convenience.[6] For this purpose a situation is to be sought, where there will be proper wood for hutting and plenty of fuel; I mean on the premises: It is scarcely necessary to add that it must be airy elevated and dry so as to secure the health of the troops and must command an ample supply of good water. About Eighty Acres will suffice.

It is desireable, if practicable, to find out more than one spot, and even to extend the inquiry lower down the Potowmack towards the Fœderal City, but on the Virginia side. You will ascertain the terms upon which each spot may be purchased or hired. A purchase will probably, be found most convenient. When you have found a place, in your opinion fit, you will immediately report it with a particular description and the terms upon which it may be had to the Commander in Chief and transmit a duplicate of your report to me; and continuing your examination in the direction which I have mentioned you will successively report in the same manner. This letter will be transmitted to him [7] to be forwarded to you with any directions he may think fit to give.

You will make arrangements for the care of the recruiting service in your absence and you will lose no time in executing this service. The late period of the season renders dispatch indispensable.

With great consideration   I am sir   Yr. Obed ser

Thomas Parker Esq
Lt. Col Comm

ADf, Hamilton Papers, Library of Congress.
    1. H misdated this letter "September 25, 1799."
    2. See H's draft of George Washington to James McHenry, first letter of December 13, 1798; McHenry to H, February 4, 1799.
    3. For Charles Cotesworth Pinckney's command, see the introductory note to H to James Gunn, December 22, 1799.
    4. See Caleb Swan to H, September 19, 1799, note 2.
    5. McHenry to H, September 20, 1799.
    6. See, for example, Washington to Thomas Hanson of Maryland, President of the Continental Congress, October 30, 1782 (*GW*, XXV, 307–08).
    7. Enclosed in H to Washington, September 23, 1799.

From Nathan Rice

Springfield [Massachusetts] Sepr. 23d 1799

Sir

On my arrival at this place application was made to me for the discharge of two recruits, being inlisted as was alledged before they were eighteen years old.[1] Capt. Ashman [2] with whom they engagd. in July, says they assured him they were 18. By certificates from the records of the Towns, which they produce to me, one of them, Asa Chamberlin was seventeen the 9th of last April. The other William Clerk 3d was 18 yesterday.[3] They appear likely young men. must they be dischargd. or not?

I understand that three of the deserters from Major Winslows district rendezvous reported to you [4] are apprehended. Two from this post also who had deserted are taken, and in confinement. One of them a great Scoundrel. I have not receivd your directions how those of this discription are to be tryed.

It was out of my power to make my return for August before I left home; as all had not been receivd from the subdistricts; it shall be forwarded on my return. My paymaster has paid to the officers all the recruiting money which he had receivd. several of them are destitute of it & some in advance to the public.

I have neglected to assemble & muster the men at the regimental rendezvous contemplating their speedy removal to winter quarters. If I have erred, will proceed to do it without delay. I am pleased with the proficiency, they have made in discipline. They are in appearance fine men. I find it now necessary to appoint my Adjutant. Permit me to nominate Lieutenant Henry Sergent.[5] You will perhaps after the high recommendations I gave Mr. Roulstone [6] wonder I did not name him. Was his penmanship equal to his other qualifications I undoubtedly should. I pray that *his* merits may be rewarded as I requested in a former letter.

I am sorry to have occasion to report two more deserters from this district. I have enclosed Major Walkers report of them.[7] I flatter myself they will be taken, as some accounts have been had of their retreat. Pray Sir are the Officers or noncommissiond. officers entitled to the premium allowed by the public for taking up Deserters? Captain Chandler [8] has in one instance promised it to a Serjeant who apprehended one. I have doubted myself whether it was proper.

The men begin to grow impatient for pay they say they were encouraged when inlisted in an expectation of receiving it at least in three months.

With great consideration,   I am Sir yr Ob Servant   Nathan Rice

PS. Please to direct your communications in future to me at Boston as from thence I receive them with more dispatch than from Hingham—when absent.   N R.

Major General Hamilton

ALS, Hamilton Papers, Library of Congress.
    1. See H to Timothy Taylor, June 21, 1799.
    2. Phineas Ashmun.
    3. For the enlistments of Chamberlain and Clark, see RG 94, Records of the Adjutant General's Office, Register of Enlistments in the United States Army, 1798–1914, Vol. 5, National Archives.
    4. See Rice to H, September 6, 1799.
    5. Sargent was a second lieutenant in the Fourteenth Regiment of Infantry.

6. See Rice to H, August 31, 1799.
7. John Walker. Walker's list contains descriptions of four deserters (AD, Hamilton Papers, Library of Congress).
8. Thomas Chandler.

To Caleb Swan

New York Sepr. 23. 1799

Sir

I regret that I did not find in your letter of the 19 instant information that you were sending a supply of money for bounty and Pay to the additional Regiments.[1] The Secy of War tells me that he had instructed you to report an estimate of what might be requisite and that he would sanction the advance.[2] In my letter,[3] to which yours is a reply, I request that two months pay may be forwarded. To this may be added a sufficient sum to make up, with what has been already furnished, the full bounty for one half the complement of the 5th 6th and 16th. and three fourths of the complement of the ⁴ and the full complement of the others. I sometime since sent to the Secretary of War, as a guide, the numbers of the several Regiments according to my information at that time.[5] I now send the present state of them agreeably to later information.

It is my duty to urge in the most serious manner that not a moment may be lost in forwarding this money. Serious inconveniences are to be apprehended from the not doing of it. When it is considered that one material form, that of the warrants of the Commanding Generals, cannot be executed for want of the requisite appointments of Deputies and that the prescribed forms of Muster and Pay Rolls were only received by me from the war Department in the course of this week—When, I say, these circumstances are taken in connection with other obvious ones incident to the creation of new corps—there ought certainly to be no hesitation any where about making reasonable advances. If within proper limits, there can be no possible risk, more than are inseperable from all public disbursements where there are intermediate Agents. I count implicitly upon your zeal and exertion. I am assured of the sanction of the Secy of War and I take it for granted there will be no obstacle from any other quarter.

I am obliged by your expressions of confidence and shall lose no time in selecting a fit character as Deputy in this Quarter. The arrival of General Pinckney makes your resort to him for another Deputy very proper. I shall consider what the law [6] permits as to other deputies and will give you my opinion as well of the regularity as of the expediency of an increase of the number.

The dispersed situation of the two Regiments of Artillery renders it difficult to designate Pay Masters by the nomination of the Officers. But I shall speedily devise a mode of effecting the object as nearly in conformity with usage as the circumstances will permit. I am clearly of opinion that all necessary organs of service ought without delay to be instituted & especially where the disbursement of money is concerned.

I request you to send me as soon as may be a statement of all the monies which have been advanced for bounty & pay to the additional Regiments and a statement of the arrears of pay now due to the four old Regts.[7] & that you will give me a monthly view of the subject.

With great consideration   I am Sir   Yr Obed ser

Caleb Swan Esq

ADf, Hamilton Papers, Library of Congress.
    1. This is a reference to the Additional Army. See the introductory note to H to James Gunn, December 22, 1798.
    2. James McHenry to H, September 16, 1799.
    3. H to Swan, September 14, 1799.
    4. Space left blank in MS.
    5. H to McHenry, August 19, 1799.
    6. See H to McHenry, September 16, 1799, note 5.
    7. This is a reference to the Regular Army. See the introductory note to H to Gunn, December 22, 1798.

To George Washington

New York Sept 23d. 1799

Dear Sir

I had the pleasure of receiving in due time your letter of the 15th. instant. The suggestions it contains will be maturely weighed. I postpone any thing definitive, till the return of General Wilkinson [1] which is momently expected. The other Documents, besides No. 8, which accompanied this letter, were not material to the consideration of its contents, or they would have been forwarded. Even Number one does nothing more than exhibit in the form of a table the propositions which are found in the letter. I was afraid of burthening you with papers, which did not necessarily require your attention, being matters of mere detail.

Inclosed is a letter of this date to Col: Parker about Winter Quarters for the Eighth Ninth and Tenth Regiments. It is late to begin, but you perceive in it the causes of the delay.

It is extremely desirable that you would be pleased to take the direction of this matter, and to have the business done in such manner as you shall deem eligible. Not having a right to presume that you would choose to take the charge of it, I have adopted the expedient of addressing my self to Colonel Parker. But perhaps you may think of some preferable Agent. In which case, you will be so good as to retain the letter and give complete directions to such other Agent. Compensation and the defraying of his Expences need not be Obstacles.

At any rate, I hope you will not find it inconvenient to instruct Colo. Parker to conclude a bargain for such place, as upon his reports to you, shall be, in your opinion eligible. It is very necessary that these young troops should be early covered. Collateral Ideas with regard to Harper's Ferry as a place for Arsenals and magazines may perhaps be combined. These will more readily occur to you than to me.

Scotch Plains near Bound Brook will be fixed upon for the 11th. 12th. & 13th. Regiments. A very eligible Spot, of about Ninety Acres, is offered there at 50 Dollars per Acre, for the fee simple.[2] It affords the advantage of a good Summer encampment also; with a prospect of a Supply, for years, of fuel and Straw at cheap rates and the convenience of a *pleasant* and *plentiful* surrounding Country.

Search has been, for some time past, making for a suitable position for the three most Northern Regiments, in the vicinity of Uxbridge in Massachusetts.[3]

With true respect & attachment   I have the honor to be   Dr. Sir yr. obedt. servt.   Alex Hamilton

General Washington

LS, George Washington Papers, Library of Congress; LS, marked "Duplicate," George Washington Papers, Library of Congress; ADfS, Hamilton Papers, Library of Congress.

1. James Wilkinson had been in New York City conferring with H from August 3, 1799, to early September, when he left New York with the intention of visiting President John Adams at Quincy, Massachusetts. See H to Wilkinson, August 3, 1799; H to Adams, September 7, 1799. On September 12, 1799, Wilkinson arrived in Newport, Rhode Island, where he stayed until September 15, at which time he left to go to Providence (*Newport Mercury*, September 17, 1799). Wilkinson presumably never did confer with Adams, and he returned to New York on October 6, 1799. See H to James McHenry, October 6, 1799.

2. Aaron Ogden selected the site for the winter quarters at Scotch Plains, New Jersey. See Ogden to H, September 19, 20, 1799; H to Ogden, September 23, 1799; H to McHenry, September 25, 1799 (all listed in the appendix to this volume).

3. See Nathan Rice to H, September 22, 1799.

General Orders [1]

New York, September 24th 1799.

The Paymaster General having arrived and entered upon his functions at the seat of government, all muster and pay rolls are, hereafter, to be transmitted to him, instead of the office of the Adjutant General, until a Deputy Paymaster General shall have been appointed and announced to the troops. They are to be sent addressed to Caleb Swan, Esquire, Paymaster General, at Philadelphia, with the usual endorsement on public service, and the name of the writer.

The Paymaster General will prescribe and transmit the forms of muster and pay rolls, and of accounts connected with them, together with instructions for carrying them into execution, which are strictly to be observed by all officers whom it may concern.

Abraham R. Ellery
Assistant Adjutant General.

LC, RG 98, Post-Revolutionary War Commands, Castle Island Records, National Archives.

1. For background to this document, see H to Caleb Swan, September 22, 23, 1799.

From James McHenry

War Department, Trenton,
September 24th: 1799.

Sir,

I have received your letter dated the 17th: instant, and shall not fail to give the project of regulations it contained, as early and deliberate a consideration as possible. You will however be pleased to direct a stop to be put to the issue of Rations to the Children of Soldiers, because such issues had grown into abuse, and I know of no law that authorizes them; they are besides extra of any Estimate. The prohibition will certainly be felt as a great hardship, in particular cases, and encrease the regrets for the want of some establishment for the support and education of Army Children.

I am Sir,   with great respect,   Your obedt: servant,

James McHenry

Major General Alexander Hamilton

LS, Hamilton Papers, Library of Congress; LS, letterpress copy, James McHenry Papers, Library of Congress.

From Caleb Swan

Trenton, September 25, 1799. "I have received your two letters of the 23rd Instant.[1] I am in the act of complying with all therein required; but as I have to apportion the sums of money to the different Regiments, and obtain seperate drafts for the same out of the Bank in Philadelphia, it will necessarily consume a few days; you may however, calculate on the whole being done and the money put in motion in the course of a week. In this business I find myself standing on uncertain ground—committed to the hazard of accident by a robbery of the Mail or other contingency—and that kind of responsibility which I have been accustomed to only, of delivering the money in person to the proper accountable officer, changed alto-gether. And from the letter of the law,[2] the tenor of my instruc-tions,[3] and the rigid adherence to rules and forms in the examining officers of the Treasury,[4] I can have but faint hopes of relief in case of accident, unless it be through your agency, which I am in hopes will never be required; yet should any loss happen, I am persuaded of your efforts in my behalf. . . ."

ALS, Hamilton Papers, Library of Congress.
1. Actually the two letters which Swan is answering in this letter are dated September 22 and 23, 1799.
2. See Section 3 of "An Act making alterations in the Treasury and War Departments" (1 *Stat.* 280 [May 8, 1792]) and Section 15 of "An Act for the better organizing of the Troops of the United States; and for other purposes" (1 *Stat.* 753 [March 3, 1799]). For the text of Section 3, see James McHenry to H, August 29, 1799. For the text of Section 15, see H to McHenry, September 16, 1799, note 5.
3. See Oliver Wolcott, Jr., to Swan, July 26, 1792 (Df, partly in Wolcott's handwriting, Connecticut Historical Society, Hartford).
4. See, for example, Wolcott to H, August 29, 1793.

From Caleb Swan

Trenton, September 25, 1799. "In the pressure of business I omitted to mention in my letter of this day, that a calculation had been made previously to the receipt of yours of the 23. instant, for sending as much money to the new Regiments at this time as would discharge all arrearages of pay and subsistence up to the 30th of this month inclusive. This will amount to rather more than two months pay to some of the officers, who have generally received four in advance. And from the best information I possess, it will not far exceed two months pay generally to the soldiers, who have in some instances been paid a moiety by the paymasters, as will appear by the schedule of advances forwarded this day. . . ."[1]

ALS, Hamilton Papers, Library of Congress.
1. On the envelope H wrote: "*approve* Press sending on the forms."

To James McHenry

New York, September 26, 1799. Encloses extract of Lieutenant Colonel John F. Hamtramck's letter of July 1, 1799, concerning his failure to be repaid for expenses incurred for the First Regiment. States: "I would request your particular Attention to this subject. You will be so good as to inform me whether the payment will be made, or if there are any special objections to the measure communicate them to me that I may be able to transmit them to Col. Hamtramck."

Df, in the handwriting of Thomas Y. How, Hamilton Papers, Library of Congress.

To William North [1]

Private   New York Sept. 26th. 1799

Dr. Sir

There is nothing to change or postpone the call for you to this City. Your presence is necessary. Several things wait for it. The whole machinery must be in motion. The disease here is wearing out and your Office is in a healthy part of the Town. But still I advise you to repair in the first instance to the encampment of the 12th. Regt. at West Chester and inform me of your being there. Do not tell my friends that I write to you from N. York.

Df, in the handwriting of Ethan Brown, Hamilton Papers, Library of Congress.
1. This letter was written in reply to North to H, September 18, 1799.

To Charles Cotesworth Pinckney

N. York Sept. 26th. 1799

My dear Sir

I have heard of your arrival at Rhode Island.[1] On the   [2] I wrote you a long letter transmitting all the Instructions which respect the recruiting service &c. Did you receive that letter? Is there any one who would act upon it in your absence? I wish you could make a visit to Trenton convenient. More Organisation is indispensable. Several things of material concern are to be arranged. I shall go there with General Wilkinson as soon as he arrives from Boston whither he lately went.[3] Your cooperation would be important. If you come with this view it must be speedy.

affectly. yrs. &c

Df, in the handwriting of Ethan Brown, Hamilton Papers, Library of Congress.
  1. See Caleb Swan to H, September 17, 1799, note 2; James McHenry to H, September 20, 1799.
  2. Space left blank in MS. H is referring to H to Pinckney, August 13, 1799.
  3. See H to George Washington, September 23, 1799, note 1.

To Ebenezer Stevens

New-York Sept. 26th. 1799

Sir

I request that you will make inquiry for a small house, with five convenient rooms, as Quarters for my military family, and inform me of the result.

I imagine such a one may be found in Broadway, not very far from my house.[1] I need not tell you that it should be in a situation, the most unexceptionably healthy.

With great consideration   I am Sir   Yr. obedt. Servt.   A Hamilton

Col. Stevens

LS, New-York Historical Society, New York City; Df, in the handwriting of Ethan Brown, Hamilton Papers, Library of Congress.
  1. See H to James McHenry, second letter of August 13, 1799, note 1.

From John F. Hamtramck

Fort Fayette (Pittsburgh), September 27, 1799. ". . . I have reviewed the Troops of this Garrison; they are a handsome set of young Men, make a good appearance, and their Cloathing is in good order, their policie does honor to . . . the Commanding Officer; but like all the other Troops are defficient in tactics; the Arms are in good order but without Gun Slings, and the Cartridge Boxes tho' clean are not fit for service; the Non Commissioned Officers & Music are without Swords, and the latter are but passable, and have no Coats, the Pickets want to be renewed, but the Barracks of both Officers and Soldiers, are in very good repair. I have Received a Letter from the Surveyor General Rufus Putnam Esqr to whom I had wrote [1] and requested he would inform me the reason why the Indian boundary line had not been run before in which he says that in May 1798 he had contracted with a Mr Ludlow [2] to run the lines, and it then appeared probable that they would have been surveyed in the following Autumn, but other Surveys which he judged necessary to be previously executed, which were connected with, and preparatory to the Surveys of the Boundary Line, and which were not compleated till the uprising of the last Spring, was the cause that it was not done before. I expect some other information through a different chanel, which shall be communicated as soon as it arrives. . . ."

LS, Hamilton Papers, Library of Congress.
  1. See H to Hamtramck, May 12, 1799.
  2. Israel Ludlow. See Oliver Wolcott, Jr., to H, May 24, 1799.

To James McHenry

New York Sepr 27. 1799

Sir

I regret that I did not find in your letter of the 23 instant some assurances, as to the future, which would have enabled me to tranquillize the minds of those Officers, who may have been rendered uneasy by the appointments which have been in discussion between us. Had this been the case, I should have gladly left the subject at rest; for certainly I have no inclination to animadvert on the past, except with the view of preventing if possible the continuance of a practice, which in my judgment is calculated to injure the service.

ADf, Hamilton Papers, Library of Congress.

It is not my desire to controvert the position which you seem desirous to establish, that what has been done is justified by the usage of the Department, and that it has been countenanced by the recommendations of the Commandants of Regiments, of General Pinckney, perhaps of myself.

Yet upon recurring to my letter,[1] in the instance you particularly cite, I do not perceive that it warrants the inference which has been drawn. That letter, reminding you of an opinion which I had before given of a contrary tendency, and which you were not understood to have adopted, only states that if a different rule was to prevail, the application of it to this case would probably be expedient; and for this conclusion it cautiously relies on the presumption that the commandant, who recommended, had not been unmindful of the probable effect of the measure on the feelings of his officers.

I have also referred to the letter of Col Hunewell,[2] on which mine is grounded, and I find this paragraph preceding that which I presume was sent to you—"The Secy of War has officially informed me that Capt Philips [3] of my Regiment has applied to *decline his acceptance* as Captain in the army &c." This phrase is incorrect and ambiguous, but I am persuaded the impression on my mind was, that he had *declined to accept*, not that he had resigned after acceptance.

But I willingly relinquish the assertion of my own consistency, and consent to share the responsibility of what ever may have been done contrary to the course which I now advocate. I am only anxious that this course, which I deem most correct in itself, and most conducive to the harmony and success of the service, may prevail in future. In determining the propriety of it, neither the past usage of the department nor the ideas, deliberate or inadvertent, of particular officers are conclusive. If these have led to an inconvenient practice, it is no reason that a better should not be substituted.

The only argument for the past practice, which in the view of expediency I find in your communications, is the greater prospect of a good selection of character. But I have a strong doubt whether

1. H to McHenry, second letter of July 10, 1799.
2. Richard Hunewell's letter to H, which H sent to McHenry in his second letter of July 10, 1799, has not been found.
3. Thomas Philips. See H to McHenry, second letter of July 10, 1799; McHenry to H, September 23, 1799.

the operation will in this respect accord with the hypothesis. In the first formation of a corps, it is natural and usual to combine various and extensive information of the characters of candidates. A careful selection, guided by adequate lights, may be presumed to be the result. When, the corps being in a state of progression, a vacancy happens, the service commonly requires that it be speedily filled. And it is often probable, that the necessity of expedition will interfere with the judiciousness of Choice.

If I may credit the representations of some of the Commandants, this supposition is verified by the fact. Inferior characters in some of the new appointments have been placed over the heads of those which were preferable.

But admitting the fact, which is the basis of the argument, it still remains to judge, whether the little more of advantage, which in that particular may be obtained will compensate for the inconveniences of the scheme.

These inconveniences have been before adverted to. They resolve themselves into the dissatisfaction of Officers; by the contravention of expectations which are naturally formed—and which are connected with the strongest motives that actuate the breasts of military men.

In addition to the more general considerations, which create those expectations, it may be observed, that when officers by their exertions have contributed to raise the men or a considerable part of them who are to compose a Regiment, they are apt to consider new persons, placed over them as Intruders, to whom the fruits of their labours have been transferred. This impression is distinct from mere military prejudice. It results from the relation which intrinsically subsists between service and recompence. The usage of the Department, as stated by you, infringes that relation.

Thus justice coincides with the prepossessions of the military state to recommend, that the discretion to introduce new characters into corps once organised should be confined within narrow limits—and should not be permitted to move within so wide a circle as you assign to it. I cannot but adhere to the opinion that the limits delineated by me in my former letter,[4] afford as much latitude as can be reconciled with propriety & the interest of the service.

I am not able to assent to the proposition that "Military Etiquette,

4. H to McHenry, September 19, 1799.

on the subject of succession is the production of rank once settled." The right of succession, is incident to every military establishment of which we have any knowlege. It is considered as the primary reward of service, and has its foundation in natural justice and
in very strong passions of the human heart. The moment a corps is
organised by the appointment of its officers, the expectation of
promotion, by succession from a lower to higher grade, arises spon-
taneously in the heart of every officer, founded in a sentiment of
right and in the analogy of practice. If the expectation is disappointed, unless in conformity with exceptions previously declared
and understood, a sense of injury is excited.

If the relative rank between the individuals of a corps is suspended in the act of appointment, though the parties must and will
resign themselves to a future decision of that point; yet they will
expect that as against all strangers to the corps, they will enjoy a
right of succession, to be applied individually among themselves as
soon as there shall be a settlement of relative rank. This, they will
consider as a principle of military right and Etiquette. With this,
they will connect the point of honor, and will be apt to think themselves degraded, if the principle be not observed towards them.

As to the *provisional* arrangement of relative rank by the Board of
General Officers on which you lay some stress—it had no other
meaning than to reserve to the Government the right of readjusting
the rank as between the Individuals who were recommended by
then. It had no eye whatever to the introduction of new men—or
to the suspension of the right of promotion in favour of persons of
this description. The caution of the Board, in recommending the express reservation of a right to change the arrangement is an indica-
tion of their sense of the strictness of the rules of rank.

You intimate that you contemplated the period of a definitive settlement of the relative rank as that at which the right of succession
should commence. This idea was for the first time intimated in your
letter, to which this is an answer, and of course could not regulate
the expectation of any officer. Besides, it is to make an important
right depend in different corps upon local collateral and casual circumstances. The commanding General was empowered to make the
definitive settlement of rank, but it was a prerequisite that he was to
acquire the necessary information. In proportion to the distance

from which this was to come, and to the dispersion of the officers over a greater or smaller extent of Country, must have been the celerity with which the settlement in each case could be made. Corps near the Quarters of the General might have been put in enjoyment of the right in a fortnight, while those at the extremities must have been postponed for months; though all were appointed at the same time. So unequal, and let me add without offence, so capricious a result cannot on mature reflection be thought a proper one.

It has happened, as well from the necessity of such an expedient, as in conformity with what was by me understood to be the sense of the Board of General Officers, that the field officers of each Regiment have been resorted to as the Agents of the readjustment of rank—reserving a discretion to approve alter or reject. In some instances through more diligence, perhaps less circumspection, or from better means of information, the field officers have executed with promptness the task confided to them. In others notwithstanding reiterated calls, the execution is still delayed, and for reasons which have too much appearance of validity to be disapproved.

Hence if the definitive arrangement is to be the criterion of the right of succession, some regiments will have been intitled to it for months past, and others may not be intitled to it for some time yet to come.

I must entreat that you will be pleased to review the considerations which I have stated, and I will allow myself to hope that the principles suggested in my last letter will appear to you solid and that they will still receive your sanction for future practice.

They are that when a new corps is organised, though vacancies by *non-acceptance* may be filled by new men, yet the right of succession shall immediately attach as to every case of *vacancy*, after acceptance of the person whose station may have become vacant.

That even as to the filling of vacancies, arising from *non acceptance*, a determinate period shall be fixed, sufficient for ascertaining who will accept and who will decline; after the expiration of which time, the right of succession shall begin to operate.

And I submit that three months from the time of organisation, by the first appointment of officers, ought to be deemed sufficient for that purpose.

General and certain rules in most affairs are of great consequence.

In whatever relates to military institutions, they are peculiarly necessary. Partial or particular conveniences, to be derived from the suspension of them, are scarcely ever to be put in competition with the aggregate of advantages which they produce. A steady system, constituted by fixed rules, is the essential basis of a good and prosperous military establishment: a maxim which cannot be too constantly borne in mind or too carefully observed.

With great respect & esteem I have the honor to be Sir   Yr Obed ser

The Secy of War

To Nathan Rice

New York Sepr. 27. 1799

Sir

Your letter of the twenty second Instant on the subject of Winter Quarters has just been delivered to me.

I am disposed to prefer the situation at Oxford as well because your opinion is in favor of that situation, as because there does not seem to be a sufficient quantity of wood for hutting and fuel at the other place.

You mention that you have entered into an agreement for the ground at Uxbridge. I presume the agreement is conditional, as you present another place for consideration, and as no powers were given to you to form a definitive contract. It is my wish that you should purchase the right of soil if it can be had at a price any way proportional to that which is demanded for the use and for the wood. You will please to complete the purchase either of the use or of the right of soil as soon as possible, and the moment I shall be informed that this has been done I will take measures for having you supplied with the necessary funds.

The diligence which you have employed upon this occasion claims my acknowledgements.

Col. Rice

Df, in the handwriting of Thomas Y. How, Hamilton Papers, Library of Congress.

From James McHenry

Private & confidential   Trenton 28 Sept. 1799

My dear Sir

I have understood this morning that the monies expended on the works which have been directed to be erected by Brig. Gen. Wilkinson at Loftus's heights have already occasioned an expenditure of above 80,000 Dolls. I can hardly beleive in the information, and yet it is sufficiently circumstantial to create no little uneasiness. The works at this place, were undertaken without orders. I shall send you copies of his instructions [1] and of two letters to him of the 2d Augt. 1798 & 31 Jany 1799.[2] What he has done may be right however notwithstanding the light in which it strikes me.

The appropriation for the defensive protection of the frontiers, by which is meant militia services & fortfications is 60,000 only.[3]

This passion for fort building, I mean permanent ones must be restrained. I believe there has also been a new one commenced on the Tom bigbee.[4]

Yours affectionately   James McHenry

Gen. Hamilton

ALS, Hamilton Papers, Library of Congress; ADf, James McHenry Papers, Library of Congress; copy, Hamilton Papers, Library of Congress.

1. McHenry to James Wilkinson, March 22, 1797 (copy, Hamilton Papers, Library of Congress). This letter was enclosed in McHenry to H, October 4, 1799 (listed in the appendix to this volume).

2. Copies, Hamilton Papers, Library of Congress. These letters were enclosed in McHenry to H, October 4, 1799 (listed in the appendix to this volume). McHenry had also sent to H on February 4, 1799, a copy of his letter to Wilkinson of January 31, 1799.

3. This is a reference to Section 1 of "An Act making appropriations for the Military establishment, for the year one thousand seven hundred and ninety-eight; and for other purposes" (1 Stat. 564 [June 12, 1798]).

4. Fort Saint Stephens was on the Tombigbee River about one hundred and forty miles southwest of what is now Montgomery, Alabama.

From James McHenry [1]

War Department
28th. September 1799

Sir,

I have received your letter dated the 21st instant, pressing that measures, may without fail, and speedily, be taken to pay the sums due to the troops of the United States.

Observations in your letter, relative to the causes, which have prevented the exhibition of muster and pay rolls, would seem to convey an idea, that in your opinion some delay or failure in this particular is attributable to me.

It becomes therefore proper that I should observe, I can discover, in whatever relates to the pay of the army, no deficiency of any organ, which it lay with this Department to appoint. If one or more Deputies are thought indispensible to the Pay Master General, it will be recollected, that the appointment lays with him,[2] not with me, and that so far as my sanction of the measure, seemed to be expected, I have readily accorded it.

It also deserves attention, that had Deputies existed, they could have made no payments to the troops regularly, but on muster and pay rolls, previously exhibitted, and your warrant.

The difficulty in my conception, has arisen from the want of muster and pay rolls only; and the forms for these were presented by the Department of the Treasury to the Paymaster General. It was his exclusive duty to communicate his instructions to the Commanding Generals, and to forward forms for use, to every Officer to whom they would be necessary. The instructions and forms originated, as by Law, they ought in another department;[3] in these I individually had no agency; having every reason to suppose the instructions to the Paymaster, and the forms used, were satisfactory in practice, since the payments to troops went on without complaints from that cause, my attention indeed was never particularly called to either, until the late difficulties presented.

It was to confirm an opinion I had entertained and expressed, viz. That one or two of the officers of a regiment or company &c were considered by the Comptroller as competent to muster the troops of their command, and sign the requisite Certificates; that I procured the instructions to the Paymaster and forwarded them to you, and for no other purpose.

I request you to believe, the preceding observations are dictated by a desire to satisfy you, that as I have not intentionally, so I am not conscious I have in fact, neglected any duty, incumbent upon me, to facilitate the payment of the troops, to effect which in future, I am extremely anxious, the most proper and decisive measures should be adopted.

I am Sir   with great respect   your obedient humble servant

James McHenry

Major General Alexander Hamilton

LS, Hamilton Papers, Library of Congress; LS, letterpress copy, James Mc-Henry Papers, Library of Congress.
    1. For background to this letter, see Caleb Swan to H, September 9, 1799; H to Swan, September 14, 1799; McHenry to H, September 16, 1799; H to McHenry, September 14, 16, 1799.
    2. This statement is in accordance with Section 15 of "An Act for the better organizing of the Troops of the United States; and for other purposes" (1 *Stat.* 749–55 [March 3, 1799]). For the text of this section, see H to McHenry, September 16, 1799, note 5.
    3. Section 9 of "An Act making alterations in the Treasury and War Departments" (1 *Stat.* 281 [May 8, 1792]) reads: "That the forms of keeping and rendering all public accounts whatsoever, shall be prescribed by the department of the Treasury."

From George Washington

Mount Vernon 29th Sepr. 1799

Dear Sir,

Your letter of the 23d. instant was received the 27th; and this day will proceed in the Mail to Winchester—the nearest Post-Town to Colo. Parker's residence, if he should be at his own house, the letter enclosed for him.[1]

There being no person in my view more eligable than Colo. Parker to carry your Instructions into effect unless Colo. Carrington had been in office as Quarter Master General,[2] I had no hesitation in forwarding your letter to him, with such sentimts. as occurred to me on the subject,[3] which differed in no essential point, from those you had given.

I confined him more pointedly than you had done, to the site near Harpers ferry for his Winter Cantonment—because very cogent reasons, in my opinion, required it, for besides possessing all the advantages enumerated in your letter to him (so far as my recollection of the spot, & information goes); being in a fertile & most abounding Country; and one of the strongest positions by nature, perhaps in America; It appeared to me, that the Encampment, and Arsenal which is established at that place, might mutually assist, & benefit each other.

If the States are wise enough to keep united, I have no doubt of this Arsenal being their principal place of Arms, and best foundary; as it is in the midst of Furnaces and Forges of the best Iron; Can receive at, & transport from it, by Inland Navigation, all its wants, & manufacture, in every direction—and is, indubitably—supposing the advantage of water transportation out of the question altogether, the great high way to the Country on the River Ohio.

For the reasons I have assigned, I did not hesitate a moment in giving the vicinity of Harpers ferry (at the confluence of the Rivers Potomac & Shenandoah) a decided preference—but if I am not mistaken, another strong inducement is afforded, namely—that there is a sufficiency of Land, purchased for the purpose of the Arsenal, to accomodate both objects. Of this I have informed Colo. Parker, but as Mr. Lear is from home (who was the Agent for the War Department in the purchase) I could not inform him with certainty.[4] If the fact however, should be as I suspect, it will prove a most fortunate circumstance, as well in the article of expence, as in the time that will be gained in completing the Huts. If it should be otherwise, I have advised Colo. Parker to hold out to view, & examine many places, while he by some Agent, is endeavouring to possess himself, by purchase, the site near Harpers Ferry; without which he might be imposed on in the price of the Land. With very great esteem & regard I remain

Dear Sir   Your Obedient and Affecte. Hble Servant

Go: Washington

Majr. Genl Hamilton

ALS, Hamilton Papers, Library of Congress; ALS, letterpress copy, George Washington Papers, Library of Congress.

1. H to Thomas Parker, September 23, 1799.
2. See H to James McHenry, August 19, 1799, note 3.
3. Washington to Parker, September 28, 1799 (ALS, letterpress copy, George Washington Papers, Library of Congress).
4. Tobias Lear was Washington's private secretary from 1786 to 1793 and his military secretary from 1798 until Washington's death in December, 1799.

On January 28, 1796, Timothy Pickering authorized Lear to purchase land at Harpers Ferry for an arsenal (ALS, Massachusetts Historical Society, Boston). In September, 1799, Lear was in Berkeley, Virginia, where his late wife, Frances Bassett Washington, and George Washington, to whom she had been related by her first marriage, owned land. Lear returned to Mount Vernon on October 13, 1799 (John C. Fitzpatrick, ed., *The Diaries of George Washington, 1748–1799* [Boston, 1925], IV, 315).

From Caleb Gibbs [1]

[*Boston, September 30, 1799.* On October 24, 1799, Hamilton wrote to Gibbs: "I have received your improper letter of the 30th. of September." *Letter not found.*]

1. Gibbs, who had been an aide-de-camp to George Washington during the American Revolution, was an indefatigable office seeker. See Gibbs to H, January 16, May 16, 1791; September 10, 1792; February 16, June 24, 1793; January 31, 1794.

To James McHenry

New York Sepr. 30th. 1799

Sir

Enquiry has been made of me by the Commandants of the several regiments [1] with respect to the construction of the last resolution in the Appendix to the Articles of War.[2] They wish to know whether this resolution gives a reward to parties of soldiers who may apprehend deserters. I would thank you for your opinion on the subject. Of the expediency of giving a reward to parties of soldiers that may be successful in the pursuit of deserters I have no doubt as it would make them zealous and active in the search, and would save expence by obviating the necessity of resorting to other means.[3]

With great respect   I am Sir

Secretary of War

Df, in the handwriting of Thomas Y. How, Hamilton Papers, Library of Congress.

1. See, for example, Nathan Rice to H, September 23, 1799.

2. This is a reference to Article 14 of the articles of war, which was called the "Administration of Justice" and printed as an appendix to the articles of war in the 1794 edition of *Rules and Articles for the Better Government of the Troops, Raised, or to be raised, and kept in pay, by and at the expence of the United States of America.* See H to Jonathan Dayton, August 6, 1798, note 11.

Article 14 reads in part: "That the Commanding Officer of any of the forces in the service of the United States shall, upon report made to him of any desertions in the troops under his orders, cause the most immediate and vigorous search to be made after the deserter or deserters, which may be conducted by a commissioned or non-commissioned officer, as the case shall require. That, if such search should prove ineffectual, the Officer Commanding the regiment or Corps to which the deserter or deserters belonged, shall insert, in the nearest gazette or newspaper, an advertisement, descriptive of the deserter or deserters, and offering a reward, not exceeding ten dollars, for each deserter who shall be apprehended and secured in any of the gaols of the neighboring States. That the charges of advertising deserters, the reasonable extra expenses incurred by the person conducting the pursuit, and the reward shall be paid by the Secretary at War, on the Certificate of the Commanding Officer of the troops" (*JCC*, XXX, 322).

3. John Adams was also interested in the question of the payment of a reward for the capture of prisoners. On August 30, 1799, Adams wrote to McHenry to inquire into the refusal of William Simmons, the accountant to the War Department, to pay Hugh McAllister, a citizen, the reward for the capture of David Gill, a deserter from Captain Edward Miller's company in the Second Regiment of Infantry (copy, Adams Family Papers, deposited in the Massachusetts Historical Society, Boston). See also the copy of a statement by McAllister, dated August 24, 1799, in the Adams Family Papers, deposited in the Massachusetts Historical Society, Boston. As a result of the letters from H and Adams, McHenry wrote to Simmons on October 14, 1799, enclosing H's letter and requesting that Simmons meet with John Steele, the comptroller of the Treasury, to determine the proper interpretation to be given to Article 14 of the articles of war (copy, Adams Family Papers, deposited in the Massachusetts Historical Society, Boston). In his response, dated October 16, Simmons wrote in part: ". . . I proceed to state what has been the prevailing custom in effecting settlements here when deserters have been pursued or apprehended. when detachments have been sent in pursuit of deserters agreeable to the directions contained in the last Resolution in the appendix to the articles of War—their reasonable expences & not the Premium has been allowed—whether they have been successful or not. That such pursuit proving ineffectual & the deserter being advertized the premium offered has in all cases been allowed whether the deserter has been apprehended by a Private citizen—a Soldier or a detachment of Soldiers. This is the rule which has heretofore governed, no difficulty has arisen relative thereto & my accots. passing at the Treasury proves that this construction of the Law was in conformity with that of the Offices of the Treasury" (LC, RG 217, Records of the General Accounting Office, Letter Books, Accountant's Office, Vol. F, May 16, 1799–February 27, 1800, National Archives; copy, Adams Family Papers, deposited in the Massachusetts Historical Society, Boston). After McHenry informed Simmons on October 16 that the accountant's letter did not answer the question of how to implement Article 14 of the articles of war (copy, Adams Family Papers, deposited in the Massachusetts Historical Society, Boston), Simmons responded on October 21

that he had consulted Steele and that it would be easier to consider the capture of deserters on an individual basis than to establish a uniform rule (LC, RG 217, Records of the General Accounting Office, Letter Books, Accountant's Office, Vol. F, May 16, 1799–February 27, 1800, National Archives; copy, Adams Family Papers, deposited in the Massachusetts Historical Society, Boston). In a letter to Adams on the same day, Simmons explained his reasons for rejecting McAllister's claim (LC, RG 217, Records of the General Accounting Office, Letter Books, Accountant's Office, Vol. F, May 16, 1799–February 27, 1800, National Archives; copy, Adams Family Papers, deposited in the Massachusetts Historical Society, Boston). McHenry, who considered Simmons's conduct insubordinate, enclosed copies of all the relevant documents in a letter to Adams on October 25, 1799. This letter concluded: "The Head of a Department is presumed to be charged with its superintendance throughout the subordinate branches, to be invested with authority to call for information from all persons employed in it, to be entitled to a respectful attention to his calls, and a sedulous endeavor to make the information given, as clear, explicit, and complete as possible. Unless this is the case, it is not possible that public business can be carried on, in an orderly, correct, expeditious or satisfactory manner, either to the Administrators, or those who apply them.

"Making only these general observations, it will be permitted to ask, whether in the opinion of the president, the answers of the Accountant to an application on my part, plain, explicit, and definite, and to questions necessary to be answered, for the government of the Military Officers of every description, are in manner respectful, and particularly the first one at all satisfactory—and also whether declining as the Accountant has done, stating the particulars applying to the claim of the Citizen, who complained of its refusal, to the Head of his Department, but reserving the same, for the president only, is not an instance of insubordination, incompatible with the due administration of the Department, with the public interest, and those of Individuals in any manner concerned in business connected with military concerns, and the insinuation that he will do so, because the representation was made by the direction of the president—a mere pretence, desultory and evasive?" (LS, Adams Family Papers, deposited in the Massachusetts Historical Society, Boston).

To James McHenry

Newyork Octor 1st. 99

Sir

I wait for your instructions concerning the regulations proposed to you with respect to objects of extra expence.[1] As soon as I receive your direction I shall issue orders for having the regulations carried into effect.

With great respect   I am, Sir

If it shall be agreeable to General Pinckney to whom I have written on the subject,[2] it is my wish to employ Major Tousard during the winter, in assisting me to prepare regulations for the service of the Artillery, and at fortifications. As this officer is now employed by you on a special commission[3] I wish to know whether there is any thing in that commission which will interefere with my wish.

Secretary of War.

Df, in the handwriting of Thomas Y. How, Hamilton Papers, Library of Congress.
   1. See H to McHenry, September 17, 1799.
   2. H to Charles Cotesworth Pinckney, October 1, 1799 (listed in the appendix to this volume). H wrote to Pinckney about this matter because Lewis Tousard was "annexed" to Pinckney's "command."
   3. For Tousard's "special commission," see McHenry to Tousard, January 16, 1799, which is printed as note 1 to Tousard to H, March 10, 1799.

From John J. U. Rivardi

Niagara October 2d. 1799

Sir,

I had the honor of receiving your letter of the 26th of August. I have been waiting with anxiety for the arrival of Major Hoops & Captain Still[1] & I begin To apprehend they met with Some accident on the way. Permit me To offer it as my opinion that before I exhibit formally charges against Captain Bruff it would be perhaps proper To wait for a final result of those which he entered against me. I shall however be directed by the instructions which the officers of the Court will have.

Having a greater Number of Sick than Usual & Doctor Muirhead ascribing it in great measure To The want of warmer dress—I issued yesterday Winter clothing To The Troops—thinking that you would not disaprove of that anticipating one month on the usual time of Issues—four or five men belonging To The infantry could get no coats that article having been Some time Since exhausted. I hope that our Supplies will arrive before Winter otherwise the Troops must experience Several Severe wants. I am much allarmed at the Account we have received of Doctor Coffin's illness

ALS, Hamilton Papers, Library of Congress.
   1. See H to Rivardi, August 26, 1799, note 1.

not only for his own Sake but also because it may prevent him from producing in time the documents which he has respecting the Quarter Master's Department.[2] This leads me naturally to renew the Subject of Medical Assistance for this Garrison. The Season approaches during which all intercourse between New Ark & Niagara will be Suspended on Account of the Ice. Should we then have any Sick, requiring attendance, their Situation would be dismal indeed. My anxiety is by no means increased at this Moment by Mrs. Rivardi's Situation—for even when we had a Doctor here, I employed at my own expense a physician of New Ark whenever She wanted one.[3] The Soldiers of this Garrison have been indiscriminately made To understand that they had no more To expect than half a Gill of Rum per ration & they are Satisfied—they have generally however received extra liquor these Six weeks past for fatigue compensation. This Garrison had no wharf—The British having constructed theirs in So Slight a Manner that they allways were carried away by the Ice. I have been occupied for Some time in erecting two which form a comodious & Safe basin for our boats which we used constantly To lose in Stormy weather; by an estimate that business would have cost at least two hundred Pounds, & To The U States it will come To a few Gallons of Rum. The Main wharf is fifty foot in front & better than Seventy near the Shore with Strong land Ties; it was Sunk in water deep enough To admit of any Vessel coming with her Side close To it. I hope that the whole will be completed in a fortnight & it will be a very considerable convenience To The place—as formerly every thing had To be brought in boats. I inclose copies of the reports made by the board appointed To examine the State of the provisions.[4] I or-

2. Dr. John Coffin had acted as quartermaster at Fort Niagara. For information on Coffin's attempts to settle his accounts, see Rivardi to H, March 21, 1799. The following letters, all of which are listed in the appendix to this volume, also refer to Coffin's accounts: Rivardi to H, July 15, 1799; H to Coffin, September 18, 1799; H to William Simmons, September 18, 1799; Simmons to H, September 21, 1799.

3. In Coffin's absence, the garrison of Fort Niagara was dependent on Canadian doctors. See Rivardi to H, July 25, September 12–16, 1799.

4. Rivardi enclosed two such reports. Both are dated September 24, 1799, and are signed by William McNabb and Nanning J. Visscher and countersigned by Rivardi (copies, Hamilton Papers, Library of Congress). These reports state that salted beef and flour issued to the garrison "are in a putrid State and not fit to be issued to the Troops."

dered the putrid meat to be thrown in the river—the damaged flour may be of use for the public cattle. I must remark on that head that I do not understand the Meaning of a letter which Coll. O'Hara wrote lately To the issuing Comissary here, directing him To receipt To The U S. for the provisions deposited at this Garrison & on hand On the first day of October. Could he be ignorant that they were already receipted for? or did he allude To The provisions brought with the last detachment from Oswego. The latter Supposition appears hardly probable as he could not So Soon be apprized of that transaction—if however he made agreements, by which what was in Store was To be considered again as United States property, the latter have Suffered no triffling loss.

The Mail arriving this time So Shortly after the close of the Month it will be impossible To prepare in time the papers of the Garrison for September but by next Post they will be forwarded. I hope also To be able To Transmit a Quarter Master's Return. I received by last mail from The Board of War a Small pamphlet containing the Rudiments of *large Fortification* [5] translated it Seems from the french. It is Too much for beginers & Too little for Such Officers as have gone Through the elements of their profession. An extract of Clairac [6] or a translation of what is to be found on that head in Belair's *Manual de l'Artilleur* [7] would in my opinion have deserved much better to be trusted To The press of Fenno's [8] & To The engraver of Thaccara. [9] In fact there is no large fortification in The United States & little appearance that there will be any Soon, or that our Officers will have To besiege a place fortified by Vauban [10] or Coehorn. [11] My fear of Committing To The press Works full of

5. This is a reference to Jonathan Williams's translation of *The Elements of Fortification*. See Williams to H, June 17, 1799.

6. Louis-André de La Mamie de Clairac, *L'Ingénieur de campagne, ou Traité de la fortification passagère* . . . (Paris: C. A. Jombert, 1749).

7. Rivardi is presumably referring to Alexandre Pierre Julienne de Belair, *Eléments de fortification . . . suivis d'un dictionnaire militaire . . . et d'une explication raisonnée de trente belles planches* . . . (Paris: F. Didot, 1792).

8. John Ward Fenno had become publisher of the *Gazette of the United States, and Philadelphia Daily Advertiser* after the death of his father, John Fenno, in September, 1798.

9. James Thackara, a resident of Philadelphia, was an engraver. In 1794 he had been the partner of John Vallance in a firm of engravers in Philadelphia.

10. Sébastien LePretre, Segneur de Vauban, was a late seventeenth-century military engineer who directed the construction of the fortresses defending France.

11. Menno, baron de Coehorn, was Vauban's contemporary.

Germanismes has deterred me hitherto from Selecting from my papers a few Small treatises which otherwise might perhaps be usefull. I fancy the most essential now would be one on Field fortifications & that of Gaudi, a Prussian Officer, with the additions made by Belair,[12] is I think the best that could be Submitted To Translation, particularly, as the author has contrived easy modes of tracing every Kind of Field Works on the ground without the necessity of recurring To Trigonometrical operations. I take the liberty of inclosing a letter for your Assistant Adjutant General [13] acknowledging the receipt of Such General orders as reached This place.

With the Most respectfull consideration I have the honor to be Sir   Your Most Obedient & Very humble Servant

J J Ulrich Rivardi

Major General A. Hamilton

12. Friedrich Wilhelm von Gaudy, *Instruction adressée aux officiers d'infanterie pour tracer et construire toutes sortes d'ouvrages de campagne, . . . par F. Gaudi, augmentée . . . par A. P. J. Belair* (Paris, 1792). Gaudy's original work is entitled *Versuch einer Anweisung für Officiers von der Infanterie, wie Feldschanzen von allerhand Art angelegt und erbauet, und wie verschiedene andere Posten in Defensiensstand gesetzt werden können* . . . (Wesel: F. J. Röder, 1767).
13. Abraham Ellery.

To John J. U. Rivardi

New York, October 2, 1799. ". . . I have been, for some time, engaged with General Wilkinson in forming a plan respecting the disposition of the western army generally which will include the posts in your quarter.[1] It is part of this plan that the garrison of Niagara be reinforced, to consist at present of two companies of infantry and half a company of artillerists. Some doubts have been suggested whether it would not be proper to relinquish the post which is now occupied, and construct a fortification on some other part of the streight. This question will in future receive a full consideration. In the meantime it is a reason for avoiding all expence except such as may be absolutely necessary to preserve valuable things from falling into ruin. Your different letters mention various expences from time to time incurred. This method of proceeding in detail tends to create difficulty. It is therefore my wish that you would, as soon as possible, present me with a general plan stating the objects which it will be of importance to accomplish, and the money that will be necessary for the purpose. Let the objects be stated distinctly with the expence of each one that they may be considered hereafter and executed in whole or in part as may be deemed adviseable. . . . I am pleased with the kind and neighborly conduct of the British officers [2] and doubt not that you will as often as occasion shall occur manifest a similiar disposition. You may, if you think proper, make known to the British Commandant [3] the sense I entertain of his polite and friendly offices. . . . I have seen the person of whom you speak [4] and have conversed with him on the subject of a carrying place. . . . I have written to Mr. Glen [5] to provide a boat for the use of the garrison. . . ." [6]

Df, in the handwriting of H and Thomas Y. How, Hamilton Papers, Library of Congress.
    1. See James Wilkinson to H, September 6, 1799; H to George Washington, September 9, 1799.
    2. This subject was discussed in Rivardi to H, July 15, 1799 (listed in the appendix to this volume).
    3. John McDonnell was the commanding officer of the British post at Niagara.
    4. This is a reference to John Laughton, a resident of Fort Schlosser, New York. Rivardi had introduced him to H in his letter of July 15, 1799 (listed in the appendix to this volume).
    5. H to Henry Glen, October 2, 1799 (listed in the appendix to this volume).
    6. Rivardi had requested such a boat in Rivardi to H, June 27, 1799.

To Lewis Tousard

New York, October 2, 1799. ". . . I am very sensible of the necessity of more organization and system on the subject of fortifications than now exist. The thing has had my attention and will continue to have it untill the object is accomplished. It is my intention, if the views of the Secretary of War shall not prevent,[1] to employ you during the winter at or near New York in assisting to prepare regulations for the service of the corps of Artillerists."

Df, in the handwriting of Thomas Y. How, Hamilton Papers, Library of Congress.
    1. See H to James McHenry, October 1, 1799.

From Daniel Bradley

Staunton [*Virginia*] *October 3, 1799.* ". . . we are in great want of a supply of recruiting money unless some is immediately forwarded we shall be obldged to desist from recruiting—as the Officers have no money of their own to advance, they nor their recruits have received a farthing of pay since we left Tennessee 1st. April, and they are labouring under great disadvantage, for the want of it."

ALS, Hamilton Papers, Library of Congress.

To James McHenry

New York October 3. 1799

Sir

The following arrangement as to Hutts [1] appears to me expedient. Each hutt to be fourteen by Sixteen feet for all but the field officers. One hut for Twelve privates or Eight non Commissioned Officers. One hut for each Captain and each of the Regimental Staff. One hut for every two subalterns. A hutt for a Lt Col of 14 by 24 feet and for each Major of fourteen by 22 feet. One hutt as a Kitchen to every mess of officers and to each field Officer.

It is contemplated that the hutts be roofed with Boards—unless where slabs can be had very cheap. The Albany board being always 14 feet in length [2] and this being from convenience a pretty common length of other boards it has had some influence in determining the size of the hutts. Boards will also be wanted for bunks. Such of the boards as can be preserved entire may be afterwards sold for nearly their cost. The slabs would be worth little more than mere fuel.

I send you an estimate of carpenters tools requisite in the opinion of General Stevens (who is a *professional* Judge) for hutting a Regiment.[3]

It is important that your sense of the matter should be received without delay as time begins to press.

In the execution of the plan slight deviations may be expedient (with reference to the kind of materials &c.) to fulfil the general views of the plan.

As soon as your sentiments shall be signified I shall proceed to order provision to be made—except of such articles as you shall inform me are already procured, or to be procured elsewhere.

I presume Carpenters sufficient will be found in each Regiment to conduct the roofing &c, but the service being irrelative to their established duty, there must be some extra compensation. It may however in some cases be necessary to engage a few additional hands of this description. In every thing however œconomy as much as possible will be consulted. With great respect

I have the honor to be   Yr. Obed ser

Js. Mc.Henry Esq Secy of W

ADf, Hamilton Papers, Library of Congress.
    1. These huts were to be used for winter quarters for the troops. H had requested Ebenezer Stevens to prepare a plan for him (H to Stevens, September 23, 1799; Stevens to H, September 23, 28, 1799 [all listed in the appendix to this volume]).
    2. The "Albany board," which was of inferior quality, was irregular in width, and contrary to H's statement it was from ten to fifteen feet in length.
    3. Stevens to H, second letter of October 2, 1799 (listed in the appendix to this volume).

From William C. Bentley

Richmond [*Virginia*] *October 4, 1799.* "A few days before my arival at this place, some of the Troops of the Regimt. of Artillerists & Engineers, of Capt. Eddins's[1] Company, stationed at this place, were guilty of a most violent and flagrant breach of Civil Authority; the Circumstances were these; One of their new recruits was discovered to be a fugitive from justice, he had been committed to a County Court jail for Horse-stealing, which he broke and fled from. The Shff of that County discouvering him among the Soldiers in Town, had him apprehended under a Warrant from a Magistrate of this City, and which in possession of the Sheriff, he was rescued by Six or Seven of Eddins's Soldiers, and Suffered to make his escape.[2] This has afforded another opportunity for the Jacobines Printers to sport with the *Standing Army*, as they call it; The paper of this place, called the Examiner [3] of which, that *Scotch Fugitive* Callender,[4] has the direction, has detailed the circumstances to the public, rather highly coloured, and has called on all his *Yoke Mates*, (using his own Words) to notice it in their papers. . . ."

ALS, Hamilton Papers, Library of Congress.

1. Samuel Eddins, a veteran of the American Revolution, was a captain in the Second Regiment of Artillerists and Engineers.

2. On October 1, 1799, the [Richmond] *Virginia Argus* reported: "The following remarkable circumstance took place at the Swan Tavern, in this city, on last Friday evening:

"Joseph Fulcher Tribble, a person who lately enlisted in the troops of the United States, quartered here, had some months ago been committed to the jail of Mechlenburg county for horse-stealing. On Friday last, this man was apprehended in Richmond, on a warrant from Dr. Foushe, by Mr. Holman, constable. By him he was given up to Mr. Speed, deputy sheriff of Mechlenburg county. This gentleman took Tribble, for the evening, to the Swan tavern, where he had provided a room for the fellow's confinement.

"In the course of the evening (we have not learned the exact time of night) Mr. Miles Carey, a Cadet belonging, it is said, to the Company of Captain Eddins, called on Mr. Speed, and obtained leave to see the prisoner. This Gentleman staid but a short time in the room. When he came out of it, one Sergeant Hacket, with seven soldiers in the federal uniform, rushed into the room and set the prisoner at liberty, the deputy and his party not being a match for eight armed men.

"Several Gentlemen, were present when this happened. Carey and Hacket have been committed to jail."

3. The [Richmond] *Examiner* was published by Meriwether Jones.

4. James Thomson Callender, a native of Scotland, was a naturalized citizen. In 1799 he joined the staff of the *Examiner*. For his earlier publications, see Oliver Wolcott, Jr., to H, July 3, 1797, note 1.

From Josias Carvel Hall

Havre de Grace [Maryland] October 4, 1799. Discusses supplies, relative rank of officers, and military routine. States: ". . . My Idea [1] of substituting hand Labor, with Ignominy to Death, for Desertion was the crude Suggestion of the moment. If it merits your Consideration you can have it carried into effect by naming the Place to which you will have them sent. Perhaps branding them on some conspicuous Part of the Face with an hot Iron would not be an improper addition. Severe Floging will never mend the Principles of a Soldier. In European Armies Desertion is punished with Death. To American Habits of thinking this appears inadequate—every alleviatiting Circumstance is laid hold of the Court, & of those condemned very few are exicuted. Tho' a very high military Crime I confess I can not discover in it much moral Turpitude. It generally arrises from Levity or that Desire of change incidental to Humanity. If Death is to be the ordinary Punishment of Desertion what is to be allotted to the high aggrevation of deserting from their Post misbehaving before the Enimy. The Spirit of the American Constitution & Laws will not admit of runing the Gantlosse &c previously I have taken the Liberty to throw out these desultary Observations in the hope, if the Subject should strike you in the same Point of view that it does me, that you will devise some more adequate Punishment from which no Hope of Escape will be left, reserving Death for Desertion with aggrevating Circumstances. . . ."

AL (incomplete), Hamilton Papers, Library of Congress.
    1. On September 11, 1799, Hall had written to H, in a letter which is listed in the appendix to this volume, to suggest that deserters be put to work on fortifications. On September 14, 1799, H had replied, in a letter which is also listed in the appendix to this volume, that he doubted "very much the efficacy of the punishment of hard labour." H then added: "However, if a Court Martial shall be disposed to try such an expedient I will not object to the measure. I have heretofore spoken to you of the frequency of desertion, and of the necessity of repressing it by severe punishment. It is not my wish to influence opinion in Any particular case, but I believe that a few examples of capital punishment, perhaps one in each regiment, will be found indispensable."

From Francisco de Miranda [1]

London ce 4 Octb. 1799.

Voici mon digne Ami, des Papiers [2] d'une grande importance pour le sort futur de ma Patrie—et tres interessants aussi pour la prosperité de la votre. Vous pouvez compter sur leur Autenticité, puisque les Origineaux sont dans mon pouvoir.

Je vous prie de les garder avec la Reserve convenable—et de me dire confidentiellement si je pourrois en tout cas trouver chez vous les petits secours dont nous avons besoin pour donner l'impulsion premiere!

à Dieu mon Cher Ami—ecrivez moi sans delay, et toujours sous envolope de notre mutuel Ami Mr. King.[3]

Truly & sincerely yours.   Miranda.

Alexr. Hamilton Esqr: &c. &c. &c.

ALS, Hamilton Papers, Library of Congress; ADfS, Academia Nacional de la Historia, Caracas, Venezuela.

1. For information on Miranda's plans for the liberation of Spanish America, see Miranda to H, April 1, 1797, February 7, April 6–June 7, August 17, October 19–November 10, 1798; H to Miranda, August 22, 1798; Rufus King to H, May 12, July 31, October 20, 1798, January 21, March 4, 9, 1799; H to King, August 22, 1798; Timothy Pickering to H, August 21–22, 1798.

2. Four of these enclosures have been found. They are: two copies (one in Spanish, one in English misdated November 21, 1799) of a letter "intercepted on board of a Spanish packet Boat, & transmitted to England by the Governor of Trinidad [Thomas Picton]," November 21, 1798 (copies, Hamilton Papers, Library of Congress); a proclamation signed on January 28, 1799, at the Venezuelan island of Margarita that Miranda annexed to the intercepted letter (copy, Hamilton Papers, Library of Congress); an English translation of a memorial, dated May 21, 1799, by Manuel Gual, Venezuelan revolutionist, to Lieutenant General Thomas Trigge, the commander in chief of the Windward Islands (copy, Hamilton Papers, Library of Congress); an English translation of a letter from Gual to Miranda, July 12, 1797 (copy, Hamilton Papers, Library of Congress).

3. Rufus King.

From Nathan Rice

Hingham [Massachusetts] Octr 4th. 1799

My dear General

Your favour Circular of 17th Sept.[1] I have receivd. I hope & trust the suggestions therein of the incautious remarks of officers were not applicable to any of my regiment. I am too sensible of the use which would be made by the soldiery of such remarks from their officers, not to have instantly checked them. You request of me a very accurate & special report of the quantity and quality of all the articles which have been receivd. I do not judge myself sufficiently informed of the quality of all the articles supplied, to make a report. I will make it a subject of my investigation but will observe that the article of Shoes is a sourse of great complaint both on account of the size & quality, my paymaster informs me of the number he has recevd. as many as one half can never be worn by the men; being so much under size & by the officers I am told they are of a very inferior quality particularly in the making.

In reply to yours of the 9th I should not have solicited Mr. Roulstons appointment to a first Lieutenantcy,[2] had I conceived it was to be made on the principle of regular promotion—but the appointments being incomplete—new ones daily making & the relative rank in the different grades unsettled; I judged no one would consider himself superseded any more than he was by the last appointments of Hastings Mackay [3] & others.

In settling the relative rank of the company officers, are we to be pointed to no principle by which we are to be governed? Is former rank & service to have no precedency? Nor the first apointments to have no priority over those appointed to vacancies happening consequent on nonacceptances. It is an unplesant & unthankfull task & I must beg, the arrangement may be considered as comeing from you or the War office.

Permit me to beg that some payment may be speedily made the Troops. It will satisfy the engaged and I think very much accelerate the filling up of the regiments.

I am with the utmost respect   your Obt. Servant   N: Rice

P.S. Are all Majors of Infantry considered of one Grade or are the first Majors a grade superior to the 2d Majors of Regiments. If they are not I am apprehensive the principle of rank will so opperate in the two Regts. of Massachutts,[4] as to induce Major Walker to resign; as it will give Roe of Colo Hunnewells rank of him.[5] I should regret it much as he is an excellent of⟨ficer⟩.

Yrs   N: Rice

ALS, Hamilton Papers, Library of Congress.
    1. "Circular to the Commandants of Regiments," September 7–17, 1799.
    2. See Rice to H, August 31, 1799.
    3. This is a reference to the fact that most of the officers in the Fourteenth Regiment of Infantry had been appointed on January 8, 1799 (*Executive Journal*, I, 299–301, 303), and that Samuel Mackay had been appointed a first lieutenant on March 3, 1799 (*Executive Journal*, I, 322, 323). For the dates of Daniel Hastings's appointments, see Rice to H, May 24, 1799, note 2. For the dates of John Roulstone's appointments, see Rice to H, August 31, 1799, note 4.
    4. This is a reference to the Fourteenth and Fifteenth Regiments of Infantry.
    5. Rice may have been confused, for both men held the same rank. John Walker was the first major and Isaac Winslow the second major in the Fourteenth Regiment of Infantry (Heitman, *United States Army*, I, 107). In the

Fifteenth Regiment, John Rowe was the first major and William Jones the second major (Heitman, *United States Army*, I, 109). On the other hand, Rice may be referring to the fact that Rowe was a veteran of the American Revolution, in which he had held the rank of ensign, while Walker had not held a military commission before his appointment in 1799 (Heitman, *United States Army*, I, 848). Walker's name, however, had been placed ahead of Rowe's on the list submitted to the Senate (*Executive Journal*, I, 299). Rice was concerned about the relative rank of the majors because, of the lieutenant colonel commandants of the Fourteenth, Fifteenth, and Sixteenth Regiments, he was senior in rank and therefore would be commandant of the brigade at their winter quarters (H to Rice, October 4, 1799, note 4).

For the rules governing relative rank, see the enclosure to James McHenry to H, July 20, 1799. See also H to McHenry, July 8, 1799; McHenry to H, September 3, 1799.

To Nathan Rice

New York October 4
1799

Sir

Inclosed is a duplicate of my letter of the   [1] by which you are instructed to purchase ground for the purpose of Winter Quarters. I am now to request that you will immediately require of the Contractors to procure on public account the number of boards or slabs or both which you shall deem requisite for the roofs doors & windows of hutts sufficient for Two complete Regiments with their Officers and for the floor of the hutts of the officers and for buncks for the non Commissioned officers and privates. It is contemplated that the latter will dispense with flooring as was done during the late war; or will make the floors out of the fragments of the wood cut from the premises; and that the commissioned officers as usual will be provided with their own camp beds and camp stools. Nails must also be procured at the rate of   pounds to a full Regiment. You are already informed [2] that three Regiments are to quarter together; but it is supposed that these during the present winter may not average more than 400 each. If it is found they will exceed the provision will be extended. Sufficient ground must be alloted in each case for a complete Regiment.

ADf, Hamilton Papers, Library of Congress.
1. This space and subsequent spaces in this letter were left blank in MS. H is referring to his letter to Rice of September 27, 1799.
2. H to Rice, first letter of August 22, 1799.

The following dimensions for hutts are conceived to be the most eligible viz. those for the non Commissioned Officers and privates   feet those for the Company Officers   those for Lt Colonels commandant   those for Majors   . One hutt is to be allowed to every Twelve corporals or privates, one to every Eight serjeants with the two Chief Musicians, one to each captain & each of the Regimental Staff one to every two subalterns one to each field officer and one as a Kitchen to each Mess of officers & to each field officer.

The number of Albany Boards of fourteen feet in length and   inches in breadth which are estimated to be necessary for the hutts of a Regiment in respect to the abovementioned particulars is   .

While this is mentioned as a guide, the number must of course vary with the dimensions of the boards, which are made in your Quarter and with the more or less of use which shall be made of slabs.

In this quarter boards have been preferred because they can be afterwards sold for nearly their first cost, while slabs (the price of which would be about two thirds of that of boards) could not be sold again but as fuel.

It is possible that in the vicinity of the place for your Quarters slabs may be obtained at so cheap a rate as to render them preferable in the view of œconomy to Boards. This is submitted to your judgment; but it would be agreeable that you should first confer on the subject with the Agent of the War Department.

The dimensions of the hutts have been somewhat influenced by the length of Albany Boards and by the desire to preserve them in order that they may be in a condition to be sold again with little or no loss.

If the size of your boards should be different you are at liberty to vary the dimensions of the hutts of the non Commissioned officers and privates with the same view. This will lead to a different distribution of persons to each hutt. The number *Twelve* however appears to me an eligible Standard for a mess. Experience in some of the European armies has proved that large messes, by promoting savings tend to the comfort of the troops. And in the formation, which I contemplate for the full complement of a Regiment, Twelve will form the smallest subdivision.

Hence I should not wish the dimensions to be altered unless for some material inducement of œconomy.

The Hutts of the Non Commissioned Officers and privates should be in one line of the Company Officers in another fifty feet distant and of the field officers in a third fifty feet distant from the last. The distances may however depend on the form of the ground. Particular care must be taken that there be no waste of Timber or wood. The present may not be the only winter in which the Troops may be quartered at the place intended. E. Stevens Esquire has been Instructed [3] to procure & forward a supply of Carpenters Tools. It is presumed that men will be found in the Regiments who can execute such parts as may require a degree of Carpenters knowlege.

The senior of the Lieutenant Colonels Commandant by the Rules lately promulged (who I presume is yourself) [4] will assume the command. If I am mistaken in supposing you to be the senior you will inform me of it. If it be another you will write to him accordingly giving him a copy of this letter for his government but you will nevertheless go on with the preparatory measures.

The men already recruited are to be drawn as fast as possible to the place of their winter Quarters and are to be put under cover without delay. Such as may be successively recruited are also to be drawn thither and for this purpose an extra provision of materials for hutts is to be made by the men who may be first on the ground. But the recruiting service is still to proceed until each regiment shall be carried to its Complement. Accordingly after assigning a proportionate number of officers to the command of the men already enlisted, the others are to continue on the recruiting service in their respective subdistricts. You will immediately inform Colonels Hunewell & Graves of the precise place of the Winter Quarters.[5]

3. H to Ebenezer Stevens, October 5, 1799.

4. This is apparently a reference to the fact that on the basis of rank before their appointments in 1799 Rice outranked Richard Hunewell, commanding officer of the Fifteenth Regiment of Infantry, and Rufus Graves, commanding officer of the Sixteenth Regiment. Graves had held no military rank before 1799, while during the American Revolution Hunewell had been a second lieutenant and Rice had been a major (Heitman, *United States Army*, I, 555, 827).

For the rules governing relative rank, see the enclosure to James McHenry to H, July 20, 1799. See also H to McHenry, July 8, 1799; McHenry to H, September 3, 1799.

5. H enclosed in the letter printed above a letter dated October 4, 1799, to Rufus Graves and Richard Hunewell. This letter, which is listed in the appendix to this volume, reads in part: "The town of Uxbridge or Oxford in the State of Massachusetts (I believe the latter) of which Col Rice will more cer-

You are already apprised that the contractors are to furnish the means of transportation by land & by Water.⁶

If you find this plan marked with a spirit of œconomy, you must recollect that a strict attention to oeconomy is not less necessary to the true interest of the Officers than to that of the country. So great is the unavoidable expence of every military establishment (greater in proportion in our country than in any other) that unless all the savings are made which can consist with propriety it will be impossible for the government to maintain the forces requisite for security or to make and continue those provisions which are really essential to the comfort and respectability of the army. These ideas are so important that they cannot be too deeply impressed upon the minds of Officers.

Yet if any thing more than is contemplated by this letter shall be necessary to a reasonable accomodation of the troops suggestions to that end will be well received & carefully examined.

---

tainly inform you is to be the Winter Quarters of the 14th. 15th & 16th Regiments. There they are to be hutted for which proper measures have been directed. You will lose no time in conveying the men who have been inlisted to that place, and when the season will permit you will cause those who may be afterwards inlisted to follow. Tents and baggage will of course accompany. You will take care to allot to these a due proportion of officers under the command of one of your Majors, continuing the others within the respective subdistricts upon the recruiting service. You will yourself continue for the present at your Regimental Rendezvous to direct that service.
"The Senior of the Commandants of the three Regiments is to command at the Winter Quarters. . . ." (ADf, Hamilton Papers, Library of Congress.)
6. H to Rice, May 31, first letter of August 22, 1799.

From John F. Hamtramck

Fort Fayette Pittsburgh Octobr the 5th 1799

Sir

as you have requested me to give you my opinion fully on the Military affairs of this Country,¹ I take the liberty of Submiting Some Observations for your Consideration.

it appears to me that the Want of Discipline in our troops is produced from the following causes. 1st. the incompleatness of the Regiments which for the want of Men never allows an officer a

Command equal to his Rank, the Consequence of which is, that after Detailing for the ordinary Duties of the Day (as mentioned in my letter of the 19th. Ult.) there are not a sufficient number of Men left for exercise & manoeuvring. 2d the Scattered, mutilated and mixed situation of the Regiments—Companies at an immense distance from their own doing duty with other Regiments, others Cut up and distributed to Different Posts, and officers for years together doing Duty with Regiments they do not belong to. These defects may be altogether attributed to the Smallness of the Establishment never full, appropriated to garrison an extensive frontier and augmented by the Delay that has been generaly made in filling vacancies and the tardiness of Officers in joining their Regiments after Receiving appointments.

To Remedy these evils and to acquire a Knowledge of Garrison Duty and the tactics of the Field, would be in my opinion to Keep the Regiments together as much as the Nature of the Service would permit by prescribing a Certain District that it Should garrison and no part of it to be taken out of the limits (except for Commands) without the most urgent Necessity—that at the Head Quarters of the Regiment there Should always be six full Companies or at least a Battalion Compleatly officered, together with the Staff, the Coll. and one of the Majors, by which Disposition it would become the Nursery & military School of the Regiment, the other Companies if possible intire, Should occupy not exceeding the limit of one year Such number of Posts within the District as would be found Necessary to Keep up, for we find that when a Detachment is too long by its Self, it is Apt (if the Expression may be Allowed) to Degenerate in to habits of private life.

I have frequently gone in to a Garrison Composed of a small Detachment where an uninterupted Silence reigned, giving it the resemblance more of a Convent (where two or three foot paths Seen thro' the grass were the only indications of its being inhabited) than a place of Arms. The Colonel of a Regiment or a Major Should in the summer time exercise all the troops off Duty twice a Day, and at least once a Month with Blank Catriges. The Garrison Should frequently be marched out a few Miles, Encamp & be employed in Making of fachines, saucissons, gabions, erect field Fortifications, Carry on lines of Approaches, Construct Batteries &c &c &c thus the officers and men in a party of pleasure would gain a Knowledge in the art of war and prepare themselves to Realize at a future Day the practice of their School. we have no Military Authors that treat on Garrison Duty exept foreign ones, and as they are without authority to us, the officers are Every Day at loss which to adopt, the Consequence is, that there is not two Garrisons whose Duty or police is alike—whether a treatise on that head is not wanted is also Submitted.

A practice of challinging members of Court Martial has frequently given the Culprit an opportunity of procrastinating his tryal: soldiers have frequently done it. I ask whether the challenger Should not be made to Shew Cause to be judged of by the Court or Commanding officer? my Reason for the question is from the Variety of opinions held up—many officers are ignerant on that Head: would it not be well to have Some good treatise upon Courts Martial bound with the articles of war and one furnished to each Company? You are also well acquainted with the Difficulty of punishing offenders in Small Detachments that have not officers Sufficient to form a Court martial by which means where an officer is *scrupulous*, offenders frequently goes unpunished to the great injury of the Service. Could not Some means be fallen on to remedy this Defect?

I believe Sir you will agree with me that no persons ever ought to Receive a Commission without at least understanding the Common Rules of Arithmetic and how to write, But Nevertheless we have had a Number without Knowing how to do either one, or the other; and in fact added to the other Obstacles to our improvements, we may fairly Count upon the Number of Miserable appointments that have been made.[2] the want of Non Commissioned Officers of fair characters and *Some* education is very injurious to the service, whether it is owing to want of sufficient pay to induce men Competent to the Business to engage or any other Cause it is probable you Can Best judge.

there appears to be as great Deficiency some where both Respecting the quality of the Clothing of the troops and the time of its arrival in this Country. the secretary of war in his Circular letter has accounted for the former.[3] But in order to use water transportation with Certainty the Clothing for the *Summer* Should always be at

Pittsburgh in March and that for the winter the latter end of May or Begining of June.

I wish to Know whether Detroit does not Come within the Discription of a Fortifyed Town. it Certainly is Stockaded at public expence to the amount of some thousand Dollars and in the Night time under the protection of the sentries of the Garrison. it has been my opinion that the inhabitans were under the Control of the Commanding Officer as far as related to the preservation of the town.

As the Regulation of the war office Relative to the Recruiting Service did not Contemplate that Foreigners who were then in Actual service Should be Discharged,[4] I have given it as my opinion that Foreigners who had served six and eight years in any of the Regiments in this Country and who wanted to Reinlist Should be taken—if I have erred in this or in the Opinion I had formed of the preservation of the Town of Detroit I beg you will excuse me and give me an early information in order to have it Corrected. I have the honor to be Sir with Very great Respect

Your Most Obedient and Very humble servent   J F Hamtramck

P.S. Since writing the above I have had the honor of your letter of the 24th September, and if Practicable the garrison of McMackinac will be withdrawn agreeably to your Direction.[5] I Shall Send an Express this Day to Detroit.   J F H

ALS, Hamilton Papers, Library of Congress.

1. H to Hamtramck, June 6, 1799.

2. In the margin opposite this sentence H wrote: "Secy of War." H sent this information to James McHenry on November 11, 1799 (letter listed in the appendix to Volume XXIV). See McHenry to H, second letter of November 25, 1799.

3. See "Circular to the Commandants of Regiments," July 22, 1799.

4. This is a reference to Article 3 of the March, 1799, pamphlet entitled *Rules and Regulations Respecting the Recruiting Service*. Article 3 was amended by a general order on June 6, 1799. For the text of this article, see "General Orders," June 6, 1799. See also H to Jonathan Dayton, August 6, 1798, note 6; McHenry to H, March 21, 1799.

5. In this letter, which is listed in the appendix to this volume, H wrote: "It is part of a general arrangement . . . that the garrison at Michillimackinac consist of a Serjeant and twelve artillerists together with a Lieut. two serjeants, and twenty four rank and file Infantry. I have therefore to request that you will take immediate measures to withdraw . . . all the troops except the number mentioned above, from that fortress. . . ."

From Charles Cotesworth Pinckney

Newport Rhode Island [October] [1] 5th: 1799

Dear Sr:

Your favour of the 26th. ultimo did not reach me till last Evening. I should have the greatest pleasure in meeting you at Trenton for the purpose you mention; but Mrs: Pinckney's health & very depressed spirits will not permitt me to quit her at present, and it is impossible for her in her actual situation to accompany me there. She is certainly better since her arrival at this place, but the swelling of her feet & legs, which commenced about three days ago, alarms her very much, tho Dr: Senter [2] declares it is not a dangerous symptom.

In the regulations you may form I wish you would attend to the officers doing duty as much as possible with the men belonging to their respective Regiments & Companies: I have Officers doing duty in Georgia whose Corps are on the Mississippi. Ought there not also to be a regular rotation in Garrison duty, that no Corps might be permanently placed in a disagreeable station, but each in their turn take the good & the bad? As the Season is now arrived when the engagements of the young Men to the Farmers & Planters in the upper part of the Southern States are expiring, I trust the Recruiting service will go on successfully. I long to see a body of Men collected on the Potowmac & on the Savannah, that I may begin to discipline them. It will be impossible to do so properly while they are in minute detachments. When I had the pleasure of seeing General Wilkinson here,[3] he mentioned that he had some valuable Maps & Plans of which he wished you to have copies, but he thought they could not be completed in the time he had to remain. I informed him of a Method which I learned when I was last in France of preparing paper to take off rapidly maps & plans of fortifications, and which is generally practised by the French Engineers and was used by myself in a late tour to the Southward. I will describe it, lest it should have escaped the General's memory. Oil the quantity of paper you have occasion for (I have done six or eight sheets at a time). Take a quantity of bran & spread it about an Inch thick evenly on a table; place a coarse cloth upon the bran, then your sheets of oiled paper the one upon the other on the cloth, cover the paper with a stratum of bran evenly laid on about half an Inch or an Inch in thickness, put on this another coarse cloth—then with a Washerwoman's Iron made very hot, but not sufficiently so as to burn, iron the upper cloth for about five or six minutes or longer if necessary: by this means the oil will be in a great measure extracted from the paper, & yet will leave it so transparent that on being placed on a map the most delicate line will be seen through it, whereby the map may be accurately copied as fast as the fingers can move. On this paper if properly prepared you may trace the plan with common or indian ink, & shade it with what colours you please; for the heat will have extracted all that part of the oil which would prevent the paper from taking readily the ink or colours.

The letter you mention to have written to me concerning the recruiting service [4] &c I have not received. I left Charleston the 1st: of sepr: & have heard from thence as late as the 13th: when no such letter had arrived. If it gets there safe, it will be acted upon in the same manner as if I was present, but for fear of a miscarriage one of your aids had better send me a duplicate.

I have applied for & obtained for my Brother's elder Son who is in his twentieth year a Lieutenancy in the first Regiment of Artillerists & Engineers,[5] as I intend to make him one of my Aids that I may immediately superintend his military studies. I will be obliged to you not to arrange him in the recruiting service. Captn: Thornton [6] the senior Captain in the 8th: Regiment is my other aid. Be assured I remain with sentiments of sincere regard & esteem

 Yours affectionately   Charles Cotesworth Pinckney

P.S: I open my letter to say your favour of the 1st: instant is this moment brought in. I transmitted a furlough for Major Bradley to the Secretary of War last week, on being informed you had referred it to me.[7] I chearfully consent to Major Toussard's being employed as you wish the ensuing winter.[8]

Major general Hamilton

ALS, Hamilton Papers, Library of Congress.

1. Pinckney misdated this letter "Decr. 5th: 1799."

2. Isaac Center, a native of Londonderry, New Hampshire, and a veteran of the American Revolution, received his medical education in Newport, Rhode Island. In 1779 he resigned from the Army and began his medical practice in Cranston, Rhode Island, from which town he was elected to the Rhode Island General Assembly. In 1784 he moved to Newport. When he died in 1799, he was one of the most prominent physicians in the United States.

3. See H to George Washington, September 23, 1799, note 1.

4. H to Pinckney, August 13, 1799.

5. Thomas Pinckney, Jr., was appointed a lieutenant in the First Regiment of Artillerists and Engineers on September 24, 1799, during the recess of the Senate. His name was submitted for confirmation on April 1, 1800 (*Executive Journal*, I, 342, 355).

6. Presley Peter Thornton was appointed a captain on January 10, 1799 (*Executive Journal*, I, 300, 305).

7. Daniel Bradley had first requested H to grant him a leave in a letter dated July 5, 1799 (listed in the appendix to this volume). Bradley repeated his request in his letter to H of August 9, 1799. H, however, refused Bradley's request because Bradley was under Pinckney's command (H to Bradley, August 22, October 1, 1799 [listed in the appendix to this volume]). H finally wrote to Pinckney about Bradley's leave on October 1, 1799 (listed in the appendix to this volume).

8. See H to James McHenry, October 1, 1799, note 2; H to Lewis Tousard, October 2, 1799.

To Ebenezer Stevens

New York October 5th. 1799

Sir:

The eleventh, twelfth and thirteenth regiments are to be quartered in hutts on Green Brook in the state of New Jersey, at a place nine miles distant from New Brunswick, and twelve miles distant from Amboy.

You will immediately make arrangements with Colonel Smith [1] for the conveyance of his regiment to it's destination in the most oeconomical mode.

The thirteenth will come by water to Staten Island or Amboy. If they land on Staten Island they will report themselves to you, and you will take measures for assisting their progress to Amboy where they will be met by the contractor for New Jersey.[2] The baggage can go by water and the men by land to the point opposite to Amboy from which they can be ferried over.

You will arrange with the contractor what may be necessary on his part for the accommodation of the troops.

You will also purchase without delay and cause to be forwarded to the place of quarters [Three thousand] Albany boards and [Three hundred] [3] pounds of nails. There being no Brigade Quarter Master these articles will be delivered to the Quarter Master of the eleventh regiment to be distributed among the regiments according to the orders of the commanding officer.

You will also open a communication with the proper officer at the seat of government for obtaining the Carpenter's tools specified in your estimate [4] not only for the three regiments above mentioned, but for the fourteenth, fifteenth and sixteenth regiments also which will be quartered during the winter in the town of Oxford in the state of Massachusetts. The best route to them will be by way of Providence. If not already provided you will endeavor to obtain permission to provide them so that there may be as little delay as possible.[5]

With great consideration I am, Sir   yr. obt. sevt.   A Hamilton

General Stevens

LS, in the handwriting of Thomas Y. How and H, New-York Historical Society, New York City.
1. William S. Smith was the commanding officer of the Twelfth Regiment of Infantry.
2. Elias B. Dayton. On September 30, 1799, James McHenry had sent H copies of the War Department contracts with Dayton (listed in the appendix to this volume).
3. The material within brackets is in H's handwriting.
4. Stevens sent this estimate in Stevens to H, October 2, 1799 (listed in the appendix to this volume).
5. Stevens's endorsement of this letter reads: "recd & and. same day." The reply has not been found.

From Ebenezer Stevens

[*New York, October 5, 1799.* On the envelope of the letter Hamilton wrote to him on October 5, 1799, Stevens wrote: "recd. & and. same day." *Letter not found.*]

From Caleb Swan [1]

Trenton, October 5, 1799. Protests against having to send money by mail to Army officers whom he does not know. States that it has always been a rule "to make a book entry of cash received or paid, at the time of the transaction, filing the voucher at the same time." Also writes: "As there is provision . . . for the travelling expences of military Officers, . . . whether in the first outset in business, it will not be advantageous as well to the public, as to the troops, for the Regimental Pay Masters . . . after the musters are made . . . [to] come for once at least to this Office. . . ." Adds: "In doing this they will get an insight into their business, which they cannot so readily acquire by barely seeing the forms."

ALS, Hamilton Papers, Library of Congress.
   1. For background to this letter, see H to Swan, September 22, 23, 1799; "General Orders," September 24, 1799; James McHenry to H, second letter of September 28, 1799.

To James McHenry

New York October 6th. 99

Sir

General Wilkinson has just returned to this city, [1] and will set out together with myself for Trenton [2] on Monday in order to settle definitively with you the requisite arrangements for the Western Army.

With great respect   I am Sir

Secretary of War

Df, in the handwriting of Thomas Y. How, Hamilton Papers, Library of Congress.
   1. James Wilkinson had been on a trip to New England. See H to George Washington, September 23, 1799, note 1.
   2. The Government had moved its offices to Trenton because of a yellow fever epidemic in Philadelphia. See McHenry to H, August 29, 1799.

To Thomas Lloyd Moore [1]

New York October 6th. 1799

Sir

It is afflicting to learn that Such a dispute as you state in your letter of the third instant should have occurred between two officers of the American army. Particular attachment to *any foreign nation* is an exotic sentiment which, where it exists, must derogate from the exclusive affection due to our own country. Partiality to France at this late date is a bad symptom. The profession of it by Captain Johnson, in my opinion, does him no honour. How far it ought to impair confidence must depend in a degree on personal character. But as often as a similar byass is manifested, the conduct of the person ought to engage the vigilant Attention of his commanding officer. I hesitate as to what my duty requires on the occasion, and must think further of the matter. You will be pleased to ascertain and inform me whether Lt. Irving be an American citizen or not.

You will receive another letter of this date on the subject of Winter Quarters.[2]

With Considr & esteem   I am, Sir   yr obt St

Col. Moore

Df, in the handwriting of Thomas Y. How, Hamilton Papers, Library of Congress.

1. This letter concerns a duel on September 12, 1799, in which Captain Andrew Johnson shot and killed Lieutenant John Sharp. Both men were members of the Tenth Regiment of Infantry, of which Moore was the commanding officer. The events leading up to this duel are discussed in Moore to H, September 17, 20, October 3, 1799; H to Moore, September 18, 30, 1799, all of which are listed in the appendix to this volume. In his letter to H of October 3, 1799, Moore wrote in part: ". . . The particular subject of the dispute between Cap. Johnston & Lt. [David] Irving was this. Cap. Johnston advocated the French nation by saying that notwithstanding the treatment we have recd. he would rather take part with it, than with Great Britain or words to this effect. The other expressed himself warmly in favor of G. Britain and (I believe) declared himself to be a British Subject. Cap. Johnston on this made use of very harsh language to Lt. Irving. It being in Lt. Sharps tent he interfered not in the political dispute but rather to protect Lt. Irving from (what he thought) In-

sult. The affair now took a turn, and some violent language passed between Cap. Johnston & Lt. Sharp, which ended as You have been informed. I ought to mention that I believe Cap. Johnston in his argument meant to speak in a friendly manner of the Nation, but did not go so far as to advocate french principles, if there can be this distinction made. And at any rate the Acct. must be confused owing to the state in which the parties were at the time. . . ."

2. This letter is listed in the appendix to this volume. In this letter H informed Moore that the winter quarters for the Tenth Infantry Regiment would be at Harpers Ferry. He ordered Moore to march to York, Pennsylvania, "the part of your Regiment assembled at your Regimental Rendezvous" and he suggested that Moore consolidate at Carlisle and York, "the ten sub-districts into two batallion-districts" for purposes of recruiting or propose another arrangement for his approval.

From Thomas Parker

Winchester [Virginia] October 6, 1799. ". . . It is with the Utmost pain that I am again Compelled to ask for a Supply of money for the Troops. Many of the men who have been enlisted between five & six months have never Recd a Shilling of pay & only part of their Bounty & the arts & Insinuations of the Enemies to our administration has had such an Effect on the minds of many of them that I do not Know what will be the Concequence If a Supply is not Shortly sent on. When Captain Bishops [1] Company were about to march they were so destitute of necessaries that I was obliged to advance them some Shoes Tents Shirts & overalls from our Regimental Store; In addition to this a pecuniary aid was found necessary and . . . a Respectable Merchant of this place agreed to advance them Two months pay. . . . A Considerable number of our men are entirely without waistcoats of any Kind & all our Coats are Expended. These articles with woolen overalls are much wanted."

ALS, Hamilton Papers, Library of Congress.
1. John Bishop of Virginia was a captain in the Second Regiment of Artillerists and Engineers.

To Charles Cotesworth Pinckney

New York, October 6, 1799. ". . . In consequence of your voyage to New Port The Secretary of War lately instructed me to take measures for providing winter Quarters in the vicinity of Harpurs

Ferry on the Potowmack for the Eighh Ninth & Tenth Regiments.[1]
I have instructed Col Parker [2] of the Eighth, under the direction of
the Commander in Chief who has consented to take charge of the
matter,[3] to provide ground and make the requisite preparations for
the purpose. This I trust will be promptly effected. The Ninth and
tenth Regiments will march without delay for their destination. And
You may be assured that nothing will be omitted on my part for
accomplishing the object with a careful regard to the comfortable
accomodation of the troops. . . ."

ADf, Hamilton Papers, Library of Congress.
  1. James McHenry to H, September 26, 1799 (listed in the appendix to this
volume).
  2. H to Thomas Parker, September 23, 1799.
  3. George Washington to H, September 29, 1799.

To James Miller [1]

New York, October 7, 1799. "General Wilkinson with one Gentleman of his family, the Adjutant General,[2] myself and Secretary
with [two or three] [3] servants [to the party] will set out, in the
course of the day, for Trenton. We shall stay the night at Elizabeth
town and arrive in Trenton perhaps on Tuesday evening but probably not before Wednesday Morning. You will please to provide
for us suitable [Quarters: We shall come in a stage.]"

Df, in the handwriting of Thomas Y. How and H, Hamilton Papers, Library
of Congress.
  1. Miller was the assistant quartermaster general or the Army.
  For background to this letter, see H to James McHenry, October 6, 1799.
  2. William North. See H to North, September 26, 1799.
  3. Material within brackets is in H's handwriting.

From Nathan Rice

Worecester [Massachusetts] Octr. 8th. 1799

My General
  I am thus far on my way to Oxford in compliance with the instructions contained in your favour of the 17th. ult. I had agreed

for the use of the land & the wood at the price I mentioned elec-
tional with Government to take it or not. The owner was then
averse to selling the soil—perhaps I shall now be able to agree with
him for the soil.

I trust it is your intention that on my compleating the contract I
should immediately move on my Regiment without waiting a particular direction therefor from you as the season is so far advanced.
Your directions will arrive by the time, or probably before they can
be on the Ground.

If the 15th and 16th. Regiments are to be united with mine for
the Winter, is it not necessary they should be under marching orders
as soon as possible considering the great distance some parts of them
are from Oxford. I do not consider myself autherised to give them
any directions without your special autherity. I will do myself the
honor of writing you immediately on my return from Oxford.[1] In
the Mean Time am with the highest respect your obt Serv   N: Rice

General Hamilton

ALS, Hamilton Papers, Library of Congress.
   1. H had already answered some of the questions raised by Rice in this letter
in H to Rice, October 4, 1799.

From Thomas Parker

Winchester [*Virginia*] *October 10, 1799.* States that with the
help of Tobias Lear he has selected ground for winter quarters for
the Eighth, Ninth, and Tenth Regiments.[1] Adds that he "made this
arrangement on a Supposition that the Troops are to Encamp in
the same manner as During the Revolution war. If I am not Correct
in my Ideas of the Business be pleased to Inform me. . . . as there
is a Scarcity of materials for Huting; that no time may be lost I
have with the advice of Mr Lear employed Mr Mackee . . .[2] Immediately to procure the necessary articles for Building. I think It
absolutely necessary that money shoud be placed in his[3] or some
other agents hands. . . ." Encloses duplicate of a letter from George
Washington.[4]

ALS, Hamilton Papers, Library of Congress.

1. On December 11, 1799, Thomas Wilson received $2,148.66 "for 196 acres and 18 perches land for the accommodation of the 8th and 9th regiments, situated near Harper's ferry in Virginia" (*A Statement of Expenditures*, 252).

2. John Mackey was agent for the War Department.

3. On March 13, 1800, Mackey was paid $2,008.60 "for expenditures for materials and tools for building huts near Harper's ferry for the troops, (made by him)" (*A Statement of Expenditures*, 253–54).

4. Washington to Parker, September 28, 1799 (ALS, letterpress copy, George Washington Papers, Library of Congress). In this letter Washington forwarded H to Parker, September 23, 1799, and discussed in detail the contents of that letter.

From Lewis Tousard

[*Newport, Rhode Island*] *October 11, 1799.* "I have to acknowledge the receipt of your letter of the 2d instant and will be ready to attend your summon for repairing to Newyork this winter; and will let you know, as soon as my presence is not necessary for the works at this place for the Season. . . ."

ALS, Hamilton Papers, Library of Congress.

To James McHenry [1]

Trenton October 12. 1799

Sir

I have the honor to transmit the plan which is conceived to be proper for the disposition of the four Regiments of the permanent establishment.[2] It is the result of communications with General

ADf, Hamilton Papers, Library of Congress.

1. H wrote this letter while he, James Wilkinson, and William North were in Trenton for a conference with James McHenry. On October 15, 1799, the *Gazette of the United States, and Philadelphia Daily Advertiser* reported: "The President of the United States arrived at Trenton from Quincy on Wednesday last [October 9]. It is expected he will remain there until the meeting of Congress.

"Same day arrived at Trenton, Major General Hamilton, from New York, and General Wilkinson of the Western Army. The latter has been to Quincy on public business with the president." See H to George Washington, September 23, 1799; H to McHenry, October 6, 1799; H to James Miller, October 7, 1799.

2. This is a reference to the Regular Army. See the introductory note to H to James Gunn, December 22, 1798.

Wilkinson and the Commander in Chief [3]—and accords with the opinion of the latter.

The principal objects of this plan are   1   The distribution of the troops by corps in contiguous or relative positions; keeping the men embodied under their own officers and enabling the commandants of Regiments and batalions to superintend their respective corps; an arrangement no less favourable to the convenience and regularity of supply than to the order and discipline of the troops.   2   The reduction of the number of posts; some of which however useful when originally occupied can under existing circumstances answer no valuable purpose but tend to subdivide too much our inconsiderable force and to increase the difficulty and expence of supply. 3   The obtaining of a reserve force, which being stationed in a central position, will bear upon various points either for succour or attack; and by its concentration, will be capable of discipline and ready for active efforts.   4   The promoting of œcononmy, by lessening the garrisons, of some of the most remote stations, and bringing a principal part of the force to a situation where it can be supplied with comparitive cheapness.

In judging of the effect of the plan in the last view, it is necessary to advert that the present low state of the corps in point of numbers is not the criterion. In the natural order of service the recruits would reinforce their several companies, and in this case the actual distribution of the troops would give to posts, in the most expensive situations, greater numbers than are allotted to them by the present plan.

The reduction of the garrison of Michilimacnac [4] in particular has been very much influenced by the consideration of œconomy. This motive was the more readily yielded to, as it is not perceived that a greater number there, if bearing any proportion to the whole force which we have to employ in the Western Quarter, would answer any better purpose than the number proposed to be continued. This number will serve to occupy the point as one of the portals of the country and to cover the few white inhabitants there settled. In a suitable fortification, especially as the scite is an Island, it may ef-

3. See James Wilkinson to H, September 6, 1799; H to Washington, September 9, 1799; Washington to H, September 15, 1799.
4. See H to David Strong, May 22, 1799; H to McHenry, May 23, 1799; H to John J. U. Rivardi, June 25, 1799; Rivardi to H, July 25, 1799; H to Washington, September 9, 1799.

fectually resist Indian attack—and any greater number which could be spared, could neither act effectively against them nor maintain themselves against serious attack from our English neighbours. In the last supposition, the increase of numbers, from the impracticability of reinforcement and succour, would only serve to increase loss.

It is not understood, that the station procures to us at the present juncture any commercial advantage; but in this respect is principally convenient to the British Traders in peltry; who in their intercourse with the neighbouring Indians have a rendezvous at this place.

The primary inducement to us to keep a post there is as before intimated to retain the occupation of what may be considered as one of the portals of our North Western territory & to avoid the appearance to the Indians of an abandonment of that part of the country. It contributes also in some degree to an influence over the tribes connected with Lake Michigan. And in time to come it may be an encouragement to the enterprises of American Trade[r]s. But all these ends will it is conceived be accomplished by a small force.

The force now upon the lower parts of the Mississippi will also be reduced.

It is conceived that the number contemplated by the plan will be sufficient to garrison and maintain the forts which ought at this time to exist in that Region, to impress with due respect the adjacent Indians, to give reasonable protection to the Inhabitants and to keep such of them as may have foreign attachment in check. A greater number would be inexpedient because any number which the scale of our Military establishment would permit to be stationed there would not be adequate to the repelling of a serious attack from our neighbours; and being out of the reach of succour would for that reason be in imminent danger of total defeat and loss; while it would be still more inadequate to an offensive operation, and, by its proximity, would be likely to create alarm and occasion reinforcement.

In the event of an invasion from below, our reserved force placed on the *Ohio*, reinforced by the Militia, to which it would be a rallying point can descend to meet it with effect, or can take such other measures as circumstances may dictate. If a rupture with Spain should induce us to become the Invaders, the force assigned to the undertaking can rapidly descend the Mississippi, and being at a great distance will have a better chance of masking its approach and of arriving unexpectedly—than if stationed at a place which by its nearness would excite jealousy and vigilance.

But I agree in opinion with General Wilkinson [5] that a strongly fortified post ought to guard our Southern extremity on the Mississippi. It will not only serve as an impediment to invasion by the Spaniards but will have an impressive influence on the powerful tribes of Indians in our South Western territory. Loftus's Height (where, you are informed, a fortification is begun) [6] according to the description and plans communicated by General Wilkinson is peculiarly designated as the proper scite of such a post. It is near our Southern line by much the highest point in an extensive district of country and commands the narrowest part of the River.

The dimensions of the summit are understood to correspond with a fort which may be defended with about two hundred men, and which would protect the bataries in advance towards the River and in other directions. I concur in the expediency of occupying this height with a regular fortification of stone or brick garnished with the proper exterior batteries. Bricks, I am assured are easily made in the vicinity. Inclosed is an estimate of the probable expence.[7] Though by no means an advocate for multiplying in the present circumstances of the Country the number of our fortifications already too great, I entertain no doubt of the expediency of the one in question and the object is well worth the probable expence.

It will be seen that a batalion is assigned to the care of this fort and of another now possessed on the Mobille.[8]

The propriety of continuing the latter post may however depend on circumstances. It is useful for the protection of an existing settlement, and will add to the influence of our establishments upon the minds of the Indians. But the supply of it is difficult and expensive and it is now effected through the Spanish territory. In case of a diminution of amity with Spain, that circumstance would compel to a removal—unless another channel can be conveniently opened. Indeed if this cannot be shortly done, it will hardly be proper to re-

5. See Wilkinson to H, September 6, 1799.
6. See McHenry to H, September 28, 1799.
7. H failed to enclose this estimate. See McHenry to H, October 16, 1799.
8. H is referring to Fort Stoddert, which was located on the Mobile River at the junction of the Tombigbee and Alabama rivers.

tain the post. The duration of the arrangement in this particular may therefore be considered as contingent.

The position which has been chosen for the reserve corps has various aspects. It looks to the succour of the more Northern as well as the more Southern Posts, and will be likely to controul efficaciously the North Western Indians; It has an eye to a cooperation with the troops in the state of Tenassee whenever a good communication shall be established, which is conceived to be an object of pressing moment. And it is convenient for a descent by the River Mississippi for offensive operations against our neighbours on the South, if future circumstances should recommend them.

But as well with a view to defence as offence it is deemed requisite to prepare and keep ready below the rapids of the Ohio—a number of boats equal to the transportation of Three thousand men with baggage stores provisions Artillery and other apparatus. Their number & the estimate of their cost will be found herewith.[9]

A firm occupation of the streights which connect the Lake Erie with the Huron and Ontario appears to me a material point. It is doubted whether the posts now on those streights are the best adapted to that end either as to local situation or construction. But unfortunately the want of a skilful engineer (a very painful circumstance in our military affairs) is an obstacle to the due examination of this point. It is nevertheless one which must be attended to as early as shall be practicable. It would seem to me desireable ere long to have on each streight a work suited to about a thousand men with an interior work in the nature of a Citadel adapted to about Two hundred. These might be expected to secure the place against a *coup de mains* with a small force, and the growth of settlement in the vicinity will soon furnish through the Militia the means of augmenting the Garrison upon a sudden emergency.

The good understanding which at this time subsists between the UStates & Great Britain justifies an arrangement less efficient than that just intimated. But the permanency of friendship between Nations is too little to be relied upon not to render it prudent to look forward to more substantial precautions than are immediately meditated.

9. H did not send this estimate with the letter printed above. See McHenry to H, October 16, 1799.

You will likewise have observed that particular attention is paid to Massac. In my opinion, very cogent & comprehensive reasons render it the policy of the UStates to secure & command the confluence of the *Tenassee* & *Cumberland* Rivers with the *Ohio* and of the Ohio with the Mississippi. To this end respectable fortifications to be gradually executed are necessary.

The leading motives to the plan, which I have the honor to transmit, have been sketched. Considerations not mentioned will readily present themselves to your reflections as having operated on parts of the plan. Among these, the maintenance of the troops on moderate terms has not been overlooked in the choice of the principal station.

Nothing particular has been said as to the Regiment allotted to General Pinckneys command,[10] because the disposition of it belongs to him.

But the plan which I offer requires your interposition to give it effect within the limits of that Officers District. There are now there a Regiment and part of another. An instruction from you is necessary to incorporate the men so as to form one full Regiment— marching the overplus to Harpurs Ferry to be sent in the Spring to the Ohio.

The fourth Regiment will naturally be that to be assigned to the Tenassee and Georgia. The men of the third now in Georgia can continue there, but transferred to the fourth. These, with those at present under Col Butler [11] in Tenassee, will make a full Regiment. And the recruits under Major Bradley [12] may at once be sent to Harpurs Ferry. In the course of the Winter the officers of the third in Georgia can repair to Harpur's Ferry and a sufficient number of those of the fourth can replace them in Georgia.

An arrangement for the officers of the four old Regiments is now submitted to your consideration. When approved no time will be lost in bringing Officers and men together at the several stations.

10. Charles Cotesworth Pinckney was stationed at Shepherdstown, Virginia. For the regiments under his command, see the introductory note to H to Gunn, December 22, 1798.

11. Lieutenant Colonel Thomas Butler, who was stationed at South West Point, Tennessee, commanded the Fourth Regiment of Infantry. See Butler to H, August 20, 1799.

12. Daniel Bradley superintended recruiting for the Fourth Regiment of Infantry. See Pinckney to H, October 1, 1799; Bradley to H, June 14, 1799 (both listed in the appendix to this volume).

At present they are extremely mingled and confused. Officers of one Regiment are with the men of another and so great is the disorder that I am assured that in one instance two companies are mustered to the same Captain—I allude to the case of Capt   .[13]

It is alike important and urgent to be enabled to carry this arrangement into execution or with such alterations as you may think fit to prescribe.

The advanced state of the season renders it necessary that General Wilkinson should depart without delay. This he cannot do until he receives my instructions and these cannot be given to him until I shall receive your answer to this communication; my antecedent authority not being commensurate with all the objects contemplated and the commander in Chief having confined himself to advice without giving directions.

With perfect respect & esteem   I have the honor to be   Sir   Yr Obed ser

The Secy of War

[E N C L O S U R E] [14]

Plan for the disposition of the four Regiments of the permanent
Establishment as the result of communications with
General Wilkinson and the Commander in Chief

One Regiment to be stationed partly in the State of Tennessee and partly in proper positions for the protection of the Frontier of Georgia, not extending farther Westward then the Apalachicole River. This Regiment to be attached to the command of General Pinckney. The part in Tenessee to be by him instructed in any great and sudden emergency to cooperate with General Wilkinson.

The other three Regiments to be under the immediate command of General Wilkinson and to be stationed as follows viz

    1 A batalion of Infantry & company and a half of Artillerists at *Niagara Detroit* and *Michilimacnac;* thus distributed

13. Space left blank in MS. The name of Samuel Tinsley should have been inserted. See Wilkinson to H, September 6, 1799, note 10.
14. ADf, Hamilton Papers, Library of Congress.

To Niagara   Two companies of Infantry & a half Company
          of Artillerists
  Detroit   Three companies of Infantry and one company
          of Artillerists; to furnish for
Michilimacnac.   A subaltern two sergeants twenty four rank and
          file infantry and a sergeant and twelve Artillerists
          2   A batalion of Infantry and a company of Artillerists
          at Fort Wayne, Fort Fayette (Pittsburgh) Massac and
          Fort Pickering. thus distributed (viz)
To Fort Wayne   A Company of Infantry and a quarter of a
          company of Artillerists
  Fort Fayette   A Company of Infantry and a quarter of a
          company of Artillerists to detach to
  Presque Isle   1 Subaltern 1 Sergeant 1 Corporal & 15 privates
  Massac   Two Companies of Infantry and half a com-
          pany of Artillerists to detach to Fort Pickering a Ser-
          geant & six Artillerists
  Fort Pickering   A Company of Infantry and a sergeant and six
          Artillerists

---

          3   A Batalion of Infantry and a company of Artiller-
          ists at Fort Adams and Fort Stoddard thus distributed
          (viz)
To Fort Adams   Four Companies of Infantry and a company of
          Artillerists, the latter to furnish a detachment for Fort
          Stoddard.
  Fort Stoddard   A Company of Infantry and A sergeant and
          twelve Artillerists.

The reserve-force consisting of A Regiment and a batalion of
Infantry two troops of horse and a half Company of Artillerists to
be stationed at some *point*, from Cincinnati to the Rapids of the
Ohio inclusively.

It is further contemplated that Two Regiments of Infantry a batalion of Riflemen and a Regiment of Cavalry of the *Eventual* army [15]
be organized in Tennessee Kentucke the North and South Western
Territory.

15. See the introductory note to H to Gunn, December 22, 1798.

To James McHenry

Trenton [1] October 12. 1799

Sir

It is now time to contemplate the distribution of the Troops of the UStates into Divisions and Brigades. The arrangement which appears to me expedient for the present is this—"That the four old Regiments shall form One Division and two Brigades [2] the twelve new ones Two Divisions and four Brigades."

The very great sphere of action to which the former are destined, including important and complicated objects, appears to me to render it expedient that not more than two Regiments shall constitute a Brigade. But the latter 'till there should be actual service, when the system supposes that the number of each Regiment would be increased, may for the mere purposes of discipline and arrangement, be conveniently formed three to a Brigade. The disposition for Winter Quarters [3] accords with this idea.

Correspondent Officers should be appointed; who are principally Generals Quarter Masters and Inspectors.

The latter are of the competency of the Inspector General who will proceed without delay to make the appointments.

If the non appointment of the Quarter Master General provided for by the Act of the 3d. of March last for the better organising of the Army [4] or the absence of the former Quarter Master General [5] be an impediment to the regular course of constituting a Deputy Quarter Master General to each Military District and Division and Brigade Quarter a substitute must be adopted.

Usage, founded on necessity in similar cases, would authorise each Commanding General to designate persons provisionly to perform the duties. But he cannot annex the extra compensation and without this or the expectation of it the business would labour.

I request your Interposition. I deem essential the immediate appointment within my command of a Deputy Quarter Master General and one Division and two Brigade Quarter Masters and I will observe incidentaly that the same thing must be requisite within the Command of General Pinckney. [6]

As to Generals, The President must decide. With the Western Army there is no Major General and only one Brigadier.[7] Two Brigadiers were appointed for the Additional Army, but no more than one is understood to have accepted.[8] I am anxious that the deficiency should be supplied. The discipline of the Troops ought to be accelerated. It must suffer more or less as often as one organ is transferred from its proper situation to another.

I entreat a prompt decision on the subject of Quarter Masters.

With great respect   I have the honor to be Sir   Yr. Obed ser

PS I beg to remind you of the appointment of ⟨a⟩ Major for the 12th. Regt.[9]

James Mc.Henry Esq

ADf, Hamilton Papers, Library of Congress.
   1. See H to McHenry, first letter of October 12, 1799, note 1.
   2. See "Organization proposed for the first Division of Infantry in the Army of the United States consisting of the 1st 2d 3d & 4th Regiments formed into two Brigades" (D, Hamilton Papers, Library of Congress). H endorsed this document "Proposed Organisation."
   3. See H's draft of George Washington to McHenry, first letter of December 13, 1798.
   4. 1 *Stat.* 749–55.
   5. This is a reference to John Wilkins, Jr.
   6. See H to McHenry, first letter of October 12, 1799, note 10.
   7. James Wilkinson.
   8. H is mistaken. Four brigadier generals were originally nominated on July 13, 1798, by President Adams: John Brooks of Massachusetts, William Washington of South Carolina, Jonathan Dayton of New Jersey, and William S. Smith of New York (*Executive Journal,* I, 292). The Senate refused to confirm Smith (*Executive Journal,* I, 293), and on July 19, 1799, William North was named in his place (*Executive Journal,* I, 293). Dayton and Brooks refused their appointments; Washington and North accepted.
   9. Christopher Hutton had declined to accept a commission as the second major in the Twelfth Regiment. Lieutenant Colonel William S. Smith had recommended first Theodosius Fowler and then Captain Dowe J. Fondey for the post. Since H and Smith disagreed over this change in Smith's recommendation, the matter was submitted to Adams. See H to McHenry, June 22, 1799, note 2.
   On June 25, 1799, McHenry sent to Adams copies of H's letters of May 7, 1799, and May 22, 1799 (listed in the appendix to this volume), together with extracts of Smith to H, May 16, June 18, 1799 (both listed in the appendix to this volume), and recommended that Fondey be given the promotion (ALS, Adams Family Papers, deposited in the Massachusetts Historical Society, Boston). On July 1, 1799, Adams wrote to McHenry: "If you believe Fonda has a shade in his favor, you are at liberty to appoint him . . ." (LC, Adams Family Papers, deposited in the Massachusetts Historical Society, Boston). Mc-

Henry acknowledged receipt of this letter on July 6, 1799 (ALS, Adams Family Papers, deposited in the Massachusetts Historical Society, Boston), but took no action on the matter until he received H's letter printed above. In his reply, October 15, 1799 (listed in the appendix to this volume), McHenry reminded H that he had recommended Fondey's promotion in his letter to H of July 8, 1799, which has not been found, and that he had been waiting for H's answer. He then stated: "As you have not advised to the contrary, I transmit to you his letter of appointment and request that you would have the same forwarded. Should you have any objection . . . you will be pleased to return it."

From Charles Cotesworth Pinckney

Newport Rhode Island Octr: 12th
1799.

Dear Sr:

I am obliged to you for your favour of the 6th: instant, which enclosed me the duplicate of yours of the 13th: of August:[1] neither the original of that, nor the Recruiting Instructions,[2] have come to hand; but as I expect they will be forwarded to me from Charleston by the first ship, I will not trouble you for a copy of them without I find they have miscarried.

I return you many thanks for the care you have taken to provide winter quarters for the 8th: 9th: & 10th: Regiments.[3] Is not the 7th: Regiment to be cantonned with them, also the battalion of artillery destined for field service, or where are they to be quartered the ensuing winter? Lieutt: Coll: Parker of the 8th: applied to me to go to the North Western Territory on business of much importance to him for four weeks. On the 10th: instant I wrote to him giving him liberty, and desiring him to arrange matters previous thereto so as to let his absence be attended with as little detriment as possible to the service; & to authorize some person to open any letters for him, that they might be acted upon in his absence. I have however written to him to day to desire he will postpone his departure till he has arranged the business relative to winter quarters committed to him by you.[4]

Mrs: Pinckney's health has so much mended lately, that I am in hopes I shall be able in about ten days to set out with her for Elizabeth Town; soon after which I shall have the pleasure of waiting on you, and also on the Secretary of War; and then proceed by easy Journeys to the vicinity of Harper's Ferry.

I have not received any money or order for money & cloathing for recruiting the third Regiment. If I should; the application shall be deferred agreeable to your desire.

In your favour of the 13th: of August you request my thoughts on the constant appearance of the officers in Uniform. Fashion has made the wearing a cockade general: it is not now solely appropriate to military men. An officer in my opinion should at all times appear as such, and he can only do so by wearing his uniform—a blue coat edged with white does not sufficiently designate him to be an officer, and as lace is prohibited on our uniforms, the facing a blue coat with red, does not add much to the expence. I therefore do not think the argument of additional expence is weighty. If however an undress is permitted, there should be some regulation on the subject to ascertain precisely what that undress should be. In the German & French Service the officers in cold & rainy weather are permitted to wear great coats, but the fashion of those coats is prescribed. We have no regulation on the subject.

I agree with you on the impropriety of the appointment of a Major of Artillery, the chief of a battalion, to be deputy Pay Master. I have written to the pay master general[5] on the subject, and will be obliged to you to peruse, seal & forward the enclosed letter to him.

I remain with great regard & esteem

Yrs. very sincerely   Charles Cotesworth Pinckney

Major General Hamilton

ALS, Hamilton Papers, Library of Congress.

1. On October 5, 1799, Pinckney wrote to H that he had not received H's letter of August 13, 1799. On October 6, 1799, in a letter which is listed in the appendix to this volume, H wrote to Pinckney: "I send you duplicate of my official letter of the 13 of August."

2. See "Circular to the Commandants of Regiments," March 26–April 17, 1799.

3. See H to Pinckney, October 6, 1799.

4. H to Thomas Parker, September 23, 1799.

5. Caleb Swan.

To Caleb Swan

Trenton,[1] *October 12, 1799.* Quotes from Thomas Parker's letter of October 6, 1799, concerning pay of the troops. States: "I would thank you to accelerate as much as possible the advances which you contemplate to the several regiments. There are some newly appointed officers in the four old regiments who stand in need of money to carry them to their posts. This is the case likewise with some old officers in those regiments who have been a long while on furlough. I know that these advances deviate from the general rule, but the necessity of the thing will justify a deviation." Adds: "I am endeavoring to fix upon persons to act as Pay Masters to the regiments of Artillerists; but untill this can be done it will be matter of necessity to pay them by companies as has been heretofore practised."

Df, in the handwriting of Thomas Y. How, Hamilton Papers, Library of Congress.

1. H wrote this letter while he, James Wilkinson, and William North were in Trenton for a conference with James McHenry. Because of a yellow fever epidemic in Philadelphia, the Government had moved its offices to Trenton. See McHenry to H, August 29, 1799; H to McHenry, October 6, 1799; H to James Miller, October 7, 1799.

From James Wilkinson

[*Trenton, October 12, 1799.* On October 31, 1799, Hamilton wrote to Wilkinson and referred to "your several communications of the 12th. 15. 19th. & 27 instant." *Letter of October 12 not found.*]

From George Washington

Private   Mount Vernon 13th Octr. 1799

Dear Sir,

Incon⟨venient as it was to⟩ [1] my finances, I have been ⟨induced⟩ to erect convenient to the ⟨Capital, in the⟩ Federal City, two houses ² which have ⟨the⟩ exterior of one, but by an ⟨arrangement of commu⟩nication may, according to the ⟨desire⟩ of the occupant, or occupants—may have all the conveniencies of one, or be entirely seperate & distinct.

For these buildings a person of the name of John Avery,³ ⟨wishes a boarding⟩ house in the building erected for the Governor of New York ⟨– – –⟩ for the occupancy of them ⟨for that⟩ purpose. In person & cha⟨racter he is⟩ a stranger to me; wherefore ⟨I take the liber⟩ty to enquire of you *confiden*⟨*tially* who⟩ the latter is, and whether you believe rent of about $1200 would be ⟨sure on his part.⟩ This information (especially ⟨since he seems⟩ to be too full of himself) wd. very much ⟨oblige⟩

My dear Sir Yrs. always   Go: Washington

Genl Hamilton

ALS, letterpress copy, MS Division, New York Public Library; ALS (photostat), George Washington Papers, Library of Congress.
   1. Material within broken brackets has been taken from *GW*, XXXVII, 392.
   2. In the margin opposite these words Washington wrote: "to aid in accomodating the members of Congress."
   3. John Avery operated a boardinghouse in New York City in 1798 and 1799. He died in October, 1799, during the yellow fever epidemic ([New York] *Commercial Advertiser*, October 25, 1799).

To James McHenry

Trenton ¹ October [14] 1799.

Sir

In consequence of the necessity of careful inquiry for a fit character previous to an appointment, I still remain with only one Aid.² Of course I have not all the regular assistance which the establishment allows to me; but the extent of my correspondence rendered it indispensable for me to find a substitute.

I could not with propriety have drawn an officer from the troops without additional compensation, besides that in the situation of the troops, hitherto, an officer could not have been detached for this purpose without inconvenience to his corps, if one could have been readily found who would have been content to be a mere copyist and drudge.

Hence I adopted the expedient of hiring a person to perform the service in quality of Assistant Secy [3] at the rate of Thirty Dollars per Month.

The Government, defraying this compensation, will be more than indemnified by the saving of the additional emoluments of an Aid. I trust therefore that it will be deemed proper to authorise the allowance out of the fund for extra compensations and contingencies. A charge for it is included in an Account of Pay &c. sent by me to the Pay Master General.[4] If not improper I request your sanction.

If not paid by the Public the money must be paid by me, & considering that as yet I have neither had Quarters servants nor till the beginning of this month fuel, it would be rather hard to be at this expence for the benefit of the public.

With great respect &c

The Secy of War

ADf, Hamilton Papers, Library of Congress.
1. See H to McHenry, first letter of October 12, 1799, note 1.
2. This is a reference to Thomas Y. How, who was H's secretary, not aide-de-camp. See H to How, July 3, 1799; H to McHenry, July 17, 1799; H to Caleb Swan, October 14, 1799.
3. This is a reference to Ethan Brown. See H to McHenry, April 4, 1798, note 8; H to Swan, October 14, 1799.
4. See the enclosure to H to Swan, October 14, 1799.

From Nathan Rice

Boston Octr 14th 1799.

My dear General

I repaired to Oxford, where I entered into an agreement for the lease of the land of which I made mention in my letter of the 22d Ulto. The owner Mr John Nichols engages to lease to the United States, the whole of said lot described by certain metes & bounds, estimated to contain fifteen acres for the purpose of erecting hutts thereon & for quartering troops therein the two ensuing winter seasons—if Government shall have occasion therefor—with the priviledge of encamping their troops on a field in front thereof, while hutting—of passing over the same for water—of opening springs—of using as many stones as are necessary for erecting chimneys &c—And also for the sale of all the Timber and wood growing thereon or as much thereof as the Government of the United States shall have occasion for for twenty Six Dollars Sixty Six Cents pr acre.[1] I also agreed. with another person in case it should be needed, for an additional quantity of Timber & Wood, at the same rate.[2] Will thank you to inform me to whom the conveyance is to be made & who will become responsible on the part of Government.

Yours of the 5th instant [3] is also just come to hand, with a Copy of your letter to Colonels Hunnewell & Graves.[4] I have written, already to those Gentlemen and requested them to march, without delay, their recruits to their winter destination. I have also issued my orders for the march of those of my own Regiment, on this day week—and shall direct the Contractor [5] to agree for the necessary Materials for the hutts. I had myself considered that both in view of œconomy, & conveniences it would be best to construct the hutts in such a manner, as that the soldiers of each company complete, might be contained in two hutts of 40 by 16 feet, with a chimney in the centre, which will give two rooms, of 16 by 18 feet allowing the Chimney & entry to take two feet out of each room. This mode will afford sufficient space at the back of the chimney for a length of Bunks & of course there may well be now enough to accommodate as many men as will be present at one time. A slight partition between the rooms will be sufficient, & a saveing of two gable ends thereby be made. This will correspond with your idea of increasing the size of the messes, of the Utility of which I agree perfectly with you, in sentiment.

The mode I have suggested will require only twenty six hutts for the non Commissioned officers & privates of a complete Regiment whereas Sixty of the dimentions of fourteen feet Square & twelve to a hutt, will not more than contain them. As to the dimentions of the boards commonly cut with us, I beleive they are variant according to the accidental length or size of the logs. You may rely however on my utmost attention to select such as shall conduce to the greatest œconomy.

Some Glass will be necessary for Windows to the officer hutts, I should suppose. Shall direct therefore the Contractor to procure as much as will be indispensable—unless you think proper to prohibit it.

With the highest respect   I am Sir your Obt. Servant   N: Rice

General Hamilton

ALS, Hamilton Papers, Library of Congress.

1. On October 25, 1799, in a letter which is listed in the appendix to this volume, H wrote to James Miller, assistant quartermaster general: "Colonel Rice informs me that he had entered into a contract for fifteen acres of land for the Winter Quarters of the fourteenth, fifteenth and sixteenth regiments. The price agree'd upon is four hundred dollars, and I would thank you to empower your agent Jonathan Jackson Esqr. to advance the money. I am inclined to think that there must be some mistake as to the sum, and you will probably do well in extending the authority of your agent as far as one thousand dollars. . . ."

On January 1, 1800, John Nichols received $260.66 for "a lot of ground containing 9 acres 3 quarters, 4 roods, situated at Oxford Massachusetts, for the accommodation of the 14th, 15th and 16th regiments" (*A Statement of Expenditures*, 252).

2. Rice also leased eight acres and fifteen roods at Oxford from Samuel Campbell, who received $215.85 on January 1, 1800 (*A Statement of Expenditures*, 252).

3. Rice is referring to H to Rice, October 4, 1799.

4. H to Rufus Graves and Richard Hunewell, October 4, 1799. For this letter, see H to Rice, October 4, 1799, note 5.

5. Either Joseph or Nathaniel Ruggles. See H to Hunewell and Rice, May 21, 1799; H to Rice, September 22, 1799.

To Caleb Swan

[Trenton, October 14, 1799]

Sir

I send you an account of pay &c due to myself my Secy and Assistant Secretary down to the last of September inclusively which I request you to put in a Train of Adjustment without delay in order that the money which is wanted may be received.

The last item not being within the establishment may require the sanction of the Secy of War to whom I have written on the subject.[1]

It may be proper to explain the charge of Postage. The Officers who regularly communicate with me are instructed to indorse their letters "On public service" with the addition of their respective names, and in all these cases the Post Master at New York keeps an account which is paid by E Stevens Esq Agent of the War Department. But numerous letters are received on public service from persons not in the usual line of communication which cannot be foreseen and consequently cannot come within that arrangement. My Assistant Secy keeps the account of this kind of postage and from time to time pays for it to the Penny-Post Man & takes his receipts. Of course the money is furnished by me [2] & is a proper charge against the UStates.

With great consideration   I am Sir   Yr. Obed ser

Caleb Swan Esq

[ENCLOSURE]

Account with the United States Government [3]

[Trenton, October 14, 1799]

The United States

To Alexander Hamilton   for pay as Major
  General from the first of April to the last
  of September inclusively 6 Months at
  166 Dollars ℔ Month   Ds. 996
  Extra allowances as Inspector General at
  50 Dollars ℔ Month   300
  Forage at 20 Dollars ℔ Month 120
  Rations at the rate of 15 ℔ day 2745 Rations at 16.1½ ℔ Ration being the Contract price at NYork for Postage of 443.31
  public letters paid by himself. 200.57 2059.88

To Thomas How   for his pay as Secy from
  the 11th. of July the time of Acceptance
  to the last of September inclusively Two
  months and twenty days at rate of 40
  Dollars ℔ Month   106.66⅔
  For Forage for the same time at 8 Drs ℔
  Month   21.33⅓

For Rations for the same time at the rate
of three *per day*, 244 Rations at 16.1½
℔ Ration   39.40
For his pay as second Lieutenant of the
11 Regiment from the 5 of August (the
time of Acceptance) to the last of September inclusively one Month & 26 days
at 25 Ds. ℔ Month   47.50
Rations for the same time at the rate of
two per day 112 Rations at 16.1½ ℔
Ration   28.08
                                                                          ────
                                                                          242.98
To Ethan A Brown as Assistant Secy from
the 1st of April to the last of September
inclusively 5 Month & 23 Days at 30
Dollars ℔ Month [4]   173
                                                                          ────
                      Total Dollars   2475.86
                                                                          ────

I hereby authorise my Secy. Lieutenant Thomas Brown [5] to receive
the amount of the within Account for the persons therein mentioned
                                                       Trenton October
                                                       1799

ADf, Hamilton Papers, Library of Congress.
 1. H to James McHenry, October 14, 1799.
 2. For example, not far from the end of H's Cash Book, 1795–1804, is a section entitled "Postage," which lists the amounts H paid during March, 1799, for
letters to and from various Army officers (AD, Hamilton Papers, Library of
Congress).
 3. ADf, Hamilton Papers, Library of Congress.
 4. On October 31, 1799, in a letter listed in the appendix to this volume,
H wrote to Swan that Brown's account "has been sanctioned at the War office,
and that the accountant has been instructed to pass it."
 5. This is a mistake. H should have written "Lieutenant Thomas How."

From James Wilkinson

[*Trenton, October 15, 1799.* On October 31, 1799, Hamilton
wrote to Wilkinson and referred to "your several communications
of the 12th. 15. 19th. & 27 instant." *Letter of October 15 not found.*]

From Nehemiah Freeman [1]

Fort Jay [New York] October 16, 1799. ". . . In August last I made out a return of clothing that would be due to my company on the first of the present month. The men . . . all are destitute of shirts, overalls, and shoes. . . . We claim arrearages of pay from the 30th. of June."

ALS, Hamilton Papers, Library of Congress.
   1. Freeman was captain in the First Regiment of Artillerists and Engineers.

From James McHenry

War Department Trenton 16~ October 1799

Sir

I have received your letter dated the 13 instant.[1] It has been communicated to the President, from whom I have received instructions to make the following reply.

The Plan you detail, for the disposition of the four regiments, on the former permanent establishment, as the result of communications with General Wilkinson, and the commander in chief, and according with the communications of the latter,[2] is esteemed Judicious in its objects.

1st. The distribution of the troops by Corps in contiguous or relative positions, keeping the men embodied under their own officers and enabling the Commandants of regiments and batalions, to superintend their respective corps—an arrangement no less favourable to the convenience, and regularity of supply than to the order, and discipline of the Troops.

2d. The reduction of the number of Posts, some of which how-

LS, Hamilton Papers, Library of Congress; LS, letterpress copy, James McHenry Papers, Library of Congress.
   1. McHenry is mistaken, for he is referring to H's letter of October 12, 1799.
   2. See James Wilkinson to H, September 6, 1799; H to George Washington, September 9, 1799; Washington to H, September 15, 1799.

ever useful when originally occupied, under existing circumstances, answer no valuable purpose, but tend to subdivide too much our inconsiderable force, and increase the difficulty and expence of supply.

3d. The obtaining of a reserve force, which being stationed in a Central Position, will bear upon various points, either for succour, or attack; and by its concentration, be capable of discipline, and ready for active, and efficient efforts.

4th. The promoting of economy, by lessening the garrisons of the most remote stations, and bringing a principal part of the force to a situation, where it can be supplied with comparative cheapness.

The duties of a Commandant of an army are infinitely extended, they embrace every thing that relates to the well being of his troops, their discipline and their positions, so as to effect the intentions of the Government which supports them, in the completest manner. He must necessarily therefore be intrusted with ample discretionary powers—and can with propriety be so intrusted, since his reputation and Honor are the securities.

It is therefore confided to you to make such a disposition of the troops in the Western Country, and to reduce such of the Posts, within your command, as in your judgment will comport best with the primary views of the Government—which are—

First—To keep possession of territory that might in the hands of a foreign power be disputed as our right.

2d. To keep up our influence with, awe, or in case of hostility check the efforts of the Indians, and conduce to cover the greatest extent of settlement from their inroads.

3d. To observe the operations of, afford a barrier in case of mis-understandings against, and having an aspect to the annoyance in such case of, our white neighbours.

4th. To secure the allegiance, and obedience to the laws, and subordination of such of our Citizens, as being remote from its seat, are less under the observation of Government—besides being exposed to the insinuations and arts of foreign emissaries or of misguided or treacherous Citizens.

5th. To protect the passage at the confluence of certain of the great rivers, as well with a military view, as to afford facilities to and excite trading enterprize.

The attainment of a reserved force so posited, as to comport with the views mentioned, by bearing upon all parts, and ready to act with the greatest practicable effect at every point, while it is not found so low down the western waters, as to give a neighbour when disposed, the power by a sudden stroke to crush it unprepared, but is itself rather to be apprehended, from the rapidity of approach, the natural current affords to it—is esteemed a judicious measure, and of primary importance.

Loftus's heights from their commanding and even imposing situation as described, and the natural advantages of the spot in a military aspect—no doubt ought to be crowned with a fortress—this has been some time contemplated. It is however proper to observe that the appropriations for such objects being very limitted—the fort was designed to be constructed at the least possible expence, the labor necessary it was supposed might have been given by the soldiers. The sanction of the President for what is understood to have been already done [3] would be premature without the estimate you proposed to enclose.

The Fort you designate as upon the Mobille, as I presume, has heretofore been spoken of in my communications with General Wilkinson and in the contract for supplies as upon the Tombigbee. This post presents difficulties to support it—but if it can be supported, advantages may result from it. It is through the military commandant, that information must be expected, whether the advantages of keeping it up, will Justify the difficulties and expence of its support, and opening a communication other than through a foreign territory, the use of which may be denied to us.

The boats, which you propose should be prepared, and kept ready below the falls of the Ohio, as well with a view to offence as defence and adequate to the transportation of three thousand men, with baggage, stores, provisions, artillery, and other apparatus, for the numbers, and expence of which you promise an Estimate, will properly be committed to the Commanding General, who keeping in view the indisposition, to incur and consequent necessity of avoiding any possible expence, will exercise his Judgment, and from a full view of circumstances, give his orders to the Quarter Master

3. See McHenry to H, September 28, 1799.

General, to prepare such transportation as he may deem indispensible should be held in readiness.

The Plan offered requires the Executive interposition, to give it effect within General Pinckney's command,[4] this will be readily and promptly accorded. It is however surmised, that the one regiment assigned to that command for the protection of Tennessee and the Frontiers of Georgia is supposed insufficient. An additional Battalion besides the two troops of Cavalry already in Georgia may perhaps appear requisite, when it is contemplated, that if the protection by regular troops in those quarters, is too inadequate a most expensive resort, will be forced upon the Government, that of the militia.

I have the Honor to be, with great respect, Sir, Your most Obedient Humble. Servant James McHenry

Major General Alexander Hamilton

4. See H to Charles Cotesworth Pinckney, October 6, 1799; H to McHenry, first letter of October 12, 1799, note 10.

From Thomas Parker

Winchester [*Virginia*] *October 16, 1799.* "I had forwarded pay & muster Rolls up to the 30th of September & was consoling myself with the hope of a Speedy Supply of money; when the post of yesterday Brought to my pay master[1] (Instead of money) a large Supply of Blank Returns. From the paymasters Communication I Know not when we may expect a Supply as he seems to think it necessary that the Regimental paymasters should Repair to his office[2] to adjust their accounts. The evils that this delay may Occasion are Incalculable. The Recruiting Business is Totally Stopped & desertion prevails in a considerable degree owing to the want of pay. Four Soldiers deserted a few nights ago But were all fortunately taken. Two of them who were most Guilty I have put in Irons as I think it absolutely necessary to make an example of them. . . . I am sorry that an Additional Supply of Cloathing has not arrived as It is Verry much wanted. Indeed it is Time that the Soldiers Shoud be furnished with their woollen overalls."

ALS, Hamilton Papers, Library of Congress.
    1. A resident of Alexandria, Virginia, Lemuel Bent was appointed a lieutenant in the Eighth Regiment of Infantry on January 10, 1799 (*Executive Journal*, I, 300, 305), and was appointed paymaster of the regiment on May 2, 1799 (Godfrey, "Provisional Army," 148).
    2. See Caleb Swan to H, October 5, 1799.

To Elizabeth Hamilton

Elizabeth Town [New Jersey]
Friday Oct 17. 1799

I am thus far, My Dear Eliza, on my way to New York.[1] But I am under a necessity of viewing the ground for Winter Quarters [2] to day—which will prevent my being with you before tomorrow. Then please God I shall certainly embrace you & my Dear John.[3]

A thousand blessings upon you   Yrs. Ever   AH

ALS, the Reverend Alexander van Cortlandt Hamilton, Norwalk, Connecticut.
    1. H was returning to New York after conferring with James McHenry, James Wilkinson, and William North in Trenton. See H to McHenry, October 6, 1799; H to James Miller, October 7, 1799.
    2. Winter quarters for the Eleventh, Twelfth, and Thirteenth Regiments were located at Scotch Plains, New Jersey. See H to Ebenezer Stevens, October 5, 1799.
    3. John Church Hamilton, H's son who was born on August 22, 1792.

From John J. U. Rivardi [1]

Niagara [New York] October 17, 1799. "Major Hoops & Captain Still arrived here on the 4th Instt. & opened the Court of Inquiry the Same day. . . . I lament that a business which I was in hopes would not last three or four days has already Taken So much Time. I yesterday only began to bring forward my own Evidences. From The Turn which The Affair has Taken I owe To myself Not to think of attacking in any maner Captain Bruff because the issue Must be the loss of one or the others Comission. . . . we experience Severely the want of a Surgeon NotwithStanding the attention paid To The Sick by the Doctors of The Brittish Troops who have again attended in consequence of the illness of Dr. Muirhead." [2]

ALS, Hamilton Papers, Library of Congress.
1. For an explanation of the contents of this letter, see Rivardi to H, March 21, 1799, note 13; H to Rivardi, August 26, 1799, note 1. See also Rivardi's "Charges which I Intend To bring against Captain Bruff" (AD, Hamilton Papers, Library of Congress).
2. See Rivardi to H, July 25, September 12–16, October 2, 1799.

From Richard Hunewell

Portland [District of Maine] October 19, 1799. "Herewith I send you a return from the Quarter Master & Paymaster,[1] of the several articles received in their Department, for the use of the 15th. Regiment with the several Articles wanting to compleat the number For the use of the Regt., together with my observations[2] of their qualities &c.—generally they are good, & of a much better quality than the troops expected; if the Army in general have been furnished with Cloathing Tents & other camp equipage, equal to that of my Regt., they have in my opinion no reason to complain & as Soldiers they have no right to."

LS, Hamilton Papers, Library of Congress.
1. Lieutenant Charles Cutler was appointed quartermaster of the Fifteenth Regiment of Infantry on May 23, 1799, and Lieutenant William Swan became paymaster of the regiment on the same day (Godfrey, "Provisional Army," 177–78).
2. "Observations on the several Articles Reced. for the use of the 15th Regt. Infy" (copy, Hamilton Papers, Library of Congress).

From Thomas Parker

Winchester [Virginia] October 19, 1799. ". . . I shall march tomorrow[1] but It is extreamly painfull to me to witness the Distress & Chagrin of the officers & Soldiers who have not money to discharge even the Claims of their washwomen. . . . a waggon arrived with a Supply of Coats Vests & Woolen overalls articles which were much wanted. In Concequence of my Request Mr Machee[2] Superintendant of the public works at Harpers ferry has procured some materials to aid us in Building. But no appropriation has been made for the payment of them. . . ."

ALS, Hamilton Papers, Library of Congress.
 1. See Parker to H, October 10, 16, 1799.
 2. John Mackey.

From Lewis Tousard

[*Newport, Rhode Island, October 19, 1799.* On November 6, 1799, Hamilton wrote to Tousard: "Your several letters of the third, fifth, ninth and nineteenth of October have been duly received." *Letter of October 19 not found.*]

From James Wilkinson

[*New York, October 19 1799.* On October 31, 1799, Hamilton wrote to Wilkinson and acknowledged receipt of Wilkinson's "several communications of the . . . 13th. 15. 19th. & 27 instant." *Letter of October 19 not found.*]

From Rufus King

[*London, October 20, 1799.*[1] *Letter not found.*]

1. "List of Letters from . . . Mr. King" to H, Columbia University Libraries.

To James McHenry

New York October 20th. 1799

Sir

It appears to me very adviseable to remit to the Pay Master General of the Western army [1] bounty money for a Regiment complete for the double purpose of reinlisting those men whose times of service are expiring and of recruiting in addition men equal to four companies as I am informed may probably be effected without much difficulty. The inlistment of men within the scene has the double advantage of procuring soldiers enured to the climate and of saving expence in transportation.

Cloathing in proportion must be forwarded, contemplating two companies to each Regiment.

If you approve and will give the requisite orders I will take measures for carrying the object into effect.

General Wilkinson states that the officers in general of his commands are without commissions. Those of the additional regiments are all in the same predicament. This circumstance apparently of little moment is known to create very unpleasant sensations among the officers. They attach an artificial importance to the possession of the commissions and are apt to regard delay in furnishing it as injurious inattention to their feelings. To accustom officers to habits of punctuality and strictness it is very material to give them examples of the same spirit in all who are placed over them. I must therefore urge a prompt attention to this subject. I am aware of no obstacle to the issuing of their commissions universally to the Officers of the old Regiments and the same may be done in regard to the company Officers at least of all the new Regiments the settlement of whose relative ranks has been reported.[2]

Permit me to reiterate a very essential idea, that in military affairs, it is of the greatest consequence to settle and fix every thing *as soon as it is in itself practicable.*

It is both proper and necessary that all boats passing our out posts on the Mississippi should be stopped and examined; to prevent their being used as a medium of desertion and of injurious communication with our neighbours. It would give great facility to this measure and would be likely to benefit the revenue, if a custom house officer was established at Loftus's height.[3] If thought expedient, from the peculiarity of situation, a military officer may be charged with the duty. Should the subject strike you in the same light, it will no doubt be proposed to the Secy of the Treasury.

General Wilkinson suggests as a matter of primary consequence the contracting with some suitable person to convey dispatches monthly from the Natches to Knoxville. The measure, in order to a regular transmission of intelligence, appears very desireable. I have an impression that you mentioned to me verbally that something of this kind had taken place; but not being certain I present the matter to your consideration, and shall be glad to be informed if any thing of the kind has been or will be adopted. The General thinks it practicable at an expence from twelve to fifteen hundred Dollars per annum.

I pray your immediate attention to these suggestions and information of your Determination.

I trust that tomorrows post will bring me a conclusion upon the matters which were the objects of my communications at Trenton.[4] Moments in this case are precious. Serious inconvenience may attend delay.

With great respect   I have the honor to be &c

The Secy of War

ADf, Hamilton Papers, Library of Congress.
    1. Samuel C. Vance. See Caleb Swan to H, September 19, 1799, note 3.
    2. See H to McHenry, second letter of August 25, 1799; McHenry to H, September 3, 1799.
    3. For the authority to establish a customhouse, see Section 16 of "An Act to regulate the collection of duties on imports and tonnage" (1 *Stat.* 637–39 [March 2, 1799].)
    4. See H to McHenry, first letter of October 12, 1799.
    H had been in Trenton from October 8 to October 17 conferring with James Wilkinson, William North, and McHenry. The Government offices had been moved to Trenton because of an outbreak of yellow fever in Philadelphia. See McHenry to H, August 29, 1799, note 1; H to McHenry, October 6, 1799; H to James Miller, October 7, 1799; H to Elizabeth Hamilton, October 17, 1799; H to Thomas Parker, October 21, 1799; H to George Washington, first letter of October 21, 1799.

To Thomas Parker

New York October 21. 1799

Sir

Your letter of the 10 instant, by reason of my absence at Trenton,[1] was not received till the 19th.

Its contents are somewhat embarrassing. A leading feature of the plan for Winter Quarters which in conformity with arrangements with the Department of War was indicated by my instructions to you is that Timber for hutting and wood for fuel should be found on the premisses.[2] The additional instruction to you from the Commander in Chief [3] appears to me to contemplate the same thing; and yet your letter informs me that the spot fixed upon does not offer this advantage and that with the advice of Mr. Lear you had employed Mr. Mackie to procure the necessary *articles* for *building*.[4]

It would seem from this as if in your arrangement the idea of *hutts* had been exchanged for that of *barracks*. This under all the circumstances of the case would be too extensive—and being contrary to my authority from the Secretary of War cannot be ratified.

Perhaps nothing more is intended than to procure rough Timber fit for hutts from some spot not distant which would not materially enhance the expence. If so—the business may proceed.

Otherwise a different course must be taken, in respect to which I have asked the favour of the Commander in Chief to give directions.[5]

You have been already informed that the Agent of the War Department, who I understand to be Mr. Mackie, the Gentleman you mention, has been authorised to procure boards for roofs &c. The Assistant Quarter Master General has been requested to furnish him with five thousand Dollars.[6]

You will of course enter into a particular explanation in your next letter.

With great consi

Col Parker

ADf, Hamilton Papers, Library of Congress.
1. H had been in Trenton from October 8 to October 17, 1799, for a conference concerning the Western Army with James McHenry, James Wilkinson, and William North. See McHenry to H, August 29, 1799, note 1; H to McHenry, October 6, 1799; H to James Miller, October 7, 1799; H to Elizabeth Hamilton, October 17, 1799; H to George Washington, first letter of October 21, 1799.
2. See H to Parker, September 23, 1799.
3. Washington to Parker, September 28, 1799 (ALS, letterpress copy, George Washington Papers, Library of Congress). See also Washington to H, September 29, 1799.
4. See Parker to H, October 10, 16, 1799.
5. The letter printed above was enclosed in H to Washington, second letter of October 21, 1799. Washington then sent it to Parker as an enclosure on October 26, 1799 (Df, in Tobias Lear's handwriting, George Washington Papers, Library of Congress; copy, in Tobias Lear's handwriting, Hamilton Papers, Library of Congress).
6. H to Miller, October 21, 1799 (listed in the appendix to this volume).

From Ebenezer Stevens [1]

New York Oct. 21. 1799

Sir

It seems the Comptroller of this State [2] has reimbursed the Corporation of this city with the Sum they borrowd of the Bank for the fortifications in this harbour. but Sir there are a number of acco'ts Still unpaid of such a nature as require immediate Settlement.

I wish'd Mr. Firman to assume them all but he refused having no funds in his hands. [3] I believe if you would write the Governor representing to him the necessity of this business, he would agree to it at once.

I feel guilty every time I meet the mechanics who have demands against the Military Committee. These acco'ts are in possession of Mr Jones—he says further Legislative aid is wanted, but it will not answer to wait. These acco'ts having already been so long standing I should not be surprized should they one & all commence a suit against me. Perhaps the Corporation might assume them.

I am wth. great consideration   Sir your. hum servt.   Eben Stevens

Major Gen Hamilton

LS, Hamilton Papers, Library of Congress; copy, New-York Historical Society, New York City.
    1. For an explanation of the contents of this letter, see James McHenry to H, June 4, 1798, note 4; John Jay to H, October 24, 1798; Stevens to H, November 17, 1798; H to Stevens, November 19, 1798. See also the introductory note to H to McHenry, June 1, 1798.
    2. Samuel Jones.
    3. See Jay to H, October 24, 1798, note 4; Stevens to H, November 17, 1798, note 2.

To George Washington

N. York Oct. 21st. 1799

Dear Sir

On my return from Trenton, the day before yesterday, I found your private letter of the 13th. as well as yr. public letter of the 15th. instant.

The News papers have probably informed you that poor Avery is dead of yellow fever.[1]

The President has resolved to send the commissioners to France notwithstanding the change of affairs there.[2] He is not understood to have consulted either of his Ministers; certainly not the Secy. of War or of Finance. All my calculations lead me to regret the measure. I hope that it may not in its consequences involve the United States in a war on the side of France with her enemies. My trust in Providence which has so often interposed in our favour, is my only consolation.

With great respect &c

General Washington

Copy, in the handwriting of Ethan Brown, Hamilton Papers, Library of Congress.
   1. See Washington to H, October 13, 1799, note 3.
   2. In February, 1799, John Adams had nominated William Vans Murray, Oliver Ellsworth, and William R. Davie as Envoys Extraordinary and Ministers Plenipotentiary to France to negotiate a new treaty with that country. Murray, as United States Minister Resident at The Hague, was in the Netherlands at the time of his nomination, and Adams had stipulated in a message to the Senate on February 25, 1799, that Ellsworth and Davie would not "embark for Europe, until they shall have received from the Executive Directory assurances, signified by their Secretary of Foreign Relations, that they shall be received in character; that they shall enjoy all the prerogatives attached to that character by the law of nations; and that a Minister or Ministers, of equal powers, shall be appointed and commissioned to treat with them" (*Executive Journal*, I, 317). In compliance with these terms, Charles Maurice Talleyrand-Périgord wrote to Murray on May 12: "Veuillez transmettre à vos collegues et acceptez vous même l'assurance franche et explicite, qu'il [Directoire Executif] recevra les Envoyés des Etats Unis dans le charactère officiel dont ils sont revêtur, qu'ils jouiront de toutes les prerogatives qui y sont attachées par le droit des gens et qu'un ou plusieurs Ministres seront duement autorisés à traiter avec eux" (copy, Massachusetts Historical Society, Boston, enclosed in Murray to Timothy Pickering, May 19, 1799 [ALS, Massachusetts Historical Society, Boston]). A translation of Talleyrand's letter is printed in *ASP, Foreign Relations*, II, 243–44. On July 31, Pickering, who opposed the mission to France, sent Murray's letter and its enclosure to Adams, along with the observation that Talleyrand's letter did not "conform to the terms used in the instructions to M. Murray" (ALS, Adams Family Papers, deposited in the Massachusetts Historical Society, Boston). Adams, however, wrote to the Secretary of State on August 6 reaffirming his intention to send the newly appointed ministers to France and requesting that Pickering prepare instructions for the diplomats and submit the document to the members of the cabinet for comments (LC, Adams Family Papers, deposited in the Massachusetts Historical

Society, Boston). See, for example, the observations of Oliver Wolcott, Jr., on the instructions, dated September 4, 1799 (Gibbs, *Wolcott*, II, 357–61). Although Adams had refused to suspend the mission, Pickering, Wolcott, and James McHenry remained opposed to the proposed negotiations with the French, and in the President's absence from the capital they worked to undermine his position. As early as July 10, Pickering had written to Murray explaining the reasons why he and others did not support the appointments of the ministers or the purpose of their mission (ALS, letterpress copy, partially in code and deciphered, Massachusetts Historical Society, Boston). On September 10, after the Government had moved to Trenton because of the yellow fever epidemic in Philadelphia, Pickering wrote to Adams (ALS, Adams Family Papers, deposited in the Massachusetts Historical Society, Boston) and enclosed a draft of the instructions for the ministers (ADf, Adams Family Papers, deposited in the Massachusetts Historical Society, Boston). On the following day, however, Pickering with the concurrence of Wolcott and McHenry recommended the suspension of the mission because of the news received from Murray concerning the *coup d'état* of June 18, 1799 (ALS, Adams Family Papers, deposited in the Massachusetts Historical Society, Boston). For the changes in the French government as a result of the *coup*, see Rufus King to H, July 15, 1799, note 1. Although Adams was reluctant to travel to Trenton (see, for example, Adams to Pickering, September 16, 1799 [LC, Adams Family Papers, deposited in the Massachusetts Historical Society, Boston]), Secretary of the Navy Benjamin Stoddert tried to convince the President that his presence was needed to overcome the opposition to the negotiations by members of his own party. On September 13, for example, Stoddert wrote to Adams: ". . . I have been apprehensive that artful designing men, might make such use of your absence from the seat of Government when things so important to restore Peace with one Country and to preserve it with another, were transacting, as to make your next election less honorable than it would otherwise be" (ALS, Adams Family Papers, deposited in the Massachusetts Historical Society, Boston). See also Stoddert to Adams, August 29, 1799 (ALS, Adams Family Papers, deposited in the Massachusetts Historical Society, Boston), and Adams to Stoddert, September 4, 21 (LC, Adams Family Papers, deposited in the Massachusetts Historical Society, Boston). Adams finally yielded to the pressure and arrived in Trenton in mid-October.

After several meetings with his cabinet, Adams on October 16 instructed Pickering to prepare and deliver to the ministers the instructions "as corrected last evening" and to direct them to sail for Europe by November 1, 1799 (LC, Adams Family Papers, deposited in the Massachusetts Historical Society, Boston). The text of the final instructions is printed in *ASP, Foreign Relations*, II, 301–06. During Adams's stay in Trenton, H met with the President to express his opposition to the mission. In 1809 Adams gave the following account of this meeting: "Mr. Hamilton, who had been some time in town and had visited me several times, came at last to remonstrate against the mission to France. I received him with great civility, as I always had done from my first knowledge of him. I was fortunately in a very happy temper and very good humor. He went over the whole ground of the victories of Suwarrow [Aleksandr Vasilyevich Suvarov] and Prince Charles, and the inflexible determination of the two imperial courts, in concert with Great Britain, to restore the house of Bourbon to their kingdon. That there was no doubt the enterprise was already accomplished, or at least it would be, before the end of the campaign. That Mr. Pitt was determined to restore the Bourbons. That the confidence of the nation in Mr. Pitt was unbounded. That the nation was never so united, and determined to support Mr. Pitt and his resolution to restore the monarchy of France. His eloquence and vehemence wrought the little man up to a degree of heat and effervescence like that which General [Henry] Knox used to describe of his conduct in the battle of Monmouth, and which General [Henry] Lee used to call his *paroxysms* of bravery, but which he said would never be of any service to his country. I answered him in general, as I had answered the heads of departments and Judge Ellsworth—but to no purpose. He repeated over and over again the unalterable resolution of Mr. Pitt and the two imperial courts, the invincible heroism of Suwarrow and Prince Charles, and the unbounded confidence of the British empire in Mr. Pitt, with such agitation and violent action, that I really pitied him, instead of being displeased. I only added, that I differed with him in opinion on every point, and that instead of restoring the Bourbons, it would not be long before England would make peace. I treated him throughout with great mildness and civility; but after he took leave, I could not help reflecting in my own mind on the total ignorance he had betrayed of every thing in Europe, in France, England, and elsewhere . . ." (*Correspondence of the Late President Adams. Originally Published in the Boston Patriot. In a Series of Letters* [Boston: Published by Everett and Munroe, 1809], 29–30).

Abigail Adams described the meeting between H and Adams in a letter to her sister, Mary Cranch, on December 30, 1799: "I think every days experience must convince the people of the propriety of sending the Envoys at the time they went. After the President had received the Letter from Talleyrand containing the assureances from the Directory which he requir'd, he would not allow it, to be made a question whether they should proceed tho he knew certain persons set their faces against it as far as they dared. Gen'll. Hamilton made no secret of his opinion. He made the P[residen]t a visit at Trenton, and was perfectly sanguine in the opinion that the Stateholder would be reinstated before Christmass and Louis the 18th upon the Throne of France. I should as soon expect, replied the P[resident], that the sun, moon & stars will fall from their orbits, as events of that kind take place in any such period, but suppose such an event possible, can it be any injury to our Country to have envoys there? It will be only necessary for them to wait for new commissions. And if France is disposed to accommodate our differences, will she be less so under a Royall than a Directorial Government? Have not the Directory Humbled themselves to us more than to any Nation or Power in contest with her? If she proves faithless, if she will not receive our Envoys, does the disgrace fall upon her, or upon us? We shall not be worse off than at Present. The people of our own Country will be satisfyed that every honorable method has been try'd to accommodate our differences. At the period the envoys went, France was loosing ground. She was defeated, and the combined powers appeard to be carrying victory with them. If they had been detained untill now, how mean and despicable should we have appeard? Reports have been circulated that the British Minister remonstrated: However dissagreable the measure might be to him, he is too old a minister, and understands the nature of his Mission too well, to have ventured upon any such step. As an independent Nation, no other has a Right to complain, or dictate to us, with whom we shall form connections, provided those connections are not contrary to treaties already made" (Stewart Mitchell, ed., *New Letters of Abigail Adams, 1788–1801* [Boston, 1947], 224–25).

To George Washington

New-York Oct. 21st. 1799

Sir

I have the honor to acknowledge the receipt two days since of your letter of the 15th. instant, at which time I also received one from Col: Parker, informing me of the selection of ground which he had made.[1]

You will see by the enclosed letter to him [2] the impression which his communication has made on my mind. I trust that it must be erroneous, since my supposition does not agree with the spirit of his instructions either from you or myself, nor with the manner in which you seem, by some expressions in your letter,[3] to understand that he has executed them. But as it is possible the mode of execution may not have been sufficiently explained to you, I cannot intirely dismiss my apprehensions.

If the plan of Barracks has in fact been substituted, I must once more intreat your interposition. You will judge whether there is yet time to rectify the mistake and procure a more suitable position, Or whether making an arrangement at the place which has been fixed upon for the 8th. Regiment Only, it will not be best to vary the destination of the others sending the 9th. to the Barracks at Frederick town in Maryland where I am very lately inform'd there are buildings sufficient for a Regiment,[4] belonging to the State, which I presume may be borrowed, and the 10th. at Carlisle in Pennsylvania where I am assured there exist buildings [5] the property of the United States which will accommodate a Regiment.

But these Regiments have been directed to march for their destination, the Ninth by way of Frederick town, and the tenth to *York town* there to receive further orders.[6]

Permit me to ask that you will be pleased to give these further Orders, according to your determination to which every thing is respectfully submitted.

Knowing that it is not agreeable to your general plan to take charge, at present, of military operations I am bound to apologize for the trouble I give you. But my unexpected and late agency in the affair and the advanced state of the Season leave me no alternative.

With perfect respect I have the honor to be Sir yr. obed Servt.   A Hamilton

General Washington

LS, in the handwriting of Ethan Brown, George Washington Papers, Library of Congress; ADf, Hamilton Papers, Library of Congress; copy, Hamilton Papers, Library of Congress.
    1. Thomas Parker to H, October 10, 1799.
    2. H to Parker, October 21, 1799.
    3. Washington to Parker, September 28, 1799, a copy of which was enclosed in Parker to H, October 10, 1799. See H to Parker, October 21, 1799, note 3.
    4. Josias Carvel Hall to H, October 12, 15, 1799 (both listed in the appendix to this volume).
    5. Thomas Lloyd Moore to H, October 3, 1799; H to Moore, October 6, 1799 (both listed in the appendix to this volume).
    6. H to Hall, October 5, 1799; H to Moore, second letter of October 6, 1799 (both listed in the appendix to this volume). For H's letter to Moore, see H to Moore, first letter of October 6, 1799, note 2.

To James McHenry

New York October 22. 1799

Sir

It give[s] me pleasure to learn from your letter of the 16 instant, which was received yesterday, that the leading principles and objects of the plan communicated in mine of the thirteenth [1] are approved.

In every disposition of the troops in the Western Country the primary views of the government as indicated by you will be carefully attended to.

The surmise as to leaving an additional batalion for the Tenesee and the Frontiers of Georgia has induced a reconsideration of that part of the plan. But my opinion continues unaltered. Our intire force, which, from the terms of engagement, can be applied to the purposes of our Northern Western and Southern frontiers, is manifestly inadequate. All that can be done is to make such a distribution of it as will bear a proportion to the different objects. Comparing those which are to be provided for on our North Western and South Western frontiers including the intermediate Country with those which demand attention in the other quarters and taking into the view the greater facility of reinforcement in the one case than in the other, a Regiment for Tenessee and the Frontiers of Georgia is an ample proportion.

If the Regiment be kept full, which can easily be done there will, I believe, be a greater real force than there has been in time past. This point of course ought to be looked to. The addition of a batalion would very essentially interfere with the idea of a reserve force on the Ohio large enough to be in any degree efficient. And this is deemed on all hands a cardinal object in the Disposition to be made.

I shall be happy to learn that these reasons are deemed satisfactory and that immediate measures will be taken in conformity. For these measures I refer to the suggestions in my former letter.

With great respect   I have the honor &c

P. S. Every moment presents in some new shape the necessity of organising the Qr. Master's Dept. I suppose also that the Depty Pay masters General shall act as *Clothiers*. I request your opinion on this point.[2]

The Secy of War

ADf, Hamilton Papers, Library of Congress.
  1. This is a mistake, for H intended to refer to his letter of October 12, 1799.
  2. The postscript is in the handwriting of Ethan Brown.

To Nathan Rice

N. York Oct. 22d 99.

Sir

At foot you will find a list of Articles of Quarters master's Supply necessary for hutting and providing fuel for a Regiment, two thirds of which, it is supposed, on account of the Regiments not being full, will suffice; which you are desired to procure without delay.

With great consideration &

Col: Rice

The Qr. Mr's Agent is Jona Jackson Esqr.

[ENCLOSURE]

List of Quarter Supplies necessary for 1 Regt.[1]

150   Axes for felling and cutting wood
  6   Board Axes
  2   Cross cut saws
  6   Hand saws
  3   files for Saws
  2   Grindstones
  2   Jointing plane
  2   Smothing or Jack planes
  4   Adzes
  2   Iron squares
  6   Augers—3 of one inch & the other 3 of ¾ inch
  6   Hammers
200   pound Nails

Df, in the handwriting of Ethan Brown, Hamilton Papers, Library of Congress.
   1. Copy, in the handwriting of Ethan Brown, Hamilton Papers, Library of Congress.

To Ebenezer Stevens

New York October 22. 1799

Sir

From the representations which have come to me from different Quarters it appears to me proper to adopt the scale at foot [1] as that by which the articles mentioned in it ought to be furnished for the purpose of hutting the troops.

But as the Regiments are not complete two thirds in each case will suffice. I request therefore that you will increase the supplies according to this rule and that no time may be lost in sending forward the additional quantities.

The axes cross cut saws files and grind stones being necessary to begin the work they must not be delayed for the purpose of procuring the others. Dispatch is very important.

With great consideration   I am Sir   Yr. Obedt. Servt.

A Hamilton

P. S. Are any and what measures in train for furnishing Medicine Quarter Master's articles for the garrison of Niagara.[2] This garrison is to consist of the Two companies of Infantry & a Company of Artillerists.

E Stevens Esq.

LS, in the handwriting of William LeConte, New-York Historical Society, New York City; ADf, Hamilton Papers, Library of Congress.

1. "List of Quarter-Master's supplies for one Regiment" is written on the back of the letter printed above. H also enclosed this list in H to Nathan Rice, October 22, 1799, and in H to James Miller, October 22, 1799 (listed in the appendix to this volume).

2. Stevens to H, October 22, 1799 (listed in the appendix to this volume), enclosed a copy of "Invoice of public stores . . . ," dated April 11, 1799, and signed by Samuel Hodgdon. This is a list of articles that Stevens had sent to Niagara. On the list is "6 kegs 1 to 6" of medicines.

To James McHenry

New York, October 23, 1799. ". . . I am induced to think, that the recruiting Service for the Sixth and Seventh Regiments will be promoted by leaving them to take their Winter Quarters within their respective States.[1] I submit this observation. It is not for me to judge, as to these Troops, whether there are reasons for adhering to the primitive plan [2] which outweigh the consideration just mention'd."

Df, in the handwriting of Ethan Brown, Hamilton Papers, Library of Congress.
1. The Sixth Regiment of Infantry was stationed in North Carolina and Tennessee; the Seventh Regiment of Infantry was stationed in Virginia.
2. The "primitive plan" as described in H's draft of George Washington to McHenry, first letter of December 13, 1798, was to station two regiments for the winter "in the vicinity of the Potomack near Harpers Ferry, . . . two other Regiments in the vicinity of Augusta." See H to Charles Cotesworth Pinckney, October 23, 1799.

To Charles Cotesworth Pinckney

New York Oct. 23d. 1799

Dr Sir

Your letter of the 12th. inst. found me at Trenton, from which place I have recently arrived.[1]

The seventh Regt. together with the 5th. & 6th. was destined for Augusta. But I am not apprised how far the arrangements for this object, have been matured, and I believe that it may be most adviseable to quarter those Regiments for the present winter within their respective States. I thought it in order to say to the Secy. of War that in my opinion this disposition would best answer the purpose of the *recruiting Service*.[2] If you agree in the general idea, it may be necessary for you to give directions accordingly.

The Battalion of Artillery for the Field is collecting at Harper's Ferry.

Your letter to the Pay Mr. General has been forwarded.

It gives me great pleasure to learn that Mrs Pinckney's health has mended. I trust you will be able to do as you mention—And by stopping at New York and taking a room with us, you will give pleasure both to Mrs Hamilton and myself. She desires to be affectionately remembered to Mrs Pinckney.

We consider our city as perfectly free from disease.

Very cordially and truly   Dr. Sir   yr

General Pinckney

Df, in the handwriting of Ethan Brown, Hamilton Papers, Library of Congress.
1. H had been in Trenton from October 8 to October 17, 1799, conferring with James Wilkinson, William North, and James McHenry. See H to Mc-

Henry, October 6, 1799; H to James Miller, October 7, 1799; H to Elizabeth Hamilton, October 17, 1799; H to George Washington, first letter of October 21, 1799.

2. H to McHenry, October 23, 1799.

To Caleb Gibbs

New York October 24. 1799

Sir

I have received your very improper letter of the 30th. of September.[1] This is not the first instance of my life in which good offices on my part have met with an ill return.

When you were informed, that The Commander in Chief (who, aided by General Pinckney & myself, made in the first instance the nomination of Officers for the twelve Regiments) had presented your name for the place of Lt Col Commandant,[2] you had an explanation of what I meant, when I wrote to you [3] that your disappointment had not proceeded from want of friendship in General washington or myself. What could I do more than cooperate in your nomination to the President? This I did and with great cordiality. What agency can I be supposed to have had after this? Evidently whatever happened subsequently is as foreign to me as to General Washington.[4]

Tis therefore as curious as it is unbecoming to interrogate me in a premptory and even censorious manner about the causes which may have *induced the President* to reject the nomination. It is true that collaterally and after the thing was determined upon, I heard what they were, but it was in a manner which did not leave me at liberty to explain to you. This I before hinted, and you must on reflection see the impropriety of your having addressed me on the subject as you have done. It is very certain that you never can nor will have an explanation from me on the point.

If any one has wickedly endeavoured to make you believe that there has been any thing uncandid or unfriendly in my conduct, you ought to dispise the author of such an attempt to impose on your understanding. If you have inferred it from the reserve in my mode of writing to you on the subject, you formed as false an estimate of what the delicacy of my situation required, as you did of my true character.

I am Sir   Yr. humble ser

Caleb Gibbs Esq
Boston

ADf, Hamilton Papers, Library of Congress.
1. Letter not found. Gibbs had written to H on three occasions asking for assistance in securing a commission. See Gibbs to H, January 21 (listed in the appendix to Volume XXII), April 25, June 10, 1799 (listed in the appendix to this volume).
2. See "Candidates for Army Appointments from Massachusetts," December 9–28, 1798. See also the enclosure to James McHenry to H, January 22, 1799.
3. Letter not found.
4. For H and McHenry's opinion of Gibbs, see H to McHenry, February 6, 1799; McHenry to H, February 8, 1799. For George Washington's involvement in Gibb's application, see Washington to McHenry, March 25, 1799 (ALS, letterpress copy, George Washington Papers, Library of Congress); Gibbs to Washington, April 21, 1799 (ALS, George Washington Papers, Library of Congress; copy, Hamilton Papers, Library of Congress); Washington to McHenry, April 23, 1799 (ALS, letterpress copy, George Washington Papers, Library of Congress); Washington to Gibbs, May 5, 1799 (ALS, letterpress copy, George Washington Papers, Library of Congress).

To James McHenry

[*New York, October 24, 1799.* The description of this letter in the dealer's catalogue reads: "Refers to 'the evils which attend the delay of money—Among the rest the keeping of the Troops out of Winter Quarters to suffer the rigours of the advancing season. . . . If the contentment and attachment of the troops are to be aimed at, there must be a material change in the plan which has hitherto been pursued.' " *Letter not found.*]

AL, sold at Swann Galleries, January 31, 1946, Item 38.

To Caleb Swan [1]

New York October 24th. 1799

Sir

The post of this morning brought me a letter from Col Parker [2] of which the inclosed is an extract. I trust his inference must be an erroneous one, as you gave me clearly to understand that with regard to arrears the money would be sent forward upon estimates without waiting for the regular Rolls in the forms of your office and that this would suffer no delay. My assurances have conformed to this idea and it would be to compromise me as well as to injure the service not to fulfil them.

I should have no apprehension, was it not that while at Trenton [3] the Secy of War let fall an observation which seemed to import that the Rolls must precede the sending of the money. I told him what I had understood from you and he made no reply.

If contrary to my expectation this idea should have been taken up, I must earnestly urge that it be relinquished. The relinquishment is due to me as well as to the service. In future, giving the necessary instructions, as much strictness as you please, but at present a relaxation is indispensable. I hope to be told by the next post after the receipt of this precisely what is doing & will be done.

With consideration   I am Sir   Yr. Obed Ser

P. S. I have just recd. a letter from Col: Hall [4] of which there is a Copy inclosed—which is another strong proof of the exigency of the case.[5]

ADf, Hamilton Papers, Library of Congress.
  1. This letter was enclosed in H to James McHenry, October 24, 1799. Mc-Henry then forwarded it to Swan.
  2. Thomas Parker to H, October 16, 1799.
  3. See H to Parker, October 21, 1799, note 1.
  4. Josias Carvel Hall to H, October 20, 1799 (listed in the appendix to this volume). In this letter Hall complained of "the Want of Pay" for the men in his regiment.
  5. The postscript is in the handwriting of Ethan Brown.

From James McHenry

War Department, Trenton, October 25, 1799. "I this morning received your Letter, dated the 23d. instant. . . . Entertaining the same opinion I request, you will accordingly give such orders as you may deem proper, and expedient, for the comfortable accomodations of both regiments at as little expence as possible, and without a purchase of Land. . . . The orders on the subject should proceed directly from you."

Df, James McHenry Papers, Library of Congress.

From James McHenry

War Department
Trenton 25~ October 1799

Sir

I this moment received your letter of the 24~ instant [1] containing one to the Pay Master General.[2] I have sent it to him with an earnest injunction that no time be lost in complying with your expectations, and desired him to engage an express to carry the money to the appropriate officers should he think it best so to do.

It is certainly my wish to keep the Troops regularly paid, and to do every thing proper to increase their contentment and attachment; but I cannot alter the instructions of the Treasury under which the Pay master acts,[3] neither ought it to be expected that I should take upon myself the responsibility in making advances which are opposed by the laws [4] and those regulations.

I have the Honor to be, with great respect, Sir Your Most Obed. Huml. Serv, James McHenry

Major General A. Hamilton

LS, Hamilton Papers, Library of Congress; LS, letterpress copy, James McHenry Papers, Library of Congress.
1. Letter not found.

2. H to Caleb Swan, October 24, 1799.

3. Oliver Wolcott, Jr., to Swan, July 26, 1792 (Df, partly in Wolcott's handwriting, Connecticut Historical Society, Hartford; copy, Hamilton Papers, Library of Congress).

4. See McHenry to H, August 29, 1799; H to McHenry, September 16, 1799, notes 4 and 5.

To James McHenry

N. York Oct. 25th. 1799

Sir

Lt. Campbel Smith has made a representation to me [1] on the subject of some claims which he has pending in the Accountant's Office, and has requested the interposition of my opinion.[2]

Thinking it due to him as an Officer now under my command I trouble you with this letter.

He states that he has claims of two kinds—One for services rendered for more than two years as judge advocate previous to the law authorising that appointment,[3] another for the legal emoluments of the Office in virtue of an appointment of the commanding General on the basis of that law [4]—that having been absent, in consequence of ill health induced by a severe wound received in the service, obstacles have occurred to the allowing of the compensation during the term of such absence—that the Atty. Genl. has given his opinion that the appointment was a regular one under the law,[5] and that he understands the opinion to have been heretofore acted upon by your Department. Upon these data I submit my ideas.

I consider it to be a principle sanctionned by usage, that when an Officer is called to exercise, in a permanent way, an office of skill in the Army (such as that of Judge advocate) for which provision is not made by law he is to receive a *quantum meruit*, by Special discretion, *for the time* he *officiates*, which in our present system would be paid out of the fund for the contingencies of the War Department.

This applies to the first claim. As to the second, this is my opinion —That considering the appointment as regularly made under the law—the emoluments continue of course until the office has been abdicated or superseded—the nonexercise of it for any period to the contrary notwithstanding.

In the Situation in which Lt Smith was placed by his wound he would seem intitled even to a liberal application of the rule of right.

With great respect &c

Secy of War

Df, in the handwriting of Ethan Brown, Hamilton Papers, Library of Congress.
1. Smith was a lieutenant in the Fourth Regiment of Infantry. He made his "representation" to H in Smith to H, May 12, 1799 (listed in the appendix to this volume).
2. On June 11, 1798, "A memorial of Campbell Smith, a Lieutenant in the Army of the United States, was presented to the House and read, praying compensation for his services as Judge Martial and Advocate General to the said Army, from the sixteenth of July, one thousand seven hundred and ninety-four, to the thirteenth of July, one thousand seven hundred and ninety-six. . . .
"*Ordered,* That the said memorial be referred to the Committee of Claims." (*Journal of the House,* III, 331).
The committee postponed consideration of the memorial until the next session of Congress, when it was again referred to the Committee of Claims (*Journal of the House,* III, 386–87, 535). On February 5, 1800, McHenry included H's letter printed above and his answer to it on November 12, 1799, in his report to Dwight Foster of Massachusetts, chairman of the Committee of Claims (*ASP, Military Affairs,* I, 145). The committee reported on February 21, 1800, and on February 28 the House "*Resolved,* That the proper accounting officers of the Treasury liquidate and settle the account of Campbell Smith, for his services as Judge Advocate to the legion of the United States, while he acted in that capacity under an appointment made by General [Anthony] Wayne, on the sixteenth of July, one thousand seven hundred and ninety-four; and that he be allowed such pay and emoluments for said services, as are allowed by law to officers acting in that capacity" (*Journal of the House, III,* 608). The Senate approved Smith's claim on March 11, 1800 (*Annals of Congress,* X, 117, 582, 683). See also *ASP, Military Affairs,* I, 144–46; "An Act for the relief of Campbell Smith" (6 *Stat.* 40 [March 29, 1800]).
3. "An Act to amend and repeal, in part, the Act intituled 'An Act to ascertain and fix the Military Establishment of the United States'" (1 *Stat.* 507–08 [March 3, 1797]).
4. Brigadier General James Wilkinson's general order of June 2, 1797, reads: "Lieut. Smith of the 4 Regiment, is appointed to do the duty of Judge advocate, until the will of the President be known" (LC, RG 94, Adjutant General's Office, General Orders, General James Wilkinson, 1796–1808, National Archives).
5. Charles Lee to McHenry, February 10, 1798 (copy, Hamilton Papers, Library of Congress). McHenry sent a copy of this opinion to H on November 12, 1799.

From Charles Cotesworth Pinckney

Elizabeth Town [New Jersey] Octr: 25th: 1799.

Dear Sr:

I arrived at this place this afternoon from Rhode Island,[1] via Paulus Hook. Mrs: Pinckney has sustained the fatigue of her Voyage & Journey better than I expected. She is however much tired, & I shall not be able to leave her tomorrow; but I trust she will be so much recovered as to enable me to pay my respects to you on sunday. If that should not be the case, I will wait upon you the first day I can with propriety do so. The envoys are then to sail.[2] I presume this must be a very deep measure; much too profound for my penetration. I always am

Yours very sincerely   Charles Cotesworth Pinckney

Major General Hamilton

ALS, Hamilton Papers, Library of Congress.
  1. The Pinckneys had arrived in Newport, Rhode Island, on September 13, 1799, and left there on October 22 (*Newport Mercury*, October 29, 1799). See also Caleb Swan to H, September 19, 1799.
  2. See H to George Washington, October 21, 1799, note 2.

From Nathan Rice

Confidential   Oxford [Massachusetts] Octr. 25th. 1799

My dear General

Agreeable to your directions, in conjunction with my Majors,[1] I have proceeded to examine the claims of the officers of my regiment, and the result thereof will appear by the inclosed list which I have taken the liberty to make. It would be difficult to state to you, all the principles which governed us in the arrangements, in the application

ALS, Hamilton Papers, Library of Congress.
  1. See "Circular to the Commandants of Regiments," March 23, 1799.

of some which we considered it our duty to establish, we were obliged to do violence to our inclinations. We proceeded on the principle that all their appointments bore a similar state. We then conceived it our duty to apply the rule which was adopted for settling the rank of the field officers, to give those who had served in the late War, priority. But here Sir, I must observe, that principle placed a Gentleman first in the Grade of Captains, who has not supported, since he left service, that kind of reputation, which places him at this period, in the most respectable point of view. I know nothing of him criminal, but a propensity to game has led him to associate with people not of the first class, has reduced him to poverty, & I fear debased his mind. He was Six years a Captain, & served with good reputation during our revolutionary war—and as the Government has given him a Company—I did not think it within our duty or right to degrade him from that rank which his services entitled him to.

Captain Emery a very deserving officer, from his services in the last war, as an Adjutant, Pay Master and Lieutenant had the next claim with us without doubt. Captain Draper was in service as a Serjeant—has commanded a company of militia for a considerable time, is a very soldierly man—his exertions in recruiting his company appeared to place him in competition with Chandler, whose public Education, Zeal & Exertions in raising & uniforming a volunteer company, which were tendered to, & accepted by the President as a part of the provisional army, & commissioned accordingly & whose activity in recruiting his present company seemed to give him the next claim. We determined their priority by Lot, which fell to Draper.

Captain Ashmun being placed first on the list which was sent from Head Quarters has led him to expect, I am informd, to hold that rank and altho I consider him a genteel man & good officer yet I conceived his pretentions not equal to either of the Gentlemen who are placed before him. Twing was in service & resigned early—was afterwards a Lieutenant in the navey—is a likely man, we placed him next. Perhaps you will consider his claim superiour to some who stand before him.

Phelps has commanded a company of Artillery in the militia for some time with reputation & is I believe a very good Character. Tolman was wounded in the army—in what capacity he served I know not. He is not a genteel man in appearance but his activity & zeal in the service—his good conduct as a recruiting officer—& the high opinion which Mr Ames, who recommended him,[2] entertains of him—led us to place him next. Captain Babbet altho a man of a public education & bred to the Law had never turned his attention to military matters, nor do I think his present engagement therein the result of inclination, but present inconvenience—of course my expectations from him are not high, still his being among the first appointments & a Citizen give him preceedence of Captain Mackay—who of course stands the youngest in the grade of Captains. I know very little of him or his claims—only that he has served in the british army as a Subaltern—was known to you previous to his appointment & of course I am led to think very favourably of him as an officer. Should you Sir however from any Knowledge which you possess of the claims & merits of my officers —or from a view of the statement I have made think a different arrangement ought to take place—I chearfully acquiesce.

We were led to place Mr Rand at the head of first Lieutenants, not from any conspicuous military traits, in his Character, but rather from the consideration of his being strongly recommended for a company, his liberal education, respectable family—& genteel Person. If you do not think those sufficient claims—I submit—Cheney's good conduct in recruiting his company gained him our esteem & confidence—but I can not say I think Flagg ought to stand before him. On reviewing the Other Characters I am of opinion they stand as properly all things considered, as it is in my power to arrange them. Will therefore trouble you no farther with my remarks on this subject.

With the most perfect consideration I am Sir your Obedient Servant   N Rice Lt Colo Com 14th Rgt

General Hamilton

2. For Fisher Ames's recommendation of John Tolman, see "Candidates for Army Appointments from Massachusetts," December 9–28, 1798, note 61.

[E N C L O S U R E]

Proposed arrangement of the officers in the 14th Regt [3]

Captains

No				
	1	John Hastings [4]		8 [5]
	2	Ephraim Emery		1
	3	Simeon Draper	the 9th 10 [6]	
	4	Thomas Chandler		2
	5	Phineas Ashmun		3
	6	Nathaniel Twing		4
	7	Solomon Phelps		5
	8	John Tolman		6
	9	Erasmus Babbit		7
	10	Samuel Mackay		9

first Lieutenant [7]

No			
	1	Isaac Rand	1
	2	Alpheus Cheney	2
	3	Samuel Flagg	3

3. AD, Hamilton Papers, Library of Congress.

4. Hastings served as a captain throughout the American Revolution. He was appointed a captain in the Fourteenth Regiment of Infantry on July 12, 1799 (Heitman, *United States Army*, I, 510).

Of the other men on the list headed "Captains," Emery, Draper, Chandler, Thwing, Phelps, Tolman, and Babbet were appointed captains on January 8, 1799 (*Executive Journal*, I, 299, 300); Ashmun was appointed a lieutenant on January 8, 1799, and a captain on March 3, 1799 (*Executive Journal*, I, 300, 303, 322, 323); Mackay was appointed a lieutenant on March 3, 1799 (*Executive Journal*, I, 322, 323), and although he appears on this list as a captain, he was not appointed to that rank until April 4, 1800 (*Executive Journal*, I, 345, 355).

In addition to Hastings, Emery and Thwing were veterans of the American Revolution, both having served as lieutenants in that war (Heitman, *United States Army*, I, 167, 960).

5. The numbers in this column were added by H and indicate what he thought should be the relative rank of the officers in the Fourteenth Regiment of Infantry. See H to Rice, November 11, 1799.

6. At the bottom of this document H wrote: "Simeon Draper to be placed the 10th. on the list."

7. Of the men listed under the heading of "first Lieutenant," Rand, Cheney, Flagg, Church, Duncan, Wheelwright, and Allen were appointed lieutenants on January 8, 1799 (*Executive Journal*, I, 300, 303), while Sargent (not Sergent), Childs (or Child), Gardner, and Barker were appointed in July, 1799 (Godfrey, "Provisional Army," 172–73; Heitman, *United States Army*, I, 190, 299, 446, 860). No record has been found that any of the men on this list had held military rank in United States armed forces before 1799.

4	James Church	4
5	Robert Duncan	5
6	Henry Sergent	8
7	John Wheelwright	6
8	Jacob Allen	7
9	Rufus Childs	9
10	William Gardner	10
11	Francis Barker	11

Second Lieutenants [8]

No	1	John Roulstone	9
	2	Thomas Durant	
	3	William Leverett	7
	4	Daniel Hastings	8
	5	James Gardner	4
	6	Charles Hunt	3
	7	Marshall Spring	5
	8	Payton Gay	
	9	Thomas Hale	

8. Of the men listed under the heading of "Second Lieutenants," Roulstone, Durant, Leverett, Hastings, Gardner, Hunt, and Spring were appointed ensigns on January 8, 1799 (*Executive Journal*, I, 301, 303), and on March 3, 1799, in accordance with Section 2 of "An Act for the better organizing the Troops of the United States; and for other purposes" (1 *Stat.* 749–55 [March 3, 1799]), they became second lieutenants. Gay and Hale were appointed second lieutenants on July 11, 1799 (Heitman, *United States Army*, I, 450, 480). No record has been found that any of the men on this list had held military rank in United States armed forces before 1799.

To Nathan Rice

[New York, October 25, 1799]

Sir

I have received your letter of the fourteenth instant, and am apprehensive that the quantity of land contracted for will hardly furnish the timber necessary for hutting and fuel. It is not my intention however to give further directions on the subject, as you are acquainted with the local circumstances, and can therefore best determine.

I have requested Mr. Miller the Assistant Quarter Master General to have the requisite funds placed in the hands of his agent Jonathan Jackson Esqr.,[1] and you will address yourself to that Gentleman on subject.

The lease may be to James McHenry Secretary of War.

You will perceive from a letter written at Trenton that the dimensions prescribed for the hutts on a reconsidn. of the subject accord in substance with the plan which you had proposed.[2]

The necessary glass you will have procured.

With great consideration

Col. Rice

Df, in the handwriting of Thomas Y. How and H, Hamilton Papers, Library of Congress.

1. See Rice to H, October 14, 1799, note 1.
2. This is a reference to H to William S. Smith, October 12, 1799 (listed in the appendix to this volume), which H enclosed to Rice. This letter reads in part: "Information which I received at Elizabeth Town of the situation and form of the ground procured for the Winter Quarters and of the kind of Timber to be found upon it has induced me to vary my view of the dimensions of the hutts for the Corporals and Privates and of their position in a single line.

"I am now of opinion that it will be found expedient to have them of the dimensions of Eighteen by sixteen feet and to unite two hutts under one roof. . . ." (ADf, Hamilton Papers, Library of Congress.)

To Nathan Rice

[*New York, October 25, 1799.* On November 6, 1799, Rice wrote to Hamilton: "In reply to your favours of the 19th. & 25th permit me to observe, that from the knowledge I have as yet obtained of the Gentlemen I can not fully recommend one for so important an office as that of Depy Pay Master General." *Second letter of October 25 not found.*]

To Ebenezer Stevens

New York Oct 25. 1799

Dr. Sir

If the Owner of the ground adjoining you will take Eight hundred pounds (£800) for sixteen acres including a parcel of the wood land and lying on the water the whole breadth, you will oblige me by concluding the bargain with him & I will pay the money as soon as a good title shall appear.[1] If he will not sell a part at this rate, I request you to ascertain whether he will take Thirty pounds an acre for the whole tract and let me know. If I like it, after another view of the premisses, I shall probably take the whole at this price. But I can only pay one half down, a quarter in six months and the remaining quarter in a twelve month. He shall be satisfied on the score of security if he desires.

Yrs. with regard   A Hamilton

General Stevens

ALS, Hamilton Papers, Library of Congress.
  1. When this letter was written, Stevens lived at 59 Beekman Street on a plot between Front and South streets overlooking the East River (Adolf Dengler, ed., *Descriptive Index of the Maps on Records in the Office of the Register of City and County of New York* [New York: Diossy & Company, 1875], 7).
  Broadus Mitchel (*Hamilton*, II, 499) states that the property in which H was interested was located on the Hudson River and that he purchased "some thirty acres" of this property for his country house, the Grange. Allan McLane Hamilton (*Intimate Life*, 337–38) also considers the letter printed above as the first step taken by H in purchasing land for the Grange. In this instance, however, both biographers appear to be mistaken.
  The property in question had no apparent connection with the Grange, for H purchased the land for the Grange in 1800. More important, the land for the Grange was located in the upper west side rather than the lower east side of Manhattan, and it overlooked the Hudson, and not the East, River. Finally, no evidence has been found that H ever purchased the land about which he is asking Stevens in the letter printed above.

From Caleb Swan

Trenton, October 25, 1799. "The secretary of war handed me your letter of the 24 instant, this morning with an authority in writing to employ an express to take money to the 8th and 9th Regiments. I am puting the business in train, and the day after tomorrow shall send the best clerk in my office, on my own horse to accomplish it. By this mode I may expect a regular account of the money on such documents as the law and my instructions require at my hands. . . ."

ALS, Hamilton Papers, Library of Congress.

From Henry Burbeck

Michilimackinac [*Territory Northwest of the River Ohio*] *October 26, 1799.* ". . . I beg leave to inform you that this Vessel is the last that can possibly come forward to this Post this year, and was expected would bring forward the Clothing for this Garrison, but not one article has arrived. The Winters here are very long and severe—and the want of Woolen Overalls, Shirts and Shoes will be very distressing to the Troops the ensuing season. It is fifteen Months since they have received Clothing and the heavy fatigues at this Post has quite destroyed those Articles. Pay of this Garrison is not equal with the other Troops. They have nine months pay due them now, and the Officers Seventeen months Subsistence. . . . I have nothing material to communicate. All is quiet in this quarter. This closes all communication with this Post until the last of May, except something material takes place."

ALS, Hamilton Papers, Library of Congress.

From Nathan Rice

Oxford [Massachusetts] Octr 26th. 1799

My General

As by your favour of the 19th ultimo [1] I am requested to select & nominate two persons, whom I should prefer to be appointed Cadets. I now do myself the honor of solliciting that appointment for Mr Edward Le Britton Wilson whom I have named before [2] & Mr Joseph Stickney—a *very genteel* young man of the Town of Worcester in the Common Wealth—as the two whom I prefer.

With great esteem I am   Sir yr obt Servant   N: Rice

PS. We can not recruit a man for want of cash.

Genl Hamilton

ALS, Hamilton Papers, Library of Congress.
    1. "Circular to the Commandants of Regiments," September 19, 1799.
    2. Rice to H, August 31, 1799.

From George Washington [1]

Mount Vernon, October 26th: 1799.

Sir,

I have duly received your letter of the 21st instant, enclosing a letter to Colo. Parker, which I have forwarded to him,[2] and at the same time repeated my instructions for *hutting* the Troops, in conformity with the idea which you originally suggested.

I presume that the impression made on your mind by Colo. Parker's letter,[3] respecting Winter Quarters for the three Regiments, must have been erroneous.

At the time when I received and transmitted your first letter to Colo. Parker on this subject, Mr. Lear was in Berkley,[4] and as he was well acquainted with the public ground at Harper's Ferry, and other situations in the vicinity of it, he informs me that Colo. Parker requested he would accompany him to that place, and give him any information and assistance in his power towards carrying into effect the orders for hutting the Troops. This was readily complied with; and upon an examination of the public ground, and making the necessary enquiries, it was determined that no situation in the vicinity of Harper's Ferry (even if it could have been obtained) was so eligable as that belonging to the United States.[5] Colo. Parker therefore fixed upon a spot which appeared, on every account, the most convenient for hutting, and determined that the huts (which were to be built by the Soldiers) should be made of rough logs, 16 feet sqr. each (to contain 12 men) and covered with slabs, which would be much cheaper than plank or boards. As the timber which could be had from the public ground might not be sufficient for more than one half the huts wanting, Colo. Parker requested Mr Mackie,[6] Agent for the War Department at Harper's Ferry, to make the necessary enquiries and engagements for procuring such further quantity of logs and slabs as might be wanting. His motive for engaging Mr. Mackie in the business was, that, as he had been in the habit of procuring articles for public use in that part of the Country, he could do it to more advantage than any other person, and his enquiries for them would not be so likely to raise the price as would those of another Agent. Had any other place been fixed upon for hutting the Troops, the purchase of timber, fuel &c. &c. would have been as necessary as at this; and in no situation proper for the Troops could they have been procured cheaper.

From the foregoing account, which is given to me by Mr Lear (to whom Colo. Parker refered me for particular information respecting the arrangements he had made for hutting the Troops) you will see that Barracks were not contemplated by Colo Parker, and that the huts were to be built in as œconomical a manner as could be expected. I have, however, as I observed before, repeated my instructions to Colo. Parker, that the Troops should be hutted in the manner they were in the late war, which he must well recollect.

Presuming that the plan of Barracks has never been substituted by Colo. Parker for that of huts, it is, in my opinion, unnecessary to make any arrangements for quartering the 9th & 10th Regiments in the places which you suggest, vizt. at Frederick town and Carlisle. From the view which I had of the Barracks at the latter place in the year 1794, I am convinced that the expence of repairing them, fit for the Soldiers during winter, would be much greater than that of building huts. What the situation of the Barracks at Frederick town is, I am unable to say; but I presume they are not much, if any, better than those at Carlisle. And, at any rate, this dispersed situation of the Troops would defeat a primary and important object, I mean that of having them in one body, where they can be under the eye of a General Officer, and where the disciplining and training the Soldiers can be much better effected than if they were in detached corps.

From the information of a Gentleman lately from Winchester, I have reason to beleive that Colo. Parker's Regiment is at Harper's Ferry before this; and I think no time should be lost in ordering the other Regiments to the same place; for there cannot be a doubt, from the circumstances mentioned in this letter, but that Colo. Parker has taken measures for hutting the Troops agreeably to our original idea; and as the Soldiers will build their own huts, it is necessary they should begin them as soon as possible.

I cannot close this letter without mentioning that I have heard of repeated complaints for want of money to pay the Troops raised in this quarter, as well as for other purposes relating to them. If these complaints are well founded, you know, as well as I do, the evils which must result from such defect, and I cannot but be astonished at it, when it is well known that appropriations are made for the pay and support of the Troops, and the money is undoubtedly in the Treasury. I would wish you to inquire into this matter, and if the complaints are founded, it would be well to know from whence proceeds the inattention or deficiency.

With very great esteem & regard,   I am Sir,   Your most Obedt. Servt   Go: Washington

Major General Hamilton.

LS, in the handwriting of Tobias Lear, Hamilton Papers, Library of Congress; Df, in the handwriting of Tobias Lear, George Washington Papers, Library of Congress.
1. This letter was enclosed in Washington to H, October 27, 1799.
2. See H to Thomas Parker, October 21, 1799, note 5.
3. Parker to H, October 10, 1799.
4. See Washington to H, September 29, 1799, note 4.
5. See Parker to Washington, October 9, 1799 (ALS, George Washington Papers, Library of Congress); Tobias Lear to Parker, October 10, 18, 1799 (ALS, George Washington Papers, Library of Congress).
6. See Parker to H, October 19, 1799; John Mackey to H, October 24, 1799 (listed in the appendix to this volume). Mackey wrote: "Colonel Thomas Parker and I having considered the means for hutting the 8th 9th & 10th Regiments and examined the sources from which the principal article could be expected, are sorry to be obliged to inform you that a supply cannot be hoped for."

To Caleb Swan [1]

Newyork October 27th 1799

Sir:

The Secretary of the Inspector General is entitled to the pay and emoluments of a captain.[2] The expression is general. It is not stated in the law whether the emoluments of a captain of cavalry, or those of a Captain of Infantry shall be the rule of allowance.[3] In a case of this kind the construction must be governed by the particular situation of the officer, and the nature of the service in which he will be engaged. My secretary will require the use of an horse, as it will be necessary for him to accompany me in my operations. It is therefore perfectly reasonable that he should receive forage, and this appears to me to be the just construction of the law.

With great consn.

Caleb Swan Eqr.

Df, in the handwriting of Thomas Y. How, Hamilton Papers, Library of Congress.

1. This letter was written in reply to Swan to H, October 26, 1799 (listed in the appendix to this volume). In this letter Swan questioned H's charges for forage for Thomas Y. How. H had included these charges in his account with the United States Government. See H to Swan, October 14, 1799.

2. Section 26 of "An Act for the better organizing of the Troops of the United States; and for other purposes" (1 Stat. 744 [March 3, 1799]) provided in part: "There shall be allowed to the inspector-general . . . a secretary to be appointed by himself, with the pay and emoluments of a captain."

3. Section 3 of the same act fixed the pay and emoluments of captains. This section reads: "A captain of cavalry, forty dollars per month, three rations per day, or an equivalent in money, and eight dollars per month for forage, when not furnished as aforesaid. A captain of artillery and infantry, forty dollars per month, and three rations per day, or an equivalent in money" (1 Stat. 750–51).

From George Washington

Mount Vernon, Octr. 27th: 1799.

Sir,

Since writing the enclosed letter to you yesterday, I have received a letter from Colo. Parker,[1] and one from Mr. Mackey,[2] Agent for the War Department at Harper's Ferry; stating the impracticability of procuring plank &c. sufficient for covering the huts intended to have been built for three Regiments at Harper's Ferry.

In consequence of this information I have again written to Colo. Parker, under this date, by Express, conforming my instructions, respecting Winter Quarters for the Troops, to the present state of things. I enclose a copy of my letter to him of this date,[3] as well as that of yesterday,[4] which will exhibit a full view of the business, and enable you to give any additional instructions you may think proper, directly to Colonel Parker.

Altho' I had determined to take no charge of any military operations, unless the Troops should be called into the field; yet, under
the present circumstances,[5] and considering that the advanced
season of the year will admit of no delay in providing Winter
Quarters for the Troops, I have willingly given my aid in this
business, and shall never decline any assistance in my power, when
necessary, to promote the good of the Service.

On the first view, I supposed that the Regiment in this State, commanded by Colo. Bentley,[6] was included in the three to be stationed
at Harper's Ferry. I find, however, that it is not. What provision is
made for the Winter Quarters of that Regiment?

I have not said anything to Colo. Parker respecting compensation,
or reimbursement of Expences he may incur by attending to
Quartering the other Regiments, if they are seperated from his. On
this subject you will be pleased to write him, if necessary.

With very great esteem & regard   I am Sir,   Your most obedt.
Servt   Go: Washington

Major Genl. Hamilton.

LS, in the handwriting of Tobias Lear, Hamilton Papers, Library of Congress;
Df, in the handwriting of Tobias Lear, George Washington Papers, Library of
Congress.
    1. Thomas Parker to Washington, October 24, 1799 (ALS, George Washing-
ton Papers, Library of Congress). In this letter Parker suggested that the Ninth
and Tenth Regiments be sent to Carlisle, Pennsylvania, where there were sufficient barracks.
    2. John Mackey to Washington, October 24, 1799 (ALS, George Washington
Papers, Library of Congress). In this letter Mackey reported that the Eighth,
Ninth, and Tenth Regiments could not be hutted at Harpers Ferry because
planks and slabs needed to cover the huts were not available.
    3. Washington to Parker, October 27, 1799 (Df, in the handwriting of Tobias
Lear, George Washington Papers, Library of Congress; copy, in the handwriting of Tobias Lear, Hamilton Papers, Library of Congress). Washington stated
that the primary purpose of quartering the three regiments at Harpers Ferry
was the advantage to be had "in training and disciplining the Soldiers." He suggested that the huts be constructed by the soldiers using logs instead of planks,
which was the practice during the American Revolution. If this were not possible, one or more regiments were to be quartered at Frederick Town, Maryland.
    4. Washington to Parker, October 26, 1799 (Df, in the handwriting of Tobias
Lear, George Washington Papers, Library of Congress; copy, in the handwriting of Tobias Lear, Hamilton Papers, Library of Congress). Washington wrote
that he had asked H to order the remaining two regiments to Harpers Ferry
in order to begin building huts.
    5. On November 5, 1799, Washington wrote to James McHenry: ". . . I
have departed from the resolution which I had formed, not to take charge of

any military operations, unless the Army should be called into the Field, so far as to order the best arrangements to be made that circumstances would permit, at this advanced season of the year, for quartering these Regiments. Knowing that no time could be lost—and that the distance of Genl. Hamilton from this part of the Country would occasion considerable delay in the necessary communications, and that the situation of Genl. Pinckney's family must prevent his personal attention to the business" (Df, in the handwriting of Tobias Lear, George Washington Papers, Library of Congress).

6. William C. Bentley commanded the Seventh Regiment of Infantry, which was stationed in Richmond, Virginia. In H to Bentley, September 28, 1799 (listed in the appendix to this volume), H stated: "Some place in the vicinity of Augusta but above the falls of the Savannah is contemplated for the winter quarters of the fifth, sixth and seventh regiments." See also H to McHenry, October 23, 1799; H to Charles Cotesworth Pinckney, October 23, 1799.

From George Washington

Private   Mount Vernon 27th Octr 1799

Dear Sir,

To my official letters I refer you for my communication, with Colo. Parker.[1] I have no conception however, that such difficulties as are ennumerated in his and Mr. Mackie's letters,[2] can exist in the erection of simple Hutts, (such as served us last war); and so I am about to inform the former.

I am averse to the seperation of the 8th. 9th and 10th Regiments under any circumstances which exist at present; and still more so to the distribution of them into *three States*. If they cannot *all* be accomodated at Harpers Ferry, the Barracks at Frederick town (if sufficient to contain two Regiments) is to be preferred, vastly, to Carlisle; for as much as that it is only twenty miles from the Arsenal which is in great forwardness at the former place; and because fuel alone, at either Frederick Town or Carlisle for the Winter, would double all the expence of the establishment at Harpers ferry. I have gone thus far into this business, and have given these opinions, because you desired it; and because, from the peculiar situation of things, it seemed, in a manner, almost indispensable. But I wish exceedingly, that the State of Mrs. Pinckney's health, and other circumstances, would permit General Pinckney [3] to come forward, and on his *own view* to decide on matters. To engage partially in Military arrangements is not only contrary to my original design, but unpleasant in its nature & operation; inasmuch as it incurs responsibility with out proper means for decision.

With respect to Major Campbell,[4] or any of those who are applying for appointments in the Inspectorate, I have no predeliction whatsoever towards them; handing in their names, with the testimonials of their merit & fitness as I receive them, for information *only*, is all I have in view.

The purport of your (private) letter of the 21st, with respect to a late decision, has surprized me exceedingly. I was surprized at the *measure,* how much more so at the manner of it? This business seems to have commenced in an evil hour, and under unfavourable auspices; and I wish mischief may not tread in all its steps, and be the final result of the measure. A wide door was open, through which a Retreat might ⟨have⟩ [5] been made from the first faux pea⟨ux; the shut⟩ting of which, to those who are not behind the Curtain, and are as little acquainted with the Secrets of the Cabinet as I am, is, from the present aspect of European Affairs, incomprehensible. But I have the same reliance on Providence which you express, and trust that matters will *end well,* howev⟨er⟩ unfavourable they may appear at present.

With very great esteem & regard   I am, My dear Sir   Your Most Obedt. & Affecte   Go: Washington

Majr. Genl. Hamilton

ALS, Hamilton Papers, Library of Congress; ALS, letterpress copy, George Washington Papers, Library of Congress.

1. See Washington to H, September 29, October 26, first letter of October 27, 1799.

2. See Washington to H, first letter of October 27, 1799, notes 1 and 2.

3. See Charles Cotesworth Pinckney to H, October 12, 1799.

4. William Campbell was a major in the Eighth Regiment of Infantry. For Campbell's request to be appointed a division inspector, see Washington to H, October 15, 1799; H to Washington, October 23, 1799 (both listed in the appendix to this volume). For letters recommending that Campbell be appointed to this post, see Thomas Butler to H, October 6, 1799; Thomas Parker to H, October 6, 1799; Edward Stevens to H, October 6, 1799; Henry Lee to H, October 16, 1799; William C. Bentley to H, October 17, 1799 (all listed in the appendix to this volume).

5. Material in brackets has been taken from the letterpress copy.

From James Wilkinson

[*New York, October 27, 1799.* On October 31, 1799, Hamilton wrote to Wilkinson and acknowledged receipt of Wilkinson's "several communications of the . . . 13th. 15. 19th. & 27 instant." *Letter of October 27 not found.*]

To James McHenry [1]

New York October 29
1799

Sir

General Wilkinson has furnished me with the inclosed estimates of the cost of the Water Battery Barracks & Magazine, which have been undertaken at Loftus's Height. And he gives it as his opinion by analogy, but without detail, that the cost of the fort proposed to be erected at the same place will about equal the sum of these Estimates say 16000 Dollars.

I send you an estimate,[2] which I have myself made aided by the information of prices which the estimates above referred to exhibit, which makes the cost considerably less.

Yet relying on General Wilkinson's better knowlege of local circumstances I have authorised him to erect the work within a limit of expence conformable to his own calculation, unless previous to his departure for the Mississippi he should receive a negative from you or by your Direction. The provision for the supplying of the fund may require your interposition. But regarding it as very urgent to have the work proceed during the cool season, I have desired him if a fund is not otherwise provided to cause the Deputy or other representative of the Qr. Master General at his Head Quarters to draw and negotiate Bills upon the Assistant Qr. Master General at the seat of Government, which Bills he is to indorse thus—

"Approved
James Wilkinson
Brigadier General"

Inclosed is likewise an estimate of the cost of boats for transporting down the Mississippi three thousand men,[3] founded on a communication from General Wilkinson. It exceeds greatly the sum I had been led to compute from anterior verbal information, and as the boats will be liable to perish I cease to recommend the measure as one immediately to be adopted. It may perhaps be hereafter deemed adviseable to pursue it in a more limited extent; but I beg leave to refer the matter to further consideration.

Every thing is doing to get ready the vessel which is to transport Artillery and Stores. A passport from the President shewing the nature of her errand is submitted as a precaution dictated by prudence. It will likewise no doubt be considered by you whether you will not direct insurance to be made. As there is to be a convoy & it is the property of Government it is probable the insurance may be effected at a moderate premium.

As the idea of an additional batalion for Georgia and Tenassee is only *surmised* in your letter & as you have not replied to my last communication on this subject, I conclude that the original plan [4] is to take effect and have framed my instructions to General Wilkinson [5] on this supposition.

General Pinckney was here yesterday. I shewed him the plan and my [6] letter to you in which it was sent.[7] He expressed without reserve his satisfaction.

With great respect   I have the honor to be   Sir   yr Obed ser

The Secy of War

ADf, Hamilton Papers, Library of Congress.
1. For background to this letter, see H to McHenry, first letter of October 12, October 22, 1799; McHenry to H, October 16, 1799.
2. "Estimate of the Cost of a Work to be erected on Loftus's Height of dimensions equal to fifty yards Square," October 29, 1799 (AD, Hamilton Papers, Library of Congress).
3. "Estimate of Boats necessary for the transportation of three thousand men with Baggage and Stores down the Mississippi," October 29, 1799 (ADS, Hamilton Papers, Library of Congress).
4. See the enclosure to H to McHenry, first letter of October 12, 1799.
5. H to James Wilkinson, second letter of October 31, 1799.
6. In MS, "by."
7. H to McHenry, first letter of October 12, 1799.

From Thomas Parker [1]

Camp Near Harpers ferry [Virginia]
30th Octr 1799

Sir,

I have this moment Received your letter of the 21st Instant Inclosed in one from the Commander in Chief.

I Cannot Recollect any expression in my letter [2] which I Conceived Coud induce you to Suppose that I meant to Build Barracks instead of Hutts. I think I Informed you that As there was not a Sufficiency of Timber on the public ground for Huting or Covering the whole of the Troops I had employed Mr Mackie [3] to procure by Purchase materials (meaning Rough Logs & Boards or plank) for the purpose.

I have heretofore Informed you that I had proceeded on that plan to Huting my Regiment Conforming to your Instructions [4] in every Respect [except] in the Size of the Hutts which the previous Cuting of the Timber prevented me from doing.[5]

Colo Lear [6] is now with me by order of the Commander in Chief to assist me in Endeavouring to procure the necessary materials for Accomodating the Other Troops. we are on Treaty for the purchase of a piece of Land adjoining to that Belonging to the public. If we Can Effect it which I hope may be done I expect we Shall be Able to Comply with his & your wishes. I will Inform you of the Result by Sundays mail.

The General expected that the Hutts woud be covered in the same manner that they were during the Revolutionary war & that It would not take the Quantity of plank that you had ordered to be purchased.

If we Coud procure proper Timber we Coud verry Readily Comply with his Expectations But It is not to be got in the neighbourhood; & you may Rest assured that the Calculation that I Inclosed you in my last letter will Rather fall Short of the Quantity of plank Requisite for the Hutts.

with the Highest Respect   I have the honor to be   Sir your Obd. Servt   Thomas Parker

ALS, Hamilton Papers, Library of Congress.

1. Parker enclosed this letter in a second letter to H of October 30, 1799 (listed in the appendix to this volume).

2. This is a reference to Parker to H, October 10, 1799.

3. John Mackey. See George Washington to H, two letters of October 27, 1799.

4. H to Parker, October 14, 1799 (listed in the appendix to this volume).

5. Parker to H, October 29, 1799 (listed in the appendix to this volume).

6. Tobias Lear.

To Caleb Swan

New York October 30. 1799

Sir

I recur to your several letters of the 19 of September 5th. 22d and 25th of October.[1]

The characters which have been brought into my view most prominently as proper for the Office of Deputy Pay Master General, within my command, are Major Huntington[2] of the 13th Regiment and Capt Williamson[3] of the Dragoons. I am well satisfied that each of these Gentlemen is qualified for and worthy of the trust. You are to make the election and ascertain the willingness to accept. I will only observe that if equally agreeable to you I had rather that a Captain than a field Officer should be taken from his corps for the purpose. Yet I am not strenuous on this point. But I am so that no time should be lost in making an appointment.

It is in my opinion most adviseable that there should be only one deputy Pay Master General to a distinct command—that is to say one to mine and one to General Pinckneys (there is already one[4] to General Wilkinson's) who ought to be an appendage of Head Quarters and who can easily arrange with detached stations. For Example—

A batalion is allotted to the lower posts on the Mississippi.[5] There the Regimental Pay Master will have his station. Money can be remitted to him in this mode (viz.)—The Deputy Pay Master General (Capt Vance) can send him from time to time bills drawn by himself upon you in favour of the Regimental Pay Master who can indorse and negotiate them. The unity of operation will then be preserved under the check of the Superior. Similar expedients will answer every where.

The appointment of Regimental Pay Masters for the two Regiments of Artillerists [6] and the Dragoons [7] has naturally relieved you from the embarrassments you mention in your letter of the 5 of October.

Lt. House has been instructed [8] under your direction to take charge of the Pay of the Infantry at Fort McHenry at Norfolk and at West Point. As to Niagara by an arrangement now making there will be there this Winter Two Companies of Infantry & half a company of Artillerists. The companies of Infantry which will include Lt. Vischers [9] party will be incorporated in the first Regiment of infantry. The Pay Master of this Regiment will naturally be the organ of Payments to those Companies.[10]

I am glad to learn from your letter of the 25 the measure which you had adopted for making Payment to the 8th. and 9th Regiments. But there is one sentence of your letter which gives me disquietude. Informing me that you are to send one of your Clerks, you add "By *this mode* I may expect a regular account of the money on *such documents as the law and my instructions require at my hands.*" It would seem from this that as to those Regiments to which you had not sent a Clerk (as the 6th 14. 15 &c) you intended to make the documents to which you allude a preliminary to the transmission of money. This, if so, is contrary to the expectation you gave me in a former letter [11] and which announced to all the Regiments—namely that money for the arrears would be forwarded upon estimate. I hope I am mistaken as to your present plan—for I should be much dissatisfied to have been made the organ of any expectation which should not be fulfilled. This must not be the case.

The temporary departure from form is now & then indispensable & right. An officer at the head of an important branch of the Military service who should lay it down as an absolute rule never to deviate would produce inconveniences nearly as great as one who should entirely disregard system. An extraordinary responsibility must sometimes be assumed. And for reasons heretofore given the present is a proper case for assuming it.

With great consideration & esteem &c

ADf, Hamilton Papers, Library of Congress.

1. Swan's letter to H of October 22, 1799, is listed in the appendix to this volume. In this letter Swan named infantry officers detached from their regular posts who were in need of pay.

2. Jabez Huntington was a major in the Thirteenth Regiment of Infantry.
3. Benjamin Williamson was a captain in the Regiment of Light Dragoons.
4. Samuel Vance. See Swan to H, September 19, 1799, note 4.
5. See the enclosure to H to James McHenry, first letter of October 12, 1799.
6. Lieutenant James House of the First Regiment of Artillerists and Engineers was appointed paymaster of the regiment on October 18, 1799 (Heitman, *United States Army,* I, 544).
   Lieutenant Theodore Meminger was the paymaster of the Second Regiment of Artillerists and Engineers ("Return of the names of the Pay Masters in the service of the United States," December 17, 1799 [DS, signed by Caleb Swan, Hamilton Papers, Library of Congress]).
7. Stephen G. Simmons, a first lieutenant in the Light Dragoons, was appointed regimental paymaster on October 28, 1799 (Heitman, *United States Army,* I, 887).
8. H to House, October 30, 1799 (listed in the appendix to this volume).
9. Nanning J. Visscher.
10. The position of paymaster of the First Regiment of Infantry was vacant because of the promotion to captain of Lieutenant Charles Hyde (*Executive Journal,* I, 320, 323; "Return of the names of the Pay Masters in the service of the United States," December 17, 1799 [DS, signed by Caleb Swan, Hamilton Papers, Library of Congress]).
11. See H to Swan, September 23, 1799; Swan to H, September 25, 1799.

To James McHenry

N. Y. Oct. 31. 1799

Sir

I have the honor to send you the arrangement which has been proposed by General Wilkinson [1] and approved by me; subject to a negative from your Department, previous to his Departure. This mode has been adopted to accelerate his return.

In a few instances, transfers of Officers from one Regiment to another are made in order to avoid as much as possible the separation of Officers from men. But care has been taken, as to preserving to the Officers respectively equal chances of promotion in the new as in the old relative Situation.

With great respect &

The Secy. of War

Df, in the handwriting of Ethan Brown, Hamilton Papers, Library of Congress.
1. See James Wilkinson to H, September 6, 1799, note 22.

[ENCLOSURE] 2

First Regiment

Field & Staff

John F. Hamtramck — Lieut. Col. Commandant
Thomas Hunt — 1st Major
— 2d. Major
Lieut. Robert Semple — Adjutant
Lieut. Yelverton Peyton — Paymaster
Lieut. Joshua S. Rogers — Quarter Master
John Elliott — Surgeon

{ — Mates

— Cadets

— Serjeant Major
— Qr. Master Serjeant
— Drum Major
— Fife-Major

Company Officers [2] [3] [4] [Thomas Marten 1]

Captains 1 Thomas Pasteur
          2 Abner Prior
          3 Daniel Britt

2. Df, Hamilton Papers, Library of Congress. The material within brackets in this document is in H's handwriting. H endorsed this document: "Proposed Arrangement Definitively."

Company Officers

[5 in 4] 4 Ross Bird
     5 JohnWhistler [6]
[7 in 4] 6 William Diven [7]
     7 Daniel Bissell [7]
     8 Charles Hyde [8]
     9 John Michael [9]
   10 Ferdinand L. Claiborne [10]

1st. Lieutenants

1. Campbell Smith <->
2 Elijah Strong [1]
3 Nicholas Rosencrantz [2]
4 Robert Torrans [4]
5 John W. Thompson [6]
6 J. A. Davidson [8]
7 George Stahl [9]
8 Charles Smith [10]
9 Phileman P. Blake [Add]
10 Moses Hook [Add]

2d. Lieuts

1 Joseph H Dwight
2 A. Van Wert
3 Peter Robinson
4 Eli B. Clemson
5 -----
6 -----
7 deficient
8 -----
9 -----
10 -----

Second Regiment

Field & Staff
David Strong Lieut. Col. Commandant

John H. Buell ‒ ‒ ‒ ‒ 1st Major
Jacob Kingsbury ‒ ‒ ‒ 2d Major
John Whipple ‒ ‒ ‒ ‒ Adjutant
James Richmond ‒ ‒ ‒ Paymaster
Peter P. Schuyler ‒ ‒ Quarter Master
William McCrosky ‒ ‒ Surgeon

‒ ‒ ‒ Mates

‒ ‒ ‒ Cadets

‒ ‒ ‒ Serjeant Major
‒ ‒ ‒ Qr Mr Serjeant
‒ ‒ ‒ Drum Major
‒ ‒ ‒ Fife-Major

Company Officers

Captains

1.	Cornelius Lyman	[1]	
2.	Richard H. Greaton	[2]	
3.	Russell Bissell	[3]	
4.	Edward Miller	[4]	
5.	Theodore Sedgwick	[6]	[Edw D Turner 5]
6.	William Ricard		
7.	Andrew McClary	[8]	[Ben Shaumberg 7]
8.	Peter Shoemaker	[9]	
9.	Jesse Lukens	[10]	

$\left[\dfrac{3^{d}}{5} \right]$

Company Officers

[Additional] 10. Nanning J. Vischer to supply the place of Turner

1st Lieuts.	[Captain 2d]	2d Lieuts	
1. Archd. Gray	[1]	1.	John Wilson
2. Rezin Webster	[2]	2.	James Dill
3. Benjamin Rand	[5]	3.	Peter Shiras
4. Samuel Allison	[6]	4.	Thomas Porter
5. George Callender	[8]	5.	Benjamin Bullett
6. John V. Glen		6.	Seymour Rannix
7. Jacob Wilson		7.	------
8. Zebulon M Pike	[9]	8.	------
9. Nathan Heald	[10]	9.	deficient
10. William Laidlie	[Add]	10.	------

$$\frac{3}{6}$$

[John Wilson additional]

Third Regiment

Field & Staff

Henry Gaither	Lieut. Col. Commandant
Jonathan Cass	1st Major
William Kersey	2d Major
1st Lieut. William Pitt Smith	Adjutant
1st Lt. William Scott	Pay Master
1. Lieut John McClary	Quarter Master
John F. Carmichael	Surgeon
John C. Wallace }	Mates

Cadets
Serjeant Major
Qr. Master Serjeant
Drum Major
Fife Major

Company Officers

Captains
1 Zebulon Pike [1]
2. John Heth [3] [Isaac Guion 2]
3. Richard Sparks [4]
4. John Wade [6] [Wm. Rickard 5]
5. Samuel C Vance [7]
6. John Bowyer [8]
7. Aaron Gregg [9]
8. John Steele [10]
[Additional] 9. Peter Marks—to supply the place of Shaumburgh B Q. M
[1-1 Lt.] 10. Charles Wright—to supply the place of Guion B. I.

1. Lieuts.
1. Hugh McCall [3]
2. George Strother [4]
3. Samuel Lane [8]
4. Patrick McCarty [9]
5. Matthew Arbuckle [10]
6. John Horton [Add]
7. John Saxon [Addition]

2. Lieuts. 1. - - - - -
2. - - - - -
3.
4.
5.
6.
7.

deficient

Company Officers

	[1 2d Lt]	8.
8. James Ryan	[2 2d Lt]	9.
9. Stephen S. Gibbs		10.
10. deficient		

Fourth Regiment

Field & Staff

Thomas Butler	Lieut. Col Commandant
William Peters	1st Major
Daniel Bradley	2d Major
George Salmon	Adjutant
Richard Chandler	Paymaster
Thomas Swaine	Quarter Master
Joseph Phillips	Surgeon
David Davis }	Mates
- - - - - -	
- - - - - -	Cadets
- - - - - -	
- - - - - -	Serjeant Major
- - - - - -	Qr. Master Serjeant
- - - - - -	Drum Major
- - - - - -	Fife-Major

Company Officers
[1]

Captains 1. Edward Butler
[1 in first] 2. Thomas Martin

$\left[\dfrac{1}{5}\right]$

3. Joseph Brock [2]
4. Alexander Gibson [3]
5. Robert Thompson [4]
6. Samuel Tinsley [6]
7. Benjamin Lockwood [8]
8. Peter Grayson [9]
9. Jonathan Taylor [10]
10. Robert Purdy

1st Lieuts

$\left[\dfrac{1}{7}\right]$

[Campbell Smith 1
1. Hartman Leitheser [2]
2. Merriwether Lewis
3. John Wallington [3]
4. Francis Johnson [4]
5. Samuel Crutchfield
☞ 6. John Campbell [8]
7. James Boneman [9]
8. John Haines [10]
9. Gabriel Jones [Add]
10. Saml. McGuire [Add]

2d Lieuts.

1. Thos. Blackburne
2. Danl. Numan
3. James Love
4. Thomas Eastland
5. James Desha
6.
7. Deficient
8.
9.
10.

To Nathan Rice

N York Octor 31st 1799

Sir:

I have received your several letters of the twenty third of September and of the fourth and eighth of October.

No particular rules were laid down for the government of the Colonels and Majors in the arrangement of relative rank as it was supposed that they wod. naturally take into consideration all circumstances which, in a military point of view, give one man the preference to another.[1] Former service is certainly to have weight, and where there is no material difference of character, is to govern the decision. Officers of a subsequent will rank after those of a prior appointment.

The Majors are all of one grade. There will be however between them a priority of rank, and this priority will be determined by the principles of rank heretofore promulged when they come to be applied to particular cases.

With great consideration

Df, in the handwriting of Thomas Y. How, Hamilton Papers, Library of Congress.

1. For the rules governing relative rank, see the enclosure to James McHenry to H, July 2, 1799. See also H to McHenry, July 8, 1799; McHenry to H, September 3, 1799.

From Caleb Swan

Trenton, October 31, 1799. "The Express was on the point of departure with Money for the 8th. & 9th. Regiments, when Major Bradley [1] arrived here and informed me that Mr. Bent [2] Pay Master to Coll. Parkers Regiment was on the way to this Place and would be here on saturday Evening, which induced me to Suspend Sending him, as he would probably have missed the Pay Master on the Road and therefore in some measure defeated the objects of both for a few days. Money will be sent by him for the 9th at the same time. I have offered Capt. Williamson the Deputy's appointment at your Head Quarters. . . ." [3]

LS, Hamilton Papers, Library of Congress.
1. Daniel Bradley.
2. Lemuel Bent. See Thomas Parker to H, October 16, 1799.
3. Benjamin Williamson. See H to Swan, October 30, 1799.

To James Wilkinson

New York Oct. 31st. 1799

Sir

In order to enable you to regulate your requisitions upon the contractor for supplies of provisions,[1] I give it as my opinion that the recruits which you may expect to reinforce your command, and which will arrive at Pittsburgh will be, in all May, Eight hundred, and in each successive month one hundred more, till your command shall be complete. Of their progress afterwards you can best judge.

Considering the high pay which is allowed to our troops, I do not perceive it to be necessary to make them extra compensation for any service immediately relative to their proper duty, which they perform *by way of tour* as the working on fortifications &c. If a Soldier, not engaged as an Artificer, is employed as such, he ought to receive an addition to his pay which will make his allowance equal to that of an Artificer on the establishment.

In cases where from the smallness of the garrison and other special circumstances, Services usually performed by *tour*, are of necessity performed for a length of time by the same persons, it is proper to allow an extra compensation; for this the rate of two Dollars per month is deemed Sufficient; And the practice ought to be restricted as much as possible.

The addition of half a gill of rum in all cases of fatigue service is an established and reasonable practice.

The above compensations, where they occur, will be properly defrayed out of the funds for the Quarter Master's Department.

The Superintendants and their Agents are to make requisitions for Indian provisions, but the ultimate controul of the supply must remain in the Military Officers, so far as to take care that the due supply of the troops is not really hazarded.

Experience has shewn that the best way of adjusting compensations, for property converted to the use of the Public, is by a specifick agreement with the proprietors, and it is commonly better to give in this way some what more than the thing is worth than to refer to arbitration, which seldom fails to do much more than justice to private owners. The Agent for making the Agreement would naturally be the representative of the Quarter Master under the direction of the commanding Officer.

If an agreement cannot be made the point may be left to three discreet men mutually chosen. But in such a submission it ought to be precisely stipulated, that nothing more is to be allowed than the *mere value* of the *ground as such*, without reference to the use to which it is dedicated by the Public; and the Arbitrators ought to be bound by oath.

It is, no Doubt, agreable to military usage that Boats passing and repassing a frontier post should be brought to & examined. This usage is so clear and the reasons for it so cogent, that though there may be question under our form of Government as to the right of the Military commander, I think it proper to give an approbation to your having the practice kept up until the Executive Government or Judicial Decisions should pronounce against its legality.

But I trust, that the establishment of a Custom house at Loftus's Heights will speedily obviate the difficulty.[2]

The construction of General Courts Martial requires absolutely a Judge Advocate. If you deem it necessary at your *Head Quarters* you may designate an Officer to officiate in this Capacity, & it must be confided that the War Department will sanction some moderate extra compensation for this special service of skill.

You think a Superintendant of the Artizans and labourers upon the works erecting, and to be erected on Loftus's height, who is not a military Officer, ought to be employed. In general the employment of extra Agents is to be avoided. But if from the Special circumstances, best known to you, you deem it a proper measure in this instance you will pursue it. I have directed the Paymaster General to furnish bounty Money,[3] and the Superintendant of military Stores,[4] Cloathing for recruiting & reinlisting within the limits of your command, to the extent of five companies.

With great consideration & Esteem I am Sir   Your obedt. Servant   A Hamilton

General Wilkinson

LS, University of Chicago Library; ADf, Columbia University Libraries.

1. On November 6, 1799, Wilkinson wrote to James O'Hara, contractor for Army provisions, outlining the quantity of provisions required by the troops under his command and specifying the time and place for delivery of the rations (copy, signed by Wilkinson, Hamilton Papers, Library of Congress).

2. H had proposed the establishment of this customhouse in H to James McHenry, October 20, 1799.

3. See H to McHenry, October 20, 1799.

4. H to Samuel Hodgdon, November 2, 1799 (listed in the appendix to Volume XXIV).

To James Wilkinson

New York October 31. 1799

Sir

The copious explanation which have been had between us in conversation on the subjects of your several communications of the 6th. of September 12th. 15. 19th. & 27 instant[1] will abrige the observations naturally connected with the plan which has been adopted as the result and which forms the object of the present instruction.

This plan, as you know, has the same basis with that which has been presented by you. As far as there may be variances in the application of principles collateral considerations have chiefly influenced.

It is contained in the inclosed paper A.[2] The letters between the Secretary of War and myself, of which B C D & E are copies,[3] exhibit the views which have reciprocally governed.

ADf, Hamilton Papers, Library of Congress.

1. None of the letters which Wilkinson wrote in October have been found.

2. The "inclosed paper A" was the "Plan for the disposition of the four Regiments . . . ," which H enclosed to H to James McHenry, first letter of October 12, 1799.

3. H to McHenry, October 12, 22, 29, 1799; McHenry to H, October 12, 1799.

In the execution of this plan many details arise which I do not enter into because they will most properly be left with you. Neither would I be understood to require a literal execution. The great outline is, under existing circumstances, to be adhered to—but you are at liberty to deviate in details which do not contravene the leading objects.

I will only remark that it is deemed material, that no greater force than the plan contemplates shall be assigned to the posts below the confluence of the Ohio with the Mississippi; and that the reserve force shall not be stationtd more Westward or Southward than the vicinity of the rapids of the Ohio.

That vicinity, as passing the obstacles of the navigation above and facilitating a communication with the posts below, presents itself to ⟨consideration⟩ in a favourable light. But there are ⟨– – –⟩ station higher up, which you will ⟨– – –⟩ your election agreeably to the final ⟨– – – –⟩ shall take of the subject.

A question arises whether the North or the South side of the Ohio should be preferred. In favour of the latter is the important consideration, that by the contract for the ensuing year [4] the ration is at least 2 Cents & 8 Milles cheaper there than on the North side. On the other hand, it is possible that the troops there may be exposed to vexations and in danger of seduction from the arts of disaffected persons which might not attend them in the opposite territory. But these inconveniencies do not appear likely to be so great as to counteract so considerable a difference in the price of the ration though they might be allowed to prevail against a small difference. Unless therefore there should be some important alteration in this particular I recommend to you the South side for the station of your Reserve-Force.

It will be my endeavour to engage the administration to organise in Tenassee, Kentucke the North and South Western territories two Regiments of Infantry a batalion of riflemen and a Regiment of Dragoons under the Act which provides for an Eventual Army.[5]

4. This is a reference to the Government contract with James O'Hara. See H to McHenry, November 8, 1799. O'Hara's contract is dated August 1, 1799, and was enclosed in McHenry to H, September 11, 1799 (listed in the appendix to this volume).

5. "An Act giving eventual authority to the President of the United States to augment the Army" (1 Stat. 725–27 [March 2, 1799]). See the introductory note to H to James Gunn, December 22, 1798.

This, if effected, may afford a powerful auxiliary for defensive or offensive measures as future exigencies may dictate.

The recruiting for the Corps of which your command is to be composed demands and has my particular attention. You are apprised, that the business is going on under Major Bradley [6] in North Carolina and Virginia, under Major Cass in the State of Delaware and under Major Buel [7] in the state of Vermont. In addition to this, I have proposed to the Secretary of War [8] to send to the Westward bounty money and cloathing for reinlisting and recruiting to the extent of a full Regiment. The troops of Dragoons contemplated by the plan ⟨proposed are⟩ to be embraced by this ⟨– –⟩ no ⟨– – – –⟩ proposition has ⟨– – – –.⟩

There are small detachments of Recruits for the Infantry of the permanent establishment at Norfolk in Virginia Frederick Town in Mary land and at West Point in the State of New York which as soon as practicable will reinforce the army under your command. And exertions, efficacious as I trust, will be made to complete the force allotted to you and to have it on the ground early in the next temperate season.

The new organisation of the Officers of the four Regiments which you have suggested [9] has been transmitted to the Secy of War [10] with an expression of my opinion in its favour. If you hear nothing to the contrary from that Officer previous to your Departure for the Mississippi, you will consider the plan as ratified & You will give it effect within your command. If however in the execution you find small deviations expedient you will make them, reporting to me the instances and the motives.

The Inspectors of Divisions and Brigades recommended by you are appointed. The affair of Judge Advocate has not yet been definitively acted upon.

The propriety of strongly fortifying Loftus's Heights being on all

6. Daniel Bradley.
7. See H to Jonathan Cass and John H. Buell, September 21, 1799 (listed in the appendix to this volume). See also "Circular to the Officers of the First Regiment of Infantry," September 20, 1799; "Circular to the Officers of the Second Regiment of Infantry," September 20, 1799 (both listed in the appendix to this volume).
8. H to McHenry, October 20, 1799.
9. Wilkinson to H, September 6, 1799, note 22.
10. See the enclosure to H to McHenry, October 31, 1799.

sides admitted,[11] so far as the force which can be allotted for this object will permit, it remains to say something concerning the kind of fortification.

Professing no skill as an Engineer, and as a consequence of the improvidence of our national policy in time past possessing no competent aid in others, I shall attempt nothing more than to offer hints. Indeed a critical view of the local situation in all its bearings, not merely as representation on paper of the part which looks towards the River, ought to guide and regulate the plan which is to be definitively adopted. This therefore must be left to you with the help of the best lights you have or can procure.

But I will observe that it appears to me adviseable to occupy the summit of the height with a Fort or Redoubt in nature of a Citadel adapted to a garrison of four hundred men and capable, as far as possible, of resisting by its construction a coup de main and of obliging an enemy not in a condition to make considerable sacrifices of men to attack it in form.

This redoubt with a battery towards the River at the point F in the plan you have furnished is as much as can be immediately undertaken. In process of time if the relative situation of Territorial boundary remains as it now is, it will probably be necessary to extend from this Citadel in different directions out works, which in conjuction with the Citadel will require a thousand men for their defence. This operation may be a successive one.

The idea of resisting a seize presupposes a work of solid materials as well as of regular design. You have stated that Brick is of easy Fabrication in the vicinity. Wood of an elastic quality, it is presumed, may also be procured with facility. A revetement of Brick with an interior of wood and earth mingled will form a strong fortress—at a moderate expence. Your Estimates of the expence of a Water Battery barracks and magazine present a total of 16024 Dollars; and you compute that a similar sum will suffice for a work such as you contemplate. I have ⟨in⟩formed the Secy of War [12] that you would be authorised by me to incur an expence not exceeding this sum—for the purpose in question unless he should signify his negative to you before your departure. But while this sum is given to you as a limit it is not believed that the object may be accom-

11. See McHenry to H, October 16, 1799.
12. H to McHenry, October 29, 1799.

plished for less and it is not doubted that you will exert yourself to have it done as cheaply as possible.

In this place, an answer to your inquiry as to the proper employment of the soldiery very fitly occurs. Doubtless utility and usage both unite to recommend the employment of the soldiery in the construction of works as far as may be practicable. Not to do it must tend to an augmentation of expence which the finances of no country can bear; besides that it is to foregoe a powerful instrument already prepared for accomplishing the object.

I do not overlook the obstacle from the climate which you mention in ref[er]ence to our Southern frontier. But for a great part of the year I must hope that this obstacle is not formidable. If the heats of July and August and the Sultry damps of September should drive us during that period to another resource; yet the residue of the year it is hoped will permit the labour of the troops to be employed with advantage. I am well informed that on the Sea board of South Carolina and Georgia the season from November to April inclusively is deemed unexceptionable for the employment of troops in laborious operations.

In the three months which have been mentioned it may be requisite to hire the labour of Negroes but even then there may be things to which that of whites can without injury be applied.

In general the idea must be to construct the works by the labour of the soldiery. The resort to a different aid must be by way of exception to be used as little as possible. Circumstances may be permitted to decide in each case whether to continue any works with the aid of blacks during the hot season or to suspend them till the return of a season favourable to the exertions of Whites.

You will find in my letter to the Secretary doubts as to the permanent maintenance of Fort Stoddard.[13] That part of the plan, which conforms to the disposition you have made, calls for your careful revision. You will ascertain the practicability of a safe and easy interior communication; without more expence to prepare it than the advantage may be worth. There is an instrinsically strong objection to the keeping of a post to which the access must be through a foreign territory.

The importance of securing and commanding the confluence of

13. H to McHenry, October 12, 1799. See also McHenry to H, October 16, 1799.

the Rivers Tenassee & Cumberland with the Ohio and of the latter with the Mississippi has been duly felt by you.[14] The selection of a spot the most eligible for a strong fort with a view to this object and the kind of work which it will be proper to establish are worthy of your early and careful attention. You must however bear in mind that it is to be successively effected by the labour of the troops. A garrison of five hundred men may be the standard of the dimensions. You will report to me the result of your investigations on this subject.

In a permanent arrangement for the Gallies [15] watermen ought to be engaged for the mass of the crew. Perhaps some soldiers may be employed as auxiliaries without inconvenience and with saving. A provision by law is requisite for the first purpose. You will order the Gallies to such situation as you judge best.

You are informed that the Artillery you have requested for Fort Adams with correspondent ammunition & stores have been ordered [16] and are to embark with you for the Miss[issi]ppi. It will be my endeavour that Such other Artillery as may be necessary in conformity with the general plan shall be forwarded as soon as possible. As to the Artillery and stores now at the several Western Posts it is your province to have them disposed of as you deem most adviseable.

I have desired E Stevens Esqr to procure the Mathematical Instruments [17] which you have requested.[18] A regular Military Academy appears to me indispensable and will command in reference to the ensuing session of Congress my best exertions for its establishment. This meets your suggestion as to Mathematical Teachers.[19]

The General Orders issued by you which you have submitted to my perusal [20] have been considered. They appear to me proper. But as I intend to prepare in the course of the Winter a code of

14. This is a reference to Fort Massac. See Wilkinson to H, September 6, 1799. See also H to George Washington, September 9, 1799; Washington to H, September 15, 1799; H to McHenry, October 12, 1799.

15. See H to McHenry, October 12, 1799; McHenry to H, October 16, 1799.

16. See H to Ebenezer Stevens, November 1, 1799 (listed in the appendix to Volume XXIV).

17. See H to Stevens, October 29, 1799 (listed in the appendix to this volume).

18. See Wilkinson to H, September 6, 1799.

19. See Wilkinson to H, September 6, 1799.

20. See Wilkinson to H, September 6, 1799, note 28.

Regulations which will embrace their objects I forbear to give any formal sanction to them at this time. They will remain in force by your authority.

Your Convention with the Spanish Governor respecting Deserters [21] considered as a temporary arrangement appears to me a measure of convenient operation. Yet it is beyond my powers to give it an authoritative sanction; and I have concluded not to ask one from the government, from the opinion that it is best it should retain the shape of a mere military arrangement between the local commanders. In this respect I do not hesitate to advise that it may continue to be executed.

I understand that arrangements have been made which will satisfy a portion of the arrears of pay [22] which you state to be due to the troops in the Western Quarter. The subject shall not cease to occupy my anxious attention. It is impossible to feel more strongly than I do the extreme impolicy of permitting large arrears to accumulate.

The affair of boats to be provided & kept ready for the transportation of troops upon an emergency will be matter of future instruction.[23]

Should the Spanish Governor or Commander object to the conveyance of your Artillery and stores to their destination—you will make a formal & peremptory requisition of free passage on the basis of Treaty [24] and persevere in it till there shall be an unequivocal refusal, when you will send back the Vessel with those Articles to Savannah in Georgia all addressed to the Commanding Officer of the Artillery of the UStates at that Place.

Your own permanent station will of course be with your reserve force; and it is expected that you will lose no time in repairing to it as early as may be after the coming Winter.

In the mean time, it is necessary for you to concenter all the upper posts under the superintendence of the Officer next in seniority [25] and to assign to him such a position as will facilitate a com-

21. See Wilkinson to H, April 15, 1799, note 12, and May 24, 1799.

22. See H to Caleb Swan, October 12, 1799.

23. See H to McHenry, October 29, 1799, note 3.

24. This is a reference to Article 4 of the Treaty of Friendship, Limits, and Navigation between Spain and the United States (Pinckney's Treaty), signed at San Lorenzo el Real, October 27, 1795 (Miller, *Treaties*, II, 321–27).

25. H is referring to John F. Hamtramck.

munication with me for the transmission of returns and information; taking care to let him understand that he is no more than your organ—an idea to which I shall be scrupulously attentive on my part.

The policy of our Government towards Spain continues as heretofore pacific and conciliatory. You will of course give the same character to your proceedings, as far as may depend upon you.

By a communication from the Secy of War, some time since received,[26] it is indicated that the management of Indian Affairs is exclusively reserved to the Superintendants and their Agents; the Military Officers to be auxiliary but only so as to imply no controul of Military Operations. It will be expedient nevertheless that all issues to Indians at Military Posts should appear in returns from them; not confounded ⟨with⟩ the issues for the Military but distinct. You will as far as may depend upon you give effect to this system, with a spirit of accommodation. Emergencies really extraordinary must always be exceptions to a general plan. These must be left to the Discretion of a Military Commander at his peril. In regard to the Citizens of the Western Country, as far as your agency may be concerned you will do every thing to foster good Will and attachment towards the Governments of the UStates. A firm and cordial Union is certainly the vital interest of every part of our Country.

I conform in an especial manner to the views of the Administration, and to the deep impressions of my own mind derived from a full consideration of the comparitive resources and necessities of our Country, when I recommend to you in every arrangement a careful regard to œconomy. Without it, our government cannot maintain the institutions or pursue the measures which are essential to its security and welfare. Without it, the Condition of its Military force can neither be respectable nor satisfactory. The interest of the army as a corps concurs with that of the public at large to enforce the practice of œconomy as a primary duty. I entertain a full confidence that your conduct will always evince a due sense of its importance, and that it will not cease to be your study in this and in every other matter to deserve the confidence and estimation of the Government.

Sir   Yr. Obed Ser

26. McHenry to H, April 30, 1799.

To Jonathan Dayton [1]

[New York, October–November, 1799] [2]

An Accurate view of the internal situation of the UStates presents many discouraging reflections to the enlightened friends of our Government and country. Notwithstanding the unexampled success of our public measures at home and abroad—notwithstanding the instructive comments afforded by the disastrous & disgusting scenes of the french Revolution, public opinion has not been ameliorated—sentiments dangerous to social happiness have not been diminished—on the contrary there are symptoms which warrant the apprehension that among the most numerous class of citizens errors of a very pernicious tendency have not only preserved but have extended their empire. Though something may have been gained on the side of men of information and property, more has probably been lost on that of persons of different description. An extraordinary exertion of the friends of Government, aided by circumstances of momentary impression, gave in the last election for members of Congress a more favourable countenance to some states than they had before worne. [3]

ADf, Hamilton Papers, Library of Congress; copy, in the handwriting of Thomas Y. How, Massachusetts Historical Society, Boston.

1. At the close of the American Revolution, Dayton, a resident of New Jersey, held the rank of captain. Following the war he studied law and entered politics. He served in the New Jersey Ratifying Convention and in the Second, Third, Fourth, and Fifth Congresses. He was speaker of the House of Representatives in the Fourth and Fifth Congresses. From March 4, 1799, to March 3, 1805, he represented New Jersey in the United States Senate. On July 19, 1798, his appointment as brigadier general was confirmed by the Senate (*Executive Journal*, I, 292, 293). Dayton, however, declined the appointment.

On the last page of the draft of this document, James A. Hamilton, H's son, wrote: "This paper in the Handwriting of Genl Hamilton was received from him by Genl Dayton of New Jersey when he was a member of Congress and by him delivered to J.A.H." On the back of the copy of this document, which is in the Theodore Sedgwick Papers, Massachusetts Historical Society, Boston, Fisher Ames wrote: "Considerations on the measures proper to be adopted 1799. 1800."

2. In *JCHW*, VI, 383, this document is dated "1799."

3. This is a reference to the increase in the number of Federalists in the South elected to the Sixth Congress. In the Fifth Congress the Federalist strength in the southern states had been three in South Carolina, one in North Carolina, and four in Virginia. In the Sixth Congress the nominal Federalists numbered two in Georgia, five in South Carolina, five in North Carolina, and eight in Virginia. See also William Heth to H, May 11, 1799, notes 2 and 3.

Yet it is the belief of well informed men that no real or desirable change has been wrought in those States. On the other hand it is admitted by close observers that some of the parts of the Union which in time past have been the soundest have of late exhibited signs of a gangrene begun and progressive.

It is likewise apparent that opposition to the government has acquired more system than formerly—is bolder in the avowal of its designs—less solicitous than it was to discriminate between the Constitution and the Administration—more open and more enterprising in its projects.

The late attempt of Virginia & Kentucke to unite the state legislatures in a direct resistance to certain laws of the Union can be considered in no other light than as an attempt to change the Government.[4]

It is stated, in addition, that the opposition-Party in Virginia, the head Quarters of the Faction, have followed up the hostile declarations which are to be found in the resolutions of their General Assembly by an actual preparation of the means of supporting them by force [5]—That they have taken measures to put their militia on a more efficient footing—are preparing considerable arsenals and magazines [6] and (which is an unequivocal proof how much they are in earnest) have gone so far as to lay new taxes [7] on their citizens.[8]

Amidst such serious indications of hostility, the safety and the duty of the supporters of the Government call upon them to adopt

4. For the Virginia and Kentucky resolutions, see H to Sedgwick, February 2, 1799, note 1.
5. See Heth to H, January 18, 1799, note 6.
6. For Virginia's proposed military expenditures, see *Journal of the House of Delegates of the Commonwealth of Virginia: Begun and Held at the Capitol, in the City of Richmond, on Monday, the Third Day of December, One Thousand Seven Hundred and Ninety-Eight* (Richmond, 1799), 76.
7. "An Act, laying Taxes for the support of Government" (*Virginia Laws,* December, 1798, Sess., Ch. III [January 23, 1799]).
8. On November 15, 1799, Sedgwick wrote to Rufus King: "It is a truth, unfortunately, but too evident that faction has, since you left the country, become more persistent & systematic; and, I believe, its leaders have decided that the duration of the government shall depend on the actual force of its friends & enemies. This appears to me evident from the conduct of the government of Virga. and its satellite Kentucky. With regard to the former, it has displayed an anxiety to render its militia as formidable as possible, and to supply its arsenals & magazines, and for those purposes it actually imposed a tax on its Citizens" (King, *The Life and Correspondence of Rufus King,* III, 147–48).

vigorous measures of counteraction. It will be wise in them to act upon the hypothesis that the opposers of the Government are resolved, if it shall be practicable to make its existence a question of force. Possessing as they now do all the constitutional powers, it will be an unpardonable mistake on their part if they do not exert them to surround the constitution with new ramparts and to disconcert the schemes of its enemies.

The measures proper to be adopted may be classed under   9
heads:

1   Establishments which will extend the influence and promote the popularity of the Government.

Under this head three important expedients occur—1   The Extension of the Judiciary system. 2   The improvement of the great communications as well interiorly as coastwise by turnpike roads. 3   The institution of a Society with funds to be employed in premiums for new inventions discoveries and improvements in Agriculture and in the Arts.

The extension of the Judiciary system ought to embrace two objects—one The subdivision of each state into small Districts (suppose Connecticut into four and so in proportion) assigning to each a Judge with a moderate salary—the other the appointment in each Country of Conservators or Justices of the Peace with only Ministerial functions and with no other compensations than fees for the services they shall perform.

This measure is necessary to give efficacy to the laws the execution of which is obstructed by the want of similar organs and by the indisposition of the local Magistrates in some states. The constitution requires that *Judges* shall have fixed salaries—but this does not apply to mere Justices of the peace without Judicial powers. Both those descriptions of persons are essential as well to the energetic execution of the laws as to the purpose of salutary patronage.

The thing would no doubt be a subject of clamour, but it would carry with it its own antidote, and when once established would bring a very powerful support to the Government.

The improvement of the roads would be a measure universally popular. None can be more so. For this purpose a regular plan should be adopted coextensive with the Union to be successively

9. Space left blank in MS.

executed—and a fund should be appropriated sufficient for the basis of a loan of a Milion of Dollars. The revenue of the Post office naturally offers itself. The future revenue from tolls would more than reimburse the expence; and public utility would be promoted in every direction.

The institution of a society with the aid of proper funds to encourage Agriculture and the arts, besides being productive of general advantage, will speak powerfully to the feelings and interests of those classes of men to whom the benefits derived from the Government have been heretofore the least manifest.

2 Provisions for augmenting the means and consolidating the strength of the Government.

A Milion of Dollars may without difficulty be added to the Revenue, by increasing the rates of some existing indirect taxes and by the addition of some new items of a similar character. The direct taxes ought neither to be increased nor diminished.

Our naval force ought to be completed to six Ships of the line Twelve frigates and twenty four sloops of War. More at this juncture would be disproportioned to our resources. Less would be inadequate to the end to be accomplished.

Our Military force should for the present be kept upon its actual footing; making provision for a reinlistment of the men for five years in the event of a settlement of differences with France—with this condition that in case of peace between Great Britain France and Spain, the UStates being then also at peace, all the Privates of twelve additional Regiments of Infantry and of the Regiment of Dragoons exceeding Twenty to a Company shall be disbanded. The corps of Artillerists may be left to retain the numbers which it shall happen to have; but without being recruited until the number of privates shall fall below the standard of the Infantry & Dragoons. A power ought to be given to the President to augment the four Old Regiments to their War Establishmt.[10]

The laws respecting volunteer Companies [11] & the *Eventual army* [12] should be rendered permanent and the Executive should proceed

10. For an account of the organization of the United States Army, see the introductory note to H to James Gunn, December 22, 1798.

11. For the Corps of Volunteers, see the introductory note to H to Gunn, December 22, 1798.

12. For the Eventual Army, see the introductory note to H to Gunn, December 22, 1798.

without delay to organise the latter. Some modifications of the discretion of the President will however be proper in a permanent law. And it will be a great improvement of the plan if it shall be thought expedient to allow the inlistment, for the purpose of instruction, of a corps of serjeants equal to the number requisite for the Eventual Army.

The Institution of a Military Academy will be an auxiliary of great importance.[13]

Manufactories of every article, the woolen parts of cloathing included, which are essential to the supply of the army ought to be established.

3 Arrangements for confirming and enlarging the legal Powers of the Government.

There are several temporary laws which in this view ought to be rendered permanent, particularly that which authorises the calling out of the Militia to suppress unlawful combinations and Insurrections.[14]

An article ought to be proposed to be added to the constitution for empowering Congress to open canals in all cases in which it may be necessary to conduct them through the territory of two or more states or through the territory of a State and that of the UStates. The power is very desireable for the purpose of improving the prodigious facilities for inland navigation with which nature has favoured this Country. It will also assist commerce and agriculture by rendering the transportation of commodities more cheap and expeditious. It will tend to secure the connection by facilitating the communication between distant portions of the Union. And it will be a useful source of influence to the Government.

Happy would it be if a clause would be added to the constitution, enabling Congress on the application of any considerable portion of a state, containing not less than a hundred thousand persons, to erect it into a separate state on the condition of fixing the quota of contributions which it shall make towards antecedent debts, if any there shall be, reserving to Congress the authority to levy within such state

13. See H to Louis Le Bègue Du Portail, July 23, 1798; Du Portail to H, December 9, 1798; H to James McHenry, December 26, 1798; H to James Wilkinson, second letter of October 31, 1799.

14. See "An Act to provide for calling forth the Militia to execute the laws of the Union, suppress insurrections, and repel invasions; and to repeal the Act now in force for those purposes" (1 *Stat.* 424–25 [February 28, 1795]).

the taxes necessary to the payment of such quota, in case of neglect on the part of the State. The subdivision of the great states is indispensable to the security of the General Government and with it of the Union. Great States will always feel a rivalship with the common head, will often be disposed to machinate against it, and in certain situations will be able to do it with decisive effect. The subdivision of such states ought to be a cardinal point in the Fœderal policy: and small states are doubtless best adapted to the purposes of local regulation and to the preservation of the republican spirit. This suggestion however is merely thrown out for consideration. It is feared that it would be inexpedient & even dangerous to propose at this time an amendment of the kind.

4 Laws for restraining and punishing incendiary and seditious practices.

It will be useful to declare that all such writings &c which at common law are libels if levelled against any Officer whatsoever of the UStates shall be cognizable in the Courts of UStates.

To preserve confidence in the Officers of the General Government, by preserving their reputations from malicious and unfounded slanders, is essential to enable them to fulfil the ends of their appointment. It is therefore both constitutional and politic to place their reputations under the guardianship of the Courts of the United States. They ought not to be left to the cold and relucant protection of state courts always temporising sometimes disaffected.

But what avail laws which are not executed? Renegade Aliens conduct more than one of the most incendiary presses in the UStates [15] —and yet in open contempt and defiance of the laws they are permitted to continue their destructive labours. Why are they not sent away? Are laws of this kind passed merely to excite odium and remain a dead letter? Vigour in the Executive is at least as necessary as in the legislative branch. If the President requires to be stimulated those who can approach him ought to do it.

15. This is a reference to foreign-born anti-Federalist newspapermen such as John D. Burk, James Thomson Callender, and Thomas Cooper. Burk, who was born in Ireland, edited the [New York] *Time Piece*. Callender, born in Scotland, was a naturalized citizen. In 1799 he joined the staff of the [Richmond] *Examiner*. For his earlier publications, see Oliver Wolcott, Jr., to H, July 3, 1797, note 1. Cooper, born in England, was also a naturalized citizen. From April through June, 1799, he attacked the Adams Administration as editor of the [Sunbury and Northumberland, Pennsylvania] *Gazette*.

APPENDIX

APRIL, 1799

From James McHenry, April 1, 1799 (ALS, Hamilton Papers,   V
Library of Congress), enclosing John Allen to McHenry,
March 25, 1799 (ALS, Hamilton Papers, Library of Congress).

From James McHenry, April 1, 1799 (LS, Hamilton Papers,   IV
Library of Congress), enclosing McHenry to Thomas Lloyd
Moore, April 1, 1799 (LS, Hamilton Papers, Library of Con-
gress).

To Horatio Dayton, April 2, 1799 (copy, in the handwriting   III
of Philip Church, Hamilton Papers, Library of Congress).

To Nathaniel Leonard, April 2, 1799 (copy, in the handwriting of   III
Philip Church, Hamilton Papers, Library of Congress).

From James McHenry, April 2, 1799 (LS, Hamilton Papers,   VIII
Library of Congress).

To William North, April 2, 1799 (sold at Anderson Galleries,   III
New York City, January 30, 1929, Lot 39). *Letter not found.*

From Lewis Tousard, April 2, 1799 (LS, Hamilton Papers, Li-   VII
brary of Congress).

To Joseph Elliott, April 3, 1799 (ADf, Hamilton Papers, Library   III
of Congress).

From Daniel Morgan, April 3, 1799 (LS, Hamilton Papers, Li-   I
brary of Congress), enclosing Archibald C. Randolph to Morgan, March 14, 1799 (copy, Hamilton Papers, Library of
Congress).

To James Wilkinson, April 3, 1799 (copy, in the handwriting of   III
Philip Church, Hamilton Papers, Library of Congress).

From Horatio Dayton, April 4, 1799 (ALS, Hamilton Papers,   IV
Library of Congress).

From John McClallen, April 4, 1799 (ALS, Hamilton Papers,   III
Library of Congress).

From James McHenry, April 4, 1799 (LS, Hamilton Papers, Li-   IV
brary of Congress; LS, letterpress copy, Hamilton Papers,
Library of Congress), enclosing George Ingersoll to McHenry,
January 15, 1799 (ALS, Hamilton Papers, Library of Congress);
general court-martial, January 10, 1799 (DS, Hamilton Papers,
Library of Congress).

From James McHenry, April 4, 1799 (LS, Hamilton Papers, Li-   VII
brary of Congress; LS, letterpress copy, James McHenry
Papers, Library of Congress).

To Thomas Brinley, April 5, 1799 (Df, in the handwriting of   II
Philip Church, Hamilton Papers, Library of Congress).

To Thomas Lloyd Moore, April 5, 1799 (copy, in the handwriting of Philip Church, Hamilton Papers, Library of Congress). III

To Aaron Ogden, April 5, 1799 (Df, misdated March 5, 1799, in the handwriting of Philip Church, Hamilton Papers, Library of Congress). VI

To Lewis Tousard, April 5, 1799 (copy and Df, both in the handwriting of Philip Church, Hamilton Papers, Library of Congress), enclosing a list of names of officers to serve at a court-martial (D, Hamilton Papers, Library of Congress). IV

From Josias Carvel Hall, April 6, 1799 (ALS, Hamilton Papers, Library of Congress). VI

From Daniel Jackson, April 6, 1799 (ALS, Hamilton Papers, Library of Congress). VI

From Nathaniel Leonard, April 6, 1799 (ALS, Hamilton Papers, Library of Congress; ALS, with slight variations, J. W. Kingsbury Collection, Missouri Historical Society, Columbia, Missouri). VII

From William S. Smith, April 6, 1799 (ALS, Hamilton Papers, Library of Congress). Acknowledges receipt of H's letter of April 3, 1799. *Letter not found.* VI

From Thomas Lloyd Moore, April 7, 1799 (ALS, Hamilton Papers, Library of Congress). IV VI

From Aaron Ogden, April 7, 1799 (ALS, Hamilton Papers, Library of Congress). VI

From Adam Hoops, April 8, 1799 (ALS, Hamilton Papers, Library of Congress). IV

From James McHenry, April 8, 1799 (ALS, Hamilton Papers, Library of Congress; ADfS, James McHenry Papers, Library of Congress). VIII

From Aaron Ogden, April 8, 1799 (ALS, Hamilton Papers, Library of Congress). V

From Jonathan Rhea, April 8, 1799 (ALS, Hamilton Papers, Library of Congress), enclosing a contract with John Bray, April 6, 1799 (copy, Hamilton Papers, Library of Congress). VII

From William S. Smith, April 8, 1799 (ALS, Hamilton Papers, Library of Congress), enclosing "Proposed rank of Officers 12th. Regt." (AD, Hamilton Papers, Library of Congress). H's endorsement reads: "Confirmed." *Letter not found.* VI

From Hezekiah W. Bissell, April 9, 1799 (ALS, Hamilton Papers, Library of Congress). III

To John F. Hamtramck, April 9, 1799 (ADf, Hamilton Papers,   VII
Library of Congress; LC, RG 94, Post-Revolutionary War
Records, Letter Book of Major Thomas Cushing, National
Archives).

From George W. Kirkland, April 9, 1799 (ALS, Hamilton Papers,   III
Library of Congress).

To William Colfax, April 10, 1799 (copy, in the handwriting of   V
Ethan Brown, Hamilton Papers, Library of Congress).

From James McHenry, April 10, 1799 (LS, Hamilton Papers, Li-   V
brary of Congress), enclosing a list of officers for North Carolina (copy, Hamilton Papers, Library of Congress).

From Ebenezer Massey, April 10, 1799 (ALS, Hamilton Papers,   III
Library of Congress), enclosing a certificate signed by John K.
Lynch, April 8, 1799 (ADS, Hamilton Papers, Library of
Congress).

From Amos Stoddard, April 10, 1799 (ALS, Hamilton Papers,   IV
Library of Congress).   V

From Thomas Ustick, April 10, 1799 (ALS, Hamilton Papers,   II
Library of Congress).

From Aaron Ogden, April 11, 1799 (ALS, Hamilton Papers, Li-   VI
brary of Congress), enclosing a list of officers for the Eleventh
Regiment of Infantry (AD, Hamilton Papers, Library of
Congress).

From Amos Stoddard, April 11, 1799 (ALS, Hamilton Papers,   VI
Library of Congress).

From Timothy Taylor, April 11, 1799 (ALS, Hamilton Papers,   V
Library of Congress).   VI

From Henry Lee, April 12, 1799 (ALS, Hamilton Papers, Library   V
of Congress), enclosing a list of divisions and subdivisions for
Virginia (copy, in the handwriting of Thomas Parker, Hamilton Papers, Library of Congress).

From James McHenry, April 12, 1799 (LS, Hamilton Papers, Li-   V
brary of Congress; LS, letterpress copy, James McHenry Pa-   VII
pers, Library of Congress).

From James McHenry, April 12, 1799 (LS, Hamilton Papers, Li-   VIII
brary of Congress; LS, letterpress copy, James McHenry Papers, Library of Congress), enclosing McHenry to John
Wilkins, Jr., April 12, 1799; McHenry to Edward D. Turner,
April 11, 1799; McHenry to Thomas Pasteur, April 11, 1799
(copies, Hamilton Papers, Library of Congress).

From Thomas Parker, April 12, 1799 (ALS, Hamilton Papers,   V
Library of Congress).

From Staats Morris, April 13, 1799 (ALS, Hamilton Papers, Li-   III
brary of Congress).

From George Davis, April 15, 1799 (ALS, Hamilton Papers, Li-   III
brary of Congress). On the verso H wrote a draft of his
acknowledgment. *Letter not found.*

From Josias Carvel Hall, April 15, 1799 (ALS, Hamilton Papers,   V
Library of Congress).   VI

To Samuel Hodgdon, April 15, 1799 (ADf, Hamilton Papers,   VII
Library of Congress).

From James McHenry, April 15, 1799 (ALS, Hamilton Papers,   VII
Library of Congress), enclosing a contract for supplies at
Woodbury, New Jersey (copy, Hamilton Papers, Library of
Congress).

To James McHenry, April 15, 1799 (ADfS, Hamilton Papers, Li-   VIII
brary of Congress).

To Lewis Tousard, April 15, 1799 (Df, in the handwriting of   VII
Philip Church, Hamilton Papers, Library of Congress).

From Jedediah Huntington, April 16, 1799 (ALS, Hamilton Pa-   III
pers, Library of Congress).

From James McHenry, April 16, 1799 (ALS, Hamilton Papers,   III
Library of Congress; ADf, James McHenry Papers, Library of
Congress).

From Aaron Ogden, April 16, 1799 (ALS, Hamilton Papers, Li-   V
brary of Congress), enclosing "A List of the Officers assigned
to the different sub-districts of the eleventh recruiting circle . . ." (DS, Hamilton Papers, Library of Congress).

From Isaac Smith, April 16, 1799 (LS, Hamilton Papers, Library   III
of Congress).

To Ebenezer Stevens, April 16, 1799 (ALS, New-York Historical   VII
Society, New York City). Stevens's endorsement reads: "Ansd."
Letter not found.

To Nathaniel Leonard, April 17, 1799 (ADf, Hamilton Papers,   VII
Library of Congress).   VIII

To Washington Morton, April 17, 1799 (copy, in the handwrit-   IV
ing of Ethan Brown, Hamilton Papers, Library of Congress).

To Aaron Ogden, April 17, 1799 (LS, in the handwriting of   V
Ethan Brown, Lloyd W. Smith Collection, Morristown Na-   VII

tional Historical Park, Morristown, New Jersey; ADf, Hamilton Papers, Library of Congress).

From William S. Smith, April 17, 1799 (ALS, Hamilton Papers, Library of Congress). IV V VII

From Frederick Weissenfels, April 17, 1799 (ALS, Hamilton Papers, Library of Congress). I

To William Yates, April 17, 1799 (ADfS, Hamilton Papers, Library of Congress). VIII

To Truman Mosely, April 18, 1799 (copy, in the handwriting of Philip Church, Hamilton Papers, Library of Congress). VI

From Thomas Parker, April 18, 1799 (ALS, Hamilton Papers, Library of Congress). V

From Nanning J. Visscher, April 18, 1799 (ALS, Hamilton Papers, Library of Congress). V

From James McHenry, April 19, 1799 (LS, Hamilton Papers, Library of Congress; LS, letterpress copy, James McHenry Papers, Library of Congress). III

From Ebenezer Massey, April 19, 1799 (ALS, Hamilton Papers, Library of Congress). III

From Aaron Ogden, April 19, 1799 (ALS, Hamilton Papers, Library of Congress). V

To Ebenezer Stevens, April 19, 1799 (ALS, New-York Historical Society, New York City; copy, in the handwriting of Philip Church, Hamilton Papers, Library of Congress). VI

To Timothy Taylor, April 19, 1799 (copy, in the handwriting of Philip Church, Hamilton Papers, Library of Congress). V

From Daniel Clymer, April 20, 1799 (ALS, Hamilton Papers, Library of Congress). III

To Horatio Dayton, April 20, 1799 (ADf, Hamilton Papers, Library of Congress). IV

From Samuel Osborn, April 20, 1799 (ALS, Hamilton Papers, Library of Congress). IV

From William Paterson, April 20, 1799 (ALS, Hamilton Papers, Library of Congress). I

From William S. Smith, April 20, 1799 (ALS, Hamilton Papers, Library of Congress). V VII

From Thomas Ustick, April 20, 1799 (ALS, Hamilton Papers, Library of Congress), enclosing a certificate by Jacob Morton, April 19, 1799 (ADS, Hamilton Papers, Library of Congress). II

APPENDIX 611

From James McHenry, April 21, 1799 (LS, Hamilton Papers, Li-   III
brary of Congress), enclosing Alexander Gibson to McHenry,   V
April 6, 1799 (copy, Hamilton Papers, Library of Congress).

From James McHenry, April 22, 1799 (LS, Hamilton Papers,   III
Library of Congress; LS, letterpress copy, James McHenry
Papers, Library of Congress), enclosing William Simmons to
McHenry, April 18, 1799 (copy, Hamilton Papers, Library of
Congress).

From Thomas Lloyd Moore, April 22, 1799 (ALS, Hamilton Pa-   V
pers, Library of Congress).

From Thomas Parker, April 22, 1799 (ALS, Hamilton Papers,   VI
Library of Congress).

To Nicholas Fish, April 23, 1799 (ADf, Hamilton Papers, Library   VII
of Congress).

To Josias Carvel Hall, April 23, 1799 (ADfS, Hamilton Papers   VI
Library of Congress).

To Thomas Lloyd Moore, April 23, 1799 (ALS, Hamilton Papers,   IV
Library of Congress).

To William S. Smith, April 23, 1799 (copy, in the handwriting of   VII
Philip Church, Hamilton Papers, Library of Congress).

From Ebenezer Stevens, April 23, 1799 (LS, Hamilton Papers,   VII
Library of Congress; LC, New-York Historical Society, New
York City).

From Stephen Van Rensselaer, April 23, 1799 (ALS, Hamilton   I
Papers, Library of Congress).

From Thomas Grosvenor, April 24, 1799 (ALS, Hamilton Papers,   I
Library of Congress).

From James McHenry, April 24, 1799 (LS, Hamilton Papers, Li-   III
brary of Congress; copy, Hamilton Papers, Library of Congress).

To James McHenry, April [24], 1799 (ADf, Hamilton Papers,   V
Library of Congress).   VII

From Richard Willing, April 24, 1799 (ALS, Hamilton Papers,   III
Library of Congress).

To James Bruff, April 25, 1799 (ADfS, Hamilton Papers, Library   VII
of Congress).

To Mahlon Ford, April 25, 1799 (ADf, Hamilton Papers, Library   III
of Congress).

From Caleb Gibbs, April 25, 1799 (ALS, Hamilton Papers, Li-   II
brary of Congress; ALS [marked "Duplicate"], Hamilton Pa-

pers, Library of Congress), enclosing an extract of Gibbs to
George Washington, April 21, 1799 (two copies, in the hand-
writing of Gibbs [one marked "Duplicate"], Hamilton Papers,
Library of Congress).

From Josias Carvel Hall, April 25, 1799 (ALS, Hamilton Papers,   V
Library of Congress), enclosing the arrangement of Maryland   VI
into recruiting districts (AD, Hamilton Papers, Library of Con-   VII
gress).

To James McHenry, April 25, 1799 (ADf, Hamilton Papers, Li-   III
brary of Congress).   V
                                                                     VII

From Thomas Lloyd Moore, April 25, 1799 (ALS, Hamilton   III
Papers, Library of Congress).

To Thomas Lloyd Moore, April 25, 1799 (ADf, Hamilton Papers,   III
Library of Congress).   V

From Aaron Ogden, April 25, 1799 (ALS, Hamilton Papers, Li-   V
brary of Congress).   VI

From Thomas Parker, April 25, 1799 (ALS, Hamilton Papers,   V
Library of Congress).

From James McHenry, April 26, 1799 (LS, Hamilton Papers,   III
Library of Congress), enclosing Peleg Wadsworth to McHenry,
April 19, 1799 (copy, Hamilton Papers, Library of Congress).

From James Simmons, April 26, 1799 (ALS, Hamilton Papers, Li-   IV
brary of Congress), enclosing Samuel C. Vance to William Simmons, April 2, 1799 (copy, Hamilton Papers, Library of Congress); a memorandum by William Simmons, April 3, 1799
(copy, Hamilton Papers, Library of Congress).

From George Tillinghast, April 26, 1799 (ALS, Hamilton Papers,   II
Library of Congress).

From Nathaniel Leonard, April 27, 1799 (ALS, Hamilton Papers,   VI
Library of Congress).   VIII

From James McHenry, April 27, 1799 (ALS, Hamilton Papers,   III
Library of Congress; ADf, James McHenry Papers, Library of
Congress).

From James McHenry, April 27, 1799 (LS, Hamilton Papers, Li-   IV
brary of Congress).

From Staats Morris, April 27, 1799 (ALS, Hamilton Papers, Li-   III
brary of Congress).

From Samuel C. Seely, April 27, 1799 (ALS, Hamilton Papers,   II
Library of Congress).

From James Wadsworth, April 27, 1799 (ALS, Hamilton Papers, Library of Congress). — I

From David S. Jones, April 28, 1799 (ALS, Hamilton Papers, Library of Congress). — III

From James McHenry, April 29, 1799 (LS, Hamilton Papers, Library of Congress), enclosing John Wilkins, Jr., to McHenry, April 19, 1799 (copy, Hamilton Papers, Library of Congress). — VIII

To James McHenry, April 29, 1799 (AL, The Indiana Historical Society Library, Indianapolis). — VIII

To Thomas Pasteur, April 29, 1799 (ADf, Hamilton Papers, Library of Congress). — VIII

From William S. Smith, April 29, 1799 (ALS, Hamilton Papers, Library of Congress). — II / V

From Ebenezer Stevens, April 29, 1799 (LS, Hamilton Papers, Library of Congress; LC, New-York Historical Society, New York City). — VII

From Timothy Taylor, April 29, 1799 (ALS, Hamilton Papers, Library of Congress), enclosing "Disposition of the Officers of the 13th Regiment to the Districts & Sub Districts for the recruiting Service in the State of Connecticut" (ADS, Hamilton Papers, Library of Congress). — III / V

To Timothy Taylor, April 29, 1799 (ADfS, Hamilton Papers, Library of Congress). — VII

From Jonathan Cass, April 30, 1799 (ALS, Hamilton Papers, Library of Congress), enclosing James Wilkinson to Cass, July 11, 1797 (ALS, Hamilton Papers, Library of Congress). — III

From Robert G. Harper, April 30, 1799 (ALS, Hamilton Papers, Library of Congress), enclosing an extract of Harper to Charles Cotesworth Pinckney, April 30, 1799 (copy, in the handwriting of Harper, Hamilton Papers, Library of Congress). — II

From Aaron Ogden, April 30, 1799 (ALS, Hamilton Papers, Library of Congress). — V / VII

From Yelverton Peyton, April 30, 1799 (ALS, Hamilton Papers, Library of Congress). — III

To Ebenezer Stevens, April 30, 1799 (ALS, New-York Historical Society, New York City; copy, in the handwriting of Ethan Brown, Hamilton Papers, Library of Congress). — VI

From Robert Troup, April 30, 1799 (ALS, Hamilton Papers, Library of Congress). — I

From Jonathan Dayton, [April, 1799] (ALS, Hamilton Papers,   V
Library of Congress).   VI

MAY, 1799

From Timothy Banger, May 1, 1799 (ALS, Hamilton Papers, Li-   VII
brary of Congress), enclosing "Return of Clothing in the Public
Store at Philadelphia . . ." (ADS, Hamilton Papers, Library
of Congress).

From James McHenry, May 1, 1799 (LS, Hamilton Papers, Li-   III
brary of Congress).

From James McHenry, May 1, 1799 (ALS, Hamilton Papers,   VIII
Library of Congress).

To James McHenry, May 1, 1799 (Df, in the handwriting of   VII
Philip Church, Hamilton Papers, Library of Congress).

To Aaron Ogden, May 1, 1799 (LS, Lloyd W. Smith Collection,   V
Morristown National Historical Park, Morristown, New Jersey;   VII
Df, in the handwriting of Philip Church, Hamilton Papers, Li-
brary of Congress).

From Alexander Richards, May 1, 1799 (ALS, Hamilton Papers,   VII
Library of Congress), enclosing Army supply contract of
William Colfax and Abraham Van Bushvik, Jr., December 28,
1798 (copy, Hamilton Papers, Library of Congress).

From Ebenezer Stevens, May 1, 1799 (LS, Hamilton Papers, Li-   VII
brary of Congress; LC, New-York Historical Society, New
York City).

To Amos Stoddard, May 1, 1799 (Df, in the handwriting of Philip   VI
Church, Hamilton Papers, Library of Congress).

To James Bruff, May 2, 1799 (ADf, Hamilton Papers, Library   V
of Congress).

To John F. Hamtramck, May 2, 1799 (copy, in the handwriting   VII
of Ethan Brown, Hamilton Papers, Library of Congress).

From Richard Hunewell, May 2, 1799 (ALS, Hamilton Papers,   V
Library of Congress).

To Jedediah Huntington, May 2, 1799 (Df, in the handwriting of   III
Philip Church, Hamilton Papers, Library of Congress).

To James McHenry, May 2, 1799 (Df, in the handwriting of   V
Philip Church, Hamilton Papers, Library of Congress).   VII

To James McHenry, May 2, 1799 (Df [two], in the handwriting   VII
of Philip Church, Hamilton Papers, Library of Congress).

To James McHenry, May 2, 1799 (ALS, Columbia University   III
  Libraries; ALS [photostat], James McHenry Papers, Library of
  Congress; copy, in the handwriting of Ethan Brown, Hamilton
  Papers, Library of Congress).

To Staats Morris, May 2, 1799 (Df, in the handwriting of Philip   III
  Church, Hamilton Papers, Library of Congress).

To Yelverton Peyton, May 2, 1799 (Df, in the handwriting of   III
  Philip Church, Hamilton Papers, Library of Congress).

To Campbell Smith, May 2, 1799 (Df, in the handwriting of   III
  Philip Church, Hamilton Papers, Library of Congress). Acknowledges receipt of Smith's letter of April 20, 1799. *Letter
  not found.*

To Richard Willing, May 2, 1799 (copy, in the handwriting of   III
  Ethan Brown, Hamilton Papers, Library of Congress).

To Justus Barnum, May 3, 1799 (Df, in the handwriting of Philip   II
  Church, Hamilton Papers, Library of Congress). Acknowledges
  receipt of Barnum's letter of April 13, 1799. *Letter not found.*

From William C. Bentley, May 3, 1799 (LS, Hamilton Papers,   V
  Library of Congress).   VII

To Edward Carrington, May 3, 1799 (ADf, Hamilton Papers,   V
  Library of Congress).

From Horatio Dayton, May 3, 1799 (ALS, Hamilton Papers,   III
  Library of Congress).

To George W. Duncan, May 3, 1799 (Df, in the handwriting of   II
  Philip Church, Hamilton Papers, Library of Congress).

From Constant Freeman, May 3, 1799 (ALS, Hamilton Papers,   III
  Library of Congress).

From James Giles, May 3, 1799 (ALS, Hamilton Papers, Library   I
  of Congress).

To Henry Lee, May 3, 1799 (Df, in the handwriting of Philip   V
  Church, Hamilton Papers, Library of Congress).

From James McHenry, May 3, 1799 (LS, Hamilton Papers, Li-   VI
  brary of Congress), enclosing Thomas Butler to McHenry,
  April 8, 1799 (extract, Hamilton Papers, Library of Congress).

From James McHenry, May 3, 1799 (LS, Hamilton Papers, Li-   VII
  brary of Congress).

To James McHenry, May 3, 1799 (ADf, Hamilton Papers, Li-   V
  brary of Congress).

To James McHenry, May 3, 1799 (ADf, Hamilton Papers, Li-   V
  brary of Congress).   VII

To James McHenry, May 3, 1799 (Df, in the handwriting of   I
Philip Church, Hamilton Papers, Library of Congress).

From Thomas Parker, May 3, 1799 (ALS, Hamilton Papers, Li-   I
brary of Congress), enclosing "Lieutt. Colo. Thomas Parkers   V
Circle for recruiting divided and subdivided into Districts" (D,   VII
Hamilton Papers, Library of Congress).

To Thomas Parker, May 3, 1799 (ADf, Hamilton Papers, Library   V
of Congress).   VII

From James Read, May 3, 1799 (ALS, Hamilton Papers, Library   V
of Congress). Acknowledges receipt of two letters of April 17,
1799, from H. *One letter not found.*

To Timothy Taylor, May 3, 1799 (Df, in the handwriting of   VI
Philip Church, Hamilton Papers, Library of Congress).

From Lewis Tousard, May 3, 1799 (LS, Hamilton Papers, Library   IV
of Congress).

To John S. Dexter, May 4, 1799 (ADf, in the handwriting of   III
Philip Church, Hamilton Papers, Library of Congress). Acknowledges receipt of Dexter's letter of April 30, 1799. *Letter
not found.*

To James McHenry, May 4, 1799 (Df, in the handwriting of   V
Philip Church, Hamilton Papers, Library of Congress).

To Aaron Ogden, May 4, 1799 (LS, Lloyd W. Smith Collection,   V
Morristown National Historical Park, Morristown, New Jersey;   VII
Df, in the handwriting of Philip Church, Hamilton Papers, Li-
brary of Congress).

To Amos Stoddard, May 4, 1799 (Df, in the handwriting of Philip   III
Church, Hamilton Papers, Library of Congress).

To Constant Freeman, May 5, 1799 (Df, in the handwriting of   III
Philip Church, Hamilton Papers, Library of Congress).

To John Lillie, May 5, 1799 (LS, in the handwriting of Ethan   II
Brown, Massachusetts Historical Society, Boston; Df, in the
handwriting of Philip Church, Hamilton Papers, Library of
Congress). Acknowledges receipt of Lillie's letter of April 27,
1799. *Letter not found.*

To James McHenry, May 5, 1799 (Df, in the handwriting of   II
Philip Church, Hamilton Papers, Library of Congress).

To Ebenezer Massey, May 5, 1799 (copy, in the handwriting of   IV
Philip Church, Hamilton Papers, Library of Congress).

To William C. Bentley, May 6, 1799 (ADf, Hamilton Papers,   V
Library of Congress).

To Mahlon Ford, May 6, 1799 (Df, in the handwriting of Philip Church, Hamilton Papers, Library of Congress).   III

From Adam Hoops, May 6, 1799 (ALS, Hamilton Papers, Library of Congress).   III

From James McHenry, May 6, 1799 (LS, Hamilton Papers, Library of Congress; LS, letterpress copy, James McHenry Papers, Library of Congress).   V

From James McHenry, May 6, 1799 (LS, Hamilton Papers, Library of Congress), enclosing Edward Miller to McHenry, March 9, 1799; Edward D. Turner to McHenry, April 26, 1799; Thomas Butler to McHenry, April 15, 1799; Butler to Daniel Bradley, April 15, 1799; Butler to Ross Bird, April 15, 1799 (copies, Hamilton Papers, Library of Congress).   V   VII

From Lewis Tousard, May 6, 1799 (ALS, Hamilton Papers, Library of Congress).   VII

From John Henry, May 7, 1799 (ALS, Hamilton Papers, Library of Congress).   III

From James McHenry, May 7, 1799 (LS, Hamilton Papers, Library of Congress; LS, letterpress copy, James McHenry Papers, Library of Congress).   III   IV

From Benjamin Brookes, May 8, 1799 (ALS, Hamilton Papers, Library of Congress).   III

From Constant Freeman, May 8, 1799 (ALS, Hamilton Papers, Library of Congress).   III

From Josias Carvel Hall, May 8, 1799 (ALS, Hamilton Papers, Library of Congress), enclosing "the last arrangement of the officers of the 9th Regt: 6 May 1799" (AD, Hamilton Papers, Library of Congress).   V   VII

To Adam Hoops (May 8, 1799 (Df, in the handwriting of Philip Church, Hamilton Papers, Library of Congress).   III

To Andrew M. Lusk, May 8, 1799 (copy, in the handwriting of Philip Church, Hamilton Papers, Library of Congress).   V

From James McHenry, May 8, 1799 (LS, Hamilton Papers, Library of Congress; LS, letterpress copy, James McHenry Papers, Library of Congress). Acknowledges H's letter of May 5, 1799. *Letter not found.*   V   VII

To David Strong, May 8, 1799 (Df, in the handwriting of Philip Church, Hamilton Papers, Library of Congress).   IV

From John De Lancey, May 9, 1799 (ALS, Hamilton Papers, Library of Congress).   I

To James Giles, May 9, 1799 (Df, in the handwriting of Philip   II
Church, Hamilton Papers, Library of Congress).

To Jedediah Huntington, May 9, 1799 (Df, in the handwriting of   VII
Philip Church, Hamilton Papers, Library of Congress). Acknowledges Huntington's letter of May 4, 1799. *Letter not
found.*

To James McHenry, May 9, 1799 (ADf, Hamilton Papers, Li-   V
brary of Congress).   VI

From William Moulton, May 9, 1799 (ALS, Hamilton Papers,   II
Library of Congress).

From Daniel Newnan, May 9, 1799 (ALS, Hamilton Papers, Li-   III
brary of Congress).

From Thomas Parker, May 9, 1799 (ALS, Hamilton Papers, Li-   V
brary of Congress).   VII

From Jonathan Jackson, May 10, 1799 (ALS, Hamilton Papers,   VII
Library of Congress), enclosing a contract between Jackson and
Joseph Ruggles et al., May 7, 1799 (copy, Hamilton Papers,
Library of Congress).

To Nathaniel Leonard, May 10, 1799 (ADf, Hamilton Papers,   VIII
Library of Congress).

To James McHenry, May 10, 1799 (ADf, Hamilton Papers, Li-   V
brary of Congress).

To James McHenry, May 10, 1799 (ADf, Hamilton Papers, Li-   III
brary of Congress).

To Ebenezer Stevens, May 10, 1799 (ALS, New-York Historical   VIII
Society, New York City; copy, in the handwriting of Ethan
Brown, Hamilton Papers, Library of Congress).

From Daniel Jackson, May 11, 1799 (ALS, Hamilton Papers, Li-   III
brary of Congress).   IV

From Thomas Morris, May 11, 1799 (ALS, Hamilton Papers, Li-   II
brary of Congress). On the verso H wrote a draft of his reply.
Letter not found.

From John Stockton, May 11, 1799 (ALS, Hamilton Papers, Li-   VII
brary of Congress), enclosing a contract between John Elliot
and the War Department, May 11, 1799 (copy, Hamilton Papers, Library of Congress).

From Adam Hoops, May 12, 1799 (ALS, Hamilton Papers, Li-   III
brary of Congress).   IV

From Campbell Smith, May 12, 1799 (ALS, Hamilton Papers, Li-   III
brary of Congress).

To Samuel Hodgdon, May 13, 1799 (copy, in the handwriting of   VII
Ethan Brown, Hamilton Papers, Library of Congress).

From James McHenry, May 13, 1799 (LS, Hamilton Papers, Li-   I
brary of Congress), enclosing John Jay to McHenry, May 7,
1799 (ALS, Hamilton Papers, Library of Congress); John T.
Bentley to McHenry, May 2, 1799 (ALS, Hamilton Papers,
Library of Congress); Hosea Moffitt, Eleazer Grant, and
John W. Schermerhorn to Jay, May 2, 1799 (DS, in Moffitt's
handwriting, Hamilton Papers, Library of Congress).

From James McHenry, May 13, 1799 (LS, Hamilton Papers, Li-   III
brary of Congress).

From Samuel Stringer [May 13, 1799] (ALS, Hamilton Papers,   I
Library of Congress).

From Thomas Parker, May 14, 1799 (ALS, Hamilton Papers, Li-   I
brary of Congress).

From John Shute, May 14, 1799 (ALS, Hamilton Papers, Library   II
of Congress).

From Amos Stoddard, May 14, 1799 (ALS, Hamilton Papers,   III
Library of Congress).

To James McHenry, May 15, 1799 (ALS [photostat], James Mc-   II
Henry Papers, Library of Congress).

From William S. Smith, May 16, 1799 (ALS, Hamilton Papers,   I
Library of Congress).   V

From John Stockton, May 16, 1799 (ALS, Hamilton Papers, Li-   VII
brary of Congress), enclosing a contract between James Mc-
Henry and Asa Freeman, May 14, 1799 (copy, Hamilton Papers,
Library of Congress).

From William C. Bentley, May 17, 1799 (ALS, Hamilton Papers,   V
Library of Congress), enclosing "Officers of the United States
Army" (AD, Hamilton Papers, Library of Congress); "Pro-
ceedings of the officers composing Col. Bentley's Regiment,"
May 16, 1799 (ADS, Hamilton Papers, Library of Congress);
"Recruiting Districts within Circle No. 7" (AD, Hamilton Pa-
pers, Library of Congress).

To Benjamin Brookes, May 17, 1799 (Df, in the handwriting of   VI
Philip Church, Hamilton Papers, Library of Congress).

From James McHenry, May 17, 1799 (LS, Hamilton Papers, Li-   III
brary of Congress; ADf, James McHenry Papers, Library of
Congress), enclosing Francis Mentges to McHenry, May 17,
1799 (copy, Hamilton Papers, Library of Congress).

To William Paterson, May 17, 1799 (copy, in the handwriting of   I
Philip Church, Hamilton Papers, Library of Congress).

From John Steele, May 17, 1799 (ALS, Hamilton Papers, Library   II
of Congress).

To Richard Hunewell, May 18, 1799 (ADf, Hamilton Papers,   V
Library of Congress).

From Benjamin Lincoln, May 18, 1799 (ALS, Hamilton Papers,   I
Library of Congress). On the verso H wrote a draft of his
answer. *Letter not found.*

From Jonathan Nichols, May 18, 1799 (ALS, Hamilton Papers,   III
Library of Congress).

From Thomas Parker, May 18, 1799 (ALS, Hamilton Papers, Li-   II
brary of Congress). Acknowledges receipt of H's letter of   V
May 6, 1799. *Letter not found.*

From Joshua Rogers, May 18, 1799 (ALS, Hamilton Papers, Li-   III
brary of Congress).

From Uriah Tracy, May 18, 1799 (ALS, Hamilton Papers, Li-   VII
brary of Congress).

From Josias Carvel Hall, May 19, 1799 (ALS, Hamilton Papers,   V
Library of Congress).

From George Ingersoll, May 20, 1799 (ALS, Hamilton Papers,   VI
Library of Congress).

From Archibald Crary, May 21, 1799 (LS, Hamilton Papers, Li-   VII
brary of Congress), enclosing a contract between John L. Boss
and James McHenry, May 21, 1799 (copy, Hamilton Papers,
Library of Congress). The endorsement on the letter reads:
"Acknowledged May 27th." *Letter not found.*

To Samuel Hodgdon, May 21, 1799 (copy, in the handwriting of   VII
Philip Church, Hamilton Papers, Library of Congress).

From Adam Hoops, May 21, 1799 (ALS, Hamilton Papers, Li-   III
brary of Congress).   IV
  VI

To Jonathan Jackson, May 21, 1799 (copy, in the handwriting of   VII
Philip Church, Hamilton Papers, Library of Congress).

To Thomas Parker, May 21, 1799 (Df, in the handwriting of   VI
Philip Church, Hamilton Papers, Library of Congress).

From David Strong, May 21, 1799 (LS, Hamilton Papers, Library   VII
of Congress).

To Lewis Tousard, May 21, 1799 (copy, in the handwriting of   VII
Philip Church, Hamilton Papers, Library of Congress).

To Ross Bird, May 22, 1799 (ADf, Hamilton Papers, Library of   V
Congress).

To Daniel Bradley, May 22, 1799 (ADf, Hamilton Papers, Li-   V
brary of Congress), enclosing "Virginia divided and subdivided
into Districts, for recruiting" (D, in the handwriting of H and
Philip Church, Hamilton Papers, Library of Congress).

To Alexander Gibson, May 22, 1799 (ADf, Hamilton Papers, Li-   III
brary of Congress).

To John McClallen, May 22, 1799 (ADf, Hamilton Papers, Li-   V
brary of Congress).

To James McHenry, May 22, 1799 (ADf, Hamilton Papers, Li-   V
brary of Congress).

To James McHenry, May 22, 1799 (ADf, Hamilton Papers, Li-   III
brary of Congress).   V

To Ebenezer Stevens, May 22, 1799 (ALS, New-York Historical   VII
Society, New York City; copy, in the handwriting of Philip
Church, Hamilton Papers, Library of Congress).

From John Stockton, May 22, 1799 (ALS, Hamilton Papers, Li-   VII
brary of Congress), enclosing a contract between James Mc-
Henry and James Caldwell, May 20, 1799 (copy, Hamilton
Papers, Library of Congress).

To Josias Carvel Hall, May 23, 1799 (Df, in the handwriting of   V
Philip Church, Hamilton Papers, Library of Congress).

To Samuel Hodgdon, May 23, 1799 (Df, in the handwriting of   VII
Philip Church, Hamilton Papers, Library of Congress).

To Adam Hoops, May 23, 1799 (copy, in the handwriting of   IV
Philip Church, Hamilton Papers, Library of Congress).

From George Ingersoll, May 23, 1799 (ALS, Hamilton Papers,   IV
Library of Congress).

From James McHenry, May 23, 1799 (LS, Hamilton Papers, Li-   I
brary of Congress; LS, letterpress copy, James McHenry Papers, Library of Congress).

To Amos Stoddard, May 23, 1799 (Df, in the handwriting of   III
Philip Church, Hamilton Papers, Library of Congress).

From Charles Williamson, May 23, 1799 (ALS, Hamilton Papers,   II
Library of Congress).

To Joseph Elliott, May 24, 1799 (copy, in the handwriting of   III
Philip Church, Hamilton Papers, Library of Congress).

From Richard Hunewell, May 24, 1799 (ALS, Hamilton Papers,   V
Library of Congress), enclosing recruiting arrangements (ADS,
Hamilton Papers, Library of Congress).

To James McHenry, May 24, 1799 (ADf, Hamilton Papers, Library of Congress). VIII

To Thomas Lloyd Moore, May 24, 1799 (copy, in the handwriting of Ethan Brown, Hamilton Papers, Library of Congress). III

From Elias Parker, May 24, 1799 (ALS, Hamilton Papers, Library of Congress). II

To William S. Smith, May 24, 1799 (ADf, Hamilton Papers, Library of Congress). III

To John Stockton, May 24, 1799 (copy, in the handwriting of Philip Church, Hamilton Papers, Library of Congress). VII

To Lewis Tousard, May 24, 1799 (ADf, Hamilton Papers, Library of Congress). VII

From William Willcocks, May 24, 1799 (ALS, Hamilton Papers, Library of Congress). V VII

From Samuel Hodgdon, May 25, 1799 (LS, Hamilton Papers, Library of Congress), enclosing "Return of Clothing forwarded for the use of the 12 Regiments now raising from 27th April to 25th May 1799," May 25, 1799 (DS, Hamilton Papers, Library of Congress). VII

To Samuel Hodgdon, May 25, 1799 (ADfS, Hamilton Papers, Library of Congress). VII

To Jedediah Huntington, May 25, 1799 (copy, in the handwritting of Philip Church, Hamilton Papers, Library of Congress). Acknowledges receipt of Huntington's letter of May 22, 1799. *Letter not found.* VII

From James McHenry, May 25, 1799 (LS, Hamilton Papers, Library of Congress). V

From James McHenry, May 25, 1799 (LS, Hamilton Papers, Library of Congress). III

To James McHenry, May 25, 1799 (copy, Hamilton Papers, Library of Congress). VII

From William S. Smith, May 25, 1799 (ALS, Hamilton Papers, Library of Congress). III

From Mahlon Ford, May 26, 1799 (ADf, Hamilton Papers, Library of Congress). VIII

To George Ingersoll, May 26, 1799 (ADf, Hamilton Papers, Library of Congress). VIII

To Thomas Parker, May 26, 1799 (copy, in the handwriting of Philip Church, Hamilton Papers, Library of Congress). V

To Ebenezer Stevens, May 26, 1799 (two LS, New-York Historical Society, New York City; ADf, Hamilton Papers, Library of Congress). — VIII

From James Bruff, May 27, 1799 (ALS, Hamilton Papers, Library of Congress). — V VII

To Adam Hoops, May 27, 1799 (ADf, Hamilton Papers, Library of Congress). — VIII

From James McHenry, May 27, 1799 (ALS, Hamilton Papers, Library of Congress), enclosing Benjamin Stoddert to McHenry, May 27, 1799 (copy, Hamilton Papers, Library of Congress). — VIII

From Timothy Taylor, May 27, 1799 (ALS, Hamilton Papers, Library of Congress). — V VII

From Jedediah Huntington, May 28, 1799 (ALS, Hamilton Papers, Library of Congress). — VII

From James McHenry, May 28, 1799 (LS, Hamilton Papers, Library of Congress; LS, letterpress copy, James McHenry Papers, Library of Congress). — IV

From Josias Carvel Hall, May 29, 1799 (ALS, Hamilton Papers, Library of Congress). — V

To Adam Hoops, May 29, 1799 (ADf, Hamilton Papers, Library of Congress). — VIII

From George Ingersoll, May 29, 1799 (ALS, Hamilton Papers, Library of Congress). — VIII

To George Ingersoll, May 29, 1799 (ADf, Hamilton Papers, Library of Congress). — IV

From James McHenry, May 29, 1799 (ALS, Hamilton Papers, Library of Congress), enclosing James Wilkinson to McHenry, March 3, 21, April 10, 1799; agreement between Manuel Gayoso de Lemos and John M. Lovell, March 1, 1799 (copies, Hamilton Papers, Library of Congress). — III VI

From James McHenry, May 29, 1799 (LS, Hamilton Papers, Library of Congress). — V VII

To James McHenry, May 29, 1799 (copy, in the handwriting of Ethan Brown, Hamilton Papers, Library of Congress). — I

To Staats Morris, May 29, 1799 (copy, in the handwriting of Ethan Brown, Hamilton Papers, Library of Congress). — III

To Timothy Taylor, May 29, 1799 (copy, in the handwriting of Ethan Brown, Hamilton Papers, Library of Congress). — V

From Benjamin Brookes, May 30, 1799 (ALS, Hamilton Papers,   V
Library of Congress). The endorsement reads: "Ansd." *Letter
not found.*

From John G. Coffin, May 30, 1799 (ALS, Hamilton Papers, Li-   III
brary of Congress).

From John McClallen, May 30, 1799 (ALS, Hamilton Papers,   I
Library of Congress).   V
    VII

To Staats Morris, May 30, 1799 (copy, in the handwriting of   IV
Ethan Brown, Hamilton Papers, Library of Congress).

From Marinus Willett, May 30, 1799 (ALS, MS Division, New   I
York Public Library).

From Edward Carrington, May 31, 1799 (ALS, Hamilton Papers,   V
Library of Congress), enclosing a printed notice of places of
rendezvous, April 27, 1799 (Hamilton Papers, Library of Congress); "Virginia divided and Subdivided into Districts for Recruiting," May 31, 1799 (AD, Hamilton Papers, Library of
Congress). On the verso H wrote the draft of his reply. *Letter
not found.*

To Josias Carvel Hall, May 31, 1799 (ADf, Hamilton Papers,   V
Library of Congress).

To Richard Hunewell, May 31, 1799 (ADf, Hamilton Papers,   V
Library of Congress).

From James McHenry, May 31, 1799 (LS, Hamilton Papers, Li-   V
brary of Congress).   VI

From James McHenry, May 31, 1799 (LS, Hamilton Papers, Li-   III
brary of Congress; LS, letterpress copy, James McHenry Papers, Library of Congress).

From James McHenry, May 31, 1799 (LS, Hamilton Papers, Li-   V
brary of Congress; LS, letterpress copy, James McHenry Papers, Library of Congress), enclosing Matthias Barton to
McHenry, May 30, 1799 (ALS, Hamilton Papers, Library of
Congress).

From James McHenry, May 31, 1799 (LS, Hamilton Papers, Li-   III
brary of Congress; LS, letterpress copy, James McHenry Papers, Library of Congress), enclosing Robert Gilmor to
Benjamin Stoddert, May 29, 1799 (ALS, Hamilton Papers, Library of Congress); Stoddert to McHenry, May 31, 1799 (AL,
Hamilton Papers, Library of Congress).

To James McHenry, May 31, 1799 (ADf, Hamilton Papers, Li-   III
brary of Congress).   V
    VII

From Francis Lynch [May, 1799] (ALS, Hamilton Papers, Library   III
of Congress).

JUNE, 1799

To Sebastian Bauman, June 1, 1799 (ADf, Hamilton Papers, Li-   VII
brary of Congress).

To William C. Bentley, June 1, 1799 (ADf, Hamilton Papers,   V
Library of Congress).   VI

From Thomas Parker, June 1, 1799 (ALS, Hamilton Papers, Li-   V
brary of Congress).

To Thomas Parker, June 1, 1799 (ADf, Hamilton Papers, Library   V
of Congress).

From Yelverton Peyton, June 1, 1799 (ALS, Hamilton Papers,   III
Library of Congress).

From Lewis Tousard, June 1, 1799 (ALS, Hamilton Papers, Li-   VII
brary of Congress).

To Ebenezer Stevens, June 2, 1799 (AL, New-York Historical   VII
Society, New York City).

From Philip Church, June 3, 1799 (ALS, Hamilton Papers, Li-   V
brary of Congress).

From George Ingersoll, June 3, 1799 (ALS, Hamilton Papers,   VII
Library of Congress).

From John Meyer and Michael Myers, June 3, 1799 (LS, in the   I
handwriting of John Meyer, Hamilton Papers, Library of Congress).

From Selah Strong, June 3, 1799 (ALS, Hamilton Papers, Library   I
of Congress).

From Adam Hoops, June 4, 1799 (ALS, Hamilton Papers, Library   VIII
of Congress).

From Richard Hunewell, June 4, 1799 (ALS, Hamilton Papers,   V
Library of Congress). Acknowledges H's letter of May 16,
1799. *Letter not found.*

From James McHenry, June 4, 1799 (LS, Hamilton Papers, Li-   V
brary of Congress).   VI
                                                                  VII

From James McHenry, June 4, 1799 (LS, Hamilton Papers, Li-   IV
brary of Congress), enclosing the proceedings of a general
court-martial of May 20, 1799 (copy, Hamilton Papers, Library
of Congress).

To Staats Morris, June 4, 1799 (ADf, Hamilton Papers, Library   VIII
of Congress).

From Aaron Ogden, June 4, 1799 (ALS, Hamilton Papers, Library of Congress).   I

From Aaron Ogden, June 4, 1799 (ALS, Hamilton Papers, Library of Congress).   VII

To Ebenezer Stevens, June 4, 1799 (LS, New-York Historical Society, New York City). Stevens endorsed this letter: "Ansd." *Letter not found.*   VII

To William C. Bentley, Richard Hunewell, and Thomas Parker, June 5, 1799 (copy, in the handwriting of Ethan Brown, Hamilton Papers, Library of Congress).   V VI

From Thomas Butler, June 5, 1799 (ALS, Hamilton Papers, Library of Congress). Acknowledges H's letter of May 2, 1799. *Letter not found.*   VI

To John Henry, June 5, 1799 (copy, in the handwriting of Ethan Brown, Hamilton Papers, Library of Congress).   III

To Samuel Hodgdon, June 5, 1799 (ADfS, Hamilton Papers, Library of Congress).   VII

From Adam Hoops, June 5, 1799 (ALS, Hamilton Papers, Library of Congress). On the verso H wrote the draft of his answer. *Letter not found.*   VII

To Adam Hoops, June 5, 1799 (ADf, Hamilton Papers, Library of Congress), enclosing H to Benjamin Brookes, June 5, 1799, *Letter not found.*   III

From James McHenry, June 5, 1799 (LS, Hamilton Papers, Library of Congress). Acknowledges two letters from H dated June 4, 1799. *Letters not found.*   III

To James McHenry, June 5, 1799 (ADf, Hamilton Papers, Library of Congress).   II

To Ebenezer Stevens, June 5, 1799 (ADf, Hamilton Papers, Library of Congress; LS, New-York Historical Society, New York City).   VII

To Lewis Tousard, June 5, 1799 (ADf, Hamilton Papers, Library of Congress).   III

From George West, Jr., June 5, 1799 (ALS, Hamilton Papers, Library of Congress).   III

Circular to Certain Recruiting Officers, June 6, 1799 (ADf, Hamilton Papers, Library of Congress).   VI

To Adam Hoops, June 6, 1799 (ADf, Hamilton Papers, Library of Congress).   VI

From John McClallen, June 6, 1799 (ALS, Hamilton Papers, Library of Congress).   VII

From James McHenry, June 6, 1799 (LS, Hamilton Papers, Library of Congress.   III
VII

From Thomas Lloyd Moore, June 6, 1799 (ALS, Hamilton Papers, Library of Congress), enclosing "List of Officers of 10 Regt" (AD, Hamilton Papers, Library of Congress).   VI
VII

To Aaron Ogden, June 6, 1799 (LS, Lloyd W. Smith Collection, Morristown National Historical Park, Morristown, New Jersey).   III

From Adam Hoops, June 7, 1799 (ALS, Hamilton Papers, Library of Congress).   III

From Adam Hoops, June 7, 1799 (ALS, Hamilton Papers, Library of Congress).   III

From James McHenry, June 7, 1799 (ALS, Hamilton Papers, Library of Congress; ADfS, James McHenry Papers, Library of Congress). Acknowledges receipt of H's second letter of June 5, 1799. *Letter not found.*   III
VII

To Thomas Lloyd Moore, June 7, 1799 (ADfS, Hamilton Papers, Library of Congress).   III

From Ebenezer Stevens, June 7, 1799 (LS, Hamilton Papers, Library of Congress).   VII

From William C. Bentley, June 8, 1799 (ALS, Hamilton Papers, Library of Congress). On the verso H wrote a draft of his reply. *Letter not found.*   III
V

From Edward Carrington, June 8, 1799 (ALS, Hamilton Papers, Library of Congress). On the verso H wrote a draft of his reply. *Letter not found.*   V

From John C. Gilbert, June 8, 1799 (LS, Hamilton Papers, Library of Congress).   II

From Samuel Hodgdon, June 8, 1799 (LS, Hamilton Papers, Library of Congress).   VII

To James McHenry, June 8, 1799 (ADf, Hamilton Papers, Library of Congress).   II
VI

To James McHenry, June 8, 1799 (ADf, Hamilton Papers, Library of Congress).   VIII

To James McHenry, June 8, 1799 (ADf, Hamilton Papers, Library of Congress).   VII

To Aaron Ogden, June 8, 1799 (LS, Lloyd W. Smith Collection,   III

Morristown National Historical Park, Morristown, New Jersey; VI
ADf, Hamilton Papers, Library of Congress).

From Ebenezer Stevens, June 8, 1799 (LS, Hamilton Papers, Li- VII
brary of Congress).

From Joseph Elliott, June 10, 1799 (ALS, Hamilton Papers, Li- III
brary of Congress).

From Caleb Gibbs, June 10, 1799 (ALS, Hamilton Papers, Library II
of Congress).

To Adam Hoops, June 10, 1799 (copy, in the handwriting of III
Ethan Brown, Hamilton Papers, Library of Congress). VI

To James McHenry, June 10, 1799 (copy, in the handwriting of III
Ethan Brown, Hamilton Papers, Library of Congress).

From Timothy Taylor, June 10, 1799 (copy, in the handwriting II
of Ethan Brown, Hamilton Papers, Library of Congress).

To Rufus Graves, June 11, 1799 (ADf, Hamilton Papers, Library V
of Congress). VI

From Francis Lynch, June 11, 1799 (ALS, Hamilton Papers, Li- III
brary of Congress).

From James McHenry, June 11, 1799 (LS, Hamilton Papers, Li- VII
brary of Congress). Acknowledges H's letter of June 6, 1799.
Letter not found.

To Aaron Ogden, June 11, 1799 (LS, Lloyd W. Smith Collection, III
Morristown National Historical Park, Morristown, New Jersey;
copy, in the handwriting of Ethan Brown, Hamilton Papers,
Library of Congress).

To James Read, June 11, 1799 (ADf, Hamilton Papers, Library V
of Congress). VI

From William S. Smith, June 11, 1799 (ALS, Hamilton Papers VI
Library of Congress).

To Walter L. Cochran, June 12, 1799 (copy, in the handwriting III
of Ethan Brown, Hamilton Papers, Library of Congress). IV

To Joseph Elliott, June 12, 1799 (ADf, Hamilton Papers, Library III
of Congress).

To George Ingersoll, June 12, 1799 (ADf, Hamilton Papers, Li- V
brary of Congress). VI

To James McHenry, June 12, 1799 (ADf, Hamilton Papers, Li- VII
brary of Congress).

To James McHenry, June 12, 1799 (ADf, Hamilton Papers, Li- VII
brary of Congress).

To Ebenezer Massey, June 12, 1799 (copy, in the handwriting of   III
Ethan Brown, Hamilton Papers, Library of Congress).   IV

From Staats Morris, June 12, 1799 (ALS, Hamilton Papers, Li-   VIII
brary of Congress).

From Adam Hoops, June 13, 1799 (ALS, Hamilton Papers, Li-   III
brary of Congress).

From James McHenry, June 13, 1799 (LS, Hamilton Papers, Li-   VII
brary of Congress).

From Campbell Smith, June 13, 1799 (ALS, Hamilton Papers, Li-   IV
brary of Congress).

From Daniel Bradley, June 14, 1799 (ALS, Hamilton Papers, Li-   III
brary of Congress).   V
                                                                       VII

To Daniel Jackson, June 14, 1799 (ADf, Hamilton Papers, Library   VI
of Congress).

From Caleb Swan, June 14, 1799 (ALS, Hamilton Papers, Library   III
of Congress).

From Aaron Ogden, June 15, 1799 (ALS, Hamilton Papers, Li-   VI
brary of Congress).

From Revell Elton, June 16, 1799 (LS, Hamilton Papers, Library   III
of Congress).

From Thomas Parker, June 16, 1799 (ALS, Hamilton Papers, Li-   V
brary of Congress), enclosing Charles M. Thurston to Parker,
June 8, 1799 (ALS, Hamilton Papers, Library of Congress).

From Elihu Egleston, June 17, 1799 (LS, Hamilton Papers, Li-   III
brary of Congress), enclosing Perez Jones to James McHenry,
May 23, 1799 (LS, Hamilton Papers, Library of Congress).

To Joseph Elliott, June 17, 1799 (ADf, Hamilton Papers, Library   III
of Congress).

To Josias Carvel Hall, June 17, 1799 (ADf, Hamilton Papers, Li-   VII
brary of Congress).

To John McClallen, June 17, 1799 (ADf, Hamilton Papers, Li-   VII
brary of Congress).

To James McHenry, June 17, 1799 (ALS [photostat], James   III
McHenry Papers, Library of Congress; copy, in the handwriting of Ethan Brown, Hamilton Papers, Library of Congress).

To James McHenry, June 18, 1799 (copy, in the handwriting of   V
Ethan Brown, Hamilton Papers, Library of Congress), enclos-

ing an extract of Richard Hunewell to H, June 4, 1799 (copy, in the handwriting of Ethan Brown, Hamilton Papers, Library of Congress).

From Staats Morris, June 18, 1799 (ALS, Hamilton Papers, Library of Congress).   IV

From William S. Smith, [June] 18, 1799 (ALS, Hamilton Papers, Library of Congress). Acknowledges H's letter of June 14, 1799. *Letter not found.*   III

From Daniel Bradley, June 19, 1799 (ALS, Hamilton Papers, Library of Congress).   VI

To Rufus Graves, June 19, 1799 (copy, in the handwriting of Ethan Brown, Hamilton Papers, Library of Congress).   V

From James McHenry, June 19, 1799 (LS, Hamilton Papers, Library of Congress).   III

To James McHenry, June 19, 1799 (ADf, Hamilton Papers, Library of Congress).   IV

To Adam Hoops, June 20, 1799 (copy, Hamilton Papers, Library of Congress).   III

From James McHenry, June 20, 1799 (LS, Hamilton Papers, Library of Congress).   V
VII

To Ebenezer Stevens, June 20, 1799 (LS, New-York Historical Society, New York City; ADfS, Hamilton Papers, Library of Congress), enclosing "Articles of Military Supply for each Regiment of Infantry," June 20, 1799 (AD, Hamilton Papers, Library of Congress; DS, New-York Historical Society, New York City).   VII

From Timothy Taylor, June 20, 1799 (ALS, Hamilton Papers, Library of Congress). Acknowledges H's letter of June 14, 1799. *Letter not found.*   VII

To Adam Hoops, June 21, 1799 (copy, in the handwriting of Ethan Brown, Hamilton Papers, Library of Congress).   IV

From George Ingersoll, June 21, 1799 (ALS, Hamilton Papers, Library of Congress), enclosing James McHenry to Ingersoll, June 17, 1799 (LS, Hamilton Papers, Library of Congress).   VII

To Daniel Jackson, June 21, 1799 (copy, in the handwriting of Ethan Brown, Hamilton Papers, Library of Congress).   VII

From James McHenry, June 21, 1799 (LS, Hamilton Papers, Library of Congress).   V

To James McHenry, June 21, 1799 (copy, in the handwriting of Ethan Brown, Hamilton Papers, Library of Congress).   III

To Staats Morris, June 21, 1799 (copy, in the handwriting of   VII
Ethan Brown, Hamilton Papers, Library of Congress).

From Thomas Parker, June 21, 1799 (ALS, Hamilton Papers, Li-   II
brary of Congress).   V

To John J. U. Rivardi, June 21, 1799 (copy, in the handwriting   III
of Ethan Brown, Hamilton Papers, Library of Congress).

From William Simmons, June 21, 1799 (ALS, Hamilton Papers,   III
Library of Congress; LC, RG 217, Records of the General Ac-
counting Office, Letter Books, Accountant's Office, Vol. F,
May 16, 1799–February 27, 1800, National Archives).

From William S. Smith, June 21, 1799 (ALS, Hamilton Papers,   V
Library of Congress).

To Thomas Butler, June 22, 1799 (copy, in the handwriting of   V
Ethan Brown, Hamilton Papers, Library of Congress).

From Jonathan Dayton, June 22, 1799 (ALS, Hamilton Papers,   II
Library of Congress).

To Revell Elton, June 22, 1799 (copy, in the handwriting of   III
Ethan Brown, Hamilton Papers, Library of Congress).

To George Fleming, June 22, 1799 (copy, in the handwriting of   VII
Ethan Brown, Hamilton Papers, Library of Congress).

To Daniel Jackson, June 22, 1799 (copy, in the handwriting of   VII
Ethan Brown, Hamilton Papers, Library of Congress).

From Samuel Lewis, Sr., June 22, 1799 (ALS, Hamilton Papers,   VII
Library of Congress).

To James McHenry, June 22, 1799 (copy, in the handwriting of   III
Ethan Brown, Hamilton Papers, Library of Congress).

To Aaron Ogden, June 22, 1799 (LS, Lloyd W. Smith Collection,   III
Morristown National Historical Park, Morristown, New Jersey;
copy, in the handwriting of Ethan Brown, Hamilton Papers,
Library of Congress).

To Thomas Parker, June 22, 1799 (ADf, Hamilton Papers, Li-   V
brary of Congress).   VI

From John Shute, June 22, 1799 (ALS, Hamilton Papers, Library   I
of Congress).

From James Watson, June 23, 1799 (ALS, Hamilton Papers,   I
Library of Congress).

To John Adlum, June 24, 1799 (copy, in the handwriting of   III
Ethan Brown, Hamilton Papers, Library of Congress).

From Samuel Eddens, June 24, 1799 (ALS, Hamilton Papers, Li-   VI
brary of Congress).

From Henry Glen, June 24, 1799 (ALS, Hamilton Papers, Library   III
of Congress), enclosing James Wilkinson to Glen, November 4,
1798; Glen to James McHenry, May 27, 1799; McHenry to
Glen, June 8, 1799 (copies, in Glen's handwriting, Hamilton
Papers, Library of Congress).

To Richard Hunewell, June 24, 1799 (copy, in the handwriting of   VII
Ethan Brown, Hamilton Papers, Library of Congress).

To Samuel Lewis, Sr., June 24, 1799 (copy, in the handwriting of   VII
Ethan Brown, Hamilton Papers, Library of Congress).

To James McHenry, June 24, 1799 (ADf, Hamilton Papers, Li-   VII
brary of Congress).

To William Simmons, June 24, 1799 (copy, in the handwriting of   III
Ethan Brown, Hamilton Papers, Library of Congress).

To Timothy Taylor, June 24, 1799 (copy, in the handwriting of   VII
Ethan Brown, Hamilton Papers, Library of Congress).

To Timothy Taylor, June 24, 1799 (copy, in the handwriting of   VII
Ethan Brown, Hamilton Papers, Library of Congress).

From Decius Wadsworth, June 24, 1799 (ALS, Hamilton Papers,   VII
Library of Congress).

From John Adlum, June 25, 1799 (ALS, Hamilton Papers, Library   III
of Congress).

To James Bruff, June 25, 1799 (copy, in the handwriting of Ethan   IV
Brown, Hamilton Papers, Library of Congress).

From Edward Carrington, June 25, 1799 (ALS, Hamilton Papers,   II
Library of Congress), enclosing John Davidson to William
Heth, May 28, 1799 (ALS, Hamilton Papers, Library of Con-
gress).

To Matthew Clarkson, June 25, 1799 (ALS, Hamilton Papers, Li-   I
brary of Congress; copy, in the handwriting of Ethan Brown,
Hamilton Papers, Library of Congress).

To Adam Hoops, June 25, 1799 (copy, in the handwriting of   III
Ethan Brown, Hamilton Papers, Library of Congress).   IV

From Daniel Jackson, June 25, 1799 (AL, Hamilton Papers, Li-   VI
brary of Congress).

From Daniel Jackson, June 25, 1799 (ALS, Hamilton Papers, Li-   VI
brary of Congress).

From Aaron Ogden, June 25, 1799 (ALS, Hamilton Papers, Li-   III
brary of Congress), enclosing James McHenry to Thomas
Reading, Jr., January 10, 1799 (LS, Hamilton Papers, Library
of Congress).

From James Read, June 25, 1799 (ALS, Hamilton Papers, Library V
of Congress; ALS [marked "Duplicate"], Hamilton Papers, VI
Library of Congress).

To Stephen Van Rensselaer, June 25, 1799 (ALS, Columbia Uni- II
versity Libraries; Df, in the handwriting of Ethan Brown,
Hamilton Papers, Library of Congress).

To Benjamin Walker, June 25, 1799 (copy, in the handwriting of II
Ethan Brown, Hamilton Papers, Library of Congress).

From Samuel Hodgdon, June 26, 1799 (ALS, Hamilton Papers, VII
Library of Congress).

To James McHenry, June 26, 1799 (copy, in the handwriting of III
Ethan Brown, Hamilton Papers, Library of Congress).

To James McHenry, June 26, 1799 (copy, in the handwriting of III
Ethan Brown, Hamilton Papers, Library of Congress).

To Aaron Ogden, June 26, 1799 (LS, Lloyd W. Smith Collection, III
Morristown National Historical Park, Morristown, New Jersey;
copy, in the handwriting of Ethan Brown, Hamilton Papers,
Library of Congress).

From Timothy Taylor, June 26, 1799 (ALS, Hamilton Papers, I
Library of Congress).

To Nanning J. Visscher, June 26, 1799 (copy, in the handwriting VII
of Ethan Brown, Hamilton Papers, Library of Congress).

From William Willcocks, June 26, 1799 (LS, Hamilton Papers, IV
Library of Congress).

To William Willcocks, June 26, 1799 (copy, in the handwriting IV
of Ethan Brown and H, Hamilton Papers, Library of Congress).

From James Bruff, June 27, 1799 (ALS, Hamilton Papers, Library IV
of Congress). VI

From John Hancock, Jr., June 27, 1799 (ALS, Hamilton Papers, V
Library of Congress). Acknowledges H's letter of June 4, 1799. VI
Letter not found.

From John Henry, June 27, 1799 (ALS, Hamilton Papers, Library IV
of Congress).

From William Willcocks, June 27, 1799 (ALS, Hamilton Papers, IV
Library of Congress), enclosing William Laidlie to Willcocks,
June 26, 1799 (ALS, Hamilton Papers, Library of Congress).

From William Willcocks, June 27, 1799 (ALS, Hamilton Papers, IV
Library of Congress).

To James Bennett, June 28, 1799 (ALS, Hamilton Papers, Library   II
of Congress).

From Adam Hoops, June 28, 1799 (ALS, Hamilton Papers, Li-   III
brary of Congress), enclosing Nathaniel Leonard to Hoops,   IV
June 27, 1799 (ALS, Hamilton Papers, Library of Congress);
"The Proceedings of a Garrison Court Martial . . . ," December 31, 1799 (DS, signed by Hoops and Frederick Frye, Hamilton Papers, Library of Congress).

From James McHenry, June 28, 1799 (Df, Hamilton Papers, Li-   VII
brary of Congress), enclosing McHenry to Benjamin Lincoln,
June 25, 1799 (copy, Hamilton Papers, Library of Congress);
McHenry to Jonathan Jackson, June 25, 1799 (copy, Hamilton
Papers, Library of Congress); Stephen Higginson to Benjamin
Stoddert, May 15, 30, 1799 (extracts, Hamilton Papers, Library
of Congress).

From James McHenry, June 28, 179[9] (LS, Hamilton Papers,   VII
Library of Congress).

From Edward D. Turner, June 28, 1799 (ALS, Hamilton Papers,   VI
Library of Congress).

From John Hamilton, June 29, 1799 (ALS, Hamilton Papers, Li-   III
brary of Congress).

From Richard Harison, June 29, 1799 (ALS, Hamilton Papers,   I
Library of Congress).

From James McHenry, June 29, 1799 (LS, Hamilton Papers,   III
Library of Congress; copy [incomplete], New-York Historical
Society, New York City), enclosing Samuel Hodgdon to Mc-
Henry, June 28, 1799 (ALS, Hamilton Papers, Library of Congress); John J. U. Rivardi to Hodgdon, May 30, 1799 (copy
[incomplete], in Hodgdon's handwriting, Hamilton Papers, Library of Congress).

From Thomas Parker, June 29, 1799 (ALS, Hamilton Papers,   VII
Library of Congress).

From Richard Varick, June 29, 1799 (ALS, Hamilton Papers,   I
Library of Congress).

From William C. Bentley, June 30, 1799 (ALS, Hamilton Papers,   I
Library of Congress).   VII

From Josias Carvel Hall, June 30, 1799 (ALS, Hamilton Papers,   VI
Library of Congress).

From John McClallen, June 30, 1799 (ALS, Hamilton Papers,   V
Library of Congress).

From Lewis Tousard, June 30, 1799 (ALS, Hamilton Papers, Li-   VI
brary of Congress), enclosing "Disposition & arrangement of
the troops composing the Battalion of Major Daniel Jackson,"
June 30, 1799 (D, signed by Tousard and Jackson, Hamilton
Papers, Library of Congress).

JULY, 1799

To James Bennett, July 1, 1799 (copy, in the handwriting of   II
Ethan Brown, Hamilton Papers, Library of Congress).

To James Bruff, July 1, 1799 (ADf, Hamilton Papers, Library of   V
Congress).   VI

From Ebenezer Huntington, July 1, 1799 (ALS, Hamilton Papers,   II
Library of Congress).

To Daniel Jackson, July 1, 1799 (ADf, Hamilton Papers, Library VII
of Congress).

To Staats Morris, July 1, 1799 (ADf, Hamilton Papers, Library   III
of Congress).

From William S. Smith, July 1, 1799 (ALS, Hamilton Papers, Li- VI
brary of Congress).

From Nanning J. Visscher, July 1, 1799 (ALS, Hamilton Papers,   VI
Library of Congress), enclosing a "Return of the Troops sta-   VII
tioned at Fort Oswego," July 1, 1799 (AD, Hamilton Papers,
Library of Congress).

From William Willcocks, July 1, 1799 (ALS, Hamilton Papers,   IV
Library of Congress).

From John Adams, July 2, 1799 (ALS, Hamilton Papers, Library   III
of Congress; LC, Adams Family Papers, deposited in the Massachusetts Historical Society, Boston).

From Sebastian Bauman, July 2, 1799 (LS, Hamilton Papers, Li-   VII
brary of Congress).

To Daniel Bradley, July 2, 1799 (copy, in the handwriting of   VII
Ethan Brown, Hamilton Papers, Library of Congress).

To Benjamin Brookes, July 2, 1799 (copy, in the handwriting of III
Ethan Brown, Hamilton Papers, Library of Congress).

To James Bruff, July 2, 1799 (copy, in the handwriting of Ethan VI
Brown, Hamilton Papers, Library of Congress).

To Henry Glen, July 2, 1799 (LS, MS Division, New York Public   III
Library; copy, in the handwriting of Ethan Brown, Hamilton,
Papers, Library of Congress).

To Josias Carvel Hall, July 2, 1799 (copy, in the handwriting of   VII
Ethan Brown, Hamilton Papers, Library of Congress).

To John F. Hamtramck, July 2, 1799 (copy, in the handwriting   VI
of Ethan Brown, Hamilton Papers, Library of Congress).

To Callender Irvine, July 2, 1799 (copy, in the handwriting of   III
Ethan Brown, Hamilton Papers, Library of Congress).

From Daniel Jackson, July 2, 1799 (ALS, Hamilton Papers, Li-   VI
brary of Congress), enclosing "An Arrangement of the Com-   VII
panies of Artillerists & Engineers to the Garrisons within my
District" (DS, Hamilton Papers, Library of Congress).

From James McHenry, July 2, 1799 (LS, Hamilton Papers, Li-   IV
brary of Congress).

From James McHenry, July 2, 1799 (LS, Hamilton Papers, Li-   VII
brary of Congress).

To James McHenry, July 2, 1799 (copy, in the handwriting of   VII
Ethan Brown, Hamilton Papers, Library of Congress).

To William North, July 2, 1799 (copy, in the handwriting of   III
Ethan Brown, Hamilton Papers, Library of Congress).

To Aaron Ogden, July 2, 1799 (LS, Lloyd W. Smith Collection,   III
Morristown National Historical Park, Morristown, New Jersey;
copy, in the handwriting of Ethan Brown, Hamilton Papers,
Library of Congress).

From John J. U. Rivardi, July 2, 1799 (ALS, Hamilton Papers,   III
Library of Congress), enclosing "Refutation of the Charges   IV
lodged by Captn Bruff against Major Rivardi" (copy, Hamilton   VI
Papers, Library of Congress).

To John J. U. Rivardi, July 2, 1799 (copy, in the handwriting of   VII
Ethan Brown, Hamilton Papers, Library of Congress).

To William S. Smith, July 2, 1799 (copy, in the handwriting of   VI
Ethan Brown, Hamilton Papers, Library of Congress).

From David Strong, July 2, 1799 (LS, Hamilton Papers, Library   VI
of Congress).

From William Willcocks, July 2, 1799 (ALS, Hamilton Papers,   IV
Library of Congress).

To Joseph Brock, July 3, 1799 (copy, in the handwriting of   III
Ethan Brown, Hamilton Papers, Library of Congress).

To James McHenry, July 3, 1799 (Df, in the handwriting of   VII
Frederick N. Hudson, Hamilton Papers, Library of Congress),
enclosing William Willcocks to Alexander Richards, July 2,

1799 (ALS, Hamilton Papers, Library of Congress); Richards to Willcocks, July 2, 1799 (ALS, Hamilton Papers, Library of Congress).

To Aaron Ogden, July 3, 1799 (ADf, Hamilton Papers, Library of Congress).   IV

To Timothy Taylor, July 3, 1799 (copy, in the handwriting of Ethan Brown, Hamilton Papers, Library of Congress).   III

From William Willcocks, [July] 3, 1799 (ALS, Hamilton Papers, Library of Congress).   VII

From Samuel Barnum, July 4, 1799 (ALS, Hamilton Papers, Library of Congress), enclosing a certificate from Valentine Seaman, July 2, 1799 (ADS, Hamilton Papers, Library of Congress); certificate from Wright Post, July 2, 1799 (ADS, Hamilton Papers, Library of Congress); certificate from Richard J. Kissam, July 3, 1799 (ADS, Hamilton Papers, Library of Congress); certificate from Samuel Borrowe, July 3, 1799 (ADS, Hamilton Papers, Library of Congress); certificate from David Hosack, July 3, 1799 (ADS, Hamilton Papers, Library of Congress); certificate from Matthew Clarkson, July 2, 1799 (DS, Hamilton Papers, Library of Congress).   I

From William C. Bentley, July 4, 1799 (ALS, Hamilton Papers, Library of Congress).   III

From Samuel Hodgdon, July 4, 1799 (LS, Hamilton Papers, Library of Congress).   VII

From Daniel Bradley, July 5, 1799 (ALS, Hamilton Papers, Library of Congress).   III

From Adam Hoops, July 5, 1799 (ALS, Hamilton Papers, Library of Congress).   III

From James McHenry, July 5, 1799 (LS, Hamilton Papers, Library of Congress), enclosing a printed form of ration contract (copy, Hamilton Papers, Library of Congress).   VII

From Staats Morris, July 5, 1799 (ALS, Hamilton Papers, Library of Congress), enclosing James Scanlan to Morris, July 5, 1799 (ALS, Hamilton Papers, Library of Congress).   VI

To Alexander Richards, July 5, 1799 (copy, in the handwriting of Ethan Brown, Hamilton Papers, Library of Congress).   VII

From Ross Bird, July 6, 1799 (LS, Hamilton Papers, Library of Congress).   V

From Daniel Jackson, July 6, 1799 (ALS, Hamilton Papers, Library of Congress), enclosing Thomas Walsh to Jackson, July 3, 1799 (ALS, Hamilton Papers, Library of Congress).   IV

From George Leonard, July 6, 1799 (ALS, Hamilton Papers, Library of Congress), enclosing a statement by Daniel Parker, July 2, 1799 (ADS, Hamilton Papers, Library of Congress).   III

From Alexander Richards, July 6, 1799 (ALS, Hamilton Papers, Library of Congress).   VII

From Jeremiah Wadsworth, July 6, 1799 (ALS, Hamilton Papers, Library of Congress).   III

To Tench Francis, July 7, 1799 (ALS, Hamilton Papers, Library of Congress).   VII

To James McHenry, July 7, 1799 (ADf, Hamilton Papers, Library of Congress).   III

To John Adlum, July 8, 1799 (LS, Hamilton Papers, Library of Congress; copy, in the handwriting of Ethan Brown, Hamilton Papers, Library of Congress).   VII

From William Heth, July 8, 179[9] (ALS, Hamilton Papers, Library of Congress).   II

From Ephraim Hunt, July 8, 1799 (ALS, Hamilton Papers, Library of Congress).   I

To Staats Morris, July 8, 1799 (ADf, Hamilton Papers, Library of Congress).   III

To Daniel Newnan, July 8, 1799 (ADf, Hamilton Papers, Library of Congress).   VIII

From Aaron Ogden, July 8, 1799 (ALS, Hamilton Papers, Library of Congress).   V

From William Willcocks, July 8, 1799 (ALS, Hamilton Papers, Library of Congress).   III

From John T. Bentley, July 9, 1799 (ALS, Hamilton Papers, Library of Congress).   I

From James Chevalier, July 9, 1799 (ALS, Hamilton Papers, Library of Congress).   I

From Thomas Parker, July 9, 1799 (ADf, Hamilton Papers, Library of Congress).   VI VII

From Samuel C. Seely, July 9, 1799 (ALS, Hamilton Papers, Library of Congress).   I

From Amos Stoddard, July 9, 1799 (ALS, Hamilton Papers, Library of Congress).   VII

From Timothy Taylor, July 9, 1799 (ALS, Hamilton Papers, Library of Congress).   III

From James Baytop [July 10, 1799] (ALS, Hamilton Papers, Library of Congress).   V

To William C. Bentley, July 10, 1799 (copy, in the handwriting of Ethan Brown, Hamilton Papers, Library of Congress).   V VI

From Benjamin Brookes, July 10, 1799 (ALS, Hamilton Papers, Library of Congress).   III

To Josias Carvel Hall, July 10, 1799 (ADf, Hamilton Papers, Library of Congress).   V VI

From James McHenry, July 10, 1799 (ALS, Hamilton Papers, Library of Congress; ADf, James McHenry Papers, Library of Congress).   III

From Griffith J. McRee, July 10, 1799 (ALS, Hamilton Papers, Library of Congress), enclosing "Contract for Supplying the Troops of the United States within this State [North Carolina] during the present year," June 21, 1799 (copy, Hamilton Papers, Library of Congress).   VII

From Thomas Parker, July 10, 1799 (ALS, Hamilton Papers, Library of Congress).   V VII

From Jonathan Trumbull, July 10, 1799 (ALS, Hamilton Papers, Library of Congress; ADfS, Connecticut Historical Society, Hartford).   I

From Benjamin Walker, July 10, 1799 (ALS, Hamilton Papers, Library of Congress).   II

From Benjamin Walker, July 10, 1799 (ALS, Hamilton Papers, Library of Congress).   II

To Richard Hunewell, July 11, 1799 (copy, in the handwriting of Ethan Brown, Hamilton Papers, Library of Congress).   II

To James McHenry, July 11, 1799 (copy, in the handwriting of Ethan Brown, Hamilton Papers, Library of Congress).   II

To Aaron Ogden, July 11, 1799 (ALS, George N. Meissner Collection, Washington University Libraries, St. Louis, Missouri; copy, in the handwriting of Ethan Brown, Hamilton Papers, Library of Congress).   III

From John J. U. Rivardi, July 11, 1799 (ALS, Hamilton Papers, Library of Congress).   III IV VII

To William S. Smith, July 11, 1799 (ADf, Hamilton Papers, Library of Congress).   III V

From Ebenezer Stevens, July 11, 1799 (LS Hamilton Papers, Library of Congress).   VII

To Ebenezer Stevens, July 11, 1799 (ALS, New-York Historical   VII
Society, New York City; copy, in the handwriting of Ethan
Brown, Hamilton Papers, Library of Congress).

From John Fergus, July 12, 1799 (ALS, Hamilton Papers, Library   III
of Congress).

To Adam Hoops, July 12, 1799 (copy, in the handwriting of   VII
Ethan Brown, Hamilton Papers, Library of Congress).

From James McHenry, July 12, 1799 (LS, Hamilton Papers, Li-   III
brary of Congress), enclosing an extract of Caleb Swan to Mc-
Henry, July 5, 1799 (copy, Hamilton Papers, Library of
Congress).

To James McHenry, July 12, 1799 (copy, in the handwriting of   III
Ethan Brown, Hamilton Papers, Library of Congress).

From Aaron Ogden, July 12, 1799 (ALS, Hamilton Papers, Li-   III
brary of Congress).

To Thomas Parker, July 12, 1799 (copy, in the handwriting of   VII
Ethan Brown, Hamilton Papers, Library of Congress).

From William S. Smith, July 12, 1799 (ALS, Hamilton Papers,   X
Library of Congress).

To Ebenezer Stevens, July 12, 1799 (ALS, New-York Historical   VII
Society, New York City).

From David Strong, July 12, 1799 (LS, Hamilton Papers, Library   VIII
of Congress).

From Rufus Graves, July 13, 1799 (ALS, Hamilton Papers, Li-   V
brary of Congress).

From Adam Hoops, July 13, 1799 (ALS, Hamilton Papers, Li-   III
brary of Congress).   IV

From James McHenry, July 13, 1799 (LS, Hamilton Papers, Li-   III
brary of Congress).

From William Macpherson, July 13, 1799 (ALS, Hamilton Pa-   VII
pers, Library of Congress).

To Daniel Bradley, [July] 14, 1799 (copy, in the handwriting of   VI
Ethan Brown, Hamilton Papers, Library of Congress).

From Josias Carvel Hall, July 14, 1799 (ALS, Hamilton Papers,   VI
Library of Congress), enclosing David Hopkins to Hall, July 7,
1799 (ALS, Hamilton Papers, Library of Congress).

From John Adlum, July 15, 1799 (ALS, Hamilton Papers, Library   VII
of Congress).

From William C. Bentley, July 15, 1799 (ALS, Hamilton Papers,   VI
Library of Congress), enclosing "A List of the Platoon Officers

of the 7th United States Regiment" (AD, Hamilton Papers, Library of Congress).

From Adam Hoops, July 15, 1799 (ALS, Hamilton Papers, Library of Congress). III

To James McHenry, July 15, 1799 (copy, in the handwriting of Ethan Brown, Hamilton Papers, Library of Congress). III

To Aaron Ogden, July 15, 1799 (LS, George N. Meissner Collection, Washington University Libraries, St. Louis, Missouri; copy, in the handwriting of Ethan Brown, Hamilton Papers, Library of Congress). III

From John J. U. Rivardi, July 15, 1799 (ALS, Hamilton Papers, Library of Congress). III IV VII

From Lewis Tousard, July 15, 1799 (ALS, Hamilton Papers, Library of Congress), enclosing Tousard to William Littlefield, July 13, 1799 (copy, Hamilton Papers, Library of Congress); Littlefield to Tousard, July 14, 1799 (ALS, Hamilton Papers, Library of Congress). VI

From James McHenry, July 16, 1799 (LS, Hamilton Papers, Library of Congress), enclosing McHenry to Archibald Crary, July 17, 1799 (LS, letterpress copy, Hamilton Papers, Library of Congress). VII

From William North, July 16, 1799 (ALS, Hamilton Papers, Library of Congress). III

From William S. Smith, July 16, 1799 (ALS, Hamilton Papers, Library of Congress). II

From Robert Heaton, Jr., July 17, 1799 (ALS, Hamilton Papers, Library of Congress). IV

From James McHenry, July 17, 1799 (ALS, Hamilton Papers, Library of Congress). III VII

From Alexander Thompson, July 17, 1799 (ALS, Hamilton Papers, Library of Congress). VII

From James McHenry, July 18, 1799 (LS, Hamilton Papers, Library of Congress), enclosing an extract of John Stockton to McHenry, July 15, 1799 (copy, Hamilton Papers, Library of Congress). VII

From John J. U. Rivardi, July 18, 1799 (ALS, Hamilton Papers, Library of Congress). IX

To John Adlum, July 19, 1799 (LS, Hamilton Papers, Library of Congress; copy, in the handwriting of Ethan Brown, Hamilton Papers, Library of Congress). III

To Abraham Archer, July 19, 1799 (copy, in the handwriting of   II
Ethan Brown, Hamilton Papers, Library of Congress).

From John McClallen, July 19, 1799 (ALS, Hamilton Papers,   V
Library of Congress), enclosing his expense report, July 15,
1799 (ADS, Hamilton Papers, Library of Congress).

From James McHenry, July 19, 1799 (LS, Hamilton Papers, Li-   V
brary of Congress).

To James McHenry, July 19, 1799 (copy, in the handwriting of   II
Ethan Brown, Hamilton Papers, Library of Congress).

To James McHenry, July 19, 1799 (copy, in the handwriting of   VII
Ethan Brown, Hamilton Papers, Library of Congress).

To Aaron Ogden, July 19, 1799 (LS, Lloyd W. Smith Collection,   III
Morristown National Historical Park, Morristown, New Jersey;
Df, in the handwriting of Ethan Brown, Hamilton Papers, Li-
brary of Congress).

To Jonathan Trumbull, July 19, 1799 (LS, Connecticut State   II
Library, Hartford; Df, in the handwriting of Ethan Brown,
Hamilton Papers, Library of Congress).

From Daniel Jackson, July 20, 1799 (ALS, Hamilton Papers, Li-   VII
brary of Congress).

From Daniel Jackson, July 20, 1799 (ALS, Hamilton Papers, Li-   VII
brary of Congress), enclosing a plan for a hospital at Castle
William, July 20, 1799 (D, signed by Jackson, Stephen Higginson, and Thomas Walsh, Hamilton Papers, Library of Congress)

From Jacob Cuyler, July 21, 1799 (ALS, Hamilton Papers, Li-   II
brary of Congress).

From John Fergus, July 21, 1799 (ALS, Hamilton Papers, Library   VII
of Congress).

From Josias Carvel Hall, July 21, 1799 (ALS, Hamilton Papers,   V
Library of Congress).   VII

From Stephen Van Rensselaer, July 21, 1799 (ALS, Hamilton   II
Papers, Library of Congress).

From John Allen, July 22, 1799 (ALS, Hamilton Papers, Library   II
of Congress).

From Thomas Billington, July 22, 1799 (ALS, Hamilton Papers,   VII
Library of Congress).

From Josias Carvel Hall, July 22, 1799 (ALS, Hamilton Papers,   IV
Library of Congress).   VI

To Ebenezer Stevens, July 22, 1799 (ALS, New-York Historical VII
Society, New York City; copy, in the handwriting of Ethan
Brown, Hamilton Papers, Library of Congress).

From Timothy Taylor, July 22, 1799 (ALS, Hamilton Papers, III
Library of Congress).

From Edward Carrington, July 23, 1799 (ALS, Hamilton Papers, V
Library of Congress). VII

From Philip Church, July 23, 1799 (ALS, Hamilton Papers, Li- V
brary of Congress).

From John F. Hamtramck, July 23, 1799 (LS, Hamilton Papers, III
Library of Congress).

From Washington Morton, July 23, 1799 (ALS, Hamilton Papers, IV
Library of Congress).

From Aaron Ogden, July 23, 1799 (ALS, Hamilton Papers, Li- VI
brary of Congress).

From William S. Smith, July 23, 1799 (ALS, Hamilton Papers, V
Library of Congress).

From William S. Smith, July 23, 1799 (ALS, Hamilton Papers, IV
Library of Congress).

From William S. Smith, July 23, 1799 (ALS, Hamilton Papers, VII
Library of Congress).

From William S. Smith, July 23, 1799 (ALS, Hamilton Papers, III
Library of Congress), enclosing Dowe J. Fondey to Smith,
July 15, 1799 (ALS, Hamilton Papers, Library of Congress);
Inhabitants of Troy, New York, to John Adams, n.d. (copy,
Hamilton Papers, Library of Congress).

From James McHenry, July 24, 1799 (LS, Hamilton Papers, Li- IV
brary of Congress), enclosing an extract of John F. Hamtramck to McHenry, July 1, 1799 (copy, Hamilton Papers,
Library of Congress); Hamtramck to Daniel Britt, May 14,
1799 (copy, Hamilton Papers, Library of Congress).

From Daniel Morgan, July 24, 1799 (ALS, Hamilton Papers, Li- III
brary of Congress).

From Rufus Graves, July 25, 1799 (ALS, Hamilton Papers, Li- VI
brary of Congress), enclosing "Return of the sixteenth Circle. . . ," July 24, 1799 (ADS, Hamilton Papers, Library of
Congress).

From Adam Hoops, July 25, 1799 (ALS, Hamilton Papers, Li- VII
brary of Congress).

To Adam Hoops, July 25, 1799 (Df, in the handwriting of Ethan   VII
Brown, Hamilton Papers, Library of Congress).

From Isaac Craig, July 26, 1799 (ALS, Hamilton Papers, Library   III
of Congress), enclosing "Return of Stores on hand received
forwarded & issued at Pittsburg by Isaac Craig Depy. Qr. Masr.
Genl. in April, May & June 1799" (DS, Hamilton Papers, Library of Congress).

From Rufus Graves, July 26, 1799 (ALS, Hamilton Papers, Li-   VI
brary of Congress).

From Rufus Graves, July 26, 1799 (ALS, Hamilton Papers, Li-   VI
brary of Congress).

From Rufus Graves, July 27, 1799 (ALS, Hamilton Papers, Li-   V
brary of Congress).

From Rufus Graves, July 27, 1799 (ALS, Hamilton Papers, Li-   II
brary of Congress), enclosing Oliver Peabody to Graves,
July 22, 1799 (ALS, Hamilton Papers, Library of Congress).

From James Read, July 27, 1799 (ALS, Hamilton Papers, Library   VI
of Congress), enclosing "Officers of the 6th Regiment of Infantry," July 27, 1799 (ADS, Hamilton Papers, Library of
Congress). Acknowledges H's letter of May 16, 1799. *Letter
not found.*

From William S. Smith, July 27, 1799 (ALS, Hamilton Papers,   VI
Library of Congress).

From William S. Smith, July 27, 1799 (ALS, Hamilton Papers,   II
Library of Congress), enclosing Dowe J. Fondey to Smith,
June 29, 1799 (ALS, Hamilton Papers, Library of Congress).

From Richard Hunewell, July 28, 1799 (ALS, Hamilton Papers,   VII
Library of Congress).

From James McHenry, July 29, 1799 (LS, Hamilton Papers, Li-   III
brary of Congress).

From Charles Cotesworth Pinckney, July 29, 1799 (ALS, Hamil-   VI
ton Papers, Library of Congress; ALS [incomplete], marked
"Duplicate," Hamilton Papers, Library of Congress).

To James Read, July 29, 1799 (copy, in the handwriting of Ethan   VII
Brown, Hamilton Papers, Library of Congress).

From John F. Hamtramck, July 30, 1799 (LS, marked "Dupli-   III
cate," Hamilton Papers, Library of Congress).

From John F. Hamtramck, July 30, 1799 (LS, Hamilton Papers,   IX
Library of Congress).

From Johannes G. Koebel, July 30, 1799 (ALS, Hamilton Papers,   III
Library of Congress).

From Thomas Parker, July 30 [-31], 1799 (ALS, Hamilton Pa-   IV
pers, Library of Congress).   V
                                                                  VI

To James Read, July 30, 1799 (Df, in the handwriting of Ethan   III
Brown, Hamilton Papers, Library of Congress).   VIII

From William S. Smith, July 30, 1799 (ALS, Hamilton Papers,   VII
Library of Congress), enclosing Henry W. Ludlow to Smith,
July 29, 1799 (ALS, Hamilton Papers, Library of Congress).

From William Willcocks, July 30, 1799 (LS, Hamilton Papers,   V
Library of Congress).

From William Willcocks, July 30, 1799 (LS, Hamilton Papers,   IV
Library of Congress).   VII

To William Willcocks, July 30, 1799 (copy, in the handwriting of IV
Ethan Brown, Hamilton Papers, Library of Congress).

To John Allen, July 31, 1799 (copy, in the handwriting of Ethan   II
Brown, Hamilton Papers, Library of Congress).

To William C. Bentley, July 31, 1799 (copy, in the handwriting   VI
of Ethan Brown, Hamilton Papers, Library of Congress).

To James Bruff, July 31, 1799 (copy, in the handwriting of Ethan VI
Brown, Hamilton Papers, Library of Congress).

To John F. Hamtramck, July 31, 1799 (Df, in the handwriting of   IV
Ethan Brown and with corrections in H's handwriting, Hamilton Papers, Library of Congress).

To James McHenry, July 31, 1799 (copy, in the handwriting of   VI
Ethan Brown, Hamilton Papers, Library of Congress).

To Griffith J. McRee, July 31, 1799 (copy, in the handwriting of VII
Ethan Brown, Hamilton Papers, Library of Congress).

From William North, July 31, 1799 (ALS, Hamilton Papers, Li-   II
brary of Congress).

To James Read, July 31, 1799 (copy, in the handwriting of Ethan   III
Brown, Hamilton Papers, Library of Congress).

From Samuel Jane [July, 1799] (ALS, Hamilton Papers, Library   III
of Congress).

AUGUST, 1799

From James Bruff, August 1, 1799 (ALS, Hamilton Papers, Li-   IV
brary of Congress).   V

From James McHenry, August 1, 1799 (LS, Hamilton Papers,   VII
Library of Congress).

From James McHenry, August 1, 1799 (LS, Hamilton Papers,   III
Library of Congress), enclosing Samuel Eddins to McHenry,
July 13, 1799 (ALS, Hamilton Papers, Library of Congress).

From Jonathan Cowdery, August 2, 1799 (ALS, Hamilton Papers,   II
Library of Congress).

From Aaron Ogden, August 2, 1799 (ALS, Hamilton Papers, Li-   V
brary of Congress), enclosing lists of recruits (AD, Hamilton
Papers, Library of Congress).

From James McHenry, August 3, 1799 (LS, Hamilton Papers,   III
Library of Congress), enclosing a list of officers in the Fifth
Infantry Regiment and a list of majors for the Sixth Infantry
Regiment (copies, Hamilton Papers, Library of Congress).

From James McHenry, August 3, 1799 (LS, Hamilton Papers,   VII
Library of Congress), enclosing an extract of Archibald Crary
to McHenry, July 25, 1799 (copy, Hamilton Papers, Library of
Congress); Isaac Senter to Crary, July 24, 1799 (copy, Hamilton
Papers, Library of Congress).

From Aaron Ogden, August 3, 1799 (ALS, Hamilton Papers,   III
Library of Congress).

From William Simmons, August 3, 1799 (LS, Hamilton Papers,   III
Library of Congress), enclosing Simmons to James McHenry,
August 2, 1799 (LS, Hamilton Papers, Library of Congress; LC,
RG 217, Records of the General Accounting Office, Letter
Books, Accountant's Office, Vol. F, May 16, 1799–February 27,
1800, National Archives).

To Ebenezer Stevens, August 3, 1799 (ALS, New-York Historical   III
Society, New York City; copy, in the handwriting of Ethan
Brown, Hamilton Papers, Library of Congress).

From John Adlum, August 5, 1799 (ALS, Hamilton Papers, Li-   III
brary of Congress).

To Adam Hoops and Daniel Jackson, August 5, 1799 (ADf,   VII
Hamilton Papers, Library of Congress).

To James McHenry, August 5, 1799 (copy, in the handwriting of   VII
Ethan Brown, Hamilton Papers, Library of Congress).

From Aaron Ogden, August 5, 1799 (ALS, Hamilton Papers, Li-   I
brary of Congress).

From William S. Smith, August 5, 1799 (ALS, Hamilton Papers,   V
Library of Congress), enclosing a certificate for Daniel Har-

rington, June 21, 1799 (DS, Hamilton Papers, Library of Congress); certificate for Isaac Slover, June 27, 1799 (DS, Hamilton Papers, Library of Congress)

From Philip Church, August 6, 1799 (ALS, Hamilton Papers, Library of Congress).   I

From William Heth, August 6, 1799 (ALS, Hamilton Papers, Library of Congress), enclosing Edmund Taylor to Heth, August 3, 1799 (ALS, Hamilton Papers, Library of Congress).   I

From William S. Smith, August 6, 1799 (ALS, Hamilton Papers, Library of Congress), enclosing Smith to Philip Courtlandt, July 16, 1799 (copy, in Smith's handwriting, Hamilton Papers, Library of Congress).   III

From Ebenezer Stevens, August 6, 1799 (LS, Hamilton Papers, Library of Congress).   III

From Vincent de Vaublanc-Lessart, August 6, 1799 (ALS, Hamilton Papers, Library of Congress).   II

From Oliver Whipple, August 6, 1799 (ALS, Hamilton Papers, Library of Congress).   I

From Samuel White, August 6, 1799 (ALS, Hamilton Papers, Library of Congress).   IV

From Benjamin Brookes, August 7, 1799 (ALS, Hamilton Papers, Library of Congress).   III

From John Duer, August 7, 1799 (ALS, Hamilton Papers, Library of Congress).   II

From Frederick Frye [August 7, 1799] (ALS, Hamilton Papers, Library of Congress).   III
   IV

From Robert LeRoy Livingston, August 7, 1799 (ALS, Hamilton Papers, Library of Congress).   IV

From James McHenry, August 7, 1799 (LS, Hamilton Papers, Library of Congress).   VII

From James McHenry, August 7, 1799 (LS, Hamilton Papers, Library of Congress), enclosing Cornelius Lyman to McHenry, July 16, 1799 (ALS, Hamilton Papers, Library of Congress).   VII

From James McHenry, August 7, 1799 (LS, Hamilton Papers, Library of Congress).   VII

From James McHenry, August 7, 1799 (LS, Hamilton Papers, Library of Congress).   III

From Staats Morris, August 7, 1799 (ALS, Hamilton Papers, Library of Congress). Acknowledges H's letter of August 3, 1799. *Letter not found.*   III

From Samuel Osborn, August 7, 1799 (ALS, Hamilton Papers,   III
Library of Congress).

From William Shepard, August 7, 1799 (ALS, Hamilton Papers,   III
Library of Congress).

From Oliver Wolcott, Jr., August 7, 1799 (ALS, Hamilton Papers,   VII
Library of Congress), enclosing "Treasury Department Circular
to the Collectors of the Customs," May 24, 1799 (copy, Hamilton Papers, Library of Congress).

From James McHenry, August 8, 1799 (LS, Hamilton Papers, Li-   III
brary of Congress), enclosing McHenry to Ebenezer Massey,
August 8, 1799 (LS, Hamilton Papers, Library of Congress).

From James McHenry, August 8, 1799 (LS, Hamilton Papers,   III
Library of Congress).   VIII

From James McHenry, August 9, 1799 (LS, Hamilton Papers,   III
Library of Congress).

To James McHenry, August 9, 1799 (ADfS, Hamilton Papers,   VIII
Library of Congress).

To William S. Smith, August 9, 1799 (copy, in the handwriting   IV
of Ethan Brown, Hamilton Papers, Library of Congress).

To Abraham Ellery, August 10, 1799 (copy, in the handwriting   IV
of Ethan Brown, Hamilton Papers, Library of Congress).

From Josias Carvel Hall, August 10, 1799 (ALS, Hamilton Papers,   V
Library of Congress).

From Daniel Jackson, August 10, 1799 (ALS, Hamilton Papers,   VI
Library of Congress), enclosing Abraham Rand's discharge,
April 1, 1799 (copy, Hamilton Papers, Library of Congress),
and supporting affidavit, July 23, 1799 (copy, in Jackson's handwriting, Hamilton Papers, Library of Congress).

From James McHenry, August 10, 1799 (LS, Hamilton Papers,   VII
Library of Congress), enclosing McHenry to William S. Smith,
August 10, 1799 (LS, letterpress copy, Hamilton Papers, Library
of Congress).

To Samuel Osborn, August 10, 1799 (copy, in the handwriting of   III
Ethan Brown, Hamilton Papers, Library of Congress).

From William S. Smith, August 10, 1799 (ALS, Hamilton Papers,   IV
Library of Congress).

To Ebenezer Stevens, August 10, 1799 (LS, New-York Historical   VII
Society, New York City; copy, in the handwriting of Ethan
Brown, Hamilton Papers, Library of Congress).

To Oliver Wolcott, Jr., August 10, 1799 (ALS, Connecticut His-   VII
torical Society, Hartford).

From William S. Smith, August 11, 1799 (ALS, Hamilton Papers,   I
Library of Congress).

To Ebenezer Stevens, August 11, 1799 (ALS, New-York His-   VII
torical Society, New York City; copy, in the handwriting of
Ethan Brown, Hamilton Papers, Library of Congress).

To Abraham Archer, August 12, 1799 (Df, in the handwriting of   I
Ethan Brown, Hamilton Papers, Library of Congress). Acknowledges Archer's letter of August 3, 1799. *Letter not found.*

To Henry Burbeck, August 12, 1799 (copy, in the handwriting of   VII
Ethan Brown, Hamilton Papers, Library of Congress).

To Daniel Jackson, August 12, 1799 (copy, in the handwriting of   III
Ethan Brown, Hamilton Papers, Library of Congress).

To John McClallen, August 12, 1799 (copy, in the handwriting of   I
Ethan Brown, Hamilton Papers, Library of Congress).

From James McHenry, August 12, 1799 (LS, New-York His-   VII
torical Society, New York City), with instructions to Ebenezer
Stevens written by H on the verso.

To James McHenry, August 12, 1799 (Df, in the handwriting of   IV
Ethan Brown, Hamilton Papers, Library of Congress).

To James McHenry, August 12, 1799 (Df, in the handwriting of   I
Ethan Brown, Hamilton Papers, Library of Congress).

From Samuel Mackay, August 12, 1799 (ALS, Hamilton Papers,   III
Library of Congress).

To Aaron Ogden, August 12, 1799 (Df, in the handwriting of   IV
Ethan Brown, Hamilton Papers, Library of Congress).

To William S. Smith, August 12, 1799 (Df, in the handwriting of   IV
Thomas Y. How, Hamilton Papers, Library of Congress).

To John Steele, August 12, 1799 (copy, in the handwriting of   III
Ethan Brown, Hamilton Papers, Library of Congress).

To David Strong, August 12, 1799 (Df, in the handwriting of   VI
Ethan Brown, Hamilton Papers, Library of Congress).

To Rufus Graves, August 13, 1799 (Df, in the handwriting of   VI
Thomas Y. How, Hamilton Papers, Library of Congress). Ac-
knowledges Graves's letters of July 25, 26, 27, August 3, 1799.
Letter of August 3, 1799, not found.

To James McHenry, August 13, 1799 (ADf, Hamilton Papers,   IV
Library of Congress).

To James McHenry, August 13, 1799 (Df, in the handwriting of Thomas Y. How, Hamilton Papers, Library of Congress).   VI

To James Read, August 13, 1799 (Df, in the handwriting of Thomas Y. How, Hamilton Papers, Library of Congress).   V VI

From William Thompson, August 13, 1799 (ALS, Hamilton Papers, Library of Congress).   I

To Richard Hunewell, August 14, 1799 (Df, in the handwriting of Thomas Y. How and H, Hamilton Papers, Library of Congress).   III VI

From James McHenry, August 14, 1799 (LS, Hamilton Papers, Library of Congress).   IV

From Aaron Ogden, August 14, 1799 (ALS, Hamilton Papers, Library of Congress).   IV

From William S. Smith, August 14, 1799 (ALS, Hamilton Papers, Library of Congress).   IV

From George Washington, August 14, 1799 (LS, Hamilton Papers, Library of Congress; copy, George Washington Papers, Library of Congress), enclosing Levin Powell, to Washington, July 29, 1799 (ALS, Hamilton Papers, Library of Congress); Thomas Parker to Washington, July 23, 1799 (ALS, Hamilton Papers, Library of Congress); Parker to Washington, July 26, 1799 (ALS, Hamilton Papers, Library of Congress); Thomas Blackburn to Washington, July 31, 1799 (ALS, Hamilton Papers, Library of Congress).   I

To James Baytop, August 15, 1799 (Df, in the handwriting of Thomas Y. How, Hamilton Papers, Library of Congress).   III

From William C. Bentley, August 15, 1799 (ALS, Hamilton Papers, Library of Congress), enclosing proceedings of a trial concerning custody of a minor, n.d. (copy, Hamilton Papers, Library of Congress).   III V

To William C. Bentley, August 15, 1799 (Df, in the handwriting of Thomas Y. How, Hamilton Papers, Library of Congress).   III

To Samuel Jones, August 15, 1799 (ALS, Hamilton Papers, Library of Congress).   I

From James McHenry, August 15, 1799 (LS, Hamilton Papers, Library of Congress).   VII

From Thomas Parker, August 15, 1799 (ALS, Hamilton Papers, Library of Congress).   VI

To James Read, August 15, 1799 (Df, in the handwriting of Thomas Y. How, Hamilton Papers, Library of Congress).   IV

From William S. Smith, August 15, 1799 (ALS, Hamilton Papers,   IV
Library of Congress).

To William S. Smith, August 15, 1799 (Df, in the handwriting of   IV
Thomas Y. How, Hamilton Papers, Library of Congress).

From Phineas Ashmun, August 16, 1799 (ALS, Hamilton Papers,   IV
Library of Congress).

From Daniel Bradley, August 16, 1799 (ALS, Hamilton Papers,   VI
Library of Congress).

From Simeon Draper, August 16, 1799 (LS, Hamilton Papers, Li-   III
brary of Congress).

From Joseph Elliott, August 16, 1799 (ALS, Hamilton Papers,   III
Library of Congress).

To Thomas Parker, August 16, 1799 (Df, in the handwriting of   V
Thomas Y. How, Hamilton Papers, Library of Congress). Ac-   VI
knowledges Parker's letters of July 6, 10, 17, 20, 24, 30, Au-   VII
gust 1, 1799. *Letter of August 1, 1799, not found.*

To John Smith, August 16, 1799 (ADf, with postscript in Ethan   VI
Brown's handwriting, Hamilton Papers, Library of Congress),
enclosing "Plan. South Carolina Georgia Kentucky divided
into the following Subdistricts for Recruiting" (copy, Hamilton
Papers, Library of Congress).

To William C. Bentley, August 17, 1799 (Df, in the handwriting   III
of Thomas Y. How, Hamilton Papers, Library of Congress).

From Peletiah Hitchcock, August 17, 1799 (ALS, Hamilton Pa-   III
pers, Library of Congress).

From James McHenry, August 17, 1799 (LS, Hamilton Papers,   VII
Library of Congress).

From James McHenry, August 17, 1799 (LS, Hamilton Papers,   III
Library of Congress).

From Thomas Lloyd Moore, August 17, 1799 (ALS, Hamilton   V
Papers, Library of Congress).

From Thomas Parker, August 17, 1799 (ALS, Hamilton Papers,   III
Library of Congress), enclosing Robert White to Parker, Au-
gust 14, 1799 (copy, in Parker's handwriting, Hamilton Papers,
Library of Congress).

From William C. Bentley, August 18, 1799 (ALS, Hamilton Pa-   VII
pers, Library of Congress).

From Rufus Graves, August 18, 1799 (ALS, Hamilton Papers,   V
Library of Congress).

To Josias Carvel Hall, August 19, 1799 (Df, in the handwriting of   VI
Thomas Y. How, Hamilton Papers, Library of Congress).

To James McHenry, August 19, 1799 (ADf, Hamilton Papers, Li-   VII
brary of Congress).

To Thomas Lloyd Moore, August 19, 1799 (Df, in the hand-   VI
writing of Thomas Y. How, Hamilton Papers, Library of Congress).

To James Read, August 19, 1799 (copy, in the handwriting of   VII
Ethan Brown, Hamilton Papers, Library of Congress).

To William Simmons, August 19, 1799 (ADf, Hamilton Papers,   VI
Library of Congress).

To Timothy Taylor, August 19, 1799 (Df, in the handwriting of   III
Thomas Y. How, Hamilton Papers, Library of Congress).

From Lewis Tousard, August 19, 1799 (ALS, Hamilton Papers,   VI
Library of Congress).   VII

From James Triplett, August 19, 1799 (ALS, Hamilton Papers,   IV
Library of Congress).

From John Adlum, August 20, 1799 (ALS, Hamilton Papers, Li-   III
brary of Congress).   IV

From Peter Carlton, August 20, 1799 (ALS, Hamilton Papers,   III
Library of Congress).

From Cornelius Lyman, August 20, 1799 (ALS, Hamilton Papers,   IX
Library of Congress), enclosing monthly return (DS, Hamilton
Papers, Library of Congress).

To James McHenry, August 20, 1799 (Df, in the handwriting of   IX
Thomas Y. How, Hamilton Papers, Library of Congress).

To James McHenry, August 20, 1799 (Df, in the handwriting of   IX
Ethan Brown, Hamilton Papers, Library of Congress).

To Aaron Ogden, August 20, 1799 (LS, in the handwriting of   I
Thomas Y. How, Lloyd W. Smith Collection, Morristown Na-   VI
tional Historical Park, Morristown, New Jersey; Df, in the
handwriting of Thomas Y. How, Hamilton Papers, Library of
Congress).

From Ninian Pinkney, August 20, 1799 (ALS, Hamilton Papers,   IX
Library of Congress).

From Benjamin Brookes, August 21, 1799 (ALS, Hamilton Papers,   III
Library of Congress), enclosing a certificate by William Beanes
(ADS, Hamilton Papers, Library of Congress).

To Josias Carvel Hall, August 21, 1799 (Df, in the handwriting of   IV
H and Thomas Y. How, Hamilton Papers, Library of Con-   VI

gress). Acknowledges Hall's letter of August 18, 1799. *Letter not found.*

From James McHenry, August 21, 1799 (LS, Hamilton Papers, Library of Congress; copy, Hamilton Papers, Library of Congress).   III

From James McHenry, August 21, 1799 (LS, Hamilton Papers, Library of Congress).   IV

From William S. Smith, August 21, 1799 (ALS, Hamilton Papers, Library of Congress).   IV

To James Wilkinson, August 21, 1799 (Df, in the handwriting of Ethan Brown, Hamilton Papers, Library of Congress).   VI

To Daniel Bradley, August 22, 1799 (Df, in the handwriting of Thomas Y. How, Hamilton Papers, Library of Congress).   VI VII

To Benjamin Brookes, August 22, 1799 (Df, in the handwriting of Thomas Y. How, Hamilton Papers, Library of Congress).   III

From Richard Hunewell, August 22, 1799 (LS, Hamilton Papers, Library of Congress).   I

To Thomas Parker, August 22, 1799 (Df, in the handwriting of Thomas Y. How, Hamilton Papers, Library of Congress).   VI

From John J. U. Rivardi, August 22, 1799 (ALS, Hamilton Papers, Library of Congress).   III VII

To William S. Smith, August 22, 1799 (ADf, Hamilton Papers, Library of Congress).   VI

To William S. Smith, August 22, 1799 (Df, in the handwriting of Thomas Y. How, Hamilton Papers, Library of Congress).   III

To Ebenezer Stevens, August 22, 1799 (LS, New-York Historical Society, New York City; ADf, Hamilton Papers, Library of Congress).   VII

From David Strong, August 22, 1799 (ALS, Hamilton Papers, Library of Congress).   VII

From Dwight Foster, August 23, 1799 (ALS, Hamilton Papers, Library of Congress).   III

To Richard Harison, August 23, 1799 (Df, in the handwriting of Ethan Brown, Hamilton Papers, Library of Congress).   IV

From James McHenry, August 23, 1799 (LS, Hamilton Papers, Library of Congress; LS, letterpress copy, James McHenry Papers, Library of Congress), enclosing: James Cochran to McHenry, August 15, 1799 (ALS, Hamilton Papers, Library of Congress); Samuel Stringer to McHenry, August 16, 1799 (ALS, Hamilton Papers, Library of Congress); John H. Doug-   I lass to McHenry, August 19, 1799 (ALS, Hamilton Papers, Library of Congress); certificate of Michael Henry, September 20, 1797 (copy, Hamilton Papers, Library of Congress); deposition by Michael Henry, September 20, 1797 (copy, Hamilton Papers, Library of Congress).

From Aaron Ogden, August 23, 1799 (ALS, Hamilton Papers, Library of Congress).   VII

From Lewis Tousard, August 23, 1799 (ALS, Hamilton Papers, Library of Congress).   VII

To John Adlum, August 24, 1799 (LS, in the handwriting of Thomas Y. How, Hamilton Papers, Library of Congress; Df, in the handwriting of Thomas Y. How, Hamilton Papers, Library of Congress), enclosing "a letter to Lieutenant [William R.] Boote." *Letter not found.*   III

To Daniel Bradley, August 24, 1799 (Df, in the handwriting of Thomas Y. How, Hamilton Papers, Library of Congress).   VI

From Josias Carvel Hall, August 24, 1799 (ALS, Hamilton Papers, Library of Congress).   IV
VII

To Daniel Jackson, August 24, 1799 (Df, in the handwriting of Thomas Y. How, Hamilton Papers, Library of Congress).   IV
VI

To John Adlum, August 26, 1799 (LS, in the handwriting of Thomas Y. How, Hamilton Papers, Library of Congress; Df, in the handwriting of Thomas Y. How, Hamilton Papers, Library of Congress).   VII

From William C. Bentley, August 26, 1799 (ALS, Hamilton Papers, Library of Congress).   I
VI

From John H. Buell, August 26, 1799 (ALS, Hamilton Papers, Library of Congress).   III

From Samuel Hodgdon, August 26, 1799 (ALS, Hamilton Papers, Library of Congress; LC, RG 94, Post-Revolutionary War Records, Letters of Samuel Hodgdon, National Archives).   VII

To Daniel Jackson, August 26, 1799 (ADf, Hamilton Papers, Library of Congress).   VII

To Ebenezer Massey, August 26, 1799 (Df, in the handwriting of Thomas Y. How, Hamilton Papers, Library of Congress).   III

To Samuel Osborn, August 26, 1799 (ALS, Henry Ford Museum and Greenfield Village, Dearborn, Michigan; Df, in the handwriting of Thomas Y. How, Hamilton Papers, Library of Congress).   IV

To James Read, August 26, 1799 (Df, in the handwriting of Thomas Y. How, Hamilton Papers, Library of Congress).   III

To Ebenezer Stevens, August 26, 1799 (LS, in the handwriting of   VII
    Thomas Y. How, New-York Historical Society, New York
    City; Df, in the handwriting of Thomas Y. How, Hamilton
    Papers, Library of Congress).

From Thomas Underwood, August 26, 1799 (ALS, Hamilton Pa-   III
    pers, Library of Congress), enclosing Benjamin Rush to James
    McHenry, August 16, 1799 (copy, in the handwriting of Un-
    derwood, Hamilton Papers, Library of Congress).

From William Armstrong, August 27, 1799 (ALS, Hamilton Pa-   I
    pers, Library of Congress).

To James Bruff, August 27, 1799 (Df, in the handwriting of   IV
    Thomas Y. How, Hamilton Papers, Library of Congress).

To Rufus Graves, August 27, 1799 (Df, in the handwriting of   VII
    Thomas Y. How, Hamilton Papers, Library of Congress).

From John Hancock, Jr., August 27, 1799 (ALS, Hamilton Pa-   III
    pers, Library of Congress).

To Adam Hoops, August 27, 1799 (ADf, Hamilton Papers, Li-   IV
    brary of Congress).

From Jesse Lukens, August 27, 1799 (ALS, Hamilton Papers, Li-   III
    brary of Congress).

To James McHenry, August 27, 1799 (ADf, Hamilton Papers,   VI
    Library of Congress).

From Aaron Ogden, August 27, 1799 (ALS, Hamilton Papers,   IV
    Library of Congress).

To Aaron Ogden, August 27, 1799 (LS, in the handwriting of   VI
    Thomas Y. How, Lloyd W. Smith Collection, Morristown Na-
    tional Historical Park, Morristown, New Jersey; Df, in the
    handwriting of Thomas Y. How, Hamilton Papers, Library of
    Congress).

From Samuel Osborn, August 27, 1799 (ALS, Hamilton Papers,   IV
    Library of Congress).

From James Read, August 27, 1799 (ALS, Hamilton Papers, Li-   III
    brary of Congress).

From William S. Smith, August 27, 1799 (LS, Hamilton Papers,   III
    Library of Congress).

From William S. Smith, August 27, 1799 (ALS, Hamilton Papers,   I
    Library of Congress).

To Ebenezer Stevens, August 27, 1799 (Df, in the handwriting of   VII
    Thomas Y. How, Hamilton Papers, Library of Congress; copy,
    New-York Historical Society, New York City).

From Nanning J. Visscher, August 27, 1799 (ALS, Hamilton Pa-   III
pers, Library of Congress).

To William C. Bentley, August 28, 1799 (Df, in the handwriting   VI
of Thomas Y. How, Hamilton Papers, Library of Congress).

To Rufus Graves, August 28, 1799 (Df, in the handwriting of   VI
Thomas Y. How, Hamilton Papers, Library of Congress).

To James McHenry, August 28, 1799 (ADf, Hamilton Papers,   V
Library of Congress).

To James McHenry, August 28, 1799 (Df, in the handwriting of   I
Thomas Y. How, Hamilton Papers, Library of Congress).

To James McHenry, August 28, 1799 (Df, in the handwriting of   III
Thomas Y. How, Hamilton Papers, Library of Congress).   VI

To James McHenry, August 28, 1799 (Df, in the handwriting of   IV
Ethan Brown, Hamilton Papers, Library of Congress).

To James McHenry, August 28, 1799 (Df, in the handwriting of   II
Thomas Y. How, Hamilton Papers, Library of Congress).

From Thomas Parker, August 28, 1799 (ALS, Hamilton Papers,   I
Library of Congress).

To Ebenezer Stevens, August 28, 1799 (LS, New-York Historical   VII
Society, New York City; Df, in the handwriting of Ethan
Brown, Hamilton Papers, Library of Congress).

To Ebenezer Stevens, August 28, 1799 (LS, in the handwriting of   VII
Thomas Y. How, New-York Historical Society, New York
City; Df, in the handwriting of Thomas Y. How, Hamilton Pa-
pers, Library of Congress).

To John Adlum, August 29, 1799 (Df, in the handwriting of   III
Thomas Y. How, Hamilton Papers, Library of Congress).

To Benjamin Brookes, August 29, 1799 (Df, in the handwriting of   III
Thomas Y. How, Hamilton Papers, Library of Congress).

To John Dover, August 29, 1799 (Df, in the handwriting of   III
Thomas Y. How, Hamilton Papers, Library of Congress).

To Daniel Jackson, August 29, 1799 (Df, in the handwriting of   III
Thomas Y. How, Hamilton Papers, Library of Congress).

To Thomas Lloyd Moore, August 29, 1799 (Df, in the hand-   III
writing of Thomas Y. How, Hamilton Papers, Library of Congress).

To James Read, August 29, 1799 (Df, in the handwriting of   VI
Thomas Y. How, Hamilton Papers, Library of Congress).

To James Read, August 29, 1799 (Df, in the handwriting of Ethan   III
Brown, Hamilton Papers, Library of Congress).

To Ebenezer Stevens, August 29, 1799 (LS, in the handwriting of VII
Ethan Brown, New-York Historical Society, New York City;
copy, in the handwriting of Ethan Brown, Hamilton Papers,
Library of Congress).

To Samuel Hodgdon, August 30, 1799 (Df, in the handwriting of VII
H and Thomas Y. How, Hamilton Papers, Library of Congress).

From Adam Hoops, August 30, 1799 (ALS, Hamilton Papers, Li- VII
brary of Congress).

To Adam Hoops, August 30, 1799 (Df, in the handwriting of III
Thomas Y. How, Hamilton Papers, Library of Congress).

From James McHenry, August 30, 1799 (LS, Hamilton Papers, III
Library of Congress; LS, letterpress copy, James McHenry Pa-
pers, Library of Congress), enclosing "List of Surgeons and
Mates" (copy, Hamilton Papers, Library of Congress).

To James McHenry, August 30, 1799 (Df, in the handwriting of I
Thomas Y. How, Hamilton Papers, Library of Congress).

From Aaron Ogden, August 30, 1799 (ALS, Hamilton Papers, Li- VII
brary of Congress).

From James Read, August 30, 1799 (ALS, Hamilton Papers, Li- I
brary of Congress), enclosing "Officers of the 6th. Regiment of VII
Infantry," August 30, 1799 (ADS, Hamilton Papers, Library of
Congress).

To Ebenezer Stevens, August 30, 1799 (LS, in the handwriting of VII
Thomas Y. How, New-York Historical Society, New York
City; Df, in the handwriting of Thomas Y. How, Hamilton
Papers, Library of Congress).

To James Triplett, August 30, 1799 (Df, in the handwriting of H IV
and Thomas Y. How, Hamilton Papers, Library of Congress).

From Daniel Jackson, August 31, 1799 (ALS, Hamilton Papers, VII
Library of Congress).

From James McHenry, August 31, 1799 (LS, Hamilton Papers, I
Library of Congress; LS, letterpress copy, James McHenry Papers, Library of Congress).

From James McHenry, August 31, 1799 (Df, partially in Mc- IX
Henry's handwriting, James McHenry Papers, Library of Congress), enclosing Arthur St. Clair to the chiefs of the different
nations of Indians on the Wabash and Mississippi rivers, August 3, 1799 (copy, Hamilton Papers, Library of Congress); the
Kaskaskia, Mississippi, and Wabash Indians to John F. Hamtramck, June 19, 1799 (copy, Hamilton Papers, Library of
Congress).

To James McHenry, August 31, 1799 (Df, in the handwriting of   IV
Thomas Y. How, Hamilton Papers, Library of Congress).

From Aaron Ogden, August 31, 1799 (ALS, Hamilton Papers, Li-   VII
brary of Congress).

SEPTEMBER, 1799

From George Thatcher, September 1, 1799 (ALS, Hamilton Pa-   I
pers, Library of Congress).

To Daniel Jackson, September 2, 1799 (Df, in the handwriting of   III
Thomas Y. How, Hamilton Papers, Library of Congress).

To William Littlefield, September 2, 1799 (Df, in the handwriting III
of Thomas Y. How, Hamilton Papers, Library of Congress).

To James McHenry, September 2, 1799 (ADf, Hamilton Papers,   IV
Library of Congress).

To Aaron Ogden, September 2, 1799 (L[S], Lloyd W. Smith   VII
Collection, Morristown National Historical Park, Morristown,
New Jersey; Df, in the handwriting of Thomas Y. How,
Hamilton Papers, Library of Congress).

From Elijah Paine, September 2, 1799 (ALS, Hamilton Papers,   VII
Library of Congress).

From Yelverton Peyton, September 2, 1799 (ALS, Hamilton Pa-   III
pers, Library of Congress).

To Ebenezer Stevens, September 2, 1799 (LS, New-York His-   VII
torical Society, New York City; Df, in the handwriting of
Thomas Y. How, Hamilton Papers, Library of Congress).

To Lewis Tousard, September 2, 1799 (ADf, Hamilton Papers,   VI
Library of Congress).   VII

From John Whistler, September 2, 1799 (ALS, Hamilton Papers,   VII
Library of Congress).

From John Adlum, September 3, 1799 (ALS, Hamilton Papers,   III
Library of Congress).

From Augustus de Grasse, September 3, 1799 (ALS, Hamilton   II
Papers, Library of Congress).

From James McHenry, September 3, 1799 (LS, Hamilton Papers,   VII
Library of Congress), enclosing Francis Mentges to McHenry,
August 28, 1799 (copy, Hamilton Papers, Library of Congress);
"Estimate of the Expences both as to Materials and Workman-
ship in repairing the public Buildings at Carlisle, August 24,
1799" (copy, Hamilton Papers, Library of Congress).

Henry to Ebenezer Stevens, September 6, 1799 (LS, letterpress copy, Hamilton Papers, Library of Congress).

To James McHenry, September 6, 1799 (Df, in the handwriting of Thomas Y. How and H, Hamilton Papers, Library of Congress).   I VII

To James McHenry, September 6, 1799 (Df, in the handwriting of Thomas Y. How, Hamilton Papers, Library of Congress).   I

From Thomas Parker, September 6, 1799 (ALS, Hamilton Papers, Library of Congress).   VI

To Thomas Parker, September 6, 1799 (Df, in the handwriting of Thomas Y. How, Hamilton Papers, Library of Congress).   I

From Alexander Richards, September 6, 1799 (ALS, Hamilton Papers, Library of Congress).   VII

To Charles Smith, September 6, 1799 (Df, in the handwriting of Thomas Y. How, Hamilton Papers, Library of Congress).   III

To William S. Smith, September 6, 1799 (Df, in the handwriting of Thomas Y. How, Hamilton Papers, Library of Congress).   VII

To Ebenezer Stevens, September 6, 1799 (Df, in the handwriting of Thomas Y. How, Hamilton Papers, Library of Congress; copy, New-York Historical Society, New York City).   VII

From Timothy Taylor, September 6, 1799 (ALS, Hamilton Papers, Library of Congress).   III IV V VII

To Lewis Tousard, September 6, 1799 (ADf, Hamilton Papers, Library of Congress).   VII

From John Adlum, September 7, 1799 (ALS, Hamilton Papers, Library of Congress), enclosing Marks Biddle to James McHenry, September 5, 1799 (ALS, Hamilton Papers, Library of Congress); proceedings of court-martial of David Gill, James Murphy, and Henry Landais, September 2, 1799 (DS, signed by Adlum and Biddle, Hamilton Papers, Library of Congress); proceedings of court-martial of George Tyson, September 2, 1799 (DS, signed by Adlum and Biddle, Hamilton Papers, Library of Congress); proceedings of court-martial of John Lewis, September 2, 1799 (DS, signed by Adlum and Biddle, Hamilton Papers, Library of Congress).   III IV

From Eli B. Clemson, September 7, 1799 (ALS, Hamilton Papers, Library of Congress).   III

From James McHenry, September 7, 1799 (LS, letterpress copy, Hamilton Papers, Library of Congress).   IX

From James McHenry, September 7, 1799 (LS, Hamilton Papers,   VII
Library of Congress; LS, letterpress copy, James McHenry Pa-
pers, Library of Congress), enclosing Timothy Darling to Mc-
Henry, August 31, 1799 (copy, Hamilton Papers, Library of
Congress).

To James McHenry, September 7, 1799 (Df, in the handwriting   VI
of Thomas Y. How, Hamilton Papers, Library of Congress).   VII

From Thomas Porter, September 7, 1799 (ALS, Hamilton Papers,   III
Library of Congress). H wrote a draft of his reply on the back
of this letter. *Letter not found.*

From James Wilkinson, September 7, 1799 (ALS, Hamilton Pa-   VI
pers, Library of Congress).

From Daniel Bradley, September 8, 1799 (ALS, Hamilton Papers,   III
Library of Congress).   VII

From Aaron Ogden, September 8, 1799 (ALS, Hamilton Papers,   VII
Library of Congress).

From James McHenry, September 9, 1799 (LS, Hamilton Papers,   VII
Library of Congress; LS, letterpress copy, James McHenry Papers, Library of Congress), enclosing McHenry to John
Wilkins, Jr., September 9, 1799 (LS, letterpress copy, Hamilton
Papers, Library of Congress); McHenry to John Harris, September 9, 1799 (LS, letterpress copy, Hamilton Papers, Library
of Congress).

To James McHenry, September 9, 1799 (Df, in the handwriting   IX
of Thomas Y. How, Hamilton Papers, Library of Congress).

To Aaron Ogden, September 9, 1799 (Df, in the handwriting of   VII
Thomas Y. How, Hamilton Papers, Library of Congress).

From William S. Smith, September 9, 1799 (ALS, Hamilton Pa-   III
pers, Library of Congress).

To John Adlum, September 10, 1799 (ALS, Hamilton Papers, Li-   VIII
brary of Congress; Df, in the handwriting of Ethan Brown,
Hamilton Papers, Library of Congress).

From Philemon Blake, September 10, 1799 (ALS, Hamilton Pa-   III
pers, Library of Congress). Refers to his letter to H of June 19,
1799. *Letter not found.*

From Eli B. Clemson, September 10, 1799 (ALS, Hamilton Papers,   III
Library of Congress).

To Walter L. Cochran, September 10, 1799 (Df, in the handwrit- VIII
ing of William LeConte, Hamilton Papers, Library of Congress).

To Timothy Darling, September 10, 1799 (Df, in the handwriting   VII
of Thomas Y. How, Hamilton Papers, Library of Congress).

To Rufus Graves, September 10, 1799 (Df, in the handwriting of   VII
Thomas Y. How, Hamilton Papers, Library of Congress).

From Samuel Hodgdon, September 10, 1799 (ALS, Hamilton Pa-   VII
pers, Library of Congress; LC, RG 94, Post-Revolutionary War
Records, Letters of Samuel Hodgdon, National Archives).

From James McHenry, September 10, 1799 (LS, Hamilton Papers,   III
Library of Congress; LS, letterpress copy, James McHenry Papers, Library of Congress).

From James McHenry, September 10, 1799 (LS, Hamilton Papers,   VII
Library of Congress; LS, letterpress copy, James McHenry Pa-
pers, Library of Congress), enclosing McHenry to Tench
Francis, September 10, 1799 (copy, Hamilton Papers, Library of
Congress).

To James McHenry, September 10, 1799 (Df, in the handwriting   VIII
of Ethan Brown, Hamilton Papers, Library of Congress).

To Lewis Tousard, September 10, 1799 (Df, in the handwriting   VIII
of Ethan Brown, Hamilton Papers, Library of Congress).

From Benjamin Brookes, September 11, 1799 (ALS, Hamilton   III
Papers, Library of Congress).

From Josias Carvel Hall, September 11, 1799 (ALS, Hamilton Pa-   IV
pers, Library of Congress).

From James McHenry, September 11, 1799 (LS, Hamilton Papers,   VII
Library of Congress; LS, letterpress copy, James McHenry Pa-
pers, Library of Congress), enclosing a contract with James
O'Hara, August 1, 1799 (copy, Hamilton Papers, Library of
Congress).

From Nehemiah Freeman, September 12, 1799 (ALS, Hamilton   III
Papers, Library of Congress).

From Daniel Jackson, September 12, 1799 (ALS, Hamilton Papers,   IV
Library of Congress), enclosing "Battalion Orders," June 16,
1799 (copy, in Jackson's handwriting, Hamilton Papers, Library
of Congress); dismissal certificate of Levi Gates, September 2,
1799 (copy, in Jackson's handwriting, Hamilton Papers, Library
of Congress), and discharge, September 10, 1799 (AD, Hamilton Papers, Library of Congress); dismissal certificate of Edward McGowen, September 2, 1799 (copy, in Jackson's handwriting, Hamilton Papers, Library of Congress), and discharge,
September 10, 1799 (AD, Hamilton Papers, Library of Congress).

From James Miller, September 12, 1799 (ALS, Hamilton Papers,   VII
Library of Congress).

From James Read, September 12, 1799 (ALS, Hamilton Papers,   V
Library of Congress), enclosing "Recruiting Arrangements for
the 6th Regt. of Infantry," September 7, 1799 (copy, Hamilton
Papers, Library of Congress); "Recruiting Orders," September 7, 1799 (copy, in Read's handwriting, Hamilton Papers, Library of Congress); "Account of the Clothing," September 7,
1799 (D, Hamilton Papers, Library of Congress).

To John Wilkins, Jr., September 12, 1799 (Df, in the handwriting   VII
of Ethan Brown, Hamilton Papers, Library of Congress).

To William C. Bentley, September 13, 1799 (Df, in the hand-   VII
writing of Thomas Y. How, Hamilton Papers, Library of Congress).

To Daniel Bradley, September 13, 1799 (Df, in the handwriting of   III
Ethan Brown, Hamilton Papers, Library of Congress).

To Eli B. Clemson, September 13, 1799 (Df, in the handwriting of   III
Thomas Y. How, Hamilton Papers, Library of Congress).

To Walter L. Cochran, September 13, 1799 (Df, in the handwrit-   III
ing of Ethan Brown, Hamilton Papers, Library of Congress).

To Dwight Foster, September 13, 1799 (Df, in the handwriting   III
of Thomas Y. How, Hamilton Papers, Library of Congress).

From John F. Hamtramck, September 13, 1799 (ALS, Hamilton   III
Papers, Library of Congress).   IX

To Samuel Hodgdon, September 13, 1799 (Df, in the hand-   VII
writing of Ethan Brown, Hamilton Papers, Library of Congress).

To James McHenry, September 13, 1799 (Df, in the handwriting   VII
of Thomas Y. How, Hamilton Papers, Library of Congress).

To James Miller, September 13, 1799 (Df, in the handwriting of   VII
Thomas Y. How and H, Hamilton Papers, Library of Congress).

From John Neilson, September 13, 1799 (ALS, Hamilton Papers,   III
Library of Congress).

From James Watson, September 13, 1799 (ALS, Hamilton Papers,   I
Library of Congress).

To Thomas Butler, September 14, 1799 (Df, in the handwriting   VII
of Thomas Y. How, Hamilton Papers, Library of Congress).

From Rufus Graves, September 14, 1799 (ALS, Hamilton Papers,   V
Library of Congress).

To Josias Carvel Hall, September 14, 1799 (Df, in the handwriting   IV
of Thomas Y. How, Hamilton Papers, Library of Congress).

To John F. Hamtramck, September 14, 1799 (Df, in the hand-   VII
writing of Thomas Y. How, Hamilton Papers, Library of Congress).

From Andrew McClary, September 14, 1799 (ALS, Hamilton Pa-   III
pers, Library of Congress)

From James McHenry, September 14, 1799 (LS, letterpress copy,   IX
James McHenry Papers, Library of Congress).

From James McHenry, September 14, 1799 (LS, Hamilton Pa-   III
pers, Library of Congress; LS, letterpress copy, James Mc-
Henry Papers, Library of Congress).

From James McHenry, September 14, 1799 (LS, Hamilton Papers,   III
Library of Congress; LS, letterpress copy, James McHenry Papers, Library of Congress).

From James McHenry, September 14, 1799 (LS, Hamilton Papers,   III
Library of Congress; LS, letterpress copy, James McHenry Pa-
pers, Library of Congress), enclosing John Bishop to Mc-
Henry, September 9, 1799 (ALS, Hamilton Papers, Library of
Congress); McHenry to Bishop, September 14, 1799 (LS, letter-
press copy, Hamilton Papers, Library of Congress).

To James McHenry, September 14, 1799 (Df, in the handwriting   VII
of Thomas Y. How, Hamilton Papers, Library of Congress).

To John Neilson, September 14, 1799 (Df, in the handwriting of   III
Ethan Brown, Hamilton Papers, Library of Congress).

To Thomas Parker, September 14, 1799 (Df, in the handwriting   I
of Ethan Brown, Hamilton Papers, Library of Congress).   VI

From Josias Carvel Hall, September 15, 1799 (ALS, Hamilton Pa-   IV
pers, Library of Congress).

From Alexander Thompson, September 15, 1799 (ALS, Hamilton   VI
Papers, Library of Congress).

To John Bishop, September 16, 1799 (Df, in the handwriting of   VIII
Thomas Y. How, Hamilton Papers, Library of Congress).

To Daniel Bradley, September 16, 1799 (Df, in the handwriting of   IV
Ethan Brown, Hamilton Papers, Library of Congress).

From Walter L. Cochran, September 16, 1799 (ALS, Hamilton   VIII
Papers, Library of Congress).

To Samuel Eddins, September 16, 1799 (Df, in the handwriting of   VIII
Thomas Y. How, Hamilton Papers, Library of Congress).

From Samuel Hodgdon, September 16, 1799 (ALS, Hamilton Pa-   VII
pers, Library of Congress; LC, dated September 17, 1799,
RG 94, Post-Revolutionary War Records, Letters of Samuel
Hodgdon, National Archives; LC, dated September 17, 1799,
RG 92, Letter Book of Samuel Hodgdon, August 27, 1799–
October 22, 1800, National Archives), enclosing a return of
clothing (DS, Hamilton Papers, Library of Congress).

From William Hosack, September 16, 1799 (ALS, Hamilton Pa-   III
pers, Library of Congress).

To George Ingersoll, September 16, 1799 (LS, in the handwriting   VII
of Ethan Brown and H, New Hampshire Historical Society,
Concord; Df, in the handwriting of Ethan Brown, Hamilton
Papers, Library of Congress).

To James McHenry, September 16, 1799 (Df, in the handwriting   VI
of Thomas Y. How, Hamilton Papers, Library of Congress).

To Thomas Lloyd Moore, September 16, 1799 (LS, in the hand-   III
writing of Ethan Brown, Hamilton Papers, Library of Congress; copy, in the handwriting of Ethan Brown, Hamilton Papers, Library of Congress).

To William S. Smith, September 16, 1799 (Df, in the handwriting   III
of Thomas Y. How, Hamilton Papers, Library of Congress).   VII

From John Adlum, September 17, 1799 (ALS, Hamilton Papers,   III
Library of Congress).

From John Heth, September 17, 1799 (ALS, Hamilton Papers,   III
Library of Congress).

From Richard Hunewell, September 17, 1799 (ALS, Hamilton Pa-   I
pers, Library of Congress).   VII

From James McHenry, September 17, 1799 (LS, Hamilton Papers,   VII
Library of Congress; LS, letterpress copy, James McHenry Papers, Library of Congress).

From James McHenry, September 17, 1799 (LS, letterpress copy,   VII
James McHenry Papers, Library of Congress).

From Thomas Lloyd Moore, September 17, 1799 (ALS, Hamilton   III
Papers, Library of Congress).

From Campbell Smith, September 17, 1799 (ALS, Hamilton Pa-   IV
pers, Library of Congress).

To William C. Bentley, September 18, 1799 (Df, in the hand-   VI
writing of Thomas Y. How, Hamilton Papers, Library of Congress).

To John G. Coffin, September 18, 1799 (Df, in the handwriting of VII
Thomas Y. How, Hamilton Papers, Library of Congress). Ac-

knowledges Coffin's letter of September 17, 1799. *Letter not found.*

From William Colfax, September 18, 1799 (ALS, Hamilton Papers, Library of Congress).   VII

To Frederick Frye, September 18, 1799 (Df, in the handwriting   III
of Thomas Y. How, Hamilton Papers, Library of Congress).

To Augustus de Grasse, September 18, 1799 (Df, in the hand-   II
writing of Thomas Y. How, Hamilton Papers, Library of Congress).

From Josias Carvel Hall, September 18, 1799 (ALS, Hamilton Pa-   III
pers, Library of Congress).

To Samuel Hodgdon, September 18, 1799 (Df, in the handwriting   VII
of Thomas Y. How, Hamilton Papers, Library of Congress).

From James McHenry, September 18, 1799 (LS, Hamilton Papers,   III
Library of Congress; LS, letterpress copy, James McHenry Papers, Library of Congress).

To James McHenry, September 18, 1799 (Df, in the handwriting   III
of Thomas Y. How, Hamilton Papers, Library of Congress).   VII

To James McHenry, September 18, 1799 (Df, in the handwriting   II
of Thomas Y. How, Hamilton Papers, Library of Congress).

To James McHenry, September 18, 1799 (ADf, Hamilton Papers,   VII
Library of Congress).

To Thomas Lloyd Moore, September 18, 1799 (Df, in the hand-   III
writing of Thomas Y. How and H, Hamilton Papers, Library of Congress).

To Aaron Ogden, September 18, 1799 (Df, in the handwriting of   VII
Thomas Y. How, Hamilton Papers, Library of Congress).

To Aaron Ogden, September 18, 1799 (LS, Lloyd W. Smith Col-   VII
lection, Morristown National Historical Park, Morristown, New Jersey).

From Thomas Parker, September 18, 1799 (ALS, Hamilton Pa-   VII
pers, Library of Congress), enclosing "Account of Cloathing received . . . by the Paymaster of the 8th Regiment of Infantry . . ." (DS, Hamilton Papers, Library of Congress).

To William Simmons, September 18, 1799 (Df, in the handwrit-   III
ing of Thomas Y. How, Hamilton Papers, Library of Congress).

To Ebenezer Stevens, September 18, 1799 (LS, in the handwriting   VII
of Ethan Brown and H, New-York Historical Society, New York City).

To Timothy Taylor, September 18, 1799 (Df, in the handwriting III
of Thomas Y. How, Hamilton Papers, Library of Congress).

To Alexander Thompson, September 18, 1799 (Df, in the hand- III
writing of Thomas Y. How and H, Hamilton Papers, Library
of Congress).

To James Wilkinson, September 18, 1799 (Df, in the handwriting VII
of Thomas Y. How, Hamilton Papers, Library of Congress).

To John A. Winans, September 18, 1799 (Df, in the handwriting II
of Thomas Y. How, Hamilton Papers, Library of Congress).
Acknowledges Winans's letter of September 16, 1799. *Letter
not found.*

To Josias Carvel Hall, September 19, 1799 (Df, in the handwriting III
of Thomas Y. How and H, Hamilton Papers, Library of Con- VIII
gress).

To Samuel Hodgdon, September 19, 1799 (Df, in the handwriting VII
of Thomas Y. How, Hamilton Papers, Library of Congress).

To James McHenry, September 19, 1799 (Df, in the handwriting VIII
of Thomas Y. How, Hamilton Papers, Library of Congress).

To James McHenry, September 19, 1799 (Df, in the handwriting VII
of Ethan Brown, Hamilton Papers, Library of Congress).

To James McHenry, September 19, 1799 (Df, in the handwriting II
of Thomas Y. How, Hamilton Papers, Library of Congress).

To Staats Morris, September 19, 1799 (Df, in the handwriting of VIII
Thomas Y. How, Hamilton Papers, Library of Congress).

From Aaron Ogden, September 19, 1799 (ALS, Hamilton Papers, VII
Library of Congress; copy, in Ogden's handwriting, MS Division, New York Public Library).

From Thomas Parker, September 19, 1799 (ALS, Hamilton Pa- VII
pers, Library of Congress).

To James Read, September 19, 1799 (Df, in the handwriting of II
Thomas Y. How, Hamilton Papers, Library of Congress).

From Ebenezer Stevens, September 19, 1799 (LS, Hamilton VII
Papers, Library of Congress; Df, New-York Historical Society, New York City), enclosing "An estimate of Military
Stores . . ." (copy, Hamilton Papers, Library of Congress;
copy, New-York Historical Society, New York City).

To Timothy Taylor, September 19, 1799 (Df, in the handwriting VI
of Thomas Y. How, Hamilton Papers, Library of Congress). VII

To Philemon Blake, September 20, 1799 (Df, in the handwriting III
of Thomas Y. How, Hamilton Papers, Library of Congress).

To John H. Buell, September 20, 1799 (Df, in the handwriting   III
of Ethan Brown, Hamilton Papers, Library of Congress).

To Jonathan Cass, September 20, 1799 (Df, in the handwriting of   III
Ethan Brown, Hamilton Papers, Library of Congress).

"Circular to the Officers of the First Regiment of Infantry," Sep-   V
tember 20, 1799 (Df, in the handwriting of Ethan Brown,
Hamilton Papers, Library of Congress).

"Circular to the Officers of the Second Regiment of Infantry,"   V
September 20, 1799 (Df, in the handwriting of Ethan Brown,
Hamilton Papers, Library of Congress).

To Eli B. Clemson, September 20, 1799 (Df, in the handwriting   III
of Thomas Y. How, Hamilton Papers, Library of Congress).

From Samuel Eddins, September 20, 1799 (LS, Hamilton Papers,   III
Library of Congress).

To John Elliott, September 20, 1799 (Df, in the handwriting of   VII
Ethan Brown, Hamilton Papers, Library of Congress).

From Mahlon Ford, September 20, 1799 (ALS, Hamilton Papers,   III
Library of Congress).

To John Heth, September 20, 1799 (Df, in the handwriting of   III
Thomas Y. How, Hamilton Papers, Library of Congress).

From Samuel Hodgdon, September 20, 1799 (ALS, Hamilton Pa-   VII
pers, Library of Congress; LC, RG 94, Post-Revolutionary War
Records, Letters of Samuel Hodgdon, National Archives).

To Andrew McClary, September 20, 1799 (Df, in the handwriting   III
of Thomas Y. How, Hamilton Papers, Library of Congress).

From James McHenry, September 20, 1799 (LS, Hamilton Papers,   VII
Library of Congress; LS, letterpress copy, James McHenry Papers, Library of Congress).

From James McHenry, September 20, 1799 (LS, Hamilton Papers,   VII
Library of Congress; LS, letterpress copy, James McHenry
Papers, Library of Congress).

To James McHenry, September 20, 1799 (Df, in the handwriting   III
of Ethan Brown, Hamilton Papers, Library of Congress).

From Thomas Lloyd Moore, September 20, 1799 (ALS, Hamilton   III
Papers, Library of Congress).

From Aaron Ogden, September 20, 1799 (ALS, Hamilton Papers,   VII
Library of Congress).

To Elijah Paine, September 20, 1799 (Df, in the handwriting of   VII
Ethan Brown, Hamilton Papers, Library of Congress).

To Campbell Smith, September 20, 1799 (Df, in the handwriting   IV
of Thomas Y. How, Hamilton Papers, Library of Congress).

To Ebenezer Stevens, September 20, 1799 (LS, in the handwriting   VII
of Thomas Y. How, New-York Historical Society, New York
City; ADf, Hamilton Papers, Library of Congress).

From John Adlum, September 21, 1799 (ALS, Hamilton Papers,   VIII
Library of Congress).

To John Adlum, September 21, 1799 (LS, The Andre deCoppet   III
Collection, Princeton University Library; Df, in the handwriting of Thomas Y. How, Hamilton Papers, Library of Congress).

To Jonathan Cass and John H. Buell, September 21, 1799 (ADf,   V
Hamilton Papers, Library of Congress).

From John G. Coffin, September 21, 1799 (ALS, Hamilton Papers,   III
Library of Congress).

To Abraham Ellery, September 21, 1799 (Df, in the handwriting   V
of Thomas Y. How, Hamilton Papers, Library of Congress).

From Rufus Graves, September 21, 1799 (ALS, Hamilton Papers,   V
Library of Congress).

From William Leverett, September 21, 1799 (ALS, Hamilton Pa-   II
pers, Library of Congress).

From James McHenry, September 21, 1799 (LS, Hamilton Pa-   III
pers, Library of Congress; LS, letterpress copy, James McHenry
Papers, Library of Congress).

To James McHenry, September 21, 1799 (ADfS, Hamilton Pa-   III
pers, Library of Congress).

To James Miller, September 21, 1799 (ADf, Hamilton Papers,   VII
Library of Congress).

From Aaron Ogden, September 21, 1799 (ALS, Hamilton Papers,   VII
Library of Congress).

To Aaron Ogden, September 21, 1799 (Df, in the handwriting of   III
Thomas Y. How, Hamilton Papers, Library of Congress).

From William Simmons, September 21, 1799 (ALS, Hamilton Pa-   VII
pers, Library of Congress; LC, RG 217, Records of the General
Accounting Office, Letter Books, Accountant's Office, Vol. F,
May 16, 1799–February 27, 1800, National Archives).

From William S. Smith, September 21, 1799 (ALS, Hamilton Pa-   VI
pers, Library of Congress), enclosing Adrian Kissam to Smith,
September 19, 1799 (copy, Hamilton Papers, Library of Con-

gress); Smith to Kissam, September 20, 1799 (copy, Hamilton
Papers, Library of Congress). Acknowledges H's letter of September 20, 1799. *Letter not found.*

To Caleb Swan, September 21, 1799 (ADf, Hamilton Papers, Li-   V
brary of Congress).

From Timothy Taylor, September 22, 1799 (ALS, Hamilton Pa-   VI
pers, Library of Congress).

To Walter L. Cochran, September 23, 1799 (Df, in the handwrit-   VII
ing of Thomas Y. How, Hamilton Papers, Library of Congress).

From Nehemiah Freeman, September 23, 1799 (ALS, Hamilton   III
Papers, Library of Congress).

From Richard Harison, September 23, 1799 (ALS, Hamilton Pa-   I
pers, Library of Congress).

From Samuel Hodgdon, September 23, 1799 (ALS, Hamilton Pa-   VII
pers, Library of Congress; LC, RG 94, Post-Revolutionary War
Records, Letters of Samuel Hodgdon, National Archives).

From James McHenry, September 23, 1799 (LS, Hamilton Papers,   I
Library of Congress).

To James McHenry, [September] 23, 1799 (Df, in the handwrit-   VII
ing of Ethan Brown, Hamilton Papers, Library of Congress),
enclosing a "Statement of ammunition," September 23, 1799
(ADf, Hamilton Papers, Library of Congress).

To Aaron Ogden, September 23, 1799 (Df, in the handwriting   VII
of Thomas Y. How, Hamilton Papers, Library of Congress).

From Ebenezer Stevens, September 23, 1799 (LS, Hamilton Pa-   VII
pers, Library of Congress).

From Ebenezer Stevens, September 23, 1799 (LS, Hamilton Pa-   VII
pers, Library of Congress).

To Ebenezer Stevens, September 23, 1799 (ALS, New-York His-   VII
torical Society, New York City).

From Alexander Thompson, September 23, 1799 (ALS, Hamilton   III
Papers, Library of Congress), enclosing a memorandum from   VII
John J. U. Rivardi (copy, in Thompson's handwriting, Hamil-
ton Papers, Library of Congress).

To John F. Hamtramck, September 24, 1799 (Df, in the hand-   VIII
writing of Thomas Y. How, Hamilton Papers, Library of Congress).

From James McHenry, September 24, 1799 (ALS, Hamilton Pa-   IV
pers, Library of Congress; ALS, letterpress copy, James Mc-
Henry Papers, Library of Congress).

To James McHenry, September 24, 1799 (Df, in the handwriting   IV
of Thomas Y. How, Hamilton Papers, Library of Congress).

To James McHenry, September 24, 1799 (Df, in the handwriting   VII
of Thomas Y. How, Hamilton Papers, Library of Congress).

From Aaron Ogden, September 24, 1799 (ALS, Hamilton Papers,   VII
Library of Congress), enclosing a certificate by Thomson Stille
and Recompense Stanbery, September 24, 1799 (DS, in Ogden's
handwriting, Hamilton Papers, Library of Congress).

From Caleb Swan, September 24, 1799 (ALS, Hamilton Papers,   V
Library of Congress).

From William C. Bentley, September 25, 1799 (ALS, Hamilton   VII
Papers, Library of Congress).

To Nehemiah Freeman, September 25, 1799 (Df, in the hand-   VI
writing of Thomas Y. How, Hamilton Papers, Library of Congress).

To Richard Hunewell, September 25, 1799 (Df, in the hand-   VI
writing of Thomas Y. How, Hamilton Papers, Library of Congress).

To John McClallen, September 25, 1799 (Df, in the handwriting   III
of Thomas Y. How, Hamilton Papers, Library of Congress).

To James McHenry, September 25, 1799 (Df, in the handwriting   V
of Thomas Y. How, Hamilton Papers, Library of Congress).

To James McHenry, September 25, 1799 (Df, in the handwriting   VII
of Thomas Y. How, Hamilton Papers, Library of Congress),
enclosing "Rough Estimate of Expenses at Carlisle and Green-
brook" (AD, Hamilton Papers, Library of Congress).

To James McHenry, September 25, 1799 (Df, in the handwriting   I
of Thomas Y. How, Hamilton Papers, Library of Congress).

From Aaron Ogden, September 25, 1799 (ALS, Hamilton Papers,   VII
Library of Congress).

To Aaron Ogden, September 25, 1799 (ALS, The Sol Feinstone   I
Collection, American Philosophical Society, Philadelphia).

To Elijah Paine, September 25, 1799 (Df, in the handwriting of   V
Ethan Brown, Hamilton Papers, Library of Congress).

From Seymour Renick, September 25, 1799 (ALS, Hamilton Pa-   III
pers, Library of Congress).

From Charles Smith, September 25, 1799 (ALS, Hamilton Papers,   III
Library of Congress).

To Jeremiah Wadsworth, September 25, 1799 (ALS, Connecticut   I
Historical Society, Hartford).

To William C. Bentley, September 26, 1799 (Df, in the hand- VII
writing of Thomas Y. How, Hamilton Papers, Library of Con- VI
gress).

To Rufus Graves, September 26, 1799 (Df, in the handwriting VII
of Thomas Y. How, Hamilton Papers, Library of Congress).

To John F. Hamtramck, September 26, 1799 (Df, in the hand- VI
writing of Thomas Y. How, Hamilton Papers, Library of Congress).

To Samuel Hodgdon, September 26, 1799 (Df, in the handwriting VII
of Thomas Y. How, Hamilton Papers, Library of Congress).

From Richard Hunewell, September 26, 1799 (ALS, Hamilton III
Papers, Library of Congress).

From James McHenry, September 26, 1799 (LS, Hamilton Papers, III
Library of Congress; LS, letterpress copy, James McHenry Pa- VII
pers, Library of Congress), enclosing Daniel Marrow to John
Adams, August 29, 1799 (ALS, Hamilton Papers, Library of
Congress).

To James McHenry, September 26, 1799 (Df, in the handwriting VII
of Thomas Y. How and Ethan Brown, Hamilton Papers, Library of Congress).

To Thomas Lloyd Moore, September 26, 1799 (Df, in the hand- III
writing of Thomas Y. How, Hamilton Papers, Library of
Congress).

From Thomas Parker, September 26, 1799 (ALS, Hamilton III
Papers, Library of Congress), enclosing "List of Company VII
Officers belonging to the 8th Regt." (DS, in Parker's hand-
writing and signed by Parker, William Campbell, and Laurence
Butler, Hamilton Papers, Library of Congress).

To Thomas L. Parker, September 26, 1799 (Df, in the handwrit- III
ing of Thomas Y. How, Hamilton Papers, Library of Con- VII
gress).

From William S. Smith, September 26, 1799 (ALS, Hamilton Pa- III
pers, Library of Congress).

To William S. Smith, September 26, 1799 (Df, in the handwriting VII
of Thomas Y. How, Hamilton Papers, Library of Congress).

To Ebenezer Stevens, September 26, 1799 (LS, New-York His- VII
torical Society, New York City; Df, in the handwriting of
Thomas Y. How, Hamilton Papers, Library of Congress).

From William C. Bentley, September 27, 1799 (ALS, Hamilton VII
Papers, Library of Congress).

From William K. Blue, September 27, 1799 (ALS, Hamilton Pa-   **II**
pers, Library of Congress), enclosing John J. Maund to Blue,   **VII**
September 15, 1799 (ALS, Hamilton Papers, Library of Congress).

From Daniel Bradley, September 27, 1799 (ALS, Hamilton Pa-   **VII**
pers, Library of Congress).

From Rufus Graves, September 27, 1799 (ALS, Hamilton Papers,   **VII**
Library of Congress).

To Samuel Hodgdon, September 27, 1799 (Df, in the handwriting   **VII**
of Ethan Brown and H, Hamilton Papers, Library of Congress).

To William Littlefield, September 27, 1799 (Df, in the handwrit-   **III**
ing of Thomas Y. How, Hamilton Papers, Library of Con-
gress).

From Staats Morris, September 27, 1799 (ALS, Hamilton Papers,   **VI**
Library of Congress), enclosing Mountjoy Bayley's receipt for
fifty French prisoners (ADS, Hamilton Papers, Library of
Congress).

To Staats Morris, September 27, 1799 (Df, in the handwriting of   **VI**
Thomas Y. How, Hamilton Papers, Library of Congress).

From Aaron Ogden, September 27, 1799 (ALS, Hamilton Pa-   **I**
pers, Library of Congress).

To Aaron Ogden, September 27, 1799 (LS, Lloyd W. Smith Col-   **VII**
lection, Morristown National Historical Park, Morristown,
New Jersey; Df, in the handwriting of Thomas Y. How,
Hamilton Papers, Library of Congress). Acknowledges Ogden's
letter of September 26, 1799. *Letter not found.*

From James Read, September 27, 1799 (ALS, Hamilton Papers,   **VII**
Library of Congress).

To Timothy Taylor, September 27, 1799 (Df, in the handwriting   **VI**
of Ethan Brown, Hamilton Papers, Library of Congress), en-   **VII**
closing "Extract of a return of the P. Mr. Genl." (Df, in the
handwriting of Ethan Brown, Hamilton Papers, Library of
Congress).

To William C. Bentley, September 28, 1799 (Df, in the handwrit-   **VII**
ing of Thomas Y. How, Hamilton Papers, Library of Con-
gress).

To Samuel Eddins, September 28, 1799 (Df, in the handwriting of   **III**
Thomas Y. How, Hamilton Papers, Library of Congress).

To Samuel Hodgdon, September 28, 1799 (Df, in the handwriting   **VII**
of Thomas Y. How, Hamilton Papers, Library of Congress).

To Samuel Hodgdon, September 28, 1799 (Df, in the handwriting VII
of Thomas Y. How, Hamilton Papers, Library of Congress).

To Daniel Jackson, September 28, 1799 (Df, in the handwriting III
of Thomas Y. How, Hamilton Papers, Library of Congress).

To William Leverett, September 28, 1799 (Df, in the handwriting II
of Thomas Y. How, Hamilton Papers, Library of Congress).

From James McHenry, September 28, 1799 (LS, Hamilton Papers, VII
Library of Congress), enclosing William Simmons to Mc-
Henry, September 28, 1799 (copy, Hamilton Papers, Library of
Congress).

To James McHenry, September 28, 1799 (Df, in the handwriting VII
of Thomas Y. How, Hamilton Papers, Library of Congress).

From James Miller, September 28, 1799 (ALS, Hamilton Papers, VII
Library of Congress).

From Thomas Lloyd Moore, September 28, 1799 (ALS, Hamilton III
Papers, Library of Congress). VI

To Aaron Ogden, September 28, 1799 (ALS, New-York His- VII
torical Society, New York City; Df, in the handwriting of
Ethan Brown, Hamilton Papers, Library of Congress).

To Thomas Parker, September 28, 1799 (Df, in the handwriting VII
of Thomas Y. How, Hamilton Papers, Library of Congress).

To Alexander Richards, September 28, 1799 (Df, in the hand- VII
writing of Ethan Brown, Hamilton Papers, Library of Congress).

From William S. Smith, September 28, 1799 (ALS, Hamilton I
Papers, Library of Congress).

From William S. Smith, September 28, 1799 (ALS, Hamilton Pa- VII
pers, Library of Congress).

To William S. Smith, September 28, 1799 (Df, in the hand- VII
writing of Thomas Y. How, Hamilton Papers, Library of Congress).

From Ebenezer Stevens, September 28, 1799 (LS, Hamilton Pa- VII
pers, Library of Congress), enclosing "Tools, Boards &c necessary for hutting a Regt." (D, Hamilton Papers, Library of Congress).

To Ebenezer Stevens, September 28, 1799 (LS, New-York His- VII
torical Society, New York City; Df, in the handwriting of
Ethan Brown, Hamilton Papers, Library of Congress).

To Caleb Swan, September 28, 1799 (Df, in the handwriting of VII
Thomas Y. How and H, Hamilton Papers, Library of Congress).

From Starling Archer, September 29, 1799 (ALS, Hamilton Papers, Library of Congress).   II

From James Read, September 29, 1799 (ALS, Hamilton Papers, Library of Congress).   V

From George Davis, September 30, 1799 (ALS, Hamilton Papers, Library of Congress).   II

To Samuel Eddins, September 30, 1799 (Df, in the handwriting of H and Thomas Y. How, Hamilton Papers, Library of Congress). Acknowledges Eddins's letter of September 23, 1799. *Letter not found.*   III

From Jacob Kingsbury, September 30, 1799 (ALS, Hamilton Papers, Library of Congress), enclosing permission from James Wilkinson for leave of absence, April 15, 1799 (DS, Hamilton Papers, Library of Congress).   III

From James McHenry, September 30, 1799 (LS, Hamilton Papers, Library of Congress; LS, letterpress copy, James McHenry Papers, Library of Congress).   VII

To Thomas Lloyd Moore, September [30, 1799] (Df, in the handwriting of Thomas Y. How and H, Hamilton Papers, Library of Congress).   III

From Aaron Ogden, September 30, 1799 (ALS, Hamilton Papers, Library of Congress).   VII

From Aaron Ogden, September 30, 1799 (ALS, Hamilton Papers, Library of Congress).   I

From William S. Smith, September 30, 1799 (ALS, Hamilton Papers, Library of Congress).   I

To William S. Smith, September 30, 1799 (Df, in the handwriting of Thomas Y. How, Hamilton Papers, Library of Congress).   VII

To Caleb Swan, September 30, 1799 (Df, in the handwriting of Thomas Y. How, Hamilton Papers, Library of Congress).   III

OCTOBER, 1799

From John Adlum, October 1, 1799 (ALS, Hamilton Papers, Library of Congress).   IV
                                                                        VI

To Daniel Bradley, October 1, 1799 (Df, in the handwriting of Thomas Y. How, Hamilton Papers, Library of Congress).   VII

From Eli B. Clemson, October 1, 1799 (ALS, Hamilton Papers, Library of Congress).   III

From Samuel Hodgdon, October 1, 1799 (ALS, Hamilton Papers,   VII
Library of Congress; LC, RG 94, Post-Revolutionary War
Records, Letters of Samuel Hodgdon, National Archives), enclosing Hodgdon to John Swan, August 29, 1799 (copy, Hamilton Papers, Library of Congress).

To Samuel Hodgdon, October 1, 1799 (Df, in the handwriting of   VII
Thomas Y. How, Hamilton Papers, Library of Congress).

To Daniel Jackson, October 1, 1799 (Df, in the handwriting of   VII
Thomas Y. How, Hamilton Papers, Library of Congress).   III

To James McHenry, October 1, 1799 (Df, in the handwriting of   VIII
Thomas Y. How, Hamilton Papers, Library of Congress).

To Charles Cotesworth Pinckney, October 1, 1799 (Df, in the   III
handwriting of Thomas Y. How, Hamilton Papers, Library of
Congress).

To James McHenry, October 2, 1799 (Df, in the handwriting of   III
Thomas Y. How, Hamilton Papers, Library of Congress).

To John J. U. Rivardi, October 1, 1799 (Df, in the handwriting   III
of Thomas Y. How, Hamilton Papers, Library of Congress).

To Caleb Swan, October 1, 1799 (Df, in the handwriting of   III
Thomas Y. How, Hamilton Papers, Library of Congress).   VII

To Caleb Swan, October 1, 1799 (Df, in the handwriting of   VII
Thomas Y. How, Hamilton Papers, Library of Congress).

To Alexander Thompson, October 1, 1799 (Df, in the handwrit-   VII
ing of Thomas Y. How, Hamilton Papers, Library of Congress).

To Nanning J. Visscher, October 1, 1799 (Df, in the handwriting   III
of Thomas Y. How, Hamilton Papers, Library of Congress).

To Henry Glen, October 2, 1799 (Df, in the handwriting of   VII
Thomas Y. How, Hamilton Papers, Library of Congress).

From Nathan Heald, October 2, 1799 (ALS, Hamilton Papers,   III
Library of Congress).

To James McHenry, October 2, 1799 (Df, in the handwriting of   VII
Thomas Y. How, Hamilton Papers, Library of Congress).

To James McHenry, October 2, 1799 (Df, in the handwriting of   III
Thomas Y. How, Hamilton Papers, Library of Congress).

To James Miller, October 2, 1799 (Df, in the handwriting of   VIII
Thomas Y. How, Hamilton Papers, Library of Congress).

From Thomas Parker, October 2, 1799 (ALS, Hamilton Papers,   VI
Library of Congress).

From William S. Smith, October 2, 1799 (ALS, Hamilton Papers,   III
Library of Congress), enclosing three accounts of James Smith,
Jr., paymaster of the Twelfth Regiment, October 1, 1799 (ADS,
Hamilton Papers, Library of Congress). Acknowledges H's
letter of September 27, 1799. *Letter not found.*

From Ebenezer Stevens, October 2, 1799 (ALS, Hamilton Papers,   VII
Library of Congress).

From Ebenezer Stevens, October 2, 1799 (AD, Hamilton Papers,   VII
Library of Congress).

From Caleb Swan, October 2, 1799 (ALS, Hamilton Papers, Li-   I
brary of Congress).

From Timothy Taylor, October 2, 1799 (ALS, Hamilton Papers,   III
Library of Congress), enclosing a return of "Arms & Accoutre-   VII
ments," September 25, 1799 (DS, Hamilton Papers, Library of
Congress); "A Return of Clothing," September 25, 1799 (DS,
Hamilton Papers, Library of Congress).

To Alexander Thompson, October 2, 1799 (Df, in the handwrit-   VII
ing of Thomas Y. How, Hamilton Papers, Library of Congress).

From Samuel Hodgdon, October 3, 1799 (ALS, Hamilton Papers,   VII
Library of Congress; LC, RG 94, Post-Revolutionary War
Records, Letters of Samuel Hodgdon, National Archives).

To Samuel Hodgdon, October 3, 1799 (Df, in the handwriting of   VII
Thomas Y. How, Hamilton Papers, Library of Congress).

To Richard Hunewell, October 3, 1799 (Df, in the handwriting   III
of Thomas Y. How, Hamilton Papers, Library of Congress).

From James McHenry, October 3, 1799 (LS, Hamilton Papers,   VII
Library of Congress; LS, letterpress copy, James McHenry Pa-
pers, Library of Congress), enclosing Thomas Billington to
Samuel Hodgdon, September 24, 1799 (copy, Hamilton Papers,
Library of Congress); McHenry to John Harris, October 3,
1799 (copy, Hamilton Papers, Library of Congress); McHenry
to John Wilkins, Jr., October 3, 1799 (copy, Hamilton Papers,
Library of Congress).

From James McHenry, October 3, 1799 (LS, Hamilton Papers,   VII
Library of Congress; LS, letterpress copy, James McHenry Papers, Library of Congress).

To James McHenry, October 3, 1799 (Df, in the handwriting of   III
Thomas Y. How, Hamilton Papers, Library of Congress).

From Thomas Lloyd Moore, October 3, 1799 (ALS, Hamilton   IV
Papers, Library of Congress).   VII

From Aaron Ogden, October 3, 1799 (ALS, Hamilton Papers, Library of Congress).   VII

To Ebenezer Stevens, October 3, 1799 (Df, in the handwriting of Ethan Brown, Hamilton Papers, Library of Congress).   VII

From Caleb Swan, October 3, 1799 (ALS, Hamilton Papers, Library of Congress).   I

To Caleb Swan, October 3, 1799 (Df, in the handwriting of Ethan Brown and H, Hamilton Papers, Library of Congress).   II

From Lewis Tousard, October 3, 1799 (ALS, Hamilton Papers, Library of Congress).   II

To Abraham Van Vechten, October 3, 1799 (Df, in the handwriting of Thomas Y. How, Hamilton Papers, Library of Congress). Acknowledges Van Vechten's letter of September 26, 1799. *Letter not found.*   I

From Daniel Bradley, October 4, 1799 (ALS, Hamilton Papers, Library of Congress).   III

From Joseph H. Dwight, October 4, 1799 (ALS, Hamilton Papers, Library of Congress).   III

"General Orders," October 4, 1799 (copy, Pierpont Morgan Library, New York City).   IV

"General Orders," October 4, 1799 (copy, Pierpont Morgan Library, New York City).   IV

To Rufus Graves and Richard Hunewell, October 4, 1799 (ADf, Hamilton Papers, Library of Congress).   VII

From Samuel Hodgdon, October 4, 1799 (ALS, Hamilton Papers, Library of Congress; LC, RG 94, Post-Revolutionary War Records, Letters of Samuel Hodgdon, National Archives).   VII

From Samuel Lane, October 4, 1799 (ALS, Hamilton Papers, Library of Congress).   III

From James McHenry, October 4, 1799 (LS, Hamilton Papers, Library of Congress; LS, letterpress copy, James McHenry Papers, Library of Congress), enclosing McHenry to James Wilkinson, March 22, 1797; January 31, August 2, 1798 (copies, Hamilton Papers, Library of Congress).   IX

To James McHenry, October 4, 1799 (Df, in the handwriting of Thomas Y. How, Hamilton Papers, Library of Congress).   III

To James McHenry, October 4, 1799 (Df, in the handwriting of Thomas Y. How, Hamilton Papers, Library of Congress).   III

To James McHenry, October 4, 1799 (Df, in the handwriting of Thomas Y. How and H, Hamilton Papers, Library of Congress).   VII

To James McHenry, October 4, 1799 (Df, in the handwriting of IX
Ethan Brown and H, Hamilton Papers, Library of Congress).

From James Miller, October 4, 1799 (ALS, Hamilton Papers, Li- III
brary of Congress).

To Aaron Ogden, October 4, 1799 (ADf, Hamilton Papers, Li- VIII
brary of Congress).

To William C. Rogers, October 4, 1799 (Df, in the handwriting III
of Ethan Brown and H, Hamilton Papers, Library of Congress).

To William S. Smith, October 4, 1799 (LS, The Sol Feinstone VII
Collection, American Philosophical Society, Philadelphia; Df, in
the handwriting of Ethan Brown and H, Hamilton Papers, Library of Congress).

To Ebenezer Stevens, October 4, 1799 (ALS, New-York His- VII
torical Society, New York City).

From Caleb Swan, October 4, 1799 (ALS, Hamilton Papers, Li- II
brary of Congress), enclosing Charles Cotesworth Pinckney to IX
Swan, September 26, 1799 (copy, in Swan's handwriting,
Hamilton Papers, Library of Congress).

From Caleb Swan, October 4, 1799 (LS, Hamilton Papers, Li- III
brary of Congress), enclosing Swan to Lemuel Gates, August 20, 1799 (copy, Hamilton Papers, Library of Congress).
On the verso H wrote the names of seven officers and where
they were stationed.

To Caleb Swan, October 4, 1799 (Df, in the handwriting of III
Ethan Brown, Hamilton Papers, Library of Congress).

From Timothy Taylor, October 4, 1799 (ALS, Hamilton Papers, III
Library of Congress).

From Timothy Taylor, October 4, 1799 (ALS, Hamilton Papers, II
Library of Congress).

From Rufus Graves, October 5, 1799 (ALS, Hamilton Papers, VI
Library of Congress).

From Josias Carvel Hall, October 5, 1799 (ALS, Hamilton Papers, I
Library of Congress). IV

From William Littlefield, October 5, 1799 (ALS, Hamilton Pa- III
pers, Library of Congress).

From James McHenry, October 5, 1799 (LS, Hamilton Papers, VII
Library of Congress; LS, letterpress copy, James McHenry Papers, Library of Congress).

To James McHenry, October 5, 1799 (Df, in the handwriting of VIII
Ethan Brown and H, Hamilton Papers, Library of Congress).

From Aaron Ogden, October 5, 1799 (ALS, Hamilton Papers,   IV
Library of Congress).

To Timothy Taylor, October [5, 1799] (ADf, Hamilton Papers,   VIII
Library of Congress).

From Lewis Tousard, October 5, 1799 (ALS, Hamilton Papers,   III
Library of Congress). Refers to H's letter of September 8,   VII
1799. *Letter not found.*

From William C. Bentley, October 6, 1799 (ALS, Hamilton Pa-   VI
pers, Library of Congress).

From Lawrence Butler, October 6, 1799 (ALS, Hamilton Papers,   I
Library of Congress).

To Walter L. Cochran, October 6, 1799 (Df, in the handwriting VIII
of Thomas Y. How, Hamilton Papers, Library of Congress).

To Daniel Jackson, October 6, 1799 (Df, in the handwriting of VIII
Thomas Y. How, Hamilton Papers, Library of Congress).

To Jonathan Jackson, October 6, 1799 (Df, in the handwriting   IX
of Thomas Y. How, Hamilton Papers, Library of Congress).

To James Miller, October 6, 1799 (LS, The Andre deCoppet Col- VIII
lection, Princeton University Library; ADf, Hamilton Papers,
Library of Congress).

To Thomas Lloyd Moore, October 6, 1799 (ADf, Hamilton Pa-   VIII
pers, Library of Congress).

From Thomas Parker, October 6, 1799 (ALS, Hamilton Papers,   I
Library of Congress).

To Charles Cotesworth Pinckney, October 6, 1799 (Df, in the   IX
handwriting of Ethan Brown, Hamilton Papers, Library of
Congress).

To James Richmond, October 6, 1799 (Df, in the handwriting of V
Thomas Y. How, Hamilton Papers, Library of Congress). Acknowledges Richmond's letter of September 25, 1799. *Letter
not found.*

From John Adlum, October 7, 1799 (ALS, Hamilton Papers, Li-   VII
brary of Congress).

From William C. Bentley, October 7, 1799 (ALS, Hamilton Pa-   VI
pers, Library of Congress).

From Frederick Frye, October 7, 1799 (ALS, Hamilton Papers,   III
Library of Congress).

From Francis Gibson, October 7, 1799 (ALS, Hamilton Papers,   III
Library of Congress), enclosing a certificate of Gibson's health

by George Dill, October 7, 1799 (ADS, Hamilton Papers, Library of Congress).

From Michael Gunkle, October 7, 1799 (LS, Hamilton Papers, Library of Congress).   VII

From James McHenry, October 7, 1799 (LS, Hamilton Papers, Library of Congress; LS, letterpress copy, James McHenry Papers, Library of Congress), enclosing Elias B. Dayton to McHenry, October 3, 1799 (extract, Hamilton Papers, Library of Congress).   VII

From Yelverton Peyton, October 7, 1799 (ALS, Hamilton Papers, Library of Congress).   III

From Peter Robinson, October 7, 1799 (ALS, Hamilton Papers, Library of Congress).   III

From William S. Smith, October 7, 1799 (ALS, Hamilton Papers, Library of Congress).   V

To Ebenezer Stevens, October 7, 1799 (ALS, New-York Historical Society, New York City).   VII

To Ebenezer Stevens, October 7, 1799 (LS, New-York Historical Society, New York City; copy, in the handwriting of Ethan Brown, Hamilton Papers, Library of Congress).   VII

From John Taylor, October 7, 1799 (ALS, Hamilton Papers, Library of Congress).   I

From Joseph Cross, October 8, 1799 (ALS, Hamilton Papers, Library of Congress).   III

From Samuel Eddins, October 8, 1799 (ALS, Hamilton Papers, Library of Congress).   III

To James Miller, October 8, 1799 (LS, Lloyd W. Smith Collection, Morristown National Historical Park, Morristown, New Jersey).   VII

To James Miller, October 8, 1799 (ADf, Hamilton Papers, Library of Congress).   VII

From Henry Muhlenberg, October 8, 1799 (ALS, Hamilton Papers, Library of Congress), enclosing a return of Maryland recruits, September 2, 1799 (DS, Hamilton Papers, Library of Congress).   III

From William S. Smith, October 8, 1799 (ALS, Hamilton Papers, Library of Congress).   VII

From William Campbell, October 9, 1799 (ALS, Hamilton Papers, Library of Congress).   II

From Edward Stevens, October 9, 1799 (ALS, Hamilton Papers,   I
Library of Congress).

From Edward Stevens, October 9, 1799 (ALS, Hamilton Papers,   I
Library of Congress).

From Lewis Tousard, October 9, 1799 (ALS, Hamilton Papers,   VII
Library of Congress).

From John A. Winans, October 9, 1799 (ALS, Hamilton Papers,   II
Library of Congress).

From John Brooks, October 10, 1799 (ALS, Hamilton Papers,   II
Library of Congress). Refers to H's letter of September 25,
1799. *Letter not found.*

From George Fleming, October 10, 1799 (ALS, Hamilton Papers,   VI
Library of Congress), enclosing a list of lieutenants in the First
Regiment of Artillerists and Engineers (AD, Hamilton Papers,
Library of Congress).

From Daniel Bradley, October 11, 1799 (ALS, Hamilton Papers,   V
Library of Congress).

To Jonathan Cass, October 11, 1799 (ADf, Hamilton Papers, Li-   V
brary of Congress).

From James Dill, October 11, 1799 (ALS, Hamilton Papers, Li-   III
brary of Congress).

From John F. Hamtramck, October 11, 1799 (LS, Hamilton   IV
Papers, Library of Congress).   VI

From Daniel Jackson, October 11, 1799 (LS, Hamilton Papers,   VIII
Library of Congress).

To John Adlum, October 12, 1799 (LS, Hamilton Papers, Library   VIII
of Congress; Df, in the handwriting of Thomas Y. How,
Hamilton Papers, Library of Congress).

To Nehemiah Freeman, October 12, 1799 (Df, in the handwriting   VIII
of Thomas Y. How, Hamilton Papers, Library of Congress).

From Josias Carvel Hall, October 12, 1799 (ALS, Hamilton Pa-   VI
pers, Library of Congress). Acknowledges H's letter of October 6, 1799. *Letter not found.*

To Samuel Hodgdon, October 12, 1799 (Df, in the handwriting   VII
of Thomas Y. How, Hamilton Papers, Library of Congress).

To Callender Irvine, October 12, 1799 (Df, in the handwriting of VIII
Thomas Y. How, Hamilton Papers, Library of Congress).

From James McHenry, October 12, 1799 (LS, Hamilton Papers,   III
Library of Congress; LS, letterpress copy, James McHenry Pa-

pers, Library of Congress), enclosing Aaron Ogden to Mc-
Henry, October 10, 1799 (ALS, Hamilton Papers, Library of
Congress).

To James McHenry, October 12, 1799 (Df, in the handwriting of   I
Thomas Y. How, Hamilton Papers, Library of Congress).

From James Miller, October 12, 1799 (LS, Hamilton Papers, Li-   VII
brary of Congress).

To James Miller, October 12, 1799 (Df, in the handwriting of   VII
Thomas Y. How, Hamilton Papers, Library of Congress).

To Thomas Parker, October 12, 1799 (Df, in the handwriting of   VI
Thomas Y. How, Hamilton Papers, Library of Congress).   VII

To Peter Shoemaker, October 12, 1799 (Df, in the handwriting   VIII
of Thomas Y. How and H, Hamilton Papers, Library of Congress).

From William S. Smith, October 12, 1799 (ALS, Hamilton Pa-   VIII
pers, Library of Congress).

To William S. Smith, October 12, 1799 (ADf, Hamilton Papers,   VII
Library of Congress).

To Aaron Ogden, October 13, 1799 (Df, in the handwriting of   VIII
Thomas Y. How, Hamilton Papers, Library of Congress).

From David Strong, October 13, 1799 (LS, Hamilton Papers, Li-   VII
brary of Congress), enclosing "Report of Provisions in Store at
Detroit the 30th of September 1799" (DS, Hamilton Papers, Library of Congress).

From Timothy Taylor, October 13, 1799 (ALS, Hamilton Papers,   V
Library of Congress).

From Mathew Arbuckle, October 14, 1799 (ALS, Hamilton Pa-   V
pers, Library of Congress; ALS [with minor differences],
Hamilton Papers, Library of Congress).

To Daniel Bradley, October 14, 1799 (Df, in the handwriting of   VI
Thomas Y. How and H, Hamilton Papers, Library of Con-   VII
gress).

To Nehemiah Freeman and Joseph Elliott, October 14, 1799   VIII
(ADf, Hamilton Papers, Library of Congress).

From Joseph Guimpé, October 14, 1799 (ALS, Hamilton Papers,   II
Library of Congress).

From Samuel Hodgdon, October 14, 1799 (ALS, Hamilton Pa-   VII
pers, Library of Congress; LC, RG 94, Post-Revolutionary War
Records, Letters of Samuel Hodgdon, National Archives), en-

closing "Invoice of Clothing," October 14, 1799 (DS, Hamilton Papers, Library of Congress).

To James McHenry, October 14, 1799 (ADf, Hamilton Papers, Library of Congress).   IV

To James McHenry, October 14, 1799 (ADf, Hamilton Papers, Library of Congress).   VI

To James McHenry, October 14, 1799 (ADf, Hamilton Papers, Library of Congress).   IV

From James Miller, October 14, 1799 (ALS, Hamilton Papers, Library of Congress), enclosing Miller to H, October 4, 1799 (copy, Hamilton Papers, Library of Congress).   III

To Thomas Parker, October 14, 1799 (ADf, Hamilton Papers, Library of Congress).   VII

From William S. Smith, October 14, 1799 (ALS, Hamilton Papers, Library of Congress).   VIII

To Caleb Swan, October 14, 1799 (Df, in the handwriting of Thomas Y. How and H, Hamilton Papers, Library of Congress).   VII

To Caleb Swan, October 14, 1799 (Df, in the handwriting of Thomas Y. How and H, Hamilton Papers, Library of Congress).   VII

To Josias Carvel Hall, October 15, 1799 (Df, in the handwriting of Thomas Y. How, Hamilton Papers, Library of Congress).   VIII

From Richard Hunewell, October 15, 1799 (LS, Hamilton Papers, Library of Congress). Acknowledges H's second letter of September 25, 1799. *Letter not found.*   I

From Richard Hunewell, October 15, 1799 (L, Hamilton Papers, Library of Congress)   VI

From Richard Hunewell, October 15, 1799 (LS, Hamilton Papers, Library of Congress), enclosing a statement on officers of Fifteenth Infantry Regiment (DS, Hamilton Papers, Library of Congress).   VI

From James McHenry, October 15, 1799 (LS, Hamilton Papers, Library of Congress; copy, The William L. Clements Library of the University of Michigan).   II

From James McHenry, October 15, 1799 (LS, Hamilton Papers, Library of Congress; LS, letterpress copy, James McHenry Papers, Library of Congress).   III

From Joseph Phillips, October 15, 1799 (ALS, Hamilton Papers, Library of Congress).   III

From Caleb Swan, October 15, 1799 (ALS, Hamilton Papers, Library of Congress), enclosing William C. Rogers to Swan, n.d. (ALS, Hamilton Papers, Library of Congress).   II

From George Washington, October 15, 1799 (LS, in the handwriting of Tobias Lear, Hamilton Papers, Library of Congress; Df, George Washington Papers, Library of Congress).   VII

From Benjamin Brookes, October 16, 1799 (ALS, Hamilton Papers, Library of Congress).   III

From James House, October 16, 1799 (ALS, Hamilton Papers, Library of Congress).   VII

From Richard Hunewell, October 16, 1799 (LS, Hamilton Papers, Library of Congress), enclosing "List of Company Officers as ranked by the Field Officers, of the 15th Regiment" (D, Hamilton Papers, Library of Congress); "List of Officers . . . in the 15th Regiment" (D, Hamilton Papers, Library of Congress).   VI

From Henry Lee, October 16, 1799 (ALS, Hamilton Papers, Library of Congress).   II

From William Wilson, October 16, 1799 (ALS, Hamilton Papers, Library of Congress).   II

From William C. Bentley, October 17, 1799 (ALS, Hamilton Papers, Library of Congress).   I

To Joseph Cross, October 17, 1799 (Df, in the handwriting of Thomas Y. How, Hamilton Papers, Library of Congress).   III

To John F. Hamtramck, October 17, 1799 (Df, in the handwriting of Thomas Y. How, Hamilton Papers, Library of Congress).   VIII

To Samuel Hodgdon, October 17, 1799 (Df, in the handwriting of Thomas Y. How, Hamilton Papers, Library of Congress).   VIII

To James House, October 17, 1799 (Df, in the handwriting of Thomas Y. How, Hamilton Papers, Library of Congress).   III

To Theodore Meminger, October 17, 1799 (Df, in the handwriting of Thomas Y. How, Hamilton Papers, Library of Congress).   III

To Ebenezer Stevens, October 17, 1799 (LS, in the handwriting of H and Thomas Y. How, New-York Historical Society, New York City; Df, in the handwriting of Thomas Y. How, Hamilton Papers, Library of Congress). Stevens's endorsement of this letter reads: "ansd." *Letter not found.*   VII

To Caleb Swan, October 17, 1799 (Df, in the handwriting of Thomas Y. How, Hamilton Papers, Library of Congress).   III

From Jonathan Cass, October 18, 1799 (ALS, Hamilton Papers,   V
Library of Congress).

From Nehemiah Freeman, October 18, 1799 (ALS, Hamilton Pa-   VIII
pers, Library of Congress).

From John F. Hamtramck, October 18, 1799 (ALS, Hamilton   VI
Papers, Library of Congress).

From Samuel Hodgdon, October 18, 1799 (ALS, Hamilton Pa-   VII
pers, Library of Congress; LC, RG 94, Post-Revolutionary War
Records, Letters of Samuel Hodgdon, National Archives).

From John W. Patterson, October 18, 1799 (ALS, Hamilton Pa-   III
pers, Library of Congress).

From Ebenezer Stevens, October 18, 1799 (ALS, Hamilton Pa-   VII
pers, Library of Congress).

From John H. Buell, October 19, 1799 (ALS, Hamilton Papers,   VIII
Library of Congress).

From Peter Shoemaker, October 19, 1799 (ALS, Hamilton Papers,   VII
Library of Congress).

To Caleb Swan, October 19, 1799 (ALS, Hamilton Papers, Li-   VI
brary of Congress).

From Timothy Taylor, October 19, 1799 (ALS, Hamilton Pa-   VIII
pers, Library of Congress).

From William C. Bentley, October 20, 1799 (ALS, Hamilton Pa-   VI
pers, Library of Congress), enclosing "Proposed Rank of the   VII
platoon Officers of the 7th United States Regiment" (AD,
Hamilton Papers, Library of Congress). Acknowledges H's letter of September 30, 1799. *Letter not found.*

From Daniel Bradley, October 20, 1799 (ALS, Hamilton Papers,   IV
Library of Congress).

From Jonathan Dayton, October 20, 1799 (ALS, Hamilton Pa-   VII
pers, Library of Congress), enclosing "Quarter Master's supplies for the 3 Regts. cantoned upon Green brook" (AD,
Hamilton Papers, Library of Congress).

From Josias Carvel Hall, October 20, 1799 (ALS, Hamilton Pa-   VI
pers, Library of Congress).

From Josias Carvel Hall, October 20, 1799 (ALS, Hamilton Pa-   VII
pers, Library of Congress).

To James House, October 20, 1799 (ADf, Hamilton Papers, Li-   III
brary of Congress).

To Theodore Meminger, October 20, 1799 (ADf, Hamilton Pa-   III
pers, Library of Congress).

To Henry Muhlenberg, October 20, 1799 (ADf, Hamilton Papers, Library of Congress). VIII

From John J. U. Rivardi, October 20, 1799 (ALS, Hamilton Papers, Library of Congress). IV

From William S. Smith, October 20, 1799 (ALS, Hamilton Papers, Library of Congress). I

From John H. Buell, October 21, 1799 (ALS, Hamilton Papers, Library of Congress). V

To James Miller, October 21, 1799 (ADf, Hamilton Papers, Library of Congress). VII

From Zebulon M. Pike, October 21, 1799 (ALS, Hamilton Papers, Library of Congress). VII

From Caleb Swan, October 21, 1799 (ALS, Hamilton Papers, Library of Congress), enclosing William C. Rogers to Swan, October 18, 1799 (ALS, Hamilton Papers, Library of Congress). III

To Lawrence Butler, October 22, 1799 (Df, in the handwriting of Ethan Brown, Hamilton Papers, Library of Congress). I

To Jonathan Cass, October 22, 1799 (Df, in the handwriting of Ethan Brown, Hamilton Papers, Library of Congress). VI

To George Ingersoll, October 22, 1799 (Df, in the handwriting of Ethan Brown, Hamilton Papers, Library of Congress). III

From James McHenry, October 22, 1799 (LS, Hamilton Papers, Library of Congress; LS, letterpress copy, James McHenry Papers, Library of Congress). VI

To James McHenry, October 22, 1799 (Df, in the handwriting of Ethan Brown, Hamilton Papers, Library of Congress). I

From James Miller, October 22, 1799 (ALS, Hamilton Papers, Library of Congress). VII

To James Miller, October 22, 1799 (Df, in the handwriting of Ethan Brown, Hamilton Papers, Library of Congress), enclosing "List of Quarter Master's Supplies for One Regt." (Df, in the handwriting of Ethan Brown, Hamilton Papers, Library of Congress). VII

To Henry Muhlenberg, October 22, 1799 (Df, in the handwriting of Ethan Brown, Hamilton Papers, Library of Congress). III

From Ebenezer Stevens, October 22, 1799 (LS, Hamilton Papers, Library of Congress), enclosing "Invoice of public stores . . . ," April 11, 1799, by Samuel Hodgdon (copy, Hamilton Papers, Library of Congress). VII

From Caleb Swan, October 22, 1799 (ALS, Hamilton Papers, Library of Congress). VII

To Benjamin Brookes, October 23, 1799 (Df, in the handwriting   III
of Thomas Y. How, Hamilton Papers, Library of Congress).

To James Dill, October 23, 1799 (Df, in the handwriting of   III
Thomas Y. How, Hamilton Papers, Library of Congress).

To James McHenry, October 23, 1799 (Df, in the handwriting   VI
of Ethan Brown, Hamilton Papers, Library of Congress).

To James McHenry, October 23, 1799 (Df, in the handwriting   III
of Ethan Brown, Hamilton Papers, Library of Congress).

To Aaron Ogden, October 23, 1799 (Df, in the handwriting of   III
Thomas Y. How, Hamilton Papers, Library of Congress).

From Peter Robinson, October 23, 1799 (ALS, Hamilton Papers,   III
Library of Congress).

To Ebenezer Stevens, October 23, 1799 (L, in the handwriting of   VII
Ethan Brown, New-York Historical Society, New York City).

From Timothy Taylor, October 23, 1799 (ALS, Hamilton Papers,   VIII
Library of Congress).

To Timothy Taylor, October 23, 1799 (ADf, Hamilton Papers,   VI
Library of Congress).

To George Washington, October 23, 1799 (ALS, George Wash-   II
ington Papers, Library of Congress; copy, Hamilton Papers,
Library of Congress).

To Russell Bissell, October 24, 1799 (Df, in the handwriting of   III
Thomas Y. How, Hamilton Papers, Library of Congress). Acknowledges Bissell's letter of October 4, 1799. *Letter not found.*

To William K. Blue, October 24, 1799 (Df, in the handwriting   III
of Thomas Y. How, Hamilton Papers, Library of Congress).

To Elias B. Dayton, October 24, 1799 (Df, in the handwriting of   VII
Thomas Y. How, Hamilton Papers, Library of Congress).

To Frederick Frye, October 24, 1799 (Df, in the handwriting of   III
Thomas Y. How, Hamilton Papers, Library of Congress).

To Michael Gunkle, October 24, 1799 (Df, in the handwriting   VII
of Thomas Y. How, Hamilton Papers, Library of Congress).

To Josias Carvel Hall, October 24, 1799 (Df, in the handwriting   VII
of Ethan Brown and H, Hamilton Papers, Library of Con-
gress).

To Daniel Jackson, October 24, 1799 (Df, in the handwriting of   VIII
Thomas Y. How, Hamilton Papers, Library of Congress).

From James McHenry, October 24, 1799 (LS, Hamilton Papers,   I
Library of Congress; LS, letterpress copy, James McHenry Papers, Library of Congress).

From James McHenry, October 24, 1799 (LS, Hamilton Papers,   III
Library of Congress; LS, letterpress copy, James McHenry Pa-
pers, Library of Congress), enclosing Joseph Elliott to Mc-
Henry, October 22, 1799 (copy, Hamilton Papers, Library of
Congress).

From John Mackey, October 24, 1799 (ALS, Hamilton Papers,   VII
Library of Congress).

From Thomas Parker, October 24 [–25], 1799 (ALS, marked   VII
"Duplicate," with postscript dated October 25, Hamilton Papers, Library of Congress; ALS, Hamilton Papers, Library of
Congress; ALS, marked "Duplicate," Hamilton Papers, Library
of Congress).

To Thomas Parker, October 24, 1799 (Df, in the handwriting of   IV
Ethan Brown and H, Hamilton Papers, Library of Congress).

To John W. Patterson, October 24, 1799 (Df, in the handwriting   III
of Thomas Y. How, Hamilton Papers, Library of Congress).

To Zebulon M. Pike, October 24, 1799 (Df, in the handwriting of VII
Thomas Y. How, Hamilton Papers, Library of Congress).

To Charles Cotesworth Pinckney, October 24, 1799 (Df, in the   IV
handwriting of Ethan Brown, Hamilton Papers, Library of
Congress).

To Peter Robinson, October 24, 1799 (Df, in the handwriting of   III
Thomas Y. How, Hamilton Papers, Library of Congress).

From Stephen Simmons, October 24, 1799 (ALS, Hamilton Pa-   III
pers, Library of Congress). Acknowledges H's letter of October 22, 1799. *Letter not found.*

From John Smith, October 24, 1799 (ALS, Hamilton Papers, Li-   VI
brary of Congress), enclosing "Selection of officers from South
Carolina Georgia and Kentucky for the 5th Regiment" (copy,
Hamilton Papers, Library of Congress); "A Report of Sundry
Articles . . . for the use of the 5th Regiment," October 24,
1799 (DS, Hamilton Papers, Library of Congress).

To John Taylor, October 24, 1799 (Df, in the handwriting of   II
Thomas Y. How, Hamilton Papers, Library of Congress).

From John Bishop, October 25, 1799 (ALS, Hamilton Papers,   V
Library of Congress).

To Walter L. Cochran, October 25, 1799 (Df, in the handwriting   VIII
of Thomas Y. How, Hamilton Papers, Library of Congress).

From Elias B. Dayton, October 25, 1799 (ALS, Hamilton Papers,   VII
Library of Congress).

From Nehemiah Freeman, October 25, 1799 (ALS, Hamilton   VIII
Papers, Library of Congress).

To Tobias Lear, October 25, 1799 (LS, George Washington Pa-   IX
pers, Library of Congress; Df, in the handwriting of H and
Ethan Brown, Hamilton Papers, Library of Congress; copy,
Hamilton Papers, Library of Congress).

To William Leverett, October 25, 1799 (Df, in the handwriting   III
of Thomas Y. How, Hamilton Papers, Library of Congress).
Acknowledges Leverett's letter of October 5, 1799. *Letter not
found.*

From James McHenry, October 25, 1799 (LS, Hamilton Papers,   VII
Library of Congress; LS, letterpress copy, James McHenry
Papers, Library of Congress).

To James McHenry, October 25, 1799 (ADf, Hamilton Papers,   IV
Library of Congress).

To James McHenry, October 25, 1799 (Df, in the handwriting of   VI
Thomas Y. How, Hamilton Papers, Library of Congress).

To James Miller, October 25, 1799 (LS, Lloyd W. Smith Collec-   VII
tion, Morristown National Historical Park, Morristown, New
Jersey; Df, in the handwriting of Thomas Y. How, Hamilton
Papers, Library of Congress).

From James Richmond, October 25, 1799 (ALS, Hamilton Pa-   III
pers, Library of Congress).

From John Ripley, October 25, 1799 (ALS, Hamilton Papers,   VIII
Library of Congress).

To John Ripley, October 25, 1799 (Df, in the handwriting of   VIII
Ethan Brown, Hamilton Papers, Library of Congress).

From Ebenezer Stevens, October 25, 1799 (ALS, Hamilton Pa-   VIII
pers, Library of Congress).

To Ebenezer Stevens, October 25, 1799 (LS, in the handwriting   VIII
of Ethan Brown, New-York Historical Society, New York
City; Df, in the handwriting of Ethan Brown, Hamilton Papers,
Library of Congress).

To Caleb Swan, October 25, 1799 (Df, in the handwriting of   III
Thomas Y. How, Hamilton Papers, Library of Congress).

To John Bishop, October 26, 1799 (Df, in the handwriting of   VIII
Thomas Y. How, Hamilton Papers, Library of Congress).

From William Bullitt, October 26, 1799 (ALS, Hamilton Papers,   III
Library of Congress).

To Joseph Elliott, October 26, 1799 (Df, in the handwriting of   VIII
Thomas Y. How, Hamilton Papers, Library of Congress).

To Samuel Hodgdon, October 26, 1799 (Df, in the handwriting   VII
of Thomas Y. How, Hamilton Papers, Library of Congress).

From Daniel Jackson, October 26, 1799 (ALS, Hamilton Papers,   VIII
Library of Congress).

To James McHenry, October 26, 1799 (Df, in the handwriting   VIII
of Thomas Y. How, Hamilton Papers, Library of Congress).

From Ebenezer Stevens, October 26, 1799 (LS, Hamilton Papers,   VII
Library of Congress), enclosing an illustrated "plan of the Uniforms" (D, Hamilton Papers, Library of Congress).

To Ebenezer Stevens, October 26, 1799 (LS, in the handwriting   VII
of Thomas Y. How, New-York Historical Society, New York
City; Df, in the handwriting of Thomas Y. How, Hamilton Papers, Library of Congress).

From Caleb Swan, October 26, 1799 (ALS, Hamilton Papers,   VII
Library of Congress).

From Henry Muhlenberg, October 27, 1799 (ALS, Hamilton Pa-   VII
pers, Library of Congress).

From William S. Smith, October 27, 1799 (ALS, Hamilton Pa-   IV
pers, Library of Congress).

From John Heth, October 28, 1799 (ALS, Hamilton Papers, Li-   III
brary of Congress).

From Samuel Hoffman, October 28, 1799 (ALS, Hamilton Papers,   IV
Library of Congress).

From John McClallen, October 28, 1799 (ALS, Hamilton Pa-   III
pers, Library of Congress). Refers to H's letter of October 18,   V
1799. *Letter not found.*

From James McHenry, October 28, 1799 (LS, Hamilton Papers,   III
Library of Congress; LS, letterpress copy, James McHenry Papers, Library of Congress).

To James McHenry, October 28, 1799 (Df, in the handwriting   VI
of Thomas Y. How, Hamilton Papers, Library of Congress).   IX

From James Miller, October 28, 1799 (LS, Hamilton Papers, Li-   VII
brary of Congress).

From Thomas Lloyd Moore, October 28, 1799 (ALS, Hamilton   VIII
Papers, Library of Congress).

To Thomas Parker, October 28, 1799 (Df, in the handwriting of   VI
Thomas Y. How and H, Hamilton Papers, Library of Congress).

From William S. Smith, October 28, 1799 (ALS, Hamilton Pa-   VII
pers, Library of Congress).

To Ebenezer Stevens, October 28, 1799 (LS, New-York Histor- VII
ical Society, New York City; Df, in the handwriting of Ethan
Brown, Hamilton Papers, Library of Congress).

From Timothy Taylor, October 28, 1799 (ALS, Hamilton Papers, V
Library of Congress).

From James McHenry, October 29, 1799 (LS, Hamilton Papers, III
Library of Congress).

From Thomas Parker, October 29, 1799 (ALS, Hamilton Papers, III
Library of Congress), enclosing "Estimate of plank necessary VII
to Cover a Regiment of 600 men" (AD, Hamilton Papers, Library of Congress).

To Ebenezer Stevens, October 29, 1799 (LS, New-York Histor- VII
ical Society, New York City; Df, in the handwriting of
Thomas Y. How, Hamilton Papers, Library of Congress).

To Ebenezer Stevens, October 29, 1799 (LS, New-York Histor- VIII
ical Society, New York City; Df, in the handwriting of
Thomas Y. How, Hamilton Papers, Library of Congress).

From Timothy Taylor, October 29, 1799 (ALS, Hamilton Papers, III
Library of Congress).

To William C. Bentley, October 30, 1799 (ALS, Hamilton Pa- IV
pers, Library of Congress). VII

To Samuel Hodgdon, October 30, 1799 (Df, in the handwriting VII
of Thomas Y. How, Hamilton Papers, Library of Congress).

To James House, October 30, 1799 (Df, in the handwriting of III
Thomas Y. How, Hamilton Papers, Library of Congress).

To Tobias Lear, October 30, 1799 (LS, in the handwriting of IX
Ethan Brown, George Washington Papers, Library of Congress;
copy, in the handwriting of Ethan Brown, Hamilton Papers,
Library of Congress).

From James McHenry, October 30, 1799 (LS, Hamilton Papers, III
Library of Congress).

To James McHenry, October 30, 1799 (Df, in the handwriting of I
Thomas Y. How, Hamilton Papers, Library of Congress). IX

To James McHenry, October 30, 1799 (Df, in the handwriting of III
Thomas Y. How, Hamilton Papers, Library of Congress).

To James Miller, October 30, 1799 (Df, in the handwriting of VIII
Thomas Y. How, Hamilton Papers, Library of Congress).

From Thomas Lloyd Moore, October 30, 1799 (ALS, Hamilton VIII
Papers, Library of Congress), enclosing Thomas Parker to

Moore, October 26, 1799 (ALS, Hamilton Papers, Library of Congress).

To Henry Muhlenberg, October 30, 1799 (Df, in the handwriting VIII
of Thomas Y. How, Hamilton Papers, Library of Congress).

From Thomas Parker, October 30, 1799 (ALS, Hamilton Papers, IV
Library of Congress).

From James Read, October 30, 1799 (ALS, Hamilton Papers, Li- IV
brary of Congress), enclosing a list of prisoners at Fort Jay
(AD, Hamilton Papers, Library of Congress).

From William S. Smith, October 30, 1799 (ALS, Hamilton Pa- III
pers, Library of Congress).

To William S. Smith, October 30, 1799 (Df, in the handwriting of VI
Thomas Y. How, Hamilton Papers, Library of Congress).

From Caleb Swan, October 30, 1799 (ALS, Hamilton Papers, Li- III
brary of Congress). VII

From James Wilkinson, October 30, 1799 (ALS, Hamilton Papers, VII
Library of Congress).

To Walter L. Cochran, October 31, 1799 (Df, in the handwriting III
of Ethan Brown and H, Hamilton Papers, Library of Congress).

To Josias Carvel Hall, October 31, 1799 (Df, in the handwriting IV
of Thomas Y. How, Hamilton Papers, Library of Congress).

From James McHenry, October 31, 1799 (LS, Hamilton Papers, III
Library of Congress; LS, letterpress copy, James McHenry Papers, Library of Congress).

From James McHenry, October 31, 1799 (LS, Hamilton Papers, III
Library of Congress; LS, letterpress copy, James McHenry Papers, Library of Congress). Refers to his letter to H of June 4,
1799. *Letter not found.*

To James McHenry, October 31, 1799 (Df, in the handwriting III
of Thomas Y. How, Hamilton Papers, Library of Congress).

From James Miller, October 31, 1799 (ALS, Hamilton Papers, Li- VII
brary of Congress).

To Thomas Lloyd Moore, October 31, 1799 (Df, in the hand- VIII
writing of Thomas Y. How, Hamilton Papers, Library of
Congress).

To Thomas Parker, October 31, 1799 (Df, in the handwriting of III
Thomas Y. How, Hamilton Papers, Library of Congress).

From John J. U. Rivardi, October 31, 1799 (ALS, Hamilton Papers, Library of Congress).   I
    III
    IV
    VII
    IX

To John J. U. Rivardi, October 31, 1799 (Df, in the handwriting   VII
of Thomas Y. How, Hamilton Papers, Library of Congress).

To Ebenezer Stevens, October 31, 1799 (LS, in the handwriting   VII
of Ethan Brown, New-York Historical Society, New York
City; Df, in the handwriting of Ethan Brown, Hamilton Papers, Library of Congress).

To Caleb Swan, October 31, 1799 (Df, in the handwriting of   III
Ethan Brown, Hamilton Papers, Library of Congress).

To Caleb Swan, October 31, 1799 (Df, in the handwriting of   III
Thomas Y. How, Hamilton Papers, Library of Congress).

INDEX

COMPILED BY JEAN G. COOKE

202, 284, 329, 340, 349, 374, 464-65, 469, 511-12, 513, 514, 525, 548, 569, 570, 572, 573, 629, Eleventh Regiment of, 11-12, 176, 229, 246, 270, 272, 281, 282, 285, 329, 340, 349, 374, 423, 437, 469, 508, 509, 538, 608, 609, Twelfth Regiment of, 89, 122, 141, 185, 198, 202, 267, 321, 322, 329, 340, 349, 361, 374, 437, 456, 458, 469, 473, 508, 509, 524, 538, 607, 677, Thirteenth Regiment of, 178, 198, 202, 206, 329, 437, 456, 458, 469, 508, 538, 578, 613, Fourteenth Regiment of, 27, 41, 83-84, 138, 142, 198, 206, 251, 296, 329, 341, 343, 368, 376, 466, 498, 499, 502, 531, 560-64, 579, Fifteenth Regiment of, 27, 138, 198, 206, 257, 296, 329, 341, 498, 499, 501, 502, 509, 514, 531, 539, 579, 684, 685, Sixteenth Regiment of, 118, 178, 198, 329, 341, 349, 499, 501, 502, 509, 514, 531, 643; inspector general, 17, 29, 52, 153 (*see also* Hamilton, Alexander), deputy, 52, 153; inspector of fortifications, 397; inspectorship department, 439; inspectors in, 523, 593; Invalid Corps, 433; issuing commissary, 92, 221; judge advocates, 346, 360-61, 371-73, 558-59, 590, 593; major generals, 72, 73, 97-98, 192, 215, 222-23, 314, 394-95, 524; medical assistance for, 434, 489; Medical Department, 424; medical supplies for, 16, 130, 352, 450-51, 551; military storekeepers, 16, 105; military supplies, 15-19, 25, 35, 52, 92, 105-6, 122, 132, 142-43, 150, 151, 154-55, 161, 166, 177, 184, 187, 188, 190, 191, 194, 198-99, 206, 213-14, 217, 249, 262, 283, 308, 320, 322, 326-27, 331-32, 332-33, 338, 346, 352, 399, 423-28, 436, 447-54, 475, 495, 596, 630, 667; minors, enlistment of, 179, 210, 344, 465-66; money for, 14-15, 17, 18, 26-27, 35, 36, 38, 39, 43, 45, 56, 81, 109, 132, 166, 177, 184, 185, 188, 189, 191, 194-95, 196, 198, 200-1, 206, 212, 216, 220, 229, 232, 250, 253, 254, 255, 285, 300, 306-7, 310, 316, 317, 318, 321, 328, 331, 339, 345-46, 352, 359-60, 367, 400, 429, 430, 450, 452, 466, 467-68, 471-72, 493, 510, 512, 526, 537, 539, 540, 555, 556, 557, 566, 570, 579, 588-89, 591, 593; mulattoes in, 438; music and musicians for, 15, 58-59, 61,

367, 400-1, 433; musterrolls and payrolls, 153-54, 191, 206, 300, 321, 328, 352, 359, 416, 422-23, 452, 453, 457, 460, 467, 470, 482-83, 510, 537, 556; non-commissioned officers, 18; oaths to, 102; observations of, 418; officers of, 35-36, 39-40, 44, 49-50, 69-71, 73-77, 82-84, 84-85, 94-95, 99, 101, 105, 134-35, 137-38, 140, 161, 174, 177, 197, 202-3, 207-8, 210, 211, 213, 259, 504, 580-88, 593, 608, 619, 627, 640-41, 644, 646, 657, 672, 682, 684, 685, 689, absent, 356, 368-69, 385-87, 389, barracks, quarters, and fuel allowance for, 369-70, circular to, 50, commissions for, 32, 541, duties of, 16, 17, 18, compensation of, 14-15, 18, 26, 50, 132, 306-7, 310, 328, 400, 401, extra allowances for, 59-61, 162-64, 360-61, 370, 371, 373, 431, nominations for, 50, 364, rank of, 50, 63, 77, 82-83, 109, 223, 238-39, 247-49, 325, 347-49, 361-64, 367, 374-75, 400, 442, 461-63, 475-80, 495, 498-99, 501, 541, 560-64, 588, 686, servants for, 253-54, 279, 285, 432-33, 438; ordnance, 382, 430, board of, 426, department of, 330-31; organization and arrangement of, 35-36, 38-39, 51, 52, 72, 80-81, 84-85, 104-5, 363, 523-24, 602; paymaster general, 17, 150, 153, 154, 359-60, 421-23, 424, 428-29, 452, 453, 456, 460-61, 470, 482, 483, 526, 537, 673 (*see also* Swan, Caleb), deputy, 17, 153, 359-60, 361, 415-16, 424, 428, 444-45, 452, 453, 456, 460-61, 467, 468, 470, 482, 550, 565, 578, 580, 589; paymasters, 11-12, 17-18, 26, 27, 28, 35, 38, 40, 43, 45, 52, 62, 82, 85, 87, 101, 108, 109, 166, 191, 198, 202, 318, 321, 322, 351, 352, 359, 367, 460-61, 466, 468, 472, 510, 527, 537, 539, 578-80, 588-89; payment of troops, 17-18, 39, 45, 56, 92, 150, 153-54, 160, 188, 191, 195, 198, 206, 216, 220-21, 247, 318, 320, 322, 328, 338, 346, 358-60, 401-2, 414, 415-16, 421-23, 428-29, 444, 452-53, 456-58, 466, 472, 482-83, 493, 498, 527, 534, 537, 556, 557, 567, 570, 579, 589, 597; Timothy Pickering on, 224; promotions in, 78-79, 210, 238-39, 247-49, 257, 296, 347-49, 361-64, 374-75, 441-43; Provisional, 99-100, 140, 223, 561; provisions for, 16, 113,

502, 508-9, 511-12, 512-13, 513-14, 514-15, 523, 525, 529-31, 538, 542-43, 548-49, 552-53, 555, 564-65, 568-70, 571-73, 577-78; Oliver Wolcott, Jr., on 98, 100, 223-24; wood for, 333, 340, 341, 346, 458-59, 464, 480, 493-94, 499-500, 509, 514, 529-30, 542-43, 577. *See also under individual states, heading* U.S. Army
United States attorney for the District: of New York, *see* Harison, Richard
United States judge for the District: of New York *see* Troup, Robert; of Pennsylvania, *see* Peters, Richard
United States marshal for the District: of New York, *see* Smith, William S.; of Pennsylvania, *see* Nichols, William
United States Navy, 223, 448; dispute in rank, 97-98, 116-18, 274-75, 295-96; Hamilton's comments on, 227-28, 295-96, 602; for Lake Erie, 381; musicians for, 433; vacancies in, filling of, 70, 95; for western rivers, 384
Upper Canada, 379
Ustick, Thomas: *letters from*, 608, 610
Uxbridge, Mass., 109, 261, 273, 341, 458, 469, 480, 501

Vado Bay, 194
Vallance, John, 490
Van Bushvik, Abraham, Jr., 614
Vance, Samuel C., 360-61, 371-72, 444-45, 540, 542, 578, 580, 585; *letter to* William Simmons, 612
Vandenbroeck, R. J., 62
Van Rensselaer, Margarita Schuyler (Mrs. Stephen), 173, 413
Van Rensselaer, Solomon, 111
Van Rensselaer, Stephen, 413; *letters from*, 611, 642; *letter to*, 633
Van Vechten, Abraham: *letter to*, 678
Van Vleck, Isaac, 62
Van Wert, Andrew, 582
Varick, Richard: *letter from*, 634
Vauban, Sébastien LePretre, Segneur de, 490
Vaublanc-Lessart, Vincent de: *letter from*, 647
Venezuela, 497
Vera Cruz, 49
Vermont: and U.S. Army, contracts

and contractors in, 262, officers for, 50, 76, 99, 177, 356, supplies for troops in, 10, recruiting in, 593
Vincennes, 378
Vining, John, 22, 23
Virginia: and Alien and Sedition Acts, 600; Court of Chancery, 277, 278; election (1799), 112; Federalists elected in, 599; legislature, 112; and George Nicholas's *A Letter*, 41-42; supervisor of the revenue for, *see* Carrington, Edward; and U.S. Army, cavalry, 140, contracts and contractors in, 262, 272, 307, 315, Eventual, 140, 174, First Regiment of Artillerists and Engineers, 73, 75, 104, 119, Infantry, 140, and minors, 344, officers for, 32, 75, 140, 325, recruiting districts in, 31, 54, 608, 621, 624, recruiting in, 98, 134, 177, 202, 222, 307, 310, 420, 465, 493, 552, 593, supplies for troops in, 10, 243, 245, 255-56, 307, 349, 464-65, 469, 484-85, 512-13, 514-15, 539, 542-43, 548-49, 552-53; troops in, 15; U.S. Representative from, *see* Marshall, John
Virginia and Kentucky resolutions, 600
Visscher, Nanning, J., 218, 219, 221, 289, 291, 489, 579-80, 584; *letters from*, 610, 635, 656; *letters to*, 633, 676

Wabash Indians: *letter to* John F. Hamtramck, 657
Wabash River, 390, 418, 657
Wade, John, 585
Wadsworth, Decius, 76; *letter from*, 632; *letter to*, 167-68
Wadsworth, James: *letter from*, 613
Wadsworth, Jeremiah: letter from, 638; *letters to*, 123-24, 671
Wadsworth, Peleg: *letter to* James McHenry, 612
Walbach, John De Barth, 111; *letter to*, 53-54
Waldron, A. W., 22
Walker, Benjamin: *letter from*, 639; *letter to*, 633
Walker, Edward, 344
Walker, John, 83-84, 138, 466-67, 498-99
Wallace, John C., 584
Wallington, John, 587